THE SEARCH FOR
MODERN
CHINA

A
DOCUMENTARY
COLLECTION

Edited by

PEI-KAI CHENG and

MICHAEL LESTZ *with*

JONATHAN D. SPENCE

W • W • NORTON & COMPANY | New York • London

THE SEARCH FOR MODERN CHINA

A DOCUMENTARY COLLECTION

The text of this book is composed in Granjon
Composition by Binghamton Valley Composition
Book design by Jack Meserole
Cover illustration: Ren Yi (1840–1896), *Shen
Luting Reading by the Lake*, 1880. Courtesy,
The Palace Museum, Beijing, China.

Library of Congress Cataloging-in-Publication Data

The search for modern China : a documentary collection / edited by
Pei-kai Cheng, Michael Lestz, with Jonathan D. Spence.
    p. cm.
  Includes bibliographical references.
  ISBN 0-393-97372-7 (pbk.)
  1. China—History—Ch'ing dynasty, 1644–1912—Sources. 2.
China—History—20th century—Sources. I. Cheng, Pei-kai. II.
Lestz, Michael Elliot. III. Spence, Jonathan D.
  DS753.86 .S33   1998
  951'.03—ddc21   98-44315
                                                         r98

W. W. Norton & Company, Inc., 500 Fifth Avenue, New York, N.Y. 10110
http://www.wwnorton.com

W. W. Norton & Company Ltd., 10 Coptic Street, London WC1A 1PU

2 3 4 5 6 7 8 9 0

FOR OUR PARENTS

HSU-TUNG CHENG AND SHU-CHEN YIN CHENG
GERALD LESTZ, EDITH ALLPORT LESTZ, AND MARGARET GORDON LESTZ

Contents

Preface

It is a daunting task to represent four hundred years of Chinese history through documents. The process of sifting through mountains of paper to discover characteristic and illuminating pages is a challenge that repeatedly tests one's sense of historical evidence and notions of relevance. To build this anthology a great wall of paper needed to be reduced to a manageable stack of documents illustrating concerns of central importance in the complex story told through this book.

One complication for us as anthologizers was that many of the documents we thought were vital for illustrating aspects of social life, political and military problems, ethical conceptions and practice, and the inner dynamics of everyday life were not available in English. To give satisfactory breadth to the documents volume, we were obliged to unearth and translate many documents that had become available only in recent years. Accordingly, more than one-third of the documents in this volume are new translations.

Another cardinal concern for this anthology was to match the documents to the chapters of Jonathan Spence's *The Search for Modern China,* Second Edition. When we started collecting documents, both of us had recently finished our graduate work at Yale. We had been teaching assistants in Jonathan Spence's huge undergraduate course on modern China and wrote dissertations under his direction. These experiences gave us a sense of the Spence approach to the history of Qing, Republican, and post-1949 China that was invaluable as we weighed the use of documents to reinforce his text.

Since our anthology was conceived as a companion work to Spence's survey, any reader of both works will notice intentional parallelism and cross-references that unite the two books. But like the matching calligraphic panels of a hanging couplet (*duilian*), the two works are original and independent in an understood framework of relatedness. Although the chapters in both books have identical titles, the anthology does not simply repeat the historical narrative in notes and documents; rather, it comments on the text and develops themes of its own in a way designed to extend the scope of historical inquiry.

One theme followed throughout this volume in many separate documents is the question of how the state defined ideal or model political behavior in its subjects or citizens. Throughout China's political history since ancient times, ruling elites have attempted to place the stamp of state orthodoxy on the ruled. Ruling groups have sought to channel and control the conduct of the ruled in both public and private settings and devised explicit standards of behavior. To do this, they borrowed from Confucian and Legalist statecraft but, as can be seen in many documents included here, a focus on right thinking and conduct was incorporated into the political practice of many different groups in ways that reflected their ideological and social credos and the tumultuous changes produced by dynastic decline, the founding of new states, imperialism, and revolution.

The Sacred Edict of the Kangxi emperor, the Ten Commandments of Hong Xiuquan who led the Taiping rebellion, the rules proposed by the New Life Promotion Society in 1934, Liu Shaoqi's speech "How To Be a Good Communist" during the war with Japan, and propaganda to encourage emulation of Lei Feng in the early 1960s all distinguished good, orderly, valuable, and healthy behavior from harmful or even hateful behavior. While this process of splitting orthodox and heterodox as a means of control was hardly unique to China's rulers, the documents compiled around this theme permit readers to glimpse a recurrent feature of China's traditional political culture. Such documents help a student of China's past to understand how the line between approved and seditious has been laid down at many moments and in an eerily similar way during the centuries since the founding of the Qing dynasty.

A related theme that we have traced with a number of documents is that of commitment to transcendent values and the willingness to endure martyrdom for a higher cause. In a society in which right and wrong were rigidly defined in a variety of contexts, identification with high ideals that defied moral or behavioral orthodoxies often resulted in acts of self-destructive courage that proved an individual's devotion to a belief system. The account of the death of Ge Xian, leader of the Suzhou silk weavers' riot in the late Ming; the description of the desperate defense of Jiangyin by the Ming loyalist Yen; descriptions of the death of "chaste women" in village society of the nineteenth century; Zou Rong's explosive attack on the Manchu rulers of China; the last speech of Wen Yiduo in Kunming; and the declaration of the student hunger-strikers in Tiananmen Square in the spring of 1989 capture the moralistic bravado that so often animated key actors in the history of modern China.

Women's history is another focal theme in this text. The struggle for women's rights and equality with men continues today throughout all of "greater China." A number of the documents assembled here provide a sense of the hardship suffered by women in their private lives and as subjects and citizens in various sociopolitical settings in the modern era. To do full justice to this theme would require another document anthology of similar length, but we have tried, nonetheless, to sketch some facets of the picture.

Each document is preceded by a short headnote that creates a sense of the historical context that produced it. In preparing these notes we avoided the temptation of writing an extensive *explication de texte* and tried, instead, simply to provide some guideposts that teachers and students might use if more work was to be done outside of class or as part of a project related to a particular document. The documents that are translated here for the first time or in new translations were translated as literally as possible. We did not attempt to embellish the style of the original documents or improve upon their internal system of logic and organizations. Instead, our intent as translators was to permit the reader to encounter each document in a form that would be immediately intelligible and yet so close to the first text that no reader of Chinese would be puzzled by the relationship of our English to the original language of the document.

Readers of this anthology will note that *pinyin* is the dominant system of transliteration in the book as it is in *The Search for Modern China*. Documents containing names according to the Wade-Giles system were left unaltered; however, when we encountered idiosyncratic systems of romanization in nineteenth- and early-twentieth-century documents we converted them, insofar as it was possible to do so, into *pinyin* for the convenience of those who will use the book.

Finally, readers of this book will notice that we have often used selections from novels, short story collections, or poetry anthologies. In deciding to select pieces of fiction to illuminate historical concerns—which are usually described in the headnote—we were guided by the Chinese adage that "history and literature cannot be divided" (*wenshi bufen*).

Acknowledgments

Our deepest debt of gratitude goes to our teacher, Jonathan Spence, who drew us into this project and worked with us in a profoundly satisfying partnership to create a collection of documents to complement *The Search for Modern China*. Both in suggesting documents we might use and assisting in the shaping of the text, Jonathan played a critical role in the making of this book. Whatever elegance of line it may display is owing in no small way to his contribution.

As the book evolved, no one could have been more supportive than our editor Steven Forman and we are also deeply thankful to him for his assistance. He, too, provided us with sound advice as we formed the architecture of the book and suggested ways of tailoring the manuscript to match it to the needs of our readers. In the final stages of the book's composition his work as an editor helped give this collection of documents an inner consistency we were striving for all along. We would also like to thank our manuscript editor at W. W. Norton, Katharine Nicholson Ings, for a thorough and attentive reading of the drafts of the manuscript and Kristin Sheerin for steering us through copyright law and obtaining the permissions for documents published elsewhere.

We were put on course toward finding individual documents by Shen Jin (formerly of the Shanghai Municipal Library and now rare book librarian in the Yenching Library at Harvard) and Trinity College librarians Jeff Kaimowitz (director of Trinity's Watkinson Library) and Pat Bunker (of the Trinity Library reference department). We thank them warmly for their support. We also acknowledge with gratitude the help of many other librarians at Yale's Sterling Library and elsewhere who helped us obtain materials now fitted into this text.

In addition, we are grateful to colleagues and friends, including Andrew Hsieh (Grinnell College), Parks Coble (University of Nebraska), Sherman Cochran (Cornell University), Lai Tse-han (Academia Sinica), Vera Schwarcz

(Wesleyan University), William Alford (Harvard Law School), and others who suggested documents or read and commented on parts of the text. Early in the project, Madeleine Zelin (Columbia University) and Michael Gasster (Rutgers University) provided a valuable critique of selected chapters of the book. Their comments, together with those of several anonymous readers who provided tough and searching judgments of our selections and the structure of the document collection as it was emerging, helped us immensely as we went forward. We also acknowledge faculty colleagues at Trinity College and Pace University who were enthusiastic about this project and helped us in large and small ways during the time we worked on it.

Finally, we would like to thank Michelle Iacino and Martha O'Rourke, who helped with the typing and preparation of the manuscript, and Gigi St. Peter, who facilitated the passage of successive drafts and versions of the galleys from Trinity and Pace to W. W. Norton.

ML
Trinity College
Hartford

PKC
Pace University
Manhattan

THE SEARCH FOR
MODERN
CHINA

A

DOCUMENTARY

COLLECTION

CHAPTER 1

The Late Ming

1.1 AND 1.2 TWO ACCOUNTS OF THE SUZHOU RIOT, 1601

In the final decades of the Ming dynasty, the throne relied heavily on eunuch advisors who won their prestige through their presence in the Forbidden City and imperial patronage. The eunuchs were despised by the scholar officials of Peking who saw their growing power as illegitimate. The result of this opposition was a series of factional battles in which eunuchs sought to consolidate their position at the expense of their literati opponents while the scholars aimed at purging the court of eunuch influence. Ultimately, the eunuchs were largely successful in obtaining their ends and continued to play a powerful role until the collapse of the Ming dynasty in 1644.

The two documents translated below trace the consequences of eunuch encroachment within the ranks of officialdom in the context of a set of riots and disturbances that occurred in Suzhou in 1601. The Wanli Emperor (1563–1620) used eunuch commissioners to fulfill a variety of official tasks and their corruption and venality reached scandalous proportions in a number of celebrated cases.

When the powerful eunuch Sun Long (d. July 2, 1601) was appointed to oversee the imperial silk works in Suzhou, one of the three factories that provided silk for the imperial household and the state, he abused his powers in ways found intolerable by local silk workers.[1] The result was the set of popular disturbances in Suzhou that are described here by the Ming

---

1. L. Carrington Goodrich and Chaoying Fang, *Dictionary of Ming Biography, 1368–1644* (New York: Columbia University Press, 1976), pp. 405, 868.

scholars and chroniclers Shen Zan (1558–1612) and Wen Bing (1609–1669). The two sources are in contradiction about the date of the Suzhou riot. Shen Zan's *Jinshi congchan* records the riot as having occurred in July 1601 while Wen Bing's *Dingling zhulue* suggests that it happened in July 1600. According to the *Ming Veritable Records*, 1601 is the correct date.

1.1 Shen Zan's Account

Ge Xian was from Kunshan. He was hired to work as a silk weaver in the prefectural seat [Suzhou]. In the sixth moon of 1601, some treacherous people presented a plan to Tax Commissioner Sun which said: "We would like to propose a new tax law. A tax of three silver cents for every bolt of silk should be paid before it is marketed. We are willing to make efforts to take charge of this matter." They gathered substantial funds from several wealthy households to bribe the tax commissioner [to allow the tax]. The plan succeeded and the Commissioner made the announcement [of the tax] and let it be practiced.

All the artisans and silk dealers suffered from this and could find no method to stop it. Ge Xian then came forward and said: "I will be the leader and will eliminate this disorder for the people of Suzhou." He led dozens of people to the Xuanmiao Temple. He made an arrangement with his followers, saying: "Let the palm-leaf fan in my hand be the signal for your actions." The crowd said: "We agree!" Thereupon, they first went to the homes of a certain Tang and a certain Xu who had first proposed the tax plan and beat them to death. Then they went to the house of an officer named Ding Yuanfu and the home of a certain rich family named Gui and burned their residences. Both Ding and Gui had helped in arranging loans to the local bullies for bribing the tax commissioner. The rioters forbade looting and nothing was taken. They split into two groups and went to the tax collection stations outside of the Lu and Xu Gates. They stopped at each station and beat all of the collectors to death. They then went in person to see the prefect and said: "We want Tax Commissioner Sun or we won't be satisfied." The prefect tried to mollify them but dared not investigate. On the second day, the crowd still would not disperse. They said: "We won't stop until we get the Tax Commissioner!" Thereupon, Sun summoned garrison troops and local militia to make a display of force before his headquarters. Ge Xian and others also gathered a mob and approached the gate of the Tax Commission office.

Fortunately, Ge Xian's followers and the troops did not confront each other. At sunset, the mob dispersed. The Tax Commissioner took this opportunity to flee away with his escort and went to Hangzhou. Ge Xian then volunteered to go to prison. The prefect asked what he wanted. He replied: "There are many mosquitoes at night. I just need a mosquito net." People in the jail and outsiders who were not afraid of the consequences often praised him and brought wine and dried meat for him every day. Ge Xian expected that he must die but a memorial was presented and an order pardoning him was sent down. He is still in prison and is well. This is a strange matter!

1.2 *Wen Bing's Account*

When the local uprising took place in Suzhou in the sixth moon of 1600, Sun Long, the Imperial Eunuch Commissioner for Silk Weaving in Suzhou and Hangzhou was concurrently in charge of tax collection. Many local hoodlums joined his entourage and were given official duties as tax collectors. At all of the gates of the city, they set up tax collection stations and not even a single chicken or bunch of vegetables was exempted. The people could not stand living this way and were so stirred up that they considered rioting.

On the sixth day of the sixth moon, twenty-seven people suddenly appeared [in Suzhou]; their hair was loose, they were barefoot, and all of them wore short, white shirts. Each of them held a palm-leaf fan in his hand and they went to the residences of every tax collector and set fire to their homes and property. They seized the collectors and beat them to death in the streets. Although only there were only twenty-seven people, they struck like a torrential storm; nobody dared resist them. When they came to high walls or tall buildings, their leader would merely wave his fan and all of them would immediately jump up on top.

The second day, they mistakenly entered a common household. This family made its living through business but was guilty of no crime. The family knelt down and welcomed them and begged to know their offense. The leader pulled a list from his belt, looked at it and said: "We have made an error!" Both this home and that of a tax collector were located beside a bean curd shop. The leader then led his men in apologizing to the family. The group then ran over to the tax collector's house. The tax collector was frightened and jumped into a canal. The men pulled him out of the canal and began beating him. The tax collector's eyes were protruding but they still continued beating him with their fists and finally killed him.

A certain person named Tong was a local judge and possessed property worth tens of thousands of taels [1 tael = $1.38]. He also served as the tax collector in charge of the Liuhe tax station. When the riot took place, he leaped into a canal to flee but died of the cold. The rioters also burned an official household. All of the members of the household hid or eluded the rioters. The son of the family, who was a local scholar, secreted himself in a chest which was left in a neighbor's house, and thereby escaped. Tax Commissioner Sun fled by night to Hangzhou to escape.

The riot continued for three days and all of the tax collectors were eliminated. On the fourth day, a large announcement was posted alongside each of the six city gates. It read: "The tax collectors wantonly committed abuses. The people could not bear it. We started this uprising to eliminate this harm for the people. Now things are settled. All residents should return to their professions and not use this as a pretext to make more trouble . . ."

For days the whole city was quiet. There were no people in the streets. On the fifth day, the circuit intendant issued an order to arrest all those responsible for starting the riot. A certain Ge Xian came forward and appeared before the officials. He said: "I started the riot. It would be enough to execute me. You should not involve other people because if you do it will start further rioting." The officials then stopped their investigation and simply tried Ge Xian. He was sentenced to be executed but later was pardoned and paroled. Thirty years later, Ge Xian was still living. When he was asked about the happenings of that time, he dodged the questions. Some said that the true instigator of the uprising was not Ge Xian. But the fact that he voluntarily submitted himself for trial to save the people was, itself, praiseworthy.

1.3 AND 1.4 A MING OFFICIAL ON THE DECLINE AND FALL OF THE DYNASTY

Song Yingxing (1600?–1646?) was a minor government official of the late Ming. He is known to history for his *Tiangong kaiwu*, an encyclopedic survey of the state of Chinese science and technology of the late Ming that was incorporated in part into the massive encyclopedia, the *Gujin tushu jicheng*, that was assembled during Kangxi's reign. The text translated here is a part of Song's 1636 work *Yeyi*, (Unofficial opinions), a long lost treatise that was rediscovered in manuscript form in Jiangxi province during the Cultural Revolution. The two selections below include Song's reflections on the troubled years that preceded the collapse of the Ming dynastic order and a comment on the crisis of late Ming financial management. The salt merchants described in the latter document were so burdened by new taxes and levies designed to support the costly military campaigns being waged against the bandits and Manchus in the north that once prosperous centers of salt production had fallen into financial ruin. It is worth noting Song Yingxing's characteristic use of parallelism to emphasize his points; in this and other pieces, translated from the literary Chinese of the late Ming or early Qing, the translation is intentionally literal to provide a sense of the organization of ideas and tone of the original document.

1.3 *The Trend of the World*

It is said: "When order is at its peak, chaos results; when chaos is at its peak, order results." This cycle of change follows the Heavenly mathematics of division and multiplication. After characters were invented and writing and cart axles were standardized, from the time of the Shang dynasty forward,[2] no dynasty other than our own has successfully created continuous order and stability for three hundred years. Presently, some people fear that winter cold is striking in midsummer. They are unaware that when chaos is at its peak, order is coming.

The disaster caused by the bandits in the northwest has already spread to the central plain.[3] Only the walled cities remain; no one knows how many villages, towns, and markets have been burned to the ground. Today, people are killed by bandit mobs; tomorrow, they may die at the hands of government troops. No one can tell how many fields have been left fallow by farmers fleeing disaster or in how many fields already-planted crops now wither under the sun. No one can count how many families have been broken apart or number the dead lying piled in ditches. Nobody can know how many walled cities have been invaded and then recovered or how many towns have been put to the torch and then rebuilt.

Those fortunate enough to live in the southeast continue to prosper, but the eyebrows of officials are knotted with concern and the foreheads of the people creased with worry. They are distressed by the bandits who are everywhere and by the scourge of flood and drought.[4] Nothing remains of the spirit of the times of Emperors Longjing [1567–1572] and Wanli [1573–1620]! But this instant, precisely when chaos is at its peak, foretells that order is coming. The affairs of the world can still be managed; do not be perplexed at the working of cosmic mathematics.

1.4 *On the Management of the Salt Gabelle*

Everyone needs to eat salt and there is great profit for the state in its administration.[5] Management fails when corruption appears and merchants are

---

2. Traditional Chinese historians believed that the standardization of written characters and cart axles occurred during the Shang instead of the Qin dynasty.

3. The rebellions of Li Zicheng and Zhang Xianzhong.

4. Here Song refers to the troubles that afflicted the north of China but which at the time he wrote had yet to affect the territories below the Yangzi River.

5. From Han times onward, a government monopoly over the production and sale of salt was an important source of revenue for the imperial state.

impoverished when management is disorderly. It is human nature to seek profit and even risk death rushing after it. Since there is profit in trading in salt, who will not exhaust himself in pursuit of it? Why is it that the same merchants who once amassed jade and gold, have today emptied their purses and piled up debts? This is because the merchants are poor and the management of salt [production, transport, and sale] is not functioning.

Half of the state's salt levy comes from the Huai region. The other half comes from Changlu, Xiechi, Liangzhe, the Sichuan wells, the Guangdong salt ponds, and the Fujian coast.[6] Although the tax levy for Changlu and other places has been increased, the merchants there can still manage to pay. But for the Huai region, an increase is unbearable. The Huai tax quota was originally 930,000 taels. Now it has been increased to one million five hundred. If salt management was as effective as it was in the times of the Chenghua [1465–1487] and Hongzhi [1488–1505] emperors and if the merchants were still as rich as they were during the reigns of Longqing and Wanli, then such an increase could be comfortably met.

The merchants with capital are primarily from Shaanxi, Shanxi, and Huizhou. During the most prosperous years of Wanli's reign, they controlled no less than thirty million taels in the Yangzhou region. Each year this capital could produce interest of nine million taels. One million taels were paid to the government and three million were used to cover the innumerable expenses related to salt production. There was enough money for both the public and private sectors. Monks, Daoist priests, beggars, and servants were benefited and bridge building projects and Buddhist monasteries also drew from the remaining five million taels. All merchants could fatten their families and themselves; their funds were inexhaustible. Presently we can only imagine how prosperous they must have been.

The decline of the merchants started at the beginning of the Tianqi era [1621–1627]. For the state, the conflagration set by the eunuchs blazed out of control; for merchants, misfortunes were brought by spendthrift sons; in various localities, profit-seeking bullies assembled; officials became increasingly corrupt; and clerks and runners devised new, wicked techniques [to extort funds]. All of these problems grew worse each day. Just as the merchants were about to maneuver their way out of their straits, the new tax levy order fell down upon them and they were afflicted by the bandit invasions. When they could not pay the tax, the merchant's family members were arrested to force them to pay. Presently, half of them are poor and in debt. Their entire assembled capital is no more than five million taels; how could such a sum produce enough interest to pay the state's quota? ... [The remaining portion of this essay provides a

6. The major sources of salt were salt fields along the coast, particularly the Huai River region in today's northern Jiangsu province (the Subei area) and inland salt mines in Sichuan and elsewhere.

detailed description of the vast array of miscellaneous taxes and duties on salt that had driven salt merchants to the brink of bankruptcy.]

1.5 BROADSHEET FROM LI ZICHENG

This rare broadsheet announced the advance of Li Zicheng's troops into Huangzhou. Its polemical analysis of the troubles of the late Ming era is an interesting match for the more measured description furnished by Song Yingxing. It is notable for its effort to reassure local officials and win them to the side of the rebels and its reassurance that the framework of professional life would remain the same. Its final line, however, makes it clear resistors will pay a heavy price.

For the calming and pacification of the people:
The fatuous and self-indulgent Emperor of the Ming dynasty was not humane. He spoiled his eunuchs, relied heavily on exam graduates, was greedy for taxes and levies, used harsh punishments, and could not save the people from calamities. Every day the army robbed the people of their wealth, raped their wives and daughters, and exploited everyone most harshly. Our army is made up of good peasants who have worked the fields for ten generations; we formed this humane and righteous army to rescue the people from destruction. We have pacified Chengtian and De'an [prefectures in Hubei] and now are personally approaching Huangzhou. Orders have been dispatched to notify scholars and commoners not to be alarmed. Each should quietly practice his profession. Any battalion that kills good people without permission will be executed to the last man. Those of you people who happily welcome our kingly divisions with horns and bugles will establish your merit and be rewarded with weighty positions. Others should not wear arms because it is hard to distinguish jade from stones. This is our announcement.

1.6 EVALUATION OF LI ZICHENG AND ZHANG XIANZHONG

The document cited below is apparently a citation from a court document that described the peasant rebellions of Li Zicheng and Zhang Xianzhong. The large armies mobilized by the Ming state to suppress rural rebellion in northern China, such as the armies of Yang Sichang (1588–1641), Song Yihe (?), and Zuo Liangyu (1598–1645), often had the opposite effect: the depredations worked by their troops added sympathizers to the rebel camp.

In 1643, the conflagration caused by Li Zicheng and Zhang Xianzhong became more serious. The Emperor frequently summoned government officials to ask their advice. Ma Shiqi made the following comment:

"Presently Li Zicheng and Zhang Xianzhong are both committing high treason. To control Zhang is easy but to control Li is difficult. This is because people fear Zhang Xianzhong while people are siding with Li Zicheng. They do not want to side with Li Zicheng but do so because of the suffering caused by the government's troops. The people first suffered from General Yang Sichang's army and could not defend their own cities. Then they suffered from General Song Yihe's army and could not protect their families or households. Next they suffered from General Zuo Liangyu's army and residents and travelers could not even defend their own lives. The bandits knew of the bitterness the people felt in their hearts and used the extermination of the army and the security of the people as slogans. For a time the foolish masses were deceived and surrendered. To consolidate support for themselves, the bandits began spreading wealth and helping the poor; they opened the granaries and gave food to relieve hunger. In the end, the people looked upon the bandits as their benefactors. Everyone forgot loyalty and righteousness.

"In fact, how was it possible for the bandits to capture so many cities and counties? It was because the counties willingly followed the bandits. Therefore, the best strategy at present is to win over the people's hearts again. Winning their hearts should begin with causing the governors and generals to control their troops. Order the army not to abuse the people and the people will not suffer from the army."

1.7–1.9 THREE ACCOUNTS OF ZHANG XIANZHONG

Zhang Xianzhong (1605–1647) was a peasant rebel who, unlike his contemporary Li Zecheng, made no pretense of having a social program. Like some of the worst warlords of the twentieth century, he ravaged the areas of north and northwestern China through which his armies passed. After holding off the Ming armies that were sent to suppress him, Zhang's rebellion was quelled by Qing armies after the foundation of the Manchu state in 1644.

The first two documents included here are colorful biographies by literati chroniclers who detested Zhang Xianzhong and were eager to gather folk recollections of his rebellion into damning accounts of his activities as a rebel commander. The third document purports to be a genuine "edict" by Zhang Xianzhong and evinces his cruel and veangeful treatment of prominent Ming families who opposed him.

took the name Daxi [The Great West] as the name of his state and his reign title was Dashun. He honored the deity Wenchang as his great ancestral progenitor.[11] He set up government offices and posts and a certain Fan was the valedictorian of the examination class. Zhang Xianzhong himself wrote an essay critically evaluating all previous emperors and kings and praised Xiang Yu as the greatest of them.[12] This essay was called: "The Emperor-Authored Ten Thousand Word Essay." He launched a great search to find all of the gentry scholars of Sichuan and brought them all to Chengdu and had them killed by slicing. He then again made an announcement of a new scholarly examination and scholars from far and near flocked to take it. When they arrived, Zhang Xianzhong attacked them with his army and some twenty-two thousand and three hundred would-be examination candidates died. Afterwards, a huge heap of brushes and inkstones were left behind. Zhang Xianzhong hated the people of Sichuan; he first slaughtered the people and then slaughtered the scholars. He even wanted to kill the Sichuanese who were soldiers in his army. Among his generals were many Sichuanese. One such commander was Liu Jinzhong; Zhang Xianzhong wanted to arrest him and kill his troops. The plan did not succeed because word leaked to a gate guard and when the army heard of it they all ran away. Thereupon, Zhang Xianzhong's generals were gone and his army was scattered. When the great [Qing] army came to Hanzhong, Liu Jinzhong joined them. When asked where Zhang Xianzhong was, Liu Jinzhong replied: "He is in Jinchuanpu of Shunqing." He guided them to Zhang Xianzhong's camp. Zhang fled and hid under some firewood. He was hit by a stray arrow and cried out. He was then dragged from his hiding place and beheaded. Some said that Zhang Xianzhong heard of Li Zicheng's fall and hid away and died of illness. This is a false tale.

1.8 A Colorful Early Qing Biography of the Bandit Leader Zhang Xianzhong

Zhang Xianzhong was from Fushi county, in Shaanxi Province. When he was a boy, he followed his father, who was a dealer in dates, to Neijiang in Sichuan. Their donkey was tied up to the pillar of a *paifang* [an ornamental archway erected to commemorate some exceptional deed] belonging to a gentry family. The donkey defecated on the stone pillar of the archway and a servant of the family cursed them and whipped Zhang Xianzhong's father. The servant then forced the father to remove the donkey shit with his own hands. Zhang

---

11. Wenchanggong was the guardian of literature honored within the pantheon of Chinese folk religion.

12. Xiang Yu was the military commander of the forces that overthrew the Qin state in the third century B.C. He called himself the "hegemon king of Western Chu" and this possibly inspired Zhang to imitate him.

Xianzhong was close by and, although he was enraged, dared not fight back. He vowed: "I will return and kill you all. Only then will my anger be appeased." Later, when he entered Sichuan, the whole population of Neijiang was wiped out.

On the tenth day of the first moon in 1644, the Bandit Xianzhong was slaughtering the population of Chengdu at the Hongshun Bridge outside of the East Gate. Just as his men's blades were poised and ready to strike, there were three claps of thunder. The Bandit pointed to Heaven and said in a fuming rage: "You allowed me to come into the world to kill people and now you dare to use thunder to scare me?!" He returned the attack of Heaven by firing three cannon shots into the sky. That day, there were so many bodies in the water of the river that they broke the supports of the Hongshun Bridge.

Previously, when Xianzhong entered the Huguang region to escape arrest, he led a group of five or six followers. At night he tried to steal a golden ornament on the top of the roof of the main temple of Wudanghsan [a Daoist retreat]. As he was climbing up, he saw the Daoist god Wang Lingguan holding a cudgel. He shouted at Zhang Xianzhong saying: "Go away! It is only because Heaven has sent you to collect lives that I do not kill you!" Because of this Zhang Xianzhong believed that he was "appointed by Heaven to kill" and put this motto on his banners and flags.

A certain Wang who was the unlawful magistrate of Jiajiang [serving under Zhang Xianzhong] presented to the Bandit a tribute of fresh lichee nuts that were cut open and marinated with salt. Zhang Xianzhong was furious about this and ordered his personal bodyguard Wang Ke to go to that county yamen to cut off the magistrate's head. After Wang Ke was dispatched, members of Zhang's entourage said: "That person [the magistrate] was just a hick. He doesn't know what he's doing. This crime is not a capital offense." Zhang Xianzhong said: "You're right!" He immediately sent an edict that read: "The Emperor who has been entrusted by Heaven with the care of the Empire orders: Wang Ke, come back. Let's spare the life of that turtle magistrate." This unlawful edict has been preserved and still exists.

In the twelfth moon of 1646, Prince Su [Haoge] of our [Qing] dynasty entered Sichuan to surpress Zhang Xianzhong. In a dense fog, Prince Su directly attacked Zhang's army. A Banner adjutant named Yabulan shot an arrow at Zhang Xianzhong and hit him in the throat. The Bandit rode off on his horse and the Adjutant Oboi came forward and captured him. As Prince Su enumerated his crimes, he was executed by slicing. His corpse was exposed before the gate of the garrison headquarters and men and women came to hack at it. It was soon reduced to ground-up meat. He was forty-one years old.

Some said that after Zhang Xianzhong was shot he pulled out the arrow and shouted: "I was born on Swallow Peak and I'm dying on Phoenix Mountain." He then fell over his arrow quiver and died. Poisonous shrubs and thornbushes grew up over the place he was buried. People who touched these plants got skin ulcers or sores. Sometimes a black tiger came out of these bushes to devour people. When the sky was dark or cloudy, nobody dared to go by this burying ground. Alas, can someone be so venomous and as harmful as this even after death? Some others said: "When the people cut up Xianzhong's body they discovered that his heart was as black as ink." Yet others said his heart was twisted to one side and he had no liver.

Zhang Xianzhong also took the name Jingxuan when he was given amnesty at Fang'gu. He loved to have friends. When he met someone he liked, he would drink with this person for a whole night. When his new friend left, Zhang Xianzhong would load him down with gifts but then send men after him to ambush him on his way home. He would have his new friend's head cut off and brought back and would keep it in a case. When he was drinking alone and felt unhappy, he would send for the case, saying: "Ask my good friend to come!" Then he would put the head on the table, raise his cup and drink as happily as though he was drinking with a living person. He called this: "Gathering heads for a party."[13]

There was a person named Zhang from Emei who was nearly killed by the bandit. His neck was cut but his head was not severed. He hid himself among a pile of bodies. When night fell and all was calm, he saw someone coming with people calling to clear the way before him. This person was very imposing and solemn; he looked like a prince or king. When he arrived, he ordered his clerks to bring the registers and called out the names of the dead. Each dead person who was called would stand up holding his own head. When all the names had been called they all left. Zhang was surprised that his name was not included. He rose and was told by the imposing figure's followers: "This is the Prefectural City God!" Subsequently, Zhang came to his senses and escaped at dawn. He was still living in 1721. A long scar was still clearly visible on his neck. People called him "Cut-neck Zhang." He had many children and grandchildren. Some of them even became scholars.

Zhang Xianzhong had a certain nephew who secreted himself among the Thirty Six Peaks of Kuan county. He was nicknamed "The Scarred Monk." When the world was again at peace he came out and traveled and described the past activities of the Bandit Zhang Xianzhong in great detail.

1.9   Edict of the Bandit Zhang Xianzhong

"Bandit Yang Sichang [a Ming minister of war] of the Zhu [the name of the imperial family] bandit gang, once deployed all of the troops of the empire and dared to resist our Heavenly army. It was Yang Sichang's good fortune to die early before I could take revenge. Now I am passing through Wuling and his household, his fields, his family tombs, are all here. That the Yangs do not come

---

13. The Chinese term *jushou huanyan* used here means "gathering people (heads) for a party." Zhang Xianzhong was making a sinister pun.

over to us and obey is already too much; but what is far worse is that they have joined together with local gentry, scholars, and commoners to form local militia groups throughout the region. It is, thus, most proper to order the execution of all the members of the Yang clan, the exhumation and demolition of the Yang ancestral tombs, and the incineration of all clan houses and buildings. All land occupied by the clan will be turned over to the poor. Anyone who captures a person with the surname Yang will be rewarded with ten silver taels. Those who capture a son, grandson, or brother of Yang Sichang will be rewarded with ten thousand taels. This order has been dispatched to the aforementioned prefecture."

1.10 SONG MAOCHENG: *THE TALE OF THE UNGRATEFUL LOVER*

This famous tale of love, treachery, and sacrificial vindication was first written in a literary Chinese version, heavily adorned with classical allusion and devices of poetic speech, during the Wanli era (1573–1620). The author, Song Maocheng, notes in the text that he first heard of the tragedy of the story's heroine, the courtesan Du Shiniang, from a friend in 1600. Subsequent retellings, including a more embroidered vernacular version by the celebrated writer Feng Menglong (1574–1646) entitled *The Courtesan's Jewel Box* continued to nourish the legend of Du Shiniang and gave her story an enduring fame in the popular culture of China.

At the heart of Du Shiniang's story are the themes of unwavering love and sincerity. Song Maocheng intentionally focuses on these qualities to construct a striking contrast between a feckless Confucian scholar and the courtesan. Scholar Li, after years of dissipation in Peking, is weak to the core. After a lifetime spent studying moralizing neo-Confucian texts in his unsuccessful pursuit of an examination title, Li is incapable of founding his life on any principle more elevated than self-interest. Du Shiniang, however, despite years spent in the courtesan quarter, radiates a natural understanding of morality and human relations. She devotes herself entirely to Scholar Li and even when she is, literally, "sold out" by him, she acts to protect his interests. Each of her actions, including her suicide, embodies elevated moral sentiments and Song Maocheng finally is obliged to classify her with the "chaste women" of the Han-era writer Liu Xiang's catalogue of model women.

For students of the late Ming, this story provides a trove of historical information. It speaks suggestively about the roles of women and men, gives a fascinating view of the quasi-official world of Peking and the city's gay quarter, and offers insight into contemporary ideals of love. But in the starkest way, it illustrates the helplessness of women, trapped in intolerable and amoral social frameworks, who yet sought to adhere to the moral standards of a Confucian society. The translation that follows is of the earliest version of the story.

During the Wanli era, a scholar named Li from eastern Zhejiang, who was the son of a provincial judicial chief, made a donation of funds and traveled to Beijing to study in the national academy.[14] He and the courtesan Du Shiniang fell deeply in love. They had a relationship for several years. Although Li's funds were depleted and the girl's 'mother' detested the frequent visits of the scholar, the friendship between the two grew even closer.[15] The girl was the most beautiful woman of her generation in the gay quarter. She also excelled as a musician, singer, and dancer. The young men of the capital all sought her out to pass their leisure moments. Du Shiniang's 'mother' was disturbed by Li's constant presence and tried to provoke him with her scolding. When Li was as humble and prudent as before, the 'mother' treated him even more harshly. The young courtesan could not endure this humiliation and vowed to marry Scholar Li.

The 'mother' considered that since the girl was not her own daughter she could go. But the convention of the gay quarter was that when a courtesan sought to leave a payment of several hundred silver taels was necessary. The 'mother' was clearly aware that Li had no money and so she conceived of a way to corner him. She sought to shame him and leave him with no means to protest so that he would gradually forget about taking Du away. And so she gestured with her hand at her 'daughter' and scolded her, saying: 'If you can urge the young gentleman to gather three hundred taels and give them to me, I will let you go wherever you please.' The young girl readily consented and replied: 'Although Scholar Li is impoverished because of his travels, it should not be difficult for him to get three hundred taels. But the money cannot be easily assembled. What will happen if the money is prepared and you break the agreement?' The mother knew that Scholar Li was poor and so she baited him by pointing laughingly at a flickering candle flame and said: 'If Scholar Li can get the money, you can go with him. The flickering candle is an omen that he will succeed in winning you.' And so, after making their agreement, they parted company.

In the middle of the night the girl cried piteously and said to Scholar Li: 'I know that you are so far away from your home that your funds are insufficient to buy my freedom. Would it be possible to receive some aid from your relatives

14. During the Ming and Qing periods, young scholars could purchase titles through "donations" and qualify for study in the national academy, a preparatory school for higher examination degrees or government offices, located in Peking.

15. The 'mother' referred to here is the madam who controlled the group of courtesans to which Du Shiniang belonged.

or friends in this emergency?' Li was surprised by the suggestion and replied: 'Oh yes, yes. I have always had this intention but did not dare to say so.' The next day, he pretended to pack his belongings to start for home and, in the meantime, begged for loans from all of his friends and relatives [in the capital]. His intimates all knew that he had been deeply involved in the life of the gay quarter for years and doubted the sincerity of his intention to travel southward. Furthermore, Scholar Li's father was angry about his son's floating life style and wrote letters to halt his return home. If loans were supplied to him they would purchase no virtue and there would be no way for them to be repaid. All those in his circle found excuses to refuse him. This went on for over one month and finally he returned with empty hands.

During the night, the courtesan sighed and said: 'And so you were finally unable to obtain any funds? There are one hundred and fifty silver taels hidden in my mattress. I hid them in the cotton ticking along the seam. Tomorrow ask a servant to take the money and secretly bring it to you. Then pay it to 'mother.' Besides this, there is nothing I can do.' The scholar was surprised and happy. He carefully arranged for the mattress to be removed. Next he took the money out of the mattress and told his friends and relatives. They sympathized with Du Shiniang's sincere intentions and all of them generously provided the scholar with funds. But the total was only one hundred taels. The scholar wept as he told the girl: 'I have exhausted my resources. Where can I get another fifty taels?' The girl jumped up gleefully and said: 'Do not worry. Tomorrow I will make arrangements with my "sisters".' The next day she obtained the fifty taels. They assembled the money and presented it to the 'mother.' The 'mother' wanted to break the agreement, but the girl cried piteously before her and said: 'In the past you demanded three hundred taels from the young gentleman. Now the money is ready but you are breaking your word. He can take the money back but I am going to die.' The 'mother' was afraid that she would lose the money and the girl and so she said: 'I will do as I agreed. You may go, but you must leave every stitch of your clothing and your jewelry behind. None of this is yours.' The girl happily agreed.

The next day, wearing cotton clothing and with no ornaments in her hair, Du Shiniang left following the young scholar. When she went to bid farewell to all of her 'sisters' in the house, they were moved to tears and said: 'Shiniang was the leading talent of the time. Now she is following her man and leaving this place in rags. Does this not shame us "sisters"?' Thereupon, they made a present to her of what they had and in a short time she was wearing entirely new hairpins, rings, clothing, and jewelry. The sisters said: 'The young gentleman and our sister are going on a long journey of one thousand li [1 li = ⅓ mile] and you have no luggage tied up for your travels. All of us would like to give you a box as a gift.' The young scholar did not know what was in the box and the girl also seemed not to know. At dusk that evening the 'sisters' tearfully bid adieu to Du Shiniang and the girl went to the scholar's lodging place. The four walls were utterly bare and the scholar was merely able to stare before him at his desk. The girl unraveled her long left silk sleeve and threw down twenty silver taels and said: 'Use this for our travel expenses.' The next day, the scholar made arrangements to obtain a carriage and horse and they left through the Chongwen Gate. When they arrived at Luhe, they boarded a postal boat, but by now their money was already exhausted. Du Shiniang then unraveled her right silk sleeve and produced thirty silver taels. She said: 'We can buy our food with this.'

The scholar felt happy and fortunate about his frequent and unforeseen good fortune. As they traveled, autumn changed to winter. They laughed at the lone wild goose in the sky and the fish who did not swim in pairs. They vowed to live together until their hair turned as white as the autumn frost. Their ardent hearts were as red as the blazing foliage of the maple. We can guess how happy they were!

When they reached Guazhou, they left the postal boat and rented a small junk with the intention of crossing the [Yangzi] river the next day. That night the moon was like a jade *bi* [a flat, round, ceremonial jade object with a hole in its center] flashing in the water of the river. It was like flying silk or writing on a mirror. The scholar said to the girl: 'Since departing the capital, we have not wanted others to notice us. Tonight we have our own boat, what is there to fear? Moreover, the water and moon of Jiangnan is different from the wind and the dust of the north. How can we be silent?' The girl, too, had hid herself and her traces for a long time. She felt the sadness of the long passage through passes and mountains and was moved by the mingling of the river and moon. She and the young scholar linked their hands in the moonlight and sat in the bow of the boat. The scholar was in high spirits and he raised his wine cup; the comely girl sang a pure song to recompense somewhat the beauty of the river and moon. The girl's song swirled and lingered in the night air; even the cry of birds or the call of monkeys could not evoke so melancholy a feeling.

On a nearby boat was a young man who was a salt merchant in Yangzhou. He was returning at the end of the year to his native place in Xin'an [Huizhou]. He was about twenty years old and was a champion heartbreaker in the gay quarter. As he was drinking he heard this song and his emotions soared. But then the melody ceased and he was unable to rest that night. At dawn, a snowstorm suspended all crossing of the river. The Xin'an man searched for the scholar's boat and knew that there must be a great beauty aboard it. He put on a cap with mink tassels and a fur coat and paid great attention to his appearance. He glimpsed something and began to sing to attract attention. The scholar pushed open the window of his boat. The snow was still and cold. The Xin'an man called to the young scholar in a friendly way and arranged to meet with him on the bank.

The two went to a wine house and talked. After they were a bit tipsy, the Xin'an man asked who sang the pure song he had heard the night before. The scholar told him the truth. The Xin'an man then asked: 'Are you crossing the river to return to your native place?' The scholar sadly told him the reason he could not return home. The beauty would travel with him among the mountains and rivers of the Wu and Yue regions. They drank cup after cup of wine and the scholar disclosed his whole history. The Xin'an man sadly said to the young scholar: 'You are traveling with a gorgeous orchid. Haven't you heard it said that when a beautiful pearl is cast down on the road all the mighty and powerful come to contend for it? Moreover, the people in Jianghan are most skilled in flirtation. When they feel affection for someone they will do anything for love. Even I, your humble friend, have the sprouts of such feeling in my heart. Is it not possible that someone so talented as your beautiful lady, who has behaved so unexpectedly in the past, might not in the future use you as a gangplank? Might she not secretly make some other agreement in the future? If this were to happen, the misty waves of Zhenzhe, the billows of Qiantang, the bellies of fish and the teeth of whales would be your tomb. I, your foolish friend, have also heard it asked: "Is a father or a woman more important?" and "Is present pleasure or future harm to yourself a more serious concern?" I hope you can give all of this some deep thought.'

The scholar then frowned and said: 'What can I do?' The Xin'an man replied: 'Your stupid friend has an excellent plan that will benefit you but I am afraid you cannot carry it out.' The young scholar said: 'What is the plan?' The Xin'an man answered: 'If you really cut off the remaining love you feel, I your humble servant, although I am not quick, am willing to give you one thousand taels for your health and long life. You can take this one thousand taels and return home to present it to your esteemed father. If you desert the beauty, you will have nothing to fear on your journey home. I sincerely hope you will give this careful thought.' The scholar had led a solitary and floating existence for years. Although he and the girl had sworn to live forever, like a pair of mandarin ducks or the entwined roots of a tree, a leisurely and comfortable existence was impossible. There was no way to achieve it. He began to feel doubt and to think about the destructive and notorious beauties of history. He became more depressed and felt as though he was crying in a dream. The young scholar lowered his head and seemed lost in thought. Then, he excused himself and said that he wanted to return to discuss all of this with his woman. He and the Xin'an man returned hand in hand to the riverfront and boarded their own boats.

The girl had lit the lamp and was waiting for the scholar to return so that they could drink wine together. The scholar's eyes moved back and forth but his mouth was dry. He was unable to say what was on his mind. Finally they went to bed and held each other tightly through the night. In the middle of the night, the scholar began sobbing. The girl quickly sat up and embraced him and said: 'We have been in love for almost three years and have traveled several thousand Li together but I have never seen you so sad. Now we are about to cross the river; we should feel happy that we will soon be tied together forever. Why are you suddenly so sad. I don't understand it. There seems to be a tone of parting in your voice. What is it?' The scholar spoke through his tears. Although his sadness was overwhelming, he finally told her whole story and wept as before. Du Shiniang released him from her embrace and said: 'Who made this plan for you? This person is a great hero! You will receive one thousand taels which you can present to your parents. I will have another man to follow and we will be unencumbered. This plan is inspired by feeling and will lead to propriety and righteousness. How brilliant! We both obtain something from it! Where is the money?' The scholar replied that because he did not know the lady's intention, the money was still in the other man's traveling chest. The girl said: 'Go over early tomorrow morning and make the agreement with him. But one thousand silver taels is a large sum. I will not go to that man's boat until the money is safely in your luggage.'

It was already past midnight. The girl asked leave to rise and put on her most lavish make-up. She said: 'I should expend great efforts on my attire and make-up today since I shall say good-bye to an old love and meet my new gentleman.' By the time she finished with her make-up, it was already dawn. The Xin'an man had previously brought his boat to the side of the Scholar Li to give it to him. Then the Xin'an man was asked to pass the wedding price to the other boat. The sum was counted and it was correct.

Thereupon, the girl stepped out of the cabin and her boat and, holding onto the gunnels, said to the Xin'an man: 'Scholar Li's travel pass is inside the make-up case we have just passed over. Please return it to us to that we can find it.' The Xin'an man hastily did as he was told. The girl then asked Scholar Li to remove one drawer. Inside it were lovely clothes made of emerald colored feathers; she took them and threw them into the water. Their value was several hundred silver taels. Scholar Li, the champion heartbreaker, and all of the boatmen of both boats were greatly surprised. She then asked the Scholar to pull out another drawer. It was full with ornaments, jewelry and jade, and golden musical instruments. It was worth several thousand taels. She again threw everything into the river. She then asked the Scholar to remove a leather purse from the case. In it were antique jade pieces and ancient gold objects. There were articles rarely to be seen in the whole world. Their value was immeasurable. The objects, too, she threw into the river. Finally, she asked the scholar to pull out another box. It was full of the finest 'night-glowing' pearls. Everyone on the boat was alarmed and the hubbub caused a crowd of people to gather on the bank. The girl again began emptying everything into the river.

Scholar Li began to feel greatly regretful. He embraced the girl and, crying loudly, tried to restrain her. Even the Xin'an man came over to try to persuade her to stop. The girl pushed the Scholar to the side. She spat on the Xin'an man and cursed him: 'You heard a song that moved you and then started flicking your tongue like a parrot. You did not care about destroying our love.[16] You will cause my bones to be stained with my pure blood. I regret that I am not stronger so that I could use a knife to kill so vulgar a person as you. With your greed for money, you tried to force me into your embrace. How are you different from a mad dog? A moment ago you came running up like the wind and wanted to seize me. When I die, my spirit will accuse you before the gods of hell and they will take your life and your human form. I used every device to hide my property and entrusted it to my 'sisters.' They secretly stored all of those precious objects for me. I was going to use these things to help Scholar Li return home to see his parents. The reason I am now no longer keeping them and have thrown them away is to let people know that Scholar Li has no eyes in his sockets! I have cried so many tears for Scholar Li that my eyes are nearly dry. I have been driven to distraction for him. Our marriage was almost completed when he forgot our relationship. He was afraid that his shoes would be stained by the morning dew. In a single moment, I am abandoned: I am less significant than scraps and leftover gravy! But now he is greedy for the leftovers and wants to collect the spilt water. How can I have face if I let him lead me by the nose again? This life is over. The sands of the Eastern Sea glisten, the millet of Western China grows over the ruins. My sorrow twists and coils around me and is unending!'

Everyone on the bank and on the boats was crying. They cursed Scholar Li as an ungrateful lover. But holding the last pearls, the girl threw herself into the river and was drowned. At that moment, all of the bystanders wanted to beat the Xin'an man and Scholar Li. Scholar Li and the Xin'an man hurriedly departed in their boats and no one knows where they went.

Alas, such a woman would not be shamed to appear before the model women described by Liu Xiang![17] Even the chastity of those women living deep in women's quarters can not exceed hers.

16. There is a reference here to an obscure story mentioned in a folk song of the Period of Disunion and a poem by Bai Juyi. The story tells of a young girl who could not marry the man of her choice because of his parents' opposition. They finally agreed that if she could draw water from a well with a silver bottle attached to a silk thread she could marry their son. The thread broke, hence the figure of speech *jiangeng loping* [breaking the thread and dropping the bottle], and the marriage plan failed.

17. This is a reference to a Han classic by Liu Xiang, the *Lienuzhuan* (Biographies of model women), which contains descriptions of the lives of paragons of Confucian virtue.

CHAPTER 2

The Manchu Conquest

2.1 NURHACI'S SEVEN GRIEVANCES

Nurhaci (1559–1626), the founder of the banner system and unifier of the Manchu people, issued these grievances against the Ming state in 1618. The grievances constituted a Manchu declaration of war on China and shortly after they were delivered to Peking the first skirmishes between Manchu armies and Ming forces began. One year later, in 1619, in a pitched battle with Ming border garrisons specially raised to defeat them, Manchu troops crushed General Yang Hao's army at Sarhu. The Manchu invasion of China was now clearly underway.

The text of the Seven Grievances translated here comes from a 1630 edict by Nurhaci's son Huang Taiji (Abahai, 1592–1643) that recalled the circumstances that lay behind his father's decision to revolt against his Ming overlords. According to Meng Sen, one of twentieth-century China's major specialists on the history of the early Qing period, this version of the Grievances contains the most reliable version of its text. Later transcriptions, including a version that appeared in the *Veritable Records* of the Qing dynasty, were doctored by court archivists intent on stressing Nurhaci's desire to be loyal to the Ming throne and to temper the blunt language of the original.

By order of the Khan of the Jin kingdom, let it be known to all officials, soldiers, and commoners:

Since the time of our ancestors, we have overseen the border region for the great Ming dynasty and for many years have shown our loyalty and obedience. Because the emperor of the southern dynasty [the Ming] inhabits the deep recesses of his palace, he is cheated and deceived by civil and military officials of the border regions and has created no policy to comfort the people. He uses power in devious ways; his strength is exerted to the ultimate degree and all possible profit is scraped off. The insults, invasions, damage, and suffering that have resulted are indescribable! Among these abuses of power, seven are most atrocious.

Our ancestors always guarded the border region and paid tribute to the southern dynasty. They were for a long period loyal and obedient to the court. Suddenly, during the Wanli reign, two of our ancestors were arrested and executed without being convicted of any crime. This is the first grievance.

In the Guisi year [1593], nine tribes, including the Nanguan, Beiguan [the Yehe], Huipa, Wula, the Mongols, and others, gathered troops to attack us. The southern dynasty did not stand with us and paid no attention. They sat watching with their hands in their sleeves. It was only owing to heaven that we defeated all of these tribes. Later our state sought revenge and attacked and defeated the Nanguan. We moved into their inner territory and took Wuerhuda of the Nanguan as our son-in-law. The southern dynasty blamed us for this invasion and ordered us to send him back. We immediately followed this order and restored him to his domain. Later when the Beiguan attacked the Nanguan, the southern dynasty did not blame them for their destruction and looting. Although our state and Beiguan are equal tribal states we were treated differently when we acted in the same way. How can we take comfort from this? This is the second grievance.

Our Khan's [Nurhaci] loyalty to the great Ming was as firm as metal or stone. Because of the slaughter of his two esteemed relatives, he feared that the Ming doubted him. The late Khan joined with Wu Xihan, Deputy Commander of Liaoyang, in the slaughter of horses and oxen and offered sacrifices to heaven and earth. They erected a tablet on the border with this inscription: "Han people who go beyond this border without permission will be killed." Later, Han people living in the border region crossed this line without permission to dig for and gather ginseng. Since our livelihood comes from such natural wealth, we reported this repeatedly to superior officials but our reports were unheeded. Although we had a grievance, there was no channel for expressing our accusation. We were then forced to follow the rules established by the inscription and began to kill and harm violators. We sought to confirm our sworn oath and stop future [violations]; we did not want to betray our original agreement. When the new [Chinese] governor took office, we followed precedent and sought to express our humble greeting. Ganguli, Fangjinna, and others were sent to show our homage. At this time the [Han] superior officials did not attempt to determine [character missing] the responsibility for the border incidents. To the contrary, they arrested those who had come to the ceremony and demanded ten barbarian [Manchu] lives in revenge. How could anyone bear such an insult? This is the third grievance.

Beiguan and Jianzhou [Manchu tribes] are both subordinate barbarian

1.7 The Career of Zhang Xianzhong

Zhang Xianzhong came from Fushi county in Shaanxi Province.[7] He was wicked and shrewd. Both his father, Zhang Kuai, who practiced a debased profession, and his mother, née Shen, died at an early age. Zhang Xianzhong became the ward of a beggar named Big Xu. Once he stole a neighbor's chicken. By chance he was seen and was scolded. Zhang Xianzhong replied: "If I have my way, all here will be killed like chickens!" His cruel nature had already sprouted in childhood. When he grew up, he became a hoodlum. When the roving bandit Wang Jiayin rebelled, Zhang Xianzhong joined him and called himself "the Eighth Great King" or "the Yellow Tiger."

In 1631, he was given amnesty and was enlisted into the Ming army by Governor General Hong Chengchou.[8] The next year he mutinied and plundered territories from Henan to Jiangbei. He then moved into the Chu region [Huguang or today's Hunan and Hubei]. There, he was given amnesty again by Superintendent Xiong Wencan.[9] Soon he rebelled again and joined with other bandits like Luo Rucai. The Bandit Pacifying General Zuo Liangyu defeated him and so Zhang fled into Sichuan. Then he moved to Xiangyuan and burned the prefectural capital. He captured a [Ming] Prince [Zhu Yiming] there and seated him in his reception hall; Zhang Xianzhong urged the Prince to drink a cup of wine and then had him bound and killed.[10] Not long after this, Luo Rucai clashed with Zhang Xianzhong and went to join Li Zicheng. Zhang Xianzhong himself left for Yunxi and gained much plunder there. His ant-like mob of adherents now numbered several hundred thousand. Zuo Liangyu again brought troops to attack him and Zhang Xianzhong was defeated and fled. Owing to Luo Rucai's intercession on his behalf, Zhang was able to

7. This is the region where the Chinese Communist Party built its headquarters after the Long March in 1935.

8. Hong Chengchou (1593–1665) was later charged with the defense of north and northeastern China. He surrendered to the Manchus in 1642 and became a general under the Qing.

9. Xiong Wencan (d. 1640) was a high military commander later executed for military failures by the last Ming emperor.

10. Another source, Zha Jizuo's *Zuiweilu*, contains a more detailed version of this story: "Xianzhong sat proudly in the palace of Prince Xiang and had the Prince prostrate himself before him. He presented him with a cup of wine and said: 'I want to borrow your head to kill Yang Sichang. Please drink up.' His intention was that the Army Commander-in-Chief [Yang] would be executed for losing an Imperial Prince. The Prince was tied up and killed and his body was thrown into a well. It happened that Henan had also fallen into the hands of Li Zicheng at this time and Prince Fu was killed there. For losing these two imperial relatives, Yang Sichang felt that a grim fate was inescapable, and hanged himself. These events occurred exactly as Zhang Xianzhong had calculated."

flee to Li Zicheng. Li was very powerful and wanted to subdue Zhang Xian-zhong but he refused to be Li's subordinate. Li Zicheng was angered and wanted to kill him but Luo Rucai secretly provided Zhang with five hundred cavalrymen and provisions and told him to go. Because of this, Zhang Xian-zhong was able to dash to the east and join another group of bandits. They sacked Bozhou, Luzhou, Liuhe, and other localities. In all of these places, they cut off the left arms of the men and the right arms of the women. He [Zhang] then entered southern Zhili and [Ming] Commanders Huang Degong and Liu Liangzuo repeatedly defeated him. Zhang Xianzhong then went westward into the Cuh region and Huang and Liu turned back. Zhang then followed the Yangtze River upstream and sacked Hanyang and approached Wuchang. On the fifth day of the first Moon of 1642, he captured Prince Chu [in Wuchang] and stole a palace treasure worth several million taels. The bandit army's carts and horses were insufficient to carry it all away. Previously, when the Prince had been asked by the Provincial Secretary of Revenue for a loan to support the [Ming] army, he had refused. Now the people of Chu hated the Prince for his stupidity. The Bandit put the Prince in a bamboo cage and sank it in West Lake. He slaughtered several million people [sic] and floating corpses covered the river.

Zhang Xianzhong occupied the Prince's palace [in Wuchang] and took the title "King of the West." He set up a spurious system of Six Boards and Five Prefectural Offices and initiated an examination system to select officials for the appointment to prefectural and county offices. Later he occupied the entire Chu region and tore down the palace of Prince Gui and moved it to Changsha and built an illegitimate imperial palace for himself. He also dispatched troops to capture part of Jiangxi but these territories were later captured back by Zuo Liangyu. Zhang Xianzhong then abandoned Changsha and retreated into Sichuan.

He captured the Fotu Pass and sacked Chongqing. The whole family of Prince Rui was killed. He arrested more than ten thousand able-bodied men and sliced off their ears and noses and cut off one hand. They were then driven to various surrounding counties to announce this policy. If the local people did not surrender when Zhang Xianzhong's troops arrived, this same order would be applied. This threw the people and officials of all of these counties into disarray.

By the tenth moon of 1644, Zhang Xianzhong had completed his plundering and slaughter in Hunan and so he advanced and sacked Chengdu. Prince Shu and all of his retainers committed suicide by throwing themselves into wells. Governor Long Wenguang resisted but his troops were defeated and he was killed. When Zhang Xianzhong entered Sichuan he wanted to kill all of its people. Sun Kewang admonished him not to do so and so he was restrained but, even so, only one or two out of every ten Sichuanese survived. . . .

On the sixteenth day of the eleventh Moon of 1644, Zhang illegitimately enthroned himself and renamed Chengdu the Western Capital [Xijing]. He groups; when our two houses clash, the southern dynasty should seek to resolve the issue fairly. Why should it send troops and firearms to Beiguan to help them resist us? This partiality is surely hurtful! This is the fourth grievance.

An old crone of the Beiguan tribe was betrothed to our late Khan and we sent our bridal presents to them. Later the engagement was broken by the Beiguan and the marriage did not take place. Because of this, they would not have dared to permit her to marry for some time. With the support of the southern dynasty, however, she was married to a Mongol. Who could stand such a humiliation? This is the fifth grievance.

The people of our tribe who have guarded the border for over two hundred years have always lived in the border region. Later the Ming listened to the slanders of the Beiguan and sent troops to force our tribe to retreat ten miles from the border. They erected a tablet, occupied this land, burned down our peoples' houses and left the crops to rot [character missing] in the fields. Our people had no food nor lodging and were left there to die. This is the sixth grievance.

Our state was always obedient and never acted out of turn. Suddenly, the Censor Xiao Bozhi was sent [to the Manchu court] wearing court garb and jade belt. He showed his authority overbearingly; his language was crude and filthy and he insulted us in hundreds of ways. Our [character missing] officials could not endure this poisonous behavior! This is the seventh grievance.

There was no means of reporting these seven grievances. The superior officials of Liaodong were like gods and addressing the Wanli Emperor was like trying to reach heaven. He [Nurhaci] hesitated and could think of no other method than report it to heaven. He revolted and captured Fushun in the hope that the Wan Li Emperor would seek to know the details of this matter and redress his [Nurhaci's] feelings of being wronged. Subsequently, he drew up a detailed list of seven grievances and circulated them among merchants of various provinces. He waited expectantly but received no reply.

...Now we are again letting this be known. We do not fear repeating in order to clearly tell the reason for our uprising and to show clearly the meaning of our acceptance of Heaven's Mandate. We fear that the people of the world are unaware of our reasons and blame us for being wild and presumptuous. Therefore, we make this announcement and let it be known to all.

2.2 AND 2.3 EXCHANGE OF LETTERS BETWEEN WU SANGUI AND DORGON

Both of these letters were reprinted in the *Qing Veritable Records*, a collection of documents concerning the reign just past, compiled at the beginning of the new Manchu dynasty. In 1627, Abahai ordered a compilation of a *Veritable Record* for the reign of Nurhaci and this precedent was followed throughout the Qing. The finished manuscript of this internal history (the *Veritable Records* were published for the first time in 1936) was then sent to the emperor for review and was regarded by successive emperors, for reasons of filiality and politics, as an important state record. Often, revisions were demanded and it is known that the early volumes, regarding the Nurhaci and Abahai periods, were revised at least three times.

The two letters translated here concern a critical turning point in the history of modern China. On April 25, 1644, Li Zicheng's army captured Peking and the last Ming emperor committed suicide in the garden next to the Forbidden City. The loss of the imperial capital threw the commanders of Ming armies still in the field into a quandary: should they remain loyal to the throne or take their armies over to the side of one of the rebellious groups opposing the central government?

For Wu Sangui (1612–1678), the commander of the most powerful Ming army still in existence, the Shanhaiguan garrison that blocked the Manchus' southern advance, the dilemma was particularly acute. He was probably wooed by both Li Zicheng and the Manchu commander Prince Dorgon (1612–1650). As these negotiations progressed, his father and his favorite concubine were held hostage by Li's army in Peking. Finally, Wu decided to accept the Manchu offer of generalship in their army and marched with the banner forces on Peking. The combined armies of Prince Dorgon and Wu Sangui met and defeated Li Zicheng's army in a huge battle near Shanhaiguan in May 1644 and by early June the capital was in Manchu hands.

In this momentous spring of 1644, both Wu and Dorgon were anxious to cement an alliance: For Wu the stake was self-preservation and the continued existence of his army; for Dorgon, it was the conquest of China. Wu Sangui's decision to join the Manchus was possibly taken because of the excellent treatment received by other former Ming generals, like Hong Chengchou, who changed sides; it has also been speculated (in popular histories) that Wu's decision not to surrender to Li Zicheng was influenced by the fact that Li's lieutenant had seized Wu's beloved concubine.

While gaps in the historical record will perhaps forever hide the full reasons for Wu Sangui's defection, it is certain that joining the Manchus improved both his immediate and future prospects and the two documents translated below provide a reliable sense of the quality of the negotiations that brought the two sides together. After the formation of the Qing state, Wu continued to lead his army in battles with Ming pretenders and other foes of the new central government. As a reward for his services, he was given the title "The Great General who Pacifies the West" in 1657 and

was ultimately permitted to rule Sichuan and Guizhou, until his clash
with Kangxi in the 1670s.

2.2 A Letter from Wu Sangui to Dorgon Sent from Shanhaiguan, Renshen Day, 4th Moon, 1644

Since I, Wu Sangui, was first selected and promoted by the late Emperor to
shoulder, with my insignificant, mosquito-like body, the heavy duty of serving
as Chief Commander of the Liaodong garrison, I have deeply admired your
majesty's power and prestige; but the historical ideal of righteousness cannot be
applied across borders and, therefore, I never dared to present my name to you.

   This was simply the appropriate behavior of a subject and I presume your
majesty understands this. Presently, our state, because of the isolation of the
Ningyuan area, has ordered Sangui to desert Ningyuan and garrison the Shanhaiguan. The purpose of this order was to defend the eastern border and consolidate the defenses of the capital. Who could guess that roving bandits would
commit treason against Heaven and attack the gates of the capital itself? How
could such a mob of dog thieves accomplish anything? But the minds of the
people of the capital wavered; treasonous parties opened the gates and presented
tribute. Our late Emperor came to an unfortunate end and the nine temples
were left in ashes! Now the bandit chief has usurped the exalted title [of
emperor]. He and his men rashly seize women and plunder; they are guilty of
the most heinous crimes. They are like the Red Eyebrows, the Greenwood
Bandits, Huang Chao, and An Lushan [all bandit leaders or usurpers of antiq-
uity]. Heaven and the people are all outraged and have withdrawn their support.
Their fall [Li Zicheng's fall] is imminent.

   Our state cultivated virtue and benevolence; praiseful thoughts remain in the
people's minds. The imperial relatives in various provinces, like Duke Wen of
Jin or Emperor Guangwu of Han, are likely to start a restoration movement.
Far and near righteous armies have risen up and military dispatches are flying.
To the left of the [Taihang] mountains and north of the [Yangzi] river, these
armies are as numerous as the stars. I, Sangui, have received great grace from
our country and feel deep compassion for the people who are suffering from
this calamity. Though I defend this border gate [Shanhaiguan], I wish to launch
a punitive expedition to comfort the people. But the garrison area east of the
capital is small and my army is not well assembled and so, crying tears of blood,
I implore your aid.

   Our country has had good relations with your northern dynasty for more
than two hundred years. Now, for no reason, we face this national catastrophe.
Your northern dynasty should consider our plight with compassion. Moreover,
these mutinous officials and bandits also cannot be tolerated by your northern

dynasty. To be rid of this violent evil will be greatly favorable to you. To rescue others from danger and support them is a great act of righteousness. To save the people from water and fire is a great act of benevolence. To raise what has perished and continue what has ended is to win great fame. To obtain authority and establish hegemony is to win a great success. Moreover, it is impossible to calculate how much wealth or the number of women the roving bandits have already accumulated; when your righteous army arrives all this will be yours and this shall be a great profit. As the world's greatest hero, your majesty has this opportunity to rip down what is withered and rotten: certainly there will never be a second chance!

I beg you to consider the loyal and righteous words of this solitary official of a destroyed kingdom and immediately summon crack troops to enter the central and western zones. I, Sangui, will lead my command to arrive at the gates of the capital. We can then destroy the roving bandits who have taken the court and make manifest great righteousness in China. Then will our dynasty repay your northern dynasty merely with wealth? We will give land as a reward and absolutely shall never betray our word. I should have sent this letter to the Emperor of the northern dynasty, but since I do not understand the rites of the northern dynasty, I dare not lightly insult his sagely wisdom. I beg that your majesty will convey this memorial.

2.3 Dorgon's Reply to Wu Sangui Sent from Xilatala, Guiyu Day, 4th Moon, 1644

We always wanted to cultivate a good relationship with the Ming and often sent you letters; however, the Emperor and officials of the Ming did not consider the chaos afflicting the state or the death of its troops and people and you never replied. Therefore, on three occasions our state launched campaigns to show your officials, troops, and common people that we wanted the Ming Emperor to make careful plans and befriend us. We shall do this no longer. We seek only to pacify the nation and give the people rest. When I heard that roving bandits attacked and captured the capital and that the Ming Emperor met a miserable end, I was unbearably angry! Hence, I am leading a righteous and compassionate army and, having "sunk my boats and broken my woks" [burned my bridges behind me], swear that I will not turn my battle standards until I have crushed the bandits and rescued the people from this disaster.

When your excellence dispatched an envoy with your letter, I was enormously happy and, therefore, am leading my army forward. Your excellence thought to repay your [Ming] lord's graciousness toward you and refused to share the same sky with the roving bandits. This is certainly the righteousness of a loyal subject! Although your excellence has always garrisoned Liaodong and was our enemy, there is now no reason for former suspicions. In ancient times, Guan

Zhong fired an arrow at Duke Huan that struck his buckler. Later, Duke Huan used Guan Zhong as a chief advisor to win hegemony. If your excellency is willing to lead your troops to us, we will enfeoff you with a domain and ennoble you as a prince. Your state will then be avenged and you and your family will be protected. Your posterity will enjoy wealth and nobility as eternal as the mountains and rivers.

2.4 A LETTER FROM DORGON TO THE MING LOYALIST SHI KEFA, 6TH MOON, 1644

Shi Kefa (1602–1645) was a leading civil official during the Ming-Qing transition period and a martyr for the cause of Ming loyalism. In 1643, he was appointed the minister of war in Nanjing and was, thus, in a key position to coordinate future resistance to the Manchus south of the Yangzi.

In 1421, when the official capital was moved to Peking, Nanjing became China's "supplementary capital" and retained in duplicate form all of the institutions of the central government. Normally, the boards and other Nanjing bureaucratic organizations had little or no real power. However, after the fall of Peking to Li Zicheng, as many imperial relatives and former Ming officials fled to Nanjing, the city became the first center of southern Ming resistance to the Manchus.

After an abortive attempt to help in the defense of Peking, Shi Kefa participated in the selection of a new emperor. His candidate for the throne was the prince of Lu (Zhu Yihai) but Ma Shiying, a powerful official of the Nanjing court, succeeded in shifting the choice to the ineffectual prince of Fu.

Subsequently, Shi Kefa was appointed commander of the Yangzhou garrison and participated in the defense of the city against Dorgon's troops in 1645. As this letter shows, the Manchu leader was eager to use the example of Wu Sangui, now the "Pacifying King of the West," and promises of position and rewards to win Shi Kefa to the side of the banners. These offers, however, were refused and the Ming garrison of Yangzhou gallantly resisted the Manchu invaders. Following the siege, Shi Kefa was taken prisoner by the Manchu forces and was executed for his unwavering loyalty to the Ming cause.

"When I was formerly in Shenyang, I was aware that your excellency was one of the most esteemed officials of Peking. Later, when I crossed the Great Wall to destroy the bandits and had contact with people in the capital, I came to know your younger brother. I asked him to send you a letter of greeting and affection and am unsure whether the letter reached you. Presently it is rumored that someone has been enthroned in Nanjing. Hatred for the murderer of one monarch dictates that one must not share the same sky with the murderer. This is the meaning of the *Spring and Autumn Annals* in which it is written that before the murderer has been punished, the dead monarch cannot be described in history as having been formally buried nor can a new ruler rightfully take the throne. In order to guard against rebellious statesmen and unfilial sons, this rule is very strict. The "Dashing Bandit," Li Zicheng, led troops in an invasion of the capital; he harmed the Emperor and no Chinese subject came to his defense. Only the Pacifying King of the West, Wu Sangui, who was then stationed on the eastern border, emulated the ancient example of Shen Baoxu.[1] Our court was moved by his loyalty and righteousness. We remembered the generations of friendly relations between our two states and overlooked the minor quarrels of recent times. We sent our most ferocious troops to his aid to drive out these vicious animals.[2] When we entered the capital, we first paid our homage to your deceased Emperor; we gave him posthumous titles of honor; and buried him in the imperial tomb. All of this was done in proper ritual fashion. Imperial princes, generals, and others were permitted to retain their original titles. Meritorious relatives and all civil and military officials were allowed to stay in the court and continue to enjoy imperial grace. Tillers of the soil and merchants were unalarmed and not a single straw was disturbed. In the fall we plan to dispatch our troops on a western expedition; we will send a declaration of war to the Jiangnan region [south of the Yangzi river] and hope to form an alliance with you to fight in the west. We can then deploy our divisions together and single-mindedly exert all of our strength to take revenge for your Emperor and state and to manifest our dynasty's virtue. I am exceedingly puzzled that you gentlemen in the southern provinces are shamefully clinging to the illusion of peace and to empty fame. You refuse to grasp the moment and forget about the actual perils.

Our state, in its pacification of Peking, seized it from the "Dashing Bandit" Li Zicheng and not from the Ming state. The bandits destroyed the ancestral temples of the Ming dynasty and humiliated the Ming ancestors; our state felt no qualms about the toil of dispatching expeditions or the expense of using tax revenues to wipe clean the shame that befell you. Any filial son or humane person should feel indebted and repay our generosity. But you are taking advantage of our liquidation of the treasonous bandits and the temporary halt of our

---

1. Shen Baoxu was an official of the state of Chu who, after the invasion of his state by Wu, journeyed to the Qin court and tearfully implored its aid to restore his state.

2. The term used here in the original text is *xiaojing*, or owls and cat-like monsters. These two creatures are deemed to be particularly evil because according to legend the owl ate its young and the mythical *jing* devoured its mother after birth.

imperial army's advance. You seek to occupy Jiangnan and enjoy benefits obtained for you by others. If reason is applied to judge this behavior, can it be called fair? Do you think that the Yangtze cannot be crossed or that by throwing down our whips we could not halt the rivers?[3] The "Dashing Bandit" was a peril only to your Ming dynasty and never offended our state. However, our sympathy for your plight and common hatred of the enemy has caused us to manifest great righteousness. But if you now claim you hold the exalted title, then there will be two suns in heaven and we will become enemies. China with its whole strength was unable to overcome the troubles caused by the rebels; you now control merely a corner of the south and yet seek, simultaneously, to face our great country and the remaining bandits. Neither straws nor turtle shells are needed to divine what the outcome will be. I have heard that a gentleman uses virtue to manifest his love for the people; a mean man is complacent. If you gentlemen truly understand the times and the will of heaven and sincerely consider your late Emperor and deeply love your capable king, it is appropriate that you advise him to relinquish his title and pledge his allegiance to us. Thus, he can maintain his eternal happiness and good fortune. Our court will treat your king as an honored guest and permit him to carry on the rituals of the Ming court and possess the rivers and mountains of his own domain. His rank will be superior to that of other princes and nobles. This will not defy the original intention of our court to manifest righteousness by pacifying the rebels and to restore what has been severed and ruined. As for you talented gentlemen in the southern provinces, should you present yourselves to us then you shall enjoy titles of nobility and will be rewarded with lands. There exists the model of the Pacifying King of the West and I can only hope that you who are in command will make plans for the benefit of all.

Recently, your scholars have been fond of establishing unreachable standards of virtue and have ignored the crisis of the state. In each moment of emergency they natter about how to set up the defenses of the house. In former times, while the people of the Song debated the course they might take, the invaders had already crossed the river. This should be a clear example for you. Your excellency is the leader of a famed circle and is charged with making state policy. You certainly understand all the implications of this moment; how could you bear to follow the vulgar trend and float listlessly at such a time? You should decide soon whether to follow us or to resist. Our army is ready; it can advance east or west. Peace or peril for your southern state depends on the course you select. I hope you gentlemen will be unified in your intention to pay

3. This figure of speech, *toubian duanliu* (throwing down whips to stop the river's flow), is an allusion to the Period of Disunity and the invasion of the north by Fu Jian of the former Qin state. He claimed to have so many troops that the mass of their whips tossed into the river together could halt the Yangzi. Since Fu Jian was, in fact, defeated, the use of this allusion in this context was less than ideal.

the bandits and will not be greedy for a transient glory that will surely prolong the interminable calamity suffered by your state. I deeply hope that you will not give rebellious statesmen and unfilial sons reason to laugh at you. It is said in the classics: "Only good men can appreciate straightforward advice." I respectfully open my mind to you and, standing on tiptoe watch the horizon, as I anxiously await words of enlightenment from you. This letter cannot fully express my meaning.

2.5 DORGON'S EDICT: A BROADSHEET FOR THE PEOPLE OF THE SOUTHERN MING, 1645

Shi Kefa's refusal to surrender his forces and the continued resistance of other southern Ming commanders brought forceful words from the regent Dorgon. Using highly suggestive language not unlike that of Nurhaci's Seven Grievances, Dorgon threatened his obdurate opponents south of the Yangzi with punishment for their "three crimes." Dorgon's harsh message continued to be tempered, however, by promises of rank and rewards for ex-Ming officials who agreed to help the Qing cause.

The edict translated below was apparently circulated as a broadsheet and was transcribed by an anonymous inhabitant of Jiangnan just after Manchu troops took Nanjing.

Let it be known to all civil and military officials, soldiers and commoners of Henan, Nanjing, Zhejiang, Jiangxi, Huguang, and other areas: You southern subjects did not dispatch a single soldier or a single arrow when the Chongzhen Emperor of the Ming dynasty faced a calamity and when the palace gates and the doors of the imperial tombs were burst open. You did not confront the roving bandits but rather hid yourselves like tigers in a cave as the state was about to be ruined. This was your first crime. When our army was sent to exterminate the bandits who were fleeing west, you in the south enthroned Prince Fu before you obtained firm information from the capital or knew the deceased Emperor 's will. This was your second crime. The roving bandits were your deadly foe but you never considered sending a punitive expedition. Your generals sought simply to conserve their own armies and harmed the people. They provoked quarrels and fought among themselves. This was your third crime. These three crimes aroused anger throughout the realm and were too grave to be pardoned by Heaven. Therefore, I have respectfully received Heaven's mandate and have set in order the army to punish your crimes.

Any local civil or military official who surrenders his district or city, depending on the degree of his merit, will be promoted one rank. Those who resist and refuse to obey will themselves be liquidated and their family members will be taken captive. If Prince Fu regrets his past wrongs and is willing to surrender to our army, his former crimes will be pardoned and he will be as well treated as other Ming Princes. If Prince Fu's trusted officials are willing to correct themselves and give their loyalty to us, they, too, will be accorded merit fitting their contribution. People residing in places where this announcement is made should not be alarmed nor should they flee. Farmers and merchants should calmly pursue their affairs; in the villages all will be as peaceful as before and in the cities not a single straw shall be disturbed. However, all necessary fodder and hay should be prepared for dispatch to the army. The Board of War shall immediately send out orders and officials, soldiers, and the people should circulate news of this [order] as early as possible so as not to delay military deployments. This is a special announcement; let all be apprised of it.

2.6 EDICT FROM DODO (PRINCE YU) FOLLOWING THE YANGZHOU MASSACRE, 1645

This edict uses the example of the Yangzhou massacre to attempt to cow southern Ming commanders into surrender. Like Dorgon's edict announcing the Manchu army's intention to move south, Dodo's message was circulated as a broadsheet and was transcribed by an inhabitant of Jiangnan. Later it was printed in a collection of historical documents entitled the *Jiangnan wenjianlu*. By now terror, along with the obligatory promises of rewards and position, had become a key Manchu tactic in suppressing southern Ming resistance.

Let it be known to all civil and military officials, soldiers and commoners of Nanjing and other places: I have received an imperial edict ordering me to lead our great army to surpass the calm disorder. Those who follow us will be offered amnesty and enlisted on our side; those who resist will be exterminated. In many places where our great army has hitherto arrived, the blades of its swords were not stained with blood. Surrendering officials presented their seals of appointment to us and many were specially promoted and invited to remain at their posts. Among the people, not a straw was disturbed and property was untouched. Recently when our great army arrived in Yangzhou and its population tried tenaciously to defend it, I felt deep compassion for the lives of the people and could not bear to launch an offensive. I feelingly made known to them the consequences of resistance but, after several days delay, the officials [of Yangzhou] continued to resist. Orders were given to attack the city and slay its inhabitants; only women and children were taken prisoner. This was not my original intention but happened because there was no other course. In the future, Yangzhou will serve as an example for officials who do not surrender when our great army arrives. Heaven and earth give men life; it is appropriate that those who seek to resist destiny should end their own lives but they should not involve others. Our dynasty has inherited the affection of Heaven; if it fights a battle it shall win, if it attacks a city it will overcome it. I am sure you are aware of this. Although virtue must be made manifest through the action of the army, compassion and righteousness are shown by amnesty. This is as clear as a mirror. Presently Prince Fu has usurped the exalted title and wallows in wine and sex; he trusts his entourage while the people suffer more each day. Civil officials toy with power; they know only how to do evil and take bribes. Military officials threaten the monarch and contemplate overawing him to usurp his powers. The government and subjects are not of one heart and the people's plight is truly terrible! When I think of this I cannot help but to sigh. Therefore, I have respectfully taken Heaven's mandate to punish these crimes and save the people from their disaster. Let all be clearly informed of this.

2.7 AND 2.8 TWO EDICTS CONCERNING THE WEARING OF THE HAIR UNDER MANCHU RULE

Manchu leaders decided even before the taking of Peking that Chinese subjects should wear their hair dressed in the Manchu tribal style. The hair was to be shaved to the middle of the skull with the remaining hair pulled back around a "cash-shaped" circle of the scalp and braided as it grew. Former Ming subjects who resisted this order symbolizing submission to China's new Manchu rulers did so at the risk of their lives. The colloquial saying: "Lose your hair or lose your head" (Liutou bu liufa, liufa bu liutou) succinctly described the dangers in store for those still sentimentally attached to the long style of hair-dress popular during the Ming period. Later in the dynasty, cutting off the queue was a symbol of resistance to the Manchus adopted by the Taiping rebels, who were sometimes called "the long-haired rebels," and early twentieth-century revolutionaries often cut off their *bianzi* as a sign of defiance. When the Qing collapsed in 1911, groups of anti-Qing activists cornered wearers of the queue in Shanghai and other cities to cut off their pigtails. The piles of *bianzi* lying in the street symbolized the fallen fortunes of the dynasty.

2.7 Regent Dorgon's Edict to the Board of War

"Now that our dynasty has established its authority in Peking, the soldiers and common people who endured recent calamities are all our children. We will save them from disasters and give them security. Send messengers to cities and forts of all regions requesting their surrender. If, on the day this message arrives, their inhabitants shave their heads and submit, all local officials shall be promoted one rank. Soldiers and common people will be exempt from deportation. Leading civil and military officials should personally collect tax registers and army rosters and immediately bring them to the capital for imperial audience. Those who claim to submit but do not shave their heads are hesitant and watchful. They should be given a deadline for compliance based on their distance from the capital and rewarded accordingly when they arrive in Peking. If they do not meet the deadline, it is clear that they are resisting and definitely should be punished; troops are to be sent to supress them. Princes with the surname Zhu [members of the Ming imperial family] who conform to this order shall not be deprived of their titles and will continue to enjoy imperial grace."

2.8 Imperial Edict to the Board of Rites

"In the past the system of dressing the hair in a queue was not uniformly enforced. People were allowed to do as they pleased because we wanted to wait until the whole country was pacified before putting into force this system. Now, within and without, we are one family. The Emperor is like the father and the people are like his sons. The father and sons are of the same body; how can they be different from one another? If they are not as one then it will be as if they had two hearts and would they then not be like the people of different countries? We do not need to mention this because we believe all subjects under Heaven must be aware of it themselves. All residents of the capital and its vicinity will fulfill the order to shave their heads within ten days of this proclamation. For Zhili and other provinces compliance must take place within ten days of receipt of the order from the Board of Rites. Those who follow this order belong to our country; those who hesitate will be considered treasonous bandits and will be heavily penalized. Anyone who attempts to evade this order to protect his hair or who uses cunning language to argue against it will not be lightly dealt with. All officials in regions that we have already pacified who insultingly advance a memorial related to this matter arguing for the continuation of the Ming system and not following the system of our dynasty will be executed without possibility of pardon. As for other apparel, unhurried change is permitted, but it cannot differ from the system of our dynasty. The aforementioned Board will immediately dispatch this message to the capital and its vicinity and to the provincial, prefectural, sub-prefectural, and county yamen and garrisons of Zhili and other provinces. Civil and military yamen officials, clerks, scholars, students, and all members of military and civilian households shall carry this out without exception."

2.9 THE SIEGE OF JIANGYIN, 1645

The hair-cutting decrees were a dramatic sign of the changing political order in China and prompted strong resistance in many parts of the south. In the city of Jiangyin, just south of the Yangzi River in Jiangsu, local scholars used this issue to muster resistance to advancing Qing armies and in August 1645 a fierce battle with Manchu forces ensued.

This account of the eighty-day siege of Jiangyin was written by Xu Chongxi, a controversial private scholar and historian of the late Ming period from Changshu. Xu was praised by some of his contemporaries for his scholarly diligence and criticized by others for his frank and outspoken commentary on the events of his time. (During the Qianlong era, Wu's history of the final years of the Ming period was a proscribed book.)

This translation is drawn from Xu's *Postscript on the Defense of Jiangyin City* (Jiangyin chengshou houji) which describes in colorful terms the struggle by Jiangyin's defenders to hold the Manchu invaders outside the walls. The document provides a vivid sense of the violence of warfare during the conquest period and suggests, as well, how the local elite in the Jiangnan region struggled to build forces of resistance to the Qing invaders. After the defeat of Jiangyin, the Manchu army, as at Yangzhou several months before, burned the city and massacred many of its inhabitants.

"In the sixth moon of 1645, Magistrate Fang of Jiangyin arrived in the city and conveyed the [Qing] edict to dress the hair in the queue. On the first day of the intercalary sixth moon,[4] a local scholar, Xu Yongde, hung a portrait of the Ming founder in the Minglun Lecture Hall [the official local academy for instruction in the classics] and led a crowd who prostrated themselves before it and cried out: "Cut off our heads, we refuse to shave our hair!" That afternoon, the local militia in the North Gate area were the first to rise up; they arrested the magistrate and jailed him in the local guest house. Tens of thousands of people within and outside the city supported them. Those in revolt requested the release of stores of weapons and ammunition and the local judge Chen Mingxuan agreed. The chief of the local reserve unit was then arrested and a search began for spies within the city. The Huizhou merchant Shao Kanggong

---

4. Intercalary months were added to the lunar calendar to keep it in harmony with the solar year.

who was a master of the martial arts was appointed as commander and enlisted soldiers for the defense of the city. Former *Dusi*[5] Zhou Ruilong stationed ships at the mouth of the river and asked Shao Kanggong to bring his troops out through the east gate so that they could combine forces at the north gate to fight the [Qing] invaders. When the battle was joined, they were successful. The enemy's force grew larger day by day and the militia men did their best to attack it and kill Manchu soldiers. Whenever they presented one head, the city rewarded them with four taels of silver. At this time, slaves and servants were in revolt against their masters and the great local families were occupied in saving themselves from death.

The Qing army first attacked the western quarter of the city and then moved to the south gate. Shao Kanggong went forward to command the defense but could not prevail. The enemy burned the eastern quarter and looted the homes of rich families living outside the city wall. The militia fought ferociously and a certain pair of brothers killed a cavalry general. . . . Zhou Ruilong boarded his boat and fled.

The former judge, Yan Yingyuan, had been promoted to Deputy Magistrate of Yingde county in Guangdong but had not yet left to fill the position because his mother was ill. When the national calamity occurred, he and his family moved to Shashan, located east of the city. Chen Mingxuan said: "My wisdom and courage are no match for Mister Yan's; he should come to take charge of this great matter." That night riders were sent to meet with Yan Yingyuan. Yingyuan accepted and led more than forty of this family's retainers to rush to defend the city. Scattered groups of enemy soldiers were burning and looting outside the city walls. The militia had fled and no reinforcements were coming.

Now the enemy concentrated on attacking the walled city. Within the city walls there were less than a thousand soldiers and about ten thousand households. No source of pay or rations existed for the troops. Yan Yingyuan gathered up household registers and set in order defense towers. He ordered each household to present X [character missing] men to mount the city wall and commanded all others remaining to assist in preparing meals. He then released munitions and firearms made by Zeng Hualong, the former military circuit intendant, and stored them in battle towers. He sent an order to the great families of the city encouraging contributions: "Contributions will not necessarily consist of money. Clothing, grain, and other materials are all acceptable." The national academy scholar Cheng Bi came forward first with a donation of twenty-five thousand silver taels and then many other donors came forward. Within the besieged city there were three hundred charges of gunpowder, one thousand *dan* [1 *dan* = 133⅓ lbs.] of lead and iron blunderbuss ammunition, one hundred cannons, one thousand fowling pieces, ten million copper cash and ten thousand *dan* of millet, wheat and beans. Wine, salt, iron, and hay was also

5. Ming military rank equivalent to commander or captain.

available. The city was divided up into sectors for its defense. The military *juren* Huang Lue guarded the east gate. A certain sub-lieutenant commanded the south gate. Chen Mingxuan guarded the west gate and Yan Yingyuan himself guarded the north gate. Patrols circulated among the four gates.

By now there were already one hundred thousand men in the Qing army that surrounded the city. They set up more than one hundred camps and dozens of rings of soldiers surrounded the city. They fired their arrows into the air and wounded some of the men on the city wall. But on the wall the defenders used catapults and crossbows and used the advantage of the wall's height to wound many of the enemy. The Qing then used large cannons to attack the city and the wall began to crack. Yan Yingyuan ordered his men to wrap wooden doors with iron sheet tied on with iron bands. These doors were then lowered to cover the cracks. Empty coffins were stuffed with soil and used to fill in collapsed areas. The Qing next attacked the northern city and one man climbed up a scaling ladder placed against the city wall. The defenders resisted him with a long spear but this officer grasped the spear with his teeth and projected himself onto the wall. A boy grabbed him and another defender cut off the enemy's head. It was said that: "This was the seventh prince." Another Qing officer wore dozens of sharp knives and climbed up by driving long, thick nails into the wall. The defenders used an iron hammer to kill him. . . .

Among the residents of Jiangyin was one Huang Yunjiang; he was a skilled maker of arrowheads. When someone was hit in the face by one of Huang's arrows fired from an incendiary crossbow, he would howl with pain and die. Chen Riu's son made wooden grenades in the prison which looked like ones made of steel. When they were dropped from the city wall they would explode in a fiery mass showering scraps of iron in all directions. People hit by this shrapnel would immediately die. Yan Yingyuan made an iron grappling hook to which was attached a long cotton rope. When it caught the enemy soldiers they were dragged up the wall into the city. They also made fire rugs and fire arrows. The enemy so feared these weapons that they camped three li from the city wall.

The enemy commander Liu Liangzuo was originally one of the four division commanders of the Hongguang court and was ennobled as the Earl of Guangchang. However, he surrendered to the Qing and was made a senior general. Liu devised an ox-hide canopy and attacked the eastern corner of the city. The crowd of defending troops threw down huge rocks and hundreds of enemy soldiers died. Then Liu Langzuo moved his camp to the Sifang Temple and ordered its monks to kneel and tearfully implore the defenders to surrender. But the defenders did not listen. Liu Langzuo then approached the city wall on horseback and shouted: "Mister Yan and I are old friends. Tell him I want to see him." Yan Yingyuan then appeared and planted himself on the city wall. Liu told him: "The Hongguang Emperor has already fled. There is no master in all of Jiangnan. If you surrender early you will keep your wealth and nobility." Yingyuan said: "I am just a local judge of the Ming dynasty. My death is of no importance! But you who were enfoeffed and ennobled by the court and appointed to serve as its chief officer in the central command could not defend the Yangtze-Huai river zone. Instead, today you come to invade and oppress us. Do you have the face to confront the righteous scholars and commoners of our country?" Liangzuo felt ashamed and departed.

Yan Yingyuan was tall and powerful; his complexion was dark and he had a light beard. His character was stern and persistent. When he gave orders he pardoned no failures in carrying them out. But he cared little for money and was generous in giving rewards. He personally bandaged the wounded and provided excellent funerals for the men who were killed. He drank libations and wept for the dead. When he spoke with his officers and troops, he called them "good brothers" instead of using their names. Chen Mingxuan was warm and generous; each time he circled the city wall he shared the labor and hardship of the soldiers and sometimes even wept with them. Therefore, these two men were able to win the hearts of their troops and the troops were happy to die for them.

One night there was a howling rainstorm and there was no light in the entire city. Suddenly a divine light illuminated the city. The enemy saw three red-clothed figures giving commands inside the walls. In fact, there was no such thing. They also saw a woman officer waving a flag and giving commands but this too was an illusion. . . .

Beneath the city walls, day by day, the number of large cannons increased. One was located every five or six feet from the next and soon flying cannon balls fell like hail. A man stood on the city wall and was decapitated by cannon shot but his body still stood there erect. Another man was struck in the chest by a ball that passed through him but he still stood as before.

On the 15th day of the eighth moon, Yan Yingyuan donated money to the soldiers and people to allow them to have a good time enjoying the beauty of the moon. His subordinates brought drinking vessels onto the city wall and hearty drinking took place. Xu Yongde composed a folk song with five variations and ordered a good singer to sing it slowly and gracefully. The sound of the song and alarm bells and bugles made a lovely harmony. This lasted for three nights.

The *beile*,[6] when he realized that the city had no intention of surrendering, ordered his troops to attack more urgently. Risking their lives, they threw up ladders against the city walls. Their armor and helmets were all made of iron; when they were hit by a knife or ax, there was a clanging sound and the blades were broken. The sound of cannon echoed day and night and places within one hundred li of the battleground were shaken by the sound. Each day there were more wounded and dead within the city and the sounds of weeping and mourn-

---

6. A title for Manchu princes; here, the degree is indeterminable.

ing were heard along its streets. But Yingyuan courageously mounted the city and was undaunted.

One morning there was a huge downpour; at midday, a thread-like red light rose from the Mud Bridge and shot toward the western quarter and soon thereafter the city fell.

Qing troops swarmed up like bees through the smoke, mist, and rain and entered the city. Yan Yingyuan, leading one hundred fearless men, fought in eight street battles and killed or wounded thousands of the enemy. Yan and his men rushed to the gate but it was closed and they could not escape. Yingyuan determined that death was unavoidable and threw himself into the water of the Qian Lake but was not drowned. Liu Langzuo ordered his troops to take Yan Yingyuan alive and so he was captured. Langzuo sat proudly in the Qianming Temple hall; when he saw Yingyuan, he jumped up and tearfully embraced him. Yingyuan laughed and said: "What are you crying for? Since things have reached this stage, all that is left for me is death!" When he saw the *beile*, Yingyuan stood upright and refused to bow. A soldier pierced his shin with a spear which broke the bone and made him topple to the ground. Toward dusk, he was carried to the Xixia Monastery and that night the monks heard him crying: "Kill me quickly!" Without ceasing his imprecations, Yingyuan died.

Chen Mingxuan dismounted and engaged in the melee. He was killed in the fighting before the Military Circuit Intendant's office. He was already mortally wounded but stood erect against a wall holding a sword and would not fall to the ground. (Some said that his entire family committed suicide by leaping into a fire.) Someone named Han, after killing three Qing soldiers, slashed his own throat. A certain local instructor Feng from Jintan, hung himself in the Minglun Lecture Hall. The Junior Imperial Secretary Qi Xun, also known as Boping, whose family was from Qingyang, entered the city to aid in its defense. He exhausted his strength fighting and wrote in large characters on the wall of his residence: "Qi Xun died here. His wife, children, and daughter-in-law all died here." Then the entire family immolated themselves. The entire family of Xu Yongde also burned themselves. Huang Yunjiang had been good at playing the *huqin*;[7] after the city fell he disguised himself as a musician and escaped. No one recognized him as the master designer of the arrows used to defend the city. The defense lasted eighty-one days.

Two hundred and forty thousand Qing troops took part and sixty seven thousand of them died during the siege. Another seven thousand died in street fighting. In all, more than seventy-five thousand soldiers were lost. The dead in the city filled every well. Sunlangzhong Pond and Chong Pond were packed with layers of corpses. Not one person surrendered.

This official historian of Jiangyin says: During the Ming dynasty officials had

---

7. A two-stringed musical instrument originally brought to China from central Asia and used in the Peking opera.

no sense of shame. Those who were high officials enjoyed great renown but they were willing to hide their faces and beg to surrender. And all of the great commanders guarding the frontiers turned their spears and advanced into China: Only Chen and Yan, these two local judges, showed righteousness in this one city. If the defense of the Jingkou fortifications had been so strong, then Jiangnan would not have been handed over to the enemy! Contemporaries remarked: "For eighty days they kept hair to show loyalty and they were outstanding among the historical figures of the seventeen reigns since the founding of the Ming by Taizu. Sixty thousand people were of one mind and died for righteousness to preserve this three hundred li of territory."

2.10   THE JINTAN SLAVE RIOTS, 1644

The disruption of the local order caused by the depredations of Zhang Xianzhong's army can be glimpsed in the following document which records an uprising of slaves against their masters in 1644. The Jintan slaves, whose rebellion is described in this early Qing account by an unsympathetic chronicler named Yu Zizhan, were obliged to tolerate their treatment so long as the local social order was preserved by Ming armies and local authorities. However, when structures of local rule began to crumble and Ming officials took flight to preserve themselves from marauding rebel bands, the slaves took advantage of the resultant chaos to assert themselves and settle scores at the expense of their former masters and local elites.

During the Ming dynasty many notable families owned slaves. Such a life of servitude often began with the collapse of a family's fortunes when destitute parents were obligated, through contractual agreements, to sell their children and sometimes themselves into slavery. But there were also entire clans who were branded with this debased status in perpetuity as a punishment for political sins against the Ming state. In either case, status as a slave became hereditary and those who suffered under the yoke of slavery or bond-servitude were often the victims of deplorable cruelty at the hands of the families who owned them.

THE MING SLAVE REBELLIONS

When the literati of the Ming were self-indulgent they had many slaves and servants. The Chu area was the most prominent center for slavery; the city of Macheng was the major locale in which it occurred. The Mei, Liu, Tian, and Li families of Macheng each had over three or four thousand male servants and slaves. They were extremely powerful and prosperous. In the twelfth moon of 1642, when Zhang Xianzhong attacked Huamei county, the gentry and literati of Macheng considered armed defense of their city and ordered their followers to form militia leagues. They sacrificed animals and formed a "Village Benevolence Society." To show their splendor and largesse, the families competed with each other in arming and clothing their retainers. In the fourth moon of 1643, Zhang Xianzhong sacked Macheng. The masses of slaves tortured the literati and even their former masters; they defected to Zhang Xianzhong and were called the "New Battalion." They were used as guides, and vicious, cunning local hoodlums of the Qi-Huang region flocked to join them. The leader of the [former] "Village Benevolent Society" was named Tang Zhi. He slaughtered more than sixty scholars but recommended that one scholar, his friend, Zhou Wenjiang, be saved to help the bandits. The bandits appointed Wenjiang as the county magistrate and Tang Zhi as the local commander and they held Macheng for several months. When Zhang Xianzhong retreated into Sichuan, Tang Zhi was executed by the government by slicing. This was the first slave rebellion.

In the fifth moon of 1644, Prince Fu usurped the title of emperor. Ma Shiying and Ruan Dacheng colluded to form an evil alliance in the Ming court. This began another time of trouble and disaster. The family slaves of the Hua family in Jiading started a riot. They were joined by slaves and servants of other families and all rose up together. They bound their masters and beat them; they sat haughtily and demanded the return of their contracts of enslavement. Tens of thousands of people gathered. At this time, Qi Biaojia of Shanyin was appointed to pacify Suzhou. Just as the riot in Suzhou was pacified, a slave riot in Jiading began. Qi Biaojia rushed there and ordered local police to arrest all of the rioters. He executed some and threw all of the others into jail. He gave this order: "Those whose former masters provide bail will be pardoned from execution." Thereupon, the mob of slaves crawled on their knees and pounded their heads on the ground to implore their former masters to pardon them. This brought an end to the calamity.

The slave riot of Jintan also began at the beginning of that month. There was a certain Pan in this county whose family for generations had served as the slaves of a large gentry family. He was very wealthy and gave donations to pay for military provisions. He was appointed an officer in the capital [Peking] garrison. When the capital fell, he surrendered to the bandits and became an illegitimate *duwei* [local military commander]. The treasonous "Dashing bandit" [Li Zicheng] tortured officials of the capital and demanded money. Former Ming officials Zhou Kuei, Zhu Chun, Chen Yan, Wei Zaode, and others were all severely tortured; they were burned with irons, their legs and ankles were squeezed with boards, and heads were compressed. Every day this was repeated. The slave Pan was frightened; he waited for the right moment and then fled to his home.

Pan was proud and overbearing. He presented his calling card and paid a visit to the local magistrate. The magistrate did not realize that he was a former slave and so he met with him. It so happened that Pan's master was passing the yamen gate and saw handsome horses and carriages gathered outside the gatehouse. When he asked about this and found out that it was the slave Pan who was visiting, he was infuriated. He [the former master] rushed in and knocked off Pan's hat, ripped his clothes, and scolded him: "You crazy slave, you are just a dog or a horse. How dare you drag yourself, with what breath you have left from beatings, to appear before the district magistrate? How dare you smear our Confucian rites and shame the entire county?" The master slapped his face and knocked out two teeth. Pan endured it and rushed out. He felt humiliated and angry. He spent his money to recruit a group of slaves to plot to kill his master. They called themselves "the Nose-cutting Band" [xiaobi].[8] Pan called himself the commander-in-chief; they raised huge banners and battle standards and felt very daring. Tens of thousands of followers flocked to join them.

Zhu Shaoji was the son of an old servant of the local Wang family. He was born with owl-like eyes and a wolf-like voice. His nature was barbaric and wild. When he drank he was proud and abusive and liked to mistreat people in the neighborhood. All of his friends were other hoodlums. His master tried to guide him with grace and trust and admonished him with gentle words. The master hoped to curb Zhu's hawk-like nature but Zhu Shaoji's ferocity and viciousness were engrained habits and there was no way to modify him. When he was finally driven out of the household, he became even more abusive and overbearing. He learned boxing and spear-fighting and banded together with four others in a group that called itself "the five tigers." They drank a blood oath of brotherhood and vowed to die together. They organized others to start the riot. The streets and alleys were packed with rioters and reverberated with a sound as loud as the rising tide. Soon after this, Magistrate X [one character missing] trained troops and arrested Pan, Zhu, and the four others and executed them in the market square. The mass of slaves did not dare to show themselves. This was the first slave and servant riot of 1644.

In the sixth moon of 1645, the yiyou year of the Shunzhi reign period, the calamity was even more serious. Prince Yu led the [Qing] army in its southern advance. On the twenty-fourth day of the fourth moon, they entered Yangzhou and on the ninth day of the fifth moon, they crossed over to the south bank of the Yangtze River. At about two o'clock in the morning on the tenth day, Prince Fu fled from Manjing. On the sixteenth day, Prince Yu approached Nanking and sent out this army to pacify the surrounding areas. On the twenty-ninth day, Jintan surrendered. On the thirteenth day of the sixth moon, powerful local slaves took advantage of the chaos to (again) form a new "Nose-cutting Band" and gathered to take an oath in the Temple of the City God. They agreed to revolt against all the masters of the entire county and to do no more servant's

---

8. A possible homophone for a local Jintan word for "slave emancipation."

work. The oath said: "Whoever joins our league and then doubts it and returns to his former master will be killed." Soon the houses of the local gentry were empty [because their servants had joined the league.]

On the sixteenth day, the local magistrate announced that no one should interfere with slaves and servants who wanted to return to their former masters. He proclaimed that if the situation became more inflamed he would call troops to exterminate the rioters. This somewhat subdued the slaves' zest for action. On the night of the seventeenth day, local gentry secretly ran off to make a report to the prefectural authorities. On the nineteenth day, the prefect led troops to the county and stationed them ten miles outside of the county seat. He rode into the city alone to see what was happening. He met with local gentry at XXXXXX [six characters missing] and saw that there were no servants or messengers to be found. Even cups of tea were served by family members. He was surprised and when he asked why this was so, discovered the facts. The prefect was furious and immediately commanded his troops to arrest the slaves. Masses of slaves were on the lookout outside the gates of the gentry houses. They watched with bulging eyes and gaping mouths and their noise filled the streets. When the troops came, they ran off like sheep in all directions. More than a hundred people were decapitated; five leaders who had beaten their masters were arrested and after severe punishment in the court were thrown into jail. On the twentieth day, it was announced that powerful slaves of large gentry families would be let off; slaves and servants of scholarly and other families were ordered to return to their duties within three days. On the twenty-first day, the troops put their weapons in order and paraded the five leaders from the East Court to the Western Market Square for execution before the Temple of the City God. A mob of slaves again gathered on a low hill on the right side of the Temple and intended to try to rescue the condemned men. The prefect was afraid that there would be trouble and so he personally followed along behind the procession. Right after they crossed the Qinghe Bridge, he ordered that the execution take place. After the execution, the mob ran away. When the execution was taking place, the prefect ordered that the noses of the condemned men be cut off before the were beheaded. Subsequently, he hung the noses and heads in front of the city gate together with a placard written in large red characters reading: 'The band's name was the 'nose-cutters' and so their noses have been cut off to show the masses.' The omen of the birds killed by lightning was thus fulfilled by the decapitation of these slaves.[9] After the prefect pacified the riot, he led the troops back to the prefectural seat. On the twenty-second day, the local magistrate announced that at the behest of their former masters, charges would be pressed against slaves who refused to return their contracts of enslavement. Serious cases would be dealt with by decapitation

9. This omen is explained in a subsequent paragraph of the document.

and public exhibition of the head on a pole. Light cases would be addressed by flogging and the wearing of the cangue.[10]

Previously, when the mass of slaves had taken its oath before the Temple of the City God, thousands of crimson birds flew about in the sunlight and the scene was suffused with rays of light as red as fire. Then it started thundering and after a huge bolt of lightning split the sky, the bodies of birds began falling down on the square. The crowd of slaves said: "This is an omen that the powerful masters will be killed. It would bring misfortune to go against heaven." They then beat gongs and started the riot. The slaves bound their former masters and ransacked their chests and cases searching for the contracts of slavery. They looted and behaved savagely. Forty to fifty thousand people were involved in this disturbance.

There was a local gentry member who dealt with his servants and slaves in a stern and cruel way. Whenever he felt slightly upset, he would use the whip. His slaves deeply hated him. Now that the slaves were organized into a mob, they tied up this gentry member and dragged him to the Temple of the City God. They beat him with heavy bamboo clubs that had ends about five inches across and one inch thick. As his previous evil deeds were enumerated, they took turns laying on the blows. With two men facing each other across his body, they hit him more than a hundred times. Blood filtered through his clothing and covered the Temple steps. His flesh was mashed and the bones protruded. He seemed dead but then came to and lay there barely breathing. This gentry scholar had always loved to taste tea. He especially loved the tea of the Azure Ravine of Xiachuan and the Heavenly Lake tea of Yangxian. When his slaves were sent to fetch tea, they were ordered to return in a very short period of time. If they were delayed or late they were beaten. Now, after this master had been flogged he was dragged out through the Temple gate and the mob urinated on him. They then filled a jar with filthy piss and forced him to drink it. They said: "Try this from the Azure Ravine spring."

There was a local custom that at the time of festivals and happy family occasions, rice was ground into a fine powder that was steamed into rice balls called *tuanzi*. They were heated up in steamers that could hold fifty or sixty piled up one on top of the next, in as many as six or seven layers. In this gentry family, if some rice balls were not, by chance, thoroughly cooked, all of the male and female slaves and servants would be forced to kneel down before the master and their hands would be struck one blow for each uncooked *tuanzi*. The slaves had wanted to settle scores with this gentry master for these beatings for a long time. Now they beat him on the hands for each beating they had received. His hands were red and pulpy and his fingers and wrist were nearly

---

10. A broad wooden board worn around a criminal's neck as a portable pillory. The criminal's offenses were recorded on the sides of the cangue.

broken. After being beaten on the hands, the master was tied up with chains around his neck and pulled through the streets. The slaves clapped their hands and shouted excitedly. The streets and marketplace were full of people. Too many incidents of this sort happened to be recorded!

But there were also some slaves who felt grateful to their former masters. They cried out to the crowd: "When we are paying back the masters, we should make a clear distinction between gratitude and hatred. For example, if so-and-so was generous and humane or so-and-so treated us with benevolence, we should repay them accordingly. If we do not show virtue the gods and people will laugh at us." Therefore, they brought out the golden banners and colored accouterments used in processions of honor and carried forward a huge eight-man sedan chair. Next they joyously invited their former masters to pass through the city in a parade. The masters humbly thanked them but respectfully asked to be excused. The slaves insisted more forcefully and the masters kept thanking them and making excuses. Finally the crowd pushed the masters into the sedan chair and with slaves leading the way on horseback and more slaves following behind, they started out. Slaves beat drums and blew horns and the splendid procession circled around the streets and corners of the city. When the slaves returned with the masters, they thanked them repeatedly and then the mob of slaves, shouting happily to each other, ran off. There were other horrible insults and killings that even the magistrate could do nothing about.

After the five leaders were beheaded and the magistrate's order was announced, runaway servants and slaves gradually began to return to their duty. Those who did not return fled like night owls opening their wings. On the twenty-sixth day, a mob of slaves again spread the word that they would start another riot by burning the East Court on the twenty-eighth. On that day, the hair-cutting decree was announced and the local magistrate resigned and departed. People in the city also began scattering into the countryside and the calamity of the 'nose-cutters' came to an end. . . . [The concluding portion of the essay ends with a moral lesson on the proper relationship between masters and slaves.]

CHAPTER 3 | # Kangxi's Consolidation

3.1 WU SANGUI ON THE EXECUTION OF THE PRINCE OF GUI

After the Manchu conquest, resistance to Qing rule continued only on the periphery of China. Remnants of the armies of Li Zicheng and Zhang Xianzhong continued to fight in the west while the navy of Koxinga resisted Qing rule on the southern coast. In the south and southwest, Ming forces loyal to the fragile regime of the prince of Gui entered unlikely coalitions to continue their struggle and held out against the Manchus until the destruction of southern Ming forces of the Yunnan-Guizhou plateau and in northern Burma.

The general who administered the coup-de-grace to the southern Ming was the celebrated turncoat Wu Sangui. After leading his own army and most of the Ming forces north of the Yangzi into the Qing camp, Wu flourished mightily. His Manchu masters rewarded him with titles and awards and encouraged him to use his army, together with the banner forces of Dodo and Haoge, to mop up the last enemies of the new Qing state.

The prince of Gui (Emperor Yongli) was the most prominent of several Ming pretenders in the decades after the conquest. He was enthroned by Ming local officials in November 1646 in Wuzhou, Guangxi, but evacuated this capital at least six times in the years that followed. Indeed, from 1646 to 1651, Yongli's "court" was forced to flee sixteen times from Manchu forces and Prince Yongli came to be called "the son of heaven in flight" (*zou tianzi*).

In 1652, however, Yongli's fortunes briefly changed as he joined with the forces of Zhang Xianzhong's erstwhile lieutenants to form a new base in the southwest on the Guanxi-Yunnan border. From this point onward, until its downfall, the southern Ming was thus defended by the same rebels who had helped dash the fortunes of the Ming.

In January 1659, Manchu troops drove the Ming army from Yunnan and Yongli was forced to move across the Chinese border into Burma. In Burma, he was placed under virtual house arrest by the Burmese king but was not mistreated. Two years later, following a coup in the Burmese court that brought to power a new king eager to mollify the Qing state, the last Ming pretender was turned over to Wu Sangui who, as the document translated below suggests, had no compunction in putting him to death. This 1662 memorial, sent to the court by Wu Sangui and Aixing, describes the capture and execution of the prince of Gui (Zhu Yulang). The memorial includes a copy of a letter from Yongli imploring Wu Sangui for mercy written before the young pretender was captured by Wu's troops.

"We were ordered to send an expedition into Burma and advanced our troops along two fronts. In the eleventh Moon of 1661, the two forces met in Mubang. The false Prince Jin, Li Dingguo, fled to Jingxian and the false Prince Gongchange, Bai Wenxuan, fled and took up a new position along the Xibo River. His troops built rafts to cross the river and Bai Wenxuan then fled to Chashan. General Ma Ning and others were sent in pursuit to Mengmao where they obtained Bai Wenxuan's surrender. As Wu Sangui and Aixing approached Miancheng they received a letter from the false Prince Yongli to Sangui which read:

> Your excellency is a meritorious official of the new dynasty and was also an important general of the previous dynasty. For generations your family has been rewarded with noble ranks and you were enfoeffed as a garrison commander in the border regions. It can be said that the late Emperor was extremely generous to you. Who could know that our country would experience the unexpected disaster brought about by Li Zicheng's bandits who rushed into our capital, ruined our country, and forced our late Emperor to meet an early death. They unleashed great evil and slaughtered many of our people. Your excellency, like Shen Baoxu who tearfully implored aid from the Qin court to restore Chu, wore mourning garb and made a vow to lead your troops to punish the criminals. Your original intention at that time cannot be condemned.
>
> But how, later, could you side with a powerful state and, like a fox walking beside a tiger, assume an overbearing demeanor? You appeared to seek revenge but secretly you sought to be an officer of the new dynasty. After the traitor [Li Zicheng] was killed and the southern territories were no longer under the control of the previous dynasty, officials of the south could not bear to see the dynasty fail and so they invited me to be enthroned in Nanyang. Who could expect that there would be no peace and that war would come again? Prince Hongguang met a tragic end and Prince Longwu was executed. At this time, your humble servant almost did not want to go on living. How could I bear to make plans for the state? After repeated urging from

my officials, I undeservingly agreed to carry on the previous imperial line. Since then, the territory of Chu was lost in one battle and the territory of eastern Guangdong was lost in another. It is hard to calculate how many times I have fled in terror.

Fortunately, Li Dingguo invited your servant to Guizhou and received me at Nan'an. I believed this would harm no one and sought no conflict with anyone in the world! However, your excellency forgot the great righteousness shown to you by your late Emperor and sought to win merit by opening new territories and by leading troops into Yunnan to overturn my little nest. Your servant, owing to this, was forced to cross the desert and strengthen his domain by seeking the support of the Burmese. In such a distant land, who could feel happy? How miserable it is! Although I have lost the rivers and mountains that generations of my family guarded, I am now shamefully resigned to preserving my humble life among a barbarian people. And yet, I feel fortunate for this! However, your excellency accepts hardships and requests this mission to come from afar with hundreds of thousands of soldiers to doggedly pursue my transient body; is this not too narrow a view of the world? Is there no space between heaven and earth where your servant can be accommodated? After being ennobled and bestowed with titles, do you still seek merit by killing your humble servant?

"I have come to think that in this empire built through struggle by our founding Emperor, there no longer remains even a single parcel of land where your excellency can win more merit. Your excellency has already ruined my family and you now seek to take away my posterity. This is like reading the poem in the *Shijing* about the owl that devours its own young. Can you not feel moved? Your excellency is the descendant of a family long honored with appointments; even if you cannot pity your servant, can you not think of the late Emperor? If you have no consideration for the late Emperor, can you not recall the Ming ancestors? If you do not recall the Ming ancestors, can you not remember your own father and grandfather? I cannot understand what sort of grace the great Qing has bestowed you or what sort of grievance your servant has given to your excellency. Your excellency considers himself clever but is actually foolish. You believe yourself to be generous but you are mean. After some time has passed, there will be biographies and historical accounts; what sort of person will future generations consider your excellency to have been?

Your servant's armies have crumbled and his strength is depleted. He stands alone and desolate and his humble life rests in your excellency's hands. If you really want your servant's head, I dare not refuse it even though it may mean my bones will be ground into fragments and my blood smeared on the grass and weeds. I do not dare to hope that disaster can be turned into good fortune or that in some remote region there is still a piece of land to maintain the state rituals. If your servant could be like the grass or trees in peaceful times which obtain rain and dew from a sage dynasty, then, even if he had millions of troops he would turn them over to your excellency and let them merely follow your excellency's commands. Your excellency now serves the great Qing as an official but [to spare me] would show that you do not forget sacrifices due your former lords nor ignore the great grace of your former Emperor. I hope you can consider this."

On the first day of the twelfth Moon, the grand army arrived at Miancheng. The chieftain of Burma, Mangyingshi, captured Zhu Yulang and presented him to the army. The false Marquis Huating, Wang Weigong, and a hundred others were killed. The region south of Yunnan is pacified.

3.2 SHI LANG'S MEMORIAL ON THE CAPTURE OF TAIWAN

Zheng Chenggong (1624–1662) was a formidable supporter of the Ming cause after 1644. He was a favorite of the pretender Zhu Yujian who bestowed upon him the imperial surname Zhu in 1645. Afterward Cheng was widely known as "Lord of the Imperial Surname" or *Guoxingye* and was erroneously called Koxinga by the Dutch who mistook this unofficial title for Zheng Chenggong's name.

From 1647 to 1661, Zheng waged an active campaign of resistance on the behalf of the southern Ming against the Manchus in the southern coastal region. His forces harassed the Manchus on numerous fronts and engaged in several huge pitched battles with Qing forces. When pressured to withdraw from the mainland of China, Zheng Chenggong moved to Taiwan where he besieged and captured the Dutch fortress of Zeelandia (Tainan) in 1662.

Zheng Chenggong died shortly after his forced relocation to Taiwan and command of his army and fleet were passed to his son Zheng Jing (d. 1681). The Zheng family controlled Taiwan for the next twenty years.

The Kangxi emperor undertook the elimination of this last base of Ming resistance and the Qing admiral Shi Lang (1621–1696) was dispatched with a huge fleet from Fujian to destroy loyalist forces on Taiwan and the Pescadores. Shi Lang had begun his career as a talented subordinate officer in the naval forces of Zheng Zhilong and Zheng Chenggong. The Shi family genealogy suggests that a dispute between Shi Lang and Zheng Chenggong led to the arrest and execution of the former's father, younger brother, and other family members. Shi Lang escaped this fate and followed Zheng Zhilong into service with the Manchus in 1646. Shi Lang's skill as a naval tactician and the blood enmity between him and the descendants of Zheng Chenggong made him a reliable choice as the leader of the Qing expeditionary force.

The document that follows vividly describes the enormous battle in the Taiwan Straits that led to the reoccupation of Taiwan in 1683. After 1683, Taiwan became a prefecture under the provincial government of Fujian.

EXPRESS MEMORIAL DESCRIBING THE GREAT VICTORY, 1683

The Junior Guardian of the Heir Apparent, Admiral of the Fujian Fleet, and Right Chief Military Commissioner, the Earl Shi Lang most carefully, via express memorial, hereby describes the great victory of our fleet which crossed the sea to conquer and capture Penghu.

From the time of the 6th Moon one year ago, your humble subject and Governor [of Fujian] Yao Qisheng, began stationing a fleet at Tongshan. When Liu Guoxuan [an admiral of the Ming loyalist group on Taiwan] was apprised of this, he returned to Taiwan but left behind an unlawful garrison of ships and soldiers to hold Penghu. Since then, he has frequently journeyed back and forth to deploy his defenses. In the 4th and 5th Moon of this year, when Liu Guoxuan learned that I planned to use the south wind to carry out my campaign of suppression, he selected a group of sturdy and daring fighters from the Taiwan bandit gang, enlisted tenant farmers and militia men, and refitted foreign vessels as warships. All private vessels belonging to the civil and military officials of the unlawful regime were set in order and gathered together off Penghu. There were more than two hundred large and small gunboats, "birdboats" [?], silk trading junks, foreign vessels, and two-masted junks and a bandit mob of over twenty-thousand men [in this area]. To strengthen their navy's resolve to fight to the death, the family members of all unlawful garrison commanders and troops were detained in the Hongmao Fort [the Red-haired City] and the Chikan Fort on Taiwan. Liu Guoxuan personally took command and left his lair with all of his followers to come to Penghu.

The bandits built two new gun batteries on Niangmagong Island, constructed one at Fengguiwei on Penghu, another on Sijiaoshan, one on Jilongshan, set up a strong of four in the Dongxishi area, four more on the west face of Neiwaiqian and Xiyutou, and put up another on the hilltop of Niuxinwan. All along the coast, wherever it was possible for a small boat to land, they threw up short mud walls and installed musket emplacements. These fortifications stretched for more than twenty *li* and a throng of bandits was dispatched to defend them to the death. Their defenseworks were scattered everywhere like stars in the sky or chessmen and were as sturdy as an iron bucket.

Your subject took command of the fleet and had the names of all of his captains written in large characters on the sails of their ships to permit convenient observation of their movements and distinguish who should be rewarded and who punished. Between 7:00 and 9:00 a.m. on the 14th day of the 6th Moon, we departed Tongshan and began our advance. On the 15th day, between 3:00 and 5:00 p.m., we reached Cat Island and Flower Island. Several dozen bandit picket ships saw our fleet coming and fled back to Penghu. Since nightfall was imminent, we moored our fleet in Shuian Bay of Bazhao Island and sent our picket boats to Jiangjun Island and Nanda Island to pacify the people.

We attacked Penghu on the morning of the 16th day and the bandits deployed their ships to face us. . . . [Here Shi includes a list of Qing fleet commanders who led the advance.] Our ships charged forward and hurled themselves into the mass of enemy vessels. They attacked two bandit gunboats, six silk trading junks and almost entirely wiped out the bandit crews. These vessels were then set on fire and destroyed. Our warships then turned their guns on one "birdboat" and two silk junks and promptly sank them. . . . [Here Shi inserts a second list of Qing commanders who distinguished themselves in a successive episode of this battle.] [The second group of commanders] used cannons to sink one bandit "birdboat" and two more silk junks. Almost all of the bandits aboard these vessels drowned.

At this time, the southward tide was surging and the ships leading our fleet were pushed by it toward the shore batteries. The bandit ships regrouped and rushed out together to encircle the [imperiled Qing] ships. Your servant feared that these ships would be trapped and dashed directly into the group of enemy ships to kill the enemy and withdraw. The Xinghua Garrison Commander, Wu Ying, followed me into the fray and we killed the false admiral Shen Cheng . . . and more than seventy other bandit commanders whose names we do not know and cannot present here. The false naval commander-in-chief Lin Sheng was hit by three arrows, two blunderbuss projectiles, and his left leg was broken by a cannon ball. He was immediately taken back to Taiwan but his wounds were surely fatal. The bandits who were killed, burned to death, or drowned totaled more than two thousand and because of this action our ships were rescued. Your subject's right eye was wounded by a piece of shot but his eyesight was not destroyed. Dusk was falling and, hence, we moored our fleet in the sea off Xiyutou.

On the morning of the 17th day, all of the ships of the fleet were gathered in the bay of Shuian of Bazhao and stern orders were made clear to all; merit and failings were evaluated and rewards and punishments doled out to the officers and men. On the 18th day, the fleet advanced and took Hujing and Tongpan Island. On the 19th day, your subject boarded a small silk trading junk and personally went to Neiwaiqian and Shinei to carefully examine their situation. On the 20th and 21st days, using the strategy of "feigning old age and weakness to make the enemy feel arrogant," we dispatched silk junks and two-masted junks in two groups to pretend to attack Shinei and Neiwaiqian and thus divide the enemy's forces.

On the 22nd day, your subject repeated his orders and launched a broad attack with various battle groups. . . . [Here, Shi Lang describes the groups and their commanders in detail.] Your subject led this powerful fleet forward to Niangmagong and then attacked all of the batteries and confronted the various enemy gunboats, "birdboats," and silk junks which ventured out from all points to attack us. A huge brass, barbarian, cannon weighing three to four thousand catties [1 catty = 1⅓ lbs.] was mounted on each bandit gunboat; on each side of the prow of their ships, were arrayed some twenty smaller guns and one to two hundred blunderbusses.

Cannon shot and arrows fell like rain; smoke and flame covered the sky. It was impossible to see even a foot beyond the ships. . . . [Another list of the attackers and the ships they served on follows.] The fighting went on from the early morning until the late afternoon. Our sailors fought without regard for their own lives and used all of their energy to attack and kill the bandits.

Eighteen of the bandits' big gunboats were set aflame and destroyed by our navy's incendiary buckets and grenades. Eight other heavy gunboats were sunk by cannon fire. Thirty-six large "birdboats," sixty-seven silk junks, and five refitted foreign ships were also burned and destroyed. Moreover, our navy used the wind to propel incendiary boats into other bandit ships; one "birdboat" and two silk junks were destroyed in this way. The rebellious bandits fought feverishly and when their forces were exhausted packed gunpowder in holds of their own ships and blew themselves up. In this way, they burned nine gunboats and thirteen "birdboats." Some bandits panicked and jumped into the sea and, in this way, we captured two "birdboats," eight silk junks, and twenty-five two masted junks. What was to be burnt was burnt; those to be killed were killed. . . . [A list of enemy commanders captured by Qing forces follows in the original text.] Members of the bandit mob who were burned to death in the fighting, killed in combat, or who blew themselves up or who jumped into the sea and were drowned totaled roughly twelve thousand. Bodies covered the surface of the sea. . . .

The surviving bandits fled north toward Houmen in three small gunboats, two little "birdboats," eleven silk junks, and fifteen two-masted junks. It was discovered that Liu Guoxuan boarded a small, swift vessel and also ran for Houmen. . . . [Shi Lang next lists the names of 165 surrendered enemy commanders and captains and states that 4,853 sailors followed their leaders into captivity.] Your subject, knowing of your majesty's love of human life, pardoned the bandit prisoners and permitted them to reform themselves. They have already been ordered to shave their heads. As a manifestation of our dynasty's dislike of killing and to set an example for others to follow, false commanders and captains of the surrendered forces were presented with robes and honorary caps and the bandit followers were given silver and food. . . . If there are some among the surrendered officers and soldiers who are willing to return to farming, your subject will investigate their original place of registry and contact that prefecture or county in order to have them accepted. The old and the weak will also be discharged. Those who seek to be enlisted in our forces must be supplied with food and wages and I beg for an imperial decree to the Board [of War?] and consultation between the Board and the local governor so that this can be provided. This will enable all who have defected to obtain what they sought and have a place to reside. This will cause the rebels on Taiwan to see the direction of the wind and surrender. After the pacification is completed we will follow this example to deal with our captives. . . .

3.3 THE TREATY OF NERCHINSK, 1689

The Treaty of Nerchinsk was China's first international agreement with a western country. Its signing grew out of a series of disputes between Cossacks, Russian fur traders and settlers, and Qing border garrisons. The

War of the Three Feudatories (the Sanfan Rebellion, 1673–1681) fought by Wu Sangui and his followers temporarily distracted the Qing government from the problems building in the northeast, but after Wu and his confederates were suppressed, an army headed by Prince Sabsu was sent in June 1685 to drive the Russians from settlements founded on Chinese soil. Banner troops met weak resistance from the Russians but fighting continued in the area of Fort Albazin (Yaksa). Eager to halt these conflicts, the Czarist government sent agents to Peking to request direct negotiations on the border issue and to announce that an envoy of Czar Peter hoped to discuss the fate of Albazin and other Russian outposts with a representative of Kangxi. Peking acceded to the Russian request for talks and they commenced on the banks of the Shilka river, opposite Nerchinsk, in July 1689.

The Russian delegation was led by Fedor A. Golovin who was instructed to attempt to set the boundary line, if possible, along the Amur and Bystra rivers. Golovin faced a Chinese delegation headed by Prince Songgotu, a key lieutenant of the Kangxi emperor, who had been instructed to grant the Russians the use of Nerchinsk as a trading post in return for a pledge that no Russian assistance would be granted to the Kalmuk raider Galdean. Songgotu was assisted by two Jesuits, Jean-Francois Gerbillon and Thomas Perieira, who served as translators and helped draft the text of the treaty. The treaty had versions in five languages (Latin, Manchu, Chinese, Mongolian, and Russian) and was a milestone in Chinese diplomatic history. It was signed on August 27, 1689.

The record of the treaty that was enacted by the boyar Fedor Alekseevich Golovin and the Ambassador of the Chinese Khan, Councilor Sumguta, and associates, at the conference on the frontier near Nerchinsk in 7197 [1689].

By the divine grace of the Great Sovereigns, Tsars and Great Princes, Ivann Alekseevich and Petr Alekseevich, Autocrats of all the Great and Little and White Russias and of the many states and lands, eastern, western, and northern; of their fathers and fore-fathers, heirs, lords and freeholders; the Great and Plenipotentiary Ambassadors of Their Royal Highnesses, the Minister of the Presence and Lieutenant Governor of Briansk, Fedor Alekseevich Golovin, and the Chamberlain and Lieutenant Governor of Elatomsk, Ivan Ostafevich Vlasov, and the clerk Semon Kornitsky, who were at the ambassadorial conference near Nerchinsk, and the Great Ambassadors of the Great Asian Countries, of the Autocratic Monarch who of all the Bogdoi lords is the Most Wise Administrator of the Law and Guardian and Glory of the affairs of the society of the Chinese people, of the Actual Bogdoi and Chinese Bugdykhan Highness: Samguta, Commander of the Imperial Bodyguard and Voevoda of the Interior Chamber and Councilor of the Kingdom, and Tumke-Kam, Voevoda of the Interior Chamber, Prince of the First Rank and Lord of the Khan's Banner, and Ilamt [Maci], the Khan's uncle and Lord of One Banner, etc., enacted and confirmed these articles of the treaty:

I

The river called Gorbitsa which going down falls into the Shilka river from the left side near the Chernaya river is decreed the boundary between both states.

Likewise, from the upper reaches of that river the power of both states is thus divided by the stone mountain chain which begins from the upper reaches of that river and extends even to the sea, along the heights of those same mountains; so that all rivers, small and great, that fall into the Amur from the southern slopes of those mountains are under the dominion of the Khin state.

Likewise, all rivers that flow from the other slopes of those mountains shall be under the power of the tsarish majesty of the Russian state. Those other rivers that lie in the middle between the river Ud under the dominion of the Russian state and the delimited mountains which are located near the Amur of the domain of the Khin state, and which fall into the sea, and every land within that area between the above-mentioned river Ud and the mountains which lie up to the frontier remain undemarcated for now, since for the demarcation of those lands, the great and plenipotentiary ambassadors, not having a decree of the tsarish majesty, will leave them undemarcated until that propitious time when, upon the return of the embassies of both sides, the tsarish majesty is pleased, and the Bugdykhan Highness agrees, to send ambassadors or envoys with amicable correspondence, and then through either embassy or letters those named undemarcated lands calmly and properly can be set to rest and demarcated.

I I

Likewise, the river called Argun which falls into the river Amur is thus decreed the frontier, so that all lands that make up the left side, going along that river to its very sources, are under the dominion of the Khin khan; likewise, all lands contained on the right side are in the domain of the tsarish majesty of the Russian state, and all buildings on the southern bank of that river Argun shall be moved to the other side of that same river.

I I I

The town of Albazin which was built by the tsarish majesty will be destroyed to its foundations and those people living there with all military and other supplies shall be returned to the side of the tsarish majesty, and none of their losses [i.e., side effects], however small the things, shall be left there.

I V

Fugitives, whether they were, up to this peace decree, from either the side of the tsarish majesty or from the side of the Bugdykhan highness, are [permitted] to be on either side without being exchanged, but those who after this decreed peace shall pass over, such fugitives shall be expelled without delay from either side and [turned over] immediately to the frontier voevodas.

V

Whatever people with [i.e., who possess] documents of passage from either side, for the [sake of the] presently inaugurated friendship, may freely come and go to both states for their affairs on either side and may buy and sell what is necessary to them and it shall be [so] ordered.

V I

Formerly, before this decreed peace, there were quarrels between those living on the frontier for trade between both states. [Now if] traders shall pass and thefts or murder will be committed, such people, having been caught, shall be sent back to that side whence they came, to the border towns, to the voevodas, and for them who commit such crimes the punishment shall be severe. [When] people band together and commit such crimes as the above-mentioned thievery, such willful ones, having been caught, shall be sent to the frontier voevodas, and for those who commit such crimes the punishment shall be death. And warfare and bloodshed shall not be resorted to by either side for such reasons or for the offenses of those living on the frontier. Instead, it shall be written about such disputes by the side on which the thieving occurs and reported to the sovereigns [of both powers], and disputes shall be settled by special diplomatic note.

Regarding these articles of the agreements about the frontier decreed by the ambassadors, if the Bugdykhan highness wishes on his part to place markers at the border and to record on them these articles, we shall allow it at the discretion of the Bugdykhan highness.

Given at the frontiers of the tsarish majesty, in the Daur lands, August 27, 7197 [1689].

This letter was written by the hand of Andrei Belobotsky in the Latin language.

Counter signature of the secretary Fedor Aprotopov on the document.

The translator, Foma Rozanov, read from the original copy.[1]

3.4 FANG BAO'S "RANDOM NOTES FROM PRISON," 1711

During the reign of the Kangxi emperor any sign of affection or nostalgia for the defunct Ming dynasty was regarded as a treasonable offense. Schol-

---

1. The Manchu prince Songottu (d. 1703?), Tong Guokang, and Maci represented the Qing court.

ars or officials who dared in their jottings or collections to mention either the Ming or southern Ming in sympathetic terms faced harsh judicial penalties.

One of the most infamous "literary inquisitions" of the Kangxi era was the case of Dai Mingshi (1653–1713), a native of Tongcheng in Anhui, who printed a set of nostalgic essays in 1701 entitled *Nanshan ji* (The southern hills collection). Subsequently, in 1711, Dai, who was then a compiler in the Hanlin Academy, was accused of treason and arrested for having used southern Ming reign titles in this work. In roundups that followed, many of Dai's relatives and friends were taken into custody and Dai himself was finally decapitated. As it was perhaps designed to do, this case created a mood of fear in the capital and set an example for the later literary purges of the Qianlong era.

One of the scholars touched by the circles of recrimination that radiated out of the *Nanshan ji* affair was Fang Bao, a Tongcheng *jinshi*, who was one of the most outstanding prose stylists of his time and a close friend of Dai Mingshi. In 1711, Fang was accused by Gali, a high Manchu official, of writing a preface for *Nanshan ji* and was cast into the Board of Punishments prison where he languished for two years. In later years, however, he was pardoned and participated in a variety of literary projects.

The document translated below is Fang Bao's description of his experience in prison. Its stark portrait of prison conditions illustrates the perils faced by those who ran afoul of the law in the early Qing era. The penal system was often depicted by Qing writers and memoirists as a hellish realm with no rules or protocols that was presided over by sadistic brutes. Passing through the prison gates, inmates slipped out of the Confucian world of *li* (righteousness) and *ren* (humane feeling) and lost all vestiges of their previous identity or position in the world. Human dignity was purposely stripped away and, as indicated by Fang Bao's account, only an unceasing flow of silver preferred to the guards and wardens by desperate relatives could save one from the worst abuses.

In the third moon of the fifty-first year of the Kangxi Emperor [1712], while I was jailed in the prison of the Board of Punishments, I saw three or four dead prisoners dumped out through a hole each day. Mr. Du, the magistrate of Hongdong [a county of Shanxi Province], stood up and said: "This comes from an epidemic. Presently things are normal and so there aren't many people who die. In the past, dozens died every day." I asked him why this was so. Mr. Du said: "This kind of illness spreads easily. Even the relatives of those who get it dare not sleep in the same room with them."

In the prison there were four old cells. Each cell had five rooms. The jail guards lived in the center with a window in the front of their quarters for light. At the end of this room there was another opening for ventilation. There were no such windows for the other four rooms and yet more than two hundred prisoners were always confined there. Each day toward dusk, the cells were locked and the odor of the urine and excrement would mingle with that of the food and drink. Moreover, in the coldest months of the winter, the poor prisoners had to sleep on the ground and when the spring breezes came everyone got sick. The established rule in the prison was that the door would be unlocked only at dawn. During the night, the living and the dead slept side by side with no room to turn their bodies and this is why so many people became infected. Even more terrible was that robbers, veteran criminals and murderers who were imprisoned for serious offenses had strong constitutions and only one or two out of ten would be infected and even so they would recover immediately. Those who died from the malady were all light offenders or sequestered witnesses who would not normally be subjected to legal penalties.

I said: "In the capital there are the metropolitan prefectural prison and the censorial prisons of the five wards. How is it then that the Board of Punishment's prison has so many prisoners?" Mr. Du answered: "In the recent times, the metropolitan prefectural prison and the censorial prisons of the five wards have not dared to take jurisdiction for the more serious cases. Furthermore, in the cases when the city garrison commander orders arrest and interrogation, the prisoners are sent to the Board of Punishments. The chiefs and deputy heads of the Fourteen Bureaus like to get new prisoners, the clerks; prison officials, and guards all benefit from having so many prisoners. If there is the slightest pretext or connection they use every method to trap new prisoners. Once someone is put into the prison his guilt or innocence does not matter. The prisoner's hands and feet are shackled and he is put in one of the old cells until he can bear the suffering no more. Then he is led to obtain bail and permitted to live outside the jail. His family's property is measured to decide the payment and the officials and clerks all split it. Middling households and those just above exhaust their wealth to get bail. Those families somewhat less wealthy seek to have the shackles removed and to obtain lodging [for the prisoner-relative] in the custody sheds outside the jail. This also costs tens of silver taels. As for the poorest prisoners or those with no one to rely on, their shackles are not loosened at all and they are used as examples to warn the others. Sometimes cellmates guilty of serious crimes are bailed out but those guilty of small crimes and the innocent suffer the most poisonous abuse. They store up their anger and indignation, fail to eat or sleep normally, are not treated with medicine, and when they get sick they often die.

"I have humbly witnessed our Emperor's virtuous love for all beings which is as great as that of the sages of the past ages. Whenever he examines the documents related to a case, he tries to find life for those who should die. But now it has come to this [state of affairs] for the innocent. A virtuous gentleman might save many lives if he was to speak to the Emperor saying: 'Leaving aside those prisoners sentenced to death or exiled to border region for great crimes, should not small offenders and those involved in a case but not convicted be placed in a separate place without chaining their hands and feet?' Some say: 'The jail used to have five rooms called temporary cells. Those who were charged but not convicted lived in them. If this old practice could be restored it would be of some help.' "

Mr. Du said: "The Emperor extends his grace by permitting [convicted] government officials to live in the custody sheds. But now the poor are imprisoned in the old cells and some important criminals live in the sheds. How is it possible to ask the details? It would be better to set up a separate ward to halt this immoral practice." My cellmate Old Zhu, Young Yu, and a certain government official named Seng who all died of illness in prison should not have been heavily punished. There was also a certain person who accused his own son of unfiliality. The [father's] neighbors [involved in the case only as witnesses] were all chained and imprisoned in the old cells. They cried all night long. I was moved by this and so I made inquiries. Everyone corroborated this account and so I am writing this document.

Whenever the death sentence is being carried out, the executioner waits outside the door and lets his confederates enter the cell to ask for money or property. This is called *siluo*. For the rich, they ask the relatives, for the poor they simply ask the condemned man himself. If slicing is the penalty, they say: "If you satisfy me, I will stab you in the heart. Otherwise, even after your four limbs have been sliced to bits, your heart will still be beating." If strangulation is imposed, they say: "If you satisfy me, you will die after the first pull of the garotte. Otherwise, three ropes and other instruments will be used and then you will die." For decapitation there is nothing they can threaten but they can hold the head hostage afterwards. Because of these threats, the rich are obliged to bribe them [the prison personnel] with many dozens of ounces of silver and the poor are forced to sell their clothes. Dealing with those who have nothing, they do as they have said they would. Those who tie up the prisoners for execution also ask for money. If their desires are not satisfied, they break the bones or sinews with the ropes. Every year at the peak time for executions [after the Autumn Assizes], thirty or forty percent of the condemned are really checked off for execution but sixty to seventy percent are spared for the year. All of the prisoners are bound and taken to the Western Market to await their destiny. If those who are spared are injured by being bound, it will take them months to recover and some have to live with the damage for life. Once I asked an old clerk, "Since there is no animosity between the prisoners and those who tie them up and since the jailers simply want to gain something, would it not be humane, if a person really has nothing, to let the bonds be looser?" He replied, "This is done to set a model for the rest and as a warning to future violators. Were this not so they would take their chances." The beaters are also the same. Among three of my cellmates who were beaten with clubs, one paid thirty taels and his bones were only slightly damaged and he was sick for two months; another paid double and his skin was hurt but he recovered in twenty days; the third paid five times more and was able to walk as usual that very night. Someone asked a beater, "Since some of the prisoners are rich and others poor but all give something, why draw a distinction in punishing them simply because of their payments?" The answer was, "If there was no difference, who would pay more?" . . .

3.5 KANGXI'S VALEDICTORY EDICT, 1717

The imperial edict below was issued by the Kangxi emperor (1654–1722) on December 23, 1717. By this time, Kangxi had ruled China for over fifty years and placed the stamp of his thoughtful and inquiring mind on the workings of the imperial state. The ambitious rivals who threatened the throne at the outset of Kangxi's reign were long since under control. Oboi, Galdan, Wu Sangui, and Koxinga were all dead and the forces they commanded in vain efforts to achieve their aims followed them into oblivion. In the final years of the emperor's life, Kangxi was the master of a powerful and unified state.

While one glimpses through this edict the emperor's sense of his own accomplishments, there are also ruminations on mortality and the concerns of ruling a state so vast and complex as seventeenth- and eighteenth-century China. One of the agonizing difficulties of the final years of Kangxi's reign was the problem of finding an appropriate successor. Until 1712, Kangxi favored his second son, Yinreng, but the erratic and conspiratorial behavior of the heir apparent made him an impossible choice. By the time of the 1717 edict, Kangxi appeared to favor Yinti, his fourteenth son, for the throne, but the document merely suggests how burdensome this problem had become and makes no explicit reference to how Kangxi intended to resolve it.[2]

When I was young, Heaven gave me great strength, and I didn't know what sickness was. This spring I started to get serious attacks of dizziness and grew increasingly emaciated. Then I went hunting in the autumn beyond the borders, and the fine climate of the Mongolian regions made my spirits stronger day by day, and my face filled out again. Although I was riding and shooting every day, I didn't feel fatigued. After I returned to Peking the Empress Dowager fell ill, and I was dejected in mind; the dizziness grew almost incessant. Since

---

2. "Unofficial histories" (*yeshi*) of the Qing era have suggested that Yinzhen (later Emperor Yongzheng), son number four (*si*), simply erased the character for ten (*shi*) in Kangxi's decree appointing the fourteenth son (*shisi*) as his heir.

there are some things that I have wanted to say to you on a normal day, I have specially summoned you today to hear my edict, face to face with me.

The rulers of the past all took reverence for Heaven and observance of ancestral precepts as the fundamental way in ruling the country. To be sincere in reverence for Heaven and ancestors entails the following: Be kind to men from afar and keep the able ones near, nourish the people, think of the profit of all as being the real profit and the mind of the whole country as being the real mind, be considerate to officials and act as a father to the people, protect the state before danger comes and govern well before there is any disturbance, be always diligent and always careful, and maintain the balance between leniency and strictness, between principle and expediency, so that long-range plans can be made for the country. That's all there is to it.

No dynasty in history has been as just as ours in gaining the right to rule. The Emperors T'ai-tsu and T'ai-tsung initially had no intention of taking over the country; and when T'ai-tsung's armies were near Peking and his ministers advised him to take it, he replied: "The Ming have not been on good terms with our people, and it would be very easy to conquer them now. But I am aware of what an unbearable act it is to overthrow the ruler of China." Later the roving bandit Li Tzucheng stormed the city of Peking, the Ming Emperor Ch'ung-chen hanged himself, and the officials and people all came out to welcome us. Then we exterminated the violent bandits and inherited the empire. In olden times, it was Hsiang Yu who raised an army and defeated the Ch'in, yet the country then passed to the Han, even though initially Emperor Han Kao-tsu was only a local constable on the Ssu River. At the end of the Yuan, it was Ch'en Yu-liang and others who rebelled, yet the country then passed to the Ming, even though initially Emperor Ming T'ai-tsu was only a monk in the Huang-chueh Temple. The forebears of our dynasty were men who obeyed Heaven and lived in harmony with other men; and the empire was pacified. From this we can tell that all the rebellious officials and bandits are finally pushed aside by truly legitimate rulers.

I am now close to seventy, and have been over fifty years on the throne— this is all due to the quiet protection of Heaven and earth and the ancestral spirits; it was not my meager virtue that did it. Since I began reading in my childhood, I have managed to get a rough understanding of the constant historical principles. Every Emperor and ruler has been subject to the Mandate of Heaven. Those fated to enjoy old age cannot prevent themselves from enjoying that old age; those fated to enjoy a time of Great Peace cannot prevent themselves from enjoying that Great Peace.

Over 4,350 years have passed from the first year of the Yellow Emperor to the present, and over 300 emperors are listed as having reigned, though the data from the Three Dynasties—that is, for the period before the Ch'in burning of the books—are not wholly credible. In the 1,960 years from the first year of Ch'in Shih-huang to the present, there have been 211 people who have been named emperor and have taken era names. What man am I, that among all those who have reigned long since the Ch'in and Han Dynasties, it should be I who have reigned the longest?

Among the Ancients, only those who were not boastful and knew not to go too far could attain a good end. Since the Three Dynasties, those who ruled long did not leave a good name to posterity, while those who did not live long did not know the world's grief. I am already old, and have reigned long, and I cannot foretell what posterity will think of me. Besides which, because of what is going on now, I cannot hold back my tears of bitterness; and so I have prepared these notes to make my own record, for I still fear that the country may not know the depth of my sorrow.

Many emperors and rulers in the past made a taboo of the subject of death, and as we look at their valedictory decrees we find that they are not at all written in imperial tones, and do not record what the emperor really wanted to say. It was always when the emperors were weak and dying that they found some scholar-official to write out something as he chose.

With me it is different. I am letting you know what my sincerest feelings are in advance.

When I had been twenty years on the throne I didn't dare conjecture that I might reign thirty. After thirty years I didn't dare conjecture that I might reign forty. Now I have reigned fifty-seven years. The "Great Plan" section of the *Book of History* says of the five joys:

> The first is long life;
> The second is riches;
> The third is soundness of body and serenity of mind;
> The fourth is the love of virtue;
> The fifth is an end crowning the life.

The "end crowning the life" is placed last because it is so hard to attain. I am now approaching seventy, and my sons, grandsons, and great-grandsons number over 150. The country is more or less at peace and the world is at peace. Even if we haven't improved all manners and customs, and made all the people prosperous and contented, yet I have worked with unceasing diligence and intense watchfulness, never resting, never idle. So for decades I have exhausted all my strength, day after day. How can all this just be summed up in a two-word phrase like "hard work"?

Those among the rulers of earlier dynasties who did not live long have all been judged in the Histories as having caused this themselves through their own wild excesses, by overaddiction to drink and sex. Such remarks are just the sneers of pedants who have to find some blemishes in even the purest and most perfect of rulers. I exonerate these earlier rulers, because the affairs of the country are so troublesome that one can't help getting exhausted. Chu-ko Liang said: "I shall bow down in service and wear myself out until death comes," but among all the officials only Chu-ko Liang acted in this way. Whereas the emperor's responsibilities are terribly heavy, there is no way he can evade them. How can this be compared with being an official? If an official wants to serve, then he serves; if he wants to stop, then he stops. When he grows old he resigns and returns home, to look after his sons and play with his grandsons; he still has the chance to relax and enjoy himself. Whereas the ruler in all his hard-working life finds no place to rest. Thus, though the Emperor Shun said, "Through non-action one governs," he died in Ts'ang-wu [while on tour of inspection]; and after four years on the throne Emperor Yu had blistered hands and feet and found death in K'uai-ch'i. To work as hard at government as these men, to travel on inspection, to have never a leisure moment—how can this be called the valuing of "non-action" or tranquilly looking after oneself? In the *I Ching* hexagram "Retreat" not one of the six lines deals with a ruler's concerns—from this we can see that there is no place for rulers to rest, and no resting place to which they can retreat. "Bowing down in service and wearing oneself out" indeed applied to this situation.

All the Ancients used to say that the Emperor should concern himself with general principles, but need not deal with the smaller details. I find that I cannot agree with this. Careless handling of one item might bring harm to the whole world; a moment's carelessness could damage all future generations. Failure to attend to details will end up endangering your greater virtues. So I always attend carefully to the details. For example: if I neglect a couple of matters today and leave them unsettled, there will be a couple more matters for tomorrow. And if tomorrow I again don't want to be bothered, that will pile up even more obstructions for the future. The emperor's work is of great importance, and there should not be delays, so I attend to all matters, whether they are great or small. Even if it is just one character wrong in a memorial, I always correct it before forwarding it. Not to neglect anything, that is my nature. For over fifty years I have usually prepared in advance for things—and the world's millions all honor my virtuous intentions. How can one still hold to "there being no need to deal with the smaller details"?

I was strong from my childhood onward, with fine muscles; I could bend a bow with a pull of 15 *li*, and fire a fifty-two inch arrow. I was good at using troops and confronting the enemy, but I have never recklessly killed a single person. In pacifying the Three Feudatories and clearing out the northern deserts, I made all the plans myself. Unless it was for military matters or famine relief, I didn't take funds from the Board of Revenue treasury, and spent nothing recklessly, for the reason that this was the people's wealth. On my inspection tours, I didn't set out colored embroideries, and the expenses at each place were only 10,000 or 20,000 taels. In comparison, the annual expense on the river conservancy system is over 3,000,000—so the cost was not even one percent of that.

When I studied as a child, I already knew that one should be careful with drink and sex, and guard against mean people. So I grew old without illness. But after my serious illness in the forty-seventh year of my reign, my spirits had been too much wounded, and gradually I failed to regain my former state. Moreover, every day there was my work, all requiring decisions; frequently I felt that my vitality was slipping away and my internal energy diminishing. I fear that in the future if some accident happened to me I would not be able to say a word, and so my real feelings would not be disclosed. Wouldn't that be regretful? Therefore I am using this occasion when I feel clear-headed and lively to complete my life by telling you all that can be revealed, item by item. Isn't that wonderful?

All men who live must die. As Chu Hsi said, "The principle of the cyclical cosmic forces is like dawn and night." And Confucius said, "Live contentedly and await Heaven's will." These sayings express the great Way of the Sages, so why should we be afraid? I have been seriously ill recently: my mind was blurred and my body exhausted. As I moved around, if no one held me up by the arms it was hard for me to walk. In the past I fixed my mind on my responsibilities to the country; to work "until death comes" was my goal. Now that I am ill I am querulous and forgetful, and terrified of muddling right with wrong, and leaving my work in chaos. I exhaust my mind for the country's sake, and fragment my spirits for the world. When you wits aren't guarding your body, your heart has no nourishment, your eyes can't tell far from near nor ears distinguish true from false, and you eat little and have a lot to do—how can you last long? Moreover, since the country has long been at peace and people have grown lazy, joy goes and sorrows mount, "peace" departs and "stagnation" comes. When the head is crammed with trifles, the limbs are indolent—until everything is in ruins and you inevitably bring down at random and together calamities from Heaven and destruction for men. Even if you want to do something, your vitality is insufficient, and by then it's too late to admit your mistakes. No more can you be roused up, and moaning in your bed you'll die with eyes open—won't you feel anguish just before you die?

Emperor Wu-ti of the Liang was a martial dynastic founder, but when he reached old age he was forced by Hou-ching into the tragedy at T'ai-ch'eng. Emperor Wen-ti of the Sui also was a founding emperor, but he could not anticipate the evil ways of his son Yang-ti and was finally unable to die in peace. There are other examples, like killing oneself by taking cinnabar, or being poisoned and eating the cakes, or the case of Sung T'ai-tsu, when people saw the candlelight from afar. There are records of all kinds of suspicious cases—are these not tracks of the past that we can see? All these happened because [the emperors] didn't understand in time. And all brought harm to country and people. Han Kao-tsu told Empress Lu about the mandate; T'ang T'ai-tsung decided on the heir apparent with Chang-sun Wu-chi. When I read such things I feel deeply ashamed. Perhaps there are mean persons who hope to use the confusion, and will act on their own authority to alter the succession, pushing someone forward in expectation of future rewards. As long as I still have one breath left, how could I tolerate that sort of thing?

My birth was nothing miraculous—nor did anything extraordinary happen when I grew up. I came to the throne at eight, fifty-seven years ago. I've never let people talk on about supernatural influences of the kind that have been recorded in the Histories: lucky starts, auspicious clouds, unicorns and phoenixes, *chih* grass and such like blessings, or burning pearls and jade in the front of the palace, or heavenly books sent down to manifest Heaven's will. Those are all empty words, and I don't presume so far. I just go on each day in an ordinary way, and concentrate on ruling properly.

Now, officials have memorialized, requesting that I set up an heir apparent to share duties with me—that's because they feared my life might end abruptly. Death and life are ordinary phenomena—I've never avoided talking about them. It's just that all the power of the country has to be united in one person. For the last ten years, I've been writing out (and keeping sealed) what I intend to do and what my feelings are, though I haven't finished yet. Appointing the heir-apparent is a great matter; how could I neglect it? The throne of this country is one of the utmost importance. If I were to relieve myself of this burden and relax in comfort, disentangling my mind from every problem, then I could certainly expect to live longer. You officials have all received great mercies from me—how can I attain the day when I will have no more burdens?

My energies have shrunk, I have to force myself to endure, and if everything finally goes awry, won't the hard work of the last fifty-seven years indeed be wasted? It is my intense sincerity that leads me to say this. Whenever I read an old official's memorial requesting retirement, I can't stop the tears from flowing. You all have a time for retiring, but where can I find rest? But if I could have a few weeks to restore myself and a chance to conclude my life with a natural death, then my happiness would be indescribable. There is time ahead of me; maybe I will live as long as Sung Kao-tsung. We cannot tell.

Not until I was fifty-seven did I begin to have a few white hairs in my beard, and I was offered some lotion to make it black again. But I laughed and refused, saying: "How many white-haired emperors have there been in the past? If my hair and whiskers whiten, won't that be a splendid tale for later generations?" Not one man is now left from those who worked with me in my early years. Those who came later to their new appointments are harmonious and respectful with their colleagues, they are just and law-abiding, and their white heads fill the Court. This has been the case for a long time, and for this I am grateful.

I have enjoyed the veneration of my country and the riches of the world; there is no object I do not have, nothing I have not experienced. But now that I have reached old age I cannot rest easy for a moment. Therefore, I regard the whole country as a worn-out sandal, and all riches as mud and sand. If I can die without there being an outbreak of trouble, my desires will be fulfilled. I wish all of you officials to remember that I have been the peace-bearing Son of Heaven for over fifty years, and that what I have said to you over and over again is really sincere. Then that will complete this fitting end to my life.

I've been preparing this edict for ten years. If a "valedictory edict" is issued, let it contain nothing but these same words.

I've revealed my entrails and shown my guts, there's nothing left within me to reveal.

I will say no more.

CHAPTER 4

Yongzheng's Authority

4.1 AND 4.2 KANGXI'S SACRED EDICT AND WANG YUPU AND YONGZHENG'S AMPLIFICATION

The purpose of Kangxi's sixteen hortatory maxims, each expressed in seven characters, was to lay down an ethical and moral framework for subjects of the Qing state. In 1724, the Yongzheng emperor issued an amplified version of his father's maxims (the *Shengyu guangxun*) in literary Chinese. An expanded third version (the *Shengyu guangxun zhijie*) was written in a homely colloquial style by Wang Yupu, a Shaanxi salt commissioner, soon thereafter. This latter version was read aloud at yamen throughout China on the first and fifteenth of each moon.

A full translation is provided below of the original Kangxi maxims. There follow portions of Wang Yupu's vernacular exposition of the Yongzheng text for those maxims marked with an asterisk. For the Confucian ruler, well-ordered families and clans were the paradigms of an orderly state and both the Kangxi and Yongzheng versions of the Edict stress this basic principle of Chinese statecraft. It is also worth noting the scorn heaped by Wang Yupu on Buddhist and Daoist practices and folk religion in general. The central government saw its subjects as ignorant and easily misled. It distrusted and feared orthodoxies other than those it imposed and "heterodox" authorities who might extract funds or loyalty from the state's own constituencies.

4.1 *The Sacred Edict of the Kangxi Emperor, 1670*

THE SIXTEEN MAXIMS (SHENGYU)

1. Strengthen filial piety and brotherly affection to emphasize human relations.
2. Strengthen clan relations to illustrate harmony.*
3. Pacify relations between local groups to put an end to quarrels and litigation.
4. Stress agriculture and sericulture so that there may be sufficient food and clothing.
5. Prize frugality so as to make careful use of wealth.
6. Promote education to improve the habits of scholars.
7. Extirpate heresy to exalt orthodoxy.*
8. Speak of the law to give warning to the stupid and stubborn.*
9. Clarify rites and manners to improve customs.
10. Let each work at his own occupation so that the people's minds will be settled.
11. Instruct young people to prevent them from doing wrong.
12. Prevent false accusations to shield the law-abiding.
13. Prohibit sheltering of runaways to avoid being implicated in their crime.
14. Pay taxes to avoid being pressed for payment.
15. Unite the *baojia* system to eliminate theft and armed robbery.
16. Resolve hatred and quarrels to respect life.

4.2 *Wang Yupu and Yongzheng's Amplification of Kangxi's Sacred Edict, 1724*

1. AMPLIFICATION OF MAXIM TWO: STRENGTHEN CLAN RELATIONS TO ILLUSTRATE HARMONY.

... The clan is like the water of a spring which branches into several streams and then dozens of streams as it emerges. But all of these branches originated from the same spring. It is also like a tree which grows a thousand branches and ten thousand leaves that all emerge from the same root. A clan whether it is divided into a branch of several dozens of able bodied men or hundreds of men comes from the same body of the same ancestor. The clan members are like the hands, feet, ears, eyes, mouth, nose, and other parts of the ancestor's body; when you put them together they are one body. Just think, if there is a sore on my body or if I sprain my ankle or break my leg, doesn't my whole body feel uncomfortable? If you try to entrap or harm a clan member or insult or cheat him and make him feel uncomfortable, can you imagine that you will feel happy? You should treat them as you would yourself. You should look at clan members as part of one body; if one place hurts then all other places will hurt. If one spot itches, all spots will itch. Only when the blood flows throughout the body will things be as they should be. Therefore, the ancients said: 'To educate the people, filial piety, brotherly affection, harmony, love, willingness to endure for others, and charity are necessary.' When it [the section of the ancient classic the *Zhouli* quoted by Yongzheng] says filial piety, next it says brotherly affection and then it says harmony and that's because clan members are descended from the same ancestor. If someone does not want harmony in his own clan he is unfilial and goes against brotherly affection. . . .

2. AMPLIFICATION OF MAXIM SEVEN: EXTIRPATE HERESY TO EXALT ORTHODOXY.

. . . What is heterodoxy? From ancient times there have been three religions. Besides Confucian scholars there are Buddhist monks and Taoist priests. These latter sects are heretical. All the Buddhist priests talk about is meditation, enlightenment, and becoming a Buddha. They also say: "If one son becomes a monk, the whole clan will ascend to heaven." Just think about it, who has ever seen a Buddha? What is a Buddha? Buddha is in the heart. What is the meaning of chanting the name of the Buddha? It is for the mind to be constantly concerned about the heart. If the heart is good this is Buddha.

Just look at their sutras. The first sutra is the Heart Sutra. All the Heart Sutra says is that the heart should be straight; it should not be twisted or devious. It should be honest and not false and lying. It should be frank and not unclean. If one can cut oneself off from greed, anger, and stupid attachments and be, in all things, like a flower in a looking glass or the moon in water, then all doubts and fears will cease and the heart will be perfect. Therefore, Master Zhu Xi of the Song dynasty said: 'Buddhism does not concern itself with anything in the four corners of the universe but is concerned simply with the heart.' This sentence goes to the bottom of Buddhism and expresses it entirely.

. . . All this talk about fasts, processions, building temples, and making idols is invented by idle and lazy Buddhists monks and Taoist priests as a plan for swindling you. But you want to believe them and not only go yourselves to burn incense and worship in their temples but also ask your wives and daughters to go to the temples to burn incense. With oiled hair and powdered faces, dressed in bright colors, they crowd and jostle shoulder to shoulder with these Taoist and Buddhists priests and riffraff. Where the 'practicing goodness' comes in nobody knows, but many vile things are done that provoke anger, vexation, and ridicule. . . .

. . . As for reciting prayers to Buddha: You say it does good and that by burning paper, offering presents, and performing services for the release of

souls, calamity may be averted, sin destroyed, happiness increased, and life prolonged. Now just consider, it has always been said: 'The wise and upright are
divine.' If someone is a divine Buddha, how can he be greedy for your contributions of silver in order to protect you. And if you don't burn paper money
and make sacrifices, and the 'divine Buddha' then gets angry and sends a calamity down upon you, is he not a mean person? Take the example of your local
official. If you attend to your own business and are a good person, even if you
don't go to flatter him, he will still naturally regard you with respect. If you do
evil and behave in a bullying and presumptuous way, even if you think of a
hundred ways to flatter him, he will still be angry with you and get rid of you
to spare the people harm. You say: 'If we repeat the Buddha's name we can be
rid of our sins.' If you do something evil and break the law and then cry out,
'Your honor,' a thousand times in a loud voice when you reach the yamen, will
he pardon you? Every time you do something, you ask several monks and
Taoists to chant the sutras and carry out rituals. It is said that chanting the
sutras secures peace, averts disaster, and prolongs happiness and life. Suppose
you don't follow the teachings in the Sacred Edict, but instead merely recite it
several thousand times or tens of thousands of times, it is unlikely that the
Emperor will be so pleased with you that you will be given an official post or
rewarded with silver.

. . . To be perfectly loyal to the Ruler and to fulfill filial duty to the utmost
is the whole duty of man and the means of obtaining the blessing of heaven. If
you do not seek happiness which is not your lot in life and do not meddle in
matters that do not concern you but simply mind your own business, you will
enjoy the protection of the gods. Farmers should look after farming. Soldiers
should go about their patrols and garrison duties. Each should attend to his
own occupation and duties and then the realm will be naturally at peace and
the people will be naturally happy. If none of you believe in heretical sects, they
will not have to wait to be driven out but will become extinct naturally.

3. AMPLIFICATION OF MAXIM EIGHT: SPEAK OF LAW TO GIVE WARNING TO THE STUPID AND STUBBORN.

. . . Is it possible that the State could enjoy beating and decapitating people? It
is only because the people do not learn to be good and do not obey instructions
that there is no other alternative than to use the penal law to control them.
Since in many cases, the people break the law because they do not know it, this
book has been compiled to instruct them to be good people and not bad people.
For those who do bad, punishment is proportional to the offense, but even
should you merely curse someone or take a blade of grass or stick of wood you
will not escape the law.

. . . The law contains a profound meaning and was originally drawn up in accordance with human nature. If everyone knew the meaning of the law, they would not break it. There would be nobody in the prisons and few litigations. It follows that it is best to warn people before they break the law and to frequently warn them rather than waiting for them to break the law and then punishing them.

But you are also aware that breaking the law is not good and yet you incessantly disobey it. What is the reason for this? It is entirely because you do not understand the law and therefore break it unconsciously. There are even cases of people who to their dying day are unaware of it. Presently the court has called upon its great officials to set in place that great Qing's laws and to organize statutes and precedents that will be set forth in detail. This is done so that you soldiers and people will understand and obey and so that you will not find yourselves in the situation of having broken the law. It is truly tender care for you that has prompted this.

But people who have grown up in country villages are unavoidably dull and stupid and soldiers who are occupied with military affairs are mostly rough and rude. Both of these groups often break the laws of the land unknowingly. Presently we especially and repeatedly instruct you: if you all understand, you will naturally be afraid of breaking the law. . . .

. . . Make it your constant practice, by means of the law of the land, to curb and control yourselves, and to admonish others. Those who fear the law, will, come what may, avoid breaking it. Those who dread punishment will surely work to not incur it. If depravity is eliminated, then wrangling will cease. The muddled will be enlightened and the stubbornly evil will be made good. The people will be happy in the fields and the soldiers will be happy in their ranks. If the penal law is not used for several hundred years, will not everyone enjoy peace together?

4.3   YONGZHENG'S EDICT ON CHANGING THE STATUS OF THE MEAN PEOPLE

From 1723 onward, Emperor Yongzheng issued edicts that successively reclassified "mean" (*jian*) households as "common" (*liang*) households. "Mean" groups had been discriminated against for centuries and were confined to narrow occupational niches. One such group were the *yuehu* or musician households. Members of this group were descended from loyal followers of the Jianwen emperor who were exiled to Shaanxi and Shanxi after Ming emperor Yongle successfully usurped the throne in 1403. The women were subsequently obliged to work as government courtesans and the men were allowed to work only as musicians. The *duomin* or "lazy households" of Zhejiang, who may have been descended from criminals or war captives of the Song dynasty, were not permitted to wear the same clothing as ordinary people and were consigned to jobs such as catching frogs and turtles; exorcising evil spirits; working as go-betweens or as midwives; and carrying sedan chairs. People who belonged to all of these and other like groups were not permitted to take the bureaucratic examinations or enter government service, were barred from marrying commoners, and were obliged to follow strict sumptuary laws.

Although the Kangxi emperor had abolished the "musical households" of Yangzhou during his reign, Yongzheng's reforms were on a far greater scale and completely eradicated the legal basis for discrimination. Some members of these households continued to follow the same professions subsequent to the reforms and continued to be looked down upon, but nevertheless the reforms led to the gradual disappearance of the cruel social distinctions of earlier eras.

The document translated below is one example of the series of edicts through which Yongzheng abolished the discrimination suffered by the *jiamin*. It refers to the abolition of the hereditary status of household slaves and retainers in Ningguo and Huizhou prefectures in Anhui in 1727. Yongzheng believed that the social categories were evil remnants of earlier eras and regimes and sought to manifest the humanity of the Qing throne by wiping them out.

Recently I heard that in the Jiangnan area there are hereditary retainers in the Huizhou prefecture and hereditary bond servants in the Ningguo prefecture. Members of these two groups are referred to in this locality as "mean people." Their household registrations and professions are base and they are regarded almost like the "musical households" and "lazy households." Worse still is that if there are two families whose villages and lives are almost identical but one family is the hereditary bond servant or retainer of the other family, then whenever the [superior] family holds a wedding or funeral the other [mean] family must go out and serve them like slaves. If the comportment [of the mean family] is not perfect, everyone can abuse and beat them. Should one ask how or when this system originated, no one has any reliable idea. In actuality, there is not distinction between high and low; these people are merely following an evil custom. This is what we have heard. If people of this sort truly exist, the [mean] status should be abolished and they should become commoners so that they can strive and improve themselves and not be burdened with a base status to the end of their lives or have it placed upon their descendants.

CHAPTER 5 | # Chinese Society and the Reign of Qianlong

5.1 Wu Jingzi: From *The Scholars* (Rulin waishi) (Fan Jin Passes the *Juren* Examination)

Rulin waishi (An unofficial history of the literati) was probably composed between 1740 and 1750. It is the greatest exemplar of the mode of satirical realism in Chinese literature and captures more clearly than any other existing novel the quality of everyday life in Qing China. Like the contemporaneous novels of Henry Fielding, *The Scholars* provides a mordantly witty portrait of the pretensions and hypocrisies of society. Its realism has drawn the attention of historians eager to understand the nature of society and culture in the Qianlong era.

The novel's author Wu Jingzi (1701–1754) was the son of a noted official family from Anhui. His greatest accomplishment as an examination scholar, despite repeated competition for higher titles, was obtaining the *xiucai* title (the lowest examination title) in 1720. Wu was apparently looked upon as a ne'er-do-well in his own village and in 1733 left it for Nanjing where, in his middle and later years, he lived a miserably impoverished existence in the company of other failed scholars.

Frustrated and disillusioned as an examination candidate, Wu Jingzi drew upon his own experiences and those of his friends to attack the suffocating formalism and the false social hierarchies produced by the examination system. In "Fan Jin Passes the *Juren* Examination," he shows how a scorned middle-aged scholar who has worked for decades to pass the exams is drastically elevated in the esteem of his fellow Cantonese by passing the middle or *juren* examination. This chapter of *The Scholars* is one frequently anthologized because of the clarity of its style and the powerful swipe it takes at the myths and false ideals of the examination system.

Soon it was time to go to the examination in the capital. Zhou Jin's traveling expenses and clothes were provided by Jin. He passed the metropolitan examination too; and after the palace examination he was given an official post. In three years he rose to the rank of censor and was appointed commissioner of education for Guangdong Province.

Now though Zhou Jin engaged several secretaries, he thought, "I had bad luck myself so long; now that I'm in office I mean to read all the papers carefully. I must not leave everything to my secretaries, and suppress real talent." Having come to this decision, he went to Canton to take up his post. The day after his arrival he burnt incense, posted up placards, and held two examinations.

The third examination was for candidates from Nanhai and Panyu Counties. Commissioner Zhou sat in the hall and watched the candidates crowding in. There were young and old, handsome and homely, smart and shabby men among them. The last candidate to enter was thin and sallow, had a grizzled beard and was wearing an old felt hat. Guangdong has a warm climate; still, this was the twelfth month, and yet this candidate had on a linen gown only, so he was shivering with cold as he took his paper and went to his cell. Zhou Jin made a mental note of this before sealing up their doors. During the first interval, from his seat at the head of the hall he watched this candidate in the linen gown come up to hand in his paper. The man's clothes were so threadbare that a few more holes had appeared since he went into the cell. Commissioner Zhou looked at his own garments—his magnificent crimson robe and gilt belt—then he referred to the register of names, and asked, "You are Fan Jin, aren't you?"

Kneeling, Fan Jin answered, "Yes, Your Excellency."

"How old are you this year?"

"I gave my age as thirty. Actually, I am fifty-four."

"How many times have you taken the examination?"

"I first went in for it when I was twenty, and I have taken it over twenty times since then."

"How is it you have never passed?"

"My essays are too poor," replied Fan Jin, "so none of the honorable examiners will pass me."

"That may not be the only reason," said Commissioner Zhou. "Leave your paper here, and I will read it through carefully."

Fan Jin kowtowed and left.

It was still early, and no other candidates were coming to hand in their papers, so Commissioner Zhou picked up Fan Jin's essay and read it through. But he was disappointed. "Whatever is the fellow driving at in this essay?" he wondered. "I see now why he never passed." He put it aside. However, when no other candidates appeared, he thought, "I might as well have another look at Fan Jin's paper. If he shows the least talent, I'll pass him to reward his perseverance." He read it through again, and this time felt there was something in it. He was just going to read it through once more, when another candidate came up to hand in his paper.

This man knelt down, and said, "Sir, I beg for an oral test."

"I have your paper here," said Commissioner Zhou kindly. "What need is there for an oral test?"

"I can compose poems in all the ancient styles. I beg you to set a subject to test me."

The commissioner frowned and said, "Since the emperor attaches importance to essays, why should you bring up the poems of the Han and Tang Dynasties? A candidate like you should devote all his energy to writing compositions, instead of wasting time on heterodox studies. I have come here at the imperial command to examine essays, not to discuss miscellaneous literary forms with you. This devotion to superficial things means that your real work must be neglected. No doubt your essay is nothing but flashy talk, not worth reading. Attendants! Drive him out!" At the word of command, attendants ran in from both sides to seize the candidate and push him outside the gate.

But although Commissioner Zhou had had this man driven out, he still read his paper. This candidate was called Wei Haogu, and he wrote in a tolerably clear and straightforward style. "I will pass him lowest on the list," Zhou Jin decided. And, taking up his brush, he made a mark at the end of the paper as a reminder.

Then he read Fan Jin's paper again. This time he gave a gasp of amazement. "Even I failed to understand this paper the first two times I read it!" he exclaimed. "But, after reading it for the third time, I realize it is the most wonderful essay in the world—every word a pearl. This shows how often bad examiners must have suppressed real genius." Hastily taking up his brush, he carefully drew three circles on Fan Jin's paper, marking it as first. He then picked up Wei Haogu's paper again, and marked it as twentieth. After this he collected all the other essays and took them away with him.

Soon the results were published, and Fan Jin's name was first on the list. When he went in to see the commissioner, Zhou Jin commended him warmly. And when the last successful candidate—Wei Haogu—went in, Commissioner Zhou gave him some encouragement and advised him to work hard and stop studying miscellaneous works. Then, to the sound of drums and trumpets, the successful candidates left.

The next day, Commissioner Zhou set off for the capital. Fan Jin alone escorted him for ten miles of the way, doing reverence before his chair. Then the commissioner called him to his side. "First-class honors go to the mature," he said. "Your essay showed real maturity, and you are certain to do well in the provincial examination too. After I have made my report to the authorities, I will wait for you in the capital."

Fan Jin kowtowed again in thanks, then stood to one side of the road as the examiner's chair was carried swiftly off. Only when the banners had passed out of sight behind the next hill did he turn back to his lodgings to settle his bill. His home was about fifteen miles from the city, and he had to travel all night to reach it. He bowed to his mother, who lived with him in a thatched cottage with a thatched shed outside, his mother occupying the front room and his wife the back one. His wife was the daughter of Butcher Hu of the market.

Fan Jin's mother and wife were delighted by his success. They were preparing a meal when his father-in-law arrived, bringing pork sausages and a bottle of wine. Fan Jin greeted him, and they sat down together.

"Since I had the bad luck to marry my daughter to a scarecrow like you," said Butcher Hu, "Heaven knows how much you have cost me. Now I must have done some good deed to make you pass the examination. I've brought this wine to celebrate."

Fan Jin assented meekly, and called his wife to cook the sausages and warm the wine. He and his father-in-law sat in the thatched shed, while his mother and wife prepared food in the kitchen.

"Now that you have become a gentleman," went on Butcher Hu, "you must do things in proper style. Of course, men in my profession are decent, high-class people; and I am your elder too—you mustn't put on any airs before me. But these peasants round here, dung-carriers and the like, are low people. If you greet them and treat them as equals, that will be a breach of etiquette and will make me lose face too. You're such an easy- going, good-for-nothing fellow, I'm telling you this for your own good, so that you won't make a laughing-stock of yourself."

"Your advice is quite right, father," replied Fan Jin.

"Let your mother eat with us too," went on Butcher Hu. "She has only vegetables usually—it's a shame! Let my daughter join us too. She can't have tasted lard more than two or three times since she married you a dozen years ago, poor thing!"

So Fan Jin's mother and wife sat down to share the meal with them. They ate until sunset, by which time Butcher Hu was tipsy. Mother and son thanked him profusely; then, throwing his jacket over his shoulders, the butcher staggered home bloated. The next day Fan Jin had to call on relatives and friends.

Wei Haogu invited him to meet some other fellow candidates, and since it was the year for the provincial examination they held a number of literary meetings. Soon it was the end of the sixth month. Fan Jin's fellow candidates asked him to go with them to the provincial capital for the examination, but he had no money for the journey. He went to ask his father-in-law to help.

Butcher Hu spat in his face, and poured out a torrent of abuse. "Don't be a fool!" he roared. "Just passing one examination has turned your head completely—you're like a toad trying to swallow a swan! And I hear that you scraped through not because of your essay, but because the examiner pitied you for being so old. Now, like a fool, you want to pass the higher examination and become an official. But do you know who those officials are? They are all stars in heaven! Look at the Chang family in the city. All those officials have pots of money, dignified faces and big ears. But your mouth sticks out and you've a chin like an ape's. You should piss on the ground and look at your face in the puddle! You look like a monkey, yet you want to become an official. Come off it! Next year I shall find a teaching job for you with one of my friends so that you can make a few taels of silver to support that old, never-dying mother of yours and your wife—and it's high time you did! Yet you ask me for traveling expenses! I kill just one pig a day, and only make ten cents per pig. If I give you all my silver to play ducks and drakes with, my family will have to live on air." The butcher went on cursing at full blast, till Fan Jin's head spun.

When he got home again, he thought to himself, "Commissioner Zhou said that I showed maturity. And, from ancient times till now, who ever passed the first examination without going in for the second? I shan't rest easy till I've taken it." So he asked his fellow candidates to help him, and went to the city, without telling his father-in-law, to take the examination. When the examination was over he returned home, only to find that his family had had no food for two days. And Butcher Hu cursed him again.

The day the results came out there was nothing to eat in the house, and Fan Jin's mother told him, "Take that hen of mine to the market and sell it; then buy a few measures of rice to make gruel. I'm faint with hunger."

Fan Jin tucked the hen under his arm and hurried out.

He had only been gone an hour or so, when gongs sounded and three horsemen galloped up. They alighted, tethered their horses to the shed, and called out: "Where is the honorable Mr. Fan? We have come to congratulate him on passing the provincial examination."

Not knowing what had happened, Fan Jin's mother had hidden herself in the house for fear. But when she heard that he had passed, she plucked up courage to poke her head out and say, "Please come in and sit down. My son has gone out."

"So this is the old lady," said the heralds. And they pressed forward to demand a tip.

In the midst of this excitement two more batches of horsemen arrived. Some squeezed inside while the others packed themselves into the shed, where they had to sit on the ground. Neighbors gathered round, too, to watch; and the flustered old lady asked one of them to go to look for her son. The neighbor ran to the market-place, but Fan Jin was nowhere to be seen. Only when he reached the east end of the market did he discover the scholar, clutching the hen tightly against his chest and holding a sales sign in one hand. Fan Jin was pacing slowly along, looking right and left for a customer.

"Go home quickly, Mr. Fan!" cried the neighbor. "Congratulations! You have passed the provincial examination. Your house is full of heralds."

Thinking this fellow was making fun of him, Fan Jin pretended not to hear, and walked forward with a lowered head. Seeing that he paid no attention, the neighbor went up to him and tried to grab the hen.

"Why are you taking my hen?" protested Fan Jin. "You don't want to buy it."

"You have passed," insisted the neighbor. "They want you to go home and to send off the heralds."

"Good neighbor," said Fan Jin, "we have no rice left at home, so I have to sell this hen. It's a matter of life and death. This is no time for jokes! Do go away, so as not to spoil my chance of a sale."

When the neighbor saw that Fan Jin did not believe him, he seized the hen, threw it to the ground and dragged his scholar back by main force to his home.

The heralds cried, "Good! The newly honored one is back." They pressed forward to congratulate him. But Fan Jin brushed past them into the house to look at the official announcement, already hung up, which read: "This is to announce that the master of your honorable mansion, Fan Jin, has passed the provincial examination in Guangdong, coming seventh in the list. May better news follow in rapid succession!"

Fan Jin feasted his eyes on the announcement, and, after reading it through once to himself, read it once more aloud. Clapping his hands, he laughed and exclaimed, "Ha! Good! I have passed." Then, stepping back, he fell down in a dead faint. His mother hastily poured some boiled water between his lips, whereupon he recovered consciousness and struggled to his feet. Clapping his hands again, he let out a peal of laughter and shouted, "Aha! I've passed! I've passed!" Laughing wildly he ran outside, giving the heralds and the neighbors the fright of their lives. Not far from the front door he slipped and fell into a pond. When he clambered out, his hair was disheveled, his hands muddied and his whole body dripping with slime. But nobody could stop him. Still clapping his hands and laughing, he headed straight for the market.

They all looked at each other in consternation, and said, "The new honor has sent him off his head!"

His mother wailed, "Aren't we out of luck! Why should passing an examination do this to him? Now he's mad, goodness knows when he'll get better."

"He was all right this morning when he went out," said his wife. "What could have brought on this attack? What *shall* we do?"

The neighbors consoled them. "Don't be upset," they said. "We will send a couple of men to keep an eye on Mr. Fan. And we'll all bring wine and eggs and rice for these heralds. Then we can discuss what's to be done."

The neighbors brought eggs or wine, lugged along sacks of rice or carried over chickens. Fan Jin's wife wailed as she prepared the food in the kitchen. Then she took it to the shed, neighbors brought tables and stools, and they asked the heralds to sit down to a meal while they discussed what to do.

"I have an idea," said one of the heralds. "But I don't know whether it will work or not."

"What idea?" they asked.

"There must be someone the honorable Mr. Fan usually stands in awe of," said the herald. "He's only been thrown off his balance because sudden joy made him choke on his phlegm. If you can get someone he's afraid of to slap him in the face and say, 'It's all a joke. You haven't passed any examination!'— then the fright will make him cough up his phlegm, and he'll come to his senses again."

They all clapped their hands and said, "That's a fine idea. Mr. Fan is more afraid of Butcher Hu than of anyone else. Let's hurry up and fetch him. He's probably still in the market, and hasn't yet heard the news."

"If he were selling meat in the market, he would have heard the news by now," said a neighbor. "He went out at dawn to the cast market to fetch pigs, and he can't have come back yet. Someone had better go quickly to find him."

One of the neighbors hurried off in search of the butcher, and presently met him on the road, followed by an assistant who was carrying seven or eight catties of meat and four or five strings of cash.[1] Butcher Hu was coming to offer his congratulations. Fan Jin's mother, crying bitterly, told him what had happened.

"How could he be so unlucky!" exclaimed the butcher. They were calling for him outside, so he gave the meat and the money to his daughter, and went out. The heralds put their plan before him, but the Butcher Hu demurred.

"He may be my son-in-law," he said, "but he's an official[2] now—one of the stars in heaven. How can you hit one of the stars in heaven? I've heard that whoever hits the stars in heaven will be carried away by the King of Hell, given a hundred strokes with an iron rod, and shut up in the eighteenth hell, never to become a human being again. I daren't do a thing like that."

"Mr. Hu!" cried a sarcastic neighbor. "You make your living by killing pigs. Every day the blade goes in white and comes out red. After all the blood you've shed, the King of Hell must have marked you down for several thousand strokes by iron rods, so what does it matter if he adds a hundred more? Quite likely he will have used up all his iron rods before getting round to beating you for this, anyway. Or maybe, if you cure your son-in-law, the King of Hell may consider that as a good deed, and promote you from the eighteenth hell to the seventeenth."

---

1. Round coins with a square hold that were strung for convenience on string.

2. A scholar who passed the provincial examination was sometimes eligible for such posts as that of a county magistrate.

"This is not time for joking," protested one of the heralds. "This is the only way to handle it, Mr. Hu. There's nothing else for it, so please don't make difficulties."

Butcher Hu had to give in. Two bowls of wine bolstered up his courage, making him lose his scruples and start his usual rampaging. Rolling up his greasy sleeves, he strode off toward the market, followed by small groups of neighbors.

Fan Jin's mother ran out and called after him, "Just frighten him a little! Mind you don't hurt him!"

"Of course," the neighbors reassured her. "That goes without saying."

When they reached the market, they found Fan Jin standing in the doorway of a temple. His hair was tousled, his face streaked with mud, and one of his shoes had come off. But he was still clapping his hands and crowing, "Aha! I've passed! I've passed!"

Butcher Hu bore down on him like an avenging fury, roaring, "You blasted idiot! What have you passed?" and fetched him a blow. The bystanders and neighbors could hardly suppress their laughter. But although Butcher Hu had screwed up his courage to strike once, he was still afraid at heart, and his hand was trembling too much to strike a second time. The one blow, however, had been enough to knock Fan Jin out.

The neighbors pressed round to rub Fan Jin's chest and massage his back, until presently he gave a sigh and came to. His eyes were clear and his madness had passed! They helped him up and borrowed a bench from Apothecary Chen, a hunchback who lived by the temple, so that Fan Jin might sit down.

Butcher Hu, who was standing a little way off, felt his hand begin to ache; when he raised his palm, he found to his dismay that he could not bend it. "It's true, then, that you mustn't strike the stars in heaven," he thought. "Now Buddha is punishing me!" The more he thought about it, the worse his hand hurt, and he asked the apothecary to give him some ointment for it.

Meanwhile Fan Jin was looking round and asking, "How do I come to be sitting here? My mind has been in a whirl, as if in a dream."

The neighbors said, "Congratulations, sir, on having passed the examination! A short time ago, in your happiness, you brought up some phlegm; but just now you spat out several mouthfuls and recovered. Please go home quickly to send away the heralds."

"That's right," said Fan Jin. "And I seem to remember coming seventh in the list." As he was speaking, he fastened up his hair and asked the apothecary for a basin of water to wash his face, while one of the neighbors found his shoe and helped him put it on.

The sight of his father-in-law made Fan Jin afraid that he was in for another cursing. But Butcher Hu stepped forward and said, "Worthy son-in-law, I would never have presumed to slap you just now if not for your mother. She sent me to help you."

"That was what I call a friendly slap," said one of the neighbors. "Wait till Mr. Fan finishes washing his face. I bet he can easily wash off half a basin of lard!"

"Mr. Hu!" said another. "This hand of yours will be too good to kill pigs any more."

"No, indeed," replied the butcher. "Why should I go on killing pigs? My worthy son-in-law will be able to support me in style for the rest of my life. I always said that this worthy son-in-law of mine was very learned and handsome, and that not one of those Zhang and Zhou family officials in the city looked so much the fine gentleman. I have always been a good judge of character, I don't mind telling you. My daughter stayed at home till she was more than thirty, although many rich families wanted to marry her to their sons; but I saw signs of good fortune in her face, and knew that she would end up marrying an official. You see today how right I was." He gave a great guffaw, and they all started to laugh.

When Fan Jin had washed and drunk the tea brought him by the apothecary, they all started back, Fan Jin in front, Butcher Hu and the neighbors behind. The butcher, noticing that the seat of his son-in-law's gown was crumpled, kept bending forward all the way home to tug out the creases for him.

When they reached Fan Jin's house, Butcher Hu shouted: "The master is back!" The old lady came out to greet them, and was overjoyed to find her son no longer mad. The heralds, she told them, had already been sent off with the money that Butcher Hu had brought. Fan Jin bowed to his mother and thanked his father-in-law, making Butcher Hu so embarrassed that he muttered, "That bit of money was nothing."

After thanking the neighbors too, Fan Jin was just going to sit down when a smart-looking retainer hurried in, holding a big red card, and announced, "Mr. Zhang has come to pay his respects to the newly successful Mr. Fan."

By this time the sedan-chair was already at the door. Butcher Hu dived into his daughter's room and dared not come out, while the neighbors scattered in all directions. Fan Jin went out to welcome the visitor, who was one of the local gentry, and Mr. Zhang alighted from the chair and came in. He was wearing an official's gauze cap, sunflower-colored gown, gilt belt and black shoes. He was a provincial graduate, and had served as a magistrate in his time. His name was Zhang Jinzhai. He and Fan Jin made way for each other ceremoniously, and once inside the house bowed to each other as equals and sat down in the places of guest and host. Mr. Zhang began the conversation.

"Sir," he said, "although we live in the same district, I have never been able to call on you."

"I have long respected you," replied Fan Jin, "but have never had the chance to pay you a visit."

"Just now I saw the list of successful candidates. Your patron, Mr. Tang, was a pupil of my grandfather; so I feel very close to you."

"I did not deserve to pass, I am afraid," said Fan Jin. "But I am delighted to be the pupil of one of your family."

After a glance round the room, Mr. Zhang remarked, "Sir, you are certainly frugal." He took from his servant a packet of silver, and stated, "I have brought nothing to show my respect except these fifty taels of silver, which I beg you to accept. Your honorable home is not good enough for you, and it will not be very convenient when you have many callers. I have an empty house on the main street by the cast gate, which has three courtyards and three rooms in each. Although it is not big, it is quite clean. Allow me to present it to you. When you move there, I can profit by your instruction more easily."

Fan Jin declined many times, but Mr. Zhang pressed him. "With all we have in common, we should be like brothers," he said. "But if you refuse, you are treating me like a stranger." Then Fan Jin accepted the silver and expressed his thanks. After some more conversation they bowed and parted. Not until the visitor was in his chair did Butcher Hu dare to emerge.

Fan Jin gave the silver to his wife. When she opened it, and they saw the white ingots with their fine markings, he asked Butcher Hu to come in and gave him two ingots, saying, "Just now I troubled you for five thousand coppers. Please accept these six taels of silver."

Butcher Hu gripped the silver tight, but thrust out his clenched fist, saying, "You keep this. I gave you that money to congratulate you, so how can I take it back?"

"I have some more silver here," said Fan Jin. "When it is spent, I will ask you for more."

Butcher Hu immediately drew back his fist, stuffed the silver into his pocket and said, "All right. Now that you are on good terms with that Mr. Zhang, you needn't be afraid of going short. His family has more silver than the emperor, and they are my best customers. Every year, even if they have no particular occasions to celebrate, they still buy four or five thousand catties of meat. Silver is nothing to him."

Then he turned to his daughter and said, "Your rascally brother didn't want me to bring that money this morning. I told him, 'Now my honorable son-in-law is not the man he was. There will be lots of people sending him presents of money. I am only afraid he may refuse my gift.' Wasn't I right? Now I shall take this silver home and curse that dirty scoundrel." After a thousand thanks he made off, his head thrust forward and a broad grin on his face.

True enough, many people came to Fan Jin after that and made him presents of land and shops; while some poor couples came to serve him in return for his protection. In two or three months he had menservants and maidservants, to say nothing of money and rice. When Mr. Zhang came again to urge him, he moved into the new house; and for three days he entertained guests with feasts and operas. On the morning of the fourth day, after Fan Jin's mother had got up and had breakfast, she went to the rooms in the back courtyard. There she found Fan Jin's wife with a silver pin in her hair. Although this was the middle of the tenth month, it was still warm and she was wearing a sky-blue silk tunic and a green silk skirt. She was supervising the maids as they washed bowls, cups, plates and chopsticks.

"You must be very careful," the old lady warned them. "These things don't belong to us, so don't break them."

"How can you say they don't belong to you, madam?" they asked. "They are all yours."

"No, no, these aren't ours," she protested with a smile.

"Oh yes, they are," the maids cried. "Not only are these things, but all of us servants and this house belong to you."

When the old lady heard this, she picked up the fine porcelain and the cups and chopsticks inlaid with silver, and examined them carefully one by one. Then she went into a fit of laughter. "All mine!" she crowed. Screaming with laughter she fell backwards, choked and lost consciousness.

5.2   A MURDER CASE FROM THE RECORDS OF THE OFFICE FOR THE SCRUTINY OF PUNISHMENTS, 1747– 1748

Many Qing murder cases grew out of minor disputes involving land or other property. When capital punishment was decided upon by a local judicial official, it was obligatory that the case be submitted through the Board of Punishments to the emperor for a final decision. Because of this regulation, the Ming-Qing archives contain an abundance of documents dealing with local violence. In the files of the Grand Secretariat for the Qianlong reign alone, under the category *tudi zaiwu* (land and property debts) of the *Xingke* (Office for the scrutiny of punishments) are stored records of more than fifty-eight thousand murder cases involving capital punishment. Three hundred and ninety-nine of these cases have been assembled in the work from which the case of Li Jinru, translated below, has been drawn.

In solving a murder, local officials often interviewed a wide range of witnesses. The magistrate was tacitly permitted to employ judicial torture to elicit confessions from uncooperative witnesses or accused felons. The confession of Li Jinru, which is recorded in this judicial document virtually in vernacular Chinese, is first summarized by the official in charge of the case. The accused's retelling of the story of the murder is remarkably vivid and detailed and provides an eerie tableau of a long-standing hatred and the violence that resulted.

A TYPICAL MURDER CASE INVOLVING A RENT DISPUTE IN HUBEI

The report of Liu Fang'ai, Surveillance Commissioner of Hubei stationed with the Surveillance Commission in Wuchang, concerning the interrogation of Li Jinru, age 55, from Xiaogan County, Hanyang Prefecture, states the following: Li Jinru was a person of vicious and brutal character. He ignored law and principled behavior. He and the murdered monk Chengyuan lived in the same neighborhood. Li Jinru normally rented two *dou* [1 *dou* = 1 decalitre, a Chinese peck; the grain production of this small plot] of land from Chengyuan and they divided the produce of the property equally. The rent was never overdue. In the 10th year of Qianlong [1745], Monk Chengyuan took the land back and used it himself and although Li Jinru wanted to rent it he was not permitted to do so. The next year, Li Jinru again asked to rent the land but Chengyuan stubbornly refused his request and strongly rebuked him. This led to a quarrel and afterwards Li Jinru harbored hatred for the monk. In the spring of the 12th year of Qianlong [1747], Chengyuan dug out some soil from Jinru's land to build up a raised pathway adjacent to his field and the two men again quarreled. Later, Li Jinru asked Chengyuan to give him some wine. Chengyuan refused his request and so Li Jinru's hatred deepened.

On the night of the twenty-sixth day of the eighth month of 1747, Jinru, following some drinking, encountered Chengyuan who was himself returning home after a late night of drinking. Li Jinru's hatred was touched off and it suddenly occurred to him to murder Chengyuan. Between 9:00 and 11:00 p.m., Li Jinru took some bark ropes and set out for the temple with the intention of strangling Chengyuan to vent his hatred. The gate of the temple was already closed and so Li Jinru used a board to help him to climb over the wall to gain entrance. He then saw a wooden club in the courtyard and took it to beat Chengyuan to death. The temple hall and the door to Chengyuan's room happened to be unlocked and so Jinru pushed open the door and crept in. The light from the lamp in the temple hall illuminated the bed and Li Jinru found Chengyuan was sleeping soundly. Jinru raised the club to strike Chengyuan but mistakenly hit the bed. He turned to strike again but this caused Chengyuan to cry out in alarm and struggle. In this struggle, Jinyuan bruised the back of Chengyuan's right hand and the rear part of his head. Jinru also scratched the left side of Chengyuan's face, his right arm, and the back of his left hand. Chengyuan held the club tightly and refused to release it and so Li Jinru then took an iron ax lying on a trunk and struck and wounded the left side of Chengyuan's head. Li also hacked at the top of Chengyuan's head and killed him. Jinru threw the ax under the bed and used the rope to tie up Chengyuan by the neck in an endeavor to make the death seem like suicide. However, because the rope was not previously tied to the beam it was impossible to raise the corpse. Li Jinru next left the corpse on the ground, took some money, a wool blanket, and fled from the scene.

The investigation is based on testimonies of Monk Xujiao and Li Jinru.

According to Monk Xujiao: "The dead monk Chengyuan was my own brother. He was 73 *sui* [years old] this year. My surname before I became a monk was Zheng. Because we were very poor, my brother joined the Chen Family Temple. He had one disciple but he died and afterwards brother did not find a new disciple. I became a monk in the Cheng Family Temple in Guangyangpu. This temple of my brother had two *dan* of land to support it. He himself planted part of it and part of it was rented to Li Nanzheng and Wei Zhouzhen. Every year they split up the produce. . . ."

According to Li Jinru: "I'm from Lijiayuan of Xiaogan County and am fifty-five years old [*sui*]. My parents and my wife died a long time ago. I have only one son named Li Yifei and he left home to be a laborer in the seventh month of last year. The house I rented was returned to the original owner and since I had no place to live, I lived by myself in my brother Li Mingzhi's place. I made a living on my own. My brother is a trader and doesn't live at home. In his family, there's only my sister-in-law and nobody else.

"Originally I rented two *dou* of land from Chengyuan. We split the grain equally and I never owed him anything. In 1745, he suddenly refused to let me rent the land. I asked him several times but he wouldn't give in and I began to hate him. In the fall of 1746, I again begged him to be able to rent but he would not agree and said I was no good. I was really angry and had a quarrel with him but still never expressed my anger. In the spring of 1747, he dug soil from my land to build up his paddy dike. We had another quarrel then. And so I hated him for a long time. Later he bought a few catties of wine to sell to others. I asked him if I could buy wine but he deliberately said he was sold out. Even though he had it, he refused to sell it to me. He was a monk! But he was an old, cunning, wicked man. He had no sense of compassion. He always insulted and bullied me. I really hated him and wanted to teach him a lesson. But because I never had a chance, I couldn't do anything until the evening of the 26th day of the 8th month of 1747. I had had some drinks and ran into Chengyuan who was coming home from drinking. I saw he was a little drunk and then remembered all the mean things he'd done to me in the past. I got furious and under the influence of the wine wanted to hurt him. I figured that since he was an old man, was drunk and slept by himself, he would go to bed early that night and would not have any protection. I tied a rope made of bark around my waist and intended to strangle him in his sleep. I went there late at night and the gate of the temple was closed. So I took a plank from a bridge behind the temple and propped it against the wall to climb in. I saw a wooden club next to the steps going into the temple hall and thought that this could kill him with one stroke. I picked it up and went on. I knew the door of the temple hall and the bedroom door well from the time I had rented land and I knew how to open them. I did not expect that Chengyuan would leave the door unlocked after he was drunk but he did and so I just lightly pushed the door and entered his room. The room was on the east and it was connected to the temple hall. There was no wall in between, just some eaves. In the temple hall there were three lamps that threw their light into the bedroom. I got close to the bed and saw that he hadn't even pulled down his mosquito netting. His head was inclined toward the east and he was sleeping soundly. I struck out with the club but had raised it too high and it caught on the canopy frame of the bed. When I got the club free, he was already awake and had sat up and started crying out. I hit out again with the club but he grabbed it tightly. I twisted it left and right and banged his hand against the bedframe and cut the skin on the back of his hand. Then I pulled it forward and pushed him back and the back of his head hit the bedboard and again scratched him but he still held on to the club. I grabbed the club and pushed him in the face and caused cuts on the left side of his face. Because I couldn't push him down, I scratched the back of his left hand and his right arm. But he would still not let go of the club. I looked around and saw that on the trunk by the west end of his bed there was an ax. Holding the club with my right hand, I grabbed the ax with my left and hit his head. He tried to turn his head away but I cut him on the left side. He yelled even more and so I hit him again on the left crown of his head. He stopped making noise and fell back on the bed. I threw the ax under the bed and tied the bark rope around his neck to make it seem like suicide. I dragged his body out from the bed but found out that since I hadn't looped the rope over the beam, I couldn't raise him up. I was confused and scared and so I just left him where he lay. When I left the room, I saw two hundred cash on the trunk and a wool blanket on a hanging rack. I grabbed them and opened the door on the west side. I closed the door behind me when I went out. I went back to the side of my brother's house and hid the wool blanket under some hay and slept by the haystack. The next morning, I found that my shirt and jacket were stained with blood and so I secretly went into my room and took out some pieces of cloth and sewing equipment I kept there and covered the blood stained jacket with patches. I took off the shirt and washed out the bloodstains. On the 28th day, I took the money and wrapped up the wool blanket and my old shirt with a rope and went to the shop of Tailor Shu in Zhujiajing. I found that a short blue shirt was for sale and so I spent one hundred and sixty cash to buy it and spent fifteen cash to buy a pair of white cloth stockings. I also left the package I'd tied with the rope in his shop. I said that I would pick everything up together when he finished making the stockings. But now all the money was gone and I couldn't get more and so I haven't gone there to pick them up. And then I was caught by the runners and taken away. Tailor Shu had no idea what was happening. All of this happened because of my old grudge with Chengyuan and not because of money. No one helped me. I dare not make any false confession. . . ."

The aforementioned official [Liu Fang'ai], after investigating the case of Li Jinru of Xiaogan County's murder of Monk Chengyuan arrived at the following sentence: Li Jinru is guilty under the statute concerning premeditated murder. He should be sentenced to death by decapitation after the Autumn Assizes and tattooed in accordance with precedent. The younger brother of the deceased should receive the stolen money and the value of the blanket and the blanket already retrieved. . . .

13th day of the 10th month, 1748

5.3 GLORIFYING THE ORIGINS OF THE MANCHUS, FROM AN ACCOUNT IN THE STATE ARCHIVE

Jiang Liangqi (1723–1789) was a 1751 *jinshi* degree holder from Guangxi who served as compiler in the state archive (*guoshiguan*). Jiang's *Donghualu* (East Flowery gate records) was a historical chronicle, based largely on the *Qing Veritable Records*, that examined the history of China from the beginning of the Qing period to the end of Yongzheng's reign in 1735. Jiang Liangqi made a broad and scrupulous selection of documents in compiling this work and even today it is a major source for the history of the early Qing reign periods.

The mythical account of the origins of the Manchus recounted here was taken most seriously by later generations and became a staple part of the education of Manchu nobles. Its wooden quality suggests the cultural divide which still separated Manchu society from the refined literary world of sixteenth- and seventeenth-century China. The Manchus' view of their own genesis, as captured in this short piece, is hardly so elaborate a declaration of the "divine light" of the Aisin-Gioro ruling clan as a contemporary Chinese scholar might have composed if given the same assignment. However, using language and images from the myth cycles of the Manchus the piece communicates a sense that the Manchus' ruling clan was divinely blessed in its enterprise to rule China.

The ancestors of our dynasty originated in the region of the Changbai Mountains. The mountains are more than two hundred li high and stretch for more than a thousand li. Set on the mountain range is a lake called Damen which is about eighty li around. The three rivers, the Yalu, the Huntong, and the Aihu, all start here. Geomancers said that this place would give birth to a sage who would unify the world. East of these mountains is Bukuli Mountain and beneath it is a lake called Buerhuli. Legends tell that three heavenly maidens, Engulun and her two younger sisters Zheng'gulun and Fogulun, were bathing in this lake and that after their bath a divine bird placed a red fruit on the clothing of Fogulun. She swallowed it and then became pregnant. Later she gave birth to a boy. When he was born he was already able to speak and his physique was extraordinary. When he grew up, his mother told him the story of his birth and said: "Heaven gave birth to you to pacify unsettled countries. You are to use Aisin-Gioro as your surname and Bukuliyongshun as your name." His mother then ascended to heaven and the son boarded a boat and rode downstream to Hebu.

When he stepped upon the bank, he broke willow branches and reeds to make a mat and sat cross-legged upon it. In this region there were three families contending for control. They formed armed bands and killed each other in their vendettas. Someone came to the river to get water and was surprised by Bukuliyongshun's appearance and returned home and told others. A crowd came to question Bukuliyongshun and he told them his name and said: "I am the son of the Heavenly Maiden Fogulun and heaven has ordered me to quell the unrest among you." The crowd was surprised and said: "You are a divine sage!" They carried him to their village and worshipped him as their lord. They lived east of the Changbai Mountains in Ye'edoli City in the Emohui region; they called their state Manzhou. After a few generations, they were betrayed by fellow-countrymen and their people were slaughtered. Only a young boy named Fancha escaped and hid in the wilderness. When his enemies pursued him, a small bird settled on his head and his pursuers mistook him for a withered tree. He was thus able to escape. After several more generations, the imperial ancestor who founded our dynasty was born. His surname was Aisin-Gioro and his given name was Dudumengtemu. He lived in the Hetuala region below Mount Hulanhada. He was very intelligent and a careful planner. He captured more than forty descendants of his ancestor's foes; he killed some and released others and completely recovered the lost lands.

5.4 AND 5.5 HESHEN: ACCUSATION AND INVENTORY

Within days of the death of Qianlong emperor in 1799, his favorite Heshen (1750–1799) was arrested and charged with twenty "great crimes" by Qianlong's successor Jiaqing. In a gesture of deference to Qianlong, the erstwhile bannerman was not executed but was granted the favor of taking his own life. His estates and property were confiscated and his relatives deprived of the high titles awarded him in Qianlong's senile last years.

During the more than twenty years that Heshen enjoyed imperial favor, he exercised great power in the Qing court. As an intimate of the emperor, he was immune from impeachment or criticism and was able to amass a huge fortune that made him an object of envy and hostility for many contemporaries. Alone among Qianlong's retainers, Heshen rode his horse in the precincts of the Forbidden City and was able to appoint or cashier high officials in the state bureaucracy. But once deprived of the protection of his imperial patron, Heshen's fall was predictably precipitous.

The Heshen scandal is often cited as a symptom of the decline of the Qing state system and a symbol of the sort of abuse of power that had become possible by the end of the eighteenth century. Relying solely on his tie to the emperor, Heshen, as the following documents show, was able to manipulate affairs of state, place his cronies in important positions, and build a regal and lavishly furnished estate for himself, his family, and his retainers. The following edict and the accompanying list of confiscated household goods reveal Heshen's offenses against the state and suggest the magnitude of his raids on the government treasury.

5.4 *The Twenty Crimes of Heshen*

Here we list the twenty crimes of Heshen and issue this special Edict to make this known to all.

1. I was specially selected as the Crown Prince by my father, the late Emperor, on the third day of the ninth month of 1795. On the day before the Imperial Edict was promulgated, Heshen presented me with a *ruyi* [an S-shaped ornamental object symbolizing good luck]. He thus revealed this great secret [the secret of the succession] and attempted to gain merit from his support of me. This was his first great crime.
2. In the first month of last year [1798], when my departed father the Emperor summoned Heshen to the Yuanmingyuan Palace, he dared to ride a horse past the Hall of Justice and Honor [a main reception hall near the entrance of the Summer Palace] and made his way to the entrance of Longevity Hill. He had no respect for his master and no crime is greater than this one. This was his second great crime.[3]
3. Owing to a sickness affecting his leg, Heshen was carried in a sedan chair directly into the Forbidden City. He entered and departed through the Shenwu Gate [the north gate] and this was witnessed by all. He never dreaded the prohibition of such behavior. This was his third great crime.
4. He took a former palace concubine as his own concubine. This was utterly shameless. This was his fourth great crime.[4]

3. Only the emperor was permitted to ride horseback or to be carried in a sedan chair on the grounds of the imperial palaces. There were no exceptions; commoners walked.

4. Imperial concubines were occasionally permitted to leave the Forbidden City but were forbidden from remarrying after their departure from the emperor's service.

5. From the time of the campaign against the White Lotus Bandits in the Sichuan and Hubei region, my late father the Emperor was so over-burdened with military dispatches that he was unable even to sleep. But Heshen deliberately delayed consideration of military memorials from the various army commands and prolonged the campaign a great deal. This was his fifth great crime.

6. At the time when the holy, sagely body of my late father the Emperor was ailing, Heshen showed no sorrow. When he entered or departed from his visits with the Emperor, he talked and joked as in normal times with other court officials. This was heartless and deranged behavior! This was his sixth great crime.

7. Last winter, my late father the Emperor struggled against his illness to write comments on memorials and on the drafts of edicts. His brush sometimes wavered and Heshen dared to suggest that these documents should be torn up. His intention was to draw up different edicts. This was his seventh great crime.

8. My late father the Emperor originally appointed Heshen to take charge of the affairs of both the Board of Personnel and the Board of Punishments. Later because there were immediate needs for expenditures in military affairs and because Heshen was experienced in this regard he was further charged with responsibility for submitting receipts to the Board of Revenue. He then usurped all the functions of the Board, changed its set rules and regulations, and refused to allow other officials of the Board to interfere. This was his eighth great crime.

9. In the twelfth month of 1798, Kuei Shu reported in a memorial that an army of more than a thousand bandits had joined together in Xunhua and Guide [two areas in Qinghai]. They were robbing lamas and merchants of their oxen and had murdered two people. Heshen turned the memorial and hid these events. He did not take border affairs seriously. This was his ninth great crime.

10. After my later father the Emperor passed away, I ordered that those Mongol princes who had not suffered from smallpox might be exempted from coming to the capital. But Heshen disobeyed my Edict and ordered all Mongol princes to come and thereby disregard our country's special consideration for border feudatories [*waifan*]. His real intentions were unknown. This was his tenth crime.

11. Grand Secretary Su-ling-a had serious hearing problems with both ears and was utterly weak and feeble. He should have been retired but simply because he was Heshen's brother He Lin's relative through marriage, the facts were hidden and not reported. Because Vice-Ministers Wu Xinglan and Li Huang and Li Guangyun, Chief of the Court of the Imperial Stud, had all tutored Heshen's family members, they were all recommended for the rank of Minister and to head educational commissioners. This was his eleventh great crime.

12. Heshen dismissed at will those who worked in the Grand Council. His abuses of power were innumerable. This was his twelfth great crime.

13. Just yesterday we confiscated and took inventory of Heshen's family property. The buildings were all built of *nanmu* [a precious wood] and were extravagant and illegally mimicked the imperial style. The patterns and designs of the buildings followed those of the Ninghsou Palace [in the Forbidden City] and the pattern of the gardens and kiosks did not differ from those of the Summer Palace. It is impossible to know what was in his heart. This was his thirteenth great crime.

14. Heshen's ancestral tombs at Jinzhou [in Hebei] were equipped with a sacrificial hall and underground tunnels. The local residents called them the He imperial tombs. This was his fourteenth great crime.

15. In his home, Heshen amassed more than two hundred pearl bracelets. This was several times more than the number of such bracelets in the palace collection. He also had giant pearls that were larger than those used in the Emperor's crown. This was his fifteenth great crime.

16. Although he was not permitted to wear a precious stone on the peak of his cap, dozens of such jewels were found hidden in his home. Moreover, he had an incalculable number of gigantic jewels unlike any found in the imperial treasury. This was his sixteenth great crime.

17. The quantities of silver, clothing, and other objects found in his home were uncountable. This was his seventeenth great crime.

18. In false double walls in his home, tens of thousands of ounces of gold were hidden. Buried in his cellars were millions of ounces of silver. In the rear chambers were huge pearls, giant gold and silver ingots, gold pagodas, and other objects. This was his eighteenth great crime.

19. In the vicinity of the capital, in Tongzhou and Jinzhou, he set up pawnshops and banks. A chief minister was competing with mean people for profit. This was his nineteenth great crime.

20. The Liu and Ma families were low-ranking slaves of the He family but after their family properties were confiscated and inventoried it was found that the property of each family was worth more than two million ounces of silver. They also had huge pearls and pearl bracelets. If this was not permitted, how could they grasp so much? This was his twentieth great crime.

5.5 An Inventory of the Household Property Confiscated from the Home of Heshen

[1. HOUSES AND LAND]
   One garden bestowed by the Emperor
   Twenty original pavilions and kiosks
   Sixteen newly added pavilions

One main residence with thirteen sections and seven hundred and thirty rooms.

One eastern residential wing with seven sections and three hundred and sixty rooms

One western residential wing with seven sections and three hundred and fifty rooms

One Huizhou style new residence with seven sections and six hundred and twenty rooms

One counting house with seven hundred and thirty rooms

One garden with sixty-four pavilions and kiosks

Eight hundred thousand *mou* [6.6 *mou* = 1 acre] of farmland

Ten banks with capital of six hundred thousand ounces of silver

Ten pawnshops with capital of eight hundred thousand ounces of silver ...

[2. GOLD, SILVER, AND COPPER CASH]

Fifty-eight thousand ounces of pure gold

Fifty-five thousand six hundred silver ingots

Five million eight hundred and thirty thousand capital-type silver ingots

Three million one hundred and fifty thousand Suzhou ingots

Fifty-eight thousand foreign silver dollars

One million five hundred thousand strings of copper cash

The value of the above was more than fifty-four million ounces of silver.

[3. GINSENG AND JADE]

Ginseng storehouse:

Individual pieces of ginseng were not counted but the total weight was six hundred catties

Jade storehouse:

Thirteen jade tripods two and a half feet high

Twenty sets of jade chimes

One hundred and thirty jade *ruyi*

One thousand one hundred and six *ruyi* decorated with jade

Forty-eight jade snuff bottles

One hundred and thirty jade buckles

Two jade screens with twenty-four panels

Thirteen settings of jade bowls

Thirty jade vases

Eighteen jade basins

Ninety-three cases of jade utensils; individual pieces not counted

Converted to silver the value of the above would be seven million ounces of silver.

In addition there were three other jade pieces not evaluated: a jade longevity Buddha three feet six inches tall, one jade Guanyin statue three feet eight inches tall, both incised with characters reading: "Presented by Governor General of Yunnan and Guizhou, and one jade horse four feet three inches long and two feet eight inches high.

[4. JEWELRY]
Pearl storehouse:
Ten giant longan shaped Eastern pearls
Two hundred and thirty pearl bracelets
Ten huge rubies weighing two hundred and eighty catties
Eighty small rubies (not weighed)
Forty blue precious stones (not weighed)
Ninety ruby cap top decorations
Eighty coral cap top decorations
Ten screens with precious stones and gold
Silver jewelry storehouse:
Seventy-two settings of silver bowls
Two hundred pairs of gold-incised chopsticks
Five hundred pairs of silver-incised chopsticks
Sixty gold teaspoons
Three hundred and eighty silver teaspoons
One hundred and eight silver mouthwashing bowls
Forty gold cloisonné mouthwashing bowls
Eighty silver cloisonné mouthwashing bowls
Antiques:
Twenty antique bronze vessels
Twenty-one antique tripods
Thirty-three bronze flat vessels
Two antique swords
Ten Song inkstones
Seven hundred and six *duan* inkstones

The total value of the above converted to silver is eight million ounces of silver.

In addition, there were three kinds of objects not evaluated in silver: Seven coral trees, three feet six inches high; four coral trees, three feet four inches high; and one gold incised jade decorated clock. . . . [The inventory next lists the furs, furniture, household furnishings, and miscellaneous other items taken from Heshen. It ends with a count of his serving men and women. The document also mentions the twenty-six thousand ounces of gold hidden behind a false wall in Heshen's residence and the one million ounces of silver buried in his cellar.]

CHAPTER 6

China and the Eighteenth-Century World

6.1 LORD MACARTNEY'S COMMISSION FROM HENRY DUNDAS, 1792

By the end of the eighteenth century, the expansion of foreign trade, and especially trade in Asia, was a central preoccupation of the Crown government. The foundations for British rule of India had been laid down by the time of the passage of the India Bill of 1784 and at the end of the eighteenth century thousands of English merchants, soldiers, and missionaries were already living on the Indian sub-continent. At the same time British East India Company had discovered that India was an ideal trading base in Asia and was regularly organizing far-flung expeditions designed to extend the radius of English trading activities.

The British East India Company (BEIC), organized in 1600 to compete with the Dutch in Asia, was a trading monopoly that completely dominated English trade with China until the dissolution of its monopoly rights in 1834. In India, the Company was both a mercantile combine and was evolving into the agency of British rule in colonial Asia. By the time of the Macartney mission, the BEIC was amassing huge profits from its traffic in Indian and Chinese tea and had already begun, albeit on a small scale, to smuggle contraband opium from Bengal to Canton where it was exchanged for silver.

From the British perspective, the framework for Indian-Chinese trading activities was far from satisfactory. The Canton system limited British ships to a single port and imposed numerous vexing conditions on trading activities. To seek remedies for these problems, Sir Henry Dundas (1742–1811), a member of William Pitt's inner circle, president of the board of the BEIC, and, in 1792, Great Britain's home minister, urged the dispatch of a mission to Peking. Subsequently, Lord Macartney, who was a personal friend of Dundas, was appointed "Ambassador Extraordinary and Plenipotentiary from the King of Great Britain to the Emperor of China" and in September 1792 set out with an eighty-four-man mission from London to make contact with the Chinese.

The document that follows was the official charge of the Home Ministry to Macartney. While it sharply outlines the Crown's hopes for the mission, it also shows a certain befuddlement about the nature of the Chinese government. It is important to note that Dundas' charge shows that Great Britain was willing to negotiate a reduction in opium imports if more important conditions were met by the throne. In the time of Qianlong (1736–1795), China was able to resist British pleas for wider relations but they were to be reasserted in an increasingly forceful way until, by the time of the Opium War, such pleas became demands backed with military might.

Whitehall 8th September 1792

My Lord.

Having to signify to your Excellency His Majesty's Commands and Instructions on the subject of the Embassy to which he has been pleased to appoint you, I shall introduce them by recalling to your attention the occasion and object of this measure.

A greater number of His Majesty's subjects than of any other Europeans, have been trading for a considerable time past in China. The commercial intercourse between several nations and that great empire, has been preceded, accompanied or followed, by special communications with its Sovereign. Others had the support of Missionaries, who from their eminence in Science or ingenuity in the arts, were frequently admitted to the familiarity of a curious and polished Court, and which Missionaries in the midst of their care for the propagation of their faith are not supposed to have been unmindful of the view and interests of their Country; while the English traders remained unaided, and as it were, unavowed, at a distance so remote, as to admit of a misrepresentation of the national character and importance, and where too, their occupation was not held in that esteem which ought to procure their safety and respect.

Under the circumstances it would become the dignity and character of his Majesty, to extend his paternal regard to these his distant subjects, even if the commerce and prosperity of the Nation were not concerned in their success; and to claim the Emperor of China's particular protection for them, with the weight which is due to the requisition of one great Sovereign from another.

A free communication with a people, perhaps the most singular on the Globe, among whom civilization has existed, and the arts have been cultivated thro' a long series of ages, with fewer interruptions than elsewhere, is well worthy, also, of this Nation, which saw with pleasure, and applauded with gratitude, the several voyages undertaken already by his Majesty's command, and at the public expense, in the pursuit of knowledge, and for the discovery and observation of distant Countries and manners.

The extent and value of the British dominions in India, which connect us in some degree with every part of that Country, point out also the propriety of establishing sufficient means of representation and transaction of business with our principal Neighbours there.

The measures lately taken by Government respecting the Tea trade, having more than trebled the former legal importation of this article into Great Britain, it is become particularly desirable to cultivate a friendship, and increase the communication with China, which may lead to such a vent throughout that extensive Empire, of the manufactures of the mother Country, and of our Indian Territories, as beside contributing to their prosperity will out of the sales of such produce, furnish resources for the investment to Europe, now requiring no less an annual sum than one million, four hundred thousand pounds.

Hitherto, however, Great Britain has been obliged to pursue the Trade with that Country under circumstances the most discouraging, hazardous to its agents employed in conducting it, and precarious to the various interests involved in it. The only place where His Majesty's subjects have the privilege of a factory is Canton. The fair competition of the Market is there destroyed by associations of the Chinese; our Supercargoes are denied open access to the tribunals of the Country, and to the equal execution of its laws, and are kept altogether in a most arbitrary state of depression, ill suited to the importance of the concerns which are entrusted to their care, and scarcely compatible with the regulations of civilized society. . . .

His Majesty from his earnest desire to promote the present undertaking and in order to give the greater dignity to the Embassy, has been graciously pleased to order one of His Ships of War to convey you and your Suite to the Coast of China. With the same view he has ordered a Military Guard to attend your Person, to be composed of chosen Men from the light Dragoons, Infantry and Artillery, with proper Officers, under the command of Major Benson, whom he has determined to raise to the rank of Lieutenant Colonel upon this occasion. This guard will add splendour and procure respect to the Embassy; the order, appearance and evolutions of the Men may convey no useless idea of our military Character and discipline, and if it should excite in the Emperor a desire of adopting any of the exercise or maneuvers, among the Troops, an opportunity thus offers to him, for which a return of good offices on his part is natural to be expected. It will be at your option to detach one of the Lieutenants of the Ship, or of your Guard, in His Majesty's uniform to accompany the Messenger whom you will send to announce at Pekin [Peking] your arrival on the coast, if you should approach that Capital by Sea.

Besides the Chinese Interpreters whom you have already procured you will perhaps meet in your progress some Portuguese, Spanish, or Italian Missionary, or other intelligent Person free from national attachments or prejudices, who may be useful to be employed in your Service.

Should your answer be satisfactory, and I will not suppose the contrary, you will then assume the Character and public appearance of His Majesty's Ambassador Extraordinary, and proceed with as much ceremony as can be admitted without causing a material delay, or incurring an unreasonable expense. You will procure an audience as early as possible after your arrival, conforming to all ceremonials of that Court, which may not commit the honour of your Sovereign, or lessen your own dignity, so as to endanger the success of your negotiation.

Whilst I make this reserve, I am satisfied you will be too prudent and considerate, to let any trifling punctilio stand in the way of the important benefits which may be obtained by engaging the favourable disposition of the Emperor and his Ministers. You will take the earliest opportunity of representing to His Imperial Majesty, that your Royal Master, already so justly celebrated in Foreign Countries on account of the voyages projected under his immediate auspices, for the acquisition and diffusion of knowledge, was from the same disposition desirous of sending an embassy to the most civilized as well as most ancient and populous Nation in the World in order to observe its celebrated institutions, and to communicate and receive the benefits which must result from an unreserved and friendly intercourse between that Country and his own. You will take care to express the high esteem which His Majesty has conceived for the Emperor, from the wisdom and virtue with which his character has been distinguished. A like compliment may be made in the event of the death of Hienlong [Qianlong], to the Prince who will be his Successor, as he has been in the management of the Public affairs for some time.

It is not unlikely that the Emperor's curiosity may lead to a degree of familiarity with you, in conversing upon the manners or circumstances of Europe and other Countries; and as despotic Princes are frequently more easy of access than their Ministers and dependents, you will not fail to turn such contingency to proper advantage. I do not mean to prescribe to you the particular mode of your negotiation; much must be left to your circumspection, and the judgement to be formed upon occurrences as they arise; but upon the present view of the matter, I am inclined to believe that instead of attempting to gain upon the Chinese Administration by representations founded upon the intricacies of either European or Indian Politicks, you should fairly state, after repeating the general assurances of His Majesty's friendly and pacific inclinations towards the Emperor, and his respect for the reputed mildness of his Administration, first the mutual benefit to be derived from a trade between the two Nations, in the course of which we receive beside other articles to the amount of twenty millions of Pounds weight of a Chinese herb, which would find very little vent, as not being in general use in other Countries, European or Asiatic, and for which we return woolens, cottons, and other articles useful to the Chinese, but a considerable part is actually paid to China in bullion.

Secondly, that the great extent of our commercial concerns in China, requires a place of security as a depot for such of our Goods as cannot be sold off or shipped during the short season that is allowed for our shipping to arrive and depart, and that for this purpose we wish to obtain a grant of a small tract of ground or detached Island, but in a more convenient situation than Canton, where our present warehouses are at a great distance from our Ships, and where we are not able to restrain the irregularities which are occasionally committed by the seamen of the Company's Ships, and those of private traders.

Thirdly, that our views are purely commercial, having not even a wish for territory; that we desire neither fortification nor defense but only the protection of the Chinese Government for our Merchants or their agents in trading or travelling thro the Country and a security to us against the encroachments of other powers, who might ever aim to disturb our trade; and you must here be prepared to obviate any prejudice which may arise from the argument of our present dominions in India by stating our situation in this respect to have arisen without our intending it, from the necessity of our defending ourselves against the oppressions of the revolted Nabobs, who entered into Cabals to our prejudice with other Nations of Europe, and disregarded the privileges granted to us by different Emperors, or by such other arguments as your own reflections upon the subject will suggest.

This topic I have reason to believe will be very necessary to enforce by every means in your power, as it is the great object of other European Nations to injure not only the Indian powers, but likewise the Emperor and Ministers of China with an idea of danger in countenancing the Subjects of Great Britain, as if it were the intention of this Country to aim at extending its territory in every quarter. As nothing can be more untrue than these representations it will not be difficult for you to find arguments which may counteract the effect of them.

If any favorable opportunity should be afforded to your Excellency it will be advisable that the difficulties with which our trade has long laboured at Canton should be represented; but in making such a representation you will endeavour to convince the Emperor that it is from His Majesty's design to attribute any act of misconduct to persons employed under the Chinese Government but with a view only to appease his Imperial Majesty that such difficulties do exist, in full confidence that from his wisdom and justice they will not hereafter be experienced.

Should a new establishment be conceded you will take it in the name of the King of Great Britain. You will endeavour to obtain it on the most beneficial terms, with a power of regulating the police, and exercising jurisdiction over our own dependents, for which competent powers would be given so as effectually to prevent or punish the disorders of our people, which the Company's Supercargos in their limited sphere of action must see committed with impunity. Should it be required that no native Chinese be subject to be punished by our jurisdiction, or should any particular modification of this power be exacted it is not material ultimately to reject either of these propositions provided British subjects can be exempted from the Chinese jurisdiction for crimes, and that the British Chief or those under him be not held responsible if any Culprit should escape the pursuit of Justice, after search has been made by British and Chinese Officers acting in conjunction. . . .

It is necessary you should be on your Guard against one stipulation which, perhaps, will be demanded from you: which is that of the exclusion of the trade of opium from the Chinese dominions as being prohibited by the Laws of the Empire; if this subject should come into discussion, it must be handled with the greatest circumspection. It is beyond a doubt that no inconsiderable portion of the opium raised within our Indian territories actually finds its way to China: but if it should be made a positive requisition or any article of any proposed commercial treaty, that none of that drug should be sent by us to China, you must accede to it, rather than risk any essential benefit by contending for a liberty in this respect in which case the sale of our opium in Bengal must be left to take its chance in an open market, or to find a consumption in the dispersed and circuitous traffic of the eastern Seas.

A due sense of wisdom and justice of the King of Great Britain, which it will be your business to impress, as well as of the wealth and power of this Country, and of the genius and knowledge of its People, may naturally lead to a preferable acceptance of a treaty of friendship and alliance with us, as most worthy of themselves; and in a political light, as most likely to be useful to them, from our naval force, being the only assistance of which they may foresee the occasional importance to them.

In case the embassy should have an amicable and prosperous termination, it may be proposed to his Imperial Majesty to receive an occasional or perpetual Minister from the King of Great Britain, and to send one on his own part to the Court of London, in the assurance that all proper honours will be paid to any person who may be deputed in that sacred character. . . .

During the continuance of the Embassy you will take every possible opportunity that may arise, of transmitting to me for His Majesty's information, an account of your proceedings, and also of communicating with Earl Cornwallis, or the Governor General of Bengal for the time being, with whose views and efforts for promoting the trade of India to the East, it is particularly desirable you should co-operate, as far as they may be consistent with the present instructions.

Sincerely wishing your Excellency a prosperous voyage and complete success in the very important objects of it, I have the honour to be with great regard, My Lord,

> Your Excellency's most obedient
> and most humble Servant
> Henry Dundas.

6.2 MACARTNEY'S AUDIENCE WITH QIANLONG

After his arrival in China in June 1793, Lord Macartney met twice with the Qianlong emperor at the Rehe summer palace. Although Macartney was treated with great courtesy by Qianlong, he was ultimately frustrated in achieving any of the concrete objects of his mission.

Despite failures in negotiating trade or diplomatic accords, Macartney was remarkably successful in piercing the veils of mystery and misconception that had hitherto prevented Europeans from grasping the nature of Qing China. The following document represents Macartney's assessment of the Qing state and is notable for its acute portrayal of many of the problems that would frustrate Manchu rulers until the abdication of Puyi in 1911. Especially prescient, in this regard, are Macartney's remarks on the frictions inherent in the system of Manchu/Han dyarchy[1] and his accurate comprehension of the dangers of peasant revolt.

Saturday, September 14. This morning at four o'clock a.m. we set out for the Court under the convoy of Wang and Chou, and reached it in little more than an hour, the distance being about three miles from our hotel. I proceeded in great state with all my train music, guards, etc. Sir George Staunton and I went in palanquins and the officers and gentlemen of the Embassy on horseback. Over a rich embroidered velvet I wore the mantle of the Order of the Bath, with the collar, a diamond badge and a diamond star.

Sir George Staunton was dressed in a rich embroidered velvet also, and, being a Doctor of Laws in the University of Oxford, wore the habit of his degree, which is of scarlet silk, full and flowing. I mention these little particulars to show the attention I always paid, where a proper opportunity offered, to oriental customs and ideas. We alighted at the park gate, from whence we walked to the Imperial encampment, and were conducted to a large, handsome tent prepared for us on one side of the Emperor's. After waiting there about an hour his approach was announced by drums and music, on which we quitted our tent and came forward upon the green carpet.

---

1. The system of double-rule practices throughout the Qing as Han Chinese and Manchu officials served together within many organs of the state bureaucracy.

He was seated in an open palanquin, carried by sixteen bearers, attended by numbers of officers bearing flags, standards, and umbrellas, and as he passed we paid him our compliments by kneeling on one knee, whilst all the Chinese made their usual prostrations. As soon as he had ascended his throne I came to the entrance of the tent, and, holding in both my hands a large gold box enriched with diamonds in which was enclosed the King's letter, I walked deliberately up, and ascending the side-steps of the throne, delivered it into the Emperor's own hands, who, having received it, passed it to the Minister, by whom it was placed on the cushion. He then gave me as the first present from him to His Majesty the *ju-eu-jou* or *giou-giou*, as the symbol of peace and prosperity, and expressed his hopes that my Sovereign and he should always live in good correspondence and amity. It is a whitish, agate-looking stone about a foot and a half long, curiously carved, and highly prized by the Chinese, but to me it does not appear in itself to be of any great value.

The Emperor then presented me with a *ju-eu-jou* of a greenish-coloured stone of the same emblematic character; at the same time he very graciously received from me a pair of beautiful enamelled watches set with diamonds, which I had prepared in consequence of the information given me, and which, having looked at, he passed to the Minister. Sir George Staunton, whom, as he had been appointed Minister Plenipotentiary to act in case of my death or departure, I introduced to him as such, now came forward, and after kneeling upon one knee in the same manner which I had done, presented to him two elegant airguns, and received from him a *ju-eu-jou* of greenish stone nearly similar to mine. Other presents were sent at the same time to all the gentlemen of my train. We then descended from the steps of the throne, and sat down upon cushions at one of the tables on the Emperor's left hand; and at other tables, according to their different ranks, the chief Tartar Princes and the Mandarins of the Court at the same time took their places, all dressed in the proper robes of their respective ranks. These tables were then uncovered and exhibited a sumptuous banquet. The Emperor sent us several dishes from his own table, together with some liquors, which the Chinese call wine, not, however, expressed from the grape, but distilled or extracted from rice, herbs, and honey. In about half an hour he sent for Sir George Staunton and me to come to him, and gave to each of us, with his own hands, a cup of warm wine, which we immediately drank in his presence, and found it very pleasant and comfortable, the morning being cold and raw.

Amongst other things, he asked me the age of my King, and being informed of it, said he hoped he might live as many years as himself, which are eighty-three. His manner is dignified, but affable, and condescending, and his reception of us has been very gracious and satisfactory. He is a very fine old gentleman, still healthy and vigorous, not having the appearance of a man of more than sixty.

The order and regularity in serving and removing the dinner was wonderfully exact, and every function of the ceremony performed with such silence and solemnity as in some measure to resemble the celebration of a religious mystery. The Emperor's tent or pavilion, which is circular, I should calculate to be about twenty-four or twenty-five yards in diameter, and is supported by a number of pillars, either gilded, painted, or varnished, according to their distance and position. In the front was an opening of six yards, and from this opening a yellow fly-tent projected so as to lengthen considerably the space between the entrance and the throne.

The materials and distribution of the furniture within at once displayed grandeur and elegance. The tapestry, the curtains, the carpets, the lanterns, the fringes, the tassels were disposed with such harmony, the colours so artfully varied, and the light and shades so judiciously managed, that the whole assemblage filled the eye with delight, and diffused over the mind a pleasing serenity and repose undisturbed by glitter or affected embellishments. The commanding feature of the ceremony was that calm dignity, that sober pomp of Asiatic greatness, which European refinements have not yet attained.

I forgot to mention that there were present on this occasion three ambassadors from Tatze or Pegu and six Mohammedan ambassadors from the Kalmucks of the south-west, but their appearance was not very splendid. Neither must I omit that, during the ceremony, which lasted five hours, various entertainments of wrestling, tumbling, wire-dancing, together with dramatic representations, were exhibited opposite to the tent, but at a considerable distance from it.

Thus, then, have I seen 'King Solomon in all his glory'. I use this expression, as the scene recalled perfectly to my memory a puppet show of that name which I recollect to have seen in my childhood, and which made so strong an impression on my mind that I then thought it a true representation of the highest pitch of human greatness and felicity.

6.3   MACARTNEY'S DESCRIPTION OF CHINA'S GOVERNMENT

The ancient constitution of China differed essentially from the present. Although the Emperor was styled despotic, and decorated with all the titles and epithets of oriental hyperbole, the power and administration of the state resided in the great councils or tribunals, whose functions were not to be violated or disturbed by court intrigue or ministerial caprice. It was government by law, and when attempts were made by their princes to render it otherwise, as often happened, rebellion was the consequence and expulsion the penalty. Hence according to history the regular succession of the crown was broken through, new sovereigns elected, and the former constitution restored. The present family on the throne is the twenty-second distinct dynasty whose hands have swayed the sceptre of China. The government as it now stands is properly the tyranny of a handful of Tartars over more than three hundred millions of Chinese.

An uninterrupted succession of four Emperors, all endowed with excellent understandings, uncommon vigor of mind and decision of character, has hitherto obviated the danger of such an enormous disproportion, and not only maintained itself on the throne, but enlarged its dominions to a prodigious extent.

Various causes have contributed to this wonderful phenomenon in the political world. When the Tartars entered China a century and a half ago, the country had long languished under a weak administration, had been desolated by civil wars and rebellions, and was then disputed by several unworthy competitors. The Tartars availing themselves of these circumstances, at first took part as auxiliaries in favour of one of the candidates but they soon became principals, and at last by valour and perseverance surmounted every obstacle to their own establishment. The spirit of the Chinese was now effectually subdued by the weight of calamity; they were wearied with contending for the mere choice of tyrants among themselves, and they less reluctantly submitted to a foreign usurpation. The conquerors, however terrible in arms and ferocious in their manners, were conducted by a leader of a calm judgement as well as of a resolute mind, who tempered the despotism he introduced with so much prudence and policy that it seemed preferable to the other evils which they had so recently groaned under. A state of tranquil subjection succeeded for some time to the turbulence and horrors of a doubtful hostility; the government, though absolute, was at least methodical and regular. It menaced but did not injure; the blow might be dreaded, but it seldom was felt. . . .

The government of China, as now instituted, may not ineptly be compared to Astley's amphitheatre, where a single jockey rides a number of horses at once, who are so nicely bitted and dressed that he can impel them with a whisper, or stop them with a hair. But at the same time he knows the consequence of mismanagement or neglect, and that if they are not properly matched, curried and fed, patted and stoked, some of them will be liable to run out of the circle, to kick at their keepers and refuse to be mounted any longer. Considering then all circumstances, the original defect of title to the inheritance, the incessant anxiety of forcible possession, the odium of a foreign yoke, the inevitable combats of passion in a sovereign's breast, when deceived by artifice, betrayed by perfidy, or provoked by rebellion, the doubtful and intricate boundaries of reward and punishment, where vigor and indulgence may be equally misapplied, the almost incalculable population, the immense extent of dominion, the personal exertions requisite in war, and the no less difficult talents of administration in peace—considering, I say, all these circumstances, the government of such an empire must be a task that has hitherto been performed with wonderful ability and unparalleled success. That such singular skill in the

art of reigning should have been uninterruptedly transmitted through a succession of four princes for upwards of a century and a half would be very
difficult to account for, if we did not constantly bear in mind a fundamental
principle of the state. All power and authority in China derive solely from the
sovereign, and they are not only distributed by him in his life time, but attest
their origin after his decease. The appointment of his successor is exclusively
vested in him. Without regard to primogeniture, without the fondness of a
parent, without the partiality of a friend, he acts on this occasion as the father
of the state, and selects the person of his family, whom he judges the most
worthy to replace him. Every choice of this kind as yet made has been unex-
ceptionably fortunate. K'ang-hsi proved as great a prince as his father; Yung-
cheng was inferior to neither, and Ch'ien-lung surpasses the glory of all his
predecessors. Who is the Atlas destined by him to bear this load of empire when
he dies is yet unknown, but on whatever shoulders it may fall, another trans-
migration of Fo-hi into the next emperor will be necessary to enable him to
sustain it on its present balance; for though within the serene atmosphere of the
Court everything wears the face of happiness and applause, yet it cannot be
concealed that the nation in general is far from being easy or contented. The
frequent insurrections in the distant provinces are unambiguous oracles of the
real sentiments and temper of the people. The predominance of the Tartars and
the Emperor's partiality to them are the common subject of conversation among
the Chinese whenever they meet together in private, and the constant theme of
their discourse. There are certain mysterious societies in every province who
are known to be dis-affected, and although narrowly watched by the government, they find means to elude its vigilance and often to hold secret assemblies,
where they revive the memory of ancient glory and independence, brood over
recent injuries, and mediate revenge.

Though much circumscribed in the course of our travels we had opportunities of observation seldom afforded to others, and not neglected by us. The
genuine character of the inhabitants, and the effects resulting from the refined
polity and principles of the government, which are meant to restrain and direct
them, naturally claimed my particular attention and inquiry. In my researches
I often perceived the ground to be hollow under a vast superstructure, and in
trees of the most stately and flourishing appearance I discovered symptoms of
speedy decay, whilst humbler plants were held by vigorous roots, and mean
edifices rested on steady foundations. The Chinese are now recovering from the
blows that had stunned them; they are awaking from the political stupor they
had been thrown into by the Tartar impression, and begin to feel their native
energies revive. A slight collision might elicit fire from the flint, and spread
flames of revolt from one extremity of China to the other. In fact the volume
of the empire is now grown too ponderous and disproportionate to be easily
grasped by a single hand, be it ever so capacious and strong. It is possible,
notwithstanding, that the momentum impressed on the machine by the vigor

and wisdom of the present Emperor may keep it steady and entire in its orbit for a considerable time longer; but I should not be surprised if its dislocation or dismemberment were to take place before my own dissolution. Whenever such an event happens, it will probably be attended with all the horrors and atrocities from which they were delivered by the Tartar domination; but men are apt to lose the memory of former evils under the pressure of immediate suffering; and what can be expected from those who are corrupted by servitude, exasperated by despotism and maddened by despair? Their condition, however, might then become still worse than it can be at present. Like the slave who fled into the desert from his chains and was devoured by the lion, they may draw down upon themselves oppression and destruction by their very effort to avoid them, may be poisoned by their own remedies and be buried themselves in the graves which they dug for others. A sudden transition from slavery to freedom, from dependence to authority, can seldom be borne with moderation or discretion. Every change in the state of man ought to be gentle and gradual, otherwise it is commonly dangerous to himself and intolerable to others. A due preparation may be as necessary for liberty as for inoculation of the smallpox which, like liberty, is future health but without due preparation is almost certain destruction. Thus then the Chinese, if not led to emancipation by degrees, but let loose on a burst of enthusiasm would probably fall into all the excesses of folly, suffer all the paroxysms of madness, and be found as unfit for the enjoyment of freedom as the French and the negroes.

6.4 AND 6.5   QIANLONG'S REJECTION OF MACARTNEY'S DEMANDS: TWO EDICTS

Qianlong's famous edicts to George III were the Qing government's response to the proposals carried to Peking by Lord George Macartney. In 1793, Qianlong ruled territories many times the size of Great Britain; indeed, China with its dependencies was the largest unified empire in the world and had been undefeated in all of the wars it had fought with its neighbors since the seventeenth century. Each year, in adherence to a schedule established by the Board of Rites, tribute emissaries from Burma, Korea, Vietnam, Japan, and other territories trekked to Peking to pay their respects to the Chinese throne. In return for obeisance and tribute, the Qing government condescended to allow these far-flung "vassal states" (*fanguo*) to enjoy trade with China and extended protection to their monarchies. Scholars in these countries learned Chinese and memorized the Chinese classics, and in Korea, Vietnam, and Japan, the lessons of Chinese political and institutional history were assiduously studied and imitated.

The Forbidden City was the center of a political world in which loyalties had been beaten into place the by hard-riding Manchu generals of the seventeenth century. But the historical roots of this polity stretched back some two millennia.

It is, thus, little wonder that the Qianlong emperor regarded Lord Maccartney as little more than a self-important tributary emissary and rejected all of his requests without discussion or debate. In the edicts that follow, Macartney's charge from Henry Dundas was refused practically article by article. On his own turf, the Chinese emperor was used to defining things in a peremptory way but also with regard to the precedents built into the Qing scheme of foreign affairs. Qianlong's logic in these edicts was solidly founded on history, power, and a belief that a tiny maritime state thousands of *li* from China was not a force to be reckoned with.

6.4 *The First Edict, September 1793*

You, O King, live beyond the confines of many seas, nevertheless, impelled by your humble desire to partake of the benefits of our civilization, you have dispatched a mission respectfully bearing your memorial. Your Envoy has crossed the seas and paid his respects at my Court on the anniversary of my birthday. To show your devotion, you have also sent offerings of your country's produce.

I have perused your memorial: the earnest terms in which it is couched reveal a respectful humility on your part, which is highly praiseworthy. In consideration of the fact that your Ambassador and his deputy have come a long way with your memorial and tribute, I have shown them high favour and have allowed them to be introduced into my presence. To manifest my indulgence, I have entertained them at a banquet and made them numerous gifts. I have also caused presents to be forwarded to the Naval Commander and six hundred of his officers and men, although they did not come to Peking, so that they too may share in my all-embracing kindness.

As to your entreaty to send one of your nationals to be accredited to my Celestial Court and to be in control of your country's trade with China, this request is contrary to all usage of my dynasty and cannot possibly be entertained. It is true that Europeans, in the service of the dynasty, have been permitted to live at Peking, but they are compelled to adopt Chinese dress, they are strictly confined to their own precincts and are never permitted to return home. You are presumably familiar with our dynastic regulations. Your proposed Envoy to my Court could not be placed in a position similar to that of European officials in Peking who are forbidden to leave China, nor could he, on the other hand, be allowed liberty of movement and the privilege of corresponding with his own country; so that you would gain nothing by his residence in our midst.

Moreover, Our Celestial dynasty possesses vast territories, and tribute missions from the dependencies are provided for by the Department for Tributary States, which ministers to their wants and exercises strict control over their movements. It would be quite impossible to leave them to their own devices. Supposing that your Envoy should come to our Court, his language and national dress differ from that of our people, and there would be no place in which he might reside. It may be suggested that he might imitate the Europeans permanently resident in Peking and adopt the dress and customs of China, but, it has never been our dynasty's wish to force people to do things unseemly and inconvenient. Besides, supposing I sent an Ambassador to reside in your country, how could you possibly make for him the requisite arrangements? Europe consists of many other nations besides your own: if each and all demanded to be represented at our Court, how could we possibly consent? The thing is utterly impracticable. How can our dynasty alter its whole procedure and regulations, established for more than a century, in order to meet your individual views? If it be said that your object is to exercise control over your country's trade, your nationals have had full liberty to trade at Canton for many a year, and have received the greatest consideration at our hands. Missions have been sent by Portugal and Italy, preferring similar requests. The Throne appreciated their sincerity and loaded them with favours, besides authorizing measures to facilitate their trade with China. You are no doubt aware that, when my Canton merchant, Wu Chao-p'ing, was in debt to the foreign ships, I made the Viceroy advance the monies due, out of the provincial treasury, and ordered him to punish the culprit severely. Why then should foreign nations advance this utterly unreasonable request to be represented at my Court? Peking is nearly 10,000 li from Canton, and at such a distance what possible control could any British representative exercise?

If you assert that your reverence for Our Celestial dynasty fills you with a desire to acquire our civilization, our ceremonies and code laws differ so completely from your own that, even if your Envoy were able to acquire the rudiments of our civilization, you could not possibly transplant our manners and customs to your alien soil. Therefore, however adept the Envoy might become, nothing would be gained thereby.

Swaying the wide world, I have but one aim in view, namely, to maintain a perfect governance and to fulfil the duties of the State; strange and costly objects do not interest me. If I have commanded that the tribute offerings sent by you, O King, are to be accepted, this was solely in consideration for the spirit which prompted you to dispatch them from afar. Our dynasty's majestic virtue has penetrated unto every country under Heaven, and Kings of nations have offered their costly tribute by land and sea. As your Ambassador can see for himself, we possess all things. I set no value on objects strange or ingenious, and have no use for your country's manufacturers. This then is my answer to your request to appoint a representative at my Court, a request contrary to our dynastic usage, which would only result in inconvenience to yourself. I have expounded my wishes in detail and have commanded your tribute Envoys to leave in peace on their homeward journey. It behooves you, O King, to respect my sentiments and to display even greater devotion an secure peace and prosperity for your country hereafter. Besides making gifts (of which I enclose a list) to each member of your Mission, I confer upon you, O King, valuable presents in excess of the number usually bestowed on such occasions, including silks and curios—a list of which is likewise enclosed. Do you reverently receive them and take note of my tender goodwill towards you! A special mandate.

6.5   The Second Edict, September 1793

You, O King from afar, have yearned after the blessings of our civilization, and in your eagerness to come into touch with our converting influence have sent an Embassy across the sea bearing a memorial. I have already taken not of your respectful spirit of submission, have treated your mission with extreme favour and loaded it with gifts, besides issuing a mandate to you, O King, and honouring you with the bestowal of valuable presents. Thus has my indulgence been manifested.

Yesterday your Ambassador petitioned my Ministers to memorialize me regarding your trade with China, but his proposal is not consistent with our dynastic usage and cannot be entertained. Hitherto, all European nations, including your own country's barbarian merchants, have carried on their trade with Our Celestial Empire at Canton. Such has been the procedure for many years, although Our Celestial Empire possesses all things in prolific abundance and lacks no product within its own borders. There was therefore no need to import the manufactures of outside barbarians in exchange for our own produce. But as the tea, silk, and porcelain which the Celestial Empire produces are absolute necessities to European nations and to yourselves, we have permitted, as a signal mark of favour, that foreign *hongs* [merchant guilds] should be established at Canton, so that your wants might be supplied and your country thus participate in our beneficence. But your Ambassador has now put forward new requests which completely fail to recognize the Throne's principle to "treat strangers from afar with indulgence," and to exercise a pacifying control over barbarian tribes, the world over. Moreover, our dynasty, swaying the myriad races of the globe, extends the same benevolence towards all. Your England is not the only nation trading at Canton. If other nations, following your bad example, wrongfully importune my ear with further impossible requests, how will it be possible for me to treat them with easy indulgence? Nevertheless, I do not forget the lonely remoteness of your island, cut off from the world by intervening wastes of sea, nor do I overlook your excusable ignorance of the usages of Our Celestial Empire. I have consequently commanded my Ministers of the mission. But I have doubts that, after your Envoy's return he may fail to acquaint you with my view in detail or that he may be lacking in lucidity, so that I shall now proceed to take your requests *seriatim* and to issue my mandate on each question separately. In this way you will, I trust, comprehend my meaning.

1. Your Ambassador requests facilities for ships of your nation to call at Ningpo, Chusan, Tientsin and other places for purposes of trade. Until now trade with European nations has always been conducted at Macao, where the foreign *hongs* are established to store and sell foreign merchandise. Your nation has obediently complied with this regulation for years past without raising any objection. In none of the other ports named have *hongs* been established, so that even if your vessels were to proceed thither, they would have no means of disposing of their cargoes. Furthermore, no interpreters are available, so you would have no means of explaining your wants, and nothing but general inconvenience would result. For the future, as in the past, I decree that your request is refused and that the trade shall be limited to Macao.

2. The request that your merchants may establish a repository in the capital of my Empire for the storing and sale of your produce, in accordance with the precedent granted to Russia, is even more impracticable than the last. My capital is the hub and centre about which all quarters of the globe revolve. Its ordinances are most august and its laws are strict in the extreme. The subjects of our dependencies have never been allowed to open places of business in Peking. Foreign trade has hitherto been conducted at Macao, because it is conveniently near to the sea, and therefore an important gathering place for the ships of all nations sailing to and fro. If warehouses were established in Peking, the remoteness of your country lying far to the northwest of any capital, would render transport extremely difficult. Before Kiakhta was opened, the Russians were permitted to trade at Peking, but the accommodation furnished them was only temporary. As soon as Kiakhta was available, they were compelled to withdraw from Peking, which has been closed to their trade these many years. Their frontier trade at Kiakhta is equivalent to your trade at Macao. Possessing facilities at the latter place, you now ask for further privileges at Peking, although our dynasty observes the severest restrictions respecting the admission of foreigners within its boundaries, and has never permitted the subjects of dependencies to cross the Empire's barriers and settle at will amongst the Chinese people. This request is also refused.

3. Your request for a small island near Chusan, where your merchants may reside and goods be warehoused, arises from your desire to develop trade. As there are neither foreign *hongs* nor interpreters in or near Chusan, where none of your ships have ever called, such an island would be utterly

useless for your purposes. Every inch of the territory of our Empire is marked on the map and the strictest vigilance is exercised over it all: even tiny islets and far-lying sandbanks are clearly defined as part of the provinces to which they belong. Consider, moreover, that England is not the only barbarian land which wishes to establish relations with our civilization and trade with our Empire: supposing that other nations were all to imitate your evil example and beseech me to present them each and all with a site for trading purposes, how could I possibly comply. This also is a flagrant infringement of the usage of my Empire and cannot possibly be entertained.

4. The next request, for a small site in the vicinity of Canton city, where your barbarian merchants may lodge or, alternatively, that there be no longer any restrictions over their movements at Macao, has arisen from the following causes. Hitherto, the barbarian merchants of Europe have had a definite locality assigned to them at Macao for residence and trade, and have been forbidden to encroach an inch beyond the limits assigned to that locality. Barbarian merchants having business with the *hongs* have never been allowed to enter the city of Canton; by these measures, disputes between Chinese and barbarians are prevented, and a firm barrier is raised between my subjects and those of other nations. The present request is quite contrary to precedent; furthermore, European nations have been trading with Canton for a number of years and, as they make large profits, the number of traders is constantly increasing. How could it be possible to grant such a site to each country? The merchants of the foreign *hongs* are responsible to the local officials for the proceedings of barbarian merchants and they carry out periodical inspections. If these restrictions were withdrawn, friction would inevitably occur between the Chinese and your barbarian subjects, and the results would militate against the benevolent regard that I feel towards you. From every point of view, therefore, it is best that the regulations now in force should continue unchanged.

5. Regarding your request for remission or reduction of duties on merchandise discharged by your British barbarian merchants at Macao and distributed throughout the interior, there is a regular tariff in force for barbarian merchants' goods, which applies equally to all European nations. It would be as wrong to increase the duty imposed on your nation's merchandise on the ground that the bulk of foreign trade is in your hands, as to make an exception in your case in the shape of specially reduced duties. In the future, duties shall be levied equitably without discrimination between your nation and any other, and, in order to manifest my regard, your barbarian merchants shall continue to be shown every consideration at Macao.

6. As to your request that your ships shall pay the duties leviable by tariff, there are regular rules in force at the Canton Custom house respecting the

amounts payable, and since I have refused your request to be allowed to trade at other ports, this duty will naturally continue to be paid at Canton as heretofore.

7. Regarding your nation's worship of the Lord of Heaven, it is the same religion as that of other European nations. Ever since the beginning of history, sage Emperors and wise rulers have bestowed on China a moral system and inculcated a code, which from time immemorial has been religiously observed by the myriads of my subjects. There has been no hankering after heterodox doctrines. Even the European [missionary] officials in my capital are forbidden to hold intercourse with Chinese subjects; they are restricted within the limits of their appointed residences, and may not go about propagating their religion. The distinction between Chinese and barbarian is most strict, and your Ambassador's request that barbarians shall be given full liberty to disseminate their religion is utterly unreasonable.

It may be, O King, that the above proposals have been wantonly made by your Ambassador on his own responsibility or peradventure you yourself are ignorant of our dynastic regulations and had no intention of transgressing them when you expressed these wild ideas and hopes. I have ever shown the greatest condescension to the tribute missions of all States which sincerely yearn after the blessings of civilization, so as to manifest my kindly indulgence. I have even gone out of my way to grant any requests which were in any way consistent with Chinese usage. Above all, upon you, who live in a remote and inaccessible region, far across the spaces of ocean, but who have shown your submissive loyalty by sending this tribute mission, I have heaped benefits far in excess of those accorded to other nations. But the demands presented by your Embassy are not only a contravention of dynastic tradition, but would be utterly unproductive of good result to yourself, besides being quite impracticable. I have accordingly stated the facts to you in detail, and it is your bounden duty reverently to appreciate my feelings and to obey these instructions henceforward for all time, so that you may enjoy the blessings of perpetual peace. If, after the receipt of this explicit decree, you lightly give ear to the representation of your subordinates and allow your barbarian merchants to proceed to Chekiang and Tientsin, with the object of landing and trading there, the ordinances of my Celestial Empire are strict in the extreme, and the local officials, both civil and military, are bound reverently to obey the law of the land. Should your vessels touch shore, your merchants will assuredly never be permitted to land or to reside there, but will be subject to instant expulsion. In that event your barbarian merchants will have had a long journey for nothing. Do not say that you were not warned in due time! Tremblingly obey and show no negligence! A special mandate!

CHAPTER 7

The First Clash
with the West

7.1–7.4 MEMORIALS, EDICTS, AND LAWS ON OPIUM

After the abolition of the British East India Company's monopoly in the China trade in 1834, the amount of Indian opium reaching Canton increased dramatically. In 1835, over sixteen thousand chests of Bengali and Malwa opium with a dollar value of $17,388,622 were imported illegally into China. The loss of silver specie paid for the drug was already a source of deep concern for the Qing court.[1] Also distressful from Peking's perspective was the failure of local authorities to quell the booming underground trade or halt the use of opium. Since each chest of opium weighed one hundred and seventy pounds and the normal user smoked only a tiny quantity of the drug, the volume of the trade was clearly already scaled to meet the needs of a huge population of habitual and casual users. The throne was also alarmed by the prospect of dealing with a useless and narcotized population dependent on foreign merchants for their "fix."

Economic and social dilemmas raised by the opium trade prompted a number of Qing officials to memorialize the throne on this question. What ensued was a carefully reasoned examination of China's existing opium laws. Some memorialists believed that opium should be legalized and paid for with trading goods. While China developed domestic sources for the drug to diminish reliance on imports, European traders could at least be forced to pay duty on shipments from abroad. Other memorialists advo-

---

1. Chang Hsin-pao, *Commissioner Lin and the Opium War* (New York: W. W. Norton, 1970), p. 223.

cated a "war on drugs" with strict prohibitions designed to dry up the supply of the drug and discourage its domestic marketing and use.

One advocate of legalization was Xu Naiji (1777–1839), an 1809 *jinshi* from Renhe County, Zhejiang, who had served as circuit intendant (*daotai*) at Canton. In the spring of 1836, while he was serving as a sub-director of the Court of Sacrificial Worship in Peking, Xu addressed his ideas to the throne in a memorial that remains controversial even today. In the memorial, reproduced below, he admitted the evil effects of opium but argued for a process of legalization whose end result would have been the elimination of the silver outflow and the dominant foreign role in the trade. The Daoguang emperor seemed to lean toward Xu's proposal but remanded it with a terse edict to Deng Tingzhen, the governor of Guangdong and Guangxi, for his consideration.

In the fall of 1836, however, other memorialists, among them Zhu Zun (1791–1862), addressed appeals to Daoguang for even tighter bans on the opium trade. Zhu, a vice-president of the Board of Rites and sub-chancellor of the Grand Secretariat, stressed the ethical importance of good prohibitory laws as a means of controlling clear social evils. His memorial, also reproduced below, was, likewise, remanded by Daoguang to Governor Deng for his perusal, but this time with an edict that indicated that the emperor was leaning toward an opium ban. Shortly, the emperor ordered Deng to devise plans for a stricter ban on opium, setting the stage for the confrontation between British traders and Commissioner Lin Zexu that erupted three years later in 1839.

7.1 Memorial on Legalizing Opium, June 10, 1836

Xu Naiji, sub-director of the sacrificial court, presents the following memorial in regard to opium, to show that the more severe the interdicts against it are made, the more widely do the evils arising therefrom spread; and that it is right urgently to request, that a change be made in the arrangements respecting it; to which end he earnestly entreats his sacred majesty to cast a glance hereon, and to issue secret orders for a faithful investigation of the subject.

I would humbly represent that opium was originally ranked among medicines; its qualities are stimulant; it also checks excessive secretions; and prevents the evil effects of noxious vapors. . . . When any one is long habituated to inhaling it, it becomes necessary to resort to it at regular intervals, and the habit of using it, being inveterate, is destructive of time, injurious to property, and yet dear to one even as life. Of those who use it to great excess, the breath becomes feeble, the body wasted, the face sallow, the teeth black: the individuals themselves clearly see the evil effects of it, yet cannot refrain from it. It is indeed indispensably necessary to enact severe prohibitions in order to eradicate so vile a practice.

On inquiry I find that there are three kinds of opium: one is called company's; the outer covering of it is black, and hence it is also called 'black earth'; it comes from Bengal; a second kind is called 'white-skin', and it comes from Bombay; the third kind is called 'red skin', and comes from Madras.[2] These are places which belong to England.

In Qianlong's reign, as well as previously, opium was inserted in the tariff of Canton as a medicine, subject to a duty of three taels per hundred catties, with an additional charge of two taels four mace and five candareens[3] under the name of charge per package. After this, it was prohibited. In the first year of Jiaqing, those found guilty of smoking opium were subject only to the punishment of the pillory and bamboo. Now they have, in the course of time, become liable to the severest penalties, transportation in various degrees, and death after the ordinary continuance in prison. Yet the smokers of the drug have increased in number, and the practice has spread throughout almost the whole empire. In Qianlong's time and the previous reigns, when opium passed through the custom-house and paid a duty, it was given into the hands of the hong merchants in exchange for tea and other goods. But at the present time, the prohibitions of government being most strict against it, none dare openly to exchange goods for it; all secretly purchase it with money. In the reign of Jiaqing there arrived, it may be, some hundred chests annually. The number has now increased to upwards of 20,000 chests, containing each a hundred catties. The 'black earth', which is the best, sells for about 800 dollars, foreign money, per chest; the 'white-skin', which is next in quality, for about 600 dollars; and the last, or 'red-skin', for about 400 dollars. The total quantity sold during the year amounts in value to ten and some odd millions of dollars; so that, in reckoning the dollar at seven mace, standard weight of silver, the annual waste of money somewhat exceeds ten million of taels. Formerly, the barbarian merchants brought foreign money to China; which, being paid in exchange for goods, was a source of pecuniary advantage to the people of all the sea board provinces. But latterly, the barbarian merchants have clandestinely sold opium for money; which has rendered it unnecessary for them to import foreign silver. Thus foreign money has been going out of the country, while none comes into it.

During two centuries, the government has maintained peace, and by fostering the people, has greatly promoted the increase of wealth and opulence among them. With you we witness the economical rule of our august sovereign,

2. Xu refers to Turkey.
3. Chinese money of account equalling 10 copper cash or 6 grains troy. "Tael": standard weight of silver and trade name for Chinese ounce with a varied value as measured against copper cash during the Qing. "Mace": ⅒ of a tael.

an example to the whole empire. Right it is that yellow gold be common as the dust.

Always in times past, a tael of pure silver exchanged for nearly about 1000 coined cash, but of late years the same sum has borne the value of 1200 or 1300 cash: thus the price of silver rises but does not fall. In the salt agency, the price of salt is paid in cash, while the duties are paid in silver: now the salt merchants have all become involved, and the existing state of the salt trade in every province is abject in the extreme. How is this occasioned but by the unnoticed oozing out of silver? If the easily exhaustible stores of the central spring go to fill up the wide and fathomless gulf of the outer seas, gradually pouring themselves out from day to day, and from month to month, we shall shortly be reduced to a state of which I cannot bear to speak.

It is proposed entirely to cut off the foreign trade, and thus to remove the root to dam up the source of the evil? The celestial dynasty would not, indeed, hesitate to relinquish the few millions of duties arising therefrom. But all the nations of the West have had a general market open to their ships for upwards of a thousand years; while the dealers in opium are the English alone; it would be wrong, for the sake of cutting off the English trade, to cut off that of all the other nations. Besides, the hundreds of thousands of people living on the sea-coast depend wholly on trade for their livelihood, and how are they to be disposed of? Moreover, the barbarian ships, being on the high seas, can repair to any island that may be selected as an entrepot, and the native sea-going vessels can meet them there; it is then impossible to cut off the trade. Of late years, the foreign vessels have visited all the ports of Fujian, Zhejiang, Jiangnan, Shandong, even to Tianjin and Manchuria, for the purpose of selling opium. And although at once expelled by the local authorities, yet it is reported that the quantity sold by them was not small. Thus it appears that, though the commerce of Canton should be cut off, yet it will not be possible to prevent the clandestine introduction of merchandise. . . .

Since then, it will not answer to close our ports against [all trade], and since the laws issued against opium are quite inoperative, the only method left is to revert to the former system, to permit the barbarian merchants to import opium paying duty thereon as a medicine, and to require that, after having passed the custom-house, it shall be delivered to the hong merchants only in exchange for merchandise, and that no money be paid for it. The barbarians finding that the amount of duties to be paid on it is less than what is now spent in bribes, will also gladly comply therein. Foreign money should be placed on the same footing with sycee silver [lumps of fine uncoined silver], and the exportation of it should be equally prohibited. Offenders when caught should be punished by the entire destruction of the opium they have, and the confiscation of the money that be found with them. With regard to officers, civil and military, and to the scholars and common soldiers, the first are called on to fulfill the duties of their rank and attend to the public good; the others, to cultivate their talents and become fit for public usefulness. None of these, therefore, must be permitted to contract a practice so bad, or to walk in a path which will lead only to the utter waste of their time and destruction of their property. If, however, the laws enacted against the practice be made too severe, the result will be mutual connivance. It becomes my duty, then, to request that it be enacted, that any officer, scholar, or soldier, found guilty of secretly smoking opium, shall be immediately dismissed from public employ, without being made liable to any other penalty. In this way, lenity will become in fact severity towards them. And further, that, if any superior or general officer be found guilty of knowingly and willfully conniving at the practice among his subordinates, such officer shall be subjected to a court of inquiry. Lastly, that no regard be paid to the purchase and use of opium on the part of the people generally. . . .

Prostrate I beg my august sovereign to give secret directions to the governor and lieut-governor of Guangdong, together with the superintendent of maritime customs, that they faithfully investigate the character of the above statements, and that, if they find them really correct, they speedily prepare a list of regulations adapted to a change in the system, and present the same for your majesty's final decision. Perchance this may be found adequate to stop further oozing out of money, and to replenish the national resources. With inexpressible awe and trembling fear I reverently present this memorial and await your majesty's commands.

7.2   Memorial on Banning Opium, October 1836

Zhu Zun, member of the council and of the Board of Rites, kneeling, presents the following memorial, wherein he suggests the propriety of increasing the severity of certain prohibitory enactments, with a view to maintain the dignity of the laws, and to remove a great evil from among the people: to this end he respectfully states his views on the subject, and earnestly entreats his sacred majesty to cast a glance thereon.

I would humbly point out, that wherever an evil exists it should be at once removed; and that the laws should never be suffered to fall into desuetude. Our government, having received from heaven, the gift of peace, has transmitted it for two centuries: this has afforded opportunity for the removal of evils from among the people. For governing the central nation, and for holding in submission all the surrounding barbarians, rules exist perfect in their nature, and well-fitted to attain their end. And in regard to opium, special enactments were passed for the prohibitions of its use in the first year of Jiaqing [1796]; and since then, memorials presented at various successive periods, have given rise to additional prohibitions, all which have been inserted in the code and the several tariffs. The laws, then, relating thereto are not wanting in severity; but there are those in office who, for want of energy, fail to carry them into execution.

Hence the people's minds gradually become callous; and base desires, springing up among them, increase day by day and month by month, till their rank luxuriance has spread over the whole empire. These noisome weeds, having been long neglected, it has become impossible to eradicate. And those to whom this duty is entrusted are, as if handbound, wholly at a loss what to do.

When the foreign ships convey opium to the coast, it is impossible for them to sell it by retail. Hence there are at Canton, in the provincial city, brokers, named 'melters.' These engage money-changers to arrange the price with the foreigners, and to obtain orders for them; with which orders they proceed to the receiving ships, and there the vile drug is delivered to them. This part of the transaction is notorious, and the actors in it are easily discoverable. The boats which carry the drug and which are called 'fast-crabs' and 'scrambling-dragons,' are all well furnished with guns and other weapons, and ply their oars as swiftly as though they were wings. Their crews have all the over-bearing assumption and audacity of pirates. Shall such men be suffered to navigate the surrounding seas according to their own will? And shall such conduct be passed over without investigation? . . .

It is said that the opium should be admitted, subject to a duty, the importers being required to give it into the hands of the hong merchants, in barter only for merchandise, without being allowed to sell it for money. And this is proposed as a means of preventing money from secretly oozing out of the country. But the English, by whom opium is sold, have been driven out to Lintin [a small island in the Pearl River estuary] so long since as the first year of Dao-guang [1821], when the then governor of Guangdong and Guangxi discovered and punished the warehousers of opium: so long have they been expelled, nor have they ever since imported it into Macao. Having once suppressed the trade and driven them away, shall we now again call upon them and invite them to return? This would be, indeed, a derogation from the true dignity of government. As to the proposition to give tea in exchange, and entirely to prohibit the exportation of even *foreign* silver I apprehend that, if the tea should not be found sufficient, money will still be given in exchange for the drug. Besides, if it is in our power to prevent the extortion of dollars, why not also to prevent the importation of opium? And if we can but prevent the importation of opium, the exportation of dollars will then cease of itself, and the two offenses will both at once be stopped. Moreover, is it not better, by continuing the old enactments, to find even a partial remedy for the evil, than by a change of the laws to increase the importation still further? As to levying a duty of opium, the thing sounds so awkwardly, and reads so unbeseemingly, that such a duty ought sorely not to be levied.

Again, it is said that the prohibitions against the planting of the poppy by natives should be relaxed; and that the direct consequences will be, daily diminution of the profits of foreigners, and in course of time the entire cessation of the trade without the aid of prohibitions. Is it, then, forgotten that it is natural to the common people to prize things heard of only by the ear and to undervalue those which are before their eyes,—to pass by those things which are near at hand, and to seek after those which are afar off—and, though they have a thing in their own land, yet to esteem more highly such as comes to them from beyond the seas? Thus, in Jiangsu, Zhejiang, Fujian, and Guangdong, they will not quietly be guided by the laws of the empire, but must needs make use of foreign money: and this foreign money, though of an inferior standard, is nevertheless exchanged by them at a higher rate than the native sycee silver, which is pure. And although money is cast in China after exactly the same pattern, under the names of Jiangsu pieces, Fujian pieces, and native or Canton pieces, yet this money has not been able to gain currency among the people. Thus, also, the silk and cotton goods of China are not insufficient in quantity; and yet the broadcloths, and comlets, and cotton goods of the barbarians from beyond the place of the empire are in constant request. Taking men generally the minds of all are equally unenlightened in this respect, so that all men prize what is strange, and undervalue whatever is in ordinary use.

From Fujian, Guangdong, Zhejiang, Shandong, Yunnan, and Guizhou, memorials have been presented by the censors and other officers, requesting that prohibitions should be enacted against the cultivation of the poppy, and against the preparation of opium; but while nominally prohibited, the cultivation of it has not been really stopped in those places. Of any of those provinces, except Yunnan, I do not presume to speak; but of that portion of the country I have it in any power to say, that the poppy is cultivated all over the hills and the open campaign, and that the quantity of opium annually produced there cannot be less than several thousand chests. And yet we do not see any diminution in the quantity of silver exported as compared with any previous period; while, on the other hand, the lack of the metal in Yunnan is double in degree to what it formerly was. To what cause is this to be ascribed? To what but that the consumers of the drug are very many, and that those who are choice and dainty, with regard to its quality prefer always the foreign article?

Those of your majesty's advisers who compare the drug to the dried leaf of the tobacco plant are in error. The tobacco leaf does not destroy the human constitution. The profit too arising from the sale of tobacco is small, while that arising from opium is large. Besides, tobacco may be cultivated on bare and barren ground, while the poppy needs a rich and fertile soil. If all the rich and fertile ground be used for planting the poppy; and if the people, hoping for a large profit therefrom, madly engage in its cultivation; where will flax and the mulberry tree be cultivated, or wheat and rye be planted? To draw off in this way the waters of the great fountain, requisite for the production of goods and raiment, and to lavish them upon the root whence calamity and disaster spring forth, is an error which may be compared to that of a physician, who, when treating a mere external disease, should drive it inwards to the heart and centre of the body. It may in such a case be found impossible even to preserve *life*.

And shall the fine fields of Guangdong, that produce their three crops every year, be given up for the cultivation of this noxious weed—those fields in comparison with which the unequal soil of all other parts of the empire is not even to be mentioned?

To sum up the matter—the wide-spreading and baneful influence of opium, when regarded simply as injurious to property, is of inferior importance; but when regarded as hurtful to the people, it demands most anxious consideration: for in the *people* lies the very foundation of the empire. Property, it is true, is that on which the subsistence of the people depends. Yet a deficiency of it may be supplied, and an impoverished people improved; whereas it is beyond the power of any artificial means to save a people enervated by luxury. In the history of Formosa we find the following passage: "Opium was first produced in Kaoutsinne [?], which by some is said to be the same as Kalapa [or Batavia]. The natives of this place were at the first sprightly and active, and being good soldiers, were always successful in battle. But the people called Hongmao [Redhairs, a term originally applied to the Dutch] came thither, and having manufactured opium, seduced some of the natives into the habit of smoking it; from this the mania for it rapidly spread throughout the whole nation, so that in process of time, the natives became feeble and enervated, submitted to the foreign rule, and ultimately were completely subjugated." Now the English are of the race of foreigners called Hongmao [Red-hairs]. In introducing opium into this country, their purpose has been to weaken and enfeeble the central empire. If not early aroused to a sense of our danger, we shall find ourselves, ere long, on the last step towards ruin. . . .

Since your majesty's accession to the throne, the maxim of your illustrious house that horsemanship and archery are the foundations of its existence, has ever been carefully remembered. And hence the governors, the lt. governors, the commanders of the forces, and their subordinates have again and again been directed to pay the strictest attention to the discipline and exercise of the troops, and of the naval forces and have been urged and required to create by their exertions strong and powerful legions. With admiration I contemplate my sacred sovereign's anxious care for imparting a military as well as a civil education, prompted as this anxiety is by desire to establish on a firm basis the foundations of the empire, and to hold in awe the barbarians on every side. But while the stream of importation of opium is not turned aside, it is impossible to attain any certainty that none within the camp do ever secretly inhale the drug. And if the camp be once contaminated by it, the baneful influence will work its way, and the habit will be contracted beyond the power of reform. When the periodical times of desire for it come round, how can the victims—their legs tottering, their hands trembling, their eyes flowing with child-like tears—be able in any way to attend to their proper exercises? Or how can such men form strong and powerful legions? Under these circumstances, the military will become alike unfit to advance to the fight, or in a retreat to defend their posts. Of this there is clear proof in the instance of the campaign against the Yao rebels in the 12th year of our sovereign's reign [1832]. In the army sent to Yongzhou [Hunan], on that occasion, great numbers of the soldiers were opium-smokers; so that although their numerical force was large, there was hardly any strength to be found among them. . . .

At the present moment, throughout the empire, the minds of men are in imminent danger; the more foolish, being seduced by teachers of false doctrines, are sunk in vain superstitions and cannot be aroused; and the more intelligent, being intoxicated by opium, are carried away as by a whirlpool, and are beyond recovery. Most thoughtfully have I sought for some plan by which to arouse and awaken all but in vain. While, however, the empire preserves and maintains its laws, the plain and honest rustic will see what he has to fear, and will be deterred from evil; and the man of intelligence and cultivated habits will learn what is wrong in himself, and will refrain from it. And thus, though the laws be declared by some to be but waste paper, yet these their unseen effects will be of no trifling nature. If, on the other hand, the prohibitions be suddenly repealed, and the action which was a crime be no longer counted such by the government, how shall the dull clown and the mean among the people know that the action is still in itself wrong? In open day and with unblushing front, they will continue to use opium till they shall become so accustomed to it, that eventually they will find it as indispensable as their daily meat and drink, and will inhale the noxious drug with perfect indifference. When shame shall thus be entirely destroyed, and fear removed wholly out of the way, the evil consequences that will result to morality and to the minds of men will assuredly be neither few nor unimportant. As your majesty's minister, I know that the laws of the empire, being in their existing state well fitted to effect their end, will not for any slight cause be changed. But the proposal to alter the law on this subject having been made and discussed in the provinces, the instant effect has been, that crafty thieves and villains have on all hands begun to raise their heads and open their eyes, gazing about, and pointing their finger, under the nation that, when once these prohibitions are repealed thenceforth and for ever they may regard themselves free from every restraint and from every cause of fear.

Though possessing very poor abilities I have nevertheless had the happiness to enjoy the favor of your sacred majesty, and have, within a space of but few years, been raised though the several grades of the censorate, and the presidency of various courts in the metropolis, to the high elevation of a seat in the Inner Council. I have been copiously imbued with the rich dew of favors; yet have been unable to offer the feeblest token of gratitude; but if there is aught within the compass of my knowledge, I dare not to pass it by unnoticed. I feel in my duty to request that your majesty's commands may be proclaimed to the governors and lieut-governors of all the provinces, requiring them to direct the local officers to redouble their efforts for the enforcement of the existing prohibitions against opium; and to impress on every one, in the plainest and strictest manner, that all who are already contaminated by the vile habit must return and become new men,—that if any continue to walk in their former courses, strangers to repentance and to reformation, they shall assuredly be subjected to the full penalty of the law, and shall not meet with the least indulgence,—and that any found guilty of storing up or selling opium to the amount of 1000 catties or upwards, the most severe punishment shall be inflicted. Thus happily the minds of men may be impressed with fear, and the report thereof, spreading over the seas (among foreigners) may even there produce reformation. Submitting to my sovereign my feeble and obscure views, I prostrate implore your sacred majesty to cast a glance on this my respectful memorial.

7.3   Imperial Edict, September 1836

The councillor Zhu Zun has presented a memorial, requesting that the severity of the prohibitory enactments against opium may be increased. The sub-censor Xu Qiu also has laid before us a respectful representation of his views; and, in a supplementary statement, a recommendation to punish severely Chinese traitors.

Opium, coming from the distant regions of barbarians, has pervaded the country with its baneful influence, and has been made a subject of very severe prohibitory enactments. But, of late, there has been a diversity of opinion in regard to it, some requesting a change in the policy hitherto adopted, and others recommending the continuance of the severe prohibitions. It is highly important to consider the subject carefully in all its bearings, surveying at once the whole field of action, so that such measures may be adopted as shall continue for ever in force, free from all failures.

Let Deng [Deng Tingzhen, the Qing governor-general of Guangdong and Guangxi] and his colleagues anxiously and carefully consult together upon the recommendation to search for, and with utmost strictness apprehend, all those traitorous natives who sell the drug, the hong merchants who arrange the transactions in it, the brokers who purchase it by wholesale, the boat-men who are engaged in transporting it, and the naval militia who receive bribes; and having determined on the steps to be taken in order to stop up the source of the evil, let them present a true and faithful report. Let them also carefully ascertain and report whether the circumstances stated by Xu Qiu in his supplementary document, in reference to the foreigners from beyond the seas be, true or not, whether such things as are mentioned therein have or have not taken place. Copies of the several documents are to be herewith sent to those officers for perusal; and this edict is to be made known to Deng and Ke, who are to enjoin it also on Wan, the superintendent of maritime customs. Respect this.

7.4 Annexed Laws on Banning Opium, July 1839

FURNACE KEEPERS OR WHOLESALE DEALERS

Whoever shall hereafter open a "furnace," and connive with and secretly buy opium of the outside barbarians, storing it up for sale, shall, if he be the principal, be decapitated immediately on conviction.

The royal authority shall be respectfully produced and the law executed, ere a report is sent to the crown. The head of the offender shall then be stuck upon a pole, and exposed upon the seacoast as a warning to all. The accomplices, advisers, participators, receivers, givers (those who deliver the drug), and boatmen who knowingly receive opium on board their boats for transport, shall be sentenced to strangulation and thrown into dungeons to wait the royal warrant for their execution. The houses and boats of these parties shall be sequestrated.

1. Any officer or soldier on the coast station who shall receive bribes to connive at opium being brought in, whether the quantity be large or small, shall immediately upon conviction be strangled. He who, knowing it to be such, allows opium to be brought in, but without receiving a bribe, shall be transported to Xinjiang [Chinese Turkestan].

2. If any persons join together and open a furnace for the purpose of selling opium, he who originates the plan shall be considered as the principal.

3. He who stores opium brought by the foreign ships shall be dealt with in the same manner as accomplices in a "furnace." He who, knowing it to be such, consents to conceal opium for any notorious dealers who may have fallen into the hands of government, shall be punished one degree less severely than the principal.

4. He who receives a bribe to release any opium seller or smoker from his custody, shall be punished in the same manner as if he were an opium seller or smoker himself. Should the amount received be considerable, he shall be held punishable under the law against "false and malicious information."

5. Any jailor who shall buy opium and supply it to the prisoners under his charge, shall be transported to the most distant and unhealthy settlements. Any guard or overseer, guilty of a similar offence, shall be transported to a nearer settlement; should the amount received for purchases be considerable, it shall be computed and the offender held punishable under the act against "False and malicious information."

6. Any soldier or policeman, or any of those idle blackguards who infest every place, who shall, without a warrant, enter a house and under pretence of searching for opium forcibly carry of other articles, or who shall,

through malice or a desire to extort money, themselves secrete opium in the house, that an accusation may be supported [against their victim], shall, whether principal or accomplice, be held punishable under the law against "false and malicious information," and transported to the most distant settlements. If the amount stolen shall exceed in value 120 taels, the principal shall be sentenced to strangulation, and kept in prison till the warrant for his execution shall arrive.

7. All persons sentenced to transportation for crimes connected with opium shall be excluded from the benefit of the law respecting "indulgence to offenders for the sake of their parents."

SECTION 2ND. KEEPERS OF RETAIL AND SMOKING SHOPS.

Any person who shall keep a shop for selling opium to be smoked on the premises, shall, if the principal, be sentenced, on conviction, to immediate strangulation, and his house shall be sequestrated. Accomplices, accessories, or those who knowing for what purpose, still consent to let their houses to such characters, shall, on purpose, still consent to let their houses to such characters, shall, on conviction, be transported to Xinjiang to be slaves to the military, and their houses sequestrated. Any soldier or policeman who shall receive a bribe for conniving at and "securing" these dens, shall receive the same punishment as a principal. "Ground-sureties" and neighbors, who know of the existence of such places and do not report the same to government, shall be punished with 100 blows, and transported for 3 years. If they shall receive hush money, the amount shall be computed, and the law respecting "False and malicious information" put in force against them.

1. Any native traitor who shall cultivate the poppy for the purpose of expressing its juice to make opium, for preparations and sale, or who shall sell either the "paste" or "mud" to the extent of 500 taels, or if, altho' the amount does not equal that sum, he shall sell at a great number of different places and times, he shall, if apprehended within the next 18 months, be sentenced to strangulation [if a principal], and thrown into prison to wait the arrival of the warrant for his execution. Accomplices shall be transported to the most distant and unhealthy places. If any are convicted of selling only once or twice, the whole amount of such sales not being taels 500—they shall be transported, if principals to Xinjiang to be slaves to the military, if accomplices they shall be transported to a distance of 4000 le. After the expiration of the 18 months, both principals and accomplices shall be sentenced to be strangled. If any soldier or policeman receives a

bribe to connive at and screen them, he shall be punished in the same manner as the principal. If the amount received be considerable, it shall be computed, and the offender punished under the law against "false and malicious information." Any landlord, who, knowing for what purpose, lets a field or house to opium dealers, or any boatman who shall knowingly hire his boat for transporting the drug, shall, if the offence take place before the expiration of one year from this time, receive a hundred blows, and be transported 2000 li—if after one year, he shall be transported to the most distant settlement, if within half a year he shall be sentenced to receive a hundred blows and three years transportation. The fields, grounds, houses, and boats, shall in all cases be sequestrated. If any dealer shall voluntarily confess his crime and cause by his information the apprehension of other dealers, he shall be pardoned, and his house, ground, or boat shall not be sequestrated. If the parties implicated by the said person's confession shall escape and elude the vigilance of government, although his crime shall be pardoned, his house, ground, field, or boat shall not be confiscated. Any "ground surety" or neighbor, who knows of the existence of such dealers and does not forthwith inform against them, shall be punished with 100 blows. If he receives hush money, the amount shall be computed and the law respecting "false and malicious information" put in force against him.

2. The law against the crime of opium smoking, shall take effect in Peking from the day the sacred commands were received; in the provinces from the day that the commands of the board were made known. These were received in the city of Canton on the 26th day of the 5th moon from which time they will date in all the cities, and towns, throughout the province. One year from that date will be allowed for all to renounce the habit. At the expiration of that period all who have *not* renounced the habit, whether they be of the nobles, the military, or vulgar, shall on conviction be sentenced to strangulation and thrown into prison to wait the arrival of the warrant for their execution. If any are apprehended *within* the year of probation, if of the vulgar, they shall be punished with 100 blows and transported to a distance of 2000 li. &c. If they are unable to say from whom they got the opium, their punishment shall be one degree more severe; they shall receive 100 blows and transported to a distance of 2500 li; if of the Tartar soldiery, the offender shall first be expelled from his banner, (or regiment) and then dealt with as one of the common people; if a government underling, a relation of an officer, a secretary or follower, the offender shall be punished one degree more severely than a common man; if an officer of government, the offender shall be sent to Xinjiang on some degrading and laborious mission; if of the provincials or general army, the offender shall be transported to a shorter distance. . . .

7.5 LORD PALMERSTON'S DECLARATION OF WAR, FEBRUARY 20, 1840

After China's seizure of British opium in Canton, Charles Elliot and the British community in Canton rejected Lin Zexu's demand for a bond requiring them not to engage in the opium trade. They fled to Macao, where, in June 1839 Elliot and the merchants separately petitioned the Tory foreign minister, Lord Palmerston, for stern measures by the Crown on the behalf of British subjects in China. Palmerston, despite his usual advocacy of British power in the international realm, was initially loathe to help the merchants and believed they should adhere to Chinese law. However, domestic pressure, in the form of letters from some thirty-nine Manchester textile firms who feared being cut out of both the Chinese and Indian markets, and energetic lobbying efforts by William Jardine in September 1839 caused the foreign minister to change his mind.

On October 18, 1839, Palmerston informed Charles Elliot that a British expeditionary force would reach China in the spring of 1840 and would endeavor to blockade the harbor of Canton and the Pearl river. Since the structures of the British Constitution provided Parliament with little control over foreign policy, the decision for war was made without parliamentary consultation. Indeed, China policy until Palmerston's departure from the government in 1841 was single-handedly shaped by the foreign minister himself. Neither Parliament nor the nation was fully informed of the circumstances of the Opium War.

The following dispatch from the pen of Lord Palmerston informs the Chinese government of Britain's intention to use force to protect the interest of its subjects in China and states Great Britain's war aims.

DESPATCH FROM LORD PALMERSTON TO THE MINISTER OF THE EMPEROR OF CHINA

F.O. London, *February* 20, 1840.

THE UNDERSIGNED, Her Britannick Majesty's Principal Secretary of State for Foreign Affairs, has the honour to inform the Minister of the Emperor of China, that Her Majesty The Queen of Great Britain has sent a Naval and Military Force to the Coast of China, to demand from the Emperor satisfaction and redress for injuries inflicted by Chinese Authorities upon British Subjects resident in China, and for insults offered by those same Authorities to the British Crown.

For more than a hundred years, commercial intercourse has existed between China and Great Britain; and during that long period of time, British Subjects have been allowed by the Chinese Government to reside within the territory of China for the purpose of carrying on trade therein. Hence it has happened that British Subjects, trusting in the good faith of the Chinese Government, have fixed themselves in Canton as Merchants, and have brought into that city from time to time property to a large amount; while other British Subjects who wished to trade with China, but who could not for various reasons go thither themselves, have sent commodities to Canton, placing those commodities in the care of some of their fellow Countrymen resident in China, with directions that such commodities should be sold in China, and that the produce of the sale thereof should be sent to the Owners in the British Dominions.

Thus there has always been within the territory of The Emperor of China a certain number of British Subjects, and a large amount of British Property; and though no Treaty has existed between the Sovereign of England and the Emperor of China, yet British Subjects have continued to resort to China for purposes of trade, placing full confidence in the justice and good faith of The Emperor.

Moreover, of late years the Sovereign of Great Britain has stationed at Canton an officer of the British Crown, no wise connected with trade, and specially forbidden to trade, but ordered to place himself in direct communication with the local Authorities at Canton in order to afford protection to British Subjects, and to be the organ of communication between the British and the Chinese Governments.

But the British Government has learnt with much regret, and with extreme surprise, that during the last year certain officers, acting under the Authority of The Emperor of China, have committed violent outrages against the British Residents at Canton, who were living peaceably in that City, trusting to the good faith of the Chinese Government; and that those same Chinese officers, forgetting the respect which was due to the British Superintendent in his Character of Agent of the British Crown, have treated that Superintendent also with violence and indignity.

It seems that the course assigned for these proceedings was the contraband trade in Opium, carried on by some British Subjects.

It appeared that the Laws of the Chinese Empire forbid the importation of Opium into China, and declare that all opium which may be brought into the Country is liable to confiscation.

The Queen of England desires that Her Subjects who may go into Foreign Countries should obey the Laws of those Countries; and Her Majesty does not wish to protect them from the just consequences of any offenses which they may commit in foreign parts. But, on the other hand, Her Majesty cannot permit that Her Subjects residing abroad should be treated with violence, and be exposed to insult and injustice; and when wrong is done to them, Her Majesty will see that they obtain redress.

Now if a Government makes a Law which applies both to its own Subjects and to Foreigners, such Government ought to enforce that Law impartially or not at all. If it enforces that Law on Foreigners, it is bound to enforce it also upon its own Subjects; and it has no right to permit its own Subjects to violate the Law with impunity, and then to punish Foreigners for doing the very same thing.

Neither is it just that such a Law should for a great length of time be allowed to sleep as a dead letter, and that both Natives and Foreigners should be taught to consider it as of no effect, and that then suddenly, and without sufficient warning, it should be put in force with the utmost rigor and severity.

Now, although the Law of China declared that the importation of Opium should be forbidden, yet it is notorious that for many years past, that importation has been connived at and permitted by the Chinese Authorities at Canton; nay, more, that those Authorities, from the Governor downwards, have made an annual and considerable profit by taking money from Foreigners for the permission to import Opium: and of late the Chinese Authorities have gone so far in setting this Law at defiance, that Mandarin Boats were employed to bring opium to Canton from the Foreign Ships lying at Lintin.

Did the Imperial Government at Peking know these things?

If it did know these things, it virtually abolished its own Law, by permitting its own officers to act as if no such Law existed. If the Chinese Government says it did not know of these things, if it says that it knew indeed that the Law was violated by Foreigners who brought in opium, but did not know that the Law was violated by its own Officers who assisted in the importation, and received fixed sums of money for permitting it, then may Foreign Governments ask, how it happened that a Government so watchful as that of China should have one eye open to see the transgressions of Foreigners, but should have the other eye shut, and unable to see the transgressions of its own officers. . . .

Now as the distance is great which separated England from China, and as the matter in question is of urgent importance, the British Government cannot wait to know the answer which the Chinese Government may give to these demands, and thus postpone till that answer shall have been received in England, the measures which may be necessary in order to vindicate the honour and dignity of the British Crown, in the event of that answer not being satisfactory.

The British Government therefore has determined at once to send out a Naval and Military Force to the Coast of China to act in support of these demands, and in order to convince the Imperial Government that the British Government attaches the utmost importance to this matter, and that the affair is one which will not admit of delay.

And further, for the purpose of impressing still more strongly upon the Government of Peking the importance which the British Government attaches to this matter, and the urgent necessity which exists for an immediate as well as a satisfactory settlement thereof, the Commander of the Expedition has received orders that, immediately upon his arrival upon the Chinese Coast, he shall proceed to blockade the principal Chinese ports, that he shall intercept and detain and hold in deposit all Chinese ports, that he shall proceed to blockade the principal Chinese ports, that he shall intercept and detain and hold in deposit all Chinese Vessels which he may meet with, and that he shall take possession of some convenient part of the Chinese territory, to be held and occupied by the British Forces until everything shall be concluded and executed to the satisfaction of the British Government.

These measures of hostility on the part of Great Britain against China are not only justified, but even rendered absolutely necessary, by the outrages which have been committed by the Chinese Authorities against British officers and Subjects, and these hostilities will not cease, until a satisfactory arrangement shall have been made by the Chinese Government.

The British Government in order to save time, and to afford to the Government of China every facility for coming to an early arrangement, have given to the Admiral and to the Superintendent, Full Powers and Instructions to treat upon these matters with the Imperial Government, and have ordered the said Admiral and Superintendent to go up to the Mouth of the Peiho River, in the Gulph of Pechelee, that they may be within a short distance of the Imperial Cabinet. But after the indignity which was offered to Her Majesty's Superintendent at Canton, in the course of last year, it is impossible for Her Majesty's Government to permit any of Her Majesty's Officers to place themselves in the power of the Chinese Authorities until some formal Treaty shall have been duly signed, securing to British Subjects safety and respect in China; and therefore the Undersigned must request that the Chinese Government will have the goodness to send on board the Admiral's Ship the Plenipotentiaries whom the Emperor may appoint to treat upon these matters with the Plenipotentiaries of The Queen of England. Those Chinese Plenipotentiaries shall be received on board the Admiral's Ship, with every honour which is due to the Envoys of the Emperor, and shall be treated with all possible courtesy and respect.

The Undersigned has further to state, that the necessity for sending this Expedition to the Coast of China having been occasioned by the violent and unjustifiable acts of the Chinese Authorities, the British Government expects and demands that the expenses incurred thereby shall be repaid to Great Britain by the Government of China.

The Undersigned has now stated and explained to the Chinese Minister, without reserve, the causes of complaint on the part of Great Britain; the reparation which Great Britain demands, and the nature of the measures which the British officer commanding the Expedition has been instructed in the first instance to take. The British Government fervently hopes that the wisdom and spirit of Justice for which The Emperor is famed in all parts of the World, will lead the Chinese Government to see the equity of the foregoing demands; and it is the sincere wish of Her Majesty's Government that a prompt and full compliance with those demands may lead to a speedy re-establishment of that friendly intercourse which has for so great a period of time subsisted between the British and Chinese Nations, to the manifest advantage of both.

The Undersigned, in conclusion, has the honour to state to the Minister of The Emperor of China that he has directed Her Majesty's Plenipotentiaries to forward to His Excellency the present Note, of which he has transmitted to the Plenipotentiaries a copy, with instructions to cause a Translation of it to be made into the Chinese language, and to forward to the Chinese Minister the Translation at the same time with the original Note.

The Undersigned avails himself of this opportunity to offer to His Excellency the Minister of The Emperor of China the assurances of his most distinguished consideration.

PALMERSTON.

CHAPTER 8

The Crisis Within

8.1 QIAN YONG ON POPULAR RELIGION, 1838

The scholar Qian Yong (1759–1844) was a specialist in etymology and bronze and stone inscriptions. He traveled throughout China serving in various yamens but never occupied a powerful position. His famous *Luyuan conghua* is a collection of miscellaneous jottings on many subjects.

In an appendix to this work, he included the following injunction against "evil customs" in south China. It was apparently written by one of Qian Yong's acquaintances and was introduced in his jottings with an approving note. It exhibits the scorn felt by the literati for folk religion and "heterodox" festivals in the years immediately preceding the Opium War, and illustrates the impulse felt by the elite to rein in the wild and unrestrained behavior of untutored peasants, villagers, and city dwellers.

GOING OUT FOR A GATHERING

There have always been religious festivals and parades in China but presently these practices are really flourishing. In the cities, the so-called "heads" of these assemblies are the scribes, clerks, and runners of the prefectural and county yamens. In the countryside, they are the chiefs of *baojia* units[1] and local idlers. Generally, those who understand to some degree the rites and codes of the society and who have family responsibilities will not take part.

Every year in the spring when there is no farm work to tend to, people feel

---

1. Mutual surveillance organizations in the countryside used to preserve order and monitor taxation.

superstitious doubts about ghosts and spirits. What happens then is called "going out for a gathering." Everyone says that this [religious processions and gatherings] can "exorcise evil and bring good fortune" or "get rid of hardship and eliminate locusts." There is a great commotion when these gatherings occur and the whole area goes wild. Tens of thousands of men and women appear to watch these parades and although local magistrates occasionally ban such activities, they grow and prosper from year to year.

Leading the processions are banners to clear the way and people banging gongs and drums. Others hold wooden placards, just like those carried by local officials, reading "silence" and "avoidance." Some of them paint their faces and carry spears or staves. Some dress up as government soldiers and carry swords and bows and arrows or fowling pieces and rattan shields. Some others pretend to be scribes and clerks of the six departments of the local yamen and carry mock documents, case files, and registration books. Still others wear chains and shackles and pretend to be prisoners guilty of serious offenses. Two false executioners, dressed in red, lead a prisoner stripped to the waist on whose back is a tablet saying that he is to be decapitated. They [the people] are accustomed to these wicked spectacles and treat them as natural. They have no sense of shame and think that this is fun. This is really ludicrous!

Recently, Scholar Li Jiantian of Jiangyin urgently commented on this and wrote "The Ten Evils of Religious Gatherings." He considered that people should only make sacrifices to ghosts and spirits of their own clans and that only community temples were appropriate to mediate between heaven and earth. Since ancient times, whenever harvest sacrifices were presented at community temples, the people merely burned paper money and beat ceremonial drums. Beneath the altar, the libations of wine were as fragrant as the spring wind and people frolicked in nearby groves of mulberry trees. It was the very image of happiness and peace! Rites and rituals were followed without error and none went astray. There was no insult to the spirits or raucous shouting in the community. There was no violation of the rites and ceremonies or injury to social customs to this great degree. Since Li Jiantian's account of the "ten evils" is clear and precisely appropriate to the problem, I have recorded it here:

1. Blaspheming the ghosts and spirits. In the *Analects* it says: "If you are unable to attend to human affairs, how can you serve the spirits?" Paying reverence to the spirits by trying to get close to them is unheard of! This is merely a means of taking other people's money so that the "heads" of the societies can eat their fill and get drunk. The stupid commoners do not know what they are doing and so they follow them. After time, all of this becomes social custom and hundreds of problems arise. This is the first reason for imposing a ban.

2. Confusing the ritual code. In every prefecture and county there are altars for the spirits of the mountains, the rivers, and the land. There are also

temples for the civil and military city gods and shrines dedicated to local sages and worthies and famous officials of former times. All of these temples are enumerated in the local ritual handbook and it is right and appropriate for officials and the people to present sacrifices at these temples in the spring and autumn. If a certain village earth god comes to be identified as having been a certain prince, marquis, general, or prime minister, this is not listed in the ritual handbook. The names and ranks are different, there is no distinction between high and low, the past and present are all topsy turvy, and the symbols and rituals are all wrong. This is a debasement of ritual practice. But the monks and Daoist priests rely on such practices to make money and women use them to disport themselves. This is the second reason for imposing a ban.

3. Squandering money. A religious festival in any area relies on the support of tens of thousands of households. Some people stretch their finances to the utmost to participate and think of hundreds of ways to borrow funds to join in the gathering. Some even pawn their clothes or sell their stores of food and, in so doing, wreck their family finances to participate. They use their limited funds for this useless expense and are unable to pay back the debts they incur or to fulfill their rent obligations. Impoverished and disconsolate, they freeze and starve without understanding how this came to be. Although these people bring this suffering on themselves it also comes about because of evil local customs. This is the third reason for imposing a ban.

4. Disrupting normal occupations. People living in a city all have their own occupations. People living in the countryside all have their own work to do. All of them should accept frugality and diligence as the root of their lives. How is it possible for them to find the leisure time for these [heterodox, religious] activities? Moreover, all of the festivals are held in the spring time and this disrupts natural timing and their professional schedules. I surely cannot understand what is in their minds! Ask yourself, are these activities designed to win fame or profit or to obtain food or clothing? That the stupidity of small people has reached such a degree is the fourth reason for imposing a ban.

5. Mixing of men and women. Whenever a village or city has such a festival, there are multitudes of spectators. How can women be prevented from coming out? Since there are many women, how can the roving flirts who follow the parades be prevented from watching these women? These flirts take the opportunities provided by this boiling mass of people to seize the fragrance so near at hand. When a smiling head is turned toward them, they mistakenly consider that this is affection. When they hear the chattering of a sweet voice, they lose their senses. They overturn ferry boats and die in their excitement; they jostle and knock over sedan chairs and loosen the hair and hair ornaments of their female occupants.

There is no worse injury to customs than this! This is the fifth reason for imposing a ban.

6. Causing fires. Whether a religious festival occurs in the city or country-side, candles and lamps are lit up in a splendid display. Incense and smoke fills the air. The fires of teahouses and wineships are constantly burning. Sometimes colorful lanterns are made for night parades and the people are asked for contributions to pay for fireworks. If something unexpected happens, it is difficult to come to the rescue. If vicious people were to take this opportunity to loot and rob, the situation would be uncontrol-lable. This is the sixth reason for imposing a ban.

7. Promoting gambling. During festivals where there are so many different types of people mixed together, it is easy for them to form groups to gamble. They play dice and make wagers on shell games. Some lose all of their money but still hope to get it back. Some find it impossible to borrow money and are trapped in a terrible situation. Some leave stripped of their clothes and some come back waving their arms to fight. This causes endless harm to an area and this is the seventh reason for imposing a ban.

8. Causing fighting. Normally, small numbers of wild hoodlums and ban-dits in villages and market towns do get together to drink and, on occa-sion, they beat and attack each other. But during festivals there are thousands of people who gather; drinking occurs in all of the shops and gambling takes place everywhere. If someone becomes angry, he is likely to behave violently and murderously. Without intervention to mediate the problem such disputes can lead to homicide. Because of this, the calamity would extend to the *baojia* and the lawsuit might burden the village community. This is the eighth reason for imposing a ban.

9. Attracting robbers and thieves. If bandits from various places mix with the masses, it is difficult to find them out but easy for them to steal. During the day, the excitement is so great that everyone becomes exhausted and in the calm of the night they sleep so deeply that they can be robbed. In an instant, the rich lose their gold and silk and the stores of grain of the poor are swept away. It is already too late to catch the thieves or to seek the return of the stolen goods. This is the ninth reason for imposing a ban.

10. Damaging social customs. The people's original nature is simple. But because of these gatherings they make all kinds of clothes. The families are mostly poor but because of these festivals they have all sorts of expenses and in both the city and countryside they come to adore luxury. In the little streets and alleys, friends and relatives are constantly coming and going and this makes the people fall into a pattern of extravagance. This damages social customs and this is the tenth reason for imposing a ban.

8.2 THE CONVERSION OF LIANG FA: *GOOD WORKS TO EXHORT THE AGE*, 1832

One of the first converts of the London Missionary Society was Liang Fa (1789–1855), a young Cantonese printer and employee of the Society's press in Malacca. In the first years of missionary work in south China, Liang Fa or, as he was known to most of his contemporaries, Liang Afa, played a vital role in the Society's effort to carry the faith to potential Chinese converts: he wrote tracts in Chinese, personally handed them out in market places and elsewhere, and helped in the Society's efforts to translate the New Testament into Chinese.

In the 1820s and 1830s, first in Canton and then in Malacca, London Missionary Society preachers and their converts published many religious tracts. Printed on fragile paper, bound with string, and covered front and back with bright yellow paper, these thin tracts were aggressively circulated in Canton and other cities and towns in south China. Some of them inveighed against opium use, others retold Bible stories, while still others consisted of catechism-like question and answer discussions (not unlike the questions posed by Liang Fa and responded to by "Mr. Mi" in this document).

One famous religious tract written by Liang Fa in 1832, *Good Words to Exhort the Age* (Chuanshi liangyan), won its later renown neither from the number of converts it produced nor from the sophistication of its theological arguments. Rather, the nine-volume set of tracts was important because of its influence on the career of the future leader of the Taiping Rebellion, Hong Xiuquan (1813–1864), who was handed a copy of it outside the provincial examination hall in Canton in 1836. Although Hong ignored the pamphlet for years after he received it, it played an important role as a theoretical source book and guide to Christianity as the Taiping leader elaborated his own highly eclectic and eccentric Christian doctrines.

In the following document, Liang Fa describes his own conversion to Christianity and provides a clear sense of the considerations that drew him into the Christian fold.

Before I received the Lord's grace, my mind was full of evil and folly and had yet to be enlightened. I still did not piously believe the Savior's true scripture and holy way and although I slightly understood that my daily behavior and words were those of a sinful person, I did not know how to seek redemption for my sins. On the first and the fifteenth of the month, early in the morning, in an airy place, I would burn incense and pay my respects to the passing immortals. I wanted to beg the passing gods for grace and mercy and to seek protection and good fortune. I also recited the "Guanyin Sutra" and the "Duoxin Sutra" one time and implored the Boddhisattva Guanyin and Buddha to pity me, protect my health, and give me spiritual peace. I also begged for wealth and fortune. I practiced this method of paying my respect to the various gods and deities for many years. Although I was physically worshipping various gods and buddhas, I still held evil and obscene notions in the heart and spoke false and deceitful words. I was filled with vicious desires that never left my heart or were far from my mouth.

At that time, every day, I listened to a certain Mr. Mi [William Milne of the London Missionary Society] preach the true and holy message of how the Savior had sacrificed himself to save mankind from its sins. Although I was physically present listening to him preach the truth, my mind was not there but racing about in contemplation of worldly things. At times I skimmed through the pages of the Holy Bible but could not understand its meaning. Even when I listened to Mr. Mi as he spoke of the truth, my mind could still not fathom the significance of what he was saying. After listening to his sermons I ignored them and despised them; I did not want to hear them. Often I talked to my friends and said: "How can this be right? Asking people not to worship various gods and buddhas? This has to be an evil and heretical teaching. Who will believe this? If we follow this kind of reasoning, then all of those people who sell gold paper, candles, and funeral money with golden flowers on it will go out of business! I am afraid that before long all of the gods and buddhas will beat people like you to death. How can you talk such nonsense!" I was working in his [Milne's] house at this time and every day he gathered all of the people in the household together to read the true Bible. Afterwards, he would explain it for a half hour or an hour and then everyone would rise to pray to God. All of the people in the household had to listen every day and at the time I too, despite myself, had to follow his will.

After more than a year, a Buddhist monk came from Yunnan and lived in a nearby temple. He asked people to donate money to build a new temple and often came to my home to talk with me. He discussed the rules for Buddhists who followed the way. I asked the monk what the benefits were for those who followed the Buddhist way. He said: "Our Buddhist way is the greatest. If one person leaves the carnal world and joins the Buddhist community to serve Lord Buddha, that person's sins and the sins of his entire family will be wiped away." I then asked: "But how are our sins pardoned?" The monk replied: "We read the sutras every day in the morning and at night. Buddha is in the Western Heaven. When he sees us sincerely reading the sutra in the morning and at night, Buddha is overjoyed and happily pardons the sins of a person's whole family. If someone donates alms to a temple, the monks of that temple recite sutras for him and after that person dies he is reincarnated in his next life into a wealthy and famous family. He does not fall into hell and suffer." When I heard the monk say that reciting the sutras would win pardon from all of one's sins, I believed it very much and happily wanted to follow him and enter the Buddhist religion. I then told the monk: "Presently, on the mornings of the first and fifteenth day of the month, I recite the Duoxin Sutra and the Guanyin Sutra one time. Is this a good way of reciting the sutras?" The monk said: "Very good!" Then the monk gave me a copy of the Shoushengqian [Karmic Debt Repayment] Sutra and taught me how to read it and meditate on it each night. If you read it once you can pay back some of the [karmic] debts of your previous lives. If you read thousands or millions of times, you can pay back all the debts of your previous lives. You won't have any calamities or difficulties in this life and after you die you will go to the Western Heaven to live in the world of ultimate joy. When I heard the monk say that things could be this good, I followed his instructions and continuously recited the Shoushengqian Sutra for dozens of nights. Suddenly one night as I was meditating, I thought to myself that from my teens to now, when I was already twenty-eight, I had been think-ing of evil, speaking evil, and doing evil every day and night. Now I was reciting the sutra alone but was not doing good or performing good deeds. Could I really be pardoned for all the evil I had done? I was really afraid that things were not so simple.

At this time my mind slowly began to change and I no longer read the Shoushengqian Sutra or went to the monk to discuss Buddhist teachings. But every day I enjoyed listening to Mr. Mi's discussion of how Jesus had sacrificed himself to redeem the sins of mankind. In my free time, I read the Holy Bible and found that the Holy Bible teaches that people should not do evil deeds or speak evil and deceitful words. They should not worship images of gods made from wood or clay or painted on paper. I slightly understood the meaning of the Holy Bible and believed it must have a mysterious and profound message. . . . It also spoke of the Savior using his holy power to heal strange and difficult illnesses. Was this not the true holy classic? From this time on, I loved to listen to Mr. Mi speak of this book of holy truth and to worship the Lord our God.

Every Sunday, when I did not need to work, I loved to read the Holy Bible. When there were things I did not understand, I would ask Mr. Mi for expla-nations. Mr. Mi also liked to explain and so I asked him how the Savior sac-rificed himself to redeem the sins of mankind and how this could save the world.

Mr. Mi said: "Our savior Jesus was the holy son of the Lord our God and is the pure spirit of the supreme being. The people of the world are confused by all sorts of idolatrous images and regard them as gods. Because they do not worship the great god who created the heaven and earth and all beings who is also the Lord our God, they sin against the law of heaven. People in all different walks of life in the world have sinned in thousands of different ways. Were they justly dealt with, the people of the whole world would be punished and wiped out. But our holy Lord who created the heaven and earth and all beings could not endure the destruction of mankind and so instead he bestowed unusual grace and mercy upon them. He ordered his holy son, Jesus, to leave his glorious and exalted position in heaven to descend to earth and placed him in the belly of a virgin and used a divine wind and holy virtue to cause him to be born as a man. When Jesus grew to manhood, he taught the people to know that only the one heavenly master who created the heaven and earth and all beings should be worshipped. Jesus also taught mankind that there is a precious soul in the physical body of every human being that is eternal and everlasting and that there are rewards and punishments in this life and the next. He [Jesus] taught people that he had come down to this world to endure pain, suffering, and death in order to take the punishment for the sins of mankind upon himself. Therefore, whoever piously believes in Jesus' mercy in taking the punishment for mankind's sins upon himself and is baptized shall be pardoned for his own sins and obtain the salvation of his soul. The sinner who refuses to piously believe will fall into hell and suffer eternal damnation."

I then asked Mr. Mi about the meaning of being baptized.

Mr. Mi said: "In baptism a bit of pure water is sprinkled on the forehead or body of the person receiving baptism. Its inner purpose is the cleansing away of all the filth of evil and sin so that one can receive the holy wind and allow it to move one's heart. After baptism, one loves good and hates evil and its significance is that one is transformed into a new man. Because all men have committed sins and had their bodies tainted by sin and their souls besmirched by sin, the baptismal water is to clean their bodies as they implore the Lord on high and send down the divine wind [*shenfeng*] to cleanse their souls."

After hearing Mr. Mi explain all of this, I asked, "Now that I know that I am a sinner, how can my sins be pardoned?"

Mr. Mi said: "If you truly believe in Jesus and are baptized, then it will be as if Jesus suffered and died for your sins. When the Lord our God considers Jesus' great accomplishment in dying for the sins of others, he can pardon your sins and accept you as good subject of the Lord. When it is time for you to die and go on to the next life, Jesus' merit also becomes your merit and you will be granted eternal happiness in heaven."

Mr. Mi's explanation was so wonderful that after I heard it I took my leave and returned to my small room to meditate [on these lessons]. I thought: "I am a sinner. If I do not rely on Jesus' merit [*gonglau*] in taking the sins of man upon himself, how can my sin simply be pardoned by the Lord our God? In believing in the way of Jesus one could be considered one of the Lord's good subjects and also enjoy the fortune of living in heaven after death. But the most fortunate thing of all was that one would not fall into hell after death and suffer eternal pain." I had now made up my mind: The following Sunday, I would accept Jesus' way, receive baptism, and enter through the gate of truth and holy reason. I went to ask Mr. Mi whether he was willing to baptize me.

Mr. Mi said: "If you will sincerely confess your sins and change your evil ways and follow the way Jesus the Savior and not worship graven images of God and Buddha but piously worship only the lord and master of heaven, earth, and all beings and eradicate all traces of the obscene and evil behavior of your past and rid yourself of deceitful and false words, then, next Sunday, on the sabbath, you may receive baptism. If you cannot do this, you may not receive baptism."

I said: "I will obey all that you have taught me." And on the following Sunday, at noontime, I went to implore Mr. Mi to baptize me. Mr. Mi asked me again whether I would confess and renounce all my evil deeds and then read with me several passages from the Holy Scriptures. He then knelt down with me to pray to the Lord our God to bestow his grace upon me and used his hand to sprinkle a bit of pure water on my head.

After I received baptism and expressed my thanks in prayer to the Lord, I then asked Mr. Mi: "What is the sign of people who believe in Jesus?"

Mr. Mi said: "To fully concentrate one's heart on doing good is the sign of people who believe in Jesus."

I thanked Mr. Mi and returned to my small room and sitting alone there felt happy in the belief that I had obtained pardon from the lord for my great sins. I then gave myself a new name: "Xueshanzhe" [the one who studies good]. This meant that in the future I would concentrate on changing my evil ways and studying the good and would not dare to do evil.

8.3 EXECUTIONS OF TAIPING REBELS AT CANTON, 1851

Under the Qing legal code, no crime, except perhaps patricide, was regarded as more serious than the crime of insurrection. Joining a rebel band was the ultimate political risk one could take under the imperial system and rebels could look forward to no quarter from government forces sent to crush them. The document that follows dates from the first year of the Guangxi insurrection and describes most vividly the punishment meted out to groups of Taiping followers sent to Canton for punishment.

In the course of the year 1851, more than 700 unfortunate persons were executed at Canton. The severity of the mandarins seemed to increase in the same proportion as the extension of the insurrection; and every day some arrest took place, and some unhappy wretch, shut up in a bamboo cage, or shackled like a wild beast, was brought from the province of Guangxi or the revolted districts of the Guangdong. Generally they had not to wait for their sentence; since, in case of insurrection, the superior authority of the province has a right to inflict capital punishment, and makes abundant use of this sanguinary privilege. An execution is a horrible thing in any country, but in China its horror is doubled by its attendant circumstances. We give here the letter of one of our friends, who had the melancholy curiosity to be present at the execution of fifty-three rebels of the Guangxi.

"On the 1st of May," he writes, "I attended an execution with three of my friends. The street in which these frightful scenes occur, is situated as you are aware, without the walled city of Canton, towards that part of the suburbs which lies to the south along the river. This narrow, dirty street, which is about 100 *meters* long and 15 wide, is called by the Europeans, the 'Potter's Field.' All the houses on each side are in fact inhabited by workmen who make common services of porcelain, and those portable furnaces which you have often seen in the poorest houses, and in the floating residences on the river. For fear that a Chinese Scholar like you may dispute names with me, I must tell you at once that this dismal place is called by the natives, Tsien-Tse-Ma-Teou [*Qianzi matou*], or the 'Quay of the Thousand Characters,' in allusion to the numerous signs which are seen there from the river.

"We arrived there at ten o'clock in the morning, and took our station in front of a shop belonging to a mender of old stockings. This was an excellent position to take a survey of the whole ceremony, and we remained there quietly till noon; at which time some soldiers and officers attached to the service of the mandarins, arrived to clear the street and thrust back the curious. As in Europe, the persons who came to see the spectacle were the vilest dregs of the populace,—dirty, ragged people, with sinister countenances, who wandered about the ensanguined soil; where most likely they had already seen the execution of a number of their companions, and perhaps of their accomplices.

"In a short time the roll of the tam tam announced to us the arrival of the whole procession. Mandarins of every degree, with the red, white, blue, or yellow ball, riding on horseback, or carried in palanquins, and followed by an escort of musicians, sbirri [police officers], and standard-bearers, alighted at a short distance from the place of execution. Contrary to their ceremonious habits, they arranged themselves in the dismal enclosure.

"Then arrived the criminals. They were fifty-three in number, each shut up in a basket, with his hands tied behind his back, his legs chained, and a board inscribed with his sentence hanging from his neck. You have often met in the Chinese streets a pair of coolies carrying a pig stretched out at its full length in a bamboo case. Well, just imagine a human being put in the place of the unclean animal, and you can form an idea of the fifty-three unfortunate creatures in their cages. When the cages were set down, they were opened and emptied, just as when a pig is turned out at a butcher's shop. I examined these unfortunate wretches with attention: they were worn out with hunger, and looked more like skeletons than living beings. It was evident that they had suffered the most dreadful privations. They were clothed in loathsome tatters, wore long hair, and the dishevelled tail attached to the crown of the head, had been reduced to a third of its usual length. They had evidently belonged to the insurgent bands, who had adopted the fashion of the Mings, and allowed all their hair to grow.

"Many of these unfortunate persons were very young: some were not sixteen years of age; while others had gray hair. Scarcely were they thrown on the ground pell-mell, when they were compelled to kneel; but the greater part of them was so debilitated from suffering, that they could not keep in this position, and rolled in the mud. An executioner's assistant then picked them up, and arranged them all in a row; while three executioners placed themselves behind them and waited the fatal moment. You doubtless recollect those horrible figures whom we have often seen together in the *cortege* [procession] of the criminal judge of Canton—those figures dressed in a red blouse, and wearing a copper crown, adorned above the cars with two long pheasant's feathers. Well! These were the executioners who now waited the signal with a rude and heavy cutlass in their hands. These enormous weapons are about two feet long, and the back of the blade is two inches thick: altogether it is a cumbrous instrument, shaped like a Chinese razor, with a rude handle of wood.

"A mandarin who closed the *cortege*, then entered the enclosure. He was adorned with the white ball, and held in his hand a board, inscribed with the order for execution. As soon as this man appeared the frightful work began. The executioner's assistants, each clothed in a long black robe, and wearing a sort of head-dress of iron wickerwork, seized the criminals from behind, and passing their arms under the shoulders of their victims, gave them a swinging movement, which made them stretch out their necks. The executioner who was now in front, holding his sword in both hands, threw all his strength into the weapon, and divided the cervical vertebra with incredible rapidity, severing the head from the body at a single blow. The executioner never had to strike twice; for even if the flesh was not completely cut through, the weight was sufficient to tear it, and the head rolled on the ground. An assistant then levelled the victim with a kick, for the corpse would otherwise have remained in a kneeling position. After three or four decapitations, the executioner changed his weapon; the edge of the blade seeming completely turned. The execution of these fifty-three wretches only lasted some minutes.

"When the last head had fallen, the mandarins retired from the scene as silent as they had come. Seeing the highest provincial officers present at the execution of these unfortunate men, I was struck with the reflection that in all countries—horrible to say—the political scaffold has been elevated instead of degraded. After the departure of the mandarins, the executioner picked up all the heads, and threw them into a chest brought for the purpose. At the same time the assistants took the chains off the victims as they lay in a pool of blood. The heads were carried away, but the bodies were left on the place of execution.

"A lamentable scene then commenced. A troop of women with dishevelled hair approached the fatal spot, shrieking aloud in wild disorder. These unhappy beings were endeavoring to distinguish their fathers, their husbands, and their children, among the headless corpses. It was a frightful scene to see them hurrying about, pondering, and constantly mistaken among these headless remains. This search continued all day, accompanied by a mournful noise; funeral dirges being mingled with cries and sobs. The women never ceased repeating that kind of chant common to all funeral ceremonies and which was composed, it is said, in the time of the Mings. It is a sort of rhythmical plaint, in which the same words constantly recur: 'Oh, misery! Oh, despair! My happiness is gone forever! Your kindness will no longer soften the bitterness of life! Alone and bereaved of all, I can only weep and die over your ashes!' and so on.

"To these details, which I saw with my own eyes, I should add some others which have been communicated to me by the Chinese. When the criminals left their prison, each was provided with a cake. This was one of those pies cooked by steam, and filled with sweetmeats, that you have often seen on the table of mandarins.

"I asked the reason of this practice, and was informed that the criminal stomach was filled for two reasons. First, that the illusion of blood should not be too copious; and, secondly, that the soul, famished by too long an abstinence, might not torment those who separated it from its mortal tenement. I give you this explanation, that nothing may be omitted. The following particular statement is curious. It was given me by a man of letters, who stood by my side during the horrid spectacle. The execution did not take place quite according to rule. Generally the culprit is brought before a kind of altar, formed of stones brought from the eighteen privines. This expiatory altar is raised on the day previous to the execution, and when all is over it is taken down. This custom—so thought my informant—is excellent. It inspires the criminal with feelings of contrition, because he seems to pay the penalty of his crime before the inhabitants of the empire."

8.4 AND 8.5 PRECEPTS AND ODES PUBLISHED BY HONG XIUQUAN IN 1852 AND 1853: "THE TEN COMMANDMENTS" AND "THE ODE FOR YOUTH"

Examinations of the Taiping movement have shown that three major sources for the rebel ideology were the *Zhou Li* and other Confucian classics, Christian tracts and translations of the Scripture published by foreign missionary societies, and the Buddhist and Daoist folk religions of south China. The documents printed below are translations of the earliest extant versions of two major Taiping documents.

The "Ten Commandments" of the Taiping were printed in the early years of the rebellion. Each commandment is followed by a commentary and a poem. The "Ode to Youth" was designed to lay out clearly and simply the roles and duties of Taiping followers.

8.4   *The Ten Commandments*

Decalogue

THE TEN CELESTIAL COMMANDMENTS WHICH ARE TO BE CONSTANTLY OBSERVED

THE FIRST COMMANDMENT
THOU SHALT HONOUR AND WORSHIP THE GREAT GOD.

Remark.   The great God is the universal Father of all men, in every nation under heaven. Every man is produced and nourished by him: every man ought, therefore, morning and evening, to honour and worship him, with acknowledgements of his goodness. It is a common saying, that Heaven produces, nourishes, and protects men. Also, that being provided with food we must not deceive Heaven. Therefore, whoever does not worship the great God breaks the commands of Heaven.

The Hymn says:
> Imperial Heaven, the Supreme God is the true Spirit (God):
> Worship him every morning and evening, and you will be taken up;
> You ought deeply to consider the ten celestial commands,
> And not by your foolishness obscure the right principles of nature,

THE SECOND COMMANDMENT
THOU SHALT NOT WORSHIP CORRUPT SPIRITS (GODS).

Remark.   The great God says, Thou shalt have no other spirits (gods) besides me. Therefore all besides the great God are corrupt spirits (gods), deceiving and destroying mankind; they must on no account be worshipped: whoever worships the whole class of corrupt spirits (gods) offends against the commands of Heaven.

The Hymn says:
> Corrupt devils very easily delude the souls of men.
> If you perversely believe in them, you will at last go down to hell.

We exhort you all, brave people, to awake from your lethargy,
And early make your peace with your exalted Heavenly Father.

THE THIRD COMMANDMENT
THOU SHALT NOT TAKE THE NAME OF THE
GREAT GOD IN VAIN.

Remark.   The name of the great God is Jehovah, which men must not take in vain. Whoever takes God's name in vain, and rails against Heaven, offends against this command.

The Hymn says:
Our exalted Heavenly Father is infinitely honorable;
Those who disobey and profane his name, seldom come to a good end.
If unacquainted with the true doctrine, you should be on your guard,
For those who wantonly blaspheme involve themselves in endless crime.

THE FOURTH COMMANDMENT
ON THE SEVENTH DAY, THE DAY OF WORSHIP,
YOU SHOULD PRAISE THE GREAT GOD FOR HIS
GOODNESS.

Remark.   In the beginning the great God made heaven and earth, land and sea, men and things, in six days; and having finished his works on the seventh day, he called it the day of rest (or Sabbath): therefore all the men of the world, who enjoy the blessing of the great God, should on every seventh day especially reverence and worship the great God, and praise him for his goodness.

The Hymn says:
All the happiness enjoyed in the world comes from Heaven;
It is therefore reasonable that men should give thanks and sing;
At the daily morning and evening meal there should be thanksgiving,
But on the seventh day, the worship should be more intense.

THE FIFTH COMMANDMENT
THOU SHALT HONOUR THY FATHER AND THY
MOTHER, THAT THY DAYS MAY BE PROLONGED.

Remark.   Whoever disobeys his parents breaks this command.
The Hymn says:
History records that Shun honoured his parents to the end of his days,
Causing them to experience the interest pleasure and delight:
August Heaven will abundantly reward all who act thus,
And do not disappoint the expectation of the authors of their being.

THE SIXTH COMMANDMENT
THOU SHALT NOT KILL OR INJURE MEN.

Remark.   He who kills another kills himself, and he who injures another injures himself. Whoever does either of these breaks the above command.

The Hymn says:

>The whole world is one family, and all men are brethren,
>How can they be permitted to kill and destroy one another?
>The outward form and the inward principle are both conferred by Heaven:
>Allow every one, then, to enjoy the ease and comfort which he desires.

THE SEVENTH COMMANDMENT
THOU SHALT NOT COMMIT ADULTERY OR ANY THING UNCLEAN.

Remark.   All the men in the world are brethren, and all the women in the world are sisters. Among the sons and daughters of the celestial hall the males are on one side and the females on the other, and are not allowed to intermix. Should either men or women practice lewdness they are considered outcasts, as having offended against one of the chief commands of Heaven. The casting of amorous glances, the forbearing of boastful imaginations, the smoking of foreign tobacco (opium), or the singing of blasphemous songs must all be considered as breaches of this command.

The Hymn says:

>Lust and lewdness constitute the chief transgression,
>Those who practice it become outcasts, and are the objects of pity,
>If you wish to enjoy the substantial happiness of heaven,
>It is necessary to deny yourself and earnestly cultivate virtue.

THE EIGHTH COMMANDMENT
THOU SHALT NOT ROB OR STEAL.

Remark.   Riches and poverty are determined by the great God; but whosoever robs or plunders the property of others transgresses this command.

The Hymn says:

>Rest contented with your station, however poor, and do not steal.
>Robbery and violence are low and abandoned practices.
>Those who injure others really injure themselves.
>Let the noble-minded among you immediately reform.

THE NINTH COMMANDMENT
THOU SHALT NOT UTTER FALSEHOOD.

Remark.   All those who tell lies, and indulge in devilish deceits, with every kind of coarse and abandoned talk, offend against this command.

The Hymn says:

>In your daily conduct do not harbour covetous desires.
>When involved in the sea of lust the consequences are very serious.
>The above injunctions were handed down on Mount Sinai;
>And to this day the celestial commands retain all their force.

THE TENTH COMMANDMENT
THOU SHALT NOT CONCEIVE A COVETOUS DESIRE

Remark. When a man looks upon the beauty of another's wife and daughters with covetous desires, or when he regards the elegance of another man's possessions with covetous desires. or when he engages in gambling, he offends against this command.

The Hymn says:

> In your daily conduct do not harbour covetous desires.
> When involved in the sea of lust the consequences are very serious.
> The above injunction was handed down on Mount Sinai;
> And to this day the celestial command retains all its force.

8.5 *Taiping Religious Verses (from "The Ode for Youth")*

ON THE WORSHIP OF GOD.

> Let the true Spirit, the great God,
> Be honoured and adorned by all nations;
> Let all the inhabitants of the world
> Unite in the worship, morning and evening.

> Above and below, look where you may,
> All thing are imbued with the Divine favour.
> At the beginning, in six days,
> All things were created, perfect and complete.

> Whether circumcised or uncircumcised,
> Who is not produced by God?
> Reverently praise the Divine favour
> And you will obtain eternal glory.

ON REVERENCE FOR JESUS.

> Jesus, his first-born Son,
> Was in former times sent by God:
> He willingly gave his life to redeem us from sin;
> Of a truth his merits are pre-eminent.

> His cross was hard to bear;
> The sorrowing clouds obscured the sun.
> The adorable Son, the honoured of Heaven,
> Died for you, the children of men.

> After his resurrection he ascended to heaven;
> Resplendent in glory, he wields authority supreme.
> In him we know what we may trust
> To secure salvation and ascend to Heaven.

ON THE HONOUR DUE TO PARENTS.

As grain is stored against a day of need,
So men bring up children to tend their old age:
A filial son begets filial children,
The recompense here is truly wonderful.

Do you ask how this our body
Is to attain to length of years?
Keep the fifth command, we say,
And honour and emolument will descend upon you.

ON THE COURT.

The imperial court is an awe-inspiring spot,
Let those about it dread celestial majesty;
Life and death emanate from Heaven's son,
Let every officer avoid disobedience.

ON THE DUTIES OF THE SOVEREIGN.

When one man presides over the government
All nations become settled and tranquilized:
When the sovereign grasps the sceptre of power
Calumny and corruption sink and disappear.

ON THE DUTIES OF MINISTERS.

When the prince is upright, ministers are true;
When the sovereign is intelligent, ministers will be honest.
E and Chow are models worthy of imitation:
They acted uprightly and aided the government. . . .

ON THE DUTIES OF A FATHER.

When the main beam is straight the joists will be regular;
When a father is strict his duty will be fulfilled;
Let him not provoke his children to wrath,
And delightful harmony will pervade the dwelling.

ON THE DUTIES OF A MOTHER.

Ye mothers, beware of partiality,
But tenderly instruct your children in virtue;
When you are a fit example to your daughters,
The happy feeling will reach to the clouds.

ON THE DUTIES OF SONS.

Sons, be patters to your wives;
Consider obedience to parents the chief duty;

Do not listen to the tattle of women
And you will not be estranged from your own flesh.

ON THE DUTIES OF DAUGHTERS-IN-LAW.

Ye that are espoused into other families,
Be gentle and yielding, and your duty is fulfilled;
Do not quarrel with your sisters-in-law,
And thereby vex the old father and mother. . . .

OF THE DUTIES OF HUSBANDS.

Unbending firmness is natural to the man,
Love for a wife should be qualified by prudence;
And should the lions roar
Let not terror fill the mind.

ON THE DUTIES OF WIVES.

Women, be obedient to your three male relatives,
And do not disobey your lords:
When hens crow in the morning
Sorrow may be expected in the family.

ON THE DUTIES OF THE MALE SEX.

Let every man have his own partner
And maintain the duties of the human relations
Firm and unbending; his duties lie from home,
But he should avoid such things as cause suspicion.

ON THE DUTIES OF THE FEMALE SEX.

The duty of women is to maintain chastity,
She should shun proximity to the other sex;
Sober and decorous she should keep at home:
Thus she can secure happiness and felicity.

ON THE CONTRACTING MARRIAGES.

Marriages are the result of some relation in a former state
The disposal of which rests with Heaven.
When contracted, affection should flow in a continued stream,
And the association should be uninterrupted.

ON MANAGING THE HEART.

For the purpose of controlling the whole body
God has given to man an intelligent mind;

When the heart is correct it becomes the true regulator
To which the senses and members are all obedient.

ON MANAGING THE EYES.

The various corruptions first delude the eye,
But if the eye is correct all evil will be avoided;
Let the pupil of the eye be sternly fixed,
And the light of the body will shine up to heaven.

ON MANAGING THE FEET.

Let the feet walk in the path of rectitude,
And ever follow it, without treading awry;
For the countless by-paths of life
Lend only to mischief in the end.

THE WAY TO GET TO HEAVEN.

Honour and disgrace come from a man's self;
But men should exert themselves
To keep the Ten Commandments,
And they will enjoy bliss in Heaven.

8.6 ZENG GUOFAN: A PROCLAMATION AGAINST THE BANDITS OF GUANGDONG AND GUANGXI, 1854

Zeng Guofan (1811–1872) was from a middle-peasant landowning family in Xiangxiang, Hunan. In 1838 he obtained his *jinshi* degree and was appointed a Hanlin Academy scholar. He was noted for his clear and practical suggestions for addressing affairs of state. In 1852, when his mother died, in accord with the traditional mourning practice, he resigned his post as the vice minister of the Board of Rites and went back to Hunan where he received the imperial order to form militia units to fight the Taiping.

The Qing efforts to repulse the Taiping were uphill struggles in the early years and Zeng's efficiency as the commander was hampered by the chronic lack of funds. His situation improved, however, when he was given official sanction to take control of the tax revenues in the provinces where his armies were operating.

Zeng Guofan's proclamation of 1854 was a powerful evocation of the scholar-literati's view of the rebels. It stressed their affinity with other rebels in Chinese history and compared them to Li Zicheng and Zhang Xianzhong. The document was notably anti-Christian and its references to the "kingly way" and the ethos of the Confucian *junzi*[2] draw a clear line between the forces of orthodox "light" and heterodox "darkness."

It has been five years since the rebels Hung Hsiu-ch'üan and Yang Hsiu-ch'ing started their rebellion. They have inflicted bitter sorrow upon millions of people and devastated more than 5000 *li* of *chou* [regions] and *hsien* [counties]. Wherever they pass, boats of all sizes, and people rich and poor alike, have all been plundered and stripped bare; not once inch of grass has been left standing. The clothing has been stripped from the bodies of those captured by these bandits, and their money has been seized. Anyone with five taels or more of silver who does not contribute it to the bandits is forthwith decapitated. Men are given one *ho* [1/10th pint] of rice per day, and forced to march in the forefront in battle, to construct city walls, and dredge moats. Women are also given one *ho* of rice per day, and forced to stand guard on the parapets at night, and to haul rice and carry coal. The feet of women who refuse to unbind them are cut off and shown to other women as a warning. The corpses of boatmen who secretly conspired to fell were hung upside down to show other boatmen as a warning. The Yüeh [Guangdong and Guangxi] bandits indulge themselves in luxury and high position, while the people in our own Yangtze provinces living under their coercion are treated worse than animals. This cruelty and brutality appalls anyone with blood in his veins.

Ever since the times of Yao, Shun, and the Three Dynasties, sages, generation after generation, have upheld the Confucian teachings, stressing proper human relationships, between ruler and minister, father and son, superiors and subordinates, the high and the low, all in their proper place, just as hats and shoes are not interchangeable. The Yüeh bandits have stolen a few scraps from the foreign barbarians and worship the Christian religion. From their bogus ruler and bogus chief ministers down to their soldiers and menial underlings, all are called brothers. They say that only heaven can be called father; aside from him, all fathers among the people are called brothers, and all mothers are called sisters. Peasants are not allowed to till the land for themselves and pay taxes, for they say that the fields all belong to the T'ien Wang [Heavenly King]. Merchants are not allowed to trade for profit, for they say that all goods belong to the T'ien Wang. Scholars may not read the Confucian classics, for they have their so-called teachings of Jesus and the New Testament. In a single day several thousand years of Chinese ethical principles and proper human relationships, classical books, social institutions and statutes have all been completely swept away. This is not just a crisis for our Ch'ing dynasty, but the most extraordinary

2. The "ideal man" imagined and described by Confucius in his *Analects*.

crisis of all time for the Confucian teachings, which is why our Confucius and Mencius are weeping bitterly in the nether world. How can any educated person sit idly by without thinking of doing something?

Since ancient times, those with meritorious accomplishments during their lifetimes have become spirits after death; the Kingly Way governs the living and the Way of the Spirits governs among the dead. Even rebellious ministers and wicked sons of the most vicious and vile sort show respect and awe toward the spirits. When Li Tzu-ch'eng reached Ch'ü-fu [Confucius' birthplace in Shandong province], he did not molest the Temple of the Sage.[3] When Chang Hsien-chung reached Tzu-t'ung, he sacrificed to Wen Ch'ang [the patron spirit of literature].[4] But the Yueh bandits burned the school at Shen-chou, destroyed the wooden tablet of Confucius, and wildly scattered the tablets of the Ten Paragons in the two corridors all over the ground.[5] Afterwards, wherever they have passed, in every district, the first thing they have done is to burn down the temples, defiling the shrines and maiming the statues even of loyal ministers and righteous heroes such as the awesome Kuan Yü and Yüen Fei.[6] Even Buddhist and Taoist temples, shrines of guardian deities and altars to local gods have all been burned, and every statue destroyed. The ghosts and spirits in the world of darkness are enraged at this, and want to avenge their resentment.

I, the Governor-General, having received His Imperial Majesty's command leading 20,000 men advancing together on land and water, vow that I shall sleep on nettles and ship gall [to strengthen my determination] to exterminate these vicious traitors, to rescue our captured boats, and to deliver the persecuted people, not only in order to relieve the Emperor of his strenuous and conscientious labors from dawn to dusk, but also to comfort Confucius and Mencius for their silent sufferings over the proper human relationships; and only to avenge the millions who have died unjust deaths, but also to avenge the insults to all the spirits.

Therefore, let this proclamation be disseminated far and near so that all may know the following: Any red-blooded hero who assembles a company of righteous troops to assist in our extermination campaign will be taken in as my personal friend, and the troops given rations. Any Confucian gentleman who cherishes the Way, is pained at Christianity running rampant over the land, and who, in a towering rage, wants to defend our Way, will be made a member of the Governor-General's personal staff and treated as a guest teacher. Any

3. Li Tzu-ch'eng (Li Zicheng) was a major rebel leader at the end of the Ming dynasty.

4. Chang Hsien-chung (Zhang Xianzhong) was another important rebel leader at the end of the Ming period. Wen Ch'ang was the God of Literature, closely associated with the literati, and with the civil service examination system.

5. The Ten Paragons were ten famous Confucians, whose tablets were arranged along corridors, east and west, in Confucian temples.

6. Two famous generals and loyal officials. Kuan Yu was deified as the God of War.

benevolent person, stirred by moral indignation, who contributes silver or assists with provisions, will be given a treasury receipt and a commission from the Board of Civil Appointments for a donation of 1000 *chin* [1 *chin* = 1⅓ lb.] or less, and a special memorial will be composed requesting a liberal reward for a donation of over 1000 *chin*. If anyone voluntarily returns after a long stay among the bandits, and kills one of their leaders or leads a city to surrender, he will be taken into the army of the Governor-General to the Emperor, will be given an official title. Anyone who has lived under the bandits' coercion for some years, whose hair has grown several inches long, but who discards his weapon when the fighting is about to commence and returns to the fold barehanded, will receive an amnesty from the death sentence, and will be given travel expenses to return home.

In the past, at the end of the Han, T'ang, Yuan, and Ming, bands of rebels were innumerable, all because of foolish rulers and misgovernment, so that none of these rebellions could be stamped out. But today the Son of Heaven is deeply concerned and examines his character in order to reform himself, worships Heaven, and is sympathetic to the people. He has not increased the land tax, nor has he conscripted soldiers from households. With the profound benevolence of the sages, he is suppressing the cruel and worthless bandits. It does not require any great wisdom to see that sooner or later they will all be destroyed.

Those of you who have been coerced into joining the rebels, or who willingly follow the traitors, and oppose the Imperial Crusade [are warned that] when the Imperial forces sweep down it will no longer be possible to discriminate between the good and evil—every person will be crushed.

I, the Governor-General, am scant in virtue and of meager ability. I rely solely on two words, trust and loyalty, as the foundation for running the army. Above are the sun and the moon, below the ghosts and spirits; in this world, the vast waters of the Yangtze, and in the other world, the souls of loyal ministers and stalwart heroes who gave their lives in battle against previous rebellions. Let all peer into my heart and listen to my words.

Upon arrival, this proclamation immediately has the force of law. Do not disregard it!

CHAPTER 9

Restoration through Reform

9.1 AND 9.2 YUNG WING ADVISES THE TAIPING AND ZENG GUOFAN

By the late nineteenth century it was clear to Chinese reformers that the very preservation of civil order could well depend on how successfully Peking could deploy naval and ground forces built up following Western models.

Yung Wing (Rong Hong) (1828–1912) was a former student of the Morrison Educational Society founded by Protestant missionaries to honor Robert Morrison (1782–1834). Yung obtained a degree from Yale University in 1854, the first Chinese to obtain an American degree, and soon returned to China where he worked for several years as an interpreter and assistant to foreign missionaries. In 1859 he decided to accept an invitation to visit the Taiping capital in Nanjing. Despite cordial and animated discussions with the "Shield King," Yung Wing was unable to persuade the Taiping to accept a reform program he drafted for them or otherwise to influence the leaders of the Kingdom of Heavenly Peace.

In 1863, Yung Wing, now head of a flourishing tea business, was invited to meet with Zeng Guofan to discuss the purchase of Western machinery and weapons for the Jiangnan Arsenal in Shanghai. In later years, the Arsenal produced warships and munitions for the Qing navy and was one of the major reform projects of Li Hongzhang. As the selection from Yung Wing's autobiography *My Life in China and America* shows, Zeng decided to commission Yung to purchase armaments. His mission to the United States was a success and in subsequent years, he became a successful advocate of reform in many spheres.

150

9.1 Yung Wing: Policy Proposals to the Taiping, 1859

1. To organize an army on scientific principles.
2. To establish a military school for the training of competent military officers.
3. To establish a naval school for a navy.
4. To organize a civil government with able and experienced men to act as advisors in the different departments of administration.
5. To establish a banking system, and to determine on [sic] a standard of weight and measure.
6. To establish an educational system of graded schools for the people, making the Bible one of the text books.
7. To organize a system of individual schools.

9.2 Yung Wing: Interview with Zeng Guofan, 1863

After winding up my business in New Keang, I took passage in a native boat and landed at Ngan Khing in September. There, in the military headquarters of Viceroy Tsang Kwoh Fan [Zeng Guofan], I was met by my friends, Chang Si Kwei, Li Sien Lan, Wha Yuh Ting and Chu Siuh Chune, all old friends from Shanghai. They were glad to see me, and told me that the viceroy for the past six months, after hearing them tell that as a boy I had gone to America to get a Western education, had manifested the utmost curiosity and interest to see me, which accounted for the three letters which Chang and Li had written urging me to come. Now, since I had arrived, their efforts to get me there had not been fruitless, and they certainly claimed some credit for praising me up to the viceroy. I asked them if they knew what His Excellency wanted me for, aside from the curiosity of seeing a native of China made into a veritable Occidental. They all smiled significantly and told me that I would find out after one or two interviews. From this, I judged that they knew the object for which I was wanted by the Viceroy, and perhaps, they were at the bottom of the whole secret.

The next day I was to make my debut, and called. My card was sent in, and without a moment's delay or waiting in the ante-room, I was ushered into the presence of the great man of China. After the usual ceremonies of greeting, I was pointed to a seat right in front of him. For a few minutes he sat in silence, smiling all the while as though he were much pleased to see me, but at the same time his keen eyes scanned me over from head to foot to see if he could discover anything strange in my outward appearance. Finally, he took a steady look into my eyes which seemed to attract his special attention. I must confess

I felt quite uneasy all the while, though I was not abashed. Then came his first question.

"How long were you abroad?"

"I was absent from China eight years in pursuit of a Western education."

"Would you like to be a soldier in charge of a company?"

"I should be pleased to head one if I had been fitted for it. I have never studied military science."

"I should judge from your looks, you would make a fine soldier, for I can see from your eyes that you are brave and can command."

"I thank Your Excellency for the compliment. I may have the courage of a soldier, but I certainly lack military training and experience, and on that account I may not be able to meet Your Excellency's expectations."

When the question of being a soldier was suggested, I thought he really meant to have me enrolled as an officer in his army against the rebels; but in this I was mistaken, as my Shanghai friends told me afterwards. He simply put it forward to find out whether my mind was at all martially inclined. But when he found by my response that the bent of my thought was something else, he dropped the military subject and asked me my age and whether or not I was married. The last question closed my first introductory interview, which had lasted only about half an hour. He began to sip his tea and I did likewise, which according to Chinese official etiquette means that the interview is ended and the guest is at liberty to take his departure.

I returned to my room, and my Shanghai friends soon flocked around me to know what had passed between the Viceroy and myself. I told them everything, and they were highly delighted. . . .

To resume the thread of my story, I was nearly two weeks in the Viceroy's headquarters, occupying a suite of rooms in the same building assigned to my Shanghai friends—Li, Chang, Wha and Chu. There were living in his military headquarters at least two hundred officials, gathered there from all parts of the Empire, for various objects and purposes. Besides his secretaries, who numbered no less than a hundred, there were expectant officials, learned scholars, lawyers, mathematicians, astronomers and machinists; in short, the picked and noted men of China were all drawn there by the magnetic force of his character and great name. He always had a great admiration for men of distinguished learning and talents, and loved to associate and mingle with them. During the two weeks of my sojourn there, I had ample opportunity to call upon my Shanghai friends, and in that way incidentally found out what the object of the Viceroy was in urging me to be enrolled in the government service. It seemed that my friends had had frequent interviews with the Viceroy in regard to having a foreign machine shop established in China, but it had not been determined what kind of machine shop should be established. One evening they gave me a dinner, at which time the subject of the machine shop was brought up and it became the chief topic. After each man had expressed his views on the subject excepting myself, they wanted to know what my views were, intimating that in all likelihood in my next interview with the Viceroy he would bring up the subject. I said that as I was not an expert in the matter, my opinions or suggestions might not be worth much, but nevertheless from my personal observation in the United States and from a common-sense point of view, I would say that a machine shop in the present state of China be of a general and fundamental character and not one for specific purposes. In other words, I told them they ought to have a machine shop that would be able to create or reproduce other machine shops of the same character as itself; each and all of these should be able to turn out specific machinery for the manufacture of specific things. In plain words, they would have to have general and fundamental machinery in order to turn out specific machinery. A machine shop consisting of lathes of different kinds and sizes, planers and drills, would be able to turn out machinery for making guns, engines, agricultural implements, clocks, etc. In a large country like China, I told them, they would need many primary or fundamental machine shops, but that after they had one (and a first-class one at that) they could make it the mother shop for reproducing others—perhaps better and more improved. If they had a number of them, it would enable them to have the shops co-operate with each other in case of need. It would be cheaper to have them reproduced and multiplied in China, I said, where labor and material were cheaper, than in Europe and America. Such was my crude idea of the subject. After I had finished, they were apparently much pleased and interested, and expressed the hope that I would state the same views to the Viceroy if he should ask me about the subject.

Several days after the dinner and conversation, the Viceroy did send for me. In this interview he asked me what in my opinion was the best thing to do for China at that time. The question came with such a force of meaning, that if I had not been forewarned by my friends a few evenings before, or if their hearts had not been set on the introduction of a machine shop, and they had not practically won the Viceroy over to their pet scheme, I might have been strongly tempted to launch forth upon my educational scheme as a reply to the question as to what was the best thing to do for China. But in such an event, being a stranger to the Viceroy, having been brought to his notice simply through the influence of my friends, I would have run a greater risk of jeopardizing my pet scheme of education than if I were left to act independently. My obligations to them were great, and I therefore decided that my constancy and fidelity to their friendship should be correspondingly great. So, instead of finding myself embarrassed in answering such a large and important question, I had a preconceived answer to give, which seemed to dove-tail into his views already crystallized into definite form, and which was ready to be carried out at once. So my educational scheme was put in the background, and the machine shop was allowed to take precedence. I repeated in substance what I had said to my friends previously in regard to establishing a mother machine shop, capable of reproducing other machine shops of like character, etc. I especially mentioned the manufacture of rifles, which, I said, required for the manufacture of their component parts separate machinery, but that the machine shop I would recommend was not one adapted for making the rifles, but adapted to turn out specific machinery for the making of rifles, cannons, cartridges, or anything else.

"Well," said he, "this is a subject quite beyond my knowledge. It would be well for you to discuss the matter with Wha and Chu, who are more familiar with it than I am and we will then decide what is best to be done."

This ended my interview with the Viceroy. After I left him, I met my friends, who were anxious to know the result of the interview. I told them of the outcome. They were highly elated over it. In our last conference it was decided that the matter of the character of the machine shop was to be left entirely to my discretion and judgment, after consulting a professional mechanical engineer. At the end of another two weeks, Wha was authorized to tell me that the Viceroy, after having seen all the four men, had decided to empower me to go abroad and make purchases of such machinery as in the opinion of a professional engineer would be the best and the right machinery for China to adopt. It was also left entirely to me to decide where the machinery should be purchased,— either in England, France or the United States of America.

The location of the machine shop was to be at a place called Kow Chang Meu, about four miles northwest of the city of Shanghai. The Kow Chang Meu machine shop was afterwards known as the Kiang Nan Arsenal, an establishment that covers several acres of ground and embraces under its roof all the leading branches of mechanical work. Millions have been invested in it since I brought the first machinery from Fitchburg, Mass., in order to make it one of the greatest arsenals east of the Cape of Good Hope. It may properly be regarded as a lasting monument to commemorate Tsang Kwoh Fan's broadmindedness as well as far-sightedness in establishing Western machinery in China.

9.3 PRINCE GONG ON THE TONGWEN COLLEGE: THREE MEMORIALS, 1861, 1865, 1866

The *Tongwenguan* or School of Combined Learning (W. A. P. Martin's translation of the name of the institution) was founded to train Chinese translators in English, French, and Russian. Operating under the aegis of the *Zongli* yamen, it absorbed the function of a moribund Russian school created in Peking during the Qianlong era to train Russian translators for the court. Initially, the object of the *Tongwenguan* was to form a group of competent linguists, well-versed in Chinese and foreign languages, who could serve as go-betweens in international affairs.

The first of the three *Zongli* yamen memorials arranged together below is an excerpt from a memorial addressed to the throne by Prince Gong in October 1861. It confronts the difficulties faced by reformers in the Court who tried vainly to persuade skeptical and also highly conservative regional officials to recommend talented young men for this experimental school. The second extracted memorial, dating from 1865, discusses the founding of a new department of science and technology within the *Tongwenguan*. This development prompted a furious response from Grand Secretary Woren, the most important neo-Confucian scholar of his time, who despised "barbarian studies" and argued that these subjects should never replace the classical curriculum. The third memorial, dated 1866, was a counterattack that argued that China would be left behind if Western learning was neglected by Chinese scholars. Taken collectively, these three memorials show the clashes provoked in the court by the creation of a curriculum for state scholars that threatened to undermine state orthodoxies and replace the mastery of Song neo-Confucian learning as the unique means of attaining high official rank in the Qing bureaucracy.

OCTOBER 1861 MEMORIAL

In the tenth year of Xianfeng (1860) we had the honor to lay before the throne a statement of new measures, rendered necessary by the events of the late war. Among other things, we stated that a knowledge of the character and institutions of foreign nations is indispensable to the conduct of intercourse. We accordingly requested your Majesty to command the viceroy and governor at Canton and Shanghai to find natives well acquainted with foreign letters, and to send them, with a good supply of foreign books, to the capital, with a view to the instruction of youth to be chosen from the Eight Banners.

The viceroy of Canton reported that there was no man whom he could recommend, and the governor of Jiangsu reported that though *one* candidate had presented himself, he was by no means deeply versed in the subject.

This explains the long delay in carrying our plan into execution. Your Majesty's servants are penetrated with the conviction that to know the state of several nations it is necessary first to understand their language and letters. This is the sole means to protect ourselves from becoming the victims of crafty imposition.

Now these nations at large expense employ natives of China to teach them our literature, and yet China has not a man who possesses a ripe knowledge of foreign languages and letters—a state of things quite incompatible with a thorough knowledge of those countries.

As therefore no native candidates were sent up from Canton and Shanghai, we have no resource but to seek among foreigners for suitable men.

1865 MEMORIAL

The school has now been in operation nearly five years, and the students have made fair progress in the languages and letters of the West. Being, however, very young, and imperfectly acquainted with the letters of their own country, their time is unavoidably divided between Chinese and foreign studies. Should we, in addition, require them to take up astronomy and mathematics, we fear they would not succeed in acquiring more than a smattering of anything.

The machinery of the West, its steamers, its firearms, and its military tactics, all have their source in mathematical science. Now at Shanghai and elsewhere the building of steamers has been commenced; but we fear that if we are content with a superficial knowledge, and do not go to the root of the matter, such efforts will not issue in solid success.

Your Majesty's servants have accordingly to propose, after mature deliberation, that an additional department shall be established, into which none shall be admitted but those who are over twenty years of age, having previously gained a degree in Chinese learning. For we are convinced that if we are able to master the mysteries of mathematical calculation, physical investigation, astronomical observation, the construction of engines, the engineering of watercourses, this, and only this, will assure the steady growth of the power of the empire.

No sooner were these proposals laid before the throne than they were made a target for bitter attack by mandarins of the old school. A second memorial replies to these objectors. In both the provision and breadth of view are truly admirable: but how lamentable that men of such intelligence should be forced by national bigotry to repudiate all sympathy with the civilization of the West!

1866 MEMORIAL

We have now to explain that in proposing these measures we have neither been influenced by a love of novelty nor fascinated by the arts of the West, but actuated solely by the consideration that to attempt to introduce the arts without the sciences would be likely to prove an abortive and useless expenditure of public funds. Those who criticize this proceeding object that it is at present not an affair of urgent necessity; that we are wrong in renouncing our own methods to follow those of the West; or, finally, that it would be a deep disgrace for China to become the pupil of the West.

Now not only do the nations of the West learn from each other the new things that are daily produced, but Japan in the Eastern seas has recently sent men to England to learn the language and science of that country. When a small nation like Japan knows how to enter on a career of progress, what could be a greater disgrace than for China to adhere to her old traditions and never think of waking up?

9.4 ZONGLI YAMEN DOCUMENT ON THE UNEQUAL TREATIES, 1878

The following document is a circular letter addressed by the *Zongli* yamen to all of China's ministers abroad in March 1878. It laid out the views of the Qing government toward many of the thorniest issues raised by the Unequal Treaties. At this time, the Russians were occupying Ili, the Tianjin Massacre was still a recent, painful memory, and the Imperial Customs of China continued to be under foreign control. Overthrowing the treaties was an impossibility, but the *Zongli* yamen could make cautious assertions designed to hold onto elements of Chinese sovereignty not as yet threatened by the Western powers. This document, with its careful, legalistic insistence on Chinese rights reflects the new diplomacy of the Tongzhi (1862–1874) and Guangxu (1875–1908) reign periods.

THE TSUNGLI YAMEN TO THE CHINESE MINISTERS ABROAD

1. Since the Treaties of Tientsin were ratified, China's relations with foreign Powers have invariably been conducted in accordance with their stipulations. Whatever complaints there may have been on the part of foreign Governments on this head have in the main been occasioned by accidents to individuals and the incidence of taxation. As regards the first class of complaints, it must be remembered that such things may occur in any country, and that no amount of foresight can effectually guard against them; while as to taxation, it is where there are no Treaty provisions, or where Treaty provisions are read two ways, that differences occur.

2. Treaties may be revised once in every ten years, and such additions, abrogations, or modifications as are introduced depend of course on the voluntary assent of the contracting Powers. The first revision of the British Treaty was concluded by the yamen and British Minister in 1869; but notwithstanding that friendly negotiations had extended over as much as two years, the British Government refused to ratify the arrangements of its representative, and the Revised Treaty has never been in force. For a year past the revision of the German Treaty has been going on; and among the proposals of the German Minister there are some to which it is impossible for China to assent; so, although there has been much discussion, no settlement has been yet arrived at. . . .

7. As regards *Jurisdiction*, i.e. *Exterritoriality*. By the Treaties foreigners in China are not amenable to the jurisdiction of the Chinese authorities, *i.e.* they are exterritorialized. If they have disputes among themselves, their own authorities are to settle them; if they commit an offence, their own

authorities are to punish them according to their own national laws. But foreigners claim much more than this: they interpret the extraterritorial privilege as meaning, not only that Chinese officials are not to control them, but that they may disregard and violate Chinese regulations with impunity. To this we cannot assent. China has not by any Treaty given foreigners permission to disregard or violate the laws of China: while residing in China they are as much bound to observe them as Chinese are; what has been conceded in the Treaties in this connection is merely that offenders shall be punished by their own national officials in accordance with their own national laws. For example, if Chinese law prohibits Chinese subjects from going through a certain passage, foreigners cannot claim to go through that forbidden passage in virtue of exterritoriality. If they go through it and thereby break a Chinese law, their own national officials are to punish them in accordance with such laws as provide for analogous cases in their own country. In a word, the true meaning of the exterritoriality clause is, not that a foreigner is at liberty to break Chinese laws, but that if he offends he shall be punished by his own national officials. Again, seeing that China has agreed that these judicial powers shall be exercised by foreign consuls within Chinese territory, foreign governments should on their side take care that none but good and reliable men are appointed to these posts. Several states, however, appoint merchant consuls. Now, in so far as concerns that part of a consul's duty which comprises the reporting and clearing of ships and the shipping and discharging of sailors, China does not object to its being discharged to merchant consuls. But in China a consul's duties comprise judicial functions as well, and the importance of such functions is such as to seem to demand the appointment of *bona fide* officials to consular posts; moreover, where cases requiring joint investigation occur, it is neither convenient nor dignified for a Chinese official to sit on the bench with a merchant consul, who may have been fined for smuggling the day before, or who, in his mercantile capacity, may perhaps be personally interested in the case at issue.

8. The *"Most favoured Nation"* is found in all the Treaties, and it is well that it should be so, for it is difficult for China to distinguish between foreigners or say which belongs to which nationality; and so much is this so, that even non-Treaty Power foreigners are treated like the others. The object of the foreign negotiator in introducing this clause was to prevent his own nationals from being placed at a disadvantage as compared with others, and to secure that all should be equally favoured. Now this is precisely what China desires. But foreign governments, although their objects in negotiating for the "most favoured nation" clause were similar to those of China, are not always fair in their interpretation of it. For example, if China *for a consideration* grants a certain country a new privilege on such and such conditions, this would be of the nature of a

special concession for a special consideration. Should other countries come forward and in virtue of the "most favoured nation" clause claim to participate in the new privilege, although China need not necessarily exact a similar consideration in return, yet it would be only just to expect that in enjoying the privileges they would consent to observe the conditions accepted by the power to which it was originally granted. But, far from this being the case, there are some who, while demanding the privilege, refuse to be bound by the conditions attached to it. This is the unfair interpretation to which China objects. In a word, as regards this "most favoured nation" clause, we hold that if one country desires to participate in the privileges conceded to another country, it must consent to be bound by the conditions attached to them and accepted by that other.

9. Over and above the four points commented on there is the *Missionary question*. China, recognizing that the object of all religious systems is to teach men to do good, has by treaty assented to missionaries coming to teach their doctrines in China, and has also guaranteed protection to them and to their converts. But among the missionaries are some who, exalting the importance of their office, arrogate to themselves an official status, and interfere so far as to transact business that ought properly to be dealt with by the Chinese local authorities; while among their converts are some who look upon their being Christians as protecting them from the consequences of breaking the laws of their own country, and refuse to observe the rules which are binding on their neighbors. This state of things China cannot tolerate or submit to. Under the exterritoriality clause foreigners are to be dealt with by their own national authorities, but as regards Chinese subjects on Chinese soil, it is only the Chinese authorities who can deal with them, and Chinese subjects, whether Christians or not, to be accounted good subjects, must render an exact obedience to the laws of China; if any offend against those laws, they must one and all, Christians or not Christians alike, submit to be dealt with by their own native authorities, and the foreign missionary cannot be permitted to usurp the right of shielding them from the consequences of their acts.

10. In order that negotiations for Treaty revision may be facilitated, what is required is reciprocal consideration and mutual forbearance. We accordingly address to Your Excellency this communication.

9.5 ZHANG ZHIDONG'S MEMORIAL ON THE ILI CRISIS, 1880

The Ili crisis grew out of the enormous Moslem rebellions in the far western province of Xinjiang in the mid-nineteenth century. Under Qing rule since 1759, Chinese Turkestan was administered as a military colony, with relations between banner garrisons and the local Uighur tribesmen strained at best. Taking advantage of the Qing government's deployment of its armed forces to crush the Taiping rebels and recapture Nanjing, Uighur leaders revolted in 1864 and were soon successful in dominating the prefecture (*fu*) of Ili located not far from China's border with Russia.

Subsequently, in July 1871, General K. P. VonKaufman, the governor-general of Russian Turkestan, ordered the invasion of Ili under the pretext of disciplining Moslem border raiders and restoring order. To assuage the fears of Peking, the invasion was portrayed as a helpful gesture designed to place Ili *fu* under Russian stewardship until Qing authorities were once again capable of restoring order in the region. It soon became apparent, however, that the Russians' real goal was to prevent any extension of British influence from Afghanistan or India into Xinjiang. In addition, the Russians were aware of the mineral and agricultural value of the Ili region. The "temporary" invasion looked more permanent with every passing year.

The Russian land-grab in the Chinese northwest inspired a passionate debate in the Chinese court. On one side were Self-Strengtheners like Prince Gong and Li Hongzhang who argued that coastal defense and the threat posed by the Japanese in the east were more urgent priorities than the fate of far-off Ili. They opposed the dispatch of a military mission to Xinjiang as too costly and risky. On the other side of the debate were scholars who advocated swift recovery of Ili and the adoption of defensive measures to prevent further encroachments.[1]

In the meantime, the Qing army of Zuo Zongtang was efficiently routing rebel forces in Xinjiang. By 1877 Zuo's forces had won back all of the Chinese Turkestan and were camped on the border of Ili. The Qing government, taking the Russians at their word in their explanation for the invasion of Ili, began diplomatic efforts to solve the border dispute.

The representative selected to carry out these delicate negotiations was Chonghou (1826–1893), a Manchu bannerman with limited experience in foreign affairs, who arrived in St. Petersburg at the end of 1878 and promptly began negotiations with Alexander II's foreign minister, Butzow. By September 1879 basic agreements had been reached and the treaty was ready to be signed. Unaccountably, however, Chonghou had not communicated the terms of this treaty, which included the cession of most of Ili to Russia, provisions for Russian navigation on the Sungari River, an indemnity, and other terms unfavorable to China, to his own diplomatic

---

1. For a full explanation of these discussions, see Immanuel C. Y. Hsu, "The Great Policy Debate in China, 1874: Maritime Defense vs. Frontier Defense," *Harvard Journal of Asiatic Studies* 25 (1965): 212–28.

superiors in the *Zongli* yamen. When he finally cabled a copy of its text to Peking, he was ordered not to sign it. Undaunted by this explicit official rejection of what came to be known as the Treaty of Livadia, Chonghou signed it anyway.

This treaty produced consternation in Peking. Many scholars attacked its provisions and wrote memorials criticizing the manner in which it was negotiated. Still others, like Li Hongzhang, defended it and argued that Chonghou had acted within his powers under the terms of the imperial edict that sent him to Russia. Although Chonghou was arrested and war between Russia and China seemed for a time an imminent possibility, a second round of negotiations in the end brought a peaceful and, from China's point of view, satisfactory solution to the Ili crisis.

In subsequent years, it became clear that the heated debates over Ili were early signs of the gap that was opening between younger scholars eager to accelerate the rate of reform and the first generation of Self-Strengtheners. Zhang Zhidong's memorial on the Treaty of Livadia, part of which follows below, was the most famous statement of the so-called *qingyi* (pure opinion) scholars who opposed acceptance of the treaty and pressed for stronger defenses along China's internal border. In this memorial, dated June 1, 1880, Zhang demanded the execution of Chonghou and renunciation of the treaty.

I have lately read in the Peking Gazette that as a treaty had been concluded with Russia, by which your Majesty's Ambassador had dishonored his commission, your Majesty has commanded the Court officials to consult together. Of this treaty, I have heard by rumor the general purport, and as I am anxious and distressed in the extreme, I beg reverently to address your Majesty and the Empresses Regent on the momentous issues of its acceptance or rejection. . . .

The Russians, in making their demands, show themselves to be plunderers and bullies of the worst type; Chonghou, in assenting, showed himself to be a blunderer and a fool in the extreme. Your Majesty and the Empresses Regent, by your burst of indignation, by calling the Ambassador to account, and by summoning your Council, show yourselves to be possessed of a most eminent wisdom and decision. The Grand Council, the Tsungli Yamen, your Majesty's officers of every class and degree, the whole country in short, unite in saying that this treaty must not be. Those who dare not speak out officially their opinion that the treaty must be altered refrain because they fear that to alter a treaty which had been once agreed to would most probably lead to a quarrel. In my opinion, there is no occasion for fear, and I say this treaty must be altered. Trouble is certain to follow, but if we do not alter it, we are not fit to be a nation.

There are four cogent reasons for my request that the treaty be altered:—

1st, a prompt decision has to be given; 2nd, a bold attitude must be taken up; 3rd, right is on our side; 4th, a plan is arranged [in case of war].

What do I mean by a prompt decision? On the above grounds, I say, execute Chonghou. This is what I mean by a prompt decision.

What do I mean by a bold attitude? The Russians deceived our unprotected and imbecile Ambassador, and browbeat him into signing a treaty by which, for every penny they spent, they got back a hundred, and yet were not satisfied. The Russians, in a loutish way, are a great nation, and one does not expect them to act in this manner. It is not China alone that is exasperated with Russia; in the estimation of the world her character is the reverse of straightforward. For the declaration of the Russian Minister at Peking, that he was to return home without waiting for your Majesty's decision in regard to the treaty, there is no warrant in Western law. It is evident that his is an empty threat. The best course for your Majesty to pursue will be to issue an Edict calling the attention of the whole official body, metropolitan and provincial, to the injustices of the Russians, and to the reasons for rejecting this treaty to which rulers and people of China alike have given public expression. To the various foreign Powers a despatch should be sent, so that they may be able to decide whether China or Russia is in the right, and to order their assemblies to insert in the newspapers an account of how China has exhausted every possible appeal to reason. Acting on the national indignation which will brook no wrong, we must hold fast to our resolution not to accept the treaty. Although Russia is a great country, since her bitter conflict with Turkey her soldiers are worn out, her resources are exhausted and her rulers and her people are estranged. Indeed, of late years there have been reports that the Sovereign has had to take precautions against attempts on his life. If in spite of all this he repudiates [our old] treaties and our friendship, by his schemes in distant lands he will burden his people, and will certainly bring upon himself "a calamity in his house," which will inevitably destroy him. How can he then attack anybody? Let your Majesty proclaim this throughout the land. This is what I call a bold attitude.

Our Ambassador certainly signed the treaty, but he never had your Majesty's permission to do so, and the instrument itself, not having been sealed with the Imperial seal, is in the position of a document (in olden days) unattested by the oath of blood. How can it be received as evidence? The moral position of the Russians is bad, and their arguments are poor. How can they fix a quarrel on us? If then we defer to another time our claims to Ili, we shall have what I have called right on our side. . . .

Military preparations are the one essential. And they must go on whether the treaty be altered or not. Our demand for the rendition of Ili must be deferred whether the treaty be altered or not, Chonghou must be executed whether the treaty be altered or not. This is not my own individual opinion, but the public sentiment of the whole country.

Co-operation in deciding the measures to be taken is the duty of all the high officers of the crown; the bold attitude I have spoken of must be maintained by the whole body of Chinese officials. . . . The question concerns the highest interests of the Empire. Sit still and look on, I cannot; remain silent, I dare not. Looking upwards I implore your Majesty to place this my memorial before the Council, that they may deliberate on what I now, in the extremity of my grief and resentment, humbly implore your Majesty to peruse.

9.6 AND 9.7   THE BURLINGAME TREATY AND THE UNITED STATES EXCLUSION ACT

In the decades after the start of the California Gold Rush in 1849, tens of thousands of Chinese immigrants arrived in the United States. By the time of the U.S. census of 1870, there were Chinese living in every state, with the largest concentration of Chinese settlers in California.

The new immigrants were initially welcomed to California's gold fields and pioneer settlements. Even when the gold rush ended there was work aplenty for the Chinese laborers, although they were often exploited by unscrupulous contractors who sold their labor for a fraction of its value. The word for these contract laborers, "coolie," is sometimes claimed to be a Chinese loan word meaning "bitter toil," and certainly the demeaning and ill-paid labor they found after coming to the "Golden Mountain" merited this appellation.

The documents below trace the changing attitude of the American government toward Chinese labor. The first document consists of two parts of an agreement, signed by Anson Burlingame in 1868, that permitted free immigration between China and the United States: Chinese were treated like any other immigrants to America. By the mid-1870s, however, this tolerance had waned and a movement was well afoot in Washington to restrict and even halt Chinese immigration to the United States. The final document in this section is the first Exclusion Act, the first American law restricting immigration on the basis of race and national origin. First applied to the Chinese, later this act would be extended to the Japanese. With the passage of the Immigration Act of 1924, the notion of exclusion was carried still further with the application of restrictive quotas to a number of "undesirable" immigrant groups.

9.6   *The Burlingame Treaty, 1868*

ARTICLE V.   The United States of America and the Emperor of China cordially recognize the inherent and inalienable right of man to change his home and allegiance, and also the mutual advantage of the free immigration and emigration of their citizens and subjects, respectively, from the one country to the other, for purposes of curiosity, of trade, or as permanent residents. The High Contracting Parties, therefore, join in reprobating any other than an entirely voluntary emigration for these purposes. They consequently agree to pass laws making it a penal offense for a citizen of the United States or Chinese subject to take Chinese subjects either to the United States or to any other foreign country, or for a Chinese subject or citizen of the United States to take citizens of the United States to China or to any other foreign country, without their free and voluntary consent, respectively.

ARTICLE VI. Citizens of the United States visiting or residing in China shall enjoy the same privileges, or exemptions in respect to travel or residence as may there be enjoyed by the citizens or subjects of the most favored nation. And, reciprocally, Chinese subjects visiting or residing in the United States shall enjoy the same privileges, immunities, and exemptions in respect to travel or residences as may there be enjoyed by the citizens or subjects of the most favored nation. But nothing herein contained shall be held to confer naturalization upon citizens of the United States in China, nor upon the subjects of China in the United States.

9.7   *The Exclusion Act, May 6, 1882*

An Act to execute certain treaty stipulations relating to Chinese.

Whereas, in the opinion of the Government of the United States, the coming of Chinese laborers to this country endangers the good order of certain localities within the territory thereof: Therefore,

Be it enacted by the Senate and House of Representatives of the United States of America in Congress assembled, That from and after the expiration of ninety days next after the passage of this act, and until the expiration of ten years next after the passage of this act, the coming of Chinese laborers to the United States be, and the same is hereby, suspended; and during such suspension it shall not be lawful for any Chinese laborer to come, or, having so come after the expiration of said ninety days, to remain within the United States.

SEC. 2. That the master of any vessel who shall knowingly bring within the United States on such vessel, and land or permit to be landed, any Chinese laborer, from any foreign port or place, shall be deemed guilty of a misdemeanor and on conviction thereof shall be punished by a fine of not more than five hundred dollars for each and every such Chinese laborer so brought, and may be also imprisoned for a term not exceeding one year. . . .

SEC. 8. That the master of any vessel arriving in the United States from any foreign port or place shall, at the same time he delivers a manifest of the cargo and if there be no cargo, then at the time of making a report of the entry of the vessel pursuant to law, in addition to the other matter required to be reported, and before landing, or permitting to land, any Chinese passengers, deliver and report to the collector of customs of the district in which such vessel shall have arrived a separate list of all Chinese passengers taken on board his vessel at any foreign port or place, and all such passengers on board the vessel at that time.

Such lists shall show the names of such passengers (and if accredited officers of the Chinese Government traveling on the business of that Government or their servants, with a note of such facts), and the names and other particulars, as shown by their respective certificates; and such list shall be sworn to by the master in the manner required by law in relation to the manifest of the cargo.

Any willful refusal or neglect of any such master to comply with the provisions of this section shall incur the same penalties and forfeiture as are provided for a refusal or neglect to report and deliver a manifest of the cargo.

SEC. 9.   That before any Chinese passengers are landed from any such vessel, the collector or his deputy shall proceed to examine such passengers, comparing the certificates with the list and with the passengers, and no passenger shall be allowed to land in the United States from such vessel in violation of law.

SEC. 10.   That every vessel whose master shall knowingly violate any of the provisions of this act shall be deemed forfeited to the United States, and shall be liable to seizure and condemnation in any district of the United States into which such vessel may enter or in which she may be found.

SEC. 11.   That any person who shall knowingly bring into or cause to be brought into the United States by land or who shall knowingly aid or abet the same, or aid or abet the landing in the United States from any vessel of any Chinese person not lawfully entitled to enter the United States, shall be deemed guilty of a misdemeanor, and shall, on conviction thereof, be fined in a sum exceeding one thousand dollars, and imprisoned for a term not exceeding one year.

SEC. 12.   That no Chinese person shall be permitted to enter the United States by land without producing to the proper officer of customs the certificate in this act required of Chinese persons seeking to land from a vessel.

And any Chinese person found unlawfully within the United States shall be caused to be removed therefrom to the country from whence he came, by direction of the President of the United States, and at the cost of the United States, after being brought before some justice, judge, or commissioner or a court of the United States and found to be one not lawfully entitled to be or remain in the United States.

SEC. 13.   That this act shall not apply to diplomatic and other officers of the Chinese Government traveling upon the business of that Government, whose credentials shall be taken as equivalent to the certificate in this act mentioned, and shall exempt them and their body and household servants from the provisions of this act as to other Chinese persons.

SEC. 14.   That hereafter no State court or court of the United States shall admit Chinese to citizenship; and all laws in conflict with this act are hereby repealed.

SEC. 15.   That the words "Chinese laborers," wherever used in this act, shall be construed to mean both skilled and unskilled laborers and Chinese employed in mining.

Approved, May 6, 1882

9.8   CHINESE ANTI-FOREIGNISM, 1892

In the last decades of the nineteenth century, as Western missionaries spread throughout China, anti-foreign activity in China became an source of tension between the Qing government and the foreign powers. As this document, a pamphlet circulated in Canton in the early 1890s, suggests, the activities of foreign missionaries were often interpreted in a strikingly polemical and unfounded way by activists eager to diminish the influence of foreign churches and remove Westerners from their communities. The clashes that resulted from such agitation resulted in a new cycle of unequal treaties and compensatory agreements forced upon Peking by Western states outraged by the treatment of their nationals.

The Roman Catholic religion had its origin from Jesus, and is practiced by all the Western countries, and taught by them to others; it exhorts men to virtue. The founder was nailed by wicked men on a cross, and cut to death. His disciples then scattered about the world to disseminate the doctrine. The Principal is called the Fa Wang Fu [the Kingly Father of the Doctrine]. Sexual congress without shame is called "a public meeting," or "a benevolent society." When they marry they use no go-between, and make no distinctions between old and young. Any man and woman who like may come together, only must first do obeisance to the bishop, and pray to Shangdi [God]. The bride must invariably first sleep with the spiritual teacher, who takes the first fruits of her virginity. . . . Two wives may not be taken, they say, because Shangdi created one man and one woman at first. In these countries therefore concubinage is not practiced, but no unchastity in other directions is forbidden. When a wife dies another may be had. When a father dies, his son may marry the mother who bore him. When a son dies, his father may marry the son's wife; and even his own daughter. Brothers, uncles, and nieces may intermarry promiscuously. Brothers and sisters of same parents also marry together.

Zhang Shoucai was a boat-tracker on the Hun river. A man named Liu informed him that by kidnapping little children and scooping out their hearts and eyes he could earn fifty taels a set.

A foreign devil at Canton went dropping poison down the wells at night.

Every one fell ill of a strange disease, which could only be cured by foreign doctors. Untold numbers died. At last the Prefect found it out, arrested over thirty people, and put them all to death.

When these [foreign] devils open a chapel, they begin with their female converts by administering a pill. When they have swallowed it, they are beguiled, and allow themselves to be defiled. Then after the priest has outraged them, he recites an incantation. The *placenta* then is easily drawn out, and is chopped up to make an ingredient for their hocussing drugs.

At Tientsin they used constantly to beguile and entice away young children in order to scoop out their eyes and hearts. When the people discovered it, they tore down their tall foreign houses, and found heaped up inside bodies of kidnapped children, boys and girls.

All these facts should make us careful not to incur similar dangers. We should unite hands and hearts to keep out the evil before it is upon us.

His Excellency the Commander-in-chief for the Canton province.

| # New Tensions in the Late Qing

10.1 SUN YAT-SEN'S REFORM PROPOSAL TO LI HONGZHANG, 1893

Before Sun Yat-sen (1866–1925) started his career as a revolutionary, he traveled north to Tianjin to seek an audience with Li Hongzhang. He hoped to enlist Li's support for a set of principles for the reform of China. Sun had no influential friends in the north to facilitate an introduction to Li, however, and he was unable to meet with the august former leader of the Huai Army or to feel certain that his letter to Li had received any serious attention. Unlike his fellow Cantonese Yung Wing (Rong Hong), Sun was never permitted to use his knowledge of the West on the behalf of the Qing state. He left north China feeling alienated and ready for other political paths.

The reform proposals that Sun drew up in 1894 resembled plans proposed by a number of his contemporaries who, like Sun, were trained in the West and heavily influenced by foreign educational or political models. It is worth noting that this 1894 plan for reform was more moderate than those being proposed by radical reformers in the state bureaucracy, a faction led by Kang Yuwei and Liang Qichao, who saw the need for large-scale constitutional and institutional reforms.

Though my family originated in eastern Guangdong, it has lived for generations in Xiangshan.[1] Having been educated as a British physician in Hong Kong and having in fact travelled abroad during my younger days, I am more

---

1. Since 1928 the county has been renamed Zhongshan Xian to commemorate Sun Yat-sen.

than familiar with the languages, political institutions, and customs of the Western countries, as well as the natural and applied sciences. As I have paid particular attention to the way in which these Western countries strengthen themselves economically and militarily and the method whereby they refine their customs, I believe that I understand the causes of the constant shift of current events, as well as the rules and laws that govern international relations. Today people from all parts of China, being more informed than they used to be, have come to the capital to present proposals on national affairs. Meanwhile the government is doing its utmost to bring about a most efficient administration and tirelessly pursues such policies as those that will bring maximum benefit to the nation. As the future of our nation brightens, I myself have often thought of presenting my views to the attention of the authorities, hoping that some of these views may be judged good enough to be adopted. Until now I have not ventured to make such a presentation, knowing in advance that from a man of unknown reputation or prestige, my voice would be too feeble to be heard.

Now that the nation is sparing no effort to make itself wealthy and strong, it will not be long before we can march side by side with Europe in terms of achievement. We have in our possession all modern inventions, such as steamships, locomotives, telegraph, and firearms, which the Westerners have used so effectively in the past to advance their interest at our expense. As new programs continue to be introduced, the authorities of our government will acquire the means of not only bringing about peace at home and resisting aggression from abroad but also putting into practice the long-range plan of enriching our nation and strengthening its armed forces. Besides, we know in advance each move foreign countries might choose to make, since we have envoys stationed abroad. How fortunate it is for an insignificant person like me to live in such a great age as this! How impudent I would appear to be if I venture to present some of my own ideas! However, there are things about which I have thought a great deal and wish to speak. Taking advantage of this opportune moment when China enjoys the brightest prospect for the future, I shall present my thoughts, however insignificant for Your Excellency's kind consideration.

I have always felt that the real reason for Europe's wealth and power lies less in the superiority of its military might than in the fact that in Europe every man can fully develop his talent, land resources are totally utilized, each object functions to its maximum capacity, and every item of merchandise circulates freely. The full development of personal talent, the total utilization of land resources, the functioning of each object to its maximum capacity, and the free circulation of merchandise—these four items are the most basic if our nation is to become wealthy, strong, and well governed. For our nation to ignore these four items while concerning itself exclusively with ships and guns is to seek the insignificant at the expense of the basic. . . .

. . . . As man continues to search for laws that govern objects and things, the utility of these laws to his well-being will become greater and greater. Among his new discoveries none is more awe-inspiring than electricity. Electricity has neither form nor substance; it is an object and yet it is not. It exists in every object, circulates freely in the universe, and provides more and wider utility to man than anything else. It can be used for illumination or communication; it can be used for turning motors, preserving food, or opening mines. The use of electricity for illumination or communication has been a wide practice for some time, but its use for turning motors will be found in the mines for the extraction of ores. As scientists continue their research, we shall not be surprised if electricity is also used for the growth of plants, including food crops.

All this shows that the future of man is determined by man, and not by nature. Electricity, until very recently, has been generated exclusively by burning coal. Now some scientists have devised a new method; the generation of electricity by waterfalls. Furthermore, the electricity thus generated can be preserved, to be used whenever and wherever it is needed. This is another way of saying that the supply of electricity is nearly inexhaustible, no matter how much man uses it. As machines gradually replace the physical strength of man, a point will be eventually reached when all that man has to do is to use his brain, leaving all the physical work to the machines. This is not idle speculation; it will soon become a reality.

As machines become more and more intricate and their applications become wider and wider, industries of all kinds will mushroom across each of the industrialized countries. They provide not only what the government, especially its military establishment, needs but also what the people want, especially the daily necessities. Machines can produce more efficiently and at a smaller cost, as compared to a situation without them. Besides, they can do kinds of work not performed by human labor. They can be used to pulverize huge rocks for the extraction of minerals, to drill wells to such a depth as hitherto unimaginable, and to spin and weave at such a lightning speed that they can complete in an hour what a thousand workers cannot do in a day. When machines are used to spin and weave silk dregs or woolen waste, they are performing a miracle by transforming unusable materials to useful products. The kinds of work they can do are too numerous to be cited one by one.

China's territory is large and her natural resources are broad and varied. If we can promote the use of machinery on a nationwide scale, the benefit to the people will be enormous. As long as machinery is not used, our natural resources will remain hidden, and our people will continue to be poor. For all of us who want our nation to become wealthy and strong, the choice is rather obvious . . .

It has been thirty years since we began to imitate the West. We have language schools, as well as military and naval academies, to train specialists in Western affairs. We have mining and textile enterprises to open up financial resources. We have steamship and railroad companies to facilitate transportation. Yet we still lag behind Europe in overall achievement. Why? The reason is that we have not, really, embarked upon the completion of the four tasks, as described above, on a nationwide basis. When we do, given China's human and natural resources, we should be able to overtake Europe in twenty years.

Look at Japan. She opened her country for Western trade later than we did, and her imitation of the West also came later. Yet only in a short period her success in strengthening herself has been enormously impressive. She succeeds because she has been able to proceed with the four tasks, as described above, on a nationwide basis, with no opposition to speak of. There is no such thing as an impossible task—a so-called impossible task will become possible if there are enough dedicated people to perform it. The difficulty with China is not only the lack of enough dedicated people to perform but also the ignorance of too many people on the importance of performance. Had our difficulty been the former and nothing else, we could certainly hire foreigners to perform for us. Unfortunately, our real difficulty has been the latter, namely, the ignorance of too many people on the importance of performance. Had there been foreigners able and willing to work for us, the ignorant among us would obstruct and sabotage and make sure that these foreigners could not succeed. Here lies the real reason why we have not accomplished much; public opinion and entrenched ideas simply will not allow it.

For four decades Your Excellency has argued vigorously and toiled tirelessly for the building of a modern navy and the construction of railroads. Despite this valiant effort, our naval force remains the Beiyang Fleet and the railroad that has been constructed so far is the Tientsin-Shanhaiguan line. If a man like Your Excellency, who enjoys unqualified support form His Imperial Majesty and enormous popularity among his colleagues, has to encounter so many difficulties in modernizing China, we can easily imagine the kind of obstruction others have to face if they try to achieve the same. Even if Yao and Shun were living today, they would not be able to do much. That is why so many patriots have become dispirited and lost hope; that is why I myself have abandoned my own specialty to seek anonymity in medicine.

Since the Restoration Your Excellency has been most concerned with the cultivation of talent. Schools have been established to enroll young men of promise, and Western specialists have been invited to teach them. Large sums of money have been spent on education; a man of talent or skill, whenever he is found, is cherished like a newly discovered gem. Your Excellency must be highly commended for placing the cultivation of talent as the first priority of the nation. It is my misfortune that so far I have not had the privilege of making Your Excellency's acquaintance.

I was born twenty-seven years ago and have studied uninterruptedly since childhood. Though I have not been able to compose the eight-legged essays[2] to

2. During the Ming-Qing period the eight-legged style (*pa-ku*) was the standard form for examination essays.

pass the civil service examination or write in such a way as to distinguish myself among the literati, I am more than familiar with the works of our ancient sages, the art of good government, and the principle whereby the livelihood of our people can be improved. Besides, I have studied Western subjects and have been more than proficient in one particular discipline [medicine]. Knowing that Your Excellency is interested in the cultivation of talent and the employment of talent whenever one is found, I would like to enlist myself as one of the candidates, at a time when all men of conscience must rise to meet the urgent challenge of our time. . . .

10.2 LI HONGZHANG NEGOTIATES WITH JAPAN, 1895

Li Hongzhang was dismissed from office and deprived of marks of imperial favor after the collapse of China's armies in Korea in 1894. When the Japanese rejected the Chinese embassy for peace and insisted on negotiating with higher ranking Chinese officials, Li Hongzhang was selected as China's plenipotentiary in the peace negotiations and was given full responsibility to cede Chinese territory to the Japanese. He arrived at Shimonoseki on March 20, 1895, and after exchanging credentials with Ito Hirobumi and Prince Mutsu, began talks the same day. Four days later Li Hongzhang was shot and slightly wounded by an ultranationalist fanatic. The public outcry aroused by the assassination attempt caused the Japanese to temper their demands and agree to a temporary armistice. Li Hongzhang returned to the bargaining table and the Treaty of Shimonoseki was signed on April 17, 1895. The unique transcript of Li and Ito's discussions at Shimonoseki that follows shows clearly that the Japanese were negotiating from a position of towering strength. The clipped exchanges between the two representatives were polite but in the end Li Hongzhang was dictated to with chilly imperiousness by Ito Hirobumi.

Japan's demands at Shimonoseki were enormous. Ito Hirobumi called for the independence of Korea; cession of Taiwan (here termed Formosa) and Pescadores; a two hundred million tael indemnity; the opening of new treaty ports; navigation rights on the Yangzi River; and the cession of part of Fengtian province. Foreign intervention (the so-called Triple Intervention of France, Germany, and Russia) caused these terms to be modified but the end result of Li and Ito's unequal discussions—the Treaty of Shimonoseki—was, by any standard, a humiliating treaty agreement that stripped away enormous tracts of Chinese territory, further opened China to Japanese economic and military penetration, and set the stage for the ferocious Sino-Japanese conflicts of the twentieth century.

Verbal Discussions During Peace Negotiations,

Between The Chinese Plenipotentiary Viceroy Li Hung-chang And The Japanese Plenipotentiaries Count Ito And Viscount Mutsu, At Shimonoseki, Japan, March-April, 1895

FIRST INTERVIEW
MARCH 20, 1895

H(is). E(xcellency) Li. Your Excellencies may be assured that if my Government had not been actuated by a sincere desire to restore peace, I would not have been sent here; and if I had not been of like mind I would not have come.

H.E. Ito. Yours is a heavy responsibility and the issue at stake—the termination of the present war and restoring cordial relations between our countries—is of paramount importance. As Your Excellency is wise and experienced we may hope that our negotiations will end happily in a Treaty of lasting peace alike beneficial to both countries.

H.E. Li. On the Asiatic continent China and Japan are close neighbors and the written language of the two nations is the same. Is it well that we should live at enmity? The conclusion of our present differences in a lasting peace should be our great concern, for prolonging hostilities will but injure China without benefitting Japan. The European Powers which maintain vast armaments nevertheless take the greatest care not to provoke war. And we, representing the principal countries of the East, should follow this example of Europe. If Your Excellency and myself thoroughly appreciate this we cannot but conclude that the last policy which should rule the Asiatic continent, is that we should establish an enduring peace in order to prevent the yellow race of Asia from succumbing to the white race of Europe.

H.E. Ito. I endorse Your Excellency's views with all my heart. While at Tientsin ten years ago I discussed with Your Excellency upon [sic] reforms in China, but I deeply regret to see that nothing whatever has been done in this direction.

H.E. Li. I very much appreciated what Your Excellency said then, and have since admired your energy in carrying out reforms in Japan; China, however, is hampered by antiquated customs which prevent desirable reforms. I remember Your Excellency advising that, in view of the vast area and population of China, administrative reforms should be effected gradually; yet, shame to say, ten years have wrought no changes—a proof of our incapacity; while Japan has organized an efficient army after Western models and is constantly perfecting the organization of her government.

When in Peking before starting on this mission I talked over these matters with our Ministers of State, and some of them fully realized that China must reform if she would hold her own.

H.E. ITO. Heaven is impartial and speeds the right. If China will but make an effort help will come from on High. Let there be the will and Heaven, who cares alike for us all, will not forsake you; thus a nation may control its own destiny.

H.E. ITO. The Japanese are not so easy to govern as the Chinese. Then, too, we have a Parliament to reckon with—a veritable thorn in the flesh for our Government.

H.E. LI. Your Parliament is like our Censorate.

H.E. ITO. Ten years ago I ventured to advise you to abolish the Censorate, and Your Excellency replied that it would be difficult because the institution dates from the Han dynasty (B.C. 206); I replied that as most of your Censors are ignorant of the needs of the times they are mere stumbling-blocks to the administration. Your Government should appoint to its important offices men of the new school, possessed of Western knowledge, and of suitable age and vigor; You must put away what is obsolete in your system of Government if you would prosper.

H.E. LI. China is not without men in all stations who know the needs of the times; but the Empire is divided into so many provinces and jurisdictions—like Japan in feudal times—that this is a great obstacle to uniform and centralized Government.

H.E. ITO. Though there are so many conflicting jurisdictions you should have one responsible head to your Zongli Yamen, as Viscount Mutsu is in sole charge of the Japanese Foreign Office.

H.E. LI. We have, it is true; many Ministers in our Zongli Yamen, yet they have a responsible chief.

H.E. ITO. Who is he now?

H.E. LI. Prince Kung. What offices do Their Excellencies Enomoto and Otori hold at present?

H.E. ITO. Enomoto is Minister for Agriculture and Trade; Otori is President of the Shi Privy Council. May I ask what has become of Yuan Shikai, your late Minister to Korea?

H.E. LI. He has returned to his home in Henan.

H.E. ITO. Does he still hold office of Military Secretary?

H.E. LI. He holds an unimportant office. . . .

SECOND INTERVIEW
MARCH 21, 1895

. . . .

H.E. ITO. War is evil, though sometimes unavoidable.

H.E. LI. Far better avoided. When General Grant, Ex-President of the

United States, visited Tientsin and we became friends, he said to me: "The loss of life in the Rebellion in my country was so terrible that after I became President I was always anxious to avert war and have ever since advised others to do so. Your Excellency won fame in suppressing the Taiping Rebellion, yet I urge you to beware of entrance to a quarrel which might lead to war." I have always tried to follow this excellent advice; Your Excellency well knows that I was opposed to this war.

H.E. ITO. War is a cruel and bloody business; yet there are times and conditions in the intercourse of States when there is no help for it.

H.E. LI. It is barbarious, and the perfection of modern weapons adds to the slaughter. I am too old to relish such things. Your Excellency is in the prime of life and feels the impulse of martial ardor.

H.E. ITO. How easily peace might have been made at the beginning!

H.E. LI. I was for peace then, but the opposition was too much for me and the opportunity was lost.

H.E. ITO. A very little yielding would have sufficed then, what a pity it was refused! We were like travellers a few miles apart; now we are separated by hundreds of miles and it is hard to turn back.

H.E. LI. Yet it must be done. It is easy for you as Premier.

H.E. ITO. Hundreds of miles apart and all to be retraced!

H.E. LI. Then why not halt now? Though you should go thousands of miles further surely you cannot expect to exterminate my nation!

H.E. ITO. We have never had such an intention. War aims at the destruction of the enemy's power—his fleets, armies, forts and war material, and so to render him helpless; it is not waged against peaceable people.

H.E. LI. As we are willing to make peace we should stop the war.

H.E. ITO. The Chinese population of Jinzhou and other places occupied by Japanese forces are more tractable than Koreans and are hard workers; Chinese are very easy to govern.

H.E. LI. The Koreans were always an indolent people.

H.E. ITO. We can't get them to work for us. We are about to attack Formosa; what are the people there like?

H.E. LI. They are emigrants from Swatow and Zhangquan (?) on the mainland—(they are) bold and hardy.

H.E. ITO. There are aborigines too.

H.E. LI. Yes, six-tenths are savages, the rest colonists. Your Excellency said that Japan will attack Formosa. This explains your objection to the Armistice. England will hardly approve of this move. You have furnished a case to point the moral of my argument about prejudice to the interests of other countries.

H.E. ITO. England will observe neutrality.

H.E. LI. But if not?

H.E. ITO. China is affected—not necessarily England.

H.E. LI. Hardly that, for you will be near the British colony of Hongkong.

H.E. ITO. The war is confined to our countries, no others will suffer.

H.E. LI. It is said that England is averse to another Power taking Formosa.

H.E. ITO. If China should present Formosa to another Power the gift would be received with thanks.

H.E. LI. Formosa has been made a province of China and cannot be ceded away. Twenty years ago when His Excellency the Japanese Ambassador Okubo passed through Tientsin on his way to Peking to make peace, while war was going on against the savages of Formosa because they had murdered Japanese merchants, he said "China and Japan are neighbors, and this affair is like a quarrel between children-enemies for one moment and better friends than ever the next." War between our countries was imminent then, but in the councils I led in advocating peace, and said that the killing of Japanese merchants by these savages did not concern us to the extent of making it an occasion for international war. . . .

FIFTH AND LAST INTERVIEW
APRIL 15, 1895

. . . .

H.E. LI. Last year the officials at Peking denounced and impeached me as being friendly with Count Ito, Prime Minister of Japan; and now that I am here negotiating a Treaty with you their suspicions of friendliness will be confirmed.

H.E. ITO. Not understanding the situation they misjudged you; but now their eyes must be opened and they will regret their rashness.

H.E. LI. And if I sign this gruesome Treaty I am certain to bring down another avalanche of curses on my head. Think of it! . . .

H.E. LI. The Chinese in Formosa [Taiwan] are unwilling to remove and are equally unwilling to sell their property. If hereafter Proclamations are issued requiring them to do so and they revolt, the Chinese Government cannot be held responsible.

H.E. ITO. My Government will assume all future responsibility.

H.E. LI. I have received a telegram from the Governor of Formosa stating that the Formosans have revolted and swear that they will not be subject to Japan.

H.E. ITO. Let them revolt. We can manage that.

H.E. LI. This is not said to alarm you. I am telling you the truth out of good-will.

H.E. ITO. I have heard of it.

H.E. LI. If the Formosans kill the officials and band together to resist, you must not blame me.

H.E. ITO. Let China transfer the sovereignty to us and the whole responsibility will be assumed by the Japanese Government. . . .

H.E. ITO. Our intention is to send troops and officials to take Formosa over within a few weeks after the Treaty has been ratified.

H.E. LI. Someone can be appointed to consult with the Governor of Formosa about all matters pertaining to the transfer.

H.E. ITO. As soon as ratifications have been exchanged the Chinese officials should proclaim the transfer to the Formosans and we will send troops and officers to take charge for the time of all war material.

H.E. LI. Will you also send Civil officers?

H.E. ITO. Yes.

H.E. LI. The transfer is a highly important matter, and rules should be made first to prevent confusion.

H.E. ITO. We cannot wait six months. As soon as ratifications are exchanged we will send our people there. . . .

H.E. LI. One month is rushing the matter. The Zongli Yamen and myself are too far removed from Formosa to know the actual situation there. It would be much better for China to delegate the Governor of Formosa to arrange with the Japanese Governor on the spot what the conditions of transfer shall be. Then, the Treaty having been exchanged, we shall be on friendly terms and arrangements can readily be made.

H.E. ITO. One month is sufficient.

H.E. LI. There are many things to consider. Two months would give us more time to arrange to mutual advantage. Why such headlong haste about Formosa? The plum is already in your mouth.

H.E. ITO. But we shall hunger for it until we have bolted it down.

H.E. LI. One would think the 200 millions enough to satisfy your cravings. After exchange of ratifications it will be necessary to ask for an Imperial Decree appointing an official. One month is too brief.

H.E. ITO. We can make it "within a month an official shall be appointed by Edict, etc."

H.E. LI. Do not mention the Edict.

H.E. ITO. Can you appoint an official within a month or not?

H.E. LI. Yes, but the arrangements for the transfer ought to be made by the Governor of Formosa.

H.E. ITO. We should specify that within two months the transfer shall be wholly accomplished.

10.3 SINO-RUSSIAN RAILWAY AGREEMENTS, 1896

The key mover behind the Triple Intervention was the Russian Count Sergius Witte (1849–1915), who sought to deny the Japanese control of Southern Manchuria and diminish the role they would play in Korea.

These anti-Japanese gestures, which were scarcely generous since they were all too apparently motivated by Russia's own desire for territorial gain, nonetheless, won the gratitude of the Qing court. Zhang Zhidong, Liu Kunyi, and Li Hongzhang, despite their different views of domestic affairs, shared the belief that China might use an alliance with Russia as a counterweight to the Japanese influence in Manchuria and Korea.

Portions of Count Witte's memoirs record his efforts to build the Triple Alliance and describe his discussions with Li Hongzhang in Saint Petersburg in 1896. The practical result of these talks was the Secret Agreement between China and Russia of June 3, 1896, that promised Russian support for China in conflicts with Japan and allowed the Trans-Siberian Railway to be extended across Manchuria to Vladivostok.

Number 1986/5.

Russia (Russo-Chinese Bank) and China.

CONTRACT FOR THE CONSTRUCTION AND OPERATION OF
THE CHINESE EASTERN RAILWAY.
SEPTEMBER 8, 1896.

Between the undersigned, His Excellency Xu Jingcheng,[3] Minister Plenipotentiary of His Majesty the Emperor of China, at St. Petersburg, acting by virtue of an Imperial Edict, dated Guangxu, 22nd year, 7th month, 20th day (August 16/28, 1896), of the one part, and the Russo-Chinese Bank, of the other part, it has been agreed as follows:

The Chinese Government will pay the sum of five million Guping taels (Guping Tls. 5,000,000) to the Russo-Chinese Bank, and will participate in proportion to this payment in the profits and losses of the bank, on conditions set forth in a special contract.

The Chinese Government having decided upon the construction of a railway line, establishing direct communication between the city of China and the Russian South Ussuri Railway, entrusts the construction and operation of this railway to the Russo-Chinese Bank upon the following conditions:

1. The Russo-Chinese Bank will establish for the construction and operation of this railway a company under the name of the Chinese Eastern Railway Company.

   The seal which this Company will employ will be given to it by the Chinese Government. The statutes of this Company will be in conformity

---

3. Xu Jingcheng [1845–1900] was Peking's representative at the railway talks in Berlin in 1896.

with the Russian usages in regard to railways. The shares of the Company can be acquired only by Chinese or Russian subjects. The president of this Company will be named by the Chinese Government, but paid by the Company. He may have his residence in Peking. . . .

2. The route of the line will be determined by the deputies of the president (named by the Chinese Government) of the Company, in mutual agreement with the engineers of the Company and the local authorities. In laying out this line, cemeteries and tombs, as also towns and villages, should so far as possible be avoided and passed by.

3. The Company must commence the work within a period of twelve months from the day on which this contract shall be sanctioned by imperial decree and must so carry it on that the whole line will be finished within a period of six years from the day on which the route of the line is definitely established and the lands necessary therefore are placed at the disposal of the Company. The gauge of the line should be the same as that of the Russian railways (5 Russian feet—about 4 feet, 2½ inches, Chinese).

4. The Chinese Government will give orders to the local authorities to assist the Company to the extent of their ability in obtaining, at current prices, the materials necessary for the construction of the railway, as also laborers, means of transport by water and by land, the provisions necessary for the feeding of men and animals, etc.

   The Chinese Government should, as needed, take measures to facilitate such transportation.

5. The Chinese Government will take measures to assure the safety of the railway and of the persons in its service against any attack.

   The Company will have the right to employ at will, as many foreigners or natives as it may find necessary for the purpose of administration, etc.

   Criminal cases, lawsuits, etc., upon the territory of the railway, must be settled by the local authorities in accordance with the stipulations of the treaties.

6. The lands actually necessary for the construction, operation, and protection of the line, as also the lands in the vicinity of the line necessary for procuring sand, stone, lime, etc., will be turned over to the Company freely, if these lands are the property of the State; if they belong to individuals, they will be turned over to the Company either upon a single payment or upon an annual rental to the proprietors, at current prices. The lands belonging to the Company will be exempt from all land taxes (*impôt foncier*).

   The Company will have the right to construct on these lands buildings of all sorts, and likewise to construct and operate the telegraph necessary for the needs of the line.

   The income of the Company, all its receipts and the charges for the transportation of passengers and merchandise, telegraphs, etc., will likewise be exempt from any tax or duty. Exception is made, however, as to mines, for which there will be a special arrangement.

7. All goods and materials for the construction, operation, and repair of the line, will be exempt from any tax or customs duty and from any internal tax or duty.

8. The Company is responsible that the Russian troops and war material; despatched in transit over the line, will be carried through directly from one Russian station to another, without for any pretext stopping on the way longer than is strictly necessary.

9. Passengers who are not Chinese subjects, if they wish to leave the territory of the railway, should be supplied with Chinese passports. The Company is responsible that passengers, who are not Chinese subjects, should not leave the territory of the railway if they do not have Chinese passports.

10. Passengers' baggage, as well as merchandise despatched in transit from one Russian station to another, will not be subject to customs duties; they will likewise be exempt from any internal tax or duty. The Company is bound to despatch such merchandise, except passengers' baggage, in special cars, which, on arrival at the Chinese frontier, will be sealed by the office of the Chinese Customs, and cannot leave Chinese territory until after the office of the Chinese Customs shall have satisfied itself that the seals are intact; should it be established that these cars have been opened on the way without authorization, the merchandise would be confiscated.

    Merchandise imported from Russia into China by the railway, and likewise merchandise exported from China into Russia by the same route, will respectively pay the import and export duty of the Chinese maritime Customs, less one-third.

    If merchandise is transported into the interior it will pay in addition the transit duty-equivalent to a half of the import duty collected—which frees it from any further charge.

    Merchandise not paying the transit tax will be subject to all the barrier and likin duties [internal transit tolls and duties] imposed in the interior.

    The Chinese Government must install customs offices at the two frontier points on the line.

11. The charges for the transportation of passengers and of merchandise, as well as for the loading and unloading of merchandise, are to be fixed by the Company, but it is obliged to transport free of charge the Chinese official letter post, and, at half price, Chinese land or sea forces and also Chinese war materials.

12. The Chinese Government transfers to the Company the complete and exclusive right to operate the line on its own account and risk, so that the Chinese Government will in no case be responsible for any deficit whatsoever of the Company, during the time allotted for the work and

thereafter for a further eighty years from the day on which the line is finished and traffic is in operation. This period having elapsed, the line, with all its appurtenances, will pass free of charge to the Chinese Government.

At the expiration of thirty-six years from the day on which the entire line is finished and traffic is in operation, the Chinese Government will have the right to buy back this line upon repaying in full all the capital involved, as well as all the debts contracted for this line, plus accrued interest.

If—in case the profit realized exceeds the dividends allowed to the shareholders—a part of such capital is repaid, that part will be deducted from the price of repurchase. In no case may the Chinese Government enter into possession of this line before the appropriate sum is deposited in the Russian State Bank.

The day when the line is finished and traffic is in operation, the Company will make to the Chinese Government a payment of five million Guping taels (Guping Tls. 5,000,000).

> Guangxu, 22nd year,
> 8th month, 2nd day.
> (Signed) Xu.
> Berlin, August 27/September 8, 1896.
> RUSSO-CHINESE BANK
> (Signed) ROTHSTEIN
> (Signed) PRINCE OUKHTOMSKY.

10.4 ZHANG ZHIDONG ON THE CENTRAL GOVERNMENT, 1898

Zhang Zhidong (1837–1909), the leading *qingyi* scholar,[4] sought to combine Chinese and Western learning in a way that would enable China to launch reforms without losing the essential qualities of the Confucian political and cultural way. In 1898 he published *Quanxuepian* (Exhortation to study) a highly influential work designed to boost the reform cause, which was issued by the Guangxu emperor for distribution to all officials and students. It was Zhang Zhidong who coined the expression "Chinese learning as the foundation, Western learning for application" (*zhongxue wei ti, xixue wei yong*), a phrase suggesting the material aspects of foreign culture were valuable to China only when fitted to a philosophical and ethical matrix that remained Chinese. After chapters devoted to national unity, travel,

---

4. Outspoken scholars of the qingyi or "pure-opinion school," who voiced reform sentiments.

study of foreign technologies, and the need to learn from Japan, Zhang turned his attention to government.

CHAPTER VI, CENTRALIZATION OF POWER

There is a class of Chinese in the country just now who have become impatient and vexed with the present order of things. They chafe at the insults offered to us by foreigners, the impotency of the mandarins in war, and the unwillingness of the high officials to reform our mercantile and educational methods: and they would lead any movement to assemble the people together for the discussion of a republic. Alas! where did they find this word that savors so much of a rebellion? A republic, indeed! There is not a particle of good to be derived from it. On the contrary, such a system is fraught with a hundred evils. These evils we will now demonstrate. The first thing necessary in a republic is a Parliament, and it is said that China ought to establish a House. Against such a proceeding we say that the Chinese officials and people are obstructive as well as stupid. They understand nothing about the affairs of the world at the present time, are utterly ignorant of the details and intricacies of civil government. They have never heard of the demand for foreign schools, governments, military tactics, and machinery. With such men as members, what a brilliant Parliament it would be! A vast amount of good would come from such a hubbub as this assembly would make, with perhaps one sensible man in the lot, and the rest a set of fools! Then the power of adopting ways and means, etc., is vested in the Lower House. Legislation and matters of that kind are effected by the Upper House. To obtain a seat in the Parliament the candidate must possess a fairly good income. Chinese merchants do not possess these qualifications. They are not wealthy, and the experience of the people in legislative matters is very limited. Now, if any important measures were to come up for discussion, army supplies for instance, in a Parliament constituted of these unqualified members, a deadlock would ensue at once. Discussion or non-discussion would be all the same, for these M.P.'s would be ignorant of the matter in hand; they would have no knowledge to carry the appropriation bill, and no money to pay the appropriation if the bill were carried. A useless institution, indeed!

Then it is said that under a republic the Chinese can establish mercantile companies and build factories. And what is to hinder them from doing this under the present Government? There is no law to hinder the launching of such enterprises. The truth is that the merchants of China are skilled in trickery, and we have again and again cases where bogus shares have been put on the market to defraud people. If there were no official power to restrain and punish these evil-doers, the company alone would realize any profit; but where would the shareholders be? Or if a manufactory was started, and there were no official power to check the counterfeiting of trade-marks, or to quiet the brawls of the workmen, who would intervene?

The same may be said about the establishment of schools. Our laws have ever encouraged the opening of colleges, schools, and benevolent institutions by wealthy *literati*, and why ask for a republic to bring about this end? But supposing these were established, and there was no official power whatever which would confer rank on the graduates or grant their stipends; with no hope of rank or stipend, who would enter any institution established on this basis?

Again, it is said that we ought to institute a republic in order to drill troops to resist the encroachments of foreigners. But we have no arsenals or dockyards, and if ships and arms were purchased abroad, they could not be brought into a Chinese port if China was a republic, for in that case there would be no officials, and they could not be classed as "official material." An army formed under these conditions would be a noisy, cowardly flock of crows, utterly incapable of fighting a single battle. But taking for granted that this Falstaff regiment could exert itself, who would levy supplies if there were no official power? And who would go security for a foreign loan if there were no government?

We confess that China is not a powerful nation, but the people under the present government get along very well by themselves; if this republic is inaugurated, only the ignorant and foolish will rejoice. For rebellion and anarchy will come down upon us like night, and massacre will seal our eternal grave. Even those who establish the republic will not escape. Murder and rapine will hold sway in city and village. The burning of churches will follow, and under the pretext of protection, the foreigners will send troops and men-of-war to penetrate the far interior of our country and slice off our territory to be foreign dependencies, which we, perforce, submissively grant. This talk about a republic is very agreeable to the adversaries of China.

Years ago the Government of France was changed from a monarchy to a republic. The common people rose against the upper class, because the rulers were vicious and the Government cruel. Our Emperor is exceedingly humane, our laws are not oppressive, and it is folly to introduce these democratic ideas to bring manifold calamities upon China. We have studied the philosophy of these republics, and find that translators of foreign books have wrongly interpreted the word "republic" by *Min Quan* [literally "people power"]. For the people in the republics of the West only have the right to *discuss* measures, and not to carry these measures into execution. Americans resident in China inform us that the ballot-box in their country is greatly abused for personal ends, and Chinese admirers of the American Republic have not minutely examined its defects.

There are many to-day who have only a smattering of Western ways, but who speak confidently of the "power of personal liberty." This is preposterous. The idea is derived from the books of the foreign religion, which say that *Shangdi* [God] bestows upon each individual certain mental and spiritual faculties, and that every man in consequence possesses intelligence and knowledge which enable him to act freely. This means, say the translators, that every human being has a personal liberty. A greater mistake was never made! All the empires and republics of the West have governments of some kind, and the duties of officials, soldiers, and workmen are clearly prescribed. They have also lawyers and judges. Both officials and people are bound by the laws. What the Court recommends can be debated by the Parliament, but what the Parliament decides can be vetoed by the Court. How then can we say that men have personal liberty? Every market town has its elder to keep the peace, every band of robbers its chief. So every Government has its rules. If each individual possessed this "liberty," every family and village would serve its personal ends. The scholar would always sit at meat and do nothing else, the farmer would pay no taxes, the merchant would grow rich beyond bounds, the workman would raise his own wages, the *sans culotte* would plunder and rob, the son would disobey the father, the student would not follow the teacher, the wife would not obey the husband, the low would not defer to the high, the strong would force the weak, and mankind would soon be annihilated. There is not such custom even among the heathen. The English word *liberty*, which means "just in everything and beneficial to all," is mistranslated. The "Liberty Club" that now exists in foreign countries should be called the "Debating Society." If we wish to make China powerful and capable of resisting foreign nations, we must cherish loyalty and righteousness and unite ourselves under the Imperial dignity and power. This is the unchangeable truth of the past and the present, both in China and abroad. If it be urged that we give up the idea of a republic, but establish the Parliament, we reply that our present system is, to all intents and purposes, a republic now. The ancient custom practically meets the case. If the Government encounters difficult questions the Great Ministers are called upon to help settle them; and the people can apprise the rulers of their needs and wants through the appointed channels. The present Dynasty is open and above-board in its dealings, and if our Chinese subjects are loving and loyal there need be no fear that the Emperor will not find out about them and supply all their real wants. The people have the right of discussing questions now, although the rulers retain the prerogative of settling them. This is done with references to the best interests of all. Why is a Parliament demanded then, when we already have this institution in effect? If it were established, pray where would the members come from? Let us wait until our educational institutions are in full swing, and the capabilities of our men are tested by daily experience, and then consider the matter. The present is not the time.

10.5 AND 10.6 BOXER MEMOIRS: ORAL ACCOUNTS OF THE BOXER REBELLION

The Boxer Rebellion was sparked in part by the disruption of life in north China brought about by Western penetration. The coming of missionaries, the building of railroads, seizures of Chinese territory in Shandong, and other aspects of imperialism outraged north Chinese peasants and caused them to organize to obliterate the foreign presence in Shandong and Hebei. Initially, Qing troops suppressed the Boxers, but in January 1900 the dynasty ordered that the Boxers should not be considered bandits. In the spring of the same year the court, now controlled by the reactionary followers of the empress dowager, suggested that it provisionally approved of the Boxers' activities.

These oral historical accounts of the Boxer Rebellion were compiled by the Modern Chinese History Section of the History Department of Shandong University, Jinan, 1980. Beginning in in 1960, the department conducted extensive field investigations, interviewing surviving Boxers and others who experienced the rebellion, until the Cultural Revolution brought the project to a close.

10.5   *Several Accounts of "The Shining Red Lantern"*

1. The Shining Red Lantern got started a little later than Spirit Boxing. Around here Spirit Boxing started in 1898. The Shining Red Lantern started either in 1899 or 1900. I just remember that it was about a year or so later. When Spirit Boxing was about finished, the Shining Red Lantern started.

   The Shining Red Lantern also set up a practice field. Majiafang had one and all the people who went were unmarried girls in their teens and twenties. They also practiced spirit possession. Fenglou had two or three sent there to learn.

   In 1900, or maybe 1899, the Shining Red Lanterns took their spears and knives and went to the county seat to register. That is to say, they wanted to report their names and villages to the county magistrate and get him to do something. But the county magistrate didn't pay any attention to them. [Reminiscence of Dong Yuyao, age 86, from Houzhang Village of the Chengguan Commune of Renping County, January, 1966.]

2. When I was ten, I went to Fenglou to watch people play with the Shining Red Lantern. Their practice ground was set up in a house and it was really exciting and crazy! Liu Laizhu's old lady was running things. She was all dressed in red and it was really dazzling. She was teaching a dozen or so seventeen or eighteen year old girls. All these big girls were dressed from head to toe in red. Their footbinding cloths were red, their socks were red, their shoes were red, their pants were red, their shirts were all red, and they wore a red hair wrapping. Why even the little string to tie on the head wrapping was red! They carried red lanterns and waved red fans. Sometimes they practiced during the day and sometimes at night. They were all girls from poor families. Some couldn't afford to buy red

clothes so they tore off strips of cloth from their bedding and dyed it to make their red costume. [Interview with Liu Shaocheng, age 73, from Wangzhuang Village, the Zhuwang Brigade of Chengguan Commune, Renping County, December 1965.]

3. Fenglou had the Shining Red Lantern. All the Shining Red Lanterns were women who dressed up completely in red. They waved red fans and carried red lanterns and they could get wind or rain or ride the clouds and call in the mist. Two women facing each other would wave their fans and while waving them they could ascend into the sky. That was the kind of thing they did. The elder sister of Wang San of Wangguang village was a Shining Red Lantern. This sister later got married to someone from Nanguan in the city. Before this woman was married, at the age of eighteen, she was a Shining Red Lantern. I used to go to watch the hustle and bustle. [Interview with Zhang Yuqi, age 82, Ma Village, Sanlitun Commune, Renping County, January 1966.]

4. The Shining Red Lanterns were all women. All of them were unmarried girls about eighteen or nineteen years old. They dressed all in red and when they waved fans or bowls they could go up to heaven. They could ride clouds in the sky and become magic fairies! [Interview with Feng Jinyu, age 84, Feng Village, Wulizhuang Commune, Renping County, January, 1966.]

5. Girls who joined the Boxers were called "Shining Red Lanterns." They dressed all in red. In one hand they had a little red lantern and in the other a little red fan. They carried a basket in the crook of their arm. When bullets were shot at them they waved their fans and the bullets were caught in the basket. You couldn't hit them! Some were also possessed by spirits and would say that they were Ma Guiying or Hu Jinchan.[5] [Interview with Zhu Yunze, age 82, Zhu village, Yeguantun Commune, Renping County, December 1965.]

6. In every village there were girls who studied the Shining Red Lantern. In my village there were eight or ten of them. They all carried a red lantern in their right hand and a red fan in the left hand. They'd wave the fans and go up into the sky. They didn't want people to watch and so they'd practice at night when it was dark. There was a song then that went:

> "Learn to be a Boxer, study the Red Lantern.
> Kill all the foreign devils and make the churches burn."

[Interview with Li Mingde, age 74, Liuli Temple, Liuli Temple Commune, Gaotang County, January 1966.]

---

5. Ma Guiying and Hu Jinchan were famous women warriors who were often portrayed in popular dramas in north China.

10.6 *Four Accounts of the Fate of Miss Han (Han Guniang)*

1. Miss Han was from Hebei. On the 27th day of the Fifth Moon [in 1900], at the time of the big hemp marketing day, she rode a horse into the town Longgu with about a dozen followers. They stayed in the town and she gave out food. There was a big drought then and so within two or three days, over a thousand people joined her Big Knife Society [Dadaohui]. She took food from wealthy households and passed it out to the masses of the Big Knife Society.

   After two or three days, there was a big rainstorm. The next day you couldn't find any Big Knife Society members; they'd all gone. To start with they'd all joined to get something to eat. When it rained, they all went home to plant their fields. [Interview with Yu Keyi, age 78, Juye County, February 1960.]

2. Miss Han was from Long'gu in Zhili [Hebei]. Her family had several hundred *mou* of land. She was invited to come from Hebei by Xu Chuan- zhong who was from Big Xu village, located southeast of Shatuji which is east of the Hezhe county seat. Miss Han came to Long'gu on the big hemp marketing day, the 27th day of the Fifth Moon, in 1900. She was riding a big horse and a dozen or so followers came with her. They entered Long'gu blowing bugles and many people ran to watch her. Her followers came from all over Long'gu; there were several thousand of them. She was short and had a long face. Her face was a yellowish ivory color. She was about twenty-five or twenty-six. It was said that she was a Shining Red Lantern. She was very skillful; she could fight with spears or a sword. When she rode on a bench, it would turn into a horse; if she rode a rope, it would change into a dragon; if she sat on a mat it would become a cloud and she could ride the cloud and fly away.

   Miss Han was invited by Xu Chuanzhong of Xu Village. She came from the west side. She stayed in Long'gu a half month or a month. After she came she set up a "Righteous Gruel Station." Since there was a big drought that year many people came into the town. But later there wasn't enough rice and so Miss Han asked some families to provide wheat to make steamed buns. Within a few days, four or five thousand people came into town. All of them were Big Knife Society members. In Long'gu, Miss Han sent people to confiscate everything from the Huang Village church and the Ma Village church. Miss Han was the leader. She stayed in town. She didn't go herself. Then there was a big rainstorm and the next day they were all gone. Some said that when she went to Maliang in Henan, they all dispersed. Some said that after the rainstorm, the whole Big Knife Society in Long'gu dispersed because all of them were farmers and they all went home to plant crops. Others said that the very night of the rainstorm they all went off toward the northwest.

Xu Chuanzhong was the Big Knife Society leader of the villages around Long'gu. He often went to these different villages to teach boxing. You'd find his disciples in all these villages. After Miss Han came to Long'gu, he also came. He stayed a few days and left.

Later Miss Han was caught by her father and elder brother. They beat her to death with a rake. [Interview with Yuan Luanyu, Juye County, 1960.]

3. After Miss Han came to Long'gu, she gathered four or five thousand people. When the converts from Ma Village heard that there were so many Big Knife Society people in Long'gu, they all ran away. Miss Han's Big Knife Society stayed in Long'gu for about a month. All the converts had fled to Huang Village and so at the beginning of the Sixth Moon, the Big Knife Society attacked it. The first time they attacked they didn't send enough people and so they were fought off. Three days later, they sent more than two thousand people but they still couldn't get into the village.

At the time Huang Village was surrounded by a wall and they had a dozen or so platform guns on it. Shi Chuangu, the head of the church from Ma Village, led the converts in the fight. There was a big drought that year and later there was a big rainstorm and Miss Han's Big Knife Society all went off to the north.

In the Fifth and Sixth Moon of 1900, several hundred Big Knife Society People came to Ma Village from Long'gu. Before the Big Knife Society came, the people of Ma Village all ran away and so they came into Ma Village without a struggle. They took away the cattle, they took things, and knocked down the church. They came just after breakfast time and left around the time people here eat their soup. After two or three days, when the Big Knife Society in Long'gu heard that the converts had all gone to Huang Village, they sent about two thousand people to attack it.

Altogether there were only a dozen or so households of converts in Ma Village. The church was a little one-story building that the converts built with money they contributed. The Huang Village church was built under Shi Chuangu's direction. After the Ma Village converts fled to Huang Village, the minister Shi Chuangu led the Ma Village converts (there were only about a dozen) in the defense of Huang Village. They all had guns, there were a dozen or so platform guns. The Big Knife Society attacked from morning to dusk and still couldn't get in. It was because Shi Chuangu had guns and a wall to defend! At that time, the people who defended Huang Village were all Ma Village converts. The Huang Village people helped them because there were no converts in Huang Village. The Big Sword Society couldn't get in and so they left. Then there was a big rainstorm and they all went off to the north west. [Interview with Huang Ruixian, Huang Village, Juye County, 1960.]

4. When I was twelve they tore down the foreign building. The leader of the Big Knife Society was a woman who people called Miss Han. When she led her troops, she carried a spear with red tassels and a big knife. They first stayed in Long'gu and then went to Caozhou to rip down churches. She carried a big knife that was four feet long and two inches thick. It had an iron hand guard. [Interview with Qiu Xinli, age 75, Qiu Village, east of Shatu Town in Heze County, 1960.]

CHAPTER 11

The End of the Dynasty

11.1 Wu Tingfang on China's Progress, 1908

In the following document, the then Chinese ambassador to the United States, Wu Tingfang (1842–1922), a reform-minded professional diplomat, discusses the policies adopted by the Qing government on the eve of the Republican revolution. Wu had grown up in Singapore and worked as a journalist and lawyer in Hong Kong before joining the Chinese government. His optimistic summary of the accomplishments of the reform movement was deliberately one-sided and made a powerful case for a China advancing peaceably toward a new sociopolitical system. There is no sense in the document that reform was a dead letter and that other more powerful forces were now stirring in Chinese political life. Still, Wu Tingfang was not one to be marooned by shifting political currents. When domestic politics brought about a drastic change in Wu's own professional identity after the 1911 Revolution, he emerged as the new republic's chief representative in negotiations with Qing authorities for the Manchu abdication.

The tenth and final meeting of THE CIVIC FORUM for the season of 1907–1908 was held on the evening of May 5, in Carnegie Hall. His Excellency Dr. Wu Ting-fang, Chinese minister to the United States, was the speaker of the evening. An audience of nearly 1,000 was present, and the interest was unflagging. General Stewart L. Woodford, formerly United States minister at the court of Spain, presided at the meeting.

THE AWAKENING OF CHINA

The mere mentioning of this subject—"The Awakening of China"—is sufficient to make my countrymen thrill with pleasure and flush with pride. China, the country which made the dying Missionary, the famous Xavier, exclaim in 1552, "O Rock, Rock, when wilt thou open?" is at last, indeed, opened, and changes are taking place in that hoary Empire, which bid fair to constitute the miracle of the Twentieth Century.

China has been dubbed "The Sick Man of the Far East," "The Sleeping Lion," "The Tottering Empire"; and other names more or less picturesque and complimentary have been bestowed upon her. With some people it is the conviction that China has only a historical interest, that her glory is of the past,— that the leopard may change its spots, but China remains forever in her ruts, the same yesterday, to-day and to-morrow.

But while this gloomy picture of the state of affairs might have been partly true of China of a few decades ago, it is no longer true now. The "Sick Man" is rapidly convalescing, the "Sleeping Lion" is awake, and the hoary and tottering Empire has had new blood injected into her system. China is moving, and she is moving with a rapidity difficult for one who has not personally witnessed the wonderful changes to understand and realize. . . .

First and foremost, is the spread of education—and by this I mean the diffusion of general knowledge, knowledge of men and of affairs of the world. It is a far cry from the time when high officials in Peking, to whom the wonderful performance of the Morse telegraph apparatus was shown and explained, expressed simply their opinion that China got along without it for four thousand years; to the present day when every official residence and department in Peking is connected by the telephone and every provincial yamen, or administrative office, is supplied with the telegraph service.

Repeated defeats at the hands of the foreign powers soon convinced our people of the futility of matching bows and arrows against modern guns and explosives, while our wooden junks went down before the onslaught of armored cruisers and battleships like wheat before the scythe. The inability of our former so-called modern army and navy to encounter those of other nations demonstrated to us clearly that modern weapons of war without the properly trained men to handle them and without scientific leaders to direct and control are of no more value than bows and arrows and wooden junks.

For several years there was loud and threatening talk of doing violence to the integrity of the Empire, and one work actually appeared under the ominous and unfortunate title of "The Breakup of China." No sooner did books and newspapers containing discussions of this subject appear than they were translated into our language, and the wild rumors of impending violence filled the minds of the people with indignation and alarm, impelling them, one may say, at the point of the bayonet to devise ways and means whereby national danger might be averted. Proofs and incidents were not lacking to warn our people that all were *not* brothers within the four seas.

Students poured into foreign countries by the hundreds, and particularly those that went to Japan devoted a large part of their time to the editing of magazines and the translation of books, a veritable flood of literature thus pouring back to their fatherland, and reaching every nook and corner of the Empire. Some of this literature, flowing from the pens of young men flushed with the new learning and burning with patriotism, was naturally somewhat violent in tone and made sensational reading, but it produced its effect on our people, who needed something unusual to wake them out of their lethargy.

Nor must I omit to mention the services of the missionary body, particularly the American branch of it, whose indefatigable efforts in the establishment of educational institutions and in the diffusion of literature of general knowledge, formed a part of the leaven which has leavened the whole Empire of China. The onward movement derived great impetus and received much encouragement from the successes of our island neighbor, Japan. They cry was that what Japan could do, China by adopting similar reforms and taking similar steps can and will do. . . .

The earnest desire of the Imperial Government to promote the welfare of its people is strikingly illustrated in its recent decrees, in which (the promulgation of) a constitution was promised and the system of local government encouraged. With the development of self-government in our country, and the establishment of municipalities, the masses have become more interested in local administration—in such questions as improvement and widening of streets, maintenance of houses and surroundings, an efficient police system; and as the standard of education in self-government is raised, a similar and wider interest is taken in national affairs. By Imperial command, self-government bureaus have been established in every provincial center, and a large number of translators are rendering into our language the constitution and the laws of different nations. Perhaps the time for a parliament has not arrived, but the Government is broadminded enough to listen more and more to the voice of the people, and measures are being adopted which will in the near future lead to the formation of a representative assembly. . . .

The anxiety of young men and women to acquire a modern education in schools at home and abroad, and the joyful sacrifice on the part of parents and elders of luxuries and comforts, to which they have been accustomed for years, in order that the younger generation may receive a liberal education, costing ten or twenty times more than the old method, affords a sight unparalleled in our history. Female education, very much neglected in the past, is recognized as work of the first importance, and the position of women is approaching, though at present slowly, the ideal of that in the West.

A movement of striking significance, on account of the remarkable success it has met, is that started by the Anti-Foot-Binding Society. Foot-binding, originally only intended to check the feet of young women from attaining abnormal and disfiguring size, grew into a most horrible custom, through the perverted ideas of beauty, until it became the exception rather than the rule for women to possess a pair of natural feet. I could never bring myself to see the beauty of human feet, compressed and arbitrarily shaped by artificial means, and from my boyhood I always expressed my strong condemnation of the absurd fashion. I remember I agitated in my early days the question by exposing the absurdity and cruelty of the practice, and with a view of its gradual discontinuance I endeavored to persuade my friends and relatives to join with me in forming a league pledging ourselves to prohibit the compression of our daughters' feet. But to my dismay I could not induce anyone to become a member of my proposed association. It was, therefore, with genuine pleasure and agreeable surprise that some years ago I learned that an anti-foot-binding society was organized by a few foreign ladies, whose object was to accomplish the same thing that I had previously aimed to do. Though the instrumentality of public meetings, pamphlets and leaflets, which were supported by official proclamations and Imperial decrees, the people in a short time have been awakened to the folly and injuriousness of the custom and the appeal has met with a response that must be gratifying to all the people who would hold their bodies as sacred. To-day, one walks the streets of the larger cities and hardly ever sees a girl of ten or under with bound feet, and ladies of middle age, whose extremities have been cramped for a score of years, deem it their patriotic duty to liberate themselves from their bondage. Recently the work of the committee of that society has been handed over to a group of prominent Chinese gentlemen, who, it was believed, could better advance the interests of the society now that it has passed its period of infancy.

Another popular movement, which has given great joy to all friends and well wishers of China, has been the efforts for the suppression of opium. No event in China has given more and better evidence of the hopeful vitality and the solid moral character of our people than the enthusiastic and energetic manner in which the vice of opium smoking is being attacked. On the part of the Government, the highest officials in Peking have been suspended from office for not curing themselves of the habit, creating a sensation in mandarindom. Decrees and proclamations have been issued commanding an annual decrease in the cultivation of the poppy, the closing of public opium dens, the registration of smokers, and other measures which will result in the wiping out of the national curse in eight or ten years. Only a few days ago, I received by cable two Imperial Decrees issued on the 7th and 10th of last month which strengthen the growing conviction that my Government is thoroughly in earnest in its efforts to suppress the opium habit. By the first decree Prince Kung and three other high officials in Peking have been appointed members of an Imperial Commission whose duty is to find out and to see that all officials addicted to the use of the drug in Peking and in all the provinces are cured of the habit, and that in case any opium-smoking official should be discovered, he and his superior for failing to report the same should be both punished. The second commands that all the members of the diplomatic and consular corps abroad must give up their noxious pipe at once, while those too old in age or too inveterate in the use of the drug to do so must retire from the service. Our people in foreign countries are also urged to exert themselves in putting an end to the use of opium. But the more encouraging feature is the attitude of the people towards the opium question. A few years ago, opium smoking was no more condemned than cigars or cigarettes, and it was the fashion for giddy youths to sleep and eat with the deadly drug. To-day, an opium smoker confesses his habit with shame, and all society regards him as more or less an outcast. And it is this healthful change in public opinion that will liberate my country from the chain of the opium devil. At the recent closing of the opium dens in the important cities, the students turned out *en masse*, with their flags and banners and musical instruments, celebrating the occasion as if it were a victory in war, and so earnest were the people in their efforts to suppress the evil that the very keepers of the dens themselves gathered together their vile instruments of smoking and made a huge bonfire of them. . . .

What does this awakening of China mean to the world? To my mind, it means, in the first place, true and lasting peace in the Far East. The moment China becomes strong enough after her awakening to maintain her sovereign rights and protect herself from aggression, the Far Eastern question will have been solved. Again, the awakening of China means the development of commerce, and the day is not distant when the Pacific Ocean will rival the Atlantic with the number of ships that sail on its surface. The world will then witness an expansion of trade never before known in its history, and this trade will also be a safeguard in the interests of universal peace.

11.2 FENG YUXIANG: FROM *MY LIFE*

Feng Yuxiang was one of the most flamboyant and well-known of China's twentieth-century warlords. His began his career as a common enlisted man in the "New Army" of Yuan Shikai, and but for the Revolution of 1911 might never have left the lower levels of the Qing military establishment. The revolution broke down preexisting hierarchies, however, and made possible Feng's elevation as an active local commander in the north. In 1924, Feng organized his own *Guominjun* or People's Army and subsequently became a force to be reckoned with in the complicated battles between rival warlords that ensued in north China in the 1920s. In 1925, his troops briefly occupied Peking and drove the Xuantong emperor and his retinue from the Forbidden City. In 1920, after a complicated set of demarches that had taken the *Guominjun* first toward and then away from Nanjing, Feng Yuxiang joined with General Yan Xishan to oppose Chiang Kai-shek. After extensive fighting in Henan and Shandong between the warlord forces and Guomindang troops, Feng was decisively defeated and his remaining units were reorganized as Guomindang armies. After 1930, Feng continued to play a role in domestic politics and was often an outspoken critic of his erstwhile "blood brother" Chiang Kai-shek. He died in 1948 in a mysterious shipboard fire that occurred while he was en route to the Soviet Union.

Feng Yuxiang had a reputation as something of a reformist. He was a devout Christian and opposed foot-binding, opium smoking, drinking, and other social ills. His *Guominjun* was better trained and disciplined than most warlord troops and had a considerable reputation as a fighting force.

The first of the excerpts from *My Life* (Wode shenghuo) translated here describes Feng Yuxiang's experiences in the Qing army during military exercises in North China in 1905. The second selection describes his emerging political consciousness soon before the 1911 Revolution. It tells of the circulation of seditious literature in the army, including proscribed texts dating from the early Qing that recounted the savage destruction of the cities of Jiading and Yangzhou at the time of the conquest, which inflamed the sentiments of Han Chinese soldiers. In the final analysis, a combination of repeated defeat, mismanagement, and political work in the ranks of the army ultimately turned Feng Yuxiang and many Qing soldiers against the state.

1. AUTUMN MANEUVERS, 1905

Toward the end of the Qing, the force of the revolution grew stronger each day. And so, in 1905 and 1906, the Qing court twice organized autumn maneuvers, respectively in the Hejian and Zhangde areas, to overawe its enemies. . . .

Our First Mixed Brigade set off from Nanyuan and was divided into two mixed regiments. En route, we carried out our own preliminary training exercises. Because the staff was immature and ignorant, all of the orders got mixed up and so the pickets got lost and the "opposing" units could not find each other. Only the units on the flanks were able to confront other flanking units. The two main forces completely missed each other. Finally, the two armies entirely wheeled around and changed their original positions; only after the South Army had become the North Army and the North Army the South could the exercise begin. General Duan Qirui was very unhappy when he saw this and immediately gave a bugler the order to sound the signal for an emergency assembly of the officers. He pointed out to them what had gone wrong and scolded them roundly for their errors. He next ordered the armies to retreat twenty *li* and recommence the exercise. By the time the second run-through was completed, it was already seven or eight o'clock. There was no time for discussion and evaluation of the day's activities and the army was ordered to bivouac at Songlindian.

It was now already pitch black and the groups of troops and horses got completely mixed up. Things became further complicated because there was only one main road to the campsite and front and rear units were jammed one on top of the other during the march. The higher ranking officers became impatient and rode off into the night leaving behind no officers above the rank of company commander. The company commanders were all new and were unwilling to take responsibility for the march. With no one to take charge, the soldiers left their units and simply wandered around on their own. By the time the army reached the campsite, it was already midnight and the rearmost units were still lagging behind.

That evening it was decided that there would be another maneuver starting at seven o'clock the following day. Who could guess that night it would begin to rain and that the rain would grow heavier and heavier. It was Brigade Commander Lu's opinion that the army should take the train to Baoding since it would be most inconvenient for the exercise if the uniforms of the officers and men were to become soaked. He went to General Duan Qirui to seek his orders and was cursed by General Duan who accused Lu of using this pretext to improve his standing with the troops. General Duan said: "How can you be afraid of getting your uniforms wet? Do you mean that you don't go to war when it rains?" The Brigade Commander thought that this was just a maneuver and not real warfare. Had it been actual war, it would have been out of the question to use the train. Infuriated by this rebuke, the Brigade Commander took sick leave and left Baoding by train. And so the order to begin the march remained in effect.

By now it was raining cats and dogs and it was simply impossible to start out. Somehow General Duan got a fantastic idea: why not use a "scientific" method to stop the rain? He ordered our artillery to fire at the sky in order to shock the heavy rain clouds and thus stop the rain. After the order was passed down everyone started firing wildly at the sky. Heaven and earth shook and the common people, not knowing the reason for the uproar, were very much alarmed. Though we fired for a long time, the rainfall failed to subside. In fact, it grew even heavier. General Duan was angry and showed his stubborn character: "Rain or no rain, we're moving out!" The order to march was immediately sent down and we started to march. Food and fodder had to be bought on the spot. Our tents originally weighed fifty to sixty catties but after being soaked through their weight rose to over a hundred catties. The woks and kitchen gear could also not be conveniently carried and the transport troops lagged behind. . . . [The remaining portion of this section describes the difficulties of the ensuing bivouac.]

2. AGITATION IN THE ARMY

I had felt dissatisfaction with the politics of the Manchus and sympathy for the revolution for some time. But the circumstances prompting my decision to take action came about during my second year at Xinminfu [1908]. . . . One day, Platoon Leader Sun Jiansheng of the Engineers Battalion came to my quarters as I was reading *The Family Letters of Zeng Guofan*. He was very unhappy and said: "Do you still want to be a loyal subject and filial son?" I replied: "What's wrong with being a loyal subject and filial son?" He said: "I do not oppose someone being a filial son but I am against someone being a loyal subject!" He also said: "Wait a moment. I'll show you two books and you will know that I am right." He fetched two books: one of them was *The Three Massacres of Jiading* and the other was *The Ten Day Massacre of Yangzhou*. I remember that when he showed me these two books his appearance was quite peculiar. He looked about carefully before removing them from inside his uniform. After he left them with me he said very sternly: "Read them only when there is no one close by. Never let anyone see you reading them! This is not something to be trifled with." After saying this, he hurriedly departed.

Even though I had known a little bit about the racial hatred between the Manchus and Han people, my concept was quite hazy. I knew nothing about the fact that the Manchus had killed and abused the Han people during the period of the conquest. After I finished reading these two books inscribed in blood and tears, I broke out in a cold sweat. When I closed my eyes I could see the cruel and bestial faces of the Tartars and could hear the miserable cries of millions of Han people who were treated worse than chickens or dogs. Involuntarily, I began grinding my teeth and swore that I would take revenge to wipe out this humiliation and restore the freedom of our race.

I was always a person with strong feelings of rebelliousness and could not quietly endure a corrupt and vile status quo. Having felt the sort of stimulation that came from reading these two books, the volcano in my heart began to erupt. My blood was heated to the boiling point and my passions could not be cooled. Within the army, other hot-blooded officers with a sense of conscience also felt indignant and deeply hated the harmful incompetence and corruption of the Manchu court. Feeling an amorphous but uniform sense of need, a few of us who were close secretly began to organize a group. We discussed issues and encouraged each other to carry out work to overthrow this corrupt government.

11.3 ZOU RONG ON REVOLUTION, 1903

Zou Rong (1885–1905) grew up in a well-to-do merchant's family in Sichuan. He resisted pressures to prepare for the imperial examinations and at an early age took part in political activities in local schools that twice resulted in his dismissal.

In the fall of 1902, Zou registered for classes at Japan's Dobun Shoin, a preparatory school for Chinese and Korean students desirous of pursuing studies in Japanese universities or specialized schools. During this year abroad, he read Rousseau's *Social Contract*, Montesquieu's *Spirit of Laws*, Carlyle's *French Revolution*, some Herbert Spencer, and other sociopolitical works. In Japan, Zou became acquainted with members of Sun Yat-sen's *Xingzhonghui* (Revive China Association) and other revolutionary expatriates; he often spoke out against the Manchu regime. In 1903, he returned to China, carrying the manuscript of *The Revolutionary Army* (Geming jun) in his valise. The book was published in Shanghai in May 1903 and became an immediate success. It was the most widely circulated revolutionary pamphlet of its time; tens of thousands of copies were reprinted and circulated in China and in overseas communities.

Zou Rong was arrested by the police of the International Settlement in Shanghai soon after the publication of his tract and died in prison, at the age of 21, in April 1905. In later years, he was regarded as a revolutionary martyr and was honored by both the Guomindang and the Communist Party.

ON REVOLUTION

Revolution is a universal rule of evolution. Revolution is a universal principle of the world. Revolution is the essence of a transitional period of struggle for survival. Revolution follows nature and corresponds to the nature of man. Revolution eliminates what is corrupt and holds on to what is good. Revolution is to advance from savagery to civilization. Revolution is to eradicate slavery and become the master.... I have heard that the English Revolution of 1688, the American Revolution of 1775, and the French Revolution of 1870 were all revolutions that followed nature and corresponded to the nature of man. They were all revolutions designed to eliminate what was corrupt and hold on to what is good and to advance from savagery to civilization. They were all revolutions to eradicate slavery and become the master. The individual was sacrificed to save the world; the nobility was sacrificed to benefit the common people and to allow everyone to enjoy the happiness of equality and freedom.

THE YANGZHOU AND JIADING MASSACRES

Before I finished reading the *Yangzhou shiriji* [Diary of ten days at Yangzhou] and the *Jiading tuchengji* [The massacre of the city of Jiading], I began crying spontaneously. Let me say these words to my fellow countrymen: Do the ten days of Yangzhou and the three massacres of Jiading represent the entire picture of how the Manchu bandits slaughtered the Han people in a prefecture and a county? The accounts in these two books merely mention two cases. Just imagine, at that time they unleashed their army to burn and loot and also issued their hair-cutting decree; wherever the horsemen of the Manchu bandits struck, the massacres and looting must have been ten times worse than in these two places. If the infamous cases of Yangzhou and Jiading occurred, there must have been thousands of other Yangzhous and Jiadings. Whenever I think of this, my heart is moved:

> On the second day of the month, it is said that the Qing army established new officials and clerks in the prefectures and counties and then set up signboards to calm the people and prevent them from panicking. They also instructed the monks in all of the temples to burn the piles of corpses. There were also a number of women hiding in the temples and some of them died of fear or hunger. If the register for the corpses burned is consulted, it can be seen that in eight days more than eight hundred bodies were destroyed. No count was made of those who threw themselves into wells or rivers or hung themselves.

Let me inform my countrymen: When the Manchu bandits came through the passes into China, weren't the people they slaughtered our ancestral grandfathers and their uncles and brothers? Were not the women raped by the Manchu bandits the wives, daughters, and sisters of our ancestral grandfathers? The *Book of Rites* says: "One must not share the same heaven with the murderer of one's father and brothers." Even a small child knows this! Therefore, when a son cannot take revenge for his murdered father or brother, he must pass this responsibility to his own son, and his own son should pass it to his son and onward to future generations. Thus, a forebear's feud is, in fact, the feud of one's own father and elder brothers. If one does not avenge the feud of his father and elder brothers but, rather, serves those who are the object of the feud while talking about filial piety and brotherly love day in and day out, I cannot understand where filial piety and brotherly love are to be found. If the spirits of our ancestors exist, they certainly cannot lie still in the underworld.

ON REVOLUTIONARY EDUCATION

If there is to be great construction, there must be destruction. For great destruction, there must first be construction. This has been an immutable and fixed principle through the ages. The revolution we are carrying on today is a revolution to destroy in order to permit construction. However, to implement destruction we should be able to construct. This was put very well by the great hero of Italian nation-building, Mazzini, who said: "Revolution and education must be carried out together." Before all of you, my countrymen, I cry out: Revolutionary education! Moreover, there must be education before the revolution and education after the revolution. . . .

CHINESE TRAITORS

Zeng Guofan, Zuo Zongtang, and Li Hongzhang were posthumously honored as Dukes Wenzheng, Wenxiang, and Wenzhong by the emperor of the great Qing dynasty. They were revered by the worthies of their time as the three heroes of the Restoration. Their ennoblement and appointment as ministers was envied by mediocre and vulgar people. They were endlessly worshipped and held up as models by later examination scholars. But I have heard that the German Prime Minister Bismarck scolded Li Hongzhang saying: "We Europeans see merit in the pacification of alien races. I have never heard of claiming merit for the slaughter of one's own people." Oh! How I wish I could raise Zeng and Zou from the underworld to hear these words. How I wish I could bring back all the Chinese traitors who lived before Zeng and Zou to hear this. How I wish I could bring together all future Chinese traitors, from those officials with full authority to the petty officials and clerks, to hear this. Zeng, Zou, and Li all claimed that they were well-read and could be compared to the sages of the past. And yet, they mercilessly slaughtered their countrymen and served as the most loyal and submissive slaves of the Manchus. . . . There is no one to compare them to. They were even worse than Li Zicheng and Zhang Zianzhong. Li and Zhang were responsible for murdering their own people and helped bring about the Manchus' conquest of China. But Li and Zhang were not learned and they were also forced to do as they did by the corrupt politics of the Ming. I can still forgive them. Zeng, Zuo, and Li were clearly aware that they belonged to the Han race. They slaughtered their own people to win noble titles for their wives and sons and permitted the Manchus to master China for a second time. I can think of no excuse that will allow me to forgive them.

ON REVOLUTIONARY INDEPENDENCE

I am a young person with little learning or refinement. I cannot really discuss the great significance of revolutionary independence but, timidly and with trepidation, I have conscientiously tried to copy the meaning of American revolutionary independence. Prostrating myself before my most respected and beloved four hundred million exalted Han Chinese countrymen, I list the following proposals for your consideration and action:

1. China belongs to the Chinese. Our countrymen should all recognize that this is the China of the Han race.
2. We will not permit any alien race to tamper with the slightest right of our China.
3. All responsibility to obey the Manchus is abolished.
4. Let us overthrow the barbaric government established by the Manchu people in Beijing [Peking].

5. Drive out Manchus who live in China or kill them to take revenge.
6. Kill the emperor set up by the Manchus in order to assure that in perpetuity there will never be another despotic monarch.
7. Oppose foreigners and Chinese who interfere with our Chinese revolutionary independence.
8. Set up a central government as the central mechanism for the entire country.
9. Divide the country into provinces and cast votes to elect a general provincial representative. From the general provincial representatives of all provinces cast votes to elect a provisional president as representative of the entire nation. Also select a vice-president. Various prefectures and counties will also elect legislators.
10. Everyone in the country, male or female, will be a citizen.
11. All men in the country will have an obligation to perform military service.
12. Everyone will have an obligation to pay national taxes.
13. All people should be loyal to the newly founded nation.
14. All citizens of the nation, male or female, will be equal and there will be no distinction between high and low, noble and base.
15. Everyone will have inalienable natural rights.
16. Life, liberty, and the pursuit of happiness are all heaven-bestowed rights.
17. Such freedoms as the freedom of speech, thought, and publication cannot be violated.
18. Everyone's individual rights should be protected. The establishment of the government should occur through public agreement and the government will fully employ its power to protect the rights of the people.
19. Whenever the government violates the rights of the people, the people should be able to make a revolution to overthrow the old government in order to satisfy their hopes for peace and happiness. When the people have attained peace and happiness, they should be able through public discussion to rearrange rights and set up a new government. That is also a right that the people should possess.

THE GOVERNMENT TO BE ESTABLISHED AFTER THE REVOLUTION

When revolutionary independence is accomplished, people will not be satisfied if there is still the bitterness of a despotic system. This is the reason we must change the national polity of the past.

1. The government will be named the Republic of China.
2. The Republic of China will be a free and independent nation.

3. This free and independent nation should enjoy equal rights with other great nations in international affairs like the declaration of war, peace negotiations, signing treaties, commercial agreements, and all necessary affairs of state.
4. The constitution will be modeled on the American constitution and will conform to China's situation.
5. Laws for self-governance should all follow American laws for self-governance.
6. Any matter involving the whole populace or an individual, diplomatic negotiations, and the domestic division of government should all follow the American model.

11.4 TONGMENG HUI REVOLUTIONARY PROCLAMATION, 1907

By 1905, nearly ten thousand Chinese students, most of them studying law or military subjects, were enrolled in Japanese institutions of higher learning. Confronted with the dramatic proof of Japan's success as a modernizing nation, many Chinese students felt great disillusionment with the Qing government's haphazard steps toward reform. The political activism of these students was stimulated by the presence of a community of mature revolutionaries, like Sun Yat-sen, who had been forced to seek asylum in Japan following violent protests mounted against the Qing state.

In the fall of 1905, the merger of radical student groups established the *Zhonghua Tongmeng hui* (Chinese Alliance Association) with Sun Yat-sen as its leader. With its headquarters in Tokyo and branches in the Chinese communities of Singapore, Saigon, Vancouver, San Francisco, and Chicago, the *Tongmeng hui* probably comprised some one thousand members in its first year of existence (1905–1906).

The document that follows was a proclamation by the *Tongmeng hui* published a year after its founding that was designed to establish its position as a "Military Government" in exile. As in many other *Tongmeng hui* writings, the major motif here was anti-Manchuism; the political program, with its stress on a three-stage passage from military to constitutional government and equalization of land rights, was visionary but vague. In later years there would indeed be a long period of military "tutelage" but it would occur in a far less orderly way and with different results than any of the authors of this proclamation envisaged.

A PUBLIC DECLARATION

Since the beginning of China as a nation, we Chinese have governed our own country despite occasional interruptions. When China was occasionally occupied by a foreign race, our ancestors could always in the end drive these foreigners out, restore the fatherland, and preserve China for future generations of Chinese. Today when we raise the righteous standard of revolt in order to expel an alien race that has been occupying China, we are doing no more than our ancestors have done or expected us to do. Justice is so much on our side that all Chinese, once familiarizing themselves with our stand, will have no doubt about the righteousness of our cause.

There is a difference, however, between our revolution and the revolutions of our ancestors. The purpose of past revolutions, such as those conducted by the Mings and the Taipings, was to restore China to the Chinese, and nothing else. We, on the other hand, strive not only to expel the ruling aliens and thus restore China to the Chinese but also to change basically the political and economic structure of our country. While we cannot describe in detail this new political and economic structure since so much is involved, the basic principle behind it is liberty, equality, and fraternity. The revolutions of yesterday were revolutions by and for the heroes; our revolution, on the other hand, is a revolution by and for the people. In a people's revolution everyone who believes in the principles of liberty, equality, and fraternity has an obligation to participate in it, and the Military Government is merely the means whereby he can fulfill this revolutionary obligation. In short, the responsibility of the people and the responsibility of the Military Government are one and the same, and the accomplishments of the Military Government are also the accomplishments of the people. Only when they cooperate fully with each other can our revolutionary goal be attained.

At this juncture we wish to express candidly and fully how to make our revolution today and how to govern our country tomorrow.

1. *Expulsion of the Manchus from China.* The Manchus of today were known as the Eastern Barbarians *Tung hu* during bygone years. Toward the end of the Ming dynasty they repeatedly invaded our border areas and caused great difficulties. Then, taking advantage of the chaotic situation in China, they marched southward and forcibly occupied our country. They compelled all Chinese to become their slaves, and those who did not wish to subjugate themselves were slaughtered, numbering millions. In fact, we Chinese have not had a country for the past two hundred and sixty years. Now that the day has finally arrived when the brutal and evil rule by the Manchus must come to an end, we do not expect much resistance when our righteous army begins to move. We shall quickly overthrow the Manchu government so as to restore the sovereignty of China to the Chinese. All the soldiers on the Manchu side, whether they are Manchus or Chinese, will be pardoned despite their past crimes if they express repentance and surrender. If they choose to resist the people's army, they will be killed without mercy. The same can be also said about the Chinese who have collaborated with the Manchu government as traitors.

2. *Restoration of China to the Chinese.* China belongs to the Chinese who have the right to govern themselves. After the Manchus are expelled from China, we will have a national government of our own. Those who choose to follow the example of Shih Ching-t'ang and Wu San-kuei will be crushed.

3. *Establishment of a Republic.* Since one of the principles of our revolution is equality, we intend to establish a republic when we succeed in overthrowing the Manchu regime. In a republic all citizens will have the right to participate in the government, the president of the republic will be elected by the people, and the parliament will have deputies elected by and responsible to their respective constituents. A constitution of the Chinese Republic will then be formulated, to be observed by all Chinese. Anyone who entertains the thought of becoming an emperor will be crushed without mercy.

4. *Equalization of landownership.* The social and economic structure of China must be so reconstructed that the fruits of labor will be shared by all Chinese on an equal basis. Every tract of land in China must be assessed to determine its fair value in monetary terms, and this value belongs of course, to the landowner. Any added value, which results from social progress after the revolution, will, however, belong to the nation as a whole and must be shared by all Chinese. The ultimate goal of a responsible society is the guarantee of a satisfactory livelihood for all of its members and everyone, whomever he happens to be, shall have his own means of support, via gainful employment or some other source. Anyone who attempts to monopolize the livelihood of others will be ostracized.

To attain the four goals as outlined above, we propose a procedure of three stages. The first stage is that of a military rule. During this stage when people all over China are responding to our righteous uprising and when all the territories are only recently freed from the Manchu control, we should strive for harmony and cooperation among all Chinese, so that jointly we can face our common enemy. It is essential that during this period of chaos and disturbance both the people and the army must be subject to military rule. While the revolutionary army is fighting in the front, people in the rear must supply it with what it needs and must not do anything that would affect adversely its security or its capacity to complete successfully its mission. In areas that have been recently taken over by the revolutionary army, local governments will be administered by the military command which shall see to it that all the political and social abuses of the past will be eliminated. By political abuses are meant governmental oppression, bureaucratic corruption, extortion by the police, marshals, and other law-enforcement personnel, cruelty in punishment, excessive taxation, and the wearing of pigtails as a symbol of submission to the Manchu government. By social abuses are meant the ownership of domestic slaves, the cruel custom of foot-binding, the smoking of poisonous opium, and the belief in geomancy and other superstitions that are an impediment to modern progress. All these abuses must be eliminated when the Manchu influence in China is eliminated.

The stage of military rule should not last for more than three years. After a district has succeeded in attaining the goals prescribed for the stage of military rule, military rule will come to an end, and the second stage, the stage of provisional constitution, will then begin. After a district has entered the second stage, a provisional constitution will have been proclaimed and put in force, since by then the military command would have already handed over the power of government to the people of that district. The people then govern themselves by electing as their representatives deputies in the district council as well as all the executive officials. The rights and obligations of the Military Government toward the people and the people's rights and obligations toward the Military Government will be prescribed in the provisional constitution and must be observed by the Military Government, the district council, and the people in the district. The party that violates the provisional constitution shall be held responsible for the redress of its action. Six years after the nation has been pacified, a constitution will be proclaimed to replace the provisional constitution as described above, and then nation then formally enters the third or final stage, the stage of constitutional rule. The Military Government relinquishes its executive power, including its control over the nation's armed forces and hands this power to the people's representatives. The President of China will be popularly elected; so will all members of the Parliament. All policies to be pursued by the nation must be in conformity with the letter and spirit of the proclaimed constitution.

In short, during the first stage the Military Government, in cooperation with the people, will eradicate all the abuses of the past; with the arrival of the second stage the Military Government will hand over local administration to the people while reserving for itself the right of jurisdiction over all matters that concern the nation as a whole; during the third or final stage the Military Government will cease to exist and all governmental power will be invested in organs as prescribed in a national constitution. This orderly procedure is necessary because our people need time to acquaint themselves with the idea of liberty and equality. Liberty and equality are the basis on which the Republic of China rests.

To the attainment of the four goals and the implementation of the three stages, as outlined above, the Military Government will dedicate itself on behalf of all the people in the nation. It will do so with loyalty, faith, and total determination. We firmly believe that all our brethren will join us in performing the difficult task ahead, so we can accomplish a great deed together. The brilliant achievements of China have been known throughout the world, and only recently has she suffered numerous difficulties. We shall overcome these difficulties and march forward. The harder the task is, the harder we shall work.

On this day of restoring China to her own people, we urge everyone to step forward and to do the best he can. As the descendants of Huang-ti, we shall regard one another as brothers and sisters and assist each other regardless of the difficulty of the circumstances. Whatever our station in society is, rich or poor, we are all equal in our determination to safeguard the security of China as a nation and to preserve the Chinese people as a race. We shall do so with one heart and one mind. When our soldiers are willing to sacrifice their lives and when everyone else is sparing no effort for the attainment of our noble goals, the revolution will succeed and the Republic of China will be established. Let each and every one of the 400 million people do his very best.

11.5   PRESS COVERAGE OF THE WUCHANG UPRISING, 1911

The 1911 Revolution started with an uprising in Wuchang, the provincial capital of Hubei, on October 10, 1911. On the night of October 9th, bombs accidentally exploded in one of the revolutionaries' secret branches in the Russian Concession in Hankou (now part of Wuhan). Police arrested dozens of revolutionaries, searched their secret meeting places, and discovered weapons, explosives, and lists of names of revolutionary converts in the New Army, which were handed over to the Qing authorities. Upon hearing the news of impending government crackdown and arrests, the revolutionaries hastily took up arms and launched their uprising. There was no coordinated plan nor structured leadership, but their efforts succeeded and the local Qing civilian and military officials were scared into flight. While battles raged on in the Wuchang-Hankou region, provincial governments all over the country, especially in south China where revolutionary and reform climates prevailed, proclaimed their independence from the Qing central government and finally forced the regents of the Xuantong emperor to agree to an announcement of abdication.

The documents selected here are reprinted from the contemporary accounts in *The Hankow Daily News*, a local English newspaper. The dating used in the first proclamation follows a calendar never officially used in China's imperial history but which was that of the Yellow emperor, the legendary progenitor of the Han Chinese. The use of this date emphasizes the beginning, after Manchu domination, of a new Chinese historical era.

PROCLAMATION

The eighth moon of the four thousand six hundred and ninth year of the Wuchang Dynasty.

"I, the Hubei General of the People's Army, am to overthrow the Manchu Government, and am here to revive the rights of the Han people. Let all remain orderly and not disobey military law.

Those who conceal any Government officials will be beheaded.

Those who inflict injuries on foreigners will be beheaded.

Those who interfere with commerce with be beheaded.

Those who indulge in wanton slaughter, burning, or adultery will be beheaded.

Those who fight against the volunteers will be beheaded.

Those who attempt to close the shops will be beheaded.

REWARDS

Those who supply the troops with foodstuffs with be rewarded.

Those who afford protection to the foreign concessions will be highly rewarded.

Those who guard the churches will be highly rewarded.

Those who lead the people to submission are to be highly rewarded.

Those who encourage the country people to join the revolution will be rewarded.

Those who give information as to the movements of the enemy will be rewarded.

Those who maintain the prosperity of commerce will be rewarded."

THE VICEROY'S ESCAPE

The above proclamation showed that the worthy General of the People's Army [the identity of the general in question is unclear] had great hopes of success and these were apparently justified by the arrival, in the morning off the Russian Bund, of the Viceroy's launch accompanied by a cruiser. It was soon learned that the Viceroy had made his escape during cover of darkness and had reached his launch without mishap, teaming over to the side of the river later on to be out of the way of an attack. At 2 p.m. the cruiser and the launch again weighed anchor, the former proceeding close to the Wuchang shore while the latter steamed up slowly in mid-stream. The cruiser was shortly joined by two torpedo boats and firing on the city was commenced, but as far as could be judged only black ammunition was used.

FIGHTING IN WUCHANG

Meanwhile heavy fighting was going on in the city, especially to the southward where the sound of field guns could be heard and an occasional prolonged rattle of small arms, while shots were also being exchanged between the soldiers inside and outside the city, and it was stated that the revolutionary troops were rapidly gaining the upper hand. These petty shop-keepers, even coolies were clamoring in their thousand for tickets to enable them to proceed anywhere away from Hankow. Two extra trains were put on and pulled out from the station crowded to their uttermost capacity, baggage being piled high on the platforms and buffers even, while a seat on the roof of a car was considered quite a luxury.

At 11 a.m. the express left, quite an empty express be it noted, there being but few passengers either native or foreign. A guard of twenty khaki-clad soldiers, revolutionaries though no white badges were visible, were stationed on the platform and these were contentedly consuming an ample morning meal of rice and beans.

OUTSIDE THE TARTAR YAMEN

The Xiao Kao Pavillion and the Tartar [Manchu] General's Yamen in the native city were found to be standing and intact, but outside the latter two heads were displayed on poles, evidently newly severed from their bodies. One of the victims was said to be the leader of a gang of looters and the other the unfortunate secretary of the Tartar General.

More decapitations for incendiarism and looting were made during the day and in all it is said some twenty lost their lives.

PROCLAMATION ISSUED

Outside the Tartar General's Yamen was a proclamation of which we give the following free translation.

"I have the honor of the Military Government to let you, my dear country men, know that our is a righteous cause. Don't be suspicious of our army as wherever the march there will be a true reason. I raise the National Army against the Manchus not for the good or merit of myself, but for us as a whole. To rescue you out from the hot fires and deep waters. To deliver you from the sufferings of Manchus just as to heal your ulcers and sores. Why have the Manchus put you under such sufferings? Because they are a different tribe, and naturally cast you away just like a bit of straw.

So far as to-day, you must have known that the Manchus are not the sons of Han. Although you have been so loyal and righteous to them, yet they pay nothing for your service.

Now I can bear it no longer so that we suddenly gather ourselves together under the righteous flag and the foremost thing we want to do is to demolish what is harmful or injurious to you, and we are perfectly willing to exert as much effort as we can only for the welfare of you. We will not allow those who are treacherous to the sons of Han and those who are the thieves of our countrymen to breathe any longer.

Formerly they ate our flesh and now we are going to eat them.

Those who are in favor of this righteous movement are requested to enroll their names. Come and consult with us about the object, how to recover our Kingdom, "Zhonghua [China]." Now is the time for us to reestablish our country and faithfully work out our due duty as the country men of Zhonghua should do.

We wish you, my dear brothers not to misunderstand each other.

You—scholars, farmers, workers and merchants should try with one accord to drive out the savages. Lastly I wish all of you to treat each other as justly as possible.

I wish you all my dear brethren to listen to my words.

By order.

Huang Dynasty 4609, 8th moon, 19th day."

THE OATH OF ENLISTMENT

The following is a copy of the official document for enlisting in the Revolutionary Army.

I, a native of ———— Xian, of Prefecture of ———— in the Province of Hubei, through the introduction of ————, enabled to understand that the aim of the People's Army Government is to drive out the Manchus, to recover the loss of the Sons of Han, to establish a government for the people and foster liberty and equality, am now self-willing to be listed as a member of the Central Association of Hubei. Hereafter I will forever obey all its constitutions and by-laws. In case of any violation, I am prepared to receive the due punishment. . . . I hope, this will be made known to the President of the People's Army Government Sun Zhongshan (sometimes known as Sung Wen.)

The name of the Introducer (signed.)

The name of the Admitted member (signed.)

Hung Dynasty 4609, 8th moon.

11.6 THE MANCHU ABDICATION EDICT

Immediately after the Wuchang Uprising, the republican forces swept through central and southern China at a pace that shocked the Manchu rulers in Peking. Incapable of handling the crisis, the imperial government showered new appointments on Yuan Shikai, who had only shortly before been forced into retirement and deprived of his authority as the most powerful leader of the Qing New Army. The Qing court hoped that the appointment of Yuan Shikai, a Han Chinese, as the chief executive of a constitutional government would halt the revolutionary trend. Through cunning maneuvers and manipulation of the uncertainties shared by both sides, Yuan finally persuaded the Qing emperor to abdicate and extracted a promise from the revolutionaries that they would elect him as the first official president of the new republic.

The documents that follow reflect the futile last-ditch effort of the Qing court to assure its survival and win favorable terms from the revolutionary government. The abdication edict shows how Yuan Shikai manipulated the crisis, mollifying both sides during the transition as a means of taking real power. The last document, often called "The Articles of Favorable Treatment of the Qing Imperial Court," stipulates the courtesies, subsidies, and residential rights to be granted to the abdicated emperor by the new Republican government.

THE NINETEEN ARTICLES
(NOVEMBER 3, 1911)

1. The Daqing Dynasty shall reign for ever.
2. The person of the Emperor shall be inviolable.
3. The power of the Emperor shall be limited by a Constitution.
4. The order of the succession shall be prescribed in the Constitution.
5. The Constitution shall be drawn up and adopted by the National Assembly, and promulgated by the Emperor.
6. The power of amending the Constitution belongs to Parliament.
7. The members of the Upper House shall be elected by the people from among those particularly eligible for the position.
8. Parliament shall select, and the Emperor shall appoint, the Premier, who will recommend the other members of the Cabinet, these also being appointed by the Emperor. The imperial Princes shall be ineligible as Premier, Cabinet Ministers, or administrative heads of provinces.
9. If the Premier, on being impeached by Parliament, does not dissolve Parliament he must reign but one Cabinet shall not be allowed to dissolve Parliament more than once.
10. The Emperor shall assume direct control of the army and navy, but when that power is used with regard to internal affairs, he must observe special conditions, to be decided upon by Parliament, otherwise he is prohibited from exercising such power.
11. Imperial decrees cannot be made to replace the law except in the event of immediate necessity in which case decrees in the nature of a law may be issued in accordance with special conditions, but only when they are in connection with the execution of a law or what has by law been delegated.

12. International treaties shall not be concluded without the consent of Parliament, but the conclusion of peace or a declaration of war may be made by the Emperor if Parliament is not sitting, the approval of Parliament to be obtained afterwards.
13. Ordinances in connection with the administration shall be settled by Acts of Parliament.
14. In case the Budget fails to receive the approval of Parliament the Government cannot act upon the previous year's Budget, nor may items of expenditure no provided for in the Budget be appended to it. Further, the Government shall not be allowed to adopt extraordinary financial measures outside the Budget.
15. Parliament shall fix the expenses of the Imperial household, and any increase or decrease therein.
16. Regulations in connection with the Imperial family must not conflict with the Constitution.
17. The two Houses shall establish the machinery of an administrative court.
18. The Emperor shall promulgate the decisions of Parliament.
19. The National Assembly shall act upon Articles 8, 9, 10, 12, 13, 14, 15 and 18 until the opening of Parliament.

EDICT OF ABDICATION
(FEBRUARY 12, 1912)

I

We (the Emperor) have respectfully received the following Imperial Edict from Her Imperial Majesty the Empress Dowager Longyu:—

As a consequence of the uprising of the Republican Army, to which the different provinces immediately responded, the Empire seethed like a boiling cauldron and the people were plunged into utter misery. Yuan Shikai was, therefore, especially commanded some time ago to dispatch commissioners to confer with the representatives of the Republican Army on the general situation and to discuss matters pertaining to the convening of a National Assembly for the decision of the suitable mode of settlement has been discovered. Separated as the South and the North are by great distances, the unwillingness of either side to yield to the other can result only in the continued interruption of trade and the prolongation of hostilities, for, so long as the form of government is undecided, the Nation can have no peace. It is now evident that the hearts of the majority of the people are in favor of a republican form of government: the provinces of the South were the first to espouse the cause, and the generals of the North have since pledged their support. From the preference of the people's hearts, the Will of Heaven can be discerned. How could We then bear to oppose the will of the millions for the glory of one Family! Therefore, observing the tendencies of the age on the one hand and studying the opinions of the people on the other, We and His Majesty the Emperor hereby vest the sovereignty in the People and decide in favor of a republican form of constitutional government. Thus we would gratify on the one hand the desires of the whole nation who, tired of anarchy, are desirous of peace, and on the other hand would follow in the footsteps of the Ancient Sages, who regarded the Throne as the sacred trust of the Nation.

Now Yuan Shikai was elected by the provisional parliament [*zizheng yuan*][1] to be the Premier. During this period of transference of government from the old to the new, there should be some means of uniting the South and the North. Let Yuan Shikai organize with full powers a provisional republican government and confer with the Republican Army as to the methods of union, thus assuring peace to the people and tranquility to the Empire, and forming to one Great Republic of China by the union as heretofore, of the five peoples, namely, Manchus, Chinese, Mongols, Mohammedans, and Tibetans together with their territory in its integrity. We and His Majesty the Emperor, thus enabled to live in retirement, free from responsibilities, and cares and passing the time in case and comfort, shall enjoy without interruption the courteous treatment of the Nation and see with Our own eyes the consummation of an illustrious government. Is not this highly advisable. . . .

II

We have respectfully received the following Imperial Edict from Her Imperial Majesty the Empress Dowager Longyu:—

On account of the perilous situation of the State and the intense sufferings of the people, We some time ago commanded the Cabinet to negotiate with the Republican Army the terms for the courteous treatment of the Imperial House, with a view to a peaceful settlement. According to the memorial now submitted to Us by the cabinet embodying the articles of courteous treatment proposed by the Republican Army, they undertake to hold themselves responsible for the perpetual offering of sacrifices before the Imperial Ancestral Temples and the Imperial Mausolea and the completion as planned of the Mausoleum of His Late Majesty the Emperor Guangxu. His Majesty the Emperor is understood to resign only his political power, while the Imperial Title is not abolished. There have also been concluded eight articles for the courteous treatment of the Imperial House, four articles for the favorable treatment of Manchus, Mongols, Mohammedans, and Tibetans. We find the terms of perusal to be fairly

---

1. This refers to the provisional national assembly brought into existence by the 1911 Revolution.

comprehensive. We hereby proclaim to the Imperial Kinsman and the Manchus, Mongols, Mohammedans, and Tibetans that they should endeavor in the future to fuse and remove all racial differences and prejudices and maintain law and order with united efforts. It is our sincere hope that peace will once more be seen in the country and all the people will enjoy happiness under a republican government.

CHAPTER 12

The New Republic

12.1 AND 12.2 YUAN SHIKAI: TWO DOCUMENTS

Soldiers and their profession were traditionally looked down upon in China, a sentiment captured in the well-worn rhyme: Good iron is not used for nails, good men do not become soldiers (*haotie bu da ding; haonan bu dangbing*). The "Soldier's Song," written by Yuan Shikai shortly after he became president of the Chinese Republic in 1912, is typical of a genre of patriotic writings in the early Republican period that attempted to expand the nationalistic consciousness of military men. Similar motivational songs had been composed for soldiers by Zeng Guofan and other commanders during the Taiping and Nien rebellions but the stress in Yuan's song on protecting the nation, patriotism, and the soldier as "citizen" was new. The soldier of the modern armies was to be an exemplar of the purest national virtues; unlike the sedentary scholar-official who despised physical exertion and suspected change, he was to be a disciplined, forceful, modern-thinking, and dynamic agent of the state.

The document that follows the "song" is Yuan Shikai's declaration of adherence to the Republic (February 11, 1912).

12.1 *Poem to the Soldiers*

(1)

Listen to me soldiers—heed what I say!
You have been called to arms to protect the nation.

Your nation and mine.
He who bears arms for his country is a patriot.
He who disturbs it,
Commits a grave crime.
To rob or assail one's own is against human nature and manhood.

(2)

In his own home, the soldier is a citizen,
Once he joins his regiment his heart and his hand belong to all citizens.
Soldiers and citizens are as one in the nation's great family.
He has old ones and young ones to support,
He has wealth and property to protect.
Compare your lot with that of others,
And your love for all the people will be reborn.

(3)

The term "soldier" is honorable.
All citizens should respect those who are called to defend the nation.
But he who becomes a soldier must learn first to respect himself.
He must be honorable, obedient, frugal, and brave.
One base act, one man who forgets home and duty,
Disgraces the name of a regiment.
It is a pride and a duty to obey orders.

(4)

After obedience comes respect for your officers,
Civilian officials, too, are enlisted to your respect.
Foreign and Chinese officials have equal claims,
To the respect and the salute of the soldier.
The winning of victory, the defeat of an enemy,
depends on the skill of the soldier.
Drill, whose hardships patience overcomes
Brings skill to the handling of arms.

(5)

He who hastens to be first in the field is a hero.
His name is forever revered and held in respect.
While he who flees from battle is disgraced,
And dies the death of a coward.
We must all one day die, so
Better is it to die bravely fighting the fight
Your deeds remembered and beloved.

12.2 *Yuan Pledges Allegiance to the Republic, February 12, 1912*

A republic is the best form of government. The whole world admits this. That in one leap we have passed from autocracy to republicanism is really the outcome of the many years of strenuous efforts exerted by you all, and is the greatest blessing to the people. The Da Qing Emperor has proclaimed his abdication by edict countersigned by myself. The day of the promulgation of this edict shall be the end of Imperial rule and the inauguration of the Republic. Henceforth we shall exert our utmost strength to move forward in progress until we reach perfection. Henceforth, for ever, we shall not allow a monarchical government in our country. I shall be most happy to come to the South and to listen to your counsels in our conference as to the methods of procedure. Only on account of the difficulty of maintaining order in the North and the existence of a large army requiring control, and the popular mind in the North and South not being united, the slightest disturbance will affect the whole country. All of you who thoroughly understand the situation will realize my difficult position. You have studied the important question of establishing a Republic, and have definite plans in your minds. I beg you to inform me as to the best means of cooperation in the work of consolidation.

[Signed] Yuan Shikai

12.3 JAPAN'S TWENTY-ONE DEMANDS, 1915

After Japan's victory over China in 1895 and the signing of the Treaty of Shimonoseki, the Japanese government pursued a policy of expanding its territorial control at the expense of Korea and China. In 1910, Korea was officially annexed into the Japanese empire as the vassal state of Chosen. At the same time, the Southern Manchurian Railroad Company, affiliated groups, and investor groups in Japan actively expanded the Japanese sphere of influence in southern Manchuria.

When the First World War broke out in Europe and all major Western powers were busy fighting on European fronts, the Japanese government moved quickly to fill the resultant power vacuum in Asia. Under the pretext of fighting the Central Powers, Japan, after joining the Allies, ousted Germany from Jiaozhou Bay in Shandong province and took control of all the colonial interests developed there by the Germans since 1898.

Japan then took advantage of China's domestic political divisions to strengthen its gains. Striking just as President Yuan Shikai conspired to betray the new republic for his monarchial enterprise, the Japanese moved to affirm their hold on Shandong and reinforce their dominance in Manchuria and inner Mongolia. On January 18, 1915, the Japanese minister to Peking, Hioki Eki, handed Yuan Shikai the Twenty-one Demands, the goal of which was to transform China into a Japanese protectorate of sorts with vast areas actually controlled by Japan and a captive government supervised by Japanese officials or appointees.

The following is the full text of the Twenty-one Demands. For Chinese opponents of this policy, the fifth group of demands, which demanded the employment of Japanese to supervise Chinese administration and other sovereign concessions, was considered a humiliating and undisguised statement of Tokyo's intention to control and conquer China.

Faced with vehement public indignation, the Yuan administration tried to negotiate for softer terms from the Japanese. Dismayed by Yuan's procrastination, the Japanese government delivered a tough ultimatum on May 7, 1915, threatening that the Imperial government would "take steps they may deem necessary" to force compliance. The second document included here shows how China helplessly succumbed to Japan's threat and accepted the demands with the condition that the fifth group be left for future negotiation.

The acceptance of the Twenty-one Demands, albeit conditionally, provoked a tide of nationwide protests and campaigns against Yuan's government's appeasement policy and prepared the ground for the unequivocally anti-imperialist and anti-government nationalist movement of subsequent years.

Japan's Twenty-one Demands, January 18th, 1915.

TRANSLATION OF DOCUMENTS HANDED TO THE
PRESIDENT YUAN SHIH-KAI BY MR. HIOKI, THE
JAPANESE MINISTER, ON
JANUARY 18TH, 1915.

I

The Japanese Government and the Chinese Government being desirous of maintaining the general peace in Eastern Asia and further strengthening the friendly relations and good neighborhood existing between the two nations agree to the following articles:

ART. 1. The Chinese Government engages to give full assent to all matters upon which the Japanese Government may hereafter agree with the German Government relating to the disposition of all rights, interests and concessions which Germany, by virtue of treaties or otherwise, possesses in relation to the Province of Shantung.

ART. 2. The Chinese Government engages that within the Province of

Shantung and along its coast, no territory or island will be ceded or leased to a third Power under any pretext.

ART. 3. The Chinese Government consents to Japan's building a railway from Chefoo or Lungkow to join the Kiaochow-Chinanfu Railway.

ART. 4. The Chinese Government engages, in interest of trade and for the residence of foreigners, to open by herself as soon as possible certain important cities and towns in the Province of Shantung as Commercial Ports. What places shall be opened are to be jointly decided upon in a separate agreement.

I I

The Japanese Government and the Chinese Government, since the Chinese Government has always acknowledged the special position enjoyed by Japan in South Manchuria and Eastern Inner Mongolia, agree to the following articles:

ART. 1. The two Contracting Parties mutually agree that the term of lease of Port Arthur and Dalny and the term of lease of the South Manchurian Railway and the Antung-Mukden Railway shall be extended to the period of 99 years.

ART. 2. Japanese subjects in South Manchuria and Easter Inner Mongolia shall have the right to lease or own land required either for erecting suitable buildings for trade and manufacture or for farming.

ART. 3. Japanese subjects shall be free to reside and travel in South Manchuria and Eastern Inner Mongolia and to engage in business and in manufacture of any kind whatsoever.

ART. 4. The Chinese Government agrees to grant to Japanese subjects the right of opening the mines in South Manchuria and Eastern Inner Mongolia. As regards what mines are to be opened, they shall be decided upon jointly.

ART. 5. The Chinese Government agrees that in respect of the (two) cases mentioned herein below the Japanese Government's consent shall be first obtained before action is taken:

(*a*) Whenever permission is granted to the subject of a third Power to build a railway or to make a loan with a third Power for the purpose of building a railway in South Manchuria and Eastern Inner Mongolia.

(*b*) Whenever a loan is to be made with a third Power pledging the local taxes of South Manchuria and Eastern Inner Mongolia as security.

ART. 6. The Chinese Government agrees that if the Chinese Government employs political, financial or military advisers or instructors in South Manchuria or Eastern Inner Mongolia, the Japanese Government shall first be consulted.

ART. 7. The Chinese Government agrees that the control and management of the Kirin-Changchun Railway shall be handed over to the Japanese Government for a term of 99 years dating from the signing of this agreement.

III

The Japanese Government and the Chinese Government, seeing that Japanese financiers and the Hanyehping Co. have close relations with each other at present and desiring that the common interests of the two nations shall be advanced, agree to the following articles:

ART. 1.   The two Contracting Parties mutually agree that when the opportune moment arrives the Hanyehping Company shall be made a joint concern of the two nations and they further agree that without the previous consent of Japan China shall not by her own act dispose of the rights and property of whatsoever nature of the said Company nor cause the said Company to dispose freely of the same.

ART. 2.   The Chinese Government agrees that all mines in the neighborhood of those owned by the Hanyehping Company shall not be permitted, without the consent of the said Company, to be worked by other persons outside of the said Company; and further agrees that if it is desired to carry out any undertaking which, it is apprehended, may directly or indirectly affect the interests of the said Company, the consent of the said Company shall first be obtained.

IV

The Japanese Government and the Chinese Government with the object of effectively preserving the territorial integrity of China agree to the following special article:

The Chinese Government engages not to cede or lease to a third Power any harbor or bay or island along the coast of China.

V

ART. 1.   The Chinese Central Government shall employ influential Japanese as advisers in political, financial and military affairs.

ART. 2.   Japanese hospitals, churches and schools in the interior of China shall be granted the right of owning land.

ART. 3.   Inasmuch as the Japanese Government and the Chinese Government have had many cases of disputes between Japanese and Chinese police which caused no little misunderstanding, it is for this reason necessary that the police departments of important places (in China) shall be jointly administered by Japanese and Chinese or that the police departments of these places shall employ numerous Japanese, so that they may at the same time help to plan for the improvement of the Chinese Police Service.

ART. 4.   China shall purchase from Japan a fixed amount of munitions of war (say 50% or more of what is needed by the Chinese Government) or that there shall be established in China a Sino-Japanese jointly worked arsenal. Japanese technical experts are to be employed and Japanese material to be purchased.

ART. 5.   China agrees to grant to Japan the right of constructing a railway connecting Wuchang with Kiu-kiang and Nanchang, another line between Nanchang and Hangchow, and another between Nanchang and Chao-chow.

ART. 6.   If China needs foreign capital to work mines, build railways and construct harbor-works (including dockyards) in the Province of Fukien, Japan shall be first consulted.

ART. 7. China agrees that Japanese subjects shall have the right of missionary propaganda in China.

China's Reply to the Ultimatum.

THE REPLY OF THE CHINESE GOVERNMENT TO THE ULTIMATUM OF THE JAPANESE GOVERNMENT, DELIVERED TO THE JAPANESE MINISTER ON THE 8TH OF MAY, 1915.

On the 7th of this month, at three o'clock, the Chinese Government received an Ultimatum from the Japanese Government together with an Explanatory Note of seven articles. The Ultimatum concluded with the hope that the Chinese Government by six o'clock on the 9th of May will give a satisfactory reply, and "it is hereby declared that if no satisfactory reply is received before or at the designated time, the Japanese Government will take steps they may deem necessary."

The Chinese Government with a view to preserving the peace of the Far East hereby accepts, with the exception of those five articles of Group V postponed for later negotiation, all the articles of Groups I, II, III and IV and the exchange of Notes in connection with Fukien Province in Group V, as contained in the revised proposals presented on the 26th of April and in accordance with the Explanatory Note of seven articles accompanying the Ultimatum of the Japanese Government, with the hope that thereby all outstanding questions are settled, so that the cordial relationship between the two countries may be further consolidated. The Japanese Minister is hereby requested to appoint a day to call at the Ministry of Foreign Affairs to make the literary improvement of the text and sign the Agreement as soon as possible.

12.4 THE RESTORATION OF 1917, FROM PUYI'S MEMOIR

Despite the debacle of Yuan's eighty-three day reign as the Hongxian emperor, the dream of monarchial restoration never waned in the hearts of Qing loyalists. Not long after Yuan's death, factional politics in Peking precipitated a major clash between President Li Yuanhong, the nominal leader of the nation, and Premier Duan Qirui, who succeeded Yuan and now commanded the allegiance of the Beiyang Army. In a miscalculated move in May 1917, President Li dismissed Premier Duan from office and summoned General Zhang Xun to protect the capital from Duan's possible military retaliation.

Nicknamed "Pigtail General" (*bianshuai jiangjun*), Zhang Xun (1854–1923) was a staunch promoter of the Qing restoration and an ultraconservative defender of the old order. To manifest his loyalty and political allegiance to the abdicated Qing court, he not only wore a long queue himself but also ordered all his soldiers to do the same. In an era when the queue had virtually disappeared in all but the remotest locales, Zhang Xun's troops came to be called the "Pigtail Soldiers" (*bianzi bing*).

When Zhang Xun's army entered the capital to defend the constitution of the Republic, Zhang Xun defied Li Yuanhong's intentions and launched a movement to restore the Qing monarchy. With the assistance of Kang Youwei and other Qing loyalists, General Zhang reinstated Aisin-Gioro Puyi to the throne and proclaimed an authentic Manchu Restoration on July 1, 1917. Horrified by this attempt to reinstate Qing rule, Premier Duan Qirui, his generals and political supporters, including Liang Qichao, immediately gathered their forces and launched a punitive attack. By July 12, 1917, they succeeded in crushing the "Pigtail Soldiers" and ended the farce of restoration.

Puyi's memoir of these events captures a sense of his bewilderment as an eleven year old boy struggling to orient himself while political intrigues swirl around him.

The news of Yuan Shih-kai's death was received with great rejoicing in the Forbidden City. The eunuchs rushed hither and thither spreading the news, the High Consorts went to burn incense to the tutelary god, and there were no lessons that day in the Yu Ching Palace.

New opinions were expressed in the palace.

"Yuan died because he wanted to usurp the throne."

"It's not that a monarchy is impracticable, it's just that the people want their old sovereign."

"Yuan Shih-kai was different from Napoleon III: he had no such ancestry on which to rely for support."

"It would be much better to return things to the old sovereign than to have a Mr. Yuan as emperor."

All these voices were in tune with the saying of my tutor that "because of the great goodness and rich benefit conferred by our dynasty the people of the whole country are thinking of the old order...."

After Yuan's death, Li Yuan-hung succeeded him as president with Tuan Chi-jui as premier. The palace sent a representative to congratulate President Li and Li Yuan-hung returned to the palace the imperial processional weapons that Yuan had taken. Some of the Ching princes, nobles and senior officials were even given Republican decorations, including a few who had been in hiding during Yuan Shih-kai's time. The Household Department was busier than ever conferring such honours as posthumous titles, the permission to ride a horse in the Forbidden City or wear a peacock's feather; bringing girls for the High Consorts to select ladies-in-waiting from; and secretly recruiting more eunuchs despite the prohibition in the Articles of Favourable Treatment. And of course there were all sorts of contacts being made that I did not know about, from private dinners to public banquets for the members of the Republic's parliament.

In short, the Forbidden City was as active as it had been in the old days; and with Chang Hsun's [Zhang Xun] audience with me in 1917 the restoration movement reached a climax.

I had not received many people in audience before then and they had all been Manchus. Those parts of my day that were not devoted to studying in the Yu Ching Palace or reading newspapers in the Mind Nurture Palace I mostly spent playing. I was very excited to see how many people wearing court clothes were always coming and going in the palace; the news of the rising of the "loyalist" troops of Prince Su and Babojab thrilled me even more, and their defeat naturally depressed me. But generally speaking I soon forgot about such matters; and while I could not help worrying about the flight of Prince Su to Lushun and his uncertain fate, the highly amusing sight of a camel sneezing was enough to make me forget all about his predicament. With my father, my tutors and my ministers to look after things what need was there for me to concern myself? When my tutors told me about any matter it meant that everything had already been discussed and agreed. So it was on June 16, 1917.

Chen Pao-shen, who had recently been granted the title of "Grand Guardian," and Liang Ting-fen, a newly appointed tutor, came into the schoolroom together that day; and before they had sat down Chen Pao-shen said, "Your Majesty will have no lessons today. A high official is coming for an audience with Your Majesty and a eunuch will be here to announce him very shortly."

"Who is he?"

"Chang Hsun, the Viceroy of Kiangsi, Kiangsu and Anhwei and Governor of Kiangsu."

"Chang Hsun? The Chang Hsun who won't cut his queue off?"

"Yes, that's the man," said Liang Ting-fen, nodding in approval. "Your Majesty's memory is very good." Liang missed no opportunity to flatter me.

This had in fact been no feat of memory as Chen Pao-shen had told me the story of Chang Hsun not long before. From the beginning of the Republic he and his troops had kept their queues. Yuan Shih-kai owed his successful crushing of the "second revolution" in 1913 to the capture of Nanking by his pigtailed soldiers. When in the sack of the city Chang Hsun's men had mistakenly injured some of the personnel of the Japanese consulate he went and apologized to the Japanese consul in person and promised to pay full damages. He announced national mourning for the death of the empress dowager Lung Yu in a telegram of condolences and went on to say that "all we Republican officials are the subjects of the Great Ching." After the death of Yuan Shih-kai another telegram of Chang's was published in the press in which he made known his political position. Its first item was "I attach the greatest importance to all of the Articles of Favourable Treatment of the Ching house." I believed that he was a loyal subject and was interested to see what he looked like.

According to the practice of the Ching house nobody else could be present when a high official was received in audience by the emperor. For this reason my tutor would have to give me some coaching and tell me what to say before I received anyone who did not come regularly. This time Chen Pao-shen told me very seriously that I must praise Chang Hsun's loyalty, that I should remember that he was the High Inspecting Commissioner for the Yangtse River and had sixty battalions of troops in the region of Hsuchow and Yenchow; I could ask him about the military situation in Hsuchow and Yenchow and was to make it very clear that I was interested in him. Finally Chen repeated two or three times, "Chang Hsun is bound to praise Your Majesty. You must remember to reply modestly so as to display Your Majesty's divine virtue."

I had tried to form a picture of what Chang Hsun looked like from the picture magazines that the eunuchs bought for me, but I had not yet succeeded when I got down from my carrying chair. Soon after I reached the Mind Nurture Palace he arrived. As I sat on the throne he knelt before me and kotowed.

"Your subject Chang Hsun kneels and pays his respects . . ."

I waved to him to sit on a chair as the court had ended the practice of having officials report in a kneeling position. He kotowed again to thank me and then sat down. I dutifully asked him about the military situation in the Hsuchow and Yenchow area, but I did not pay any attention to his reply. I was somewhat disappointed at the appearance of this "loyal subject" of mine. He was dressed in a thin silk jacket and gown, his face was ruddy and set with very bushy eyebrows, and he was fat. The sight of his short neck made me think that but for his whiskers he would have looked like one of the eunuch cooks: he was far from perfect. I looked carefully to see if he had a queue and indeed he did: a mottled grey one.

Then he started to talk about me and, as Chen Pao-shen had expected, spoke in very respectful terms.

"Your Majesty is truly brilliant," he said.

"I am not up to much," I replied. "I am young and I know very little."

"Emperor Sheng Tsu of this dynasty (Kang Hsi) acceded to the throne when of tender years. He was only five."

"How can I be compared with my august ancestor? He was my ancestor, after all . . ."

This audience was not much longer than an ordinary one, and he went after five or six minutes. I found his speech rather coarse and reckoned that he was probably not a second Tseng Kuo-fan: I was not very excited by him. But when Chen Pao-shen and Liang Ting-fen came to me the next day beaming with smiles to tell me that Chang Hsun had praised my modesty and intelligence I was very pleased with myself. I did not ask myself why Chang had come for an audience, or why my tutors were so visibly excited, or why the Household Department had given him such lavish presents, or why the High Consorts had held a banquet for him.

About a fortnight later, on July 1, my tutors Chen Pao-shen, Liang Ting-fen and the newly arrived Chu Yu-fan came to the schoolroom together with very grave faces. Chen Pao-shen spoke first.

"Chang Hsun is here . . ."

"Has he come to pay his respects?"

"No, he has not just come for that. All preparations have been made and everything has been settled. He has come to bring Your Majesty back to power and restore the Great Ching."

Seeing that I was startled he went on to say, "Your Majesty must allow Chang Hsun to do this. He is asking for a mandate on behalf of the people; heaven has complied with the wishes of the people."

I was stunned by this completely unexpected good news. I stared at Chen Pao-shen in a daze, hoping that he would go on to tell me a little about how to be a "true emperor."

"There is no need to say much to Chang Hsun. All you have to do is to accept." Chen Pao-shen spoke with great confidence. "But it wouldn't do to accept at once; you must refuse at first and only finally say, 'If things are so then I must force myself to do it.'"

I returned to the Mind Nurture Palace and received Chang Hsun in audience again. What Chang Hsun said was much the same as had been written in his memorial requesting a restoration, except that it was less elegantly expressed.

"The empress dowager Lung Yu was not prepared to inflict a disaster on the people for the sake of one family's illustrious position, so she issued a decree ordering that a republic be organized. But who would have thought it, it was run so badly that the people have no way to make a living . . . A republic does not suit our country. . . . Only Your Majesty's restoration will save the people."

When he had finished gabbling I said, "I am too young; I have neither talent nor virtue. I could not undertake so great an office." He lavished praises on me and droned on about how Emperor Kang Hsi had come to the throne at the age of five. While he talked I thought of a question: "What about their President? Will we give him favourable treatment?"

"Li Yuan-hung has already memorialized asking that he be allowed to resign. All that is necessary is for Your Majesty to grant his request."

"Ah. . . ." Although I did not understand what was going on I thought that my tutors must have settled everything and that I had better end this audience quickly. "If things are so I must force myself to do as you say." With this I regarded myself as the emperor of the "Great Ching Empire" again.

After Chang Hsun's departure hosts of people came to kowtow to me, some to pay their respects, some to thank me, and some both to thank me and pay their respects. After this a eunuch brought in a pile of nine "imperial edicts" that had already been written out. The first of these proclaimed my return to the throne, and another created a board of seven regents, including Chang Hsun and Chen Pao-shen.

Old Pekinese remember how on that morning the police suddenly told all the households in the city to hang out imperial dragon flags; the people had to improvise them with paper and paste. Then Ching clothes that had not been seen for years reappeared on the streets worn by people who looked as if they had just stepped out of their coffins. The papers brought out special issues for the restoration at a higher price as usual; so that amid the strange sights one could hear news-vendors shouting as they sold the "Edicts of Hsuan Tung," "Antiques, six cash only! This nonsense will be an antique in a few days—six cash for an antique—dead cheap."

Some of the shops outside the Chien Men Gate did a booming trade in those days. Tailors sold Ching dragon flags as fast as they could make them; the second-hand clothes shops found that newly appointed officials were struggling to get hold of Ching court dress; and theatrical costumiers were crowded with people begging them to make false queues out of horsehair. I still remember how the Forbidden City was crowded with men wearing court robes with mandarins' buttons and peacock feathers on their hats. From the back of everyone's head dangled a queue. When later the Army to Punish the Rebels approached Peking one could pick up real queues all over the place: these were said to have been cut off by Chang Hsun's pigtailed soldiery as they fled. . . .

In the first few days of the restoration I spent half of my time in the Yu Ching Palace. Although my lessons were suspended I was obliged to see my tutors as I had to follow their directions in whatever I did. For the rest of my time I looked over the "imperial edicts" that were to be issued, read the official papers of the cabinet, and received homage and salutations, apart from this I would watch ants crawling from one hole to another or tell the eunuchs of the Imperial Stables to bring out some camels for my entertainment. But before five days of this kind of life were up the bombs dropped by the aircraft of the Army to Punish the Rebels changed things completely. Nobody came to kowtow to me any longer, there were no more "imperial edicts," and all my regents had disappeared except for Chen Pao-shen and one other, Wang Shih-chen.

On the day of the air-raid I was sitting in the schoolroom talking to my tutors when I heard an aeroplane and the unfamiliar sound of an explosion. I was so terrified that I shook all over, and the colour drained from my tutors' faces. With everything in chaos eunuchs hustled me over to the Mind Nurture Palace as if my bedroom were the only safe place. The High Consorts were in an even worse state, some of them lying in the corners of their bedrooms, and some of them hiding under tables. The air was filled with shouts and the whole palace was in confusion. This was the first air-raid in Chinese history and the first time a Chinese air force was used in civil war. Here are the first air-raid precautions, for what they may be worth: everyone lay down in their bedrooms and the bamboo blinds in the corridors were let down. As far as the knowledge of the eunuchs and the palace guard went, these were the wisest measures they could take. Fortunately the pilot did not mean business and gave us nothing worse than a fright, dropping only three tiny bombs about a foot long. One of them fell outside the Gate of Honouring the Ancestors (Lung Tsung Men) wounding one of the carriers of sedan-chairs; one fell into a pond in the Imperial Garden, damaging a corner of the pond; and the third fell on the roof of one of the gateways in the Western Avenue of the palace striking dread into the hearts of a crowd of eunuchs who were gambling there although it failed to explode.

Soon after this the sound of approaching gunfire was heard in the Forbidden City. Wang Shih-chen and Chen Pao-shen did not come to court and the palace had no more contact with the outside world. A little later a false report was brought from the commander of the palace guard that Tuan Chi-jui's Republican army had been defeated by Chang Hsun's men, but the next morning the news of Chang Hsun's flight to the Dutch embassy swept away the smiles of the day before.

My father and Chen Pao-shen now appeared, dejection written all over their drooping faces. Reading the abdication edict that they had drafted both frightened and saddened me, and I wept out loud. The decree ran like this:

> On the twentieth day of the fifth month of the ninth year of Hsuan Tung the Cabinet receives this Imperial Edict: Formerly we followed the memorials of Chang Hsun and others who, saying that the nation was a state of fundamental disorder and that the people longed for the old way, advised us to resume the government. As our years are tender and we live deep in the Forbidden City we have heard nothing about people's livelihood and the affairs of the nation. Remembering with reverence the great benevolence and the instructions of the late August Empress Hsiso Ting Ching (Lung Yu) who yielded the government out of pity for the people, we had not the least intention of treating the world as our private property; it was only because we were asked to save the nation and the people that we forced ourselves to accede to the requests made of us and assume power.
>
> Now yesterday Chang Hsun reported armed risings in every province, which may lead to military insurgencies in a struggle for power. Our people have been suffering hardships for years, and their state is as desperate as if they were being burned or drowned. How could we then compound their miseries with war? Thinking upon this we were disturbed and unable to rest. We therefore resolved that we would not keep this political power for ourselves and thus besmirch the living soul of the August Empress Hsiao Ting Ching by turning our back on her abundant virtue.
>
> Let Wang Shih-chen and Hsu Shih-chang inform Tuan Chi-jui at once, that the transfer of power may be arranged and the present troubles brought to an end, so calming the people's hearts and avoiding the calamity of war.
>
> By the command of the Emperor.

12.5–12.7 THREE SOLDIERS

General Cai Tingkai won national renown in China for his gallant defense of Shanghai in January 1932. Later his troops rebelled against the Nanjing government and Cai, together with other generals of the 19th Route Army and a group of politicians hostile to Chiang Kai-shek, launched the short-lived "Chinese Republican People's Revolutionary Government" in Fujian.

The selection from Cai's memoirs, *The Autobiography of Cai Tingkai* (Cai Tingkai zizhuan), translated here, dates from 1916. Through it one glimpses the expanding intellectual horizons of a bright Cantonese in the late Qing and early Republican period.

12.5 *Cai Tingkai: Reading the Newspaper, 1916*

... One day, Commander He told us: "If you have free time, why don't you read the newspaper? You can learn a lot from reading the news." After this, I began to learn to read newspapers and found all sorts of interesting news about society and other things. I told Chen Shun [Cai's closet friend at this time]: "When I was in the New Army, discipline was very stern and I learned a great deal but none of my superiors then could compare with our commanding officer now. He has even taught us how to read newspapers. In the three years I spent as an armed military guard, I never learned anything. I just became lazy. It was really not worthwhile."

Chen Shun said: "Commander He is terrific. He led recruits and was in charge of logistics in Gaozhou. He was very good in military science."

Then I said: "Since Commander He taught us how to read the newspaper, I have read it everyday. It is very interesting but I have trouble following the articles; I don't know how to read them and where to start from."

Chen Shun said: "There's all sorts of international, national, and local news in a newspaper. There's even news about thefts and fights. I've heard that to read the newspaper you should first read the international and national news about political affairs. You should particularly read the editorials. I said: "Although I attended school for three years, I still can't quite get the gist of what is published in the newspaper."

Chen Shun said: "If you don't understand it you can ask the company clerk."

After this, whenever I was free I read the papers and asked my colleagues or the clerk when I didn't understand. Sometimes we discussed the news that appeared and so reading the paper become a daily task for me. Everyday I would read the paper from front to cover, even including the advertisements and my knowledge was thus steadily improved and my life was not so pointless as before. ...

During this time the war in Europe was going on and things in our country were also quite confused. Long Jiguang [a pro-Yuan Shikai general] controlled Guangdong province and was slaughtering revolutionaries right and left. I read in the newspapers and also heard it rumored that in Beijing [Peking] Yuan Shikai was bribing and forcing the legislators of the National Assembly to elect him as emperor and was planning to submit to the Twenty-one Demands of the Japanese. Cai E escaped from Beijing [Peking] and went to Yunnan and joined with Tang Jiyao to plan an uprising for the independence of the province. People felt very uncertain. In the fall, Long Jiguang sent his brother Long Jinguang westward toward Yunnan at the head of an army group. Later the Guangxi army began moving eastward and was stationed at Zhaoqing and Sanshui. There were new rumors every day and the situation seemed very confused. I was only a soldier at the time and all of my news came from the newspapers and hearsay. . . .

[In mid-December] the newspaper reported that Yuan Shikai was planning to enthrone himself in Peking. Sun Yatsen, Cai E, Tang Jiyao and others entirely opposed this. According to one paper, Cai and Tang had already claimed independence in Yunnan and sent their troops to attack Sichuan. Another paper said Cai and Tang had already been defeated. We had no idea which news was true and groped in the dark for answers. We were young and naive and had no political experience or foresight. We did not know what the political parties or cliques represented or who belonged to which of them. I didn't like the fact that Yuan Shikai, after already becoming president, was now colluding with the Japanese to become emperor. I only knew that Long Jiguang was not doing good in Guangdong and wished that native Guangdongese could control political power in the province. As for what was "feudal" or what was "democratic," I had no idea whatsoever.

12.6 FENG YUXIANG: PRAISING THE LORD

Feng Yuxiang was converted to Methodism in 1914 and, thereafter, energetically proselytized his faith in the ranks of his army. Foreign missionaries welcomed his efforts to build a Christian army and were frequent visitors to Feng's headquarters at Nanyuan in Hebei. They applauded his mass baptisms of soldiers, the army's Spartan training and drill, and supported Feng's efforts to halt opium smoking, gambling, and drinking. For some of them, Feng Yuxiang was a dream come true: a charismatic native Christian leader who could produce the mass conversions that had eluded several generations of missionaries.

The following description of Feng Yuxiang's army by missionary George T. B. Davis provides a sense of the life of the soldiers in the

Guominjun (ca. 1919) and vividly demonstrates how hymns, prayer meetings, fiery sermons, and conversions were utilized by Feng and his subordinate commanders both as motivating tools and a means to attract foreign support for his endeavors.

There is a strict schedule of work and study from the rising bugle in the morning, to "lights out" at night. In the summer the men rise at 4 A.M. The first order of the day after dressing, is a bit of spiritual drill. They assemble by companies in the open air in the quiet of the early dawn. The captain leads in the singing of a gospel hymn. Then all heads are reverently bowed while an officer or corporal or private soldier prays earnestly for God's blessing upon the army and the duties of the day.

Physical drill follows spiritual. The men go out for a twenty minutes run, and clamber up and down curious little mounds with steps, to make them fit for mountain climbing, and for the day's program of study and work. Then comes military drill, followed by various forms of physical training, industrial work, study of Chinese, moral lectures, a noon prayer meeting, and so on. From morning until night there is a varied program of study and work and worship.

The army is up-to-the-minute in physical fitness, as might be expected where there is an absence of immortality, wine drinking, and cigarette smoking. The men are alert, athletic, clear-eyed, strong-muscled. Sir James Startin, a retired Admiral of the British Navy, who recently visited Peking, was much impressed with the fine physique of the men. He was also delighted with the feats they performed on the horizontal bars. The other day I saw a soldier do the full swing nearly a dozen times in succession just in their ordinary practice.

A striking feature of the army-school is its industrial branch. This was started by Gen. Feng in order that many of the men might learn a trade while in the army, and have a means of support on their return home. As you pass through one room after another you see the young men busily engaged in making shoes and clothes, knitting stockings, weaving rugs, boiling soap, and making chairs and other articles of furniture. When one set of men have learned a trade, another lot takes their place.

But the most interesting and striking phase of the army life is its spiritual side. In my early visits to the camp the thing that most impressed me was the sight of a hundred or more men standing outside a mess-room before a meal singing a gospel hymn. Then all heads were bowed while someone led in prayer; not a few formal phrases, but an earnest petition, often of some length. And imagine my surprise when calmly informed that this was the custom throughout the entire army before each of the two meals of the day!

Later I witnessed a still more striking scene that occurs at noon each day. At twelve o'clock a gun is fired. At ten minutes past twelve the men gather by companies outside their various quarters for half an hour of Bible reading and prayer. Sometimes the meeting is conducted by the captain; sometimes the companies are divided into smaller groups in charge of a corporal. First a hymn is sung; then a chapter in the New Testament is read verse about, often with brief explanations, followed by a number of earnest petitions from the men as well as the officers. It is really Family Worship for the day. Just as a father gathers his family about him for Bible reading and prayer; so the captains and corporals of the army conduct the service for those committed to their care.

And it is a singing, as well as a Bible-reading and praying, army. How the men love to sing the old hymns that are favorites at home! They sing the first thing in the morning; they sing at noon; they sing the last thing at night. They sing at meetings, they sing before meals, they sing as they march. The favorite hymn of the army is "Onward Christian Soldiers." Some others that the troops especially enjoy are: "Stand Up, Stand Up for Jesus!" "Ye Soldiers of the Cross"; "Room for Thee"; "All People That on Earth Do Dwell"; and "O Happy Day."

12.7 ZHANG ZONGCHANG: WITH PLEASURE RIFE

Not all warlords shared the pious worldview of Feng Yuxiang. Many were opportunists of the first order who capitalized on the multiple crises of the post-1911 era to advance themselves, indulge their vices, and carve out independent kingdoms where their power was absolute. Many of the warlords of this type were oblivious to the welfare of the Republican "citizens" they ruled. For them, like the soldiers so disparaged by Chinese of other eras, the people were an inert mass who they taxed, exploited, and killed as they saw fit.

One such warlord was Zhang Zongchang (1881–1932), the "Dogmeat General" of Shandong. The following satirical sketch of Zhang Zongchang was written by Lin Yutang (1895–1976), one of China's most well-known twentieth-century humorists, shortly after Zhang's demise.

So General Chang Tsung-ch'ang, the "Dog-meat General," has been killed, according to this morning's report. I am sorry for him, and I am sorry for his mother, and I am sorry for the sixteen concubines he has left behind him and the four times sixteen that had left him before he died. As I intend to specialize in writing 'in memoriams' for the bewildering generals of this bewildering generation, I am going to begin with the Dog-meat General first.

So our Dog-meat General is dead! What an event! It is full of mystic significance for me and for China and us poor folk who do not wear boots and carry bayonets! Such a thing could not happen every day, and if it could there would be an end to all China's sorrows. In such an eventuality you could abolish all the five Yuan, tear up the will of Dr. Sun Yat-sen, dismiss the hundred odd members of the Central Executive Committee of the Guomindang, close up all the schools and universities of China, and you wouldn't have to bother your head about Communism, Fascism, and Democracy, and universal suffrage, and emancipation of women, and we poor folk would still be able to live in peace and prosperity.

So one more of the colorful, legendary figures of medieval China has passed into eternity. And yet Dog-meat General's death has a special significance for me, because he was the most colorful, legendary, medieval, and unashamed ruler of modern China. He was a born ruler such as modern China wants. He was six feet tall, a towering giant, with a pair of squint eyes and a pair of abnormally massive hands. He was direct, forceful, terribly efficient at times: obstinate and gifted with moderate intelligence. He was patriotic according to his lights, and he was anti-communist, which made up for his being anti-Guomindang from convictions, but by accident. He didn't want to fight the Guomingdang: it was the Guomindang that wanted to fight him and grab his territory, and, being an honest man, he fought rather than turn tail. Given a chance, and if the Guomindang would return him his Shantung, he would join the Guomindang, because he said that the Sanmin doctrine can't do any harm.

He could drink, and he was awfully fond of 'dog-meat,' and he could swear all he wanted to and as much as he wanted to, irrespective of his official superiors and inferiors. He made no pretence to being a gentleman, and didn't affect to send nice-sounding circular telegrams, like the rest of them. He was ruthlessly honest, and this honesty made him much loved by all his close associates. If he loved women he said so, and he could see foreign consuls while he had a Russian girl sitting on his knee. If he made orgies he didn't try to conceal them from his friends and foes. If he coveted his subordinate's wife he told him openly, and wrote no psalm of repentance about it like King David. And he always played square. If he took his subordinate's wife he made her husband the chief of police of Jinan [Shandong]. And he took good care of other people's morals. He forbade girl students from entering parks in Tsinan, and protected them from the men-gorillas who stood at every corner and nook to devour them. And he was pious, and he kept a harem. He believed in polyandry as well as polygamy, and he openly allowed his concubines to make love with other men, provided he didn't want them at the time. He respected Confucius. And he was patriotic. He was reported to be overjoyed to find a bed-bug in a Japanese bed in Beppo, and he never tired of telling people of the consequent superiority of Chinese civilization. He was very fond of his executioner, and he was thoroughly devoted to his mother.

Many legends have been told about Dog-meat's ruthless honesty. He loved a Russian prostitute and his Russian prostitute loved a poodle, and he made a whole regiment pass in review before the poodle to show that he loved the prostitute that loved the poodle. Once he appointed a man magistrate in a certain district in Shantung, and another day he appointed another man to the same office and started a quarrel. Both claimed that they had been personally appointed by General Dog-meat. It was agreed, therefore, that they should go and see the General to clear up the difficulty. When they arrived it was evening, and General Chang was in bed in the midst of his orgies. "Come in," he said, with his usual candor.

The two magistrates then explained that they had both been appointed by him to the same district.

"You fools!" he said, "can't you settle such a little thing between yourselves, but must come to bother me about it?"

Like the heroes of the great Chinese novel *Shui Hu*, and like all Chinese robbers, he was an honest man. He never forgot a kindness, and he was obstinately loyal to those who had helped him. His trousers-pockets were always stuffed with money, and when people came to him for help he would pull out a bank-roll and give a handful to those that asked. He distributed hundred-dollar notes as Rockefeller distributed dimes.

CHAPTER 13

"A Road Is Made"

13.1 AND 13.2 QING FEMALE CHASTITY

The New Culture Movement (1917–1923) was a declaration of war on Chinese cultural forms. The New Culture intellectuals questioned the fundamental underpinnings of Confucian ethics and the daily practice of traditional morality. Old virtues, such as loyalty to superiors, filial piety and women's chastity, were all criticized as disguised means of control imposed on the ruled by the power elite.

The discussion by cultural critics of Chinese women's chastity, a subject too sensitive and freighted with accepted values even to be raised in previous eras, illustrates most graphically the clash of the new and old cultural forces.

The first part of the two selections that follow contains two biographies of chaste women dating from the nineteenth century. They are true stories of the abuse and martyrdom suffered by many "chaste women" (*lienu*) throughout the Ming-Qing period, and serve as examples of what Lu Xun, writing in the early twentieth century, deemed as the sacrifices demanded by a "man-eating" society.

The author of these biographies, Lu Yitian (1801–1865), was a *jinshi* scholar and later a prefectural instructor in Hangzhou. In the six months prior to his death in 1865 he was a teacher in the prestigious Ziyang Academy.

Lu Xun's essay was first published in 1918 in *New Youth*. It was one of a group of essays on women's chastity solicited by the journal's editorial board in hopes of promoting the idea of women's liberation in China. Lu Xun's brother Zhou Zuoren and Hu Shi also made contributions to the project, but Lu Xun's piece was far superior to other articles in its command of historical knowledge and its persuasive power. The essay is also marked by its incisive style and satirical tone, which reflect the author's scorn for Confucian traditions.

13.1 *Lu Yihan, Two Biographies*

1. CHASTE WOMAN WU: CHASTITY AND SUICIDE

Chaste Woman Wu was from the village of Luxiawan located near Lake Tai in Huzhou Prefecture. Because of the poverty of her own family, she was raised in the family of her husband. Her husband's name was Li Shixin. He helped his father Li Jiugao manage a family store in Hubei. And so Woman Wu lived alone in the house with her mother-in-law.

The mother-in-law was having an adulterous relationship with a distant clan relative named Big Gun Li [Li Dapao] who came to the house frequently to drink wine. Woman Wu was ordered to wait on them but she refused. The mother-in-law was furious and pinched the woman cruelly all over her body. Big Gun Li and the mother-in-law conspired to rape her to prevent her from speaking out later about their relationship. And so the mother-in-law used sweet-sounding words to tempt her: "Big Gun has earned favor from your husband. If you treat him well, your husband will think it virtuous that you have returned a favor." The mother-in-law took out a gold bracelet and gave it to Woman Wu saying: "This is a gift from the Big Gun." The woman took it and threw it on the ground. It was the sixth day of the sixth moon. The custom of the area was to eat noodle soup at this time. The mother-in-law and Big Gun made some noodles together and ordered Woman Wu to cook them. She refused to cook them and so the mother-in-law sat down to eat and invited Woman Wu to join them. She refused but Big Gun forced a portion down her throat and she cried and ran away.

At dusk, when the woman was bathing in the house, Big Gun leapt forward out of the dark. She wanted to run away but the door was already closed. She climbed out of a rear window and flung herself into the water. An old woman neighbor rescued her. Woman Wu was barely breathing but by midnight she had come to her senses. Thereupon, she again jumped into the water and died.

The members of the clan reported this to the county yamen and accused Big Gun of "forcible rape resulting in death." The county magistrate, Zhuang Youyi, was unable to unravel any matter and was nicknamed "Mixed-up Zhuang" by the local people. When the investigation took place, the mother-in-law insisted that Big Gun was not guilty of "rape resulting in death." Eventually, the case closed with the verdict that the deceased had slipped into the water and died. This happened in the thirty-sixth year of Qianlong's reign [1771].

Two years later, a robbery occurred in Zhenzhe county and Big Gun was convicted and sentenced to beheading for the crime. This slightly vented the indignation felt by the local people but the case of "rape resulting in death" had already been closed and there was no way to overturn the former verdict. The chaste woman could thus not be rewarded with imperial praise. In the thirtieth year of Daoguang [1850], the local people again submitted the matter to local officials and sought imperial praise.

2. CHASTE WOMAN NI

Chaste Woman Ni was the daughter of Wang Tongfu of Renhe. At the age of seventeen, she married to Ni Dechang of Dongli. After three months she was widowed and afterwards unceasingly and with great care served her parents-in-law. After eight years, her parents-in-law, because of the family's poverty, sought to marry her. They secretly accepted marriage gifts and secretly set a date for the wedding to occur. The day before the marriage they told Woman Ni. She pretended to agree and gave her mother-in-law a short sleeved blouse and an earring saying: "This should be sufficient to support you for a few days." At midnight she jumped into the river and died.

The next morning, Woman Ni's father arrived. He said that he and his wife had dreamed that their daughter had come to tell them that she was dead. Moreover, she said that god had appointed her to be a river goddess and that she was not suffering. They all felt shocked and frightened. In the village the news was spread that a corpse, its face concealed by long hair, had been discovered under the Taiping Bridge. The clothes were tightly sewn together. They looked and found it to be Woman Ni.

When men drown, they lie in the water face down but when women drown, they lie in the water face up. This woman was lying face down and everyone was greatly surprised. This happened during the fourth moon of the eighth year of Daoguang [1828]. The next year, an edict of imperial praise adorned the gate of this family. The village people buried her under Xixia Hill near Nanjing.

13.2   Lu Xun: "My Views on Chastity," 1918

'The world is going to the dogs. Men are growing more degenerate every day. The country is faced with ruin!'—such laments have been heard in China since time immemorial. But 'degeneracy' varies from age to age. It used to mean one thing, now it means another. Except in memorials to the throne and the like, in which no one dares make wild statements, this is the tone of all written and spoken pronouncements. For not only is such carping good for people; it removes the speaker from the ranks of the degenerate. That gentlemen sigh when they meet is only natural. But now even murderers, incendiaries, libertines, swindlers, and other scoundrels shake their heads in the intervals between their crimes and mutter: 'Men are growing more degenerate every day!' . . .

Chastity used to be a virtue for men as well as women, hence the references to 'chaste gentlemen' in our literature. However, the chastity which is extolled today is for women only—men have no part in it. According to contemporary moralists, a chaste woman is one who does not remarry or run off with a lover after her husband's death, while the earlier her husband dies and the poorer her family the more chaste it is possible for her to be. In addition, there are two other types of chaste women: one kills herself when her husband or fiance dies; the other manages to commit suicide when confronted by a ravisher, or meets her death while resisting. The more cruel her death, the greater glory she wins. If she is surprised and ravished but kills herself afterwards, there is bound to be talk. She has one chance in ten thousand of finding a generous moralist who may excuse her in view of the circumstances and grant her the title 'chaste'. But no man of letters will want to write her biography and, if forced to, he is sure to end on a note of disapproval. . . .

Only a society where each cares solely for himself and women must remain chaste while men are polygamous, could create such a perverted morality, which becomes more exacting and cruel with each passing day. There is nothing strange about this. But since man proposes and woman suffers, why is it women have never uttered a protest? Because submission is the cardinal wifely virtue. Of course a woman needs no education: even to open her mouth is counted a crime. Since her spirit is as distorted as her body,[1] she has no objection to this distorted morality. And even a woman with views of her own has no chance to express them. If she writes a few poems on moonlight and flowers, men may accuse her of looking for a lover. Then how dare she challenge this 'eternal truth'? Some stories, indeed, tell of women who for various reasons would not remain chaste. But the story-tellers always point out that a widow who remarries is either caught by her first husband's ghost and carried off to hell or, condemned by the whole world, becomes a beggar who is turned away from every door till she dies a wretched death.

This being the case, women had no choice but to submit. But why did the men let it go at that? The fact is that after the Han dynasty most mediums of public opinion were in the hands of professional Confucians, much more so from the Song and Yuan dynasties onwards. There is hardly a single book not

1. This refers to the practice of binding women's feet.

written by these orthodox scholars. They are the only ones to express opinions. With the exception of Buddhists and Taoists who were permitted by imperial decree to voice their opinions, no other 'heresies' could take a single step into the open. Moreover, most men were very much influenced by the Confucians' self-vaunted 'tractability'. To do anything unorthodox was taboo. So even those who realized the truth were not prepared to give up their lives for it. Everyone knew that a woman could lose her chastity only through a man. Still they went on blaming the woman alone, while the man who destroyed a widow's reputation by marrying her or the ruffian who forced her to die unchaste was passed over in silence. Men, after all, are more formidable than women, and to bring someone to justice is harder than to utter praise. A few men with some sense of fair play, it is true, suggested mildly that is was unnecessary for girls to follow their betrothed into the grave; but the world did not listen to them. Had they persisted, they would have been thought intolerable and treated like unchaste women; so they turned 'tractable' and held their peace. This is why there has been no change right up till now. . . .

Are women themselves in favour of chastity? The answer is, No, they are not. All human beings have their ideals and hopes. Whether high or low, their life must have a meaning. What benefits others as well as oneself is best, but at least we expect to benefit ourselves. To be chaste is difficult and painful, of profit neither to others nor to oneself; so to say that women are in favour of it is really unreasonable. Hence if you meet any young woman and in all sincerity beg her to become a martyr, she will fly into a passion, and you may even receive a blow from the respected fist of her father, brothers, or husband. Nevertheless this practice persists, supported as it is by tradition and numbers. Yet there is no one but fears this thing 'chastity'. Women fear to be crucified by it, while men fear for their nearest and dearest. That is why I say no one is in favour of it.

On the basis of the facts and reasons stated above, I affirm that to be chaste is exceedingly difficult and painful, favoured by no one, of profit neither to others nor oneself, of no service to the state or society, and of no value at all to posterity. It has lost any vigor it had and all reason for existing.

Finally I have one last question.

If chastity has lost any vigor it had and all reason for existing, are the sufferings of chaste women completely in vain?

My answer is: They still deserve compassion. These women are to be pitied. Trapped for no good reason by tradition and numbers, they are sacrificed to no purpose. We should hold a great memorial service to them.

After mourning for the dead, we must swear to be more intelligent, brave, aspiring, and progressive. We must tear off every mask. We must do away with all the stupidity and tyranny in the world which injure others as well as ourselves.

After mourning for the dead, we must swear to get rid of meaningless suffering which blights our lives. We must do away with all the stupidity and tyranny which create and relish the sufferings of others.

We must also swear to see to it that all mankind know true happiness.

July 1918

13.3 LI DAZHAO: *THE VICTORY OF BOLSHEVISM*, 1918

Li Dazhao (1889–1927) was one of the co-founders of the Chinese Communist Party in 1921. He was a professor of philosophy and chief librarian at Peking University and an active participant in the New Culture Movement. In September 1918 he organized a "Marxist Research Society" and was one of the first Chinese intellectuals to hail the significance of the Bolshevik Revolution. The article translated here captures the spirit of Li Dazhao's first forays into Marxist theory and is an artifact of the earliest period of Communism in China.

When Li wrote *Bolshevism de shengli* (The victory of Bolshevism) there was, as yet, no numerically significant Communist organization in China, and most theoretical works by Marx and his followers had yet to be translated into Chinese. It is worth noting as well, that this article predates the announcement in spring 1919 of the Versailles peace settlement and the subsequent May 4th Movement. In the fall of 1918, Li Dazhao was already skeptical of the significance of the Allied victory in Europe and critical of those who interpreted it as a victory for China.

"Victory! Victory! Victory to the Allies! Surrender! Surrender! The Germans have surrendered!" On the doors of homes everywhere hang national flags and people all over are crying out "Wansui" [Long live!] Voices and the colors all seem to be expressions of these words. Men and women from the Allied countries run back and forth on the streets celebrating their victory; soldiers of the Allied countries loudly sing their victory songs in the cities. Suddenly there is the sound of breaking glass as the store windows of German merchants are broken and of a crash as the monument to Von Ketteler is pulled down.[2] And these sounds mix together with the noise of happy celebration. It goes without saying that foreign nationals of the Allied powers resident in our

---

2. Clemens von Ketteler was the German minister in Peking at the time of the Boxer Rebellion. He was shot by a soldier on June 20, 1900, when he ventured out to attempt negotiations with the Boxers. After the rebellion, per provision of the Boxer Protocol, a marble memorial arch was built to commemorate his death.

country are exceedingly happy. Even people in our country who had little to do with the changing situation in the world have felt obliged to engage in obsequious displays of happiness as they take the joy and glory of others as their own. In academic circles there are lantern parades, politicians hold celebratory meetings, and generals who never led a single soldier in the year or so that China participated in the war, review parades of troops and are awe-inspiringly martial. Political hacks who once wrote histories of the European war which argued that Germany must inevitably win and who then turned around to declare war on Germany now claim all merit for themselves and print articles in newspapers that advertise their own activities and declaim those of others. Little people like us in the world can only follow along and join in the commotion, celebrating the victory and shouting *wansui*. This is the situation as the Allied victory has been celebrated recently in Peking.

However, let us carefully consider all of this from our standpoint as members of the world's human race: In the final analysis, whose victory is this and who has really surrendered? Who has accomplished this task and who are we celebrating for? If we consider these questions, our generals who never led troops and yet flaunt their marital prowess and the shameless politicians who claim all merit for themselves, are truly disgraceful. It is also meaningless for the people of Allied counties to say that the war was a victory of Allied arms over the military forces of Germany. Their boasts and celebrations are totally meaningless for it is probable that their political hacks will soon share the same fate as German militarism.

In fact, the victory of Allied military strength over German military strength was not the true cause of the conclusion of this war; the real cause for victory was German socialism's defeat of German militarism. The German people were not obliged to surrender by Allied armed force; in actuality, Germany's emperor, warlords, and militarism were forced to surrender by the tide of world affairs. It was not the Allies who defeated German militarism but rather the spirit of the awakened people of Germany. The failure of German militarism was the failure of Germany's Hohenzollern family (the German imperial family) and not the failure of the German people. As for the victory over German militarism, it was not the victory of the Allies and it certainly was not the victory of either the military men in our country who are scrabbling to claim merit for their participation or the politicians who are opportunistically and cunningly promoting themselves. This was the victory of humanitarianism, pacifism, justice, freedom, democracy, and socialism. This was the victory of Bolshevism, the red flag, the working class of the world, and the victory of the new tide of the twentieth century. This accomplishment belongs not so much to Wilson and others as to Lenin, Kollontai, Leibknecht, Scheidemann, and Marx. This should not be a celebration merely for one country or a group within a certain country; rather, it should be a celebration of a new dawn for world mankind. It should be a celebration not of the victory of one side's military forces over the other but a celebration of democracy and socialism's triumph over monarchy and militarism. . . .

From the facts of what the "Bolsheviki" are doing, it is possible to see that their doctrine is revolutionary socialism and their party is a revolutionary socialist party. They honor the German socialist economist Marx as the founder of their doctrine. Their goal is to break down the national boundaries which today are the obstacle blocking socialism. They seek to destroy the monopoly capitalist system of production. The true cause of the war was the destruction of national boundaries because the expanded productive force of capitalism could not be contained by the national boundaries of today. The territories enclosed by national boundaries are too constricted to permit the development of productive force. Therefore, the capitalists depend on war to break down these boundaries and they want to create a global economic organization that will tie together all parts. Socialists agree with capitalists that international borders should be broken down, but the hope of capitalist governments is to give benefits to the middle classes of their countries. These governments depend on the global economic development of the capitalist class of the victorious countries of the world. They do not rely the humanistic and rational coordination and mutual help of the producers of the world. The victorious countries of this kind will because of this war advance and change in the future from powerful countries to imperialistic countries. The "Bolsheviki" observed this and cried out and announced that this war was the Czar's war, the Kaiser's war, a war of kings, a war of emperors, a war of capitalist governments, but not their war. Their war is class war. It is a war of the proletariat of the entire world against the capitalists of the world. Although they oppose war, they are not afraid of war. They believe that everyone, male or female, should work and that all workers should belong to a union. Every union should have a central governing council and such a council should be the basic organization for all the governments of the world. There will be no congresses, no parliaments, no presidents, no premiers, no cabinets, no legislative branches, and no rulers. Only councils of labor union will exist and they will decide everything. All industries will belong to the people working there; there will be no private ownership. The Bolsheviki will unite the proletariat of the entire world and use to the utmost their power and force of resistance to create a land of freedom and they will first create a democratic federation in Europe as the basis of a world federation. These are the new beliefs of the Bolsheviki and the new doctrine of world revolution in the twentieth century. . . .

Up to now, . . . there have been revolutions in Austria-Hungary, Germany, Bavaria, and there are rumors that revolutionary socialist parties are launching uprisings in Holland, Sweden, and Spain. The revolutionary situation in these countries is basically similar to that of Russia. Red flags are flying everywhere. Labor unions are being established one by after another. It can be said that this is a Russian-style revolution or it can be said that this is a twentieth-century-style revolution. The crashing waves of revolution cannot be halted by today's capitalist governments because the mass movements of the twentieth century have brought together world humankind into one great mass. Each person within this great mass unconsciously follows the motion of the mass and all are pulled together into a great, irresistible social force. When this global force begins to rumble, the wind roars throughout the whole world, clouds surge, there is a pounding in the mountains, and valleys echo with the sound. In the face of this global, mass movement, historical remnants—such as emperors, noblemen, warlords, bureaucrats, militarism, capitalism—and all other things that obstruct the advance of this new movement will be crushed by the thunderous force. When confronted by this irresistible tide, these remnants of the past are like withered leagues facing the bitter autumn wind; one by one they will drop to the ground. On all sides one sees the victorious banners of Bolshevism and everywhere one hears the victorious songs of Bolshevism. Everyone says that the bells are ringing! The dawn of freedom is breaking! Just take a look at the world of the future, it is sure to be a world of red flags!

I said once: "History is the general psychological record of people. People's lives are closely connected and linked with one another like parts of a big mechanism. The future of an individual corresponds to the future of all of mankind. The portents revealed by one event are interrelated with portents of the entire world situation. The French Revolution of 1789 was not merely a sign of the changed mentality of the French. It was actually a sign of the general changing mentality of 19th century man. The Russian Revolution of 1917 is not only an obvious omen of the changing mentality of 20th century man." The Russian Revolution is the first fallen leaf [sic] that warns the world of the coming of autumn. Although the word Bolshevism was coined by Russians, its spirit is a spirit of enlightenment that every member of mankind can share. Therefore, the victory of Bolshevism is the victory of the new spirit of enlightenment that all mankind can share in the twentieth century.

13.4 AND 13.5 TWO LETTERS ON THE WORK-STUDY PROGRAM IN FRANCE

The Société Franco-Chinois d'Education was organized in 1915 by Cai Yuanpei and other Chinese living in Paris and Toulouse. The goal of the program was to enable large numbers of Chinese "work-study" students to pursue studies in France while paying a large part of their living costs through labor in French workshops and factories. About two thousand Chinese students, largely from Hunan and Sichuan, participated in the program in its earliest phases; a French language school was set up in

Paris and arrangements were made with the College de Montargis, south of Paris, to admit "work-study" students to its classes.

The letters below trace the involvement of young Hunanese leftists of the *Xinmin Xuehui* (New People's Study Association) with the "work-study" program. In 1918, members of this organization, including Mao Zedong and Cai Hesen, left Hunan for Peking where, stimulated by contacts with Li Dazhao, Chen Duxiu, and other leaders of the New Culture Movement and by the political activism that grew out of the May 4th student strikes, they began forming the nucleus of China's Communist Party.

In these early stages of study and organization, would-be Chinese Communists were eager to broaden their understanding of Marxism-Leninism. In 1919 and 1920, works by Kautsky, Lenin, and *The Communist Manifesto* itself appeared in Chinese translation, and a variety of interpretations of Marxism, appeared in the pages of *New Youth, Construction* (Jianshe zazhi),[3] and other journals.

Mao Zedong's letter to fellow *Xinmin xuehui* member Tao Yi illustrates the hunger for new ideas, for knowledge of the world, and for an understanding of the European left that obsessed the young intellectuals who constituted China's proto-Communist movement in the year before the party was actually formed. The first of Cai Hesen's two letters from France describes in a homely way the conditions "work-study" students found when they arrived in Montargis and is full of enthusiasm for the experience of study abroad.

13.4   *Mao Zedong: Letter from Peking, 1920*

There is another important question and that is the question of "the allocation of these who will study abroad and those who will work [in China]." If we want to reach a kind of goal (reform), we must carefully consider the appropriate methods; one of these methods concerns the allocation of people involved. At a time like the present when it is difficult to find able people, we must be extremely economic in the use of talent. Otherwise, there will be overlaps, duplication, and waste. Some of our comrades in Paris are wildly dragging people off to France. It's a good thing to pull ordinary people off to study there but a mistake to take more comrades [of the New People's Society.] Our comrades should disperse to all parts of the world to carry out their investigations. People should go off to the ends of the earth but should not pile up together in a single place. The best thing would be for one person or several people to

3. Jianshe Zazhi was a theoretical organ of the Guomindang. It published a number of articles on Marxism written by major figures in Sun Yat-sen's political movement.

take responsibility for opening a new front. Our "battle formations" should be opened up in all areas and on all fronts a vanguard should sent forth.

Our few dozen members came to know each other quite late and it hasn't been long since we've been acquainted. [The New People's Society was formed in April 1918.] Thus, we have not been able to study these questions thoroughly (or never studied them at all). As for me, I was always too muddle-headed to be of much use and I am not very learned. On this trip [Mao refers to his first journey from Changsha to Peking], I have observed many things, met quite a few people, and pondered some matters. I feel that these questions are all very much worth studying. Many people in various places, like myself, have not studied very deeply and, like me, are still slumbering in the dark. How one sighs to think of it! You are very far-sighted and a person with great goals and I wonder what you think of what I have just said? I guess that you have already been aware of this for some time.

What I just said is still empty; let's be more specific.

The members of the New People's Society and the members of the Morning Sun Society should frequently hold discussion meetings to discuss our mutual goals and the methods to reach these goals. Members going abroad or working ought to be allocated in an appropriate way and take some responsibility in order to make this a consciously organized activity. In terms of our end goals, we should have a prearranged plan: How will we open up a new front in that situation? How can we introduce and recruit new members? How can we create a new life for ourselves? It's like this for you and it's also like this for our friends Wei, Zhou, and Lao. Other comrades in Changsha or those who have left Changsha should also be like this. In the future, I too, also want to follow this rule.

Above, I have sketched out some rough ideas. Let me follow with some trivial notes.

Our member Zhang Guoji has already arranged to go to southeast Asia and I entirely agree that he should go. Xiao Zizhang and a dozen or so others in Shanghai have already arranged to go to France. That is also good. Peng Huang and some others organized a work-study mutual aid group in Shanghai. That is also a good thing. Peng Huang and I do not want to go to France but have arranged to go to Russia. He Shuheng wants to study in France. I have urged him not to go to France and said that it is better to study in Russia. My own plan is that I will leave here after a week for Shanghai. After things in Hunan have calmed down, I will return to Changsha. I want to work together with our comrades to form "Free Study Society" (or it could be named Self-Cultivation University). It is foreseen that in one or two years we will be able to have a clear, basic sense of old, new, foreign, and Chinese ideas, and will be able to use them as tools for investigations (otherwise you can't make such investigations). Then we organize a team to study in Russia and go to Russia for work-study. As for women who want to go to Russia, there is no obstacle and I expect that Russian female comrades will especially welcome them. It would be possible to have a "Women's Work-Study Society in Russia" that could be modeled on the "Women's Work-Study in France." I am presently discussing this matter (studying in Russia) with Mr. Li Dazhao and others. I have heard that Mr. Tang Shoujun, the Fudan professor in Shanghai, the former president of the Institute of Commerce, also wants to go. Because of this matter, my mind is filled with joy and hope. Therefore, I have especially written to tell you. . . .

Mao Zedong
February, 1920, Beijing [Peking]

13.5   Cai Hesen: Letter from France, 1920

I have been away from you for more than three months. We are now living in two separate parts of the earth! I guess you are all still living in Changsha. We have been here in Montargis for just one month. We spent thirty-five days on the ship, two days in Marseille, and five days in Paris. . . . Montargis is a district of France located about two hundred kilometers from Paris. We live in the district capital. The school where I live is the local middle school (Li Shizeng, Cai Yuapei, and Wang Jingwei all graduated from here). The school where mother and sister are living is the local girls' middle school. The two schools are about two or three hundred paces from one another and so we see each other everyday. Our tuition and boarding charges are extremely cheap. It costs four hundred francs each for the three months of preparatory study. One Chinese silver dollar can be exchanged in Paris for twenty francs at the Chinese-French Industrial Bank. Every month each of us spends slightly more than six [Chinese] dollars (which includes laundry and sundry other things). As we see it now, everyday life in France is not much different from life in China. It's enough for each of us to spend one franc a day on bread and one franc for vegetables and meat. Village life in France is even cheaper than in China; forty francs a month are enough to cover room and board.

We plan to stay in these two schools for three months. Then Xianxi will go to work in the beancurd [doufu] factory and I will also go to a factory to work. Working conditions in the doufu factory are as follows: forty-eight hours of work a week, five days a week, therefore, nine hours of work per day. The wages depend on your output. The daily wages of the works range from six or seven francs to twenty francs. There are three types of work: 1. making dry bean cakes . . . ; 2. putting the beancurd in tubes . . . ; and 3. putting the beancurd into cardboard boxes.

On February 4th, we visited the doufu factory and we saw more than thirty French women workers and one Chinese woman worker (from Sichuan). Seven or eight of them were thirteen or fourteen. The ages of the rest ranged from seventeen or eighteen to thirty or forty. All three types of work are non-skilled labor. The day we visited the factory, Xiang Jingyu [Cai's fiance and later his wife] and I had a discussion with the manager, Mr. Qi, and made an arrangement to go and work there.

Mr. Qi was very excited about the prospect of selling Chinese embroidery in France and so he asked the eight newcomers whether any of them could do embroidery. He also mentioned that if those who come here in the future know embroidery, he is willing to sell the goods. The Women's Work-Study Society in the future should depend on embroidery for its development. Therefore, we hope very much that sisters Ajie and Liangjie can come over as soon as possible. Ren Peidao from Xupu Girls' School will definitely come this summer. I think it would be best for the whole family to come to France. . . .

The Société Franco-Chinoise d'Education bought a splendid big building in Paris. If it were in China it would cost at least fifty thousand Chinese dollars. But it cost only seventy thousand francs or so here and it can be paid for by installments for the next ten years. When I was in Shanghai, every one hundred Chinese dollars could be exchanged for twelve hundred francs. Afterwards, I heard that this amount could be exchanged for fifteen hundred francs. Now at the Chinese-French Industrial Bank, every one hundred Chinese dollars can be exchanged for more than two thousand francs. Therefore, when you bring money here in the future, don't exchange it in Shanghai. It's worth more in Paris. But the best currency is the silver dollar with Yuan Shikai's head on it. If Ajie gets two thousand dollars from her and comes to France, her money will be worth more than forty thousand francs and she can become a middle level capitalist.

The working situation here is generally quite good. Heavy labor pays more than twenty francs a day. Mechanics make twelve to thirty francs. Zhang Kundi now makes fourteen francs a day. If you exclude the money paid for food, he can save eleven to twelve francs a day. Every year he can save four thousand francs and when the value of the franc goes up in the future his savings will be more valuable. (When the franc is high the rate of exchange is two francs for one Chinese dollar.) If Brother Lu comes, he can do heavy labor or work as a mechanic. To do mechanical work takes three months of apprenticeship in the factory. During the period, the pay is eight to nine francs a day. If Liangjie can work things out with the land, father and Brother Qing can all come to France. The tailor in Buli village who once made the fur lined coat for me came to France last July. Now he has opened the Xiehe Restaurant in Paris and business is booming. If Brother Lu wants to come, there many things opportunities like this.

We hope that Ajie, Liangjie, and Li Zefen, Liu Jingyu, and Hu Yicheng can all come with the second group. . . . When you come bring a lot of rice powder, dried vegetables, and dried meat. The bread served on the boat is not as delicious

as what you get in France. If you get seasick, don't worry because no one dies
from seasickness. . . .

Hesen
Montargis, March 8, 1920

13.6 AND 13.7 THE NORTH CHINA FAMINE, 1920–1921

In 1920 and 1921 a famine devastated the agricultural economy of the
entire north China plain, virtually the same area that had been struck by
the massive drought and famine of 1876–1879 and little had been done
since then to correct the underlying problems that had aggravated the
social effects of the long dry spell of those years. Denuded hills, twisters of
loessial dust, wrecked irrigation works, and rutted and impassable roads
still bore testimony in 1920 to the patterns of overpopulation, land overuse,
and governmental neglect that had help wreck the economy of the region
forty years before.

In 1920 as in 1876, the crisis was precipitated by lack of rainfall before
the fall harvest. In the already densely inhabited agricultural counties of
the famine zone, where population often exceeded 1200 persons per
square mile, almost all peasants were entirely dependent on the grain
crop for their livelihood. Deprived of grain, they were driven to take the
few desperate steps that were available to peasants when a crop failed:
they bartered the valuable wooden parts of their houses or their livestock
for food; they took loans at interest rates of 3–5% per month; and, when
no other recourse was available, they sold their land at ruinous rates to
still well-to-do families and land speculators. As natural conditions grew
desperate in Zhili (Hebei), Henan, Shanxi, Shaanxi, and part of Shandong, social and economic ills easily visible even in ordinary times were
accentuated. The excerpts that follow were published originally in the
report of the Peking United International Famine Relief Committee.
During the north China famine, the Famine Relief Committee took
direct charge over relief efforts in west Zhili (Hebei) and played a coordi-
nating role in much of the rest of the disaster area. In 1920, many fewer
lives were lost than in the 1876–1879 famine, but as the first excerpt on
the "Severity of the Famine" shows, millions of peasants were nonetheless
left starving and destitute. The second document, part of a guide for
relief workers prepared by the famous educator Henry Fenn, warns of
the pitfalls awaiting famine workers seeking to distribute free relief rice
in the famished villages of north China. In this terrible landscape of
destruction with its armies, destitute sufferers there were also, those who
found devious means of manipulating the crisis for personal gain, as it is

possible to see if we read between the lines of Fenn's guide. Natural disasters in troubled times made the countryside a social tinder-box that could be set aflame by the slightest spark.

13.6 *Report on the North China Famine, 1922*

SEVERITY OF FAMINE

Much must be taken into consideration in discussing famine conditions in China. In the Western world, famine means something unusual—a most rare calamity. In semi-arid North China, it is a state more or less chronic. Thus in certain districts, like those about Tingchow or Shuntefu in Chihli, famine is almost a permanent condition and times of the most intense suffering are different from normal only in degree. There are no seven fat kine[4]—rather only seven lean kine and then seven a little more lean. The casual observer, going into such a district, is apt to say, "Oh, but this is almost the ordinary state." And so the report goes out that there is not famine and that we are but feeding beggars. On the other hand, someone not realizing the great resistance of the Chinese to hardship may go into the same district and jump to the conclusion that half the population is going to die, and propaganda for relief is started fully as undependable as the former report that there is no famine at all. Again one county may be fertile and prosperous owing to water supply, while its next neighbour is barren and destitute. For instance, a worker from the Shaho Chiao District states that there were no cases of severe privation in the immediate district but investigation of the outlying towns showed the people to be without any food other than bark and leaves. Thus no county can be taken as a clue to conditions in a province, nor even one or two villages as a standard of conditions in a county.

There is however no doubt that the famine of 1920–21 has been a real one. Workers in Shantung report intense privation. In Chanhwa County, 50 percent of the people in 250 villages were absolutely destitute. In Yucheng, the young crops died close to the earth in the fields which were as dry as the roads, and the starving poor were known to go out and dig up the wheat sprouts, still in the ground, in the fields of the more prosperous neighbors. In Lin Yi County, where throughout the last six years there had been but one year of good crops, there had been but one year of good crops, there were in the entire county, but a few pecks of grain and those been imported. Even chaff had been brought in from other regions. From the province of Zhili, similar reports are made. In the district about Shentefu 1/3 of a population of 1,093,000 were in direct need and there were 31,286 deaths from hunger and cold. In Tinghsein, the early

---

4. Plural of "cow" (archaic).

summer harvest was 30% of what it should have been. In a period of three weeks, last winter, investigation showed an average of 110 deaths a week, steadily increasing, in a district of half a million people. Workers throughout the Hantan District report a percentage of destitute varying from 5% in a few lightly stricken sections to 80%. In this district, a fair sample of suffering is the town of Yang Chao Chuang, of whose 100 homes, sixty contained no food except straw and leaves. There had been at least 100 farm animals and there were then but five. One fifth of the mud houses had the roofs torn off and all timbers sold. The area about Siao Chang was very badly hit. In Tsaochiang County investigation showed that undoubtedly 50% of the people would have starved and in Nankung County 75% but for the prompt arrival of relief.

There are many safe ways of determining the severity of a famine. One is by investigation of food supplies in a house to house canvass. Such an investigation throughout the entire famine area showed the following bill of fare for all the famine sufferers:—

Kang, mixed wheat blades
Flour made of ground leaves
Fuller's earth
Flower seeds
Poplar buds
Corn cobs
Hung Chin Tsai (steamed balls of some wild herb)
Sawdust
Thistles
Leaf dust
Poisonous tree bean
Kaoliang husks
Cotton seeds
Elm bark
Bean cakes (very unpalatable)
Peanut hulls
Sweet potato vines, ground (considered a great delicacy)
Roots
Stone ground up into flour to piece out the ground leaves.

Some of this food was so unpalatable that children starved, refusing to eat it. Yet so common was dependence on this food that in many districts the relief workers investigating thousand of homes, very rarely found any store of grain commonly used in food. It is very true, that many millions of people were able to eke out their existence by the reliance on food such as above.

Another test was the economic crippling of the people. Almost every worker reporting from Siao Chang District speaks of the numbers of formerly fine farms, with houses now roofless, the straw in the mud thatch having been used as fuel, every bit of timber either sold or burned, no stocks of fuel in the courtyards, the absence of all animals. In Ling Hsien, Shantung, 138 houses in 24 villages had been completely torn down. The decrease of land values among an agricultural people, shows how disheartened they have become by the long failure of crops. Near Lin Ming Kuan in Hantan District, land worth formerly $100.00 per mou, is now selling for $3.00 to $4.00 per mou. In stricken districts of Shantung, ground formerly worth 100,000 cash would not sell now for 20,000 cash with the wheat actually planted. Farm implements are unsalable except when they are of wood and can be used as fuel.

A further test was the large migration of people from affected districts. Many workers remark the absence of younger men in the villages. They have all gone away to find work in new places or perhaps even to beg in the large cities. One worker in the Tsinan District speaks of "whole villages entirely deserted." In Feihsiang Hsien in the Hautan District, 3,000 men left their homes, (in this hsien also 5,000 children were sold.) From Shang Kwong in the same district, all the younger people had gone, both men and women. Almost every writer in the Techow District in Shantung mentions the numbers of homes plastered up from which the families have fled. Techow itself was crowded with refugees. About the stations where grain was being unloaded the frantic people would crowd so close to the cars in the hope that a little grain would be spilled, that many accidents and deaths were caused. All day, people in rags huddled in the streets scraping up the dust of the road in search of a grain of food. In Paotingfu, great hardship was caused among the poor whose friends came to stay with them and among the rickshaw coolies because the influx of men meant more competition and a decrease of income. In Tingchow, refugees slept in the streets by the score and every worker mentions seeing deaths by starvation among these people.

There must have been at least a million people who thus left their homes and went to other parts. They journeyed up and down the railroads, going as far as Mongolia, and the North district of Manchuria. They poured through the passes into the Provinces of Shansi and Shensi, an already affected area in the hope of finding means of livelihood. To a lesser degree they went South to the rice growing regions. One other strange fact is that people under such circumstances migrated to the cold North rather than to the warm South.

Another test of the severity of the famine was the number of children sold. One worker who has been twenty years in Honan Province states that never in all that time has he seen such an unprecedented sale of children. In Shang Kwong near Hantan, a town of some 250 people, 40 to 50 children were sold. In the district of Shuntefu, 25,443 children were sold. Children were sold into various positions—sometime as servants, sometimes as concubines or into the cities as prostitutes, sometimes to be secondary wives. One father in Chingehow in Shantung sold his son for 150 catties of corn, but in this case, the child was to be the son and heir of a rich man so the father could be well pleased. It is to be remembered that these famine sufferers are not beggars but sturdy, self-respecting industrious farmer folk, who think highly of their children and would only part with them in case of the greatest suffering.

Finally the intensity can be shown by the death rate. There are no reliable statistics on this matter and any statement is merely a guess. One of the most conservative committees in their estimate of destitute report a death rate of 100 a day in each Hsien of their district before a large measure of relief went in. A low estimate of the loss of life due to starvation would be half a million people. This was kept down by the wonderful ability of the Chinese people to adapt themselves to starvation conditions and live on things no other nation would deem fit for use as food, by the mild winter which cut down the deaths from cold, and by the lack of large epidemics of typhus due to the policy of keeping people in their homes, instead of concentrating them in camps. But the largest factor is undoubtedly the action of the relief committees and Government in taking measures to alleviate conditions. Had it not been for this, there would have been a higher death rate, probably equalling that of the earlier years.

13.7 Henry C. Fenn: "Notes on Field Work in the Distribution of Grain Tickets in Shundeh Fu"

1. Personal Investigation Method.
   1. Travel preferably in pairs.
   2. On arrival at a village find one of these:
      a. Ts'un Cheng—the village chief
      b. Ts'un Fu—the vice-chief
      c. Ti Fang—the sheriff
   3. Ask him to lead you to the desperately needy homes only.
   4. Inspect hastily, noting the following:
      a. Do the people keep animals?
      b. Do the rolls of bedding correspond to the number of mouths the family claims?
      c. Are there any locked doors? A lot of hurried concealment took place when you entered the village.
      d. Look for the dog's bowl and see what he eats.
      e. Did the guide bring you to this house of his own accord or because someone called to him in passing?
      f. Is there more than one family in the court? If so, do they seem to be parts of one family broken up for the occasion?
      g. Are there signs of flour on

the sifter which probably hangs on the wall in the central room?

h. Look in the "kwoa" and see what the people eat.

i. The man is probably out—may be just outside the court listening. His wife will tell you she is a widow.

j. Don't let anyone talk unless spoken to.

k. Is the house regularly inhabited or fixed up?

   1. A genuine house is not likely to be very clean, a fake is newly swept.

   2. In a genuine house, the pegs from which door curtains hang have dust on top.

   3. In a genuine house there is a "kwoa" and signs of recent fire.

   4. A genuine house smells as though it were inhabited. A fake is cold and clammy.

5. Have extra buildings been torn down and their timbers sold or burned?

6. Beware:

   a. Invitations to eat. Accept food and you accept an obligation. Don't accept anything but tea.

   b. Paying the slightest attention to a pleader. You will be mobbed.

   c. Accepting anything on hearsay. Go and see for yourself.

   d. Changing your mind. Once you have written a ticket don't change it. You will be mobbed by applicants.

CHAPTER 14

The Fractured Alliance

14.1 SUN YAT-SEN OPENS THE WHAMPOA ACADEMY, 1924

The Whampoa Military Academy was formed in the spring of 1924 on the former site of a Qing naval school. Guomindang leaders and their Comintern advisers hoped that over time graduates of the school would create a cadre of highly motivated young officers who could promote the cause of revolution and help train a reliable party army. Soviet financial aid and advice was of vital importance in launching this project, which was heavily influenced by models drawn from the experience of the Red Army. In the ranks of Whampoa's training staff were skilled political workers and talented soldiers who built a framework for military education that made the school the most advanced of its type in China.

At the time of Whampoa's founding, Chiang Kai-shek was named commandant of the academy and Liao Zhongkai was its political representative; working under their direction were such luminaries as Wang Jingwei, Hu Hanmin, Zhou Enlai, He Yingqin, Deng Yanda, and Ye Jianying. In future years early graduates of Whampoa, often former classmates, would lead the armies of both the Guomindang and the Communist Party in the bloody struggles of the civil war and play central roles in the life of their respective political parties.

Sun Yat-sen's speech at the opening ceremonies of the Whampoa Academy on June 16, 1924, expresses the exalted hopes Guomindang leaders invested in military training and the drama of this moment in the history of Republican China. Martyrdom, unselfishness, adherence by military men to the dictates of a revolutionary party, the notion that revolution begins in the human heart, and other themes found in this speech were

already cliches in the political rhetoric of 1924 but this would not deprive
them of merit as terms of exhortation in the eyes of party spokesmen of
later years.

Honored guests, faculty, and students, today marks the opening of our academy. Why do we need this school? Why must we definitely open such a school?
You all know that the Chinese Revolution has gone on for thirteen years;
although these years have been counted as years of the Republic there has been,
in reality, no Republic. After thirteen years of revolution, the Republic is just
an empty name and, even today, the revolution is a complete failure.

How have revolutions elsewhere in the world that began after our revolution
fared? Six years ago, during the European War, in a neighboring country, a
country larger than China, a country that shares a border of more than ten
thousand *li* with China and that touches both Asia and Europe, a revolution
broke out some six years after our revolution. What country was this? It was
Russia. Despite the fact that the Russian Revolution took place six years after
that of China, they have thoroughly succeeded in obtaining revolutionary
results. . . .

We can obtain a great lesson from tracing the causes for the difference
between the results of the Russian and Chinese revolutions. And it is because
we understand this lesson that we have come together to begin this school today.
What is the lesson? When the revolution broke out in Russia, revolutionary
party members served as the vanguard in the struggle against the Russian Czar.
After the success of the revolution, they immediately organized a revolutionary
army that continuously struggled for the revolution, it achieved success in a
short period of time despite the numerous obstacles it encountered.

Because of the struggle of revolutionary martyrs in China, when the revolution broke out in Wuchang, the various provinces responded, overthrew the
Manchu dynasty, and established the Republic. Our revolution, then, was par-
tially successful. But later there was no revolutionary army to continue the goals
of the revolutionary party and, therefore, although there was a partial success,
warlords and bureaucrats continue today to usurp the power of the Chinese
Republic. As for the basis of our Republic, there is none. Simply speaking, the
reason is that our revolution is supported by the struggle of a revolutionary
party but not by the struggle of the revolutionary army. Because we lack the
struggle of a revolutionary army, bureaucrats and warlords are able to control
our republic and our revolution is incapable of completely succeeding.

What is our hope is starting this school today? Our hope is that from today
on we will be able to remake our revolutionary enterprise and use the students
of this school as the foundation of a revolutionary army. You students will be
the basic cadres of the revolutionary army of the future. With such excellent
cadres as soldiers of the revolutionary army, our revolutionary enterprise will
definitely succeed. Without a good revolutionary army, the Chinese revolution

is doomed to failure. Therefore, in opening this military academy here today, our sole hope is to create a revolutionary army to save China from extinction!

What is a revolutionary army? What sort of resolve should those of you who have come to this school to study possess to become revolutionary soldiers? What qualifications should you have to call yourselves revolutionary soldiers? To become revolutionary soldiers, you should take the martyrs of the revolution as your models, you should learn from revolutionary party members, and you should study the revolutionary struggle of the party. Only when the struggle of the party and army are the identical is there a revolutionary army. None of the armies that have taken part in China's revolutionary struggles in the last thirteen years have shared the same goals as the revolutionary party. I venture to say that in these years there has been no revolutionary army. Quite a few armies in Guangdong have worked with us in the struggle of our revolutionary party, but none of them can be called a revolutionary army. But if these armies have worked with our revolutionary party, why do I dare not call them revolutionary armies? The reason I cannot call these armies revolutionary armies is that the elements who make them up are too complicated, have had no revolutionary training, and have no revolutionary foundation. What is a revolutionary foundation? A revolutionary foundation is something that inspires the same behavior as that of martyrs of the revolution. . . .

You gentlemen who have come to study here from the far corners of China, were no doubt aware even before you arrived that it is our goal to build a kind of revolutionary army. To join our revolutionary enterprise, you must surely possess a sort of powerful resolve. Where should the starting point of the revolutionary enterprise be? It should be in your own heart. You should eradicate from your hearts all bad thoughts and habits; you should eliminate all animalistic or evil traits of character that are not in keeping with humanity and righteousness. Therefore, if you want to make a political revolution you should start by making a revolution in your hearts. If you can revolutionize your hearts, there is hope that you will succeed in the political revolution. If you cannot make a revolution in your hearts, even though you study military science in this fully equipped military academy, you cannot become a revolutionary soldier in the future or accomplish the revolutionary enterprise. Therefore, if you gentlemen want to make a revolution you must have a revolutionary will and if you have this revolutionary will, then in the future you can become the commanders and generals of the revolutionary army. If we want to succeed in our revolution, we must resolve today that for our whole lives we will not have the idea of "becoming officials and making money." We seek only to save the people and the nation and to enact the Three People's Principles and the Five Power Constitution. Only by wholeheartedly pursuing revolution can we reach the goals of the revolution. Otherwise, even if you gentlemen start your own armies, win many battles, obtain much land, and control tens of thousands of people, you still can not be called revolutionary soldiers. . . .

Whether an army can make revolution depends upon whether its generals and soldiers have a revolutionary resolve; it does not depend on how good its weapons are. . . . In the future, when you graduate and organize a revolutionary army you should be willing to give up your lives to overcome obstacles facing the Republic and have the spirit of one person fighting to overcome one hundred. What is the source of such a spirit? What sort of person should you use as a model to be a revolutionary soldier? Simply put, you should use the martyrs of the revolution as your model and study their behavior. Like them you should sacrifice yourselves for humanity and singlemindedly sacrifice all of your rights to save the country. Only then can you become a revolutionary soldier with no fear of death. . . . Death is something we welcome. To die before the bullets and shells of the enemy is something we especially welcome. With such great courage and resolve, one can defeat one hundred. The enemy believes that to live is to be happy; we believe that to die is to be happy and that when we die we reach our goals. There is such an enormous difference regarding life and death between the enemy and us that they are no match for us and we are invincible.

14.2 A. I. Cherepanov on Life in Whampoa

The Soviet Union played an instrumental role in the foundation of the Whampoa Academy in the spring of 1924. Comintern funds were used to subsidize the Academy and Russian advisers were brought to China to supervise the training of the cadets corps.

One of the first three Russian officers to work at Whampoa was A. I. Cherepanov, a former enlisted man in the Czarist army and veteran of the Red Army during the Russian Civil War, who arrived in Canton in January 1924. Cherepanov, who later became a general in the Soviet Army, worked directly under the leadership of Michael Borodin and after the death of Stalin publicly credited Borodin for his keen grasp of a complex political milieu in China that baffled other Russian advisers.

In these excerpts from Cherepanov's memoirs, *As Military Adviser in China*, written some forty years after the opening of Whampoa, he describes the first months of his mission to China and some of the difficulties encountered in building the foundations for a new "party army."

By November 1924, there were 1,500 people in the Whampoa School including 62 teachers and officers, 131 administrative workers, 950 cadets, 120 messengers and 237 service personnel.

It was agreed with Sun Yat-sen that the school would mostly provide training for a period of 6 months. In addition, there were special classes offered: artillery

(60 cadets—9 to 12 months), engineer (130 cadets—9 months), signal (30 cadets—9 months), and logistics (60 cadets—6 months). The machine-gun class provided a 20-hour course for 120 infantry cadets.

Later, training of political officers was organized at the school, and it was officially called the Central Military Political School.

The school also had classes in Russian (25 cadets), fencing and gymnastics.

The teachers were chosen from among officers with sufficiently high general qualifications, but with different military education: some finished military school abroad, mostly in Japan, others were trained in the old Chinese military school in Baoding or provincial schools with the private armies of individual warlords.

Of course, in our daily work at the Whampoa School we constantly encountered resistance on the part of officers from the warlords, armies and the Guomindang members who ostensibly supported Sun Yat-sen's death. Whampoa had grown strong enough as a revolutionary center on its own, and, in addition, two and a half months following Sun's death, a powerful revolutionary movement initiated by the Shanghai proletariat (the May Thirtieth Incident) began.

On the whole, the Whampoa School under Sun Yat-sen became his armed foothold.

The cadets had mostly been students of secondary and higher schools in Guangzhou, Shanghai and other cities. These young people had already passed through the revolutionary school of student struggle and were resolved to fight for the ideals personified in Sun Yat-sen.

Whereas there were 39 Communists in the first graduating class, there were almost no workers. Later, special courses were set up at the school for uneducated volunteers from among the common people, largely peasants and the urban poor. The government set about to train military and revolutionary personnel from among the inhabitants of all the provinces in China. This task was accomplished.

In 1925, 2,500 cadets were graduated in the third year of the Whampoa School.

They included 25 Koreans and 10–15 Vietnamese. This reflected the desire of Sun Yat-sen, the revolutionary wing of the Guomindang, and the Communist Party of China to help the peoples of neighboring countries in training personnel.

Ho Chi Minh, who was in Guangzhou in 1924–1925, maintained relations with the Vietnamese cadets in the Whampoa School and supervised their education.

I had happened to meet Ho Chi Minh several times at Borodin's, but at the time I had no way of knowing that he would become the leader of the Vietnamese working people, founder of the Vietnam Workers' Party and the first president of the Democratic Republic of Vietnam.

By their social origin the cadets may be broken down as follows: 1,640 peasants, 1090 workers, 400 merchants, 400 students, 10 soldiers, 15 employees and 12 intellectuals.

The fourth graduating class was approximately the same.

In those years, military personnel was being trained not only in the south of China, but also in Soviet Russia. Many future outstanding leaders of Chinese Communists of the 1920's were trained in Soviet schools and colleges.

At the Whampoa School we distributed duties in the following manner: Vladimir Polyak was senior adviser and dealt with training. He worked directly with General Wang Mayou. Nikolai and I supervised drill, rifle practice and tactical training and dealt with General He Yingqin in our work.

The principal difficulty we first encountered was the absence of interpreters. We spoke English and Chinese very poorly, and for that reason were unable to check the theoretical knowledge or the lectures of the teachers and introduce the necessary changes. To an even less extent were we able to conduct an independent course.

Due to the different levels of knowledge among the teaching staff, the cadets received uneven training. The first problem that we solved successfully was the more or less sensible allocation of time between the different subjects. Taking into account the limited time allowed for the course (only six months), we decided to allot the most time to practical training.

However, on this issue, we immediately encountered General Wang Mayou's stubbornness. We had to spend a lot of time trying to persuade him, and at times we failed altogether.

The teachers proved to be just as stubborn in opposing everything new. In all their lectures the narrative prevailed over the demonstration. Even the company and platoon commanders had this shortcoming. With time, however, they began to accept and implement our suggestions. Generally speaking, the commanders were more democratic. Many of them, if not all, were displeased with the high-handed manners of the "gods" from among the teaching staff. Therefore, the commanders listened to our advice more readily and began to work according to our programmes.

14.3–14.5   R E A C T I O N S   T O   T H E   M A Y   T H I R T I E T H   I N C I D E N T

After the formation of the United Front in 1924, demonstrations of anti-imperialism were actively encouraged by spokesmen of the Nationalist and Communist Parties. Renunciation of the Unequal Treaties became a central goal of the Canton government. Boycotts of foreign goods and massive parades through the streets of Treaty Port cities signaled that anti-imperialism could draw popular support for the Nationalist revolution. Simultaneously, labor organizers in China's major industrial cities, many

of them Chinese Communists, adeptly capitalized on anti-imperialist sentiment to organize strikes and marches that dramatized the hellish plight of
Chinese workers in foreign factories.

On May 30, 1925, a march in Shanghai to protest the murder of a
worker in a Japanese textile mill was met by British police, who killed
eleven Chinese and wounded scores of others. This murder of innocents
inflamed popular opinion, and in the weeks that followed sympathetic protests erupted throughout China. The May Thirtieth Incident and its aftermath aggravated the tensions already present in the Nationalist coalition.
The Chinese Communist Party used the passions inspired by May Thirtieth to add thousands of new members to its ranks. For the first time in
the history of the United Front it began to emerge as a credible political
force. The Nationalists, in contrast, issued strident declarations but worried that the mass demonstrations, if carried too far, might have incalculable effects.

The three documents that follow give a sense of how the May Thirtieth
disturbances were perceived by contemporary observers and participants.
The outraged manifesto of the Peking professors, dated June 9, 1925,
shows the kind of political and moral conclusions that the Chinese intelligentsia drew from May Thirtieth. Consul General J. W. Jamieson's cool
and self-serving description of the Shameen massacre of June 23, 1925, in
which fifty-two Chinese were killed with no fatalities on the British side,
is in striking contrast to the veteran Guomindang politician Zou Lu's fiery
polemic on the same topic. Chinese national aspirations, whether adopted
by the left or right, were clearly on a collision course with imperialism.
Machine guns, sand bags, and strands of concertina wire were temporarily
sufficient to rout the impassioned demonstrators of 1925, but enduring battle lines of principle and theory had been drawn.

14.3   *Peking Professors on the Shameen Massacre*

The tragedy which has taken place in the International Settlement of Shanghai
has filled the Chinese nation with horror and indignation. However, facts have
been invariably distorted by different agencies for different purposes. Seeing
that misrepresentations would not only aggravate the injustice done to the dead
and the living, but may also tend to ferment other grave conflicts between the
Chinese and foreigners, we feel it our duty to give the facts for the information
of the world at large. Those who think with us that international harmony and
justice are desirable will not fail, we trust, to pay due attention to the matter.
The facts are clear enough. Strikes of Chinese workers, demanding the increase
of wages, had been going on for some time in the Japanese cotton factories at
Tsingtao and Shanghai, and a striker was shot and killed by the Japanese with-

out any justifiable cause. Against this brutal act some Chinese students, who were merely young boys and girls, paraded as a manifestation of protest in the streets of Shanghai on May 30 last. They were armed with nothing more than pamphlets and handbills. The police of the International Settlement, who are practically under the complete control of British officials and Consul not only saw fit to prohibit the demonstration but also arrested a number of the students taking part in it. Then the rest of the students went to the police station demanding the release of their fellow students. The police ordered the former to disperse. As they refused to go a British police inspector ordered "Shoot to kill." Six of the boys were killed on the spot and over forty severely wounded. This did not, however, prevent the defenseless students from repeating their demonstration, so the firing of rifles and machine guns continued by the British controlled police for at least six days. The exact number of casualties is still unacertainable, but most reports show that at least seventy were killed and 300 wounded. They were all Chinese, and not a single British or any other national appears on the casualty list. Would any right-minded people regard these boys and girls as rioters and treat them with bullets and rounds of machine guns? Could their manifestation be reasonably interpreted as "anti-foreign" or "Bolshevised" as some foreign-owned news agencies suggested? Were not the acts of the authorities deliberately committed, considering the fact that they did not cease for a period of six days? Why did not the British and Japanese Ministers in Peking give instructions to stop the killing immediately, if they did not approve or countenance it? These are the questions we want only to submit and not to answer. People in Europe and America might think it unbelievable that officials of civilized Governments could ever commit or countenance such infernal acts, but explanations can be easily found if one realizes that foreigners in China have long been privileged by stipulations of unjust treaties, and thereby have lost such sense of moral and legal responsibilities as their fellow-men hold in their home lands. Now bitter feelings prevail among all classes of the Chinese people; strikes in British and Japanese factories and boycotts against British and Japanese goods are spreading throughout the country. The Ministers and Consuls of Great Britain and Japan are still trying and may continue to try to uphold their prestige by their rifles and gunboats, but would their fellow men at home allow them to go on with this kind of atrocity? Would not the common conscience of mankind demand to have the wrongdoers punished and the wrongs righted?

14.4 *British Consul J. W. Jamieson on the Shameen Massacre*

In the forenoon of the 23rd, knowing that a monster demonstration was going to take place in the course of the day, the naval and civilian defense units of the British and French concessions took up their allotted posts with strict instructions—at least on this side—to keep, in so far as it was possible to do so, out of sight and all persons not on duty were forbidden to appear on the back creek opposite to the road along which the procession was to pass, so that nothing which might be construed as provocation could be charged against us. These orders were strictly observed. Through a British subject, recently engaged as liaison police officer by the city police, a request was the previous evening addressed to the French consulate that permission be given for the procession to enter Shameen by the French bridge and to leave by the British bridge, which request was of course not entertained.

At 11 a.m. two motor cars passed along the Shakee Street, on the other side of the canal, and distributed leaflets, signed by the cadets of the military school of the Guangdong army, calling upon all and sundry to eject the foreigner. At about 2:30 p.m. the procession was at the end of the Shakee Street, which commences at the gate of the French bridge, and proceeded along the north bank of the canal. The only persons in the vicinity of our bridge were myself, the British senior naval officer, the superintendent of Shameen police, one or two naval officers, a member of my staff and some unarmed Chinese police, who, being Hakkas, had not walked out with the rest of the Chinese on the island on the 21st. (The customs employees left on the 23rd and the post office employees on the 24th.) Unarmed Chinese police lined the road on the other side at intervals of about 50 yards and a company of armed soldiers took up positions under the verandas of Chinese shops in the neighbourhood of the bridge. Three-quarters of the procession, consisting of labour, agricultural and other unions, marched along in an orderly manner with flags and banners, and I was actually on the point of leaving to send a telegram that all had passed off peacefully, when the senior naval officer remarked to me that perhaps it would be as well to wait until the students came along. In the course of a few minutes bodies of male and female students came in sight, and, on crossing the invisible line separating the British from the French concession, started to raise what I assumed to be college yells, and, in so far as I could understand, calling for cheers for the Kuo Min Tang. In other respects they did not differ from those preceding them.

Immediately following on was a body of armed military cadets dressed in dark bluish-grey uniforms, who halted at a point some 50 yards east of the bridge-head. I had in the meantime noticed a man get on a box at the mouth of Shoe Lane, which debouches on the canal side, and wave a fan, and at the same time an excited person waving a flag shouted derision at our party.

Some members of the procession fell out, as I thought, to listen to what was being said, when suddenly a rifle shot was heard, and the procession broke up in disorder, rushing for shelter. Half a minute afterwards a volley was fired on to Shameen, and it was only when I found bullets spattering all around me that I realized that an attack was contemplated and beat a hasty retreat, as did those with me. Finding the senior naval officer and myself under fire, which was likewise affecting them, one of our posts in a building to the west of the bridge returned the fire, which was stopped on Commander Maxwell-Scott reaching it. As, however, firing at the island still continued, the other posts opened fire likewise, as did the French posts. This is all I personally witnessed.

Firing from our side lasted intermittently for about 10 minutes, until the orders to cease fire could reach the further posts, all ways of communication being under fire. After this occasional shots were necessary to deal with snipers, who were very persistent on the other side. Even this was soon stopped by orders not to reply unless they became too dangerous. About 4:30 all firing on both sides stopped. The casualties on Shameen were 1 French non-combatant killed, 7–8 Europeans and Japanese wounded, including 1 British subject—also non-combatant—comparatively seriously, and the Commissioner of Customs slightly. The casualties on the other side are reported to be 37 killed, including 1 woman, 4 students of the Canton Christian College and a teacher, and about 80 wounded.

A despatch on subsequent developments follows.

I have, &c.

J. W. JAMIESON.

14.5 *The President of Guangzhou University on the Shameen Massacre*

Since the day our country was forced to sign the unequal treaties by the Imperialists, she has suffered a good deal through the eighty long years of foreign political and economic aggression. Through sheer love of peace our people have maintained from first to last, a tolerant and yielding attitude. Unexpectedly, the more magnanimous we are in our attitude of tolerance, the greater the pressure of the Imperialists becomes. Since May of the present year, successive massacres of Chinese by the British, Japanese, and French have actually taken place. Those responsible for the massacre make use of xenophobia as a pretext for exciting international ill will so as to conceal their own evil acts and prolong their brutal conduct, thereby jeopardizing constantly the lives of our Chinese citizens. That the nations of the world may get a true view of the case and the real aims of our people, we now undertake to lay before you the cases relating to the massacre of Chinese by the British, Japanese, and French Imperialists since last May so that in the future similar massacres may be effectively prevented. . . .

On the 23rd of June, there again occurred the Great Shaki Massacre in Canton. On the day in question, the labourers, peasants, merchants, students, and men from every walk of life, held a mass meeting to express their sorrow for the labourers and students of Shanghai and Hankow, who were wantonly massacred by the Japanese and British, and unanimously passed the proposal for the abolishment of unequal treaties. A solemn and orderly parade followed.

When they arrived at Shaki Road, which runs parallel to Shameen, (a small island used by the foreigners as residential and business quarters) and is separated from it by a creek from 70 to 100 feet wide, the British and French soldiers and policemen suddenly swept the paraders and bystanders with machine guns. The French gunboat anchoring near by a also opened fire against the crowd. More than 60 persons were killed and over a hundred wounded on the spot. The whole affairs was so sudden that the military cadets in the rear had to rush forward its rescue. But for this timely assistance, the casualties would exceed the present number. After this, the British Consul in fraudulent language with a view to extricating himself from guilt alleged that the Chinese started fire first. According to the order of the procession on that day, the labourers and peasants came first, next came the merchants, then came the boy and girl students of the various schools, and the military cadets brought up the rear. Those first fired upon by the British troops were the unarmed boy and girl student in the front group, and the men, women, and children who stood on both sides of the street. If the military students were the first to open fire, followed by a reply from the British and French, then the casualties on the part of the paraders would be among the military cadets. Why should the unarmed students and citizens in front be the ones to fall? What fight could such a dense unarmed crowd put up when passing along a narrow street, and how could they intrude upon Shameen with its gates and bridges securely bolted and with a body of water in between? Moreover, there were many policemen and others holding white banners and maintaining order so that there should be no room for any misunderstanding.

Subsequent investigation after these events revealed the fact that the British had several gun-boats sent up and had Shameen piled up with sand-bags and mounted with guns and rifles. Had they no murderous intent wherefore such stern preparations? Moreover, the bullets used against the crowd were dum-dum bullets and the like, which are severely prohibited by International Law. These bullets pierce into the flesh and cause fearful gashes, tearing the flesh at the other end ten times larger than at the first entrance, causing the seriously wounded ones to die immediately and rendering the slightly wounded incurable. Such is the extent of the brutality and inhumanity. Therefore, the American, German, and Russian people residing in Canton, have all raised their voices against such barbarous acts. This act shows that justice is still present in the human mind. . . .

CHOW LU [Zou Lu], President
National Kwangtung University,
Canton, dated July 14, 1925.

14.6–14.8   PURGING THE CCP: THREE DOCUMENTS

The purge of the Communists from the United Front in the spring of 1927 drastically altered the character of the Guomindang. The party began almost immediately to retreat from the radical social programs and politics of confrontation it had grudgingly lent its name to since 1924. Instead, it sought to promote the Three People's Principles as a panacea for all of China's ills and forsook the path of class struggle for good. In the weeks that followed Chiang's attack on his erstwhile allies, civilian and military spokesmen for the Guomindang were obliged to justify their actions, whip up enthusiasm for the purge policy, and send warnings to workers and others who still admired and supported the Communists.

The three documents that follow, all published within days of the start of roundups and summary executions of Communists in Shanghai and Guangzhou, show how the Nationalists attempted to carry out these political goals. The party statement outlines the rationale for expulsion, the slogans are designed to motivate correct thought, and the army division's proclamation provides ominous suggestions of the fate awaiting Chinese workers who forsake "endurance and obedience" to take part in strikes, walkouts, and other political activities.

14.6   *Official Statement by the Guomindang, April 1927*

To understand clearly the objects of the movement for the purification of the Guomindang Party, it is necessary to know first the actual conditions of the present time. We have not yet accomplished the aims of the Revolution. We are only at the beginning of the task; and while victory is already in sight, it is of the utmost importance at this juncture to carry on the Revolution to a successful end. We must stand together and face the common cause with a united mind. The slightest neglect on our part will not only defeat the Revolution, but will also make it impossible to attain the objects of liberty and equality for the Chinese nation.

Therefore, all members of the party must know the gravity of their responsibility. At this critical moment, the undesirable elements are unscrupulously and untiringly doing the work of destruction, and if we do not check it in an effective manner, it will not only mean the fall of the Party but also the failure of the Revolution. With this in view, we adopt the following for the purification of the Party. First, to purge the Party of the Communists, and Secondly, to purge the Party of the opportunists and other undesirable elements.

It will be remembered that when Dr. Sun Yat-sen admitted members of the

Communist Party into the Guomindang, he was quite aware of the fact that Communism was not fit for China. But as the Communist Party members were ready to give up their Communistic belief, and willing to be directed by the Guomindang in order to co-operate in the work of the Revolution, it was only natural that they should be admitted into the Party. But since the beginning of the Northern Expedition, while members of the Guomindang have been labouring faithfully either on the field of battle or elsewhere, and while the militarists of the country have been gradually eliminated, the Communists, taking advantage of our success, have seized important cities as their centres for propaganda and usurped the power of the Party. Our military successes are being utilized by them to inflame the undesirable sections of the populace to undermine our forward move and to create disturbances in the rear.

Aside from the Communistic members who are to be condemned, there are also the opportunists and other undesirable elements in the Party. It is they who shamefully steal the name of the Party for their selfish gains, and it is also they who falsely use the power of the party for their personal activities and aggrandizement. Theirs is a crime no less serious than that of the Communists.

For the welfare of the Revolution as well as that of the Guomindang, we are forced to adopt this strong measure to purge the Party of all the undesirable elements.

14.7 *"Purge the Party" Slogans for the Chinese People, May 1927*

THE FOLLOWING SLOGANS, PREPARED BY THE PUBLICITY COMMITTEE OF THE GUANGDONG PROVINCIAL SPECIAL GUOMINDANG, ARE AN EMBODIMENT OF THE AIMS AND SPIRIT OF THE NATIONALIST MOVEMENT.

(MAY 1927.)

1. Down with the Chinese Communist Party, which is treacherous to our late director, Dr. Sun Yat-sen.
2. Down with the Chinese Communist Party which is against the San-Min. Chu-I, "The Three Principles of the People."
3. Down with the Chinese Communist Party which is destroying the People's Revolution.
4. Down with the Chinese Communist Party which is undoing the work of the Northern Expedition.
5. Down with the Chinese Communist Party which is utilizing bandits and labor usurpers to oppress the Peasants and Labourers.
6. Down with the Chinese Communist Party which is insulting and disgracing our late Director, Dr. Sun.

7. Down with the Chinese Communist Party which is plotting the downfall and destruction of the Guomindang.
8. To be against "The Three Principles of the People" is to be a Counter-Revolutionary.
9. To be against the Guomindang is to be a Counter-Revolutionary.
10. All power and authority belong to the Guomindang.
11. All true and loyal comrades of the Guomindang must unite and rise.
12. Down with all Counter-Revolutionaries.
13. Down with all Opportunists.
14. Concentrate the powers of the Guomindang.
15. Down with all forms of Imperialism.
16. Down with the Fengtien clique of Militarists.
17. Eradicate all corrupt officials, greedy gentry, and unscrupulous merchants.
18. Purge the Guomindang of all anti-revolutionists.
19. To call a Strike against the Guomindang is Counter-Revolutionary.
20. Those who refuse to come under the direction and guidance of the Guomindang are not Revolutionaries.
21. The masses of the people must rise and clean up the Counter-Revolutionary Chinese Communist Party.
22. The masses of the people must rise and support the Chinese Guomindang.
23. Support the Central Government at Nanking.
24. Support the advancing Nationalist Forces.
25. Down with the bogus governments at Wuhan and at Peking. . . .

14.8 *A Proclamation, Headquarters of the Twenty-sixth Nationalist Army, April 22, 1927*

Our Chinese workmen have been admired by the world for their endurance and obedience, but with the increase in industrial activity there has come a menace in the form of strikes and walkouts.

When Shanghai was recently taken by our armies, many workmen were induced or forced by mutineers to leave their employment and to parade and join various unlawful associations, and to otherwise countenance unlawful activities.

Through my advice to workers and other steps which have been taken many factories are again running. These are cases, however, where simple-minded workers are still deluded by agitators. To them I wish to offer this advice:

1. The manufacturing and commercial conditions of China are quite different from those of Europe and America. Because of this difference the treatment accorded to workmen must be different. Chinese workmen,

consequently, cannot expect the same treatment as that accorded to workmen in other countries.

2. Chinese workmen are fortunate in that they can if they wish make China a real industrial nation by gaining full knowledge of the industries with which they are affiliated. This fact has apparently been lost sight of in following professional agitators who are very selfish and who are seeking to sacrifice the laboring classes only for their own benefit.

3. If, in following the advice of these agitators and law violators, a strike occurs, the loss of valuable time and the money which that valuable time would bring to the workmen is the only result. Although some of the workmen who go on strike have money for the rainy day, others have not. These last starve themselves and starve their families. It is absolutely foolish to strike, for it is both unlawful and a loss of livelihood.

4. When a strike is in effect the factories are closed. Consequently the Nationalist government and the Nationalist armies are forced to buy foreign made goods merely because there are no native productions. This is death not only to the country's commerce, but to patriotism as well.

From the above four points it is plain that strikes are not only harmful, but they have not a single advantage.

The Nationalist Government is now facing and executing the task of clearing away the bacteria which causes the disturbances in the laboring classes—and making the source of this disturbance clear.

Hereafter when professional agitators or others in the laboring classes plan to induce otherwise good workmen to strike, commit unlawful acts, or violence we ask that the factories and the good workmen report them to the headquarters of this army that they may be severely punished. Only by doing this may we be able to protect the good workmen and see that they are well treated.

> April 22, 1927.
> Chow Vung Chee,
> Commander of the Twenty-Sixth
> Nationalist Army; and
> Vice-Commander of the Shanghai
> and Sungkiang Defence Area.

14.9 MADAME SUN YAT-SEN DEFENDS THE LEFT, AUGUST 1927

After the collapse of the Wuhan government, the Left Guomindang disintegrated into a collection of squabbling factions. Madame Sun Yat-sen and others who had supported the *Liane Ronggong* (Unite with Russia, Accept the Communist Party) policy were dismayed when Wuhan leaders started their own purge of Communists in July 1927. They expressed their opposition to the direction taken by the various anti-Communist groups within the Guomindang by following Borodin and other Comintern representatives into exile in the U.S.S.R.

Madame Sun Yat-sen (Soong Ch'ing-ling, 1892–1981) was nearly thirty years younger than her late husband. In the struggles that overcame the Guomindang following Sun's death she became an increasingly outspoken critic of Chiang Kai-shek and Guomindang rightists whom she believed were attempting to appropriate her husband's name and ideas to justify their own political program. As her public statement issued on August 22, 1927, in Shanghai shortly before she left for Moscow indicates, Madame Sun believed that the Party was now commanded by "pseudo-leaders," narrow-minded militarists and political hacks.

If China is to survive as an independent country in the modern struggle of nations, her semi-feudal conditions of life must be fundamentally changed and a modern state created to replace the medieval system which has existed for more than a thousand years. This task needs to be done by the method of revolution, if only because the alternative method of gradualness postulates a period of time which is denied the nation by both the cancerous force of Chinese militarism eating from inside and foreign imperialism ravaging from outside.

To forge a fit instrument of revolution, Sun Yat-sen reorganized the Guomindang on a revolutionary basis in the winter of 1924, and reinforced the Three People's Principles by formulating the Three Great Policies of action. The first of these policies calls for the inclusion and support of the nation's workers and peasants in the work of the revolution. These two massive elements of the national population—one carrying on and sustaining the life of organized society and the other producing food on which man lives—represent nearly 90 percent of the nation. And, in view of their numerical strength and the fact that the masses ought to be the chief beneficiaries of the revolution, they must be drawn into it if there is to be life and reality in the movement.

The second of the policies laid down by Sun recognizes the necessity of cooperation between the Guomindang and members of the Chinese Communist Party during the period of revolutionary struggle with Chinese militarism and foreign imperialism. The Chinese Communist Party is indubitably the most dynamic of all internal revolutionary forces in China; and its influence over the masses and power of propaganda enabled the Guomindang to control its military elements and subordinate them to the civil authorities.

The third of Sun Yat-sen's policies deals with the profoundly important question of the connection of the Soviet Union with the Guomindang. The connection is sometimes justified on the ground that the Soviet Union has no unequal treaties with China. This, however, was a minor consideration in Sun's view of the matter. In formulating the third policy, he was moved by larger reasons. Just as he regarded the Chinese Communist Party as the most active revolutionary force in China, so he envisaged the Soviet Union as the most powerful revolutionary force in the world; and he believed that a right correlation by the Guomindang of these two outstanding revolutionary forces would signally assist the revolution to realize national independence for China. Sun was not afraid or ashamed to avow this revolutionary thesis, since he knew that the revolutionary role played by France, in the person of Lafayette, in the American revolution was repeated in many a chapter in the history of freedom.

It was a statesmanlike application of these three policies of Sun and the correlation of the forces deriving from them that enabled the Guomindang power to put an end to ten years of disorder and confusion in Canton, and to create and finance revolutionary armies that conquered their way to the historic line of the Yangtze and—after shattering the main force of the Fengtien army[1] in Honan—penetrated to the bank of the Yellow River. Besides its striking administrative work at Canton and the great military achievement of the Northern Expedition, the Guomindang scored memorable successes in a field in which China has always known defeat and humiliation. It raised the international status of China to a point never attained before, compelling the representatives of great powers to meet the foreign minister of Nationalist China as an equal in council, and causing men in high as well as in the scattered places of the earth to heed his statements on Nationalist aims and aspirations. In those days—it is but three months since—the Guomindang may have been hated and even feared, but none dared to despise it.

Today it is otherwise. The famous name of the Nationalist Government is now sunk to the level of other semi-feudal remnants in the North; and those who have been entrusted by the revolution with leadership are allowing the new militarist clique in the Yangtze to capture and utilize the Guomindang; and they themselves are now becoming or are about to become, the secretaries and clerks of the new Caesar. No one fears and no one respects the Guomindang, which is now despised even by foes who used to blanch and flee at the sound of its armies on the march.

What is the cause for this startling change in values and in men's opinions? The answer is to be found in the work of the reaction in Canton, in Nanking and Shanghai, in Changsha, and lastly in Wuhan. Peasants and their leaders, workers and their leaders, Communists and their leaders, who labored in order that the Guomindang power might reach the Yangtze, have been ruthlessly and wantonly killed; and Soviet workers who gave of their best to the Guomindang and who men, in later and juster days, will adjudge to have deserved well of Nationalist China, have been forced to leave, because so-called "leaders" of the Guomindang—petty politicians reverting to type—believe that they can violate

1. Manchurian warlord army under Zhang Zuolin.

Sun Yat-sen's Three Policies and rely on the new militarism to carry out the stupendous task of the revolution.

They will fail and go the way of those before them who have sought to rule in like fashion. But they must not be permitted to involve in their own ultimate ruin the heritage left to us by Sun. His true followers must seek to rescue the real Guomindang from the degradation of becoming a mere secretariat of the new militarist clique emerging out of the intrigues and disloyalties now afoot.

My own course is clear. Accepting the thesis that the Three Policies are an essential part of the thought and technique of the revolution, I draw the conclusion that real Nationalist success in the struggle with Chinese militarism and foreign imperialism is possible only by a right correlation, under Guomindang leadership, of the revolutionary forces issuing from the Three Policies. As the reaction led by pseudo-leaders of the Guomindang endangers the Third Policy, it is necessary for the revolutionary wing of the Guomindang—the group with which Sun would today be identified had he been alive—to leave no doubt in the Soviet mind that, though some have crossed over to reaction and counter-revolution, there are others who will continue true and steadfast to the Three Policies enunciated by him for the guidance and advancement of the work of the revolution.

I go, therefore, to Moscow to explain this in person.

CHAPTER 15

The Guomindang in Power

15.1 AND 15.2 LAW IN THE NANJING DECADE

During the Nanjing decade (1928–1937), Chiang Kai-shek's government strove to build a monolithic Party dictatorship. The Party's main goals were to strengthen the central armies, enforce ideological unity, and take back territories controlled by anti-Nationalist groups. To achieve these aims the Nationalists formed an extensive civil and military internal security apparatus and established judicial and military courts with maximum flexibility to punish and suppress the party's enemies during the period of "Political Tutelage" that officially commenced in March 1929.

Hu Shi's article on the "failure of law" was published originally in the liberal journal *Xinyue* (The crescent moon) in the spring of 1929 and was reprinted almost simultaneously in Shanghai's *North China Herald*. It criticized the imprecision of Guomindang (GMD) definitions of legal and human rights and suggested that the party government had created a legal framework that invited arbitrary manipulation. The judiciary was far from independent of party control, equality before the law remained an unrealized aspiration, and soldiers and police were encouraged by the laxity of legal structures to "improvise" when dealing with offenders who had confronted or offended Nationalist party bosses. The article that follows was one of a series of sharply critical pieces that Hu Shi published on this topic. Cumulatively, they aroused the ire of GMD authorities and resulted in a temporary ban on Hu Shi's writings.

The "Emergency Law for the Suppression of Crimes Against the Safety of the Republic" is a specimen of the special or provisional legislation used by the Nanjing government to facilitate its "Extermination Campaigns"

270

against the Communists. In March 1928 the national government promulgated a "Temporary Law for the Punishment of Counterrevolutionaries" but some Guomindang leaders believed that it was insufficiently rigorous. After extensive discussion, a new "Emergency Law" was finalized and published in January 1931. By this time, the alliance of warlords Yan Xishan (1883–1960) and Feng Yuxiang (1882–1948) had been defeated and the primary targets of the new martial law decree were clearly the Communist "rebels" of the Jiangxi Soviet. The intentionally imprecise language and the harsh punishments prescribed by this law gave Nationalist jurists the broadest discretion in disposing of cases involving "counterrevolutionaries."

15.1 *Hu Shi Appeals for Legal Rights, 1929*

Failure of Law in Nationalist China

RIGHTS OF THE INDIVIDUAL DESTROYED UNDER THE
PROVISIONAL CONSTITUTION
BY DR. HU SHI

The National Government on April 20, 1929, promulgated a decree aiming at the protection of the Rights of Man. The decree reads:

'In all countries in the world the Rights of Man receive the protection of law. The tutelage period having now commenced, a solid foundation should be laid for government by law. No persons, individual or corporate body residing within the domain of the National Government of China, shall, by an illegal act, be permitted to violate another man's person, liberty and property. Any violation of this kind shall be severely punished according to law. Let all governmental organs, executive and judicial, publish this order for general observance.'

The above order issued at the present period during which personal rights are being least respected, cannot but be welcomed by the people. When, however, our first enthusiasm for its reception is over and when we scrutinize the order in a more sober state of mind, we are greatly disappointed in at least three aspects:

SOME NOTABLE OMISSIONS

(1) While the order recognizes the rights of man under three headings—person, liberty and property—these rights are not defined. For instance, under liberty, the order omits to say what kinds of liberty, nor does it say

what will be the form of guarantee which will be given to property. The absence of definition of any sort is a serious defect.

(2) This order only forbids violation of these rights by a private individual or a corporation but fails to restrict governmental organs. It is true that a private person or a corporation must be prohibited from attempting acts of encroachment upon another man's person, liberty and property, but the country is suffering very much more through and from illegal acts of the governmental organs, or acts done in the name of the government and the party. For example, all interference with the liberty of speech and publication, confiscation or private property, and recent attempts at nationalization (which is another form of confiscation) of electrical and industrial plants in several cities—all these have been done in the name of some government organ. The order in question seems to have accorded no protection or guarantee to the people against these acts of the government itself. "A public officer may indeed start a conflagration, but the people must not light their tiny lamps."

(3) The order is of a mandatory nature carrying a penalty, "according to law." It omits to state what law, or kind of law will be applicable in a case of this sort. There is indeed a special provision in the criminal code for an offence against personal liberty. But should an act of unlawful violation be perpetrated under and in the name of the government or the party, then the aggrieved party would be without a redress of guarantee.

NOT AFFECTED BY THE ORDER

Shortly after the promulgation of the order, the local press in Shanghai began to question whether or not the activities of the Anti-Japanese Boycott Society would be covered by it. The Japanese press answered the question in the affirmative, but Chinese papers like the "Shishi Xinbao" argued that this order did not cover the acts of the patriotic boycotters.

The Anti-Japanese Boycott Society is not the only exception. All those who are branded as "Reactionaries," "Local Bullies and Wicked Elders," "Counter-Revolutionaries" and "Suspected Communists" are not within it, so that their persons may be insulted, liberty curtailed, and property seized at pleasure. These acts would not be illegal. Any publication may be banned as reactionary and the banning would be no violation of the liberty of thought or the press. A foreign-controlled school may be closed down as an organ of "cultural invasion," and a Chinese-controlled school may meet the same fate, if someone sees fit to style it a reactionary center. Are these not acts of unlawful violation of personal rights? What guarantee do people have against such unlawful acts of encroachment?

DEMAND FOR MORE RIGOUR

On March 26, 1929, the Shanghai papers contained in their telegram columns, a report that Mr. Chen Decheng[1] of the Shanghai Municipality had submitted a proposal before the Third Congress of the Party, in which Mr. Chen moved for a stronger policy in dealing with the counter-revolutionaries. Mr. Chen felt that the courts of justice had been too lenient, having, in his opinion, too much regard for proof and were inclined to technicalities, thus enabling many counter-revolutionaries to escape from their merited punishments. The proposal he submitted was that anyone who had been certified by a provincial branch of the Guomindang, or of a special Municipality as a counter-revolutionary, should be accepted as such by all courts of justice with the local GMD's certification as conclusive evidence of his guilt without further evidence being adduced. On his appeal against the judgment, a similar certificate issued by the Central Guomindang Party would constitute a sufficient ground for dismissing the appeal. In other words, Mr. Chen wanted to vest in the Party judicial authority to determine the question of guilt of one who is charged with being a counter-revolutionary, and the court had only to perform its ministerial duty in the execution of the Party's order. Such a suggestion is preposterous and totally inconsistent with the doctrine of government by law.

A LETTER THAT WAS BANNED

After reading the press report, I immediately wrote a letter addressed to Dr. Wang Zhonghui, President of the Judicial Council, asking his opinion on the subject, and inquiring if he, with his profound knowledge of the legal history of the world, had known of anything like it in the history of jurisprudence in any civilized country. I considered Mr. Chen's proposal as something deserving public attention, so I sent a copy of my letter to the Guowen News Agency for publication.

The agency after a few days wrote back saying that the latter had been duly forwarded to various newspapers, but its publication had been banned by the censor, and the copy was therefore returned. I failed to see any legal groups justifying the censor to suppress the publication of a document having no reference whatsoever in military affairs. It was written in my own name for which

1. Chen Decheng was the head of the Propaganda Department of the Guomindang Headquarters in Shanghai. He and Hu Shi were frequently at odds in 1929 as Hu became a vocal critic of elements of Sun Yat-sen's Three Principles of the People and, as in this document, Guomindang experiments in controlling dissent through draconian laws and state mandates. See Jerome Grieder, *Hu Shih and the Chinese Revolution, Liberalism and the Chinese Revolution, 1917–1937* (Boston: Harvard University Press, 1970), pp. 240–241.

I was prepared to assume full responsibility. Why may not a private citizen discuss a question of national importance and interest when he is prepared to take the responsibility? What protection have we against this kind of unreasonable interference? . . .

NEED OF A CONSTITUTION

If there is a real desire to protect the rights of man and to have a true government by law the first prerequisite should be a Constitution of the Chinese Republic. The least . . . should be the promulgation of a Provisional Constitution for the period of tutelage.

Dr. Sun Yat-sen in his work entitled *Revolutionary Tactics* [1906] divided his national construction program into three distinct periods: (1) the Military Era, scheduled to last for three years, (2) the era of the Provisional Constitution, which is to last six years during which all the rights and obligations of the military government towards the people as well as the people's rights and obligations towards the government shall be definitely fixed by the Provisional Constitution. This law should be rigidly obeyed by the military government and the local assemblies as well as private citizens, [and] (3) the era of Constitutional Rule.

. . . In 1919 when Dr. Sun wrote his *Sun Wen's Philosophy* the author in no mistakable manner repeatedly emphasized the importance of the transitional stage during which "the government should rule in accordance with the Provisional Constitution in order to guide the people towards local self-government." In his later work, *The History of Chinese Revolution*, published in January 1923, the second stage assumed a new name and was termed "the transitional stage," which, said Dr. Sun,

> "is an era of rule under the Provisional Constitution (not the one promulgated in Nanjing in 1912). This stage shall devote itself to instituting local self-government, and to the development of popular government. Taking a *hsien* as a unit, each *hsien* or district shall see to it that as soon as all disbanded soldiers are expelled and all miliary operations ceased, the Provisional Constitution shall be proclaimed and enforced, in which people's rights and obligations as well as the authority of the revolutionary government shall be clearly defined. This era is to have a duration of three years, on expiration of which, the people shall elect their own district officials. The revolutionary government shall only exercise a tutelage supervision, within the limits of the Provisional Constitution, over all self-government functionaries."

FUNDAMENTAL LAW INDISPENSABLE

One year later, in 1924, when Dr. Sun commenced writing his *Program for National Construction*, he again divided the rehabilitation into three stages. The second stage was now called the tutelage era, but no mention was made of the Provisional Constitution nor of the length of the tutelage period. Unfortunately, another year later, Dr. Sun died. People who read the last *Program* without a knowledge of his previous works, are likely to think that the tutelage era may be prolonged indefinitely, and may not need any convention or constitution. This I think is a grave mistake....

What we want to-day is a Provisional Constitution or convention, the kind which, in the words of Dr. Sun, "would define the rights and obligations of the people as well as the governmental powers of the revolutionary government." We want some law to fix the proper limits of the government beyond which all acts become illegal. We ask for a convention that will define and safeguard man's person, liberty, and property. Any violator of these rights, be he the Chairman of the National Government, or the Colonel of the 152nd Brigade, may be prosecuted and adjudicated by law.

15.2 Guomindang "Emergency Laws," 1931

(I)

Emergency Law for the Suppression of Crimes Against the Safety of the Republic

PROMULGATED BY THE NATIONAL GOVERNMENT ON JANUARY 31ST OF THE 20TH YEAR OF THE REPUBLIC OF CHINA (1931) AND ENFORCED ON MARCH THE SAME YEAR.

ARTICLE I. Whoever, with a view to subvert the Republic, commits one of the following acts, shall be punished by death:

1. Disturbing peace and order,
2. Entering into a secret relationship with a foreign country in order to disturb peace and order,
3. Associating with rebels in order to disturb peace and order,
4. Instigating a military person to commit a non-disciplinary [*sic.*, insubordinate] act or cause him to fail in the performance of his duty, or to associate with rebels.

ARTICLE 2. Whoever, with a view to subvert the Republic, commits one of the following acts, shall be punished with death or life imprisonment:

1. Instigating another person to disturb peace and order or to associate with rebels,

2. Conducting a campaign of propaganda against the State by writing, sketching, or speech-making.

ARTICLE 3.   Whoever, with a view to subvert the Republic, commits one of the following acts, shall be punished by life imprisonment, or imprisonment for more than ten years:

1. Committing a non-disciplinary [*sic.*, insubordinate] act, failing in the performance of his duty, or associating with rebels on the instigation of the criminal indicated in 4 of Article 1,
2. Disturbing peace and order or associating with rebels on the instigation of the criminal indicated in Part I of Article 4,
3. Conducting propaganda on the instigation of the criminal indicated in Part 2 of Article 2.

Whoever, having committed one of the crimes specified in the preceding paragraphs, on immediately and voluntarily reporting, shall receive an attenuation or exoneration or the penalty.

ARTICLE 4.   Whoever, having knowledge that a certain individual is a rebel, shelters him without giving notification to the competent authorities, shall be punished by imprisonment or more than five years.

Whoever, having committed the crime specified in the preceding paragraph, immediately and voluntarily reports, shall receive an attenuation or exoneration of the penalty.

ARTICLE 5.   Whoever, with a view to subvert the Republic commits one of the following acts, shall be punished with death, or life imprisonment or imprisonment for more than ten years:

1. Obtaining or transporting military supplies for rebels,
2. Revealing or transmitting to rebels military and political secrets,
3. Destroying means of communication.

ARTICLE 6.   Whoever, with a view to subvert the Republic organizes associations or unions or spreads doctrines incompatible with the *"Three Principles of the People,"* shall be punished by imprisonment of from five to fifteen years.

ARTICLE 7.   Whoever, commits one of the crimes specified by the present law in a region under a state of siege shall be tried by the highest military organ in that region: If he commits the crime within the limits of the suppression of banditry, he shall be tried by a provisional court composed of the magistrate of the district and two judicial officials.

The provisional court shall be established in the district and the magistrate shall be designated as the president of the court.

ARTICLE 8. In case a suspect is tried by a military organ in conformity with the present law, that organ shall submit a statement of the trial to the competent superior military organ and the sentence shall be executed only after approval by the latter. If the suspect is tried by a provisional court, the court shall submit a statement of the trial to the superior court and the sentence shall be executed only after approval by the latter; the case shall also be reported to the provincial government for reference.

The competent superior military organ or the superior court, if it doubts the judgment passed by the organ which is its subordinate, can give to that organ an order for re-examination, or designate a special delegate to be present at the reconsideration of the judgment.

ARTICLE 9. The military organ or police which arrests a person suspected of having committed one of the infractions specified by the present law, shall report the matter immediately to the interested competent authorities.

ARTICLE 10. To all offenses that do not fall within the limits of the present law, the provisions of the Penal Code are applicable.

ARTICLE 11. The duration of the application of the present law and the date of its enforcement shall be fixed by ordinance.

The provisional law suppressing anti-revolutionary plots shall be repealed from the date of the enforcement of the present law.

15.3–15.5 THE MUKDEN INCIDENT AND MANCHUKUO

After the Sino-Japanese War (1894–1895) Manchuria became a key zone of international competition. Its vast resources and strategic position made it a tempting target for both Russian and Japanese expansion, and the Qing government was forced to strike compromises with both sides to retain its sovereignty over the region. After its defeat of Russia in 1905, Japan greatly expanded its military position in Manchuria, establishing the southern part of the region as a Japanese "sphere of influence."

Following the signing of the Portsmouth Treaty on September 5, 1905, Japan's Guandong Army (Kantō gun) was posted to Manchuria, ostensibly to guard the Southern Manchurian Railroad (SMR). It soon became the dominant army in China's northeast. By the time the Guandong Army moved its headquarters from Port Arthur to Mukden in 1928, the proximity of other Japanese units and support facilities in Chosen (the Japanese colony in Korea) and the dense rail network controlled by the SMR made its position virtually unassailable. Protected by this overseas army, Japanese banks and lumber, chemical, manufacturing, and mining concerns established footholds throughout China's three northeastern provinces. Civilian and military proponents of a "positive" policy in Manchuria began to sug-

gest that Japan seize these territories from China and weld them to the
Japanese colonial empire.

To justify war against the Chinese garrisons in Manchuria, the Guandong Army needed a pretext. The first document, excerpted from a Japanese foreign ministry report on the Manchurian Incident, lucidly describes
a provocation that never occurred. In fact, the bombing incident this document describes was entirely invented by conspirators of the Guandong
Army. The "bomb" was a tiny explosive charge planted by Captain Imada
Shintaro of the Guandong Army's Special Service Agency. It caused little
physical damage to the SMR tracks—soon after the detonation a south-
bound express rolled over the damaged railbed and arrived on time in
Mukden—but it gave the conspirators of the Guandong Army the
"emergency" they needed to launch their invasion of Manchuria. Soon
nearly one-sixth of the land mass of China, at least as it existed prior to
1911, was controlled by Japan.

The League of Nation's response to Japan's activity in southern Man-
churia was far less forceful than Nationalist politicians hoped it would be.
In December 1931 the League organized a commission headed by Lord
Lytton, the acting viceroy of India, to investigate the Manchurian Incident.
During this investigation, Japanese spokesmen did their best to justify the
takeover of Manchuria. They invited the last reigning emperor of the
Qing dynasty, Henry Puyi, to come to Mukden to claim the throne of the
"independent" state of Manchukuo, and tried to round up international
recognition for the new government. Surrounded and coached by ultraconservative ex-Qing officials, Japanese politicians and soldiers, and Manchu
clansmen, Puyi took a predictably ultraconservative approach to rule. His
statement, made at the time of his installation as "Chief Executive" of
Manchukuo, pledged, in stilted and archaic language, to bring about
"benevolent rule" and the "kingly way." This enabled Japanese politicians
to create a veneer of political legitimacy for the new Manchurian state.

The satirical poem "The Naughty Japanese," published in Mukden
shortly after the foundation of Manchukuo, expressed what for the Japanese was a real grudge: other countries, including France, Britain, and the
United States had built up their colonies without a word of condemnation
but when Japan attempted to do likewise it became the whipping boy of
the international community.

In the Lytton Commission's report, issued in October 1932 and accepted
by the League's members in February 1933, the Commission advocated, in
carefully measured terms, a return to the *status quo ante bellum* with no
recognition of the new Japanese-sponsored state of Manchukuo. However,
it made no threat of multilateral use of force to reverse Japan's aggression
nor did it advocate economic sanctions. The Japanese, outraged by even

the feeble rebuke of the Lytton Commission and the disapproval of the international community, withdrew from the League of Nations in February 1933 and set about transforming Manchukuo into a model of what some Japanese politicians and soldiers hoped they could accomplish for all of Asia.

Matsuoka Yosuke's (1880–1946) speech in New York in 1934 provided a rationale for Japan's defiant attitude and suggested what he and many other contemporary Japanese believed their country could do to secure law and order in the Chinese northeast. Matsuoka, who had been educated in the United States, served as the vice-president of the Southern Manchurian Railroad from 1927 to 1929. He entered politics as a member of the Diet in 1930 and played a leading role as an advocate of the Seiyukai party's "positive" policy for the Chinese mainland. As Japan's chief delegate to the League in 1933, Matsuoka walked out after the acceptance of the Lytton Commission's report. From 1935 to 1938 he served as president of the Southern Manchurian Railway, a cabinet advisor, and, in 1940, as Japan's minister. In this capacity, he helped bring about the Tokyo-Rome-Berlin Axis. At the end of the Second World War he was arrested and brought to trial as a class A war criminal.

The Manchurian Incident opened a new era in China's political life. Throughout the years that preceded the outbreak of the war in China, this issue dominated Chinese domestic politics and compromised the Nationalist government's attempts to bring about reform. Manchukuo was an open wound, a source of indignation, a banner around which to rally. Chiang Kai-shek's opponents of the 1930s rarely failed to remind him that a huge portion of sovereign territory and some thirty million Chinese were living under Japanese occupation.

In a larger sense, the Manchurian Incident can be seen as the first warning signal that the territorial status quo in the world set in place in 1919 was now under siege. The League's torpid reaction to aggression in 1932 would inspire other ambitious powers to test its collective will as the decade continued.

15.3 *Japan on the Mukden Incident*

A few minutes past 10 o'clock on the evening of September 18, a lieutenant and six privates of the railway guards stationed at Hushitai were proceeding southward on patrol practice along the railway track. When they reached a point about six or seven hundred meters south of the North Barracks of the Fengtien army, they suddenly heard the sound of an explosion in the rear. They hurriedly retraced their steps to the spot where the explosion had occurred, and found a number of Chinese soldiers running in the direction of the North Barracks after destroying a section of the track.[2] They gave chase to them, when they were suddenly fired upon by Chinese troops, four or five hundred strong, appeared in *gaoliang* fields to the north of the North Barracks and opened a fierce fire upon them. They hurried 120 men to the scene and engaged and defeated the enemy, who fled into the North Barracks pursued by the Japanese troops. Upon attempting to enter the barracks, they were greeted with a hail of bullets and shells from rifles, machine-guns and infantry guns, but succeeding occupying part of the barracks. They had, however, to fight hard for a time as they were pitted against overwhelming numbers, until they were reinforced by the main strength of the battalion then stationed at Mukden. Subsequently with the help of reinforcements hurried from Tieling the Japanese succeeded in clearing the North Barracks of their assailants by daybreak of the following day.

Now that regular troops of Japan and China had thus come to an armed collision, it was at once realized that it was quite different in nature from encounters of our railway guards with Manchurian bandits, such as had very frequently taken place in the past,—that the situation was extremely critical, and that in view of the attitude the Chinese troops in Mukden were adopting against our army and fellow country-men prior to the present occurrence, the Chinese troops in other places would also commence active hostilities. The total strength of the Japanese army in service in Manchuria at that time was only 10,400, while that of the Chinese was as high as 220,000 (of the 330,000 officers and men constituting the total strength of Zhang Xueliang's[3] army, 110,000 were then in service in North China inside the Great Wall). If, therefore, the Chinese army attacked ours, not only would our men find it difficult to discharge their duty of defending the Guandong Leased Territory and protecting 1,100 kilometres of the South Manchuria Railway, but the lives of one million Japanese subjects resident in Manchuria would be exposed to great danger. For this reason it was imperative for the Japanese army to act promptly, to concentrate the troops scattered about in small numbers at various points of strategic importance and to forestall the hostile forces by taking advantage of the efficient training of the men and the railway facilities that could be commanded. In other words, it was the only course left open to our army, in confronting the

2. Cases of obstruction done by Chinese to the operation of the South Manchuria Railway have occurred frequently of late, cases of heavy stones being laid on the track, stones thrown at passenger trains, rivets of rails or sleepers removed, sticks inserted in the points, etc., having been experienced one after another. In spite of the vigilant watch kept by the railway guards and the employees of the South Manchuria Railway Company such attempts at dislocating the traffic service were gradually on the increase in recent years causing delay of the service and endangering the lives of passengers.

3. Commander of the pro-Guomindang Fengtian Army (b. 1898).

numerically far superior hostile forces, to attack them first and eliminate the troops immediately opposed to it as quickly as possible, and to find a means of discharging its duties by securing scope for active operations. Accordingly as soon as a report of the incident reached them, the higher command of our army promptly commenced operations for removing all causes of danger by disarming the Chinese troops in its vicinity.

After helping their comrades who had come to a collision with Chinese troops to drive the latter away from the North Barracks, our troops in Mukden promptly occupied all points of strategic importance in that city such as the Government offices, arsenal and wireless station. On the other hand our troops stationed at Tieling, Kaiyuan, Sipingkai and Liaoyang moved to Mukden on the 19th, leaving skeleton forces at their respective posts. The headquarters of our army at Port Arthur were also removed to Mukden the same day.

At various places along the South Manchuria Railway . . . our troops for the purpose of removing immediate danger, as well as for the defence of the railway zone and the protection of Japanese subjects resident in their neighbourhood, disarmed the Chinese troops and police and occupied the strategic points. . . . It was reported that simultaneously with the occupation of various points, our army proclaimed military administration and seized customs-houses. This report is, however, absolutely devoid of foundation. Only in Mukden and one or two other cities, the Chinese authorities having fled, our army, in cooperation with leading Chinese citizens, took temporary charge of the preservation of peace and order, but in no instance did it interfere with Chinese local administration.

15.4 *Japan's Expansion: A Satirical Poem*

THE NAUGHTY JAPANESE

> *I am bad*
> *All others good;*
> *O wherefore should this be?*
> *Strong nations have their lovers*
> * —Except the Japanese.*

Look upon the cheery Indo-Chin,
For brunet Senegal spare but a glance;
Syria too considers with a grin
How deep her debt to kindly rule of France.

> *For I am bad*
> *All others good;*
> *O wherefore should this be?*
> *There's place for you in heaven*
> * —But not the Japanese.*

Children of the jewel Irish Isle
Johnny Bull their tender homage give;
Ghandi's natives likewise fondly smile,
Grateful they have still a right to live.
    Yes I am bad
    All others good;
    O wherefore should this be?
    Make way for all the righteous
      —This bars the Japanese.
Mongol Herder murmurs "Vive La Russe"!
Master's voice is heard at every campfire.
Who would care to make the smallest fuss.
In Soviet Union's gentle empire?
    I am bad
    All others good;
    O wherefore should this be?
    Hell is closed to everyone
      —Except the Japanese.
Benevolent the pious hand of Sam:
Europe for his loans is full of praise;
Hawaii, Haiti, blacks in Alabam
Bless his rule that brings delirious days.
    Ugh! I am bad
    All others are good;
    O wherefore should this be!
    Faultless are the empires
      —Except the Japanese.
Destiny has marked us on the stage,
Villain part as foil against the rest;
How else could sanctified and sage
Except by contrast rate themselves the best!
    So I am bad
    All others are good;
    O wherefore should this be?
    All mankind's in union
      —But the naughty Japanese.

15.5 *Puyi's Proclamation*

CHIEF EXECUTIVE'S PROCLAMATION

Mankind should respect Morality. Since there exists racial discrimination, one race attempts to exalt itself by oppressing the others; thus comes about the weakness of Morality.

Benevolence should be highly esteemed by mankind. But on account of international strife, one nation strives to benefit herself at the expense of others, which causes Benevolence to lose its value.

Our new State is established on Morality and Benevolence. As a result of the removal of racial discrimination and the termination of international strife, this State will, as a matter of course, become a land of peace and happiness under "Wang-tao", the Way of Benevolent Rule.

Endeavor, therefore, all people for the attainment of these noble objectives.

Pu Yi
Chief Executive of Manchukuo
9th March, the First Year of Tatung (1932).

15.6 JAPAN DEFENDED AT THE CHAMBER OF COMMERCE, 1934

At present China, despite her gigantic military forces, is no menace to Japan, but she has been in past centuries and may be in the future, and we Japanese cannot forget the past nor ignore the future as easily as nations far away from China, across the oceans or the plains of Asia. We are China's immediate neighbor.

The charge that we want to take control of China is false, but Western persons have persisted so long in heeding and disseminating it that, generally speaking, they believe it. If we had wanted to do this we could have found many opportunities in the last twenty-three years of China's civil war. In this period there have been many provocations of which Western nations similarly situated would have taken advantage.

If we had wanted to annex Manchuria we could easily have done so two years ago, and need not have set up an independent government there. But it seems useless to make such statements any longer; the Western nations reject the obvious facts of the Far East. Japan is, therefore, compelled to act at times in disregard of their views.

The trouble in Eastern Asia, is fundamentally of Western making. The record is a long and often unfortunate one—particularly unfortunate for China. It was not Japan that provoked the aggression upon China; for decades Japan endeavored to prevent these aggressions, on one occasion waging a life-or-death struggle against Russia for this purpose. For a hundred years, even before Japan opened her doors to the Western World (at American request) invasions of China had been going on, and but for Japan they would be, in all probability, continuing today.

ACTIVITIES OF RUSSIANS

It was not only the Russia of the Czar that attempted conquests in Chinese territory; Soviet Russia, too, has done this, Outer Mongolia—which borders on

Inner Mongolia and Manchuria—has been incorporated in the Soviet Union in the last ten years, and in 1925, by agreement with China's leading revolutionary, Dr. Sun Yat-sen, the Moscow Government sent money, arms, military instructors and trained propagandists to China in an effort to Sovietize the entire country.

PERPLEXITY OVER ATTITUDE

It seems strange to Japanese that though the United States and the League of Nations took no notice of Soviet Russia's annexation of Outer Mongolia and made no protest against her bloody attempt to Sovietize all of China only seven years ago, they vigorously protested against Japan's action in Manchuria, ignoring the bandit character of the government there and the vital interests of Japan, both economically and strategically.

If the action of the League and of the American Government had been of a friendly diplomatic character, Japan would have dealt with it with similar courtesy, but, though the purpose was declared to be peaceful, it was made in the nature of brow-beating, accompanied by saber-rattling. Men in the League spoke of the application of "sanctions," of bringing economic and financial pressure upon Japan, and the American navy was concentrated at Hawaii. The Japanese Government and people cannot be dealt with in this manner.

The methods of Western countries in dealing with Japan for some years have been partisan. Without protest, Germany could take territory in China, establish a naval base at Tsingtao and create a "sphere of influence" in Shantung (as she did in 1898); but when Japan drove the Germans out of that province, during the World War, the American Government objected to Japan's assumptions of the German rights.

France could seize the extensive territory of Indo-China and extend her "sphere of influence" up into the Province of Yunnan, in China proper, and no criticism comes for Europe of America. But when Japan objects to French extension of possession to two small sparsely populated islands off the Indo-China Coast, from which our people have long obtained guano [bird dung], American and European newspapers charge that we plan to create an airplane base on these islands and state that this is further evidence of our aggressive intentions.

Britain may hold Hongkong and lay claim to a "sphere of influence" throughout the Yangtse Valley, but when Japan seeks railway and other concessions of less importance we are charged with dangerous designs.

The United States may obtain rights for Christian missionaries to own land in any province in China, but if we were to require similar rights for Buddhists there would be pan-Christian objections.

America may acquire the Philippine Islands, an Asiatic territory 6,000 miles away from her shores, but when Japan takes control of Korea, a country smaller in territory than the Philippines and only 100 miles away from her island borders, the action is denounced.

DISTINCTIONS ARE MADE

To the Western mind it would seem what Europe or America does in Asia is in the nature of duty and in the line of human progress, while what we do is in the nature of selfish interest. But, in fact, we, being Asiatics, are far more capable of dealing with other Asiatics in their best interests than are Americans or Europeans. For example, in bringing order out of chaos in Korea we killed far fewer people than the Americans killed in suppressing the independence movement in the Phillippines. Yet independence was the key-word in the making of America.

GAINS IN GOVERNMENT

In Manchuria now there is better government than exists in any part of China proper. None of the score or more military dictatorships in China is as considerate of the people as the government of Manchukuo under that country's legitimate ruler, the Emperor Kang The. No comparison can be made between the orderly condition prevailing in Manchukuo and the terror that holds sway in even the provinces of China controlled by the so-called National Government.

The capital of Manchukuo, Hsinking, is an orderly, thriving city, while Nanking, the Chinese capital, is a wreck in which no Chinese banker or merchant of importance, unless affiliated with the government and personally protected by it, dares invest his money. The independent Chinese bankers, merchants and newspapers have crowded for existence into the foreign protected and French and International Settlements in Shanghai, where American, French, British and Japanese naval vessels lie constantly at anchor.

NO UTILITY NOW EXISTS

As a result of civil wars in China since the republic was proclaimed in 1911, the great majority of the people are in desperate condition. Tens of millions of men have the alternatives only of actual starvation or service under one of the military leaders. A rising of the people against these leaders is impossible. Unarmed men with empty stomachs cannot fight today against troops, as they did in the French Revolution; the machine gun protects the dictator, who is safe as long as his army is loyal.

That explains why today, as before the independence of Manchuria, the Chinese peasants are flocking to that country, often selling their daughters into slavery or prostitution to get the money to enable them to take their sons up into the cold northern territory beyond the Great Wall, where the presence of

Japanese troops makes life and property safe and enables the Manchukuo Government to function.

EFFORTS TO AID CHINESE

We Japanese have striven to help the Chinese if only in our own selfish interest—and we could have accomplished much for them had our efforts not been opposed by Westerners. China could have been made relatively unified and orderly and peaceful today had our efforts not been opposed and thwarted; and not only the Chinese people, but those of Western countries would have profited. . . .

15.7 POLITICS OF POWER: GENERAL VON FALKENHAUSEN'S ADVICE TO CHIANG KAI-SHEK, 1936

Between 1934 and 1937, the Nanjing regime developed a close relationship to the Third Reich of Adolf Hitler. China, like Germany, was attempting to establish a state unified around a single party and a single leader, and the German model seemed an attractive paradigm to many of Chiang Kai-shek's followers and, quite probably, to the Generalissimo himself. Many adherents of the Guomindang, including Chiang's own son, were sent to Germany to receive military, police, and other sorts of training in this era. There were those who surely dreamed that China's "Revival Society" (*Fuxingshe*), a paramilitary group also known as the Blueshirts, would ultimately emerge as an elite political clique that would wield great power in the Guomindang.

Another symbol of the mutual interest and sympathy of Germans and Chinese in the 1930s was the arrival of numerous German advisors in China. Several Germans in sequence served as Jiang's chief foreign military advisers; Captain Walter Stennes trained Chiang Kai-shek's personal bodyguard; and Colonel-General Hans von Seeckt and General Alexander von Falkenhausen, both outstanding staff officers of the First World War, were the architects of the positional warfare tactics that led to the destruction of the Jiangxi Soviet in October 1934. Von Falkenhausen, as this top secret memorandum to Chiang Kai-shek indicates, also had fixed ideas in the political realm and was anxious to see Chiang emerge as a president with powers similar to those enjoyed by Mussolini and, of course, Hitler.

Office of the General Adviser
Tbg. No. 5972/I.
Top Secret!
Nanjing, September 6, 1936

.... The history of all times has taught us that leaders are needed by states and nations in times of distress, when only the concerted application of *all* state and national power can provide the necessary control over their destiny. Absolute power made possible the great deeds of such historical figures, from Julius Caesar to Genghis Khan, such as Cromwell, Frederick the Great, and Napoleon I. Though history has examples of leadership shared by several persons, *one* person always was clearly in the leadership, and the others subordinate; such as recently Bismarck who, with the support of the King, found in Moltke and Roon the necessary complement to himself.

Limited power, however, or a division of power, but also the inadequacy of the leader, have almost invariably brought struggles for national existence to an unsuccessful end; from Hannibal to the Great War of 1914–18....

The recent period has everywhere shown tendencies to return to practical absolutism. For example in Italy and Germany, but also in Russia, all power is concentrated in one hand, while in some instances no constitutions even exist, and no control organ such as, legally, in Italy the King and in Germany Hindenburg until his death.

Therein lies the natural striving to have a personality at the head of the state endowed with ultimate responsibility, a person independent from elections, party politics, and public mood, and capable to provide a stability immune to the turnover of individual personalities. But this is the essence of monarchy.

[But] we must distinguish leaders [Führer] from dictators. Leaders are those who command the allegiance of the masses of the people and who provide for some check through occasional plebiscites. Dictators derive authority from material power, supported by a minority. Dictators can nevertheless be historically justifiable at a time when no consensus is possible among the people and the state is in need of firm guidance in order to survive.

Most dictators come to a violent end, unless they found a dynasty (Ming Dynasty). ... For in every pure dictatorship there comes the moment when the dictator has become blind to the signs of the time, or is no longer in the position to heed them. What is missing is control through a healthy, objective opposition. For this reason, Bismarck once said, that in the absence of an opposition he would create one. The dictator who has no responsibility but to himself needs a source of control that is independent without interfering with his freedom of making the final decision in times of great emergency. *The opposition also, must be selfless and national-minded* in order to fulfill purpose in the state....

In applying the supreme power of command of the President care must be taken not to limit the instruments of power of the state to the traditional armed forces on land, sea, and air, but to note that modern warfare requires the combined strength of the whole state and its people, down to the smallest detail.

As a precaution, the whole nation must be prepared for war; this is the only way to provide for its security in its entirety. This consideration must apply to every state measure concerning the economy, finances, and above all popular education and propaganda. Every powerful modern state today does this; they represent "nations in arms." Most states have laws regulating in every detail the "mobilization of the nation in case of war."

This fact leads naturally to the preeminent importance of military consideration in all government actions, and requires that the leading statesman possess unfettered powers in this so vital area for the state and nation. Generally speaking, this task no longer can be left to the individual government departments. Instead, it calls for firm consolidation and single-minded leadership.

"War is the continuation of politics by other means." Policies must be coordinated with the realities of the state's power, its "potential de guerre." This means: the state's policies must be based on a just assessment of the power instruments available, and the instruments of power must be so ordered to suit the political situation.

Thus the ideal is a chief of state who is both statesman and commander in chief (e.g. Frederick the Great, Pilsudski, Mustapha-Kemal-Atatürk, et al.), and who *already in time of peace so organizes and staffs the national instruments of power* that the whole machine functions smoothly at all times.

At the same time we must remember that no single person in today's world has the energy to direct and lead everything. As division of labor becomes necessary, the unity of concept and the loyal cooperation of all must be secured above all.

Thus the whole organization of the state must be basically adapted to modern warfare in time of peace, for modern warfare requires that everything be prepared in peace time down to the smallest detail, so that it can automatically begin to function at the outbreak of hostilities.

Three major areas are affected:

a) All branches of the armed forces, on land, water, and in the air must be organically coordinated, also their missions.
b) The whole task of preparing for national economic mobilization.
c) The [need for an] unanimous attitude on the part of the true public, i.e., unanimous national support.

To subordinate the three areas—armed forces, economy, people—to the supreme leader is the ultimate end of all preparation for mobilization. They are closely related to one another. . . .

We [in China] have also tried centralization through the person of the Generalissimo and the creation of the National Military Commission. But since the highest offices of the armed forces continue to exist unchanged, there is in practice a lack of clarity in the division of spheres of competence and responsibility. This gives rise to duplication of work, interferes with cooperation, leads to higher expenditures.

Thus to create a clear and unitary organization is important. It must assure in peace time the shaping and the coordination of all the direct and indirect elements that make up the state and the nation's defensive capacity, so that they work automatically in time of war. . . .

CHAPTER 16

Communist Survival

16.1 COMMUNIST SURVIVAL: THE TALE OF THE LUDING BRIDGE, 1935

Between 1928 and 1934, the Nanjing government launched five "Bandit Extermination" (*jiaofei*) campaigns against the Jiangxi Soviet. The first four of these campaigns were successfully countered by the guerilla tactics of the Red Army. In the Fifth Extermination Campaign in the late summer and fall of 1934, however, Nanjing mobilized an army of nearly two million men and adopted a strategy of encirclement that steadily reduced the size of the Jiangxi Soviet.

To escape the ring of steel that was closing down on them in Jiangxi, Bo Gu, then the general secretary of the Communist party, and the German adviser Otto Braun decided to launch a breakout. In October 1934, some one hundred thousand men and women fought their way through a vulnerable part of the Nationalist lines and began the famous Ten Thousand Li Long March to safety in northwestern China. In a grim, year-long epic of endurance, most of the Long Marchers died. Reduced by combat with Guomindang troops and some six thousand miles of forced marching over some of the most rugged and desolate terrain in China, only ten thousand survivors arrived in Shaanxi in the fall of 1935. But through their relocation to Yan'an, Communism in China survived, as a movement and an idea. Later, in a celebrated reference to the Long March, Mao Zedong wrote that it was "a manifesto, a propaganda force, a seeding-machine." As years passed the epic story of the Long March, with its episodes of heroism and self-sacrifice, was evoked again and again, particularly by the survivors of the March who now led the party, to symbolize, with almost mythic force, the commitment, the courage, and the inner vitality of the Chinese Communist party and its army.

In this selection, Yang Chengwu, a Red Army regimental commander in 1935 and later the chief of staff of the Chinese Air Force, describes an especially hair-raising moment during the Long March. Although his account undoubtedly embroiders the Communist army's heroism, it nonetheless captures the drama and risk of this episode in the Long March. Less than a century before, a Taiping army had been destroyed at the Anshunchang crossing and the Communist army might have faced a similar fate if the Luding Bridge had not been secured through resourceful leadership and suicide tactics, the Communists were able to make a perilous crossing of the Luding Bridge and continue their meandering journey to Yan'an.

On May 25, 1935, the First Regiment of the Red Army's First Division made a successful crossing of the Dadu River at Anshunchang. The current was too rapid to permit the building of a bridge there, and it would take many days to transfer our thousands of men to the other side, as only a few small boats were available to serve as ferries.

Chiang Kai-shek had ordered Yang Sen and other Szechuan warlords to rush up their troops and prevent our crossing. . . . Decades before, the famous general of the Taiping Revolution, Shih Dakai, and his army had been annihilated by the Ching soldiers at Anshunchang. Chiang Kai-shek had dreams of causing the Red Army to meet a similar fate. It was imperative to capture the bridge at Luding and ensure swift crossing of the river to prevent encirclement by the enemy. At such a critical moment, this task was given to the vanguard Fourth Regiment of our left-route army. The First Division, our right-route army, which had already crossed the river, would advance north along the east bank of the river in co-ordination with our efforts to capture Luding Bridge. . . .

After we had occupied several buildings and a Catholic church to the west of the bridge, our men prepared for the coming battle. When Regimental Commander Wang and I went out with the battalion and company officers to study the location, we were taken aback by the difficulties to be overcome. The reddish waters, cascading down the mountain gorges of the river's upper reaches, pounded against ugly boulders rising from the river bed and tossed white foam high into the air. The roar of the rushing torrent was deafening. In such a current even a fish could not keep steady for long. Fording or crossing in boats was out of the question.

We examined the bridge. It was made of 13 iron chains, each link as thick as a rice bowl. Two chains on each side served as hand-railings, while the other nine formed a cat-walk. Planks had originally been laid across the nine chains but were now gone, taken away by the enemy, and only the black swinging chains remained. At the head of the bridge two lines of a poem were inscribed on a stone slab:

> *Towering mountains flank Luding Bridge,*
> *Their summits rising a thousand li into the clouds.*

The town of Luding was built half along the shore and half on the mountain slope, located directly beyond the eastern end of the bridge and surrounded by a wall more than seven meters high. Its west gate faced the end of the bridge. Luding was garrisoned by two enemy regiments, and strong fortifications had been built along the mountain slope. Machine-gun emplacements close to the bridge kept us in continual fire, and mortar shells rained down on us.

The enemy soldiers were confident that their position was impregnable and yelled sneeringly: "Let's see you fly over! We'll give you our arms if you can do it!"

Our soldiers shouted back: "We don't want your weapons. It's the bridge we want!"

Back from our survey we soon set a battalion in position to seal off the narrow path and prevent the movement of any enemy reinforcements on the eastern bank of the river. That was the only path between the mountainside and the river along which they could come. Then we went among our companies to begin our battle rallies. Enthusiasm ran high, each company submitting a list of volunteers for an assault party, and each wanting the men of their particular unit to be given the task of taking the bridge.

All the officers of the regiment met in the church at noon to decide on the composition of the assault party. Discussion had just started when enemy mortar shells blew a big hole in the roof of the building where we gathered. Shell fragments and bits of broken tile showered down on us, but not one of us moved.

"The enemy is urging us on," I said. "We must drive across the bridge immediately. Now let's decide which company shall be responsible for the assaults."

Liao Ta-chu, commander of the Second Company, jumped to his feet. A taciturn man, he forced himself to speak, his dark, sunburned face flushed with the effort, and his short wiry frame trembled with excitement as he said:

"The First Company was commended as a model for their forced crossing of the Wuchiang River. We'd like to emulate them and distinguish ourselves in the battle to take Luding Bridge."

"You've got to give the assault mission to the Third Company," interrupted Wang Yu-tsai, the quick-tempered commander of that company, spluttering like a machine-gun. "Our Third Company has done well in every battle. We guarantee to take Luding Bridge." Standing as solid as an iron turret, he added plaintively, "If you do not give the assault mission to the Third Company, I dare not go back and face my men."

A heated debate followed, no company willing to yield to another. It was left to the leaders to decide. Commander Wang and I talked it over. Then he stood up and announced that the Second Company would be given the mission. I then rose and said:

"If it's fighting you want, there's plenty more to come. You'll each get your chance. At the Wuchiang River it was the First Company that led off; this time we'll let the Second Company start. The assault party will be formed of twenty-two men, Communists and non-Party activists, and will be led by Company Commander Liao. It seems like a good arrangement to me. What do the rest of you think?"

The response was a burst of applause from all present. Commander Liao jumped for joy. Only the Third Company commander was not satisfied. "The Third Company's job is not easy either," I assured him. "You have to go over directly behind the Second Company and lay planks across those chains so that the rest of the men can charge into the town. Is that all right?" The commander smiled.

Men fight better on a full stomach, so I told the company commanders to give each man a good meal. After the meeting, Lo Hua-sheng, secretary of the general Party branch, went to the Second Company to help with their preparations for the assault.

The attack began at four in the afternoon. The regimental commander and I directed it from the west end of the bridge. The buglers of the regiment gathered together to sound the charge, and we opened up with every weapon we had. The blare of the bugles, the firing and the shouts of the men reverberated through the valley. The 22 heroes, led by Commander Liao, crept across on the swaying bridge chains in the teeth of intense enemy fire. Each man carried a tommy-gun or a pistol, a broadsword and 12 hand-grenades. Behind them came the men of the Third Company, each carrying a plank in addition to full battle gear. They fought and laid planks at the same time.

Just as the assault party reached the bridgehead on the opposite side, huge flames sprang into the sky outside the town's west gate. The enemy was trying to throw a fire barrier across our path. The blaze, reddening the sky, licked fiercely around the end of the bridge.

The outcome of the attack hung by a hair. Our assault party hesitated for a few seconds and the men standing by the regimental commander and me shouted in unison: "It's a critical moment, comrades! Charge in! The enemy is crushed!" The shouts gave the heroes courage, confidence and strength. With the clarion call of the bugles, our assault party swiftly plunged into the flames. Commander Liao's cap caught fire. He threw it away and fought on. The others also dashed through the flames, closely behind Liao. In the street fighting that followed, the enemy brought their full weight to bear, determined to wipe out our assault party. Our gallant men fought until all their bullets and grenades were spent. There was a critical pause as the Third Company came charging to their rescue. Then Regimental Commander Wang and I sped across the bridge with our reinforcements and entered the town. Within two hours we had destroyed the greater part of the two enemy regiments while the remainder fled in panic. By dusk we had completely occupied the town of Luding and were in control of the bridge.

16.2–16.4 THREE ACCOUNTS OF THE NEW LIFE MOVEMENT

The New Life movement was launched with a torchlight parade in the streets of Nanchang on February 19, 1934. This date was specially selected by Guomindang planners to coincide with the Lantern Festival and the start of the new lunar year. In a 1936 article describing New Life, a party spokesman named Chen Hanming described the international context for this effort in the following terms:

> Mr. Franklin Delano Roosevelt, President of the United States, has given to the people of America a New Deal. Il Duce, Signor Benito Mussolini, has given the Italian people his New Deal in the form of Fascism. The Reichsfuhrer, Herr Adolf Hitler, is beloved by the people of Germany because he has given them his New Deal—National Socialism. The Union of Soviet Socialist Republics and several other nations have also received their New Deals....
>
> And now, in China, the Chinese people are being given a New Deal in the form of New Life Movement by the Chairman of the Executive Yuan and Generalissimo of the Nationalist Forces of China, General Chiang Kai-shek."[1]

One of the cherished goals of the New Life movement was to carry propriety, righteousness, incorruptibility, and a sense of shame (*liyilianchi*) to all Chinese. These clichéd neo-Confucian virtues, now carried to the masses for the first time in Chinese history by radio, in propaganda broadsides, slogans, and via other mechanisms at the disposal of the party state, were to be the formulae for national revival. Guomindang planners believed that these and other New Life moral and behavioral notions, once assimilated by ordinary Chinese, would transform China into a healthy and forward-looking nation state.

Madame Chiang Kai-shek's idiosyncratic description of the meaning

1. Walter Hanming Chen, "The New Life Movement," *Information Bulletin*, vol. 11, no. 11 (Nanjing: Council of International Affairs, December 21, 1936): 189.

and application of *liyilianchi* was designed to persuade American readers of the 1930s, in terminology they could identify with, of the high purposes of New Life.

During the heyday of the New Life movement, the slogan was thought to be a particularly potent way of conveying political and social information. To help this occur, the Nanchang headquarters drew up hundreds of slogans in 1934 and 1935 that could be conveniently memorized and chanted by middle and high school students, army trainees, and others whom the party hoped to inspire with its message.

C. W. H. Young's elegiac description of the accomplishments of the New Life movement in Jiangxi suggests how it was perceived by some members of the large American missionary community active in China in the mid-1930s. For Young and others, the spectacle of Communists reforming to match their behavior to New Life slogans under the direction of Guomindang officials was proof of the vigor of the movement and the sacrifices it could inspire. Like some Americans who visited Yan'an in the same era and returned to write glowing descriptions of what they had seen, Young was clearly inclined to emphasize features of social reform that accorded with his own perspective that, like New Life, placed enormous stress on renunciation of past sins and conversion to a wholesome spiritual worldview.

16.2 *Mme. Chiang on the New Life movement, 1935*

China, like almost every other nation during the past few years, has felt the tremendously enervating effects of world depression. Each nation, according to its lights, has sought to find a way out of stagnation into normalcy. Italy has its Fascism, Germany its Nazism, the Soviet Union its first and second five-year plans, and America its New Deal. The primary aim of each is to solve the economic problems involved and to bring material prosperity to the people. China, like the rest of the nations, is confronted with a similar problem, added to which is the necessity of rescuing the people from the cumulative miseries of poverty, ignorance, and superstition, combined with the after effects of communistic orgies and natural calamities, and last but not least, the grave consequences of external aggression.

To this end, what is known as the New Life movement has been launched, to strike at the very roots of the several evils. . . .

FOUR ANCIENT VIRTUES

The idea of the New Life movement became crystallized in the mind of Generalissimo Chiang Kai-shek during the anti-communist campaign. He realized that military occupation of recovered territory was not enough; that it must be followed up by social and economic reconstruction in the divested areas; and that, to be effective, a national consciousness and spirit of mutual co-operation must be aroused. He saw that the immediate need was the development of the vitality of the spirit of the people, which seemed to have been crushed. He contemplated the perspective of history in the light of existing conditions about him; he realized how much depended upon the people's consciousness of their heritage from the past and conviction came to him that the four great virtues of old China, *Li, I, Lien*, and *Chih* constituted a remedy that could rescue the country from stagnation and ruin, because at the time when those principles were practiced, China was indeed a great nation. He decided then and there to base a New Life movement upon them, to try to recover what had been lost by forgetfulness of this source of China's greatness. For it has become obvious that mere accumulation of wealth is not sufficient to enable China to resume her position as a great nation. There must also be a revival of the spirit, since spiritual values transcend mere material riches.

What significance lies behind these four principles which hold so much good in them for China, if they can be carried out in the spirit intended?

First the *Li*, which in the ordinary and most accepted form of translation means courtesy. And by courtesy is meant that which emanates from the heart—not a formality which merely obeys the law.

The second is *I*, which, roughly translated, means duty or service, toward the individual's fellow men and toward himself.

The third is *Lien*, meaning a clear definition of the rights of the individual and of the degree in which those rights may be enforced without infringing upon those of others. In other words, honesty. A clear demarcation between what is public and what is private, what is yours and what is mine.

The fourth is *Chih*, which denotes high-mindedness and honor.

Some people have criticized the New Life movement on the ground that, since there is not sufficient food for everyone in the land, it is useless to talk about or seek spiritual regeneration. We reject the argument by pointing out the very evident fact that, if everyone from the highest official to the lowest wheel-barrow-man would conscientiously practice these principles in everyday life, there would be food for all. If we have the right conception of *Li*, we recognize not outward pomp but the sterling native qualities in our fellow men. If we practice *I*, we feel an obligation not to hold wealth and enjoy it wastefully while our fellow countrymen may be on the verge of starvation or suffering from sickness or other misfortunes. Again with *Lien*: if officials recognize the rights of the people under them, they do not try to benefit themselves at the expense of the people just because the latter are too powerless and ignorant to fight in their own defense. And, if *Chih* is a reality, no one is shameless or stoops to mean or underhanded deeds.

Being a realist, the Generalissimo recognized that conditions in China are entirely different from what they were centuries ago when China was a great nation. At that time China could well afford to stand aloof, shut herself within the confines of her own boundaries, and keep out all intruders; but today she is part of a worldwide scheme of things, and, in order to maintain and improve her present position, she must keep in step with world progress.

So the New Life movement is based upon the preservation of these four virtues, and it aims to apply them to actual, existing conditions, in order that the moral character of the nation shall attain the highest possible standard. The Generalissimo observed that communism crushed the spirit of the people in addition to robbing them of material things; that it struck at all the fundamental principles of moral character. He found the people bereft of ideas or ideals concerning either humanity in general or their fellow men in particular. Communism was, indeed, the last abrasive in the destruction of a sense of law and order, unselfishness, loyalty, and those other qualities necessary for the development of human kindness and the maintenance of a high national consciousness. It tortured and degraded the status of man and dispossessed human life of value. In the face of this dismal prospect, the Generalissimo decided that the New Life movement could sow the first seeds of an effort to awaken in the people an urge for a more satisfying life.

THE MOVEMENT SPREADS

Not content with organizations specially delegated to these divested areas to work toward a better community life, the Generalissimo, before the end of the spring school season, called a meeting of all the middle-school students in Nanchang. He spoke at length to them of the conditions in the country at large and particularly in their own districts. He pointed out to them the necessity of recognizing the sacrifices their parents were making to give them educations and the fact that such sacrifices entailed a proportionate responsibility on the part of the students to repay the community for what they were receiving. . . .

As a direct result of this talk the students pledged themselves to return to their homes to take active part in giving a practical impetus to the principles of the New Life movement. Some pledged themselves to open up kindergartens for the village children; others, to teach night classes for the adults; others, to lecture on hygiene and sanitation; and still others, to make fly swatters and to rid their communities of breeding places of insects which carry malarial infections. The reports have just arrived, and these show that the students take their work seriously.

Out of all this is emerging a new citizen, a contented farmer and artisan, on the one hand, and, on the other, a teacher with new ideals, born of the contentment he is producing. The response of the people to the new movement on their behalf has been significant. Finding that those who have come so suddenly to work among them are working for them, they cooperate to the full and have complete confidence in their leaders. Progress is noticeable immediately. The neglect and filth which characterized the villages go quickly. Personal cleanliness is replacing erst-while indifference to dirt and disease, and the villagers' participation in the many schemes for their good develops a feeling of happiness. Corruption is being fearlessly exposed when detected; soldiers have been shorn of domineering attitudes by strict punishment for proved offenses.

The New Life movement has already come within the reach of the humblest citizen and had much to contribute to the most enlightened. As it operates in Jiangxi, so it is spreading and flourishing all over the country. In the twelve provinces recently toured by the Generalissimo, noticeable advances were seen in the general cleanliness and orderliness of the cities as well as in the recovery of spirit by the people and in a new sense of responsibility in officials. They, in contradistinction to other days, are manifesting lively concern for the well-being of the people and contributing in every way possible to the effective application of the principles of the New Life movement.

In the large centers, the missionary bodies were assembled and were addressed by the Generalissimo and by myself. In every case they signified an immediate wish to work with the leaders of the movement in their respective regions, and joint committees were at once formed under the chairmanship of the Governor of the Province. While the government is enforcing stringent measures for opium suppression, these committees will do their part in establishing opium-curing clinics and teaching the people its evil effects. They will carry on campaigns against foot-binding, tuberculosis, trachoma, and other more local evils.. . . .

In conclusion let me quote from a letter just received from one of the foreign missionaries, now in Jiangxi, on his reaction to the work sponsored there by the New Life movement:

> "The suppression of the communist-bandits and the work of the New Life Movement are proving to be the first stage of a long battle against ignorance, dirt, carelessness, unsuitable dwellings, and the corruption that has for so long cost so much in human suffering. Like the program of Christ this movement is concerned with the poor, the oppressed, the sick, and the little children who have never been given a chance to enjoy life. Out of it will come a strong and united China, which will command the respect of the world, and that new China, like the very old one, will be based firmly upon the four cardinal virtues, with the addition of those desirable elements which go to make a modern world."

16.3   *"New Life" in Brief*

RULES FOR BEHAVIOR
Clothing should be tidy and clean.
Buttons should be well buttoned.

Hats should be worn straight.
Shoes should be worn correctly.
Food should be eaten in an orderly manner.
Sit upright.
Do not throw food on the ground.
Bowls and chopsticks should be set in order.
Do not make noise while eating and drinking.
Rooms should be kept clean.
Do not write on walls.
Furniture should be simple.
The home should be tranquil.
Walk and sit with erect posture.
Be punctual for appointments.
Speak after others have finished speaking.
Help your neighbor if a fire breaks out.
Do not laugh when others have funerals.
Try to mediate the quarrels of others.
Aid others who have fallen.
Keep silent in meetings or at the theater.
Do not scold, swear at, or hit others.
Do not laugh or talk loudly on boats or in buses.
Do not call out in restaurants or teahouses.
Be polite in conversation.
Keep to the left when walking on the street.
Do not overtake others while walking.
Stay in line at the station when buying tickets.
Stay in line when entering a public place.
Say good morning to others every morning.
Say goodbye when you leave your friends.
Do not gamble or visit prostitutes.
Do not smoke opium.
If you pick up something on the street, return it to its owner.
Be careful of public property and try to make use of scrap materials.
Salute the national flag when it is raised and brought down.
Stand while singing the Party song or the National anthem.
Salute your elders.
Be polite and courteous to women and children.
Help old people, women, and the weak in getting off boats and buses.
Be filial to your parents and love your brothers and sisters.
Take off your hat in meeting places.
Do not wear your hat indoors.
Be loyal to your friends.
Be fair in business transactions.

Reduce the number of meaningless parties or gatherings.
Be frugal at weddings, funerals, and on festive occasions.

HYGIENE
Go to bed early and rise early.
Keep your face clean.
Keep your hands clean.
Wash out your mouth and keep your hair clean.
Breathe fresh air.
Comb your hair.
Cut your nails frequently.
Clothes should be kept clean.
Holes in clothing should be patched.
Bedding should frequently be washed and dried outdoors.
Children should be kept clean.
Do not eat snacks.
Do not eat unclean food.
Do not drink unboiled water.
Do not get drunk.
Do not smoke.
Sweep and clean your rooms frequently.
Drain ditches and gutters frequently.
Keep windows open as often as possible.
Keep tables and chairs clean.
Keep bowls and chopsticks clean.
Keep bathrooms clean.
Exterminate flies.
Exterminate mosquitoes.
Exterminate rats.
Do not spit on the ground.
Do not urinate as you please.
Dump garbage in garbage cans.
Do not throw waste paper on the street.
Do not throw fruit peels on the street.
Do not hang your clothes and dry them on the street.
Do not post advertisements everywhere.
Get vaccinated.
Keep bus stations and docks clean.
Keep parks and theaters clean.
Restaurants, hotels, and tea houses should be clean.
Bath houses and barber shops should be clean.
Every household should clean the street in front of its door each day.
Everyone should keep himself clean all the time.

16.4 "New Life" for the Reds

VARIOUS PHASES OF NEW LIFE MOVEMENT

The New Life movement, the aim of which is the social regeneration of China, is within reach of the humblest citizen but it has contributed much towards the most enlightened. It is reconstruction through a widespread social movement that promises rapidly to remold the life of the entire Chinese people. Progress is achieved through discipline and order, rather than through violent revolution.

It is concerned with the materials out of which life is made and it further stresses the use that shall be made of these materials. In doing so, it emphasizes both the material and spiritual in life and desires a happy blending of the two. Respect for personality and a desire to prevent the exploitation of man by man— these are the factors that are at the heart of the movement.

In the province of Jiangxi, the heart of the movement, New Life has penetrated government offices, public utilities, schools, bus lines, wharves, railways, and even the army. It will first establish itself in the heart of the administration and gradually it will extend its influence to the people. Indeed, it has already made considerable headway towards influencing the masses.

On the trains and motor buses, and on the ferries, I found cleanliness and orderliness that one hardly expected to find in the heart of an interior province. Members of the staffs were extremely courteous and gave the passengers every assistance possible: indeed, they were comparable in their courtesy to the staffs of some of the best run trains in western countries. They were courteous not because they wanted to be "tipped" ("tipping" being a practice which is not encouraged) but because they had been influenced by the New Life movement. . . .

The train between Jiujiang and Nanchang is, as a result of the operation of the New Life movement, probably the best train in the whole of China. It always keeps to time, except, of course, in case of accidents. It starts punctually on time and its third class carriages and conveniences are as scrupulously clean as the first-class. It is a train run for the benefit of the people, as a whole, not for the privileged classes alone. . . .

REFORM PROGRAM FOR CONVERTED REDS

Many have heard of what the Generalissimo and Madame Chiang Kai-shek are doing and have been doing for the past two years towards bringing about the reformation of Communists who have surrendered but few actually know the lines on which this program is being carried out as those in charge of the "repentance" camps which have been established at Jiujiang have been reluctant to discuss their activities with outsiders, much less with members of the press.

Hence, nothing has appeared in print concerning this aspect of the Generalissimo's fine work.

In the Red camp, the inhabitants and soldiers are given to believe that, should they escape from the Communist areas and flee to Government territory, they will immediately be slaughtered for aiding the Soviets. Nothing could be further from the truth, as inmates of the repentance camps will tell you. As a matter of fact, the contrary is the case.

Those who have fled into Government territory have been agreeably surprised to find that they are received with open arms, like the Prodigal Son of the Biblical tale.

As soon as they surrender, they are at once taken to the repentance camps. Here they are informed that the Government has pardoned them for their former "faults" and they are given small rewards for surrendering their arms, if they possess any.

In these camps, they are taught the error of their former ways and emphasis is placed on the fact that the Communist doctrine is one which is not suitable for China and the Chinese people. They are taught a way of earning a livelihood and, at the end of their term, they may elect either to return to their native homes or remain in the service of the Government. Not a few choose the latter alternative and they are now bitter enemies (to use their own words) of Communism and devoted followers of the Generalissimo. They are taught to see things in a new light and their policy of "first realize your own faults, then try to teach others to realize theirs. Love others as yourselves," is one which they are attempting to put into practice.

REPENTANCE CAMPS

Here in these repentance camps, they are given an elementary education, a factor which apparently was omitted from the Soviet "equality" program and they are taught to become good citizens in every sense of the word.

The repentance camps, well arranged and well equipped, luxurious from a Red viewpoint, have been established in the barracks of the huge military field at Jiujiang. All of the buildings are built on western lines and contain many commodious class-rooms, sanitary bed-rooms and bath-rooms. Emphasis is placed on the word sanitation and not a thing has been left undone to ensure that absolutely clean conditions prevail. In addition to the rooms mentioned, there are rooms for laundry work, hair-dressing saloons, clinics and a hospital, a number of recreation halls (for games, such as ping-pong, etc.), a gymnasium, several libraries and a cinema hall. In addition, the huge drill ground in front is utilized for football, basket-ball, volley-ball and other outdoor games, as well as Chinese boxing and calisthenics.

Clean and wholesome food is provided for all inmates. True, this is not elaborate but it is thoroughly appetizing and most palatable. The old rags worn in the Communist districts have been discarded and the inmates appear distinctive in neat uniforms presented by the Generalissimo himself.

INTELLECTUAL IMPROVEMENT

The living quarters are very good indeed and those visiting the camps consider that they look like superior Chinese village hotels, with the exception that conditions are much cleaner. Each inmate is provided with a bed, matting, pillows, and blankets. In addition, they are supplied with towels, soap, socks and shoes, things which, they say, are seldom to be seen in the Communist territories.

Along the lines of education, the inmates are, as already mentioned, given elementary lessons with books provided by the Special Educational movement of Jiangxi under Mr. Zheng Shigui, and lectures are given on the New Life Movement and other worthy subjects, capable of transforming the erstwhile Red men and women into useful citizens of China. Debates and discussions on useful subjects are held regularly in which all are expected to take part. Prizes are offered at regular intervals for the best literary efforts and everything is done to improve these talents and to improve the intellects of those in the camps.

The instructors are all men and women of experience and education, who, at a great sacrifice, give of their time and effort in order to make the inmates independent and good citizens. The majority of these teachers receive a small salary, which is only a percentage of what they could earn elsewhere, but they are a happy group, happy to be able to do something for their country. They believe the work they are doing is for the good of their country and their fellow-citizens.

MANUAL TRAINING

Manual training is a section of the work which must not be overlooked as it is from these classes that many graduate and return to their homes, there to take up the work which they have learned in the repentance camps. Here we find carpenters, there are shoe-makers, on the other side umbrella makers, and so on. Thus, former Reds are armed to go out into the world as independent men and women instead of forcing themselves on the communities as burdens. The better educated, instead of being given manual training, are given instruction in the big chemical laboratory.

I have already mentioned that there is a hospital and several clinics in the camp for the care of the wounded and the ill. These are all well-equipped and adequately supplied and the hospitals are as good as are to be found in any branch of the Chinese military service. All the doctors are men possessing degrees from universities and medical colleges and the nurses are members of the Chinese Nurses Association, all properly trained for the work in which they are engaged.

At the present time, there are some 9,000 former Communists in the repentance camps and others are being admitted at the rate of about a hundred a day.

Each inmate must, upon admission, undergo a physical examination. Tuberculars and others suffering from contagious or communicable diseases are segregated, the seriously wounded are removed to the military hospitals, and those suffering from slight wounds or illness of a minor nature are given clinical treatment.

HAIR CUTS COMPULSORY

It is compulsory for the former Reds to have daily baths and three hair-cuts a month, their comrades acting as barbers.

Every morning, at the call of the bugle, they are called up to drill, after which they attend lectures and other educational classes. Classes continue in the afternoon after which there is a period for recreation and then manual training. A further lecture on the New Life Movement completes the day's work and the inmates are free either to use the libraries, recreation halls, or the gymnasium.

The inmates, apart from showing a keenness to learn reading and writing and some sort of handicraft, have shown a fondness for physical culture, Chinese boxing taking the chief place. Men and women are to be seen during the recreation hours "doing their turns" and they appear to be quite adept at the Chinese art of self defence. . . .

Sunday is a camp holiday, the only compulsory item on the program on that day being that inmates should rise before eight o'clock in the morning to salute the national flag. . . .

16.5 THE STUDENTS DEMONSTRATE, DECEMBER 16, 1935

After the Japanese occupation force succeeded in creating the puppet state of Manchukuo in 1932, it moved on to its second project in conquering China: the formation of an "autonomous" north China. From 1932 to 1936, the Japanese army made impressive progress in extending its control in Inner Mongolia and north China, while the Chinese Central Government under Chiang Kai-shek's leadership had other, more urgent, priorities. Preoccupied with the Communist guerilla activities in Jiangxi and other border bases, the Guomindang government adopted a policy of "internal consolidation first, expulsion of foreign encroachments later" (*xian annei, hou anwai*) and concentrated on its "Bandit Suppression" campaigns. The Japanese were thus given a comparatively free hand as they

worked to create pro-Japanese local governments that would be the prelude for a nominally "autonomous" north China in the future.

Growing Japanese encroachment on north China and the Chinese
appeasement policy greatly alienated the Chinese intelligentsia and college
students who saw such a policy as a "selling out of the country" (*maiguo*).
Forbidden by party authorities and press censors from publicly voicing
patriotic anti-Japanese sentiments, the intelligentsia was obliged to nurse
its grievances in secret and gradually to form an opposition force. These
opponents of Nanjing believed that national resistance against the Japanese
invasion was an urgent national priority and bided their time before taking to the streets to express their hostility to Chiang's policy.

The outburst of a series of student demonstrations in December 1935,
which caught the government off guard, was thus actually the end product
of a long period of indignation and frustration over the fate of China.
Although the Chinese Communist Party (CCP) underground agents did
help students organize the demonstrations in Peking, the prime moving
force of the student movement of this decade, in which thousands of students took part, was unmistakenly patriotic and nationalistic.

The document selected here is an account from the local *Damei Evening
News* of the second major student demonstration on December 16, which
was also the most massive rally following the December 9 outburst.
Through such radical action, modern Chinese students were able to
reclaim some of the leadership role, against a new power elite represented
by the Guomindang, as the vanguard and conscience of the people in Chinese political culture, which had been traditionally played by the Confucian elite.

After eleven o'clock all of the students from the various schools converged from
all directions on Tianqiao.[2] There were no fewer than ten thousand people
present. [The vast majority of the marchers came from thirteen universities and
colleges and thirty-one middle schools.] The Citizen's Congress was declared
open and its chairman was elected by the students. The following resolutions
were passed: (1) Organize the masses, including the workers, merchants, students, peasants, soldiers, and police, to resist the enemy! (2) Let the masses arm
themselves! (3) Oppose to the death the Japanese imperialists' invasion of China!
and (4) Let students go to the Foreign Affairs Building and the Municipal
Government to inquire how it is that the local authorities are betraying the
country! They then resolved to carry out a demonstration march.

The marchers were divided into two columns with four people walking
abreast in each column. There were more participants than in any demonstra-

2. A famous marble bridge, located south of Tiananmen Square, that was known as the
Bridge of Heaven. Visitors crossed it en route to the Temple of Heaven.

tion that has occurred for the last ten years or so. The enthusiasm of the masses was also unprecedentedly high. The columns of marchers stretched for over two li. Qinghua University students led the way raising high a huge banner and flags that read: "Oppose the Hebei-Chahar Political Council!,"[3] "Down with all Chinese traitors!," "Down with Japanese imperialism." All of the other schools followed in order and waved the banners that remained after the attacks of the police. On the flanks were each school's student marshals and the bicycle communication teams. As they marched, the students cried out: "Down with Chinese traitors!," "Oppose all false organizations!," "Down with Japanese imperialism!," "Expand the national revolutionary war!" They also passed out leaflets and pasted slogans on electrical poles.

When the marchers arrived at Qianmen (the Zhengyang Gate), they found that the police had shut one of the huge doors of the gate (the other door was broken and could not be shut). The Special Service Police brandished the sabres they had used at the battle of Xifengkou[4] and dashed in among the marchers as though they were confronting a strong enemy with whom they had decided to fight to the death. When the students arrived here the police suddenly fired dozens of shots and as the crowd looked for cover the rear portion of the march unit was thrown into chaos. The police continued to fire shots and all of the shopkeepers along the street began to close up their shops and pedestrians ran wildly in all directions. In the melee three rickshaws were overturned and crushed. The marchers then turned back and went into the empty square in front of the Pinghan Railroad Station. Many of the students were now badly hurt and the two sides were locked in a tense face-off for a long time. Gradually, however, things began to quiet down. Then the students began to negotiate informally with the police. The students said to the policemen: "You are Chinese, why are you helping people to beat up other Chinese. We are not your enemy." A small number of police showed some sympathy but the face-off was maintained.

In the meantime, on Qianmen Avenue a crowd of about ten thousand people had gathered. Everyone wanted to know the reason for the shooting. Everywhere the students had put up posters and slogans, scores of people gathered around to read them in order to understand what was going on. After Qianmen was sealed off, many pedestrians were not permitted to pass through it and so gradually about two hundred people gathered before the gate. They raised a great clamor and opposed the police's opening fire on the students. Some police

---

3. Sponsored by Nanjing and set up in Peking in December 1935 to counter the Japanese "autonomist" organization in East Hebei.

4. A battle between Song Zheyuan's Chinese army and the Japanese outside the Great Wall. Song (1885–1940) was a former subordinate of Feng Yutiang who, by mid-1930, served the Nanjing government. On July 7, 1937, Song's troops clashed with the Japanese near the Marco Polo Bridge, which led to the outbreak of large-scale fighting in China.

went over to hold them in check and the crowd roared: "Beat them! Beat the running dogs!" Because there were only a few police, they felt scared and scuttled back to their lines. More police were sent and they used clubs and their belts to disperse the masses.

It was already three o'clock in the afternoon. Student representatives began negotiating with the police. The police insisted that they would not permit all of the students to pass through the Zhengyan Gate. Early that morning many policemen had been posted to guard the Hebei-Chahar Political Council Building but they were still afraid that the students would attempt to destroy it. The police then permitted the students to divide themselves into three groups; a small group could enter the city through the Zhengyang Gate while the majority would enter through the Shunzhi Gate (the West Gate). The remaining students would wait where they were until the other two groups dispersed and then a decision would be made about them. Moreover, they were not permitted to circulate leaflets.

As the students were negotiating with the police, they declared the opening of a student congress and elected a chairman on the spot. They used three bicycles to form an impromptu speaker's platform and student marshals protected it on all sides. They passed the following eight resolutions: (1) "Autonomy" or any political "autonomist" organization[5] is not in accord with the will of the people; (2) The government must apologize to and compensate students who were wounded and beaten, or stabbed; (3) The government must refuse Japan's political and economic demands; (4) Telegrams should be sent to students of the entire nation asking them to go on strike immediately and stay on strike until the government meets student demands; (5) Oppose the government's recognition of the Three Principles of Hirota;[6] (6) Demand that the government immediately halt the civil war and abolish the Hebei-Chahar Political Council; (7) Expand the people's revolutionary war; (8) Swear to fight to the death for absolute freedom to be a patriot.

After the meeting, the chairman and student leaders led the crowd in shouting slogans. When the gathering dispersed, one group of five or six hundred students from Peking University, Zhicheng Middle School, and other schools passed through Qianmen Gate and entered the city. They passed Rongxian *hutong* [narrow alleys] and as they walked they shouted slogans and passed out

5. The formation of a Japanese-sponsored "autonomist" organization in north China and Inner Mongolia was seen by Peking students as an attempt by Tokyo to gain further control of north China through pulling Hebei, Chabar, Suiyuan, and Shandong into the Eastern Hebei Autonomous Council, organized in the winter of 1935.

6. Hirota Koki (1878–1948), foreign minister of Japan in 1934. He proposed three principles (the so-called *sangensoku*) for Manchuria and north China in October 1935, including the formation of a Japan-China-Manchukuo block, the quelling of anti-Japanese activities in China, and the formation of a Sino-Japanese front to combat communism.

leaflets. After one more attack by the police, they arrived at Shunzhi Gate. The students' original intention was to join forces with other students who were to enter the city through the Shunzhi Gate but when they arrived at the gate it was still closed. It was already four o'clock and soon the more than two thousand students who were marching here from the Pinghan Railroad Station arrived. The sound of slogans shouted from inside and without the city walls echoed and re-echoed.[7]

The one thousand or so students who were outside Qianmen, insisting that they would certainly be tricked, refused to be led into the city by the police. They returned, instead, to Tianqiao and continued their speeches for about half an hour before they were again stopped by the police. They then turned about and walked to the outer side of Shunzhi Gate and joined forces with the other students already there. At five o'clock, the police and city firemen rushed up and again used sabres and bayonets to slash at the students and, finally, to force them to disperse. Three wounded girl students were all junior students from the Second Girl's Middle School. . . . There were many male students whose clothing was slashed to ribbons and who had been cut on the arms or head. They were all taken to Shoushan Hospital and Peking Union Hospital. The majority of the wounded students, however, simply returned home.

The students outside the Shunzhi Gate, feeling terribly cold and hungry, waited until eight o'clock or so but the authorities still refused to open the gate. The students from Yanjing University and Jingde Middle School then left the city through Xibian Gate. (But according to a report from the Yanjing University student union, only a few of these students had returned by the morning of the seventeenth. . . . According to students who telephoned from the city, a large number were wounded and still trapped inside the city.) . . .

Students from Yanyi Middle School and the middle school affiliated with Peking Normal University and local residents formed various relief teams to send water, rolls, and steamed buns to the hungry students [gathered at the city gate]. At nine thirty it was decided that they would go to the Normal University and spend the night there. The chill wind cut at them like a knife and the police watched them attentively. The students continued to behave as they had before and some new students, hearing of all of this, came to join them. When their march passed the Chunming Girl's Middle School, the police again swept the student's ranks with fire hoses and swarmed out with sabres and clubs from all directions to attack them. The students were already so tired and hungry they seemed about to topple over and many of them simply fell to the ground. It was already the middle of the night; there were very few passersby and the police beat them even more brutally than they had during the day. Pounding

7. The activity described here took place on the edge of the "Tartar City." The Shunzhi Gate was one of the gates of the city wall southwest of Tiananmen (the Gate of Heavenly Peace). The Pinghan Railroad Station was the terminus of the Peking-Hankow railroad line.

them with frenzied blows, the police pursued them in all directions and innumerable students were wounded. This finally halted at about ten o'clock. When the Peking Union Hospital heard of this, they immediately sent four ambulances to the rescue. They were halted, however, and constrained to return. According to reports on the 17th, thirteen students were carried to Union Hospital but there were no clear reports from other hospitals. It is impossible to calculate how many students were arrested.

16.6 AND 16.7 XI'AN 1936: THE GENERALS' DEMANDS AND CHIANG KAI-SHEK'S REPLY

The CCP survived the Long March and reached Shaanxi in October 1935. It was, however, by no means safe from the Extermination Campaign policy of the Guomindang that Chiang Kai-shek pledged to carry out under his personal direction until all Communists were eliminated. The only troops loyal to Nanjing stationed in the northwest region that could be used to carry out the suppression campaign were the soldiers of the Northeastern (Manchurian) Army under the command of Young Marshal Zhang Xueliang and those of the Northwestern Army led by Yang Hucheng. These troops, however, were reluctant to fight the Red Army. Domestic and international events had eroded their support for Chiang Kai-shek's policy of internal consolidation. Leaders and men of the armies in Shaanxi were more concerned with "National Salvation" and the threat posed by the Japanese. The Manchurian soldiers of Zhang Xueliang's army, who had been forced out of their native land by the Japanese in 1931 and 1932, were particularly susceptible to the new "National Resistance" program of the CCP, which advocated cessation of the civil war and the formation of a new united front to fight Japanese encroachments on China's territory.

Worried about the length of the suppression campaign and a possible weakening of the army's will to fight, Chiang Kai-shek flew to Xi'an on December 3, 1936, to supervise Generals Zhang and Yang as they dispatched their armies in a new offensive against the communists. On December 12, 1936, three days after massive student demonstrations in Xi'an commemorating the anniversary of the December Ninth movement, a mutiny broke out and Chiang was placed under house arrest by his field commanders in the northwest. This event stunned China and the world and led directly to the Second United Front between the GMD and the CCP.

The first document selected here, a telegram sent out to the nation by

Zhang and Yang immediately after Chiang's arrest, suggests the motives and demands of the mutinous generals. Conspicuous in this document is a tone of patriotism and selfless devotion to national goals. The second document, an excerpted passage from Chiang's admonition of Yang and Zhang issued after the Generalissimo's sudden release on Christmas 1936, was intended to rectify any "misunderstanding" of Chiang's strategic sagacity and to underline his uncompromising commitment to the recovery of China's lost territories.

16.6   *Zhang Xueliang and Yang Hucheng's Eight-Point Program*

It is now over five years since Japan occupied China. National sovereignty has been infringed upon, and more and more of our territory lost to the enemy. The humiliating Shanghai Armistice Agreement of early 1932 was followed by the signing of the Tang'gu and He-Umezu Agreements.[8] All our fellow countrymen feel distressed at these events. Recently, a great change has taken place in the international situation with some forces working hand in glove to make a sacrifice of our country and people. The start of fighting in east Suiyuan has thrown the whole country into a ferment and the morale of our troops has never been so high.

At this very moment, the central authorities should do their utmost to encourage the army and people to launch nationwide resistance against Japan. But while our officers and men are engaged in bloody fighting against the enemy at the front, our diplomats have been doing their best to reach a compromise with alien invaders. The imprisonment of the Shanghai patriots has shocked the whole world besides paining the entire Chinese nation. It distresses everyone to see patriots treated as criminals. Generalissimo Chiang, misled by mean officials and divorced from the masses of people, has made our nation suffer greatly. We—Zhang Xueliang and Yang Hucheng—have repeatedly offered him our earnest remonstrances, only to be harshly reproached. When the students in Xi'an demonstrated for national salvation, police were ordered to open fire at these patriotic youths. Anyone with a conscience could not have let things go so far! Having for long years been colleagues of the Generalissimo, we could hardly sit by idly. So we offered him our last remonstrance for the sake of his personal safety and in order to stimulate his awakening.

Now the army and people in northwest China unanimously demand:

1. Reorganize the Nanjing government to admit representatives of all parties and groups to jointly share the responsibility of saving the nation;

8. The Tang'gu Truce of May 1933 and the He-Umezu Agreement of June 1935 removed Nationalist armies from Hebei and were seen by opponents of appeasing the Japanese as stripping north China of appropriate cover.

2. End all civil war;
3. Immediately release all the imprisoned leaders of the patriotic movement in Shanghai;
4. Release all political prisoners in the country;
5. Give a free hand to the patriotic mass movement;
6. Safeguard the political freedom of the people, including the freedom of assembly;
7. Earnestly carry out Dr. Sun Yat-sen's Will; and
8. Immediately convene a conference on national salvation.

The above eight points are what we and the army and people in the northwest stand for with respect to national salvation. It is hoped that all of you, in compliance with public opinion, will endorse the aforesaid in true earnest so that there will be a ray of hope for the nation, and past wrongs will be righted. For the sake of this our just cause, we feel duty-bound to act, our sole purpose being the thorough implementation of the program of national salvation which, we believe, will benefit our nation. As for ourselves, we leave it to our compatriots to judge whether our act is a merit or crime.

Anxiously we look forward to your response.
Zhang Xueliang
Yang Hucheng

16.7 Chiang Kai-shek's Admonition to Zhang Xueliang and Yang Hucheng

"This coup d'état is an act which gravely affects both the continuity of Chinese history of five thousand years and the life and death of the Chinese nation, and it is a criterion whereby the character of the Chinese race may be judged. Since today you have shown due regard for the welfare of the nation and have decided to send me back to Nanjing and no longer try to make any special demands or force me to make any promise or give any orders, it marks a turning point in the life of the nation and is also an indication of the high moral and cultural standard of the Chinese people.

"It is an ancient Chinese saying that a gentleman should correct his mistakes as soon as he realizes them. The present outcome of the coup d'état shows that you are both ready to correct your own mistakes, and that is creditable to you as well as auguring a bright future for the Chinese race. Since you are now so convinced by my sincerity towards you that you have the courage to acknowledge your wrongdoing you are entitled to remain as my subordinates. Furthermore, since you can be so readily converted it will certainly be easier for your subordinates to follow suit.

"Formerly you were deceived by reactionaries and believed that I did not treat the people fairly and squarely and that I was not loyal to our revolutionary ideals. But now you have read my private diary for this whole year, the public and private telegrams and documents numbering some fifty thousand words that have passed through my hands during the past two months as well as my plans for the salvation of the nation and those relating to internal administration, foreign affairs, military finance and education, numbering some one hundred thousand words, you must now know that there is not a single word which could condemn me of any self-interest or insincerity on my part.

"In fact since I took military command and began to take charge of military training there are two principles which I have always emphasized to my students and subordinates, namely:

"(1) That if I have any selfish motives or do anything against the welfare of the country and the people, then anybody may consider me a traitor and may shoot me on that account.
"(2) If my words and deeds are in the least insincere and I neglect the principles and revolutionary ideals, my soldiers may treat me as their enemy and may also shoot me.

"From my diary and the other documents you can see whether you can find one word which is to the detriment of the revolution. If you can find one such word here I am still in Xi'an and you are at liberty to condemn and kill me. On my part I am glad that I have always done what I have taught other people to do, namely, to be sincere and disinterested, and I can say in all confidence that I have done nothing of which I need be ashamed.

"The responsibility of this coup d'état naturally rests with you two, but I consider myself also responsible for the causes which led up to the crisis. I have always worked for the country and always believed that my sincerity and teaching would reach all my subordinates. Hence I have not paid any attention to my personal safety. I have taken no precautions on that account and have therefore tempted the reactionaries to take advantage of the situation. Everything has its remote causes. My own carelessness was the remote cause of this coup d'état and gave rise to this breakdown of discipline, causing the Central government as well as the people much worry and the nation much loss. On this account I feel I am to be blamed and must apologize to the nation, the party and the people.

"A country must have law and discipline. You two are military officers in command of troops, and when such a coup d'état has taken place you should submit to the judgment of the Central government. However, I recognize that you were deceived by propaganda of reactionaries and misjudged my good intentions to be bad ones. Fortunately immediately after the coup you realized that it was harmful to the country and expressed your deep remorse to me. Now you have further realized your own mistake in listening to reactionaries and are now convinced that not only have I had no bad intentions towards you, but that I have always had every consideration for you.

"I have always told my subordinates that when they make mistakes their superiors must also be blamed for not having given them adequate training. As I am in supreme command of the army, your fault is also my fault, and I must ask for punishment by the Central Authorities. At the same time I will explain to them that you sincerely regret what you have done. As you have rectified your mistake at an early stage, the crisis has not been prolonged, and I believe the Central Authorities should be able to be lenient with you. . . .

"The policy of the Central government for the last few years has been to achieve peace in and unification of the country and to increase the strength of the nation. Nothing should be done to impair this strength. During the present crisis, as you engineered the coup, you are responsible for bringing about warfare in the country. But as you have expressed remorse, I shall recommend the Central government to settle the matter in a way that will not be prejudicial to the interests of the nation.

"In short you now know the situation of our country as well as my determination to save it. I always give first thought to the life and death of the nation as well as the success or failure of the revolution and do not pay any attention to personal favours or grudges. Questions of personal danger or loss are of no interest to me. I have had the benefit of receiving personal instruction from Dr. Sun concerning broad-mindedness, benevolence and sincerity, and am not vindictive with regard to things that have passed. As you felt remorse very early, it shows that you know that the welfare of the nation is above everything else. That being the case, you ought to obey unreservedly the orders of the Central government and carry out whatever decisions it may make. This is the way to save the nation from the dangers it is facing, and this is the way to turn a national calamity into a national blessing."

CHAPTER 17

World War II

17.1 AND 17.2 JAPAN AT WAR

When the Japanese army launched its all-out attack on Chinese troops in north China after the Marco Polo Bridge Incident on July 7, 1937, the uneasy peace between Nanjing and Tokyo came to a definitive end. Despite the initiation of hostilities, a declaration of war was never issued by the invader and in the early phase of the war, both sides diplomatically referred to the state of war existing between them as the "Sino-Japanese conflict" or "Far Eastern conflict" to leave room for possible negotiations and a mutually agreeable compromise that might conclude the fighting. During this state of "conflict," however, major battles were waged in north and central China, tens of thousands of civilian Chinese were brutally massacred in Nanjing, province after province was lost to the Japanese occupation army, and the Chinese government was forced to move its capital to the interior mountain city of Chongqing. From this wartime capital, Chiang Kai-shek continued to resist Japan without substantial foreign help until after Japan's attack on Pearl Harbor.

In the historical perspective of Sino-Japanese relations since the late nineteenth century, the outbreak of the war seemed to many contemporary Chinese an inevitable consequence of Japan's long-term expansionist policy in Asia. It was true, as Japan's prime minister Prince Konoe argues in the first document selected here, that Japan did not originally intend to use military force against China as long as the latter was willing to eliminate all anti-Japanese sentiments and accept the constraints Japan set on China's sovereign rights. But Konoe's claim that "the right of self-defence as well as the cause of righteousness and humanity" justified Japan's invasion of China was a deception.

The second document, written by Horosi Saito, then Japanese ambassador to the United States, follows this line of justification and attributes the cause of war to China's century-old xenophobic attitude. Saito, in an attempt to dissuade Western nations, principally the U.S., from helping China, suggests that conditions for foreigners anxious to live or trade in China would be more secure under Japanese rule. Saito also condemns rampant political corruption in China and its leaders' stubborn refusal to follow the Western way of life as the source of the sufferings that afflicted the Chinese people. For the Japanese, he implies, the war was a great sacrifice of national resources and human lives designed to foster the welfare of the Chinese people and the "peace and security in the Far East."

17.1 Prince Konoe's Address, September 1937

ADDRESS

OF

PRINCE AYAMARO KONOYE, PRIME MINISTER
AT THE 72ND SESSION OF THE IMPERIAL DIET
—SEPTEMBER 5, 1937—

I am profoundly moved to say that His Imperial Majesty's most gracious message regarding the China affair was granted us at the opening of the Imperial Diet yesterday. It is my humble desire that we shall be able to set His Majesty's heart at rest by our loyal and devoted service to the Throne in accordance with the august will of our Sovereign.

Since the outbreak of the affair in North China on July 7th, the fundamental policy of the Japanese Government toward China has been simply and purely to seek the reconsideration of the Chinese Government and the abandonment of its erroneous anti-Japanese policies, with the view of making a basic readjustment in relations between Japan and China. This policy has never undergone a change; even today it remains the same. The Japanese Government has endeavored to save the situation by preventing aggravation of the incident and by limiting its scope. This has been repeatedly enunciated; I trust that is fully understood by you.

The Chinese, however, not only fail to understand the true motives of the Government, but have increasingly aroused a spirit of contempt and have offered resistance toward Japan, taking advantage of the patience of our Government. Thus, by the outburst of uncontrolled national sentiment, the situation has fast been aggravated, spreading in scope to Central and South China. And now, our Government, which has been patient to the utmost, has acknowledged the impossibility of settling the incident passively and locally, and has been forced to deal a firm and decisive blow against the Chinese Government in an active and comprehensive manner.

In point of fact, for one country to adopt as its national policy the antagonizing of and the showing of contempt for some particular country, and to make these the underlying principles of national education by implanting such ideas in minds of the young, is unprecedented in the history of the world. Thus, when we consider the outcome of such policies on the part of China, we feel grave concern not only for the future of Sino-Japanese relations, but for the peace of the Orient and consequently for the peace of the entire world. The Japanese Government, therefore, has repeatedly requested the Chinese Government to reconsider and to change its attitude, but all in vain. This failure of the Chinese Government has finally caused the present affair.

We firmly believe that it is in accordance with the right of self-defence as well as with the cause of righteousness and humanity that our country has determined to give a decisive blow to such a country, so that it may reflect upon the errors of its ways.

For the peoples of East Asia, there can be no happiness without a just peace in this part of the world. The Chinese people themselves by no means form the objective of our actions, which objective is directed against the Chinese Government and its army who are carrying out such erroneous, anti-foreign policies. If, therefore, the Chinese Government truly and fully reexamines its attitude and in real sincerity makes endeavors for the establishment of peace and for the development of culture in the Orient in collaboration with our country, our Empire intends to press no further.

At the present moment, however, the sole measure for the Japanese Empire to adopt is to administer a thoroughgoing blow to the Chinese Army so that it may lose completely its will to fight. And if, at the same time, China fails to realize its mistakes and persists in its stubborn resistance, our Empire is fully prepared for protracted hostilities. Until we accomplish our great mission of establishing peace in the Orient, we must face many serious difficulties, and, in order to overcome them, we must proceed steadily with our task, adhering to the spirit of perseverance and fortitude in one united body. . . .

17.2   The Japanese Ambassador Explains, 1937

I

The conflict in the Far East is by no means as simple in origin as some Europeans and Americans seem to think. The trouble did not begin last July. It is a result of the condition of China, which has caused the invasion of foreign armies for more than a century and is the reason for the presence there today of British, French, Italian, Dutch and American troops. If China's house were in order there would be no need for the presence of these foreign forces or of Japan's present action. In fact, if law and order were maintained in China, if China were a unified and stabilized nation, it would be able to "drive all foreigners into the sea"—which has been the objective of many of its anti-foreign movements.

Who is to blame for the condition of China? Is it Great Britain, which sought for decades to help successive Chinese governments to organize their two principal sources of revenue, the Maritime Customs and the Salt Gabelle,[1] and administer them without corruption? Is it France, which has sent more missionaries and teachers to them than to all other backward nations combined? Is it Japan, which almost staked her existence in a war with Russia to prevent "the break-up of China"—a disaster expected throughout the world at the time of the Boxer Rising in 1900? It is difficult for many Japanese to understand how so many people of the West can fail to see that the trouble is not of foreign but of Chinese making.

It might be well at this point to review the circumstances which placed Japanese troops in North China. Japan, like Great Britain, France, Italy and the United States, keeps a permanent garrison in the Peking-Tientsin area. The right to do so was established by the agreements with China which followed the Boxer outrage in 1900. When the trouble began there again this summer, the Japanese garrison numbered one soldier for every four Japanese residents in the area. The European and American garrisons provided one soldier for every two of their nationals. Surely, if our Government had contemplated aggression or even anticipated a serious conflict our forces would not have been but six or eight thousand men.

The fighting at Shanghai was begun a month later by circumstances similar to those in the North. In an editorial on this point, *The Christian Science Monitor* said some weeks ago, "Belief that China forced the issue at Shanghai is not restricted to Japanese spokesmen and apologists. A number of foreign observers have expressed the opinion that the swift increase in the number of disguised Chinese troops in the region which was supposedly covered by the truce of 1932 was a main factor in precipitating hostilities."

The 1932 truce-agreement, which set up a demilitarized zone around Shanghai in which no Chinese troops were to be stationed, was concluded by Japanese and Chinese officials and countersigned by the representatives of the United States, Great Britain, France and Italy. This agreement was designed to prevent the recurrence of fighting in or around Shanghai. In direct violation of it thousands of regular Chinese army soldiers were sent into the demilitarized zone disguised as peasants and gendarmes, and by early August the 30,000 Japanese civilians in Shanghai were in grave danger of mass murder. Japan's defense force of 3,000 marines faced 30,000 Chinese soldiers. This made it nec-

---

1. The Qing monopoly on the production and sale of salt.

essary to strengthen the Japanese squadron on the river. The Chinese opened hostilities by attempting to bomb the Japanese naval vessels and the Japanese Consulate-General. As is well known, their aim was so bad that several of the bombs fell in the most crowded section of the International Settlement, killing thousands of Chinese and several foreigners, including my good American friend, Dr. Reischauer.

The present conflict has been forced upon Japan, and Japan wants to end it as quickly as possible. But she is determined to end it in a way so decisive that a situation like the present can never recur. Our objective, therefore, is a genuine change-of-heart on the part of those in power at Nanjing. We insist that the organized campaign to stir up hate against Japan be discontinued and that the Central Government renounce the union with Communism which was solemnized at Xi'an, in Shaanxi Province, when General Chiang Kai-shek was released from imprisonment last Christmas Day.

Premier Konoye, Foreign Minister Hirota and War Minister Sugiyama, have all stated that Japan is not bent on conquest and has no desire to detach or annex any part of China. What our government and people want is peace and security in the Far East. If only in our own selfish interests we seek the welfare of the colossal nation beside which we must continue to live for all time.

In a number of North China cities temporarily local governments have grown up to replace the military administrations which have disappeared with the retreating Chinese armies. These "Peace Preservation Committees," formed by local Chinese leaders, are successfully maintaining civil order. But they have been given to understand that Japan will not support them in any move to secede from the rest of China. Indeed, the commanders of the Japanese garrisons not only permitted but encouraged the people of North China to celebrate what the Chinese call the "Double-Tenth" holiday on October 10, the anniversary of the founding of the Chinese Republic. This is evidence of our intentions. . . .

. . . . With China's millions Japan has no quarrel—nor have those millions anything to fear from Japan. In fact, even at this moment several thousand Chinese students are attending Japanese schools and tens of thousands of Chinese businessmen are conducting their trades as usual in Japan. At no time since the present trouble began has there been a single case of violence against any Chinese living in Japan.

The underlying accord of our peoples prompts in me high hope that when the leaders of the Nanjing regime and the Chinese Nationalist Party adopt a reasonable policy toward Japan, it will not take long to spin close ties of friendship and harmony of incalculable benefit to both China and Japan, and of much also to the rest of the world. With permanent peace between Japan and China, progress will be made in East of Asia that will redound to the benefit of others in a spread of the feeling of security and an expansion of general and profitable trade and cultural relations. The progress of Japan has brought an enormous increase of trade to Western Counties, particularly the United States, and the peace of China cannot fail to bring progress to the industrious and well-meaning masses of her people.

17.3 CHIANG REPLIES, 1938

Toward the end of 1938, the Japanese army controlled the eastern half of China, having pressed the Chinese resistance forces into the less populated and economically backward interior. In the eyes of Japanese militarists, the fall of Canton and Wuhan marked a "turning point" in the Sino-Japanese "conflict." The Chinese government under Chiang Kai-shek was stripped, by the reality of the Japanese invasion, of its legitimacy as the Central Government of China and converted into a "local government." Japan now encouraged the Chinese to start serious collaboration efforts with the Japanese occupation army. Since Chiang Kai-shek was adamant in his promise to carry on a resistance war to the end, the Japanese began to place their hope on a split within the Guomindang and the establishment of a separate collaborationist government under Japanese control.

Statements of the Japanese government laid out the theoretical foundation for the Japanese wartime project of a "Greater East Asia Co-Prosperity Sphere," a euphemism for Japanese rule throughout east and southeast Asia. Accusing the Guomindang government of being not only anti-Japanese but also procommunist, the Japanese hoped to strengthen support for the war policy at home and deflect the hostile public opinion of the West.

In response to Japan's new call for Chinese collaboration, Chiang Kai-shek, in an address before a meeting at the Central Guomindang Headquarters in Chongqing on December 26, 1938, sought to expose Japan's design of subjugating China and dominating east Asia. The address specifically attacks a statement made by Prince Konoe on December 22, 1938, which, Chiang believed, illuminated the true intentions of Japan's new policy.

GENERALISSIMO CHIANG ASSAILS PRINCE KONOYE'S STATEMENT

Comrades, our resistance has now entered a new phase. I have recently pointed out on several occasions that the past eighteen months may be called the first period of our resistance of the preliminary period. We have now entered upon the second or latter period. At present, on both northern and southern warfronts the excellence of our soldiers' morale and fighting spirit provides an auspicious sign unprecedented since the war commenced. Our soldiers are fully aware that in this war our enemy is bent on subjugating China completely and that we must take the most drastic measures to save our country. Their determination is, therefore, extraordinarily strong and their spirit roused to the uttermost.

Our people also understand that the enemy will not pause until he has fully realized his malevolent designs and the ultimate aim of his aggression in the destruction of China. If we do not seek life by braving death we cannot expect to survive in any fortuitous way. . . .

Konoye's statement is intrinsically nothing more than sheer wearisome repetition of canting phrases. Solemnly engaged in our resistance as we are, it would seem unnecessary for us to pay any attention to it, let alone refute it. Considering it, however, together with the enemy's deeds and words of the past months, we perceive that the statement, though superficially vague and incoherent, has a keen edge hidden beneath. It might be called, in short, a complete exposure of the fantastic Japanese programme to annex China, dominate East Asia and further even to subdue the world. It is also a complete revelation of the contents of the enemy. . . .

What I wish to draw the attention of all to is the barbarism of the Japanese militarists, their insanity, their practice of deceiving themselves and others, and their gross ignorance. What is most urgent is that all should realize that Japan is determined to swallow China entirely. Taking Konoye's statement on December 22 as the pivot for my observations, I shall now recall what Japanese popular sentiment has championed during the past few months and what cabals and slogans have been actually put into practice. By analysis, a comprehensive understanding may be gained. For convenience of narration I shall first draw attention to the following four points:—

(1) THE SO-CALLED "CREATION OF A NEW ORDER IN EAST ASIA!"

The Japanese take special pride in this slogan. According to the Japanese Foreign Minister, Arita, in his explanation of December 19: "The new order in East Asia consists in Japan, Manchukuo, and China assisting and co-operating with each other closely in politics, economics and culture to combat the Red Peril, to protect Oriental civilization, to remove economic barriers, and to help China rise from her semi-colonial status so as to secure peace in the Far East." On December 14, Konoye also said: "The ultimate objective of the China Incident lies not merely in achieving military triumph but in a rebirth of China and the erection of a new order in East Asia. This new order will be based on tripartite cooperation of a new China with Japan and Manchukuo."

Let all observe that what he meant by a China reborn was that independent China was to perish and in its place an enslaved China created, which would abide by Japan's word from generation to generation. The so-called new order would be based on the intimate relations that would tie the enslaved China to the Japanese-created Manchukuo and Japan herself. What is the real aim? Under the pretext of opposition to the "Red Peril," Japan seeks to control China's military affairs; claiming to uphold Oriental civilization, Japan seeks to uproot China's racial culture; and by urging the elimination of economic barriers, she aspires to exclude American and European influence and dominate the Pacific. Again, the so-called "economic unity" of Japan, Manchukuo and China is the instrument she intends to use for obtaining a strangle-hold on China's economic arteries. Let us try to realize the immense evils with which the words "creation of a new order in East Asia" are pregnant. In a word, it is a term for the overthrow of international order in East Asia, and the enslavement of China as the means whereby Japan may dominate the Pacific and proceed to dismember other states of the world.

(2) THE SO-CALLED "UNITY OF EAST ASIA," "INDIVISIBILITY OF JAPAN, MANCHUKUO AND CHINA," "LINKED RELATIONS OF MUTUAL ASSISTANCE BETWEEN JAPAN, MANCHUKUO AND CHINA."

To make a "homogeneous body" of East Asia has been a much-touted Japanese slogan during the past few months. The application of this slogan is broader, vaguer and more general than that of the so-called "economic unity" or "economic bloc."

Advancing the theme of an "indivisibility of Japan, Manchukuo and China," the Japanese aim to absorb China politically, economically, and culturally into one body with their own country. Japanese periodicals have maintained that the structural relationship of the "East Asia unity" should be vertical with Japan at the summit, and not in any sense horizontal; the system of relationship should be patriarchal, with Japan as patriarch and Manchukuo and China as offspring. In other words, the former is to be the governor and master while the latters are to be the governed and underlings.

What is it if it is not annexation? What is it if it is not the total extinction of China? Konoye's phrase, "the establishment of linked relations of mutual assistance in matters political, economic and cultural between Japan, Manchukuo and China," puts me in mind only of links and manacles and shackles. His "linked relations" would be the forged chains which would drag us down into a pit from which we would never escape.

(3) THE SO-CALLED "ECONOMIC UNITY" AND "ECONOMIC BLOC."

This has been promoted for many years by the Japanese, and the thesis has recently been as prevalent as ever and has even made rapid headway. It is essential to the proposed "homogeneity of East Asia." They have rung many changes on the wording of the slogan: they have called it on occasion "economic reciprocity" and "economic co-operation." In the manifesto of the Japanese Government issued on November 3, it was described as "economic union." In the latter part of November enemy newspapers printed the headline "Japan, Manchukuo and China are to form an economic unity and henceforth share a common fate." Subsequently Arita in his statement of December 19 said: "Japan has resolved to convene an economic conference to bring about an intimate economic confederation between Japan, Manchukuo and China and to invigorate the resulting economic monad."

Japan has, in fact, already installed such instruments of economic aggression as the "North China Development Company" and the "Central China Development Company." Economic conversations have already been held more than once by self-styled representatives of Manchukuo and China with those of Japan. What the Japanese call their "Planning Bureau" adopted, two days after Konoye's statement was made, a resolution urging "the expansion of the productive capacity of Japan, Manchukuo and China." The "economic bloc" is designed to be the means of not only taking control over our customs revenue and finance and of monopolizing our production and trade, but also of gradually limiting the individual freedom of our people even in regard to what they eat and wear, where they live and whither they move. The Japanese are to do as they please: to have power among us over life and death, the power of binding and losing; we are then to become their slaves and cattle, and the whole of our nation will thus be dissolved beneath the lash of tyranny.

(4) THE CREATION OF THE SO-CALLED "ASIATIC DEVELOPMENT BUREAU."

This organ was introduced after much agitation for a medium through which to deal with China. A "China Bureau" was once projected, which has now given way to this "Asia Development Bureau." The former term is insulting and dreaded enough, but the comprehensiveness of the latter is a flagrant insult to all the peoples of Asia. Japan is set not only on ruining and dismembering China alone, but her ambition embraces the entire Asiatic Continent.

On the day before the official inauguration of this "Asia Development Bureau" on December 15, Konoye stated that "a new executive organ should be constituted for creating a new order in East Asia: this organ in conjunction with other organs abroad will maintain coherent relations between Japan and China: it will become the key to executing our China policy, the fulfillment of which is our final object in regard to the China Incident." This should serve to acquaint all with the true function of the organ: to be the means of executing a policy designed to destroy China. For it may be described as Japan's highest special service organ combining all the special service branches long set up all over China for the working of all manner of villainy, which formerly operated with the greatest stealth because it was regarded premature to work openly. Now, however, they boldly unmask themselves and are accorded official status. By establishment of the "Asia Development Bureau" a concentrated light is thrown upon the means and ends of Japanese policy; the tortuous and obscure devices pursued for years are seen with their supreme aim openly confessed. All concealment is at an end. . . .

On our part, the war for a year and a half has laid for us a solid foundation for national regeneration. We fear no problems, nor are we concerned over impending dangers. We merely lament the fate of Japan, the present status of which was brought about by the hard efforts and sacrifices of her reformist patriots. To-day, her people are powerless, her throne without prerogative, and her politicians without integrity and knowledge, thus allowing a few hot-headed young militarists to do as they please. They are sapping Japan's national strength, shaking her national foundations and advancing savagely on the infamous road of self-seeking at the expense of others. In the eyes of these young Japanese militarists, China does not exist, nor do the other countries of the world. They have regard neither for discipline, nor for law, nor yet for their own government. Guided by their greed, cruelty, and violence, they do as they please. If such conduct be allowed to continue, the future of Japan is indeed full of danger. Although we are sworn enemies of the Japanese militarists, yet we are still neighbors to the Japanese people, who share with us a language of a common origin. Reviewing Japan's history and looking forward to her future, we not only see danger in her path but lament her lot. . . .

China as a state is founded on the principle of not oppressing the undefended, nor fearing the aggressive. More particularly, she is not willing to violate pacts or break faith and thus destroy the righteous principles governing the relations of mankind. I remember the meeting of Tanaka and our late Tsungli (Dr. Sun Yat-sen) in Shanghai in the third year of the Republic which coincided with the outbreak of the Great War in Europe. Tanaka proposed that East Asiatics should at the time denounce all rationed relations with foreign countries and erect a new order in East Asia. Dr. Sun queried: "Would it not involve the breaking of international treaties?" To which Tanaka retorted: "Is not the denunciation of treaties and termination of unequal obligations advantageous to China?" "Unequal treaties should be terminated by straightforward and legitimate procedure," solemnly declared Dr. Sun, "and China is not prepared to become a party to the illegal denunciation of treaties even though advantageous to our country." Comrades, such is China's spirit. It is also the spirit of the Three People's Principles. We have relied on this spirit to resist invasion; we have depended on this spirit to resist all forms of domination, force and violence. We should be sustained by this spirit to restore order in East Asia and offer it as a contribution towards enduring world peace. . . .

A Chinese proverb says: "Virtue never lacks company; it will ever find support." The force of world justice will rise, and men of goodwill ultimately cooperate in the interests of rectitude. On our part, we should hold fast to our goal, and be firm in our determination. Our firmness should increase with greater difficulties, and our courage should rise with prolonged resistance. The entire nation should carry on with oneness of heart. The final victory will be ours. I urge my comrades, our army, and our people to redouble their efforts in order to attain success.

17.4 AND 17.5 THE RAPE OF NANJING

On December 13, 1937, one month after the Japanese Army had taken Shanghai, the first elements of General Iwane Matsui's attacking forces entered Nanjing. A few days before, in a message calling upon the Chinese garrison commander of the Nationalist capital to surrender, Matsui had declared: "Though harsh and relentless to those who resist, the Japanese troops are kind and generous to noncombatants and to Chinese troops who entertain no enmity to Japan." In reality, the officers and men of the Imperial Army were to show neither kindness nor generosity to the hapless citizenry of Nanjing. Their capture of the city was the prelude for a month-long reign of terror in the streets and outskirts of the erstwhile center of Guomindang power. During this time, unarmed Chinese prisoners of war were used as living targets for bayonet and rifle practice; drunken mobs of Japanese infantry roamed the streets looting, murdering, and raping; and large parts of Nanjing were burned to ground by fires that were deliberately set by the invading forces. By the time martial law was finally imposed by the Japanese command, the once bustling city of Nanjing, its streets in ruins and its prewar population of nearly one million decreased to less than two hundred thousand, was practically a ghost town.

The following letter from an anonymous foreign resident of Nanjing and some excerpts of a diary kept by the same author during the grim days of December 1937, were both reprinted in a volume on the "Rape of Nanjing" compiled by H. J. Timperley, China correspondent for the *Manchester Guardian*. They provided foreign readers with an eyewitness account of the consequences of the arrival of the Japanese invasion force. These accounts of the takeover of Nanjing describe a violence that was at once random and deliberate. The slaying of groups of panicked refugees, the rapes, and the burning were all part of a policy of violence that also countenanced deliberate roundups and executions of captured Nationalist troops.

In an appendix, Timperley also reprinted copies of two short articles published respectively on December 7 and 14, 1937, by the *Japan Advertiser*, an English daily printed in Tokyo, that described the competition between two young Japanese officers to kill Chinese and reflected too clearly the small price placed by the Imperial Army on Chinese lives.

17.4 *Bearing Witness*

On Tuesday the 14th [December 1937] the Japanese were pouring into the city—tanks, artillery, infantry, trucks. The reign of terror commenced, and it was to increase in severity and horror with each of the succeeding ten days. They were the conquerors of China's capital, the seat of the hated Chiang Kai-shek government, and they were given free reign to do as they pleased. The proclamation on the handbills which airplanes scattered over the city saying that the Japanese were the only real friends of the Chinese and would protect the good, of course meant no more than most of their statements. And to show their 'sincerity' they raped, looted and killed at will. Men were taken from our refuge camps in droves, as we supposed at the time for labor—but they have never been heard from again, nor will they be. A colonel and his staff called at my office and spent an hour trying to learn where the "six thousand disarmed soldiers" were. Four times that day Japanese soldiers came and tried to take our cars away. Others in the meantime succeeded in stealing three of our cars that were elsewhere. On Sone's[2] they tore off the American flag, and threw it on the ground, broke a window and managed to get away all within the five minutes he had gone into Prof. Stanley's[3] house. They tried to steal our trucks—did succeed in getting two,—so ever since it has been necessary for two Americans to spend most of their time riding trucks as they delivered rice and coal. Their experience in dealing daily with these Japanese car thieves would make an interesting story in itself. And at the University Hospital they took the watches and fountain pens from the nurses. . . .

At our staff conference that evening word came that soldiers were taking all 1,300 men in one of our camps near headquarters to shoot them. We knew there were a number of ex-soldiers among them, but Rabe[4] had been promised by an officer that very afternoon that their lives would be spared. It was now all too obvious what they were going to do. The men were lined up and roped together in groups of about a hundred by soldiers and bayonets fixed; those who had hats had them roughly torn off and thrown on the ground,—and then by the light of our headlights we watched them marched away to their doom.

2. Reverend Hubert L. Sone, American, Nanjing Theological Seminary.
3. Professor C. Stanley, American, Nanjing Theological Seminary.
4. Hans Rabe was a German businessman who tried to protect Chinese civilians in Nanjing. He left an illuminating diary which describes the sacking of the city.

Not a whimper came from the entire throng. Our own hearts were lead. Were those four lads from Canton who had trudged all the way up from the south and yesterday had reluctantly given me their arms among them, I wondered; or that tall, strapping sergeant from the north whose disillusioned eyes, as he made the fatal decision, still haunt me? How foolish I had been to tell them the Japanese would spare their lives! We had confidently expected that they would live up to their promises, at least in some degree, and that order would be established with their arrival. Little did we dream that we should see such brutality and savagery as has probably not been equalled in modern times. For worse days were yet to come.

The problem of transportation became acute on the 16th, with the Japanese stealing our trucks and cars. I went over to the American Embassy where the Chinese staff were still standing by, and borrowed Mr. Atcheson's car for Mills[5] to deliver coal. For our big concentrations of refugees and our three big rice kitchens had to have fuel as well as rice. We now had twenty-five camps, ranging from two hundred to twelve thousand people in them. In the University buildings alone there were nearly thirty thousand and in Ginling College, which was reserved for women and children, the three thousand were rapidly increased to over nine thousand. In the latter place even the covered passageways between buildings were crowded, while within every foot of space was taken. We had figured on sixteen square feet to a person, but actually they were crowded in much closer than that. For while no place was safe, we did manage to preserve a fair degree of safety at Ginling, to a lesser degree in the University. Miss Vautrin,[6] Mrs. Twinem[7] and Mrs. Chen[8] were heroic in their care and protection of the women.

That morning the cases of rape began to be reported. Over a hundred women that we knew of were taken away by soldiers, seven of them from the University library; but there must have been many times that number who were raped in their homes. Hundreds were on the streets trying to find a place of safety. At tiffin [tea] time Riggs,[9] who was associate commissioner of housing, came in crying. The Japanese had emptied the Law College and Supreme Court and taken away practically all the men, to a fate we could only guess. Fifty of our policemen had been taken with them. Riggs had protested, only to be roughly handled by the soldiers and twice struck by an officer. Refugees were searched for money and anything they had on them was taken away, often to their last

5. Reverend W. P. Mills, American, Northern Presbyterian Mission.

6. Miss Minnie Vautrin, American, Ginling College.

7. Mrs. Paul DeWitt Twinem, formerly American but now a Chinese citizen, University of Nanjing.

8. Mrs. Chen, matron and superintendent of Dormitories, Ginling College.

9. Charles H. Riggs, American, University of Nanjing.

bit of bedding. At our staff conference at four we could hear the shots of the execution squad nearby. It was a day of unspeakable terror for the poor refugees and horror for us. . . .

Friday, Dec. 17. Robbery, murder, rape continued unabated. A rough estimate would be at least a thousand women raped last night and during the day. One poor woman was raped thirty-seven times. Another had her five months infant deliberately smothered by the brute to stop its crying while he raped her. Resistance means the bayonet. The hospital is rapidly filling up with the victims of Japanese cruelty and barbarity. Bob Wilson, our only surgeon, has his hands more than full and has to work into the night. Rickshas, cattle, pigs, donkeys, often the sole means of livelihood of the people, are taken from them. Our rice kitchens and rice shop are interfered with. We have had to close the latter.

After dinner I took Bates[10] to the University and McCallum[11] to the hospital where they will spend the night, then Mills and Smythe to Ginling, for one of our group has been sleeping there each night. At the gate of the latter place we were stopped by what seemed to be a searching party. We were roughly pulled from the car at the point of the bayonet, my car keys taken from me, lined up and frisked for arms, our hats jerked off, electric torches held to our faces, our passports and purpose in coming demanded. Opposite us were Miss Vautrin, Mrs. Twinem and Mrs. Chen, with a score of refugee women kneeling on the ground. The sergeant, who spoke a little French (about as much as I do), insisted there were soldiers concealed there. I maintained that aside from about fifty domestics and other members of their staff there were no men on the place. This he said he did not believe and said he would shoot all he found beyond that number. He then demanded that we all leave, including the ladies, and when Miss Vautrin refused she was roughly hustled to the car. Then he changed his mind: the ladies were told to stay and we to go. We tried to insist that one of us should stay too, but this he would not permit. Altogether we were kept standing there for over an hour before we were released. The next day we learned that this gang had abducted twelve girls from the school.

Saturday, Dec. 18. At breakfast Riggs, who lives in the Zone a block away but has his meals with us, reported that two women, one a cousin of a Y.M.C.A. Secretary, were raped in his house while he was having dinner with us. Wilson reported a boy of five years of age brought to the hospital after having been stabbed with a bayonet five times, once through his abdomen; a man with eighteen bayonet wounds, a women with seventeen cuts on her face and several on her legs. Between four and five hundred terrorized women poured into our headquarters compound in the afternoon and spent the night in the open.

10. Dr. M. S. Bates, American, University of Nanjing.
11. Reverend James H. McCallum, American, University of Nanjing Hospital.

Sunday, Dec. 19. A day of complete anarchy. Several big fires raging today, started by the soldiers, and more are promised. The American flag was torn down in a number of places. At the American School it was trampled on and the caretaker told he would be killed if he put it up again. The proclamations placed on all American and other foreign properties by the Japanese Embassy are flouted by their soldiers, sometimes deliberately torn off. Some houses are entered from five to ten times in one day and the poor people looted and robbed and the women raped. Several were killed in cold blood, for no apparent reason whatever. Six out of seven of our sanitation squad in one district were slaughtered; the seventh escaped, wounded, to tell the tale. Toward evening today two of us rushed to Dr. Brady's[12] house (he is away) and chased four would-be rapers out and took all women there to the University. Sperling is busy at this game all day. I also went to the house of Douglas Jenkins[13] of our Embassy. The flag was still there; but in the garage his house boy lay dead, another servant, dead, was under a bed, both brutally killed. The house was in utter confusion. There are still many corpses on the streets. All of them civilians as far as we can see. The Red Swastika Society would bury them, but their truck has been stolen, their coffins used for bonfires, and several of their workers bearing their insignia have been marched away.

Smythe and I called again at the Japanese Embassy with a list of fifty-five additional cases of violence, all authenticated, and told Messers, Tanaka[14] and Fukui[15] that today was the worst so far. We were assured that they would 'do their best' and hoped that things would be better 'soon,' but it is quite obvious that they have little or no influence with the military whatever, and the military had no control over the soldiers. . . .

Wednesday, Dec. 22. Firing squad at work very near us at 5 a.m. today. Counted over a hundred shots. The University was entered twice during the night, the policeman at the gate held up at the point of a bayonet, and a door broken down. The Japanese military police recently appointed to duty there were asleep. Representatives of the new Japanese police called and promised order by January 1. They also asked for the loan of motorcars and trucks. Went with Sperling to see fifty corpses in some ponds a quarter of a mile east of headquarters. All obviously civilians, hands bound behind backs, one with the top half of his head cut completely off. Were they used for sabre practice? On the way home for tiffin stopped to help the father of a Y.M.C.A. writer who was being threatened by a drunken soldier with the bayonet, the poor mother

---

12. Dr. Richard F. Brady, American, acting superintendent of the University of Nanjing Hospital.
13. Douglas Jenkins, Jr., third secretary, American Embassy.
14. Sueo Tanaka, attache, Japanese Embassy (now Consul).
15. Kiyoshi Fukui, Japanese consul-general, Nanjing.

frantic with fear, and before sitting down had to run over with two of our fellows to chase soldiers out of Gee's[16] and Daniel's[17] houses, where they were just about to rape the women. We had to laugh to see those brave soldiers trying to get over a barbed wire fence as we chased them!

Bates and Riggs had to leave before they were through tiffin to chase soldiers out of the Sericulture building—several drunk. And on my arrival at office there was an S.O.S. call, which Rabe and I answered, from Sperling and Kroeger who were seriously threatened by a drunk with a bayonet. By fortunate chance Tanaka of the Embassy together with some general arrived a the same moment. The soldier had his face soundly slapped a couple of times by the general but I don't suppose he got any more than that. We have heard of no cases of discipline so far. If a soldier is caught by an officer or M.P. he is very politely told that he shouldn't do that again. In the evening I walked home with Riggs after dinner—a woman of fifty-four had been raped in his house just before our arrival. It's cruel to leave the women to their fate, but of course it is impossible for us to spend all our time protecting them. Mr. Wu, engineer in the power plant which is located in Hsiakwan, brought us the amusing news that forty-three of the fifty-four employees who had so heroically kept the plant going to the very last day and had finally been obliged to seek refuge in the International Export Company, a British factory on the river front, had been taken out and shot on the grounds that the power plant was a government concern—which it is not. Japanese officials have been at my office daily trying to get hold of these very men so they could start the turbines and have electricity. It was small comfort to be able to tell them that their own military had murdered most of them.

17.6 *The Nanjing "Murder Race"*

SUB-LIEUTENANTS IN RACE
TO FELL 100 CHINESE
RUNNING CLOSE CONTEST

Sub-lieutenant Toshiaki Mukai and Sub-lieutenant Takeshi Noda, both of the Katagiri unit of Kuyung, in a friendly contest to see which of them will first fell 100 Chinese in individual sword combat before the Japanese forces completely occupy Nanjing, are well in the final phase of their race, running almost neck to neck. On Sunday when their unit was fighting outside Kuyung, the

16. C. T. Gee, Chinese, resident architect and engineer, University of Nanjing.
17. Dr. J. H. Daniel, American, superintendent, University of Nanjing Hospital.

"score," according to the newspaper the *Asahi*, was: Sub-lieutenant Mukai, 89, and Sub-lieutenant Noda, 78.

On December 14, 1937, the same paper published the following additional report:

CONTEST TO KILL FIRST 100 CHINESE WITH SWORD EXTENDED WHEN BOTH FIGHTERS EXCEED MARK

The winner of the competition between Sub-lieutenant Toshiaki Mukai and Sub-lieutenant Takeshi Noda to see who would be the first to kill 100 Chinese with his Yamato sword has not been decided, the *Nichi Nichi* reports from the slopes of Purple Mountain, outside Nanjing. Mukai has a score of 106 and his rival has dispatched 105 men, but the two contestants have found it impossible to determine which passed the 100 mark first. Instead of settling it with a discussion, they are going to extend the goal by 50.

Mukai's blade was slightly damaged in the competition. He explained that this was the result of cutting a Chinese in half, helmet and all. The contest was "fun," he declared, and he thought it a good thing that both men had gone over the 100 mark without knowing that the other had done so.

Early Saturday morning, when the *Nichi Nichi* man interviewed the sub-lieutenant at a point overlooking Dr. Sun Yat-sen's tomb, another Japanese unit set fire to the slopes of Purple Mountain in an attempt to drive out the Chinese troops. The action also smoked out Sub-lieutenant Mukai and his unit, and the men stood idly by while bullets passed overhead.

"Not a shot hits me while I am holding this sword on my shoulder," he explained confidently.

17.6 WANG JINGWEI: ON COLLABORATION, 1941

It was a sad irony that Wang Jingwei's career as a revolutionary and Chinese patriot ended in shameless collaboration with the forces of the Japanese occupation. After the Mukden Incident, Wang was briefly one of the most violent and outspoken critics of Chiang Kai-shek's policy of nonresistance to Japanese aggression. However, after he joined the Guomindang government as head of the Executive Yuan in January 1932, he ceased his attacks on Chiang and accommodated his position to fit that of the party.

After the Marco Polo Bridge Incident and the Japanese occupation of much of coastal China, Wang urged Chiang Kai-shek to open negotiations with the Japanese but was ignored. Convinced that the war policy of the Chongqing government would bleed China dry, Wang Jingwei decided to act on his ideas and in December 1938 he fled to Hanoi where he announced his support for a negotiated settlement to the war. Starting in mid-1939, he entered into talks with the Japanese in Hanoi and then Shanghai to prepare a secret memorandum defining relations between the two countries. In March 1940, he agreed to head a collaborationist "national" government in Shanghai.

One of the first fruits of Wang's cooperation with Tokyo was the Sino-Japanese Treaty signed on November 30, 1940. As the text of this treaty shows, Wang's government was willing to make the most sweeping concessions to conciliate its Japanese masters. Not since Yuan Shikai's acceptance of the Twenty-one Demands in 1915 had any Chinese government signed so humiliating a document.

After 1940, the Faustian bargain that Wang Jingwei had struck with the Japanese repeatedly threw him into grotesque and self-abasing postures. By June, 1941, as the Tokyo radio address that the follows illustrates, the brave and often visionary rhetoric that had once distinguished Wang Jingwei was now replaced by the language of submission. Although Wang Jingwei's defenders have maintained that Wang secretly continued to serve and fight for the interests of his countrymen, his public stance was akin to that of other *quislings* (collaborationist leaders) during the war years.

RADIO ADDRESS BY MR. WANG JINGWEI, PRESIDENT OF THE CHINESE EXECUTIVE YUAN BROADCAST ON JUNE 24, 1941

I am deeply moved as I speak to you today in Tokyo, the capital of your great country. I studied in your country 38 years ago. My stay then was short, and due particularly to my limited abilities I could not master your language and learning. However, if, fortunately, I know something, I owe it to my old teachers and classmates. I can never forget what they have done for me. To have been able to come to your great country again and meet you, the people of Japan, is like meeting my old teachers and classmates and I am filled with the warm feeling. . . .

When the slogan of "the construction of a new order in East Asia" was heard in your country, our people found a gleam of hope in the darkness. When the Konoe Statement was issued, in particular, how the two nations can cooperate was made clearly and concretely known to us, and we have been led to take steps looking to the realization of the hope.

The significance of the construction of a new order in East Asia lies, on the one hand, in endeavoring to eliminate from East Asia the evils of Western economic imperialism from which this part of the world has suffered for the past century and, on the other, in checking the rising tide of Communism which has been threatening our prosperity for these twenty years. Japan was the only country in the East who could shoulder the responsibility for such undertakings single-handedly. Although we have Dr. Sun Yat-sen's Pan-Asianism, his followers and compatriots have failed to make united efforts for the attainment of that ideal.

There may be causes for the recent unfortunate conflict between our two countries. If, however, we examine ourselves as to why we have failed in our efforts to purge the country of the evils of Western economic imperialism and to check the rise of Communism, thereby leaving the country to deteriorate into a semi-colonial status and the people in the deepest distress, we cannot but blame ourselves. When we heard of the slogan of the construction of a new order in East Asia put forth by Japan, we immediately opened our eyes to the fact that it was not time for quarreling among ourselves, and realized that we should revert to our essential character founded upon the moral principles of the East, breaking down the old order consisting of a chain of pressures brought to bear upon us by economic imperialism and Communism, and establish a new order based on independence, freedom, co-existence and co-prosperity. China could not but hesitate to take up such a heavy responsibility when she thought of her limited spiritual and material resources. Moreover, the conditions in which she found herself were too difficult for her to readily undertake such a heavy responsibility. This hesitation, however, was overcome when she heard the Konoe Statement; she knew for the first time that Japan had already surmounted such difficulties on behalf of China.

The most important significance of the Konoe Statement, I believe, lies in the fact that Japan will give aid to China in providing such conditions as are necessary for her development into a modern State if China herself will participate with determination and sincerity in the construction of a new order in East Asia. The reason why Japan adopted this definite policy was that if Japan and China unite and proceed with the construction, it will result not only in the establishment of permanent peace between the two countries but also in the reconstruction of East Asia. . . .

I and my colleagues in the National Government of China have never failed to examine ourselves constantly as to our responsibilities for increasing strength; and at the same time we are making efforts to induce Chungking leaders to join in the peace movement. As a matter of fact, we have been and are ceaselessly making every effort to induce them through various channels to join us in the peace movement; we will continue to do so in the future.

I should like to add that not only number but also quality is important in the development of the peace movement. The basic objective of peace is to realize Pan-Asianism and to establish a new order in East Asia. In our efforts to attain that objective the peace movement should be purified in quality as it grows in numbers; its quality should not be changed or weakened by an increase in numbers. Not to give economic imperialism any chance to recover its influ-

ence and not to give Communism an opportunity to succeed are two main points
which we should not neglect.

I was deeply moved when I paid a visit to His Imperial Minister, the
Emperor, who granted me His gracious words concerning Sino-Japanese friendship. Yesterday Prime Minister Prince Konoe and I issued a joint statement as
a result of our conversations for several days. We are firmly determined to strive
hereafter for the accomplishment of the purpose in accordance with the statement. I want to tell you tonight of this inflexible determination of mine, and
taking this occasion I want to express my deep appreciation of your expectations
for our future and for your warmest sympathy for and powerful aid to our
cause. Certainly I am moved by your kindness; I shall never forget to the end
of my life all that you have done for me. At the same time, however, I cannot
but be ashamed to think of the fact of how little I have accomplished; I am not
worthy of all your kindness. Only let me take back with me your kindness and
sympathy to the people at home, so that they may fully appreciate your earnest
wishes for Sino-Japanese friendship. All our people will unite with you, I am
sure, for the performance of the high task to which the peoples of East Asia
are called. My friends, no one knows what new developments may take place
tomorrow in the international situation. Whatever happens, the attitude of our
two countries to reconstruct East Asia in the friendly relationship of co-existence
and co-prosperity will be forever unchangeable.

In conclusion, let me wish you health and prosperity. *Banzai* for the Empire
of Japan! *Banzai* for the Republic of China!

17.7 LIU SHAOQI: HOW TO BE A GOOD COMMUNIST, 1939

During the war years the Chinese Communist party, like other governments, parties, and protogovernments in China's history, labored to devise
an ideal model for behavior with which to inspire its followers. The invasion of China's coastal regions had driven millions of refugees into the hin-
terlands of China and the new recruits who had come to Yan'an from
Shanghai, Tianjin, Peking, and other parts of China had to be taught to
adhere to party discipline and to serve as reliable cogs in the political
machinery being constructed in the Liberated Zones. Many of the refugees
from urban areas were intellectuals who may have worked on the fringes
of clandestine leftist organizations but were by no means accustomed to
behaving in docile accord with party dictates.

In July 1939, in lectures delivered at the Institute of Marxism-Leninism,
one of the party's major cadre schools in Yan'an, Liu Shaoqi, a former
Shanghai labor organizer and senior party official, attempted to synthesize

notions of what was meant by a "good Communist" for newcomers to the ranks of the party and also for veteran party members.

The short excerpt from Liu's long theoretical speech on the theme of being a good communist that is included here stresses self-cultivation and a mode of personal remolding very much in harmony with traditional Confucian mores. Communist and revolutionary standards replaced, of course, the benchmarks provided by the neo-Confucian tradition but the idea of creating individual behavior in perfect harmony with ethical models provided by the party and state was all too familiar.

WHY COMMUNISTS MUST UNDERTAKE SELF-CULTIVATION

Why must Communists undertake to cultivate themselves?

In order to live, man must wage a struggle against nature and make use of nature to produce material values. At all times and under all conditions, his production of material things is social in character. It follows that when men engage in production at any stage of social development, they have to enter into certain relations of production with one another. In their ceaseless struggle against nature, men ceaselessly change nature and simultaneously change themselves and their mutual relations. Men themselves, their social relations, their forms of social organization, and their consciousness change and progress continuously in the long struggle which as social beings they wage against nature. In ancient times, man's mode of life, social organization, and consciousness were all different from what they are today, and in the future they will again be different.

Mankind and human society are in process of historical development. When human society reached a certain historical stage, classes and class struggle emerged. Every member of a class society exists as a member of a given class and lives in given conditions of a class struggle. Man's social being determines his consciousness. In class society the ideology of the members of each class reflects a different class position and different class interests. The class struggle constantly goes on among these classes with their different positions, interests, and ideologies. Thus it is not only in the struggle against nature but in the struggle of social classes that men change nature, change society and at the same time change themselves. . . .

When we say that Communists must remold themselves by waging struggles in every sphere against the counter-revolutionaries and reformists, we mean that it is through such struggles that they must seek to make progress, and must enhance their revolutionary quality and ability. An immature revolutionary has to go through a long process of revolutionary tempering and self-cultivation, a long process of remolding, before he can become a mature and seasoned revolutionary who can grasp and skillfully apply the laws of revolution. For in the first place a comparatively immature revolutionary, born and bred in that old society, carries with him remnants of the various ideologies of that society (including its prejudices, habits, and traditions), and in the second he has not been through a long period of revolutionary activity. Therefore he does not yet have a really thorough understanding of the enemy, of ourselves, or of the laws of social development and revolutionary struggle. In order to change this state of affairs, besides learning from past revolutionary experience (the practice of our predecessors), he must himself participate in contemporary revolutionary practice, and in this revolutionary practice and the struggle against all kinds of counter-revolutionaries and reformists, he must bring his conscious activity into full play and work hard at study and self-cultivation. Only so can he gradually acquire deeper experience and knowledge of the laws of social development and revolutionary struggle, acquire a really thorough understanding of the enemy and ourselves, discover and correct his wrong ideas, habits and prejudices, and thus raise the level of his political consciousness, cultivate his revolutionary qualities and improve his revolutionary methods.

Hence, in order to remold himself and raise his own level, a revolutionary must take part in revolutionary practice from which he must on no account isolate himself. He cannot do so, moreover, without subjective effort, without self-cultivation and study, in the course of practice. Otherwise, it will still be impossible for him to make progress. . . .

Tempering and self-cultivation in revolutionary practice and tempering and self-cultivation in proletarian ideology are important for every Communist, especially after the seizure of political power. The Communist Party did not drop from heaven but was born out of Chinese society. Every member of the Communist Party has come from this society, is living in it today, and is constantly exposed to all its evils. It is not surprising then that Communists, whether they are of proletarian or non-proletarian origin and whether they are old or new members of the Party, should carry with them to a greater or lesser extent the thinking and habits of the old society. In order to preserve our purity as vanguard fighters of the proletariat and to enhance our revolutionary quality and working ability, it is essential for every Communist to work hard to temper and cultivate himself in every respect. . . .

CHAPTER 18

The Fall of the Guomindang State

18.1 WEN YIDUO: THE POET'S FAREWELL, 1946

Wen Yiduo (1899–1946) was one of twentieth-century China's most important poets. Some of his earliest poems, such as "The Laundryman's Song," were critical of the racial discrimination he experienced during his time as a student at the Art Institute in Chicago during the 1920s. In general, however, Wen Yiduo was largely apolitical prior to the outbreak of the Second World War. He led a reclusive scholarly life, served as a professor of Chinese literature at Qinghua University in Peking, and concentrated on the study of Chinese and Western art, ancient poetry, and Chinese mythology.

After the outbreak of the war, Wen Yiduo followed Qinghua University when it moved to Changsha and then to Kunming in flight from the advancing Japanese. This long journey, much of it by foot, renewed Wen Yiduo's interest in art and drew him back to the realities of life for the common people of China.

Toward the end of the war, disillusioned by the corruption of the Nationalist government, Wen became actively engaged in reform politics. He argued eloquently for democracy and mass mobilization to defeat the Japanese. As a writer, editor, and public speaker he often attacked the Guomindang, which nicknamed him "Wenyiduofu" (the added *fu* made Wen's name sound like the transliteration of a Russian name).

After the war, Wen Yiduo actively opposed the resumption of the civil war. He was outraged when his friend Li Gongpu, a longtime political opponent of the Guomindang and leading member of the Democratic League, was assassinated by Nationalist secret police on July 9, 1946. Six days later, at a memorial service for Li Gongpu, Wen Yiduo delivered a fiery address attacking all *tewu* (special service agents) in the audience and condemning the moral bankruptcy of the Chiang government. Returning to his home following this gathering, Wen was shot by government agents on a street corner not far from his own doorstep.

Intellectuals throughout China were outraged by this cold-blooded political assassination. During the years of the civil war and later, Wen's manner of death was alluded to often by speakers eager to prove the despotic character of the Guomindang. Reproduced below is the text of Wen Yiduo's final speech at Li's memorial service as it was recorded by a contemporary listener.

A few days ago, as we are all aware, one of the most despicable and shameful events of history occurred here in Kunming. What crime did Mr. Li Gongpu commit that would cause him to be murdered in such a vicious way? He merely used his pen to write a few articles, he used his mouth to speak out, and what he said and wrote was nothing more than what any Chinese with a conscience would say. We all have pens and mouths. If there is a reason for it, why not speak out? Why should people be beaten, killed, or, even worse, killed in a devious way? [Applause]

Are there any special agents [Guomindang spies] here today? Stand up! If you are men, stand up! Come forward and speak? Why did you kill Mr. Li? [Enthusiastic applause] You kill people but refuse to admit it and even circulate false rumors that the murder happened because of some sexual scandal or as the result of Communists killing other Communists. Shameless! Shameless! [Applause] This is the shamelessness of the Guomindang but the glory belongs to Mr. Li. Mr. Li participated in Kunming's democratic movement for a number of years. Now he has returned to Kunming and sacrificed his own life. This is Mr. Li's glory, it is the glory of the people of Kunming!

Last year, at the time of the December 1st Incident, the young students of Kunming were slaughtered for demonstrating against the civil war and that was a case of the younger generation sacrificing its precious lives. Now, Mr. Li, striving for democracy and peace, has also suffered assassination by the reactionaries. Let me proudly say, an old comrade-in-arms has now sacrificed his precious life for my generation. Both of these incidents happened here in Kunming and this will be an eternal glory for Kunming. [Applause]

After the news of the reactionary's assassination of Mr. Li spread, everyone was indignant and outraged. I certainly can't understand the heart of those shameless creatures; under these circumstances how can they fabricate false rumors to insult Mr. Li? But in fact it is very simple. The reason they are madly creating terror is because they themselves are in a panic! They are afraid! They create terror because they feel terrified!

Special agents, think about it, how many days are left for you?

Do you really think that if you hurt a few or kill a few, that you can intimidate the whole people? In fact, you cannot beat all of the people or kill all of the people. For every Li Gongpu you kill, hundreds of millions of Li Gongpus will stand up! [Applause] In the future you will lose the support of hundreds of millions of people.

The reactionaries believe that they can reduce the number of people participating in the democratic movement and destroy its power through the terror of assassination. But let me tell you, our power is great, our power is enormous! [Applause] Look! All of these people today are our people and their power is our power. [Applause]

The power of the people will win and truth will live forever! [Applause] Throughout history, all who have opposed the people have been destroyed by the people! Didn't Hitler and Mussolini fall before the people? Chiang Kai-shek, you are so rabid, so reactionary, turn the pages of history, how many days do you think you have left? You're finished! It is over for you! [Enthusiastic applause]

Bright days are coming for us. Look, the light is before us. Just as Mr. Li said as he was dying: "Daybreak is coming!" Now is that darkest moment before dawn. We have the power to break through this darkness and attain the light! The coming of our light marks the final moment for the reactionaries! [Applause]

Mr. Li's blood was not shed in vain! Mr. Li gave his life and we shall demand a price in return. We have this confidence and we must have this confidence. . . .

Reactionaries, you have seen one man fall but have you seen hundreds of millions stand up?

Justice can never be killed because truth lives forever! . . . [Applause]

To attain democracy and peace, we must pay a price. We are not afraid of making sacrifices. Each of us should be like Mr. Li. When we step through the door, we must be prepared never to return. [Long, enthusiastic applause]

18.2 GENERAL MARSHALL: THE MEDIATOR'S VIEW, 1947

After VJ (Victory over Japan) Day, the United States government was eager to bring about a coalition government uniting the Guomindang and the Chinese Communist party. General George Marshall, the wartime U.S. chief of staff, was sent to China by President Truman in mid-December 1945 to attempt to work out a cease-fire and the formation of a Political Consultative Conference (PCC) that might set in place the foundations for one national government and army. Initially, Marshall believed that both sides were receptive to the concept of a unity government; he was received cordially by Chiang and Mao and steps were already underway in January 1946 to build the PCC.

In the end, however, the decades of political opposition, civil war, and deep feelings of mutual suspicion foreordained the failure of the Marshall Mission. Intractable opponents to a unity government worked against Marshall in both the Nationalist and Communist camps. By the spring of 1946 armed clashes had already broken out between the two parties. Marshall continued his attempts to forestall civil war during the summer of 1946 but by the end of that year he was obliged to acknowledge the futility of further American efforts to stave off war.

The statement below was released on January 7, 1947, just before Marshall's return to the United States. It reflected his conviction that efforts to unite the Nationalists and Communists were doomed by their intransigence and the lack of any moderate force in Chinese politics capable of acting as a buffer between them in a coalition government. When Marshall was, subsequently, appointed secretary of state, he adopted a wait-and-see policy for the United States that precluded an active search for solutions to the deepening crisis in China.

The greatest obstacle to peace[in China] has been the complete, almost overwhelming suspicion with which the Chinese Communist Party and the Guomindang regard each other.

On the one hand, the leaders of the Government are strongly opposed to a communistic form of government. On the other, the Communists frankly state that they are Marxists and intend to work toward establishing a communistic form of government in China, though first advancing through the medium of a democratic form of government of the American or British type.

The leaders of the Government are convinced in their minds that the Communist-expressed desire to participate in a government of the type endorsed by the Political Consultative Conference last January had for its purpose only a destructive intention. The Communists felt, I believe, that the government was insincere in its apparent acceptance of the PCC resolutions for the formation of the new government and intended by coercion of military force and the action of secret police to obliterate the Communist Party. Combined with this mutual deep distrust was the conspicuous error by both parties of ignoring the effect of the fears and suspicions of the other party in estimating the reason for proposals or opposition regarding the settlement of various matters under negotiation. They each sought only to take counsel of their own fears. They both, therefore, to that extent took a rather lopsided view of each situation and were susceptible to every evil suggestion or possibility. . . .

I think the most important factors involved in the recent breakdown of negotiations are these: On the side of the National Government, which is in effect the Guomindang, there is a dominant group of reactionaries who have been opposed, in my opinion, to almost every effort I have made to influence the formation of a genuine coalition government. This has usually been under the cover of political or party action, but since the Party was the Government, this action, though subtle or indirect, has been devastating in its effect. They were quite frank in publicly stating their belief that cooperation by the Chinese Communist Party in the government was inconceivable and that only a policy of force could definitely settle the issue. This group includes military as well as political leaders.

On the side of the Chinese Communist Party there are, I believe, liberals as well as radicals, though this view is vigorously opposed by many who believe that the Chinese Communist Party discipline is too rigidly enforced to admit of such differences of viewpoint. Nevertheless, it has appeared to me that there is a definite liberal group among the Communist ideology in the immediate future. The dyed-in-the-wool Communists do not hesitate at the most drastic measures to gain their end as, for instance, the destruction of communications in order to wreck the economy of China and produce a situation that would facilitate the overthrow or collapse of the Government, without any regard to the immediate suffering of the people involved. They completely distrust the leaders of the Guomindang and appear convinced that every Government proposal is designed to crush the Chinese Communist Party. I must say that the quite evidently inspired mob actions of last February and March, some within a few blocks of where I was then engaged in completing negotiations, gave the Communists good excuse for such suspicions.

However, a very harmful and immensely proactive phase of the Chinese Communist Party procedure has been in the character of its propaganda. I wish to state to the American people that in the deliberate misrepresentation and abuse of the action, policies and purposes of our Government this propaganda has been without regard for the truth, without any regard whatsoever for the facts, and has given plain evidence of a determined purpose to mislead the Chinese people and the world and to arouse a bitter hatred of Americans. It has been difficult to remain silent in the midst of such public abuse and wholesale disregard of facts, but a denial would merely lead to the necessity of daily denials, an intolerable course of action for an American official. In the interest of fairness, I must state that the Nationalist Government publicity agency has made numerous misrepresentations, though not of the vicious nature of the Communist propaganda. Incidentally, the Communist statements regarding the Anping incident[1] which resulted in the death of three Marines and the wounding of twelve others were almost pure fabrication, deliberately representing a carefully arranged ambuscade of a Marine convoy with supplies for the main-

1. A clash between U.S. Marines and Communist troops that occurred near Tianjin, on July 29, 1946.

tenance of Executive Headquarters and some UNRRA supplies, as a defence against a Marine assault. The investigation of this incident was a tortuous procedure of delays and maneuvers to disguise the true and privately admitted facts of the case.

Sincere efforts to achieve settlement have been frustrated time and again by extremist elements of both sides. The agreements reached by The Political Consultive Conference a year ago were a liberal and forward-looking charter which then offered China a basis for peace and reconstruction. However, irreconcilable groups within the Guomindang, interested in the preservation of their own feudal control of China, evidently had no real intention of implementing them. Though I speak as a soldier, I must here also deplore the dominating influence of the military. Their dominance accentuates the weakness of civil government in China. At the same time, in pondering the situation in China, one must have clearly in mind not the workings of small Communist groups or committees to which we are accustomed in America, but rather of millions of people and an army of more than a million men. . . .

Between this dominant reactionary group in the Government and the irreconcilable Communists who, I must state, did not so appear last February, lies the problem of how peace and well-being are to be brought to the long-suffering and presently inarticulate mass of the people of China. The reactionaries in the Government have evidently counted on substantial American support regardless of their actions. The Communists by their unwillingness to compromise in the national interest are evidently counting on an economic collapse to bring about the fall of the Government, accelerated by extensive guerrilla action against the long lines of rail communications—regardless of the cost of suffering to the Chinese people.

The salvation of the situation, as I see it, would be the assumption of leadership by the liberals in the Government and in the minority parties, a splendid group of men, but who as yet lack the political power to exercise a controlling influence. Successful action on their part under the leadership of Generalissimo Chiang Kai-shek would, I believe, lead to unity through good government.

In fact, the National Assembly has adopted a democratic constitution which in all major respects is in accordance with the principles laid down by the all-party Political Consultative Conference of last January. It is unfortunate that the Communists did not see fit to participate in the Assembly since the constitution that has been adopted seems to include every major point that they wanted.

Soon the Government in China will undergo major reorganization pending the coming into force of the constitution following elections to be completed before Christmas Day 1947. Now that the form for a democratic China has been laid down by the newly adopted constitution, practical measures will be the test. It remains to be seen to what extent the Government will give substance to the form by a genuine welcome of all groups actively to share in the responsibility of government.

The first step will be the reorganization of the State Council and the executive branch of Government to carry on administration pending the enforcement of the constitution. The manner in which this is done and the amount of representation accorded to liberals and to non-Guomindang members will be significant. It is also to be hoped that during this interim period the door will remain open for Communists or other groups to participate if they see fit to assume their share of responsibility for the future of China.

It has been stated officially and categorically that the period of political tutelage under the Guomindang is at an end. If the termination of one-party rule is to be a reality, the Guomindang should cease to receive financial support from the Government.

I have spoken very frankly because in no other way can I hope to bring the people of the United States to even a partial understanding of this complex problem. I have expressed all these views privately in the course of negotiations; they are well known, I think, to most of the individuals concerned. I express them now publicly, as it is my duty, to present my estimate of the situation and its possibilities to the American people who have a deep interest in the development of conditions in the Far East promising an enduring peace in the Pacific.

18.3 CHIANG STEPS DOWN

Chiang Kai-shek was obliged to "retire" from office three times in his political career: in 1927, in 1931, and in 1949. In the first two cases, Chiang was forced by political opponents to retreat to his hometown of Fenghua in Zhejiang but was later able to defeat opponents and to place himself again at the helm of the Nationalist party.

In 1949, however, following the Manchurian campaign and the catastrophic defeat at Xuzhou in November 1948, Chiang's army was broken and many of his erstwhile generals sat in Communist prisons. In the meantime, civil society, afflicted by runaway inflation and chronic shortages, was clearly beyond Nanjing's control. Under these circumstances, Chiang was again obliged to give up the leadership of the Nationalist government. This time he abdicated control to his vice president Li Zongren. Li, a Guangxi warlord and ancient political enemy, had, ironically, been instrumental in pushing Chiang from office at the time of his first "retirement" in 1927. After abandoning the presidency to Li, Chiang continued to move troops and economic resources to Taiwan but deliberately left Li Zongren out of the planning process. By now, Guomindang control of the mainland was utterly fragmented and many civil and military personnel loyal to Nanjing actively searched for means to depart China.

After the fall of the mainland, Li Zongren departed for exile in the United States but Chiang Kai-shek proved a more long-lived feature of the Chinese political scene. Having evacuated some two million troops to Taiwan and other offshore islands, Chiang again took office as the president of the Republic of China on Taiwan on March 1, 1950, and would serve in this capacity until his death in 1975. The two documents reproduced here reflect the complex political maneuvering that took place on the eve of the Nationalist defeat and the sense of enormous confusion in the GMD camp prior to the transition to Communist power.

PRESIDENT CHIANG'S STATEMENT ON RETIREMENT (JANUARY 21, 1949)

Since I issued my New Year message urging the restoration of peace, the entire nation, with one accord, has echoed its unreserved support. However, although more than two weeks have now elapsed, warfare has not yet drawn to a close and the ultimate aim of achieving peace has not been realized. Consequently an end to the people's suffering still is not in sight.

With the hope that the hostilities may be brought to an end and the people's suffering be relieved, I have decided to retire. As from Jan. 21, Vice-President Li Zongren will exercise the duties and powers of President in accordance with Article 49 of the Constitution which provides that "in the event the President, for any reason, is unable to perform his functions, his duties and powers shall be exercised by the Vice-President." I hope the entire nation, including both the military and civilian populations, as well as the various Government departments and agencies, will unreservedly, and with on heart, support Vice-President Li in order that a lasting peace may be achieved.

I have devoted my entire life to the work of the people's revolution, observing strictly the Three Principles of the People. From the fifteenth year of the Republic when we set out from Canton on the Northern Punitive Expedition to the time when national unity was achieved, I never for a moment failed to consider it my sacred duty to implement the principle of nationalism, give effect to the principle of democracy and improve the livelihood of the people.

At the same time, I have always realized that it is absolutely necessary to secure peace for the country before a sound foundation can be laid for the improvement of the nation's political and economic life. That is why for more than twenty years, while I was sometimes forced to resort to military measures in dealing with domestic affairs, I have always been prepared to make personal sacrifices and concessions. The only exception was the war of resistance against

Japanese aggression, in which case I was determined to fight to the bitter end. This is a record well borne out by facts.

My earnest prayers will have been answered if the Communist Party henceforth comes to the full realization of the grave situation confronting the country, orders a cease-fire, and agrees to commence peace talks with the Government. Thus the people will be spared their intense sufferings, the spiritual and material resources of the nation preserved and its territorial integrity and political sovereignty maintained. Thus, also, the continuity of the nation's history, culture and social order will be perpetuated and the people's livelihood and freedom safeguarded.

VICE-PRESIDENT LI'S STATEMENT (JANUARY 21, 1949)

In consideration of the difficulties on confronting the nation and the hardships suffered by the people and with a view to promoting the early realization of peace, President Chiang Kai-shek has decided to retire from office. In accordance with Article 49 of the Constitution, I as Vice-President, shall exercise the duties and powers of the President.

It is with great diffidence that I accept such heavy responsibilities. I have worked for more than twenty years for the consummation of the revolution under the leadership of the President. In these years, I have gained an intimate knowledge of the great care the President exercised in performing the duties of his high offices and the emphasis he always placed upon the welfare of the nation and the people. In matters relating to his personal position, he has always exercised great prudence and shown extreme sincerity. Once a decision is made, he never changes his mind.

In the circumstances, I have found it impossible to decline the performance of the duties thus entrusted to me. I can only do my best to serve the country with loyalty, hoping to maintain the continuity of the affairs of state and to complete the President's mission in bringing about the salvation of the nation and the people.

It is my hope that all the people of the nation will extend to me their sincere cooperation, that all civil and military officials will remain at their respective posts and that one and all will, in accordance with the policy of peace and reconstruction, exert their concerted effort for the attainment of democracy and freedom.

18.4–18.5 MAO TAKES CHARGE

The rapid advance of Mao's armies after the surrender of Peking brought many cities and regions that had never experienced Communist administration under the control of the CCP. On April 21, 1949, the Communist armies forced their way across the Yangzi River and by April 23, Nanjing fell to the Second Field Army led by Liu Bocheng and Deng Xiaoping. In the months that followed, the entire lower Yangzi River basin, once the bastion of Guomindang power, was captured by the Red Army. It was clear by the beginning of the summer of 1949 that victory in the civil war belonged to the Communists.

A Chinese saying tells that "an army in defeat falls like a mountain" (*bingbai ru shandao*) and certainly this was true of Chiang Kai-shek's army. Despite huge quantities of superior weapons and material, the Guomindang was unable to resist the Communist onslaught; the military ineptness of Chiang Kai-shek and his coterie of Whampoa generals and the low morale of many of the troops they commanded ultimately spelled defeat for the Nationalist army. In the final analysis, the Communist victory was both a political victory and a triumph of arms. Superior military organization and training, the higher motivation of Red Army troops, and excellent generalship were the decisive elements of Communist victory in the civil war. Like the Manchus in the seventeenth century, the Communists experienced the euphoria of unifying China through their military victories.

The two documents that follow capture the mood in the Communist camp as their troops advanced to take the Guomindang capital of Nanjing on April 23, 1949. Like Prince Dorgon in 1644, Chairman Mao was no longer obliged to coddle his enemies. The outcome of the war was clearly in sight and rhetoric of compromise or conciliation was no longer necessary. Instead, Mao sought to reassure erstwhile enemies of his good intentions and promised a quick restoration of order. Simultaneously, knowing that a rapid victory in the southeast would prevent the demolition of the industrial base built by the GMD, he spurred on Red Army commanders to complete the military consolidation of China.

18.4 *The Army Advances*

ORDER TO THE ARMY FOR THE COUNTRY-WIDE ADVANCE (APRIL 21, 1949)

Comrade commanders and fighters of all field armies, comrades of the People's Liberation Army in the guerrilla areas of the south!

The Agreement on Internal Peace, drafted after long negotiations between the delegation of the Communist Party of China and the delegation of the

Nanjing Guomindang government, has been rejected by that government. The responsible members of the Nanjing Guomindang government have rejected the agreement because they are still obeying the orders of U.S. imperialism and Chiang Kai-shek, the chieftain of the Guomindang bandit gang, and because they are trying to block the progress of the cause of the Chinese people's liberation and prevent the internal problem from being solved by peaceful means. The Agreement on Internal Peace, comprising eight sections with twenty-four articles formulated by the two delegations in the negotiations, is lenient on the problem of war criminals, is lenient towards the Guomindang officers, soldiers and government personnel and provides appropriate solutions for other problems, all proceeding from the interests of the nation and the people. The rejection of this agreement shows that the Guomindang reactionaries are determined to fight to the finish the counter-revolutionary war which they started. The rejection of this agreement shows that in proposing peace negotiations on January 1 of this year the Guomindang reactionaries were only trying to check the advance of the People's Liberation Army and thus gain a breathing space for a later comeback to crush the revolutionary forces. The rejection of this agreement shows that the Li Zougren government at Nanjing was utterly hypocritical in professing to accept the Chinese Communist Party's eight terms for peace as the basis for negotiations. Inasmuch as the Li Zongren government had already accepted such fundamental terms as the punishment of war criminals, the reorganization of all the reactionary Guomindang troops on democratic principles and the handing over of all power and authority by the Nanjing government and its subordinate governments at all levels, it had no reason to reject the specific measures which were drawn up on the basis of these fundamental terms and which are most lenient. In these circumstances, we order you as follows:

1. Advance bravely and annihilate resolutely, thoroughly, wholly and completely all the Guomindang reactionaries within China's borders who dare to resist. Liberate the people of the whole country. Safeguard China's territorial integrity, sovereignty and independence.
2. Advance bravely and arrest all the incorrigible war criminals. No matter where they may flee, they must be brought to justice and punished according to law. Pay special attention to arresting the bandit chieftain Chiang Kai-shek.
3. Proclaim to all Guomindang local governments and local military groups the final amended version of the Agreement on Internal Peace. In accordance with its general ideas, you may conclude local agreements with those who are willing to cease hostilities and to settle matters by peaceful means.
4. After the People's Liberation Army has encircled Nanjing, we are willing to give the Li Zongren government at Nanjing another opportunity to

sign the Agreement on Internal Peace if that government has not yet fled and dispersed and desires to sign it.

> Mao Zedong
> Chairman of the Chinese People's
> Revolutionary Military Commission

> Chu De
> Commander-in-Chief of the Chinese
> People's Liberation Army

18.5 *Takeover Details*

PROCLAMATION OF THE CHINESE PEOPLE'S LIBERATION ARMY
(APRIL 25, 1949)

The Guomindang reactionaries have rejected the terms for peace and persist in their stand of waging a criminal war against the nation and the people. The people all over the country hope that the People's Liberation Army will speedily wipe out the Guomindang reactionaries. We have ordered the People's Liberation Army to advance courageously, wipe out all reactionary Guomindang troops who dare to resist, arrest all the incorrigible war criminals, liberate the people of the whole country, safeguard China's territorial integrity, sovereignty and independence, and bring about the genuine unification of the country, which the whole people long for. We earnestly hope that people in all walks of life will assist the People's Liberation Army wherever it goes. We hereby proclaim the following eight-point covenant by which we, together with the whole people shall abide.

1. Protect the lives and property of all the people. People in all walks of life, irrespective of class, belief or occupation, are expected to maintain order and adopt a co-operative attitude towards the People's Liberation Army. The People's Liberation Army on its part will adopt a co-operative attitude towards people in all walks of life. Counter-revolutionaries or other saboteurs who seize the opportunity to create disturbances, loot or sabotage shall be severely dealt with.
2. Protect the industrial, commercial, agricultural and livestock enterprises of the national bourgeoisie. All privately owned factories, shops, banks, warehouses, vessels, wharves, farms, livestock frames and other enterprises will without exception be protected against any encroachment. It is hoped that workers and employees in all occupations will maintain production as usual and that all shops will remain open as usual.

3. Confiscate bureaucrat-capital. All factories, shops, banks, and warehouses, all vessels, wharves and railways, all postal, telegraph, electric light, telephone and water supply services, and all farms, livestock farms and other enterprises operated by the reactionary Guomindang government and the big bureaucrats shall be taken over by the People's Government. In such enterprises the private shares held by national capitalists engaged in industry, commerce, agriculture or livestock raising shall be recognized, after their ownership is verified. All personnel working in bureaucrat-capitalist enterprises must remain at their posts pending the take-over by the People's Government and must assume responsibility for the safekeeping of all assets, machinery, charts, account books, records, etc., in preparation for the check-up and take-over. Those who render useful service in this connection will be rewarded; those who obstruct or sabotage will be punished. Those desiring to go on working after the take-over by the People's Government will be given employment commensurate with their abilities so that they will not become destitute and homeless.

4. Protect all public and private schools, hospitals, cultural and educational institutions, athletic fields and other public welfare establishments. It is hoped that all personnel in these institutions will remain at their posts; the People's Liberation Army will protect them from molestation.

5. Except for the incorrigible war criminals and counter-revolutionaries who have committed the most heinous crimes, the People's Liberation Army and the People's Government will not hold captive, arrest or subject to indignity any officials, whether high or low, in the Guomindang's central, provincial, municipal and county governments, deputies to the "National Assembly," members of the Legislative and Control Yuans, members of the political consultative councils, police officers and district, township, village and *pao-chia*[2] officials, so long as they do not offer armed resistance or plot sabotage. All these persons are enjoined, pending the take-over, to stay at their posts, abide by the orders and decrees of the People's Liberation Army and the People's Government and assume responsibility for the safekeeping of all the assets and records of their offices. The People's Government will permit the employment of those among them who can make themselves useful in some kind of work and have not committed any grave reactionary act or other flagrant misdeed. Punishment shall be meted out to those who seize the opportunity to engage in sabotage, theft or embezzlement, or abscond with public funds, assets or records, or refuse to give an accounting.

6. In order to ensure peace and security in both cities and rural areas and to

---

2. *Pao-chia* was an administrative system by which the Guomindang enforced rule at the primary level. On August 1, 1932, Chiang Kai-shek promulgated the Regulations for the Organization of *Pao and Chia*. Neighbors were required to watch and report each other's activities to the authorities, and all were punishable when one was found guilty.

maintain public order, all stragglers and disbanded soldiers are required to report and surrender to the People's Liberation Army or the People's Government in their localities. No action will be taken against those who voluntarily do so and hand over their arms. Those who refuse to report or who conceal their arms shall be arrested and investigated. Persons who shelter stragglers and disbanded soldiers and do not report them to the authorities shall be duly punished.

7. The feudal system of landownership in the rural areas is irrational and should be abolished. To abolish it, however, preparations must be made and the necessary steps taken. Generally speaking, the reduction of rent and interest should come first and land distribution later; only after the People's Liberation Army has arrived at a place and worked there for a considerable time will it be possible to speak of solving the land problem in earnest. The peasant masses should organize themselves and help the People's Liberation Army to carry out the various initial reforms. They should also work hard at their farming so as to prevent the present level of agricultural production from falling and should then raise it step by step to improve their own livelihood and supply the people of the cities with commodity grain. Urban land and buildings cannot be dealt with in the same way as the problem of rural land.

8. Protect the lives and property of foreign nationals. It is hoped that all foreign nations will follow their usual pursuits and observe order. All foreign nationals must abide by the orders and decrees of the People's Liberation Army and the People's Government and must abide by the orders and decrees of the People's Liberation Army and the People's Government and must not engage in espionage, act against the cause of China's national independence and the people's liberation, or harbour Chinese war criminals, counter-revolutionaries or other law-breakers. Otherwise, they shall be dealt with according to law by the People's Liberation Army and the People's Government.

The People's Liberation Army is highly disciplined; it is fair in buying and selling and is not allowed to take even a needle or a piece of thread from the people. It is hoped that the people throughout the country will live and work in peace and will not give credence to rumors or raise false alarms. This proclamation is hereby issued in all sincerity and earnestness.

Mao Zedong
Chairman of the Chinese People's
Revolutionary Military Commission

Chu De
Commander-in-Chief of the Chinese
People's Liberation Army

18.6 DEMOCRATIC DICTATORSHIP

During the last days of civil war and on the eve of the twenty-eighth anniversary of the founding of the party, Mao Zedong took time to reflect on the turbulent pattern of modern Chinese history and the revolutionary experiences that he and others of his generation had shared. The product of these ruminations was his famous essay "On the People's Democratic Dictatorship."

This work, like Lenin's *The State and the Revolution*, was the expression of a lifetime of sacrifice and labor on the behalf of the revolutionary ideal. The practical problems of bringing about revolution and the unification of China were at an end and the time was at hand for construction of the revolutionary state that party visionaries had dreamed of since the formation of the earliest Marxist study groups in China.

Mao suggested that it was the "correct world outlook" of the Communist Party that enabled it to triumph in the historical process; its understanding of "the laws governing the existence and development of things" had led the party to victory in its contest with the lingering forces of Chinese feudalism and the Guomindang. In the future, this "scientific" understanding of history would provide the framework of CCP rule and the dictatorship of the Party would lead the way to a classless society and the extinction of parties, governments, and, of course, social classes. Enemies of the revolutionary order would be silenced and democracy would be the property of "the people" i.e., the peasantry, the working class, the national bourgeoisie, and the urban petty bourgeoisie. The dialectic process had foretold the demise of the CCP's enemies and dictatorship would henceforth be an instrument to crush the landlord class, Nationalist reactionaries, and bureaucratic capitalists.

In subsequent years, the Communist party would succumb to the temptation of using the dictatorship proclaimed by Mao in 1949 in cruel and capricious ways. The political movements and struggles of the first decades of Communist rule would lead to a repeated amendment and expansion of the category of enemies to include "rightists," "revisionists," "social imperialists," the "five black categories," and "turbulent counterrevolutionary elements." But in the summer of 1949, the abuses to which a monopoly of political power and single-party rule could lead were only dimly glimpsed. The war was at an end, Chiang Kai-shek had skulked off to Taiwan, U.S. and British imperialism were at bay, and Chairman Mao and his comrades-in-arms strode forward to place their imprint on the future of China.

On The People's Democratic Dictatorship

IN COMMEMORATION OF THE TWENTY-EIGHTH
ANNIVERSARY OF THE COMMUNIST PARTY OF CHINA
JUNE 30, 1949

The first of July 1949 marks the fact that the Communist Party of China has already lived through twenty-eight years. Like a man, a political party has its childhood, youth, manhood and old age. The Communist Party of China is no longer a child or a lad in his teens but has become an adult. When a man reaches old age, he will die; the same is true of a party. When classes disappear, all instruments of class struggle—parties and the state machinery—will lose their function, cease to be necessary, therefore gradually wither away and end their historical mission; and human society will move to a higher stage. We are the opposite of the political parties of the bourgeoisie. They are afraid to speak of the extinction of classes, state power, and parties. We, on the contrary, declare openly that we are striving hard to create the very conditions which will bring about their extinction. The leadership of the Communist Party and the state power of the people's dictatorship are such conditions. Anyone who does not recognize this truth is no communist. Young comrades who have not studied Marxism-Leninism and have only recently joined the Party may not yet understand this truth. They must understand it—only then can they have a correct world outlook. They must understand that the road to the abolition of classes, to the abolition of state power and to the abolition of parties is the road all mankind must take; it is only a question of time and conditions. Communists the world over are wiser than the bourgeoisie, they understand the laws governing the existence and development of things, they understand dialectics and they can see farther. The bourgeoisie does not welcome this truth because it does not want to be overthrown. To be overthrown is painful and is unbearable to contemplate for those overthrown, for example, for the Guomindang reactionaries whom we are now overthrowing and for Japanese imperialism which we together with other peoples overthrew some time ago. But for the working class, the laboring people and the Communist Party the question is not one of being overthrown, but of working hard to create the conditions in which classes, state power and political parties will die out very naturally and mankind will enter the realm of Great Harmony. We have mentioned in passing the long-range perspective of human progress in order to explain clearly the problems we are about to discuss.

As everyone knows, our Party passed through these twenty-eight years not in peace but amid hardships, for we had to fight enemies, both foreign and domestic, both inside and outside the Party. We thank Marx, Engels, Lenin and Stalin for giving us a weapon. This weapon is not a machine-gun, but Marxism-Leninism.

In his book *"Left-Wing" Communism, an Infantile Disorder* written in 1920, Lenin described the quest of the Russians for revolutionary theory. Only after several decades of hardship and suffering did the Russians find Marxism. Many things in China were the same as, or similar to, those in Russia before the October Revolution. There was the same feudal oppression. There was similar economic and cultural backwardness. Both countries were backward, China even more so. In both countries alike, for the sake of national regeneration progressives braved hard and bitter struggles in their quest for revolutionary truth.

From the time of China's defeat in the Opium War of 1840, Chinese progressives went through untold hardships in their quest for truth from the Western countries. Hung Hsiu-chuan, Kang Yu-wei, Yen Fu and Sun Yat-sen were representative of those who had looked to the West for truth before the Communist Party of China was born. Chinese who then sought progress would read any book containing the new knowledge from the West. The number of students sent to Japan, Britain, the United States, France, and Germany was amazing. At home, the imperial examinations were abolished and modern schools sprang up like bamboo shoots after a spring rain; every effort was made to learn from the West. In my youth, I too engaged in such studies. They represented the culture of Western bourgeois democracy, including the social theories and natural sciences of that period, and they were called "the new learning" in contrast to Chinese feudal culture, which was called "the old learning". For quite a long time, those who had acquired the new learning felt confident that it would save China, and very few of them had any doubts on this score, as the adherents of the old learning had. Only modernization could save China, only learning from foreign countries could modernize China. Among the foreign countries, only the Western capitalist countries were then progressive, as they had successfully built modern bourgeois states. The Japanese had been successful in learning from the West, and the Chinese also wished to learn from the Japanese. The Chinese in those days regarded Russia as backward, and few wanted to learn from her. That was how the Chinese tried to learn from foreign countries in the period from the 1840's to the beginning of the 20th century.

Imperialist aggression shattered the fond dreams of the Chinese about learning from the West. It was very odd—why were the teachers always committing aggression against their pupil? The Chinese learned a good deal from the West, but they could not make it work and were never able to realize their ideals. Their repeated struggles, including such a country-wide movement as the Revolution of 1911, all ended in failure. Day by day, conditions in the country got worse, and life was made impossible. Doubts arose, increased and deepened. World War I shook the whole globe. The Russians made the October Revolution and created the world's first socialist state. Under the leadership of Lenin and Stalin, the revolutionary energy of the great proletariat and laboring people of Russia, hitherto latent and unseen by foreigners, suddenly erupted like a volcano, and the Chinese and all mankind began to see the Russians in a new light. Then, and only then, did the Chinese enter an entirely new era in their thinking and their life. They found Marxism-Leninism, the universally applicable truth, and the face of China began to change.

It was through the Russians that the Chinese found Marxism. Before the October Revolution, the Chinese were not only ignorant of Lenin and Stalin, they did not even know of Marx and Engels. The salvoes of the October Revolution brought us Marxism-Leninism. The October Revolution helped progressives in China, as throughout the world, to adopt the proletarian world outlook as the instrument for studying a nation's destiny and considering anew their own problems. Follow the path of the Russians—that was their conclusion. In 1919, the May 4th Movement took place in China. In 1921, the Communist Party of China was founded. Sun Yat-sen, in the depths of despair, came across the October Revolution and the Communist Party of China. He welcomed the October Revolution, welcomed Russian help to the Chinese and welcomed cooperation of the Communist Party of China. Then Sun Yat-sen died and Chiang Kai-shek rose to power. Over a long period of twenty-two years, Chiang Kai-shek dragged China into ever more hopeless straits. In this period, during the anti-fascist Second World War in which the Soviet Union was the main force, three big imperialist powers were knocked out, while two others were weakened. In the whole world only one big imperialist power, the United States of America, remained uninjured. But the United States faced a grave domestic crisis. It wanted to enslave the whole world; it supplied arms to help Chiang Kai-shek slaughter several million Chinese. Under the leadership of the Communist Party of China, the Chinese people, after driving out Japanese imperialism, waged the People's War of Liberation for three years and have basically won victory.

Thus Western bourgeois civilization, bourgeois democracy and the plan for a bourgeois republic have all gone bankrupt in the eyes of the Chinese people. Bourgeois democracy has given way to people's democracy under the leadership of the working class and the bourgeois republic to the people's republic. This has made it possible to achieve socialism and communism through the people's republic, to abolish classes to render a world of Great Harmony. Kang Yu-wei wrote Tatungshu, or the *Book of Great Harmony*, but he did not and could not find the way to achieve Great Harmony. There are bourgeois republics in foreign lands, but China cannot have a bourgeois republic because she is a country suffering under imperialist oppression. The only way is through a people's republic led by the working class.

All other ways have been tried and failed. Of the people who hankered after those ways, some have fallen, some have awakened and some are changing their ideas. Events are developing so swiftly that many feel the abruptness of the change and the need to learn anew. This state of mind is understandable and we welcome this worthy desire to learn anew.

The vanguard of the Chinese proletariat learned Marxism-Leninism after the October Revolution and founded the Communist Party of China. It entered at once into political struggle and only now, after a tortuous course of twenty-eight years, has it won basic victory. From our twenty-eight years' experience we have drawn a conclusion similar to the one Sun Yat-sen drew in his testament from his "experience of forty years"; that is, we are deeply convinced that to win victory, "we must arouse the masses of the people and unite in a common struggle with those nations of the world which treat us as equals." Sun Yat-sen had a world outlook different from ours and started from a different class standpoint in studying and tackling problems; yet, in the 1920's he reached a conclusion basically the same as ours on the question of how to struggle against imperialism.

Twenty-four years have passed since Sun Yat-sen's death, and the Chinese revolution, led by the Communist Party of China, has made tremendous advances both in theory and practice and has radically changed the face of China. Up to now the principal and fundamental experience the Chinese people have gained is twofold:

(1) Internally, arouse the masses of the people. That is, unite the working class, the peasantry, the urban petty bourgeoisie and the national bourgeoisie, form a domestic united front under the leadership of the working class, and advance from this to the establishment of a state which is a people's democratic dictatorship under the leadership of the working class and based on the alliance of workers and peasants.

(2) Externally, unite in a common struggle with those nations of the world which treat us as equals and unite with the peoples of all countries. That is, ally ourselves with the Soviet Union, with the People's Democracies and with the proletariat and the broad masses of the people in all other countries, and form an international united front.

"You are leaning to one side." Exactly. The forty years' experience of Sun Yat-sen and the twenty-eight years' experience of the Communist Party have taught us to lean to one side, and we are firmly convinced that in order to win victory and consolidate it we must lean to one side. In the light of the experiences accumulated in these forty years and these twenty-eight years, all Chinese without exception must lean either to the side of imperialism or to the side of socialism. Sitting on the fence will not do, nor is there a third road. We oppose the Chiang Kai-shek reactionaries who lean to the side of imperialism, and we also oppose the illusions about a third road.

"You are too irritating." We are talking about how to deal with domestic and foreign reactionaries, the imperialists and their running dogs, not about how to deal with anyone else. With regard to such reactionaries, the question of irritating them or not does not arise. Irritated or not irritated, they will remain the same because they are reactionaries. Only if we draw a clear line between reactionaries and revolutionaries, expose the intrigues and plots of the reactionaries, arouse the vigilance and attention of the revolutionary ranks, heighten our will to fight and crush the enemy's arrogance can we isolate the reactionaries, vanquish them or supersede them. We must not show the slightest timidity before a wild beast. We must learn from Wu Sung on the Chingyang Ridge.[3] As Wu Sung saw it, the tiger on Chingyang Ridge was a man-eater, whether irritated or not. Either kill the tiger or be eaten by him—one or the other. . . .

"You are dictatorial." My dear sirs, you are right, that is just what you are. All the experience the Chinese people have accumulated through several decades teach us to enforce the people's democratic dictatorship, that is, to deprive the reactionaries of the right to speak and let the people alone have that right.

Who are the people? At the present stage in China, they are the working class, the peasantry, the urban petty bourgeoisie and the national bourgeoisie. These classes, led by the working class and the Communist Party, unite to form their own state and elect their own government; they enforce their dictatorship over the running dogs of imperialism—the landlord class and bureaucrat-bourgeoisie, as well as the representatives of those classes, the Guomindang reactionaries and their accomplices—suppress them, allow them only to behave themselves and not to be unruly in word or deed. If they speak or act in an unruly way, they will be promptly stopped and punished. Democracy is practiced within the ranks of the people, who enjoy the rights of freedom of speech, assembly, association and so on. The right to vote belongs only to the people, not to the reactionaries. The combination of these two aspects, democracy for the people and dictatorship over the reactionaries, is the people's democratic dictatorship.

Why must things be done this way? The reason is quite clear to everybody. If things were not done this way, the revolution would fail, the people would suffer, the country would be conquered.

"Don't you want to abolish state power?" Yes, we do, but not right now; we cannot do it yet. Why? Because imperialism still exists, because domestic reaction still exists, because classes still exist in our country. Our present task is to strengthen the people's state apparatus—mainly the people's army, the people's police and the people's courts—in order to consolidate national defence and protect the people's interests. Given this condition, China can develop steadily, under the leadership of the working class and the Communist Party, from an

3. Mao here refers to a celebrated episode from the Ming novel *Water Margin* (early sixteenth century) by Luo Guanzhong. This novel was one of Mao Zedong's favorites as a boy and it is characteristic of him that Wu Sung's single-handed struggle to defeat a ravenous tiger should be remembered here as a metaphor for the CCP's struggle against its enemies.

agricultural into an industrial country and from a new-democratic into a social-ist and communist society, can abolish classes and realize the Great Harmony. The state apparatus, including the army, the police and the courts, is the instru-ment by which one class oppresses another. It is an instrument for the oppression of antagonistic classes; it is violence and not "benevolence." "You are not benev-olent!" Quite so. We definitely do not apply a policy of benevolence to the reactionary classes. Our policy of benevolence is applied only within the ranks of the people, not beyond them to the reactionaries or to the reactionary activities of reactionary classes.

The people's state protects the people. Only when the people have such a state can they educate and remold themselves by democratic methods on a country-wide scale, with everyone taking part, and shake off the influence of domestic and foreign reactionaries (which is still very strong, will survive for a long time and cannot be quickly destroyed), rid themselves of the bad habits and ideas acquired in the old society, not allow themselves to be led astray by the reactionaries, and continue to advance—to advance towards a socialist and communist society.

Here, the method we employ is democratic, the method of persuasion, not of compulsion. When anyone among the people breaks the law, he too shall be punished, imprisoned or even sentenced to death; but this is a matter of a few individual cases, and it differs in principle from the dictatorship exercised over the reactionaries as a class.

As for the members of the reactionary classes and individual reactionaries, so long as they do not rebel, sabotage or create trouble after their political power has been overthrown, land and work will be given to them as well in order to allow them to live and remold themselves through labour into a new people. If they are not willing to work, the people's state will compel them to work. Propaganda and educational work will be done among them too and will be done, moreover, with as much care and thoroughness as among the captured army officers in the past. This, too, may be called a "policy of benevolence" if you like, but it is imposed by us on the members of the enemy classes and cannot be mentioned in the same breath with the work of self-education which we carry on within the ranks of the revolutionary people.

Such remolding of members of the reactionary classes can be accomplished only by a state of the people's democracy dictatorship under the leadership of the Communist Party. When it is well done, China's major exploiting classes, the landlord class and the bureaucrat-bourgeoisie (the monopoly capitalist class), will be eliminated for good. There remain the national bourgeoisie; at the pres-ent stage, we can already do a good deal of suitable educational work with many of them. When the time comes to realize socialism, that is, to nationalize private enterprise, we shall carry the work of educating and remolding them a step further. The people have a powerful state apparatus in their hands—there is no need to fear rebellion by the national bourgeoisie.

The serious problem is the education of the peasantry. The peasant economy is scattered, and the socialization of agriculture, judging by the Soviet Union's experience, will require a long time and painstaking work. Without socialization of agriculture, there can be no complete, consolidated socialism. The steps to socialize agriculture must be co-ordinated with the development of a powerful industry having state enterprise as its backbone. The state of the people's democratic dictatorship must systematically solve the problems of industrialization. Since it is not proposed to discuss economic problems in detail in this article, I shall not go into them further. . . .

To sum up our experience and concentrate it into one point, it is: the people's democratic dictatorship under the leadership of the working class (through the Communist Party) and based upon the alliance of workers and peasants. This dictatorship must unite as one with the international revolutionary forces. This is our formula, our principal experience, our main programme.

Twenty-eight years of our Party are a long period, in which we have accomplished only one thing—we have won basic victory in the revolutionary war. This calls for celebration, because it is the people's victory, because it is victory in a country as large as China. But we still have much work to do; to use the analogy of a journey, our last work is only the first step in a long march of ten thousand *li*. Remnants of the enemy have yet to be wiped out. The serious task of economic construction lies before us. We shall soon put aside some of the things we know well and be compelled to do things we don't know well. This means difficulties. The imperialists reckon that we will not be able to manage our economy; they are standing by and joking on, awaiting our failure.

We must overcome difficulties, we must learn what we do not know. We must learn to do economic work from all who know how, no matter who they are. We must esteem them as teachers, learning from them respectfully and conscientiously. We must not pretend to know when we do not know. We must not put on bureaucratic airs. If we dig into a subject for several months, for a year or two, for three or five years, we shall eventually master it. At first some of the Soviet Communists also were not very good at handling economic matters and the imperialists awaited their failure too. But the Communist Party of the Soviet Union emerged victorious and, under the leadership of Lenin and Stalin, it learned not only how to make the revolution but also how to carry on construction. It has built a great and splendid socialist state. The Communist Party of the Soviet Union is our best teacher and we must learn from it. The situation both at home and abroad is in our favour, we can rely fully on the weapon of the people's democratic dictatorship, unite the people throughout the country, the reactionaries excepted, and advance steadily to our goal.

CHAPTER 19

The Birth of the People's Republic

19.1 TREATY WITH THE SOVIET UNION, FEBRUARY 1950

Throughout the first decade of Communist rule, the Soviet Union was the primary ally of the People's Republic of China (PRC). The legal basis for Sino-Soviet cooperation was set in place in 1949 and 1950 in a series of diplomatic and economic accords. After the proclamation of the new Chinese state, thousands of Soviet advisers were dispatched by Moscow to assist in the construction of socialist China. In this era of cordial relations with the USSR, Stalinist models were adopted in almost every sphere of Chinese life, including industry, law, education, and art. Even the Chinese system of collectivized agriculture was influenced by the model of the Soviet *kolhoz* or collective farm.

The Treaty of Friendship of February 1950 was cornerstone of the Sino-Soviet alliance. It tied China's international interests to those of the Soviet Union and would serve as a defining framework after the outbreak of the Korean War in June 1950. For cold-war warriors in the West, already hostile to "people's China," this treaty substantiated the existence of an "international communist conspiracy," with the Soviet Union and China parts of a monolithic communist bloc.

358

TREATY OF FRIENDSHIP, ALLIANCE AND MUTUAL ASSISTANCE BETWEEN THE UNION OF SOVIET SOCIALIST REPUBLICS AND THE PEOPLE'S REPUBLIC OF CHINA

(FEBRUARY 14, 1950)

The Presidium of the Supreme Soviet of the Union of Soviet Socialist Republics and the Central People's Government of the People's Republic of China.

Being determined, by strengthening friendship and co-operation between the Union of Soviet Socialist Republics and the People's Republic of China, jointly to prevent the revival of Japanese imperialism and the repetition of aggression on the part of Japan or any other State that might in any way join with Japan in acts of aggression.

Being anxious to promote a lasting peace and general security in the Far East and throughout the world in accordance with the purposes and principles of the United Nations.[1]

Being firmly convinced that the strengthening of good-neighborly and friendly relations between the Union of Soviet Socialist Republics and the People's Republic of China is in accordance with the fundamental interests of the peoples of the Soviet Union and China.

Have decided for this purpose to conclude the present Treaty and have appointed as their plenipotentiaries:

The Presidium of the Supreme Soviet of the Union of Soviet Socialist Republics: Andrei Yanuarevich Vyshinsky, Minister of Foreign Affairs of the USSR;

The Central People's Government of the People's Republic of China: Chou En-lai, Chairman of the State Administrative Council and Minister of Foreign Affairs of China.

The two plenipotentiary representatives, having exchanged their full powers, found in good and due form, have agreed as follows:

ARTICLE 1. The two Contracting Parties undertake to carry out jointly all necessary measures within their power to prevent a repetition of aggression and breach of the peace by Japan or any other State which might directly or indirectly join with Japan in acts of aggression. Should either of the Contracting Parties be attacked by Japan or by States allied with Japan and thus find itself in a state war, the other Contracting Party shall immediately extend military and other assistance with all the means at its disposal.

The Contracting Parties likewise declare that they are prepared to participate, in a spirit of sincere co-operation, in all international action designed to safe-

---

1. Although China was not a member of the United Nations, the USSR, as a founding member, presumed the new Peking government would fill the seat held by the Republic of China on Taiwan.

guard peace and security throughout the world, and will devote all their energies to the speediest realization of these aims.

ARTICLE 2. The two Contracting Parties undertake, by common agreement, to strive for the conclusion at the earliest possible date, in conjunction with the other Powers which were their Allies during the Second World War, of a Peace Treaty with Japan.

ARTICLE 3. Neither of the Contracting Parties shall enter into any alliance directed against the other Party, or participate in any coalition or in any action or measures directed against the other Party.

ARTICLE 4. The two Contracting Parties shall consult together on all important international questions involving the common interests of the Soviet Union and China, with a view to strengthening peace and universal security.

ARTICLE 5. The two Contracting Parties undertake, in a spirit of friendship and cooperation and in accordance with the principles of equal rights, mutual interests, mutual respect for State sovereignty and territorial integrity, and non-intervention in the domestic affairs of the other Party, to develop and strengthen the economic and cultural ties between the Soviet Union and China, to render each other all possible economic assistance and to effect the necessary economic co-operation.

ARTICLE 6. This Treaty shall come into force immediately upon ratification;[2] the exchange of the instruments of ratification shall take place at Peking.

This Treaty shall remain in force for thirty years. If neither of the Contracting Parties gives notice one year before they expiration of the said period that it wishes to denounce the Treaty, it shall remain in force for a further five years and shall thereafter be continued in force in accordance with this provision.

DONE at Moscow, on 14 February 1950, in two copies, each in the Russian and Chinese languages, both texts being equally authentic.

By authorization of the Presidium of Supreme Soviet of the Union of Soviet Socialist Republics:
(Signed) A. Y. Vishinsky

By authorization of the Central People's Government of the People's Republic of China:
(Signed) Chou En-lai

19.2 NEW LAWS: MARRIAGE AND DIVORCE, MAY 1950

During the civil war, the Chinese Communist Party enlisted millions of women into the revolutionary struggle. Party workers encouraged peasant

2. Came into force April 11, 1950.

women to throw off the shackles of feudal society and strove to promote a liberalized vision of women's rights in rural areas. With the Communist victory in 1949, local women's associations were formed throughout China to carry the party's message of liberation to women.

Influenced by legislation applied in the liberated areas and also by Soviet experience, the Communist party invoked law to redefine the role women could play in the workplace and household after 1949. Through the Marriage Law of 1950, which was the first law proclaimed by the new government, the party, in cooperation with the Women's Federation, established a legal foundation women could rely upon as they challenged the traditional social order. The law provided guarantees for women's control of property; abolished concubinage, arranged marriages, and child marriages; and announced a basic reformation of the institution of divorce. In the first year after the promulgation of this law there were nearly a million divorces in China as women took advantage of the party's legislation to leave unhappy marriages. In subsequent years, there was much resistance to this law by men who argued that it was "an unequal treaty against men" but the law prevailed and continued to be an inspiration for the women's movement in China.

The Marriage Law of the People's Republic of China

PROMULGATED BY THE CENTRAL PEOPLE'S GOVERNMENT
ON MAY 1, 1950

CHAPTER ONE: GENERAL PRINCIPLES

ARTICLE 1. The arbitrary and compulsory feudal marriage system, which is based on the superiority of man over woman and which ignores the children's interest is abolished.

The New Democratic marriage system, which is based on free choice of partners, on monogamy, on equal rights for both sexes, and on protection of the lawful interests of women and children, shall be put into effect.

ARTICLE 2. Polygamy, concubinage, child betrothal, interference with the remarriage of widows and the exaction of money or gifts in connection with marriage shall be prohibited.

CHAPTER TWO: CONTRACTING OF MARRIAGE

ARTICLE 3. Marriage shall be based upon the complete willingness of the two parties. Neither party shall use compulsion and no third party shall be allowed to interfere.

ARTICLE 4. A marriage can be contracted only after the man has reached twenty years of age and the woman has reached eighteen years of age.

ARTICLE 5. No man or woman in any of the following instances shall be allowed to marry:

(a) Where the man and woman are lineal relatives by blood or where the man and woman are brother and sister born of the same parents or where the man and woman are half-brother and half-sister. The question of prohibiting marriage between collateral relatives by blood within the fifth degree of relationship is to be determined by custom.

(b) When one party, because of certain physical defects, is sexually impotent.

(c) Where one party is suffering from venereal disease, mental disorder, leprosy, or any other disease which is regarded by medical science as rendering the person unfit for marriage.

ARTICLE 6. In order to contract a marriage, both the man and the woman shall register in person with the people's government of the subdistrict or village in which they reside. If the marriage is found to be in conformity with the provisions of this law, the local people's government shall, without delay, issue a marriage certificate.

If the marriage is found to be incompatible with the provisions of this law, no registration shall be granted.

CHAPTER THREE: RIGHTS AND DUTIES OF HUSBAND AND WIFE

ARTICLE 7. Husband and wife are companions living together and shall enjoy equal status in the home.

ARTICLE 8. Husband and wife are in duty bound to love, respect, assist, and look after each other, to live in harmony, to engage in production, to care for the children, and to strive jointly for the welfare of the family and for the building up of a new society.

ARTICLE 9. Both husband and wife shall have the right to free choice of occupation and free participation in work or in social activities.

ARTICLE 10. Both husband and wife shall have equal rights in the possession and management of family property.

ARTICLE 11. Both husband and wife shall have the right to use his or her own family name.

ARTICLE 12. Both husband and wife shall have the right to inherit each other's property.

CHAPTER FOUR: RELATIONS BETWEEN PARENTS AND CHILDREN

ARTICLE 13.   Parents have the duty to rear and to educate their children; the children have the duty to look after and to assist their parents. Neither the parents nor the children shall maltreat or desert one another.

The foregoing provision also applies to stepparents and stepchildren. Infanticide by drowning and similar criminal acts are strictly prohibited.

ARTICLE 14.   Parents and children shall have the right to inherit one another's property.

ARTICLE 15.   Children born out of wedlock shall enjoy the same rights as children born in lawful wedlock. No person shall be allowed to harm or to discriminate against children born out of wedlock.

Where the paternity of a child born out of wedlock is legally established by the mother of the child, by other witnesses, or by other material evidence, the identified father must bear the whole or part of the cost of maintenance and education of the child until it has attained the age of eighteen.

With the consent of the natural mother, the natural father may have custody of the child.

With regard to the maintenance of a child whose natural mother marries, the provisions of Article 22 shall apply.

ARTICLE 16.   A husband or wife shall not maltreat or discriminate against a child born of a previous marriage.

CHAPTER FIVE: DIVORCE

ARTICLE 17.   Divorce shall be granted when husband and wife both desire it. In the event of either the husband or wife insisting upon divorce, it may be granted only when mediation by the subdistrict people's government and the subdistrict judicial organ has failed to bring about a reconciliation.

In the case where divorce is desired by both the husband and wife, both parties shall register with the subdistrict people's government in order to obtain a certificate of divorce. The subdistrict government, after establishing that divorce is desired by both parties and that appropriate measures have been taken for the care of children and property, shall issue the certificate of divorce without delay.

When only one party insists on divorce, the subdistrict people's government may try to effect a reconciliation. If such mediation fails, it should, without delay, refer the case to the district or city people's court for decision. The subdistrict people's government shall not attempt to prevent or to obstruct either party from appealing to the district or city people's court. In dealing with a divorce case, the district or city people's court must, in the first instance, try to bring about a reconciliation between the parties. In case such mediation fails, the court shall render a verdict without delay.

In the case where, after divorce, both husband and wife desire the resumption of matrimonial relations, they should apply to the subdistrict people's government for a registration of remarriage. The subdistrict people's government should accept such a registration and issue a certificate of re-marriage.

ARTICLE 18.   The husband shall not apply for a divorce when his wife is with child. He may apply for divorce only one year after birth of the child. In the case of a woman applying for divorce, this restriction does not apply.

ARTICLE 19.   The spouse of a member of the revolutionary army on active service who maintains correspondence with his (or her) family must first obtain his (or her) consent before he (or she) can ask for a divorce.

As from the date of the promulgation of this law, divorce may be granted to the spouse of a member of the revolutionary army who does not correspond with his (or her) family for a subsequent period of two years. Divorce may also be granted to the spouse of a member of the revolutionary army who has not maintained correspondence with his (or her) family for a further period of one year subsequent to the promulgation of the present law.

CHAPTER SIX: SUPPORT AND EDUCATION OF CHILDREN AFTER DIVORCE

ARTICLE 20.   The blood ties between parents and children do not end with the divorce of the parents. No matter whether the father or the mother acts as guardian of the child or children, they still remain the children of both parties.

After divorce, both parents still have the duty to support and educate their children.

After divorce, the guiding principle is to allow the mother to have custody of a baby still being breast-fed. After the weaning of the child, if a dispute arises between the two parties over the guardianship and an agreement cannot be reached, the people's court shall render a decision in accordance with the best interests of the child.

ARTICLE 21.   After divorce, if the mother is given custody of a child, the father shall be responsible for the whole or part of the necessary cost of the maintenance and education of the child. Both parties shall reach an agreement regarding the amount of the cost of the duration of such maintenance and education. In the case where the two parties fail to reach an agreement, the people's court shall render a decision.

Payment must be made in cash, in kind, or by tilling the land allocated to the child.

Such an agreement reached between the parents or decision rendered by the people's court in connection with the maintenance and educational expenses for a child shall not prevent the child from requesting either parent to increase the amount above that fixed by agreement or by judicial decision.

ARTICLE 22. In the case where a divorced woman remarries and her husband is willing to pay the whole or part of the cost of maintenance and education for the child or children by her former husband, the father of the child or children is entitled to have such cost of maintenance and education reduced or is entitled to be exempt from bearing such cost in accordance with the circumstances.

CHAPTER SEVEN: PROPERTY AND MAINTENANCE AFTER DIVORCE

ARTICLE 23. In case of divorce, the wife shall retain such property as belonged to her prior to her marriage. The disposal of other household properties shall be subject to agreement between the two parties. In the case where an agreement cannot be reached, the people's court shall render a decision after taking into consideration the actual state of the family property, the interests of the wife and the child or children, and the principle of benefiting the development of production.

In the case where the property allocated to the wife and her child or children is sufficient for the maintenance and education of the child or children, the husband may be exempt from bearing further maintenance and education costs.

ARTICLE 24. After divorce, debts incurred during the period of marriage shall be paid out of the property acquired by husband and wife during this period. In the case where no such property has been acquired or in the case where such property is insufficient to pay off such debts, the husband shall be held responsible for paying these debts. Debts incurred separately by the husband or wife shall be paid off by the party responsible.

ARTICLE 25. After divorce, if one party has not remarried and has difficulties in maintenance, the other party should render assistance. Both parties shall work out an agreement with regard to the method and duration of such assistance; in case an agreement cannot be reached, the people's court shall render a decision.

ARTICLE 26. Persons violating this law shall be punished in accordance with law. In the case where interference with the freedom of marriage has caused death or injury, the person guilty of such interference shall bear criminal responsibility before the law.

ARTICLE 27. This law shall come into force from this date of its promulgation. In regions inhabited by national minorities, the Military and Political Council of the Administrative Area of the provincial people's government may enact certain modifications of supplementary articles in conformity with the actual conditions prevailing among national minorities in regard to marriage. But such measures must be submitted to the Government Administration Council for ratification before enforcement.

19.3 DING LING'S FICTION: THE POWER OF THE PEOPLE

In the summer of 1946, the Chinese Communist party issued a detailed directive concerning land reform and dispatched thousands of its cadres to the countryside in the liberated zones to lead reform efforts. During this campaign, the famous woman writer Ding Ling accompanied her husband Chen Ming to the Chahar countryside northwest of Peking and there observed early land-reform efforts first hand. Later, she used this material as the basis of her novel *The Sun Shines over the Sanggan River* which was published first in 1948. This novel was a vivid party-sanctioned description of the land-reform efforts and in 1951 it became the first Chinese novel to win a Stalin Prize.

One aspect of land reform was the "speak bitterness" (*suku*) meeting. In these meetings, peasants were encouraged to confront the landlords and rich peasants who once abused them and in some cases these class enemies were beaten to death in the tumultuous airing of grievances that followed. Nothing like this had ever happened in the context of rural China; ordinarily, peasants "ate bitterness" (*chiku*) and the whole notion of passionate confrontation of the powerful and the open expression of angry or aggressive feelings by the powerless was both novel and intensely stimulating. As the floodgates opened and peasants realized that it was safe for them to make public display of their pain, the meetings sometimes slipped out of the control of the young land reform cadres which were supposed to direct them. In these meetings it is possible to detect parallels with similar confrontations brought about in Chinese history as social groups clashed in the context of local revolts or peasant rebellions. It is also possible to see distinct similarities between such meetings and the political struggle and exposure meetings of the 1950s and 1960s in which political antagonists of the party were exposed to similar pressures and public attacks.

Chapter 50 of Ding Ling's *Sanggan River* described a *suku* meeting in a village called Nuanshui. Here, the "enemy of the people" is a certain local bully named "Schemer Qian" and, as often happened, the meeting passes from order to disorder. In this piece and others, it is possible to glimpse the depths of rural dissatisfaction, and the energies that the Chinese Communist party was able to harness as it built its revolutionary movement. By legitimating personal vengeance as it strove to destroy the pre-1949 rural

order, the party persuaded millions of peasants that it understood them
and was willing to use its doctrine of class struggle to permit the settling
of long standing scores of China's rural society.

THE SUN SHINES OVER THE SANGGAN RIVER

When they heard the footsteps of the children who had followed the militia
out, the men on the stage glanced at each other, knowing what it meant. The
crowd stood still, straining their necks for a sight. The militia looked even
sterner, and stopped talking. Yumin, Orchard-keeper Li and Young Guo posted
themselves in the middle of the stage and Freckles Li started shouting slogans:
"Down with the local despots!" "Down with feudal landlords!" The crowd
shouted too, at the same time pressing forward, watching and waiting in an
agony of impatience, so that when they were not shouting slogans they were
absolutely still.

With a smart movement the militia obeyed the order to stack their rifles,
and the crowd's tension increased even more. Then three or four militiamen
took Schemer Qian up to the platform. He was wearing a lined gown of grey
silk and white trousers, his hands tied behind him. His head was slightly lowered, and his small beady eyes were screwed up, searching the crowd. Those
reptilian eyes of his which used to strike fear into people's hearts still cast a
blight and quelled many of those present. His pointed mustaches made him
look more sinister. Nobody said a word.

Members of the presidium looked at each other anxiously. Old Dong and
other members of the work team exchanged anxious glances too and looked
expectantly at Freckles Li, who in turn was looking expectantly at the members
of the crowd. The crowd was looking at Schemer Qian, and still not a word
was said.

For thousands of years the local despots had the power. They had oppressed
generation after generation of peasants, and the peasants had bowed their necks
under their yoke. Now abruptly they were confronted with this power standing
before them with bound hands, and they felt bewildered, at a loss. Some who
were particularly intimidated by his malevolent look recalled the days when
they could only submit, and now, exposed to this blast, wavered again. So for
the time being they were silent.

All this time Schemer Qian, standing on the stage gnawing his lips, was
glancing round, wanting to quell these yokels, unwilling to admit defeat. For
a moment he really had the mastery. He and his many years of power had
become so firmly established in the village it was difficult for anyone to dislodge
him. The peasants hated him, and had just been cursing him; but now that he
stood before them they held their breath and faltered. It was like the pause

before two game-cocks start fighting, each estimating the other's strength. The longer the silence lasted, the greater Qian's power became, until it looked as if he were going to win.

At this point a man suddenly leapt out from the crowd. He had thick eyebrows and sparkling eyes. Rushing up to Schemer Qian he cursed him: "You murderer! You trampled our village under your feet! You killed people from behind the scenes for money. Today we're going to settle all old scores, and do a thorough job of it. Do you hear that? Do you still want to frighten people? It's no use! There's no place for you to stand on this stage! Kneel down! Kneel to all the villagers!" He pushed Qian hard, while the crowd echoed: "Kneel down! Kneel down!" The militiamen forced him to kneel down properly.

Then the masses' rage flared up, they tasted power and stirred indignantly. A child's voice was heard: "Put on the hat! Make him wear the hat!"

Young Guo jumped forward and asked: "Who'll put it on? Whoever'll put it on, come up here!"

While the crowd was shouting, "Make him wear the hat! Put on the hat!" a boy of thirteen or fourteen jumped up, lifted the hat and set it on Schemer Qian's head, at the same time spitting at him and cursing: "Here you are, Qian!" Then he jumped down amid laughter.

By now Qian had lowered his head completely, his malevolent eyes could no longer sweep their faces. The tall paper hat made him look like a clown. Bent basely from the waist, screwing up his eyes, he had lost all his power, had become the people's prisoner, a criminal against the masses.

The man who had cursed Qian turned now to face the crowd, and they all saw that it was Young Cheng, the chairman of the peasants' association.

"Friends!" said Young Cheng. "Look at him and look at me! See how soft and delicate he is: it's not cold yet but he's wearing a lined gown. Then look at me, look at yourselves. Do we look like human beings? Hah, when our mothers bore us, we were all alike! We've poured out blood and sweat to feed him. He's been living on our blood and sweat, oppressing us all these years; but today we want him to give back money for money, life for life, isn't that right?"

"Right! Give back money for money, life for life!"

"Don't let's be afraid of him any longer. Today we poor people are standing up! Let's forget our personal likes and dislikes. I'm chairman of the peasants' association. A few days ago I wasn't keen to struggle. I'm ashamed of myself, I forgot myself! I let all of you down. You can spit at me or beat me if you like and I won't say a word. I've seen light at last, and I want to settle scores with him. Since I was a child my mother and I went hungry. And all for what? In order to toil like a beast for him and become his running dog! It's no go! I must tell you—last night he even sent his wife to bribe me. Look, what do you think this is!" Young Cheng opened the white cloth bundle and shook out one title deed after another. Another roar rose from below, mingled with cries of amazement, rage, sympathy and approval.

"No! I'm not like that! I want to have a thorough settlement with that beast who feeds on human flesh! I've only one thought: I'm a poor man, I'm traveling with the poor. I'll follow Chairman Mao to the end of my way!"

"We peasants must unite! We must wipe our feudalism from the face of the earth!" Freckles Li had rushed to the front of the stage. The crowd shouted at him.

Yumin shook his fist too, and shouted: "Young Cheng is a good example for us all!"

"All peasants are brothers!" "Support Chairman Mao!" "Follow Chairman Mao to the end!" Shouts sounded from the stage and from the crowd.

Then people rushed up to the stage, stumbling over each other to confront Schemer Qian. Mrs. Qian stood with tear-stained cheeks behind her husband, pleading with them all: "Good people, have pity on my old man! Good people!" Her hair was disheveled, there were no longer flowers in it, but the traces of black varnish could still be seen. She was like a female clown in the theatre, making a fine couple with her husband. She had echoed him all her life, and now she still clung to him, unwilling to separate their fates.

One accusation was brought after another. Liuman kept leading the crowd to shout slogans. Some peasants were so carried away that they climbed onto the stage and struck at Schemer Qian as they questioned him, while the crowd backed them up: "Beat him, beat him to death!"

Qian was helpless. Trying to extricate himself, he said: "Good people, I was guilty in every way. I admit everything, whether I did it or not. I only ask you to be generous!"

His wife too said tearfully: "For the sake of our son in the Eighth Route Army, don't be too hard on him!"

"Damn it!" Liuman jumped up. "Have *I* wronged *you*! Say, did you trick my father into starting that mill or not?"

"Yes, I did," Qian had to admit.

"Did you have my eldest brother conscripted or not?"

"Yes, I did."

"Did you drive my second brother mad or not?"

"Yes, yes."

"Have I condemned you wrongly?"

"No."

"Damn it! Then why should you say 'whether I did it or not'? Let's ask him what injustice there's been! What does he want us to take him for, damn him! Let me tell you, I'm going to thrash this out with you: you give me back my father, give me back my eldest brother. Give me back my second brother!"

"Let him pay with his life!" someone shouted. "Put him to death!"

Peasants surged up to the stage, shouting wildly: "Kill him!" "A life for our lives!"

A group of villagers rushed to beat him. It was not clear who started, but one struck the first blow and others fought to get at him, while those behind who could not reach him shouted: "Throw him down! Throw him down! Let's all beat him!"

One feeling animated them all—vengeance! They wanted vengeance! They wanted to give vent to their hatred, the sufferings of the oppressed since their ancestors' times, the hatred of thousands of years; all this resentment they directed against him. They would have liked to tear him with their teeth.

The cadres could not stop everyone jumping onto the stage. With blows and curses the crowd succeeded in dragging him down from the stage and then more people swarmed towards him. Some crawled over across the heads and shoulders of those in front.

Schemer Qian's silk gown was torn. His shoes had fallen off, the white paper hat had been trampled into pieces underfoot. All semblance of order was gone and it looked as though he was going to be beaten to death, when Yumin remembered Comrade Pin's last instructions and pushed his way into the crowd. Having no other way of stopping them, he shielded Qian with his body, and shouted: "Don't be in such a hurry to beat him to death! We've got to ask the county authorities!" Then the militiamen started checking the people.

The crowd was furious at seeing Yumin shelter Schemer Qian. They pressed forward together. Yumin was considerably knocked about but still he said to them: "I swear, there was a time I was afraid we couldn't get the better of him! Now you want to beat him to death, of course I'm pleased. I've long wanted to beat him to death to clean up our district! Only, there's been no order from our superiors and I don't dare. I daren't take the responsibility. A man can only be executed with the county court's approval. I'm asking you to delay it for a few days. Do it as a favour for me! Don't kill him yet; we'll punish him suitably later."

By now quite a few others had come over to help him keep the crowd back, and they said: "Yumin's quite right. A sudden end is too good for him. Let's make him suffer." A lot of people were persuaded, feeling that it was best to consult the county court before killing anyone, and since it was certain the county would grant the people's request, it did not matter waiting a few days. But still some of them were dissatisfied. "Why can't we kill him? The people want to kill him, what's to stop them?"

Old Dong stepped forward and addressed the crowd:

"Schemer Qian owes you money and lives. Just killing him won't make it up to you, will it?"

"If he died several deaths he couldn't make it up," someone said.

By this time Qian had already been carried back onto the stage. He lay there panting like a dying dog, and someone said: "Kill the dog."

"Bah! Killing's too good for him. Let's make him beg for death. Let's humble him for a few days, how about it?" Old Dong's face was red with excitement. He had started life as a hired labourer. Now that he saw peasants just like himself daring to speak out and act boldly, his heart was racing wildly with happiness.

"Right," someone agreed.

"If you don't pull the roots, a weed will always make trouble," another said.

"Are you still afraid of him? Don't be afraid. As long as we're united like today we can keep him in order. Think of a way to deal with him."

"Yes, I've a proposal. Let's have the whole village spit at him, what about that?"

"I say his property should be divided up among us all."

"Make him write a statement, admitting his crimes, and if he opposes us again, we'll have his life."

"Yes, let him write a statement. Make him write it himself."

Schemer Qian crawled to his feet again and kneeled to kowtow to the crowd. His right eye was swollen after his beating so that the eye looked even smaller. His lip was split and mud was mixed with his blood. His bedraggled mustache drooped disconsolately. He was a wretched sight, and as he thanked the villagers his voice was no longer clear and strong, but he stammered out: "Good people! I'm kowtowing to you good folks. I was quite wrong in the past. Thank you for your mercy . . ."

A group of children softly aped his voice: "Good people! . . ."

Then he was dragged over to write a statement. He took the brush in his trembling hand and wrote line by line. Then everyone discussed the question of confiscating his property and decided to appropriate all, including that of Qianli. But they could not touch Yi's twenty-four *mou* [1 mou = 1/6 acre]. The peasants were dissatisfied, but this was an order from above, because Yi was a soldier in the Eighth Route Army! So they had to put up with it.

By now the sun was sinking. Hunger made some of the children so restless, they were kicking pebbles at the back of the meeting, and some of the women went quietly home to prepare a meal. The presidium urged Schemer Qian to hurry up and finish writing, saying everybody was tired of waiting for him, and asking where his usual ability had gone to.

When the chairman started reading the statement the crowd grew tense again, and shouted, "Let him read it himself!"

Qian knelt in the middle of the stage, his lined gown hanging in shreds, shoeless, not daring to meet anyone's eyes. He read: "In the past I committed crimes in the village, oppressing good people! . . ."

"That won't do! Just to write 'I' won't do! Write 'local despot, Qian.'"

"Yes, write 'I, local despot Qian.'"

"Start again!"

Schemer Qian started reading again: "I, Qian, a local despot, committed crimes in the village, oppressing good people, and I deserve to die a hundred times over; but my good friends are merciful . . ."

"Who the devil are you calling your good friends?" An old man rushed forward and spat at him.

"Go on reading! Just say all the people of the village."

"No, why should he call us his people."

"Say all the gentlemen."

"Say all the poor gentlemen. We don't want to be rich gentlemen! Only the rich are called gentlemen."

Qian had to continue: "Thanks to the mercy of all the poor gentlemen in the village . . ."

"That's no good. Don't say poor gentlemen; today we poor people have stood up. Say 'the liberated gentlemen,' and it can't be wrong."

"Yes, liberated gentlemen."

Someone chuckled. "Today we're liberated gentlemen!"

"Thanks to the mercy of the liberated gentlemen, my unworthy life has been spared . . ."

"What? I don't understand." Another voice from the crowd interrupted Qian. "We liberated gentlemen aren't going to pass all this literary stuff. Just put it briefly: say your dog's life has been spared."

"Yes, spare your dog's life!" the rest agreed.

Qian had to go on: "Spare my dog's life. In future I must change my former evil ways completely. If I transgress in the slightest or oppose the masses, I shall be put to death. This statement is made by the local despot, Qian, and signed in the presence of the masses. August 3."

The presidium asked the crowd to discuss it, but very few further amendments were proposed, although a few people still felt he was getting off too lightly and they ought to beat him some more.

Schemer Qian was allowed to go back. He was only permitted to live in Yi's house for the time being. All his property apart from his land was to be sealed up immediately by the peasants' association. As to the question of how much should be left him, that was left to the land assessment committee to decide.

Last of all a land assessment committee was elected. Everybody shouted Liuman's name. Young Guo was elected too. Orchard-keeper Li had made quite a good chairman, and he was elected too. Quan was an old peasant who knew more than anyone else about the acreage in the village, so he was also elected. He rubbed his bristling mustaches and said with embarrassment: "If you don't think I'm too old, and want me to do a job, how can I refuse!"

Co-op Tian was elected too, because he was good at using the abacus and quick-witted. Without him they would be in the soup with their accounts. Young Hou could calculate too, and he was young and not afraid of offending people, so he was nominated and elected. Last of all they elected the chairman of the peasants' association, Young Cheng. Cheng had refused Schemer Qian's bribe, staunchly leading them all in the struggle; they all supported such a peasants' association chairman.

By now land reform here could be considered as well under way. Although the peasants still had certain reservations, at least they had passed one large hurdle, and overthrown their greatest enemy. They intended to continue the struggle against the bad powers in the village, settling accounts with each in turn. They meant to stand up properly. They had the strength, as the events of the day made them realize. Their confidence had increased. Nuanshui was no longer the same as the previous day. As the meeting broke up they shouted for joy, a roar like thunder going up into the air. This was an end, it was also a beginning.

19.4 HU SIDU AND HU SHI: THE SON AND THE FATHER

Hu Shi (1891–1962) was one of the major proponents of Anglo-American democracy in China. Throughout his career as an educator, writer, and diplomat he maintained a distance between himself and the two contending political parties. In the 1920s and 1930s, Hu was frequently in conflict with both the reactionaries in the Nanjing government who proclaimed their preference for a dictatorial system and Marxist revolutionaries who argued that their ideology of class struggle was the solution to China's problems.

Despite his differences with Chiang Kai-shek's government, Hu did serve in a series of official and quasi-official positions. From 1938 to 1941, Hu served as Chongqing's ambassador to the United States and later acted as an adviser to the Executive Yuan. He came to be seen as belonging to the most liberal group loyal to the Nationalist government. Throughout his life, until his death on Taiwan in 1962, he remained an advocate of incremental democratic and legal reform.

Hu's position on reform and his willingness to bestow upon the Guomindang government his friendship and occasional support caused left-wing intellectuals and the Communists to dislike him. After the Communist victory on the mainland, Hu fled first to the United States, but his son, Hu Sidu, remained in China and underwent "thought reform" to purge himself of his erstwhile bourgeois worldview.

"Thought reform" or "brainwashing," as this process was called by critics outside of China, was a common Party practice in the early 1950s. The technique of changing people's thoughts by administering a rough and ready political education was a product of the Communist party's long years of opposition, during which it was obliged to absorb millions of people into the revolutionary movement. After 1949, the new Peking regime felt obliged to perform this transformation on an even more massive scale. Party cadres worked overtime to convert erstwhile liberal intellectual opponents and neutral intellectuals who had hitherto abjured playing a political role into sympathetic allies. The objects of "thought reform" were encouraged to reflect on their lives and write long, critical self-confessions. They also read Marxist and Maoist classics and were frequently tested to see if they had shed their previous worldview.

Hu Sidu's 1950 criticism of his father was, thus, part of what was already a familiar genre of self-criticism. In it, he "drew a line" between himself and his father and promised to serve the people and the People's Republic. Although the Communist party denied any element of vengefulness in the process of "thought reform," it is not difficult to imagine the satisfaction Hu Shi's erstwhile enemies must have felt in reading Hu's second son's denunciation of his father as a "public enemy."

HU SIDU'S DENUNCIATION OF HIS FATHER

In the old society, I considered my father as an "aloof" and "clean" good man. Even after the liberation I felt deeply insulted whenever my father was being criticized. Within my heart I strongly objected to Premier Zhou Enlai's calling my father a man who never understood what imperialism means. After I had read the *History of Social Development, State and Revolution, History of Chinese Revolution* and many other books written by Communists, my concept of my father began to change. Now I shall analyze his effect on historical development.

My father came from a fallen family of bureaucrats. He was a student from 1904 to 1910. When he went to the United States at the age of 20, the American material and spiritual civilization dazzled him and swiftly conquered him. His educational environment changed him as a man from a semi-feudal, semi-colonial country to a bourgeois. His article on "The Improvement of Chinese Literature" won him popularity in China because it was anti-feudalistic. He was considered as a progressive.

When he returned in 1917, China was under the despotic rule of Yuan Shi-kai and Duan Qirui. He made up his mind "not to talk politics in 20 years" and buried himself in books. But during the period of "May 4" he could no longer escape from politics. So he published his *Problem and Doctrine*, to attack the growing socialistic ideas with evolutionism. He believed that China could have progress without making fundamental changes. His opinion represented the entire class of bourgeois intellectuals when confronted with the "May 4," and "June 3" movements. What he objected to was a revolution that would demolish the war lords, bureaucrats, landlords, and state machine.

THE WRONG WAY

After 1919 he drifted farther down the wrong way. He praised Ibsenism and battled materialism with experimentalism. He himself was wandering among the rulers of those days, hoping his "evolutionism" would be adopted by them. Weak capitalist intellectuals never dared resist the "government." Hu Shi, like all other members of his class bowed his head to the reactionary government, and turned to Chiang Kai-shek to practice his doctrine of reforms.

...[In 1931] he voluntarily became the dean of the Arts School of Peking University. It was in that job that he laid down his foundation as a political and cultural ruler. He became one of the pillars of the Rockefeller Foundation and the Sino-American Cultural Fund Society. He turned out to be the docile tool of the imperialists.

GREATER POWER

When the reactionary government was campaigning against the Communists, he praised it as a "good men's government." Wang Wenhao and Jiang Tingfu[3] under his "inspiration" all joined the reactionary government. The people who had long suffered under the oppression of the reactionaries thought that the government might change for the better after such "liberal" professors had joined it. The reason why my father refused to become the Minister of Education under Chiang at that time was because he thought that by remaining "aloof" he would enjoy greater power.

In 1937, when the Japanese invading hordes began to storm into East and South China and the rich compradores of the Anglo-American imperialists were forced to take up their cudgel against the aggressor, the interests of his class were gravely threatened. In 1938, he finally became Chiang's ambassador to the United States. In his post as the ambassador to the American imperialists, he signed all kinds of trade agreements and was greatly instrumental in obtaining loans from the American government to fight the Communists.

BOOMING TIDE

In 1946, when the booming tide of the people's revolution was threatening the ruling class, he considered it as a sacred duty to serve for his class. He returned to his country and worked faithfully for the Chiang government. At that time he was carrying out the orders of the reactionary government as the president of the Peking University on the one hand and was deceiving the people by writing middle-of-the-road articles on the other. He more or less had given the people an impression of a "worldly man."

But his loyalty to the reactionary government had not saved the common enemy of the people from extinction. At a time when final victory was about

3. Important associates of Hu Shi and leading intellectual figures of the 1930s. Both men served on the editorial board of the famous journal *The Independent Critic* (Duli pinglun) published in Peking from 1932 to 1937 and joined the Guomindang government in 1935.

to descend to the people, he left Peking and China to become a "White Chinese" living a life of exile.

Today, after my education in the Party, I begin to recognize his true qualities. I have come to know that he is a loyal element of the reactionary class and an enemy of the people. Politically, he has never been progressive. After his publication of *Problem and Doctrine*, in 1919, he wandered on the road in indecision. For 11 years, he groped in the labyrinth of darkness. In 1930, he began to participate actively in the work of strengthening of the reactionary government.

This time he went to the United States in an endeavor to form a third party and took care of the U.S. $4,000,000 relief fund for Chinese students in the United States on behalf of the American State Department. He was willing to serve for the United States and for those reactionary individualistic students.

ENSLAVEMENT EDUCATION

In the past, I was subjected to a long period of enslavement education by the reactionaries, and I was ignorant about the policies of the people. A friend of mine who came to Peking from Hong Kong on business asked me what attitude I would adopt toward my father. I replied that perhaps he could never learn about "group doctrine" and would probably stay in the United States.

Today I realize the lenient policy of the People's government. It gives a chance to all those who have acted against the interests of the people to live down their past and start life anew, only if they can come to realize their past misdeeds.

Until my father returns to the people's arms, he will always remain a public enemy of the people, and an enemy of myself. Today, in my determination to rebel against my own class, I feel it important to draw a line of demarcation between my father and myself. . . .

19.5 CHIANG KAI-SHEK: BACK TO THE MAINLAND, OCTOBER 10, 1954

The Korean War and the consequent posting of the U.S. Seventh Fleet to the Taiwan Strait thwarted the reunification of Taiwan with China and gave a new lease of life to Chiang Kai-shek's government-in-exile. After Chiang consolidated his control over Taiwan, he purged dissident elements in his officer corps and began rebuilding his shattered armies. Institution for institution, the Nanjing government was reconstituted in Taipei and a separate provincial government for Taiwan was set up in the city of Taizhong.

Throughout the remaining years of Chiang Kai-shek's life, the Peking regime of Mao Zedong was regarded by Taipei as a temporary "bandit" government that would be replaced when Chiang returned to the mainland in triumph with his armies. Each year on the Double Ten anniversary of the founding of the Republic of China, Chiang would reiterate the legitimacy of his government as the government of all of China and would restate his promise to rescue the Chinese people from Communist bondage. For decades after 1949, Chiang promised the people of Taiwan and the mainland that the "decisive phase" of the war to reclaim China was at hand, and, as in this document, he excoriated Communist mismanagement of natural disasters (here flooding), social reform, and a panoply of other dilemmas. But despite cries in some quarters in the United States for the "unleashing" of Chiang, no American support was forthcoming for new Nationalist military adventures on the mainland. And, in lieu of more than rhetorical American support, Chiang's fulminations sounded increasingly hollow, even to followers on Taiwan, as years passed without the promised recapture of the mainland.

PRESIDENT CHIANG KAI-SHEK'S MESSAGE TO THE NATION ON NATIONAL DAY (OCTOBER 10, 1954)

Fellow Countrymen and Members of the Armed Forces:

It is 60 years since the founder of the Chinese Republic, Dr. Sun Yat-sen, started the national revolution and organized the Xingzhonghui [Revive China Society].[4] It is 43 years since the revolution of 1911 and, today, we find ourselves engaged in an anti-Communist and resist-Russia struggle. It is a struggle that will decide the outcome of our national revolution. It is also a struggle which will decide whether we as a nation are to survive or perish. This struggle has now entered into its crucial stage. The Chinese people must stand united as one and demonstrate their patriotism by dedicating themselves to the achievement of final victory in order to make this day a glorious occasion to be remembered as the National Day of the Republic of China.

On this National Day, the thing that comes to our mind is that millions of our compatriots, including our own parents, our children, our relatives and our friends on the mainland, are being subjected to greater suffering than ever before at the hands of the Russian and Chinese Communist bandits. This thought has filled our hearts with pain and sorrow.

In the last five years, the Communist bandits have, in their propaganda, been boasting that they had benefited from the experience of the Russian Communists and that they had undertaken a great piece of engineering work in water conservancy along the Huai, the Yellow and the Yangtze Rivers. They claimed

4. Sun Yat-sen's first revolutionary organization, formed in November 1894.

that they had succeeded in harnessing these rivers and that floods had become a thing of the past. But last summer, the basins of the Yangtze, the Huai, the Yellow and the Han Rivers were all inundated by floods of unprecedented ferocity. Breaches in the dikes of these rivers have resulted in the flooding of twelve provinces, making millions of our compatriots homeless and starving. What is the cause of such unprecedented natural and man-made calamities? This is, as the Communists have been telling people, the "miracle" created by the Communist party, "which, by representing and safeguarding the vital interest of the people, would lead the people to a life of freedom and happiness." This is also what they have been boasting as "the grand achievement of farm irrigation and conservancy" and "raising the standard of living of the people."

As is to be expected, the Communist bandits under Zhu De and Mao Zedong have shown no sympathy for the hapless flood victims. The surprising thing is that they have seen fit at this particular moment to compel our compatriots on the mainland to toe what they call "the general line of the transition period." By using such phrases as "transition period" and "general line," it is their intention to drive our compatriots on the mainland further along the road to create a tightly integrated "unbreakable alliance between the USSR and the People's Republic of China." In other words, it is the intention of Zhu De and Mao Zedong to hand over our people and territory on the mainland to the Russian imperialists. Fellow Countrymen: Can we allow "transition" to come to pass? Can we bear to see the ruin of our country and the extermination of our race? No, we must stand united; we must rise up and work for the downfall of both the Russian and Chinese Communist bandits.

In the past five years, we have not relaxed our efforts in prosecuting the war against the Communists in the Taiwan Straits and along the mainland coast. But these on and off operations are merely small-scale engagements of a long-term all-out war. Now the Communist bandits are about to embark on a new adventure and start a new war. They have initiated hostile action against Quemoy and Tachen [islands] off the mainland coast and have boasted about their determination to "liberate" Taiwan. The Russian Communist bosses have openly stated they would do their best to support the Chinese Communists. They have said that the Soviet Union is deeply concerned with the "liberation" of Taiwan. Why is Soviet Russia so much concerned with this war? The answer is that it might thwart her attempt to enslave 1,100,000,000 people in Asia. This why the Russian Communist bosses stated emphatically that they would support the Chinese Communist bandits to fight for further consolidation and development. It is possible that the objective of the Russian Communist is not limited to the "liberation" of Taiwan. It will in due course include the "liberation" of all the nations in Asia and eventually the entire human race. The "liberation" of Taiwan is but a foretaste of what the Russian Communists have in store for the world. . . .

Fellow Countrymen: The Communist bandits have started hostile action against the islands off the mainland. They are in fact knocking on the front door of this island. All our military forces and civilians must be mobilized for war. We must intensify our mobilization and speed up our preparation for our counter-offensive, in order to discharge our heavy responsibility to recover our country and save the people.

Now I would like to take this opportunity to acquaint our compatriots on the mainland with the fundamental principles by which the Government will be guided upon the recovery of the mainland. First, we shall safeguard all freedoms and rights of the people in accordance with the Constitution of the Republic of China—especially freedom of the person, freedom of speech, freedom of press, freedom of assembly and freedom of religious belief. We shall establish local self-government. We shall safeguard the people's rights to live, to work, to own property, to elect their own representatives, and to be elected to office. Secondly, we shall allow the farmers to continue to work on the land on which they have been working, and we shall safeguard their income. We shall settle all their disputes in fairness and in accordance with the land-to-the-tiller principle. We shall see to it that everyone shall have land, employment and the chance of education and lead a secure and happy life. The land now held by the Communist usurpers shall be given to the soldiers who have retired from the service. Thirdly, we shall extend assistance to the trade unions, safeguard the interests of both labor and capital, help develop industries and trade and increase production and promote social welfare. These are principles laid down in the Three People's Principles and the Five Power Constitution and carried out in Taiwan Province. They shall be carried out in all provinces of China upon the recovery of the mainland. We shall see to it that freedom of marriage and religion be respected. The Government shall wipe out the last vestige of tyranny left by the Communist bandits on the mainland. The Government shall do away with excessive taxation, oppression, false accusations, liquidation's, struggles, persecutions, brainwashing and other forms of thought reform. We shall claim back our lost territories from the Russians and our freedom from the Communist bandits Zhu De and Mao Zedong.

Fellow Countrymen: We are now approaching the decisive phase in our revolutionary war. We must be prepared to fight with grim determination and give our all to the cause of the anti-Communist and resist-Russia struggle. Everyone in Free China or overseas should heighten their political consciousness in order to wreck the evil designs of the Communist bandits and defeat every word and move of the Russian imperialistic aggressor. But that is not all. Those who are living under the Communists on the mainland must fortify themselves and wait for the proper occasion to come forth. They should join the "retaliation movement" to take vengeance on the Russians and their Communist puppets under Zhu De and Mao Zedong for the murder of their parents, children, brothers, sister, relatives and friends. They should seek to extend the "go-slow movement" and, more positively, instigate "resistance movements." They should augment their guerrilla forces, establish administrative organs behind enemy lines and synchronize their actions with the counterattack of our regular army. Let all people in the country, military and civilians, join in the fight regardless of the cost. Then we shall be able to regain our freedom and recover our country. Let us be loyal and faithful to our cause. Let us unite all anti-Communist and patriotic elements, whether they be in China or overseas and regardless of political affiliations or past grievances, to fight the common fight against the Communist bandits and the Russians. Let us continue to work for the recovery of our country and the liberation of our people. Let us strive to accomplish the glorious historical mission bequeathed to us by our great leader, Dr. Sun Yatsen, and those of his followers who have given their lives to the revival of the country and the creation of the Republic of China.

Let us arise and shout:

Long live the Republic of China!

Long live the Three People's Principles!

Long Live the victory for the cause of Anti-Communism and Resistance to Russia!

Long live the success of the National Revolution!

CHAPTER 20

Planning the New Society

20.1 AND 20.2 A-BOMBS AND PAPER TIGERS

Following the Korean War, China was almost entirely isolated in international affairs. Outside of the socialist bloc of countries, few states recognized the People's Republic and China's diplomats strove to broaden recognition for the country among neutral or nonaligned countries in the Third World. The five major themes of Chinese foreign policy were set in place by Zhou Enlai at the Bandung conference in Indonesia in 1955. They included mutual respect for territorial sovereignty; mutual nonaggression; mutual noninterference in domestic affairs; equality of relationships and mutual benefit; and peaceful coexistence.

At the same time, U.S. imperialism was seen as the greatest threat to China and world peace. America's growing arsenal of nuclear weapons made it clear that a war would place China at a great disadvantage. Mao Zedong, however, was not awed by America's superiority in weaponry and often argued, as in the following two documents, that China's vast manpower and the multitude of America's enemies in global landscape of socialist societies and peoples at war to defeat colonialism and Western domination made the American technological edge irrelevant. According to Mao, the United States was a "paper tiger" that would soon be toppled by the irresistible forces of world revolution.

20.1 Mao Zedong: "The Chinese People Cannot Be Cowed by the Atom Bomb," January 28, 1955

Today, the danger of a world war and the threats to China come mainly from the warmongers in the United States. They have occupied our Taiwan and the Taiwan Straits and are contemplating an atomic war. We have two principles: first, we don't want war; second, we will strike back resolutely if anyone invades us. This is what we teach the members of the Communist Party and the whole nation. The Chinese people are not to be cowed by U.S. atomic blackmail. Our country has a population of 600 million and an area of 9,600,000 square kilometres. The United States cannot annihilate the Chinese nation with its small stack of atom bombs. Even if the U.S. atom bombs were so powerful that, when dropped on China, they would make a hole right through the earth, or even blow it up, that would hardly mean anything to the universe as a whole, though it might be a major event for the solar system.

We have an expression, millet plus rifles. In the case of the United States, it is planes plus the A-bomb. However, if the United States with its planes plus the A-bomb is to launch a war of aggression against China, then China with its millet plus rifles is sure to emerge the victor. The people of the whole world will support us. As a result of World War I, the tsar, the landlords and the capitalists in Russia were wiped out; as a result of World War II, Chiang Kai-shek and the landlords were overthrown in China and the East European countries and a number of countries in Asia were liberated. Should the United States launch a third world war and supposing it lasted eight or ten years, the result would be the elimination of the ruling classes in the United States, Britain and the other accomplice countries and the transformation of most of the world into countries led by Communist Parties. World wars end not in favour of the warmongers but in favour of the Communist Parties and the revolutionary people in all lands. If the warmongers are to make war, then they mustn't blame us for making revolution or engaging in "subversive activities," as they keep saying all the time. If they desist from war, they can survive a little longer on this earth. But the sooner they make war, the sooner they will be wiped from the face of the earth. Then a people's united nations would be set up, maybe in Shanghai, maybe somewhere in Europe, or it might be set up again in New York, provided the U.S. warmongers had been wiped out.

20.2 Mao Zedong: "U.S. Imperialism Is a Paper Tiger," July 14, 1956

The United States is flaunting the anti-Communist banner everywhere in order to perpetrate aggression against other countries.

The United States owes debts everywhere. It owes debts not only to the countries of Latin America, Asia and Africa, but also to the countries of Europe and Oceania. The whole world, Britain included, dislikes the United States. The masses of the people dislike it. Japan dislikes the United States because it oppresses her. None of the countries in the East is free from U.S. aggression. The United States has invaded our Taiwan Province. Japan, Korea, the Philippines, Viet Nam and Pakistan all suffer from U.S. aggression, although some of them are allies of the United States. The people are dissatisfied and in some countries so are the authorities.

All oppressed nations want independence.

Everything is subject to change. The big decadent forces will give way to the small new-born forces. The small forces will change into big forces. The small forces will change into big forces because the majority of the people demand this change. The U.S. imperialist forces will change from big to small because the American people, too, are dissatisfied with their government.

In my own lifetime I myself have witnessed such changes. Some of us present were born in the Qing Dynasty and others after the 1911 Revolution.

The Qing Dynasty was overthrown long ago. By whom? By the party led by Sun Yat-sen, together with the people. Sun Yat-sen's forces were so small that the Qing officials didn't take him seriously. He led many uprisings which failed each time. In the end, however, it was Sun Yat-sen who brought down the Qing Dynasty. Bigness is nothing to be afraid of. The big will be overthrown by the small. The small will become big. After overthrowing the Qing Dynasty, Sun Yat-sen met with defeat. For he failed to satisfy the demands of the people, such as their demands for land and for opposition to imperialism. Nor did he understand the necessity of suppressing the counter-revolutionaries who were then moving about freely. Later, he suffered defeat at the hands of Yuan Shih-kai, the chieftain of the Northern warlords. Yuan Shih-kai's forces were larger than Sun Yat-sen's. But here again this law operated: small forces linked with the people become strong, while big forces opposed to the people become weak. Subsequently Sun Yat-sen's bourgeois-democratic revolutionaries co-operated with us Communists and together we defeated the warlord set-up left behind by Yuan Shih-kai.

Chiang Kai-shek's rule in China was recognized by the governments of all countries and lasted twenty-two years, and his forces were the biggest. Our forces were small, fifty thousand Party members at first but only a few thousand after counter-revolutionary suppressions. The enemy made trouble everywhere. Again this law operated: the big and strong end up in defeat because they are divorced from the people, whereas the small and weak emerge victorious because they are linked with the people and work in their interest. That's how things turned out in the end.

During the anti-Japanese war, Japan was very powerful, the Guomindang troops were driven to the hinterland, and the armed forces led by the Communist Party could only conduct guerrilla warfare in the rural areas behind the enemy lines. Japan occupied large Chinese cities such as Peking, Tianjin, Shanghai, Nanjing, Wuhan and Canton. Nevertheless, like Germany's Hitler the Japanese militarists collapsed in a few years, in accordance with the same law.

We underwent innumerable difficulties and were driven from the south to the north, while our forces fell from several hundred thousand strong to a few tens of thousands. At the end of the 25,000-*li* Long March we had only 25,000 men left. . . .

Now U.S. imperialism is quite powerful, but in reality it isn't. It is very weak politically because it is divorced from the masses of the people and is disliked by everybody and by the American people too. In appearance it is very powerful but in reality it is nothing to be afraid of, it is a paper tiger.

History as a whole, the history of class society for thousands of years, has proved this point: the strong must give way to the weak. This holds true for the Americas as well.

Only when imperialism is eliminated can peace prevail. The day will come when the paper tigers will be wiped out. But they won't become extinct of their own accord, they need to be battered by the wind and the rain.

When we say U.S. imperialism is a paper tiger, we are speaking in terms of strategy. Regarding it as a whole, we must despise it. But regarding each part, we must take it seriously. It has claws and fangs. We have to destroy it piecemeal. For instance, if it has ten fangs, knock off one the first time, and there will be nine left; knock off another, and there will be eight left. When all the fangs are gone, it will still have claws. If we deal with it step by step and in earnest, we will certainly succeed in the end.

Strategically, we must utterly despise U.S. imperialism. Tactically, we must take it seriously. In struggling against it, we must take each battle, each encounter, seriously. At present, the United States is powerful, but when looked at in a broader perspective, as a whole and from a long-term viewpoint, it has no popular support, its policies are disliked by the people, because it oppresses and exploits them. For this reason, the tiger is doomed. Therefore, it is nothing to be afraid of and can be despised. But today the United States still has strength, turning out more than 100 million tons of steel a year and hitting out everywhere. That is why we must continue to wage struggles against it, fight it with all our might and wrest one position after another from it. And that takes time.

It seems that the countries of the Americas, Asia and Africa will have to go on quarreling with the United States till the very end, till the paper tiger is destroyed by the wind and the rain.

To oppose U.S. imperialism, people of European origin in the Latin-American countries should unite with the indigenous Indians. Perhaps the white immigrants from Europe can be divided into two groups, one composed of rulers and the other of the ruled. This should make it easier for the group of oppressed white people to get close to the local people, for their position is the same.

Our friends in Latin America, Asia and Africa are in the same position as we and are doing the same kind of work, doing something for the people to lessen their oppression by imperialism. If we do a good job, we can root out imperialist oppression. In this we are comrades.

We are of the same nature as you in our opposition to imperialist oppression, differing only in geographical position, nationality and language. But we are different in nature from imperialism, and the very sight of it makes us sick.

What use is imperialism? The Chinese people will have none of it, nor will the people in the rest of the world. There is no reason for the existence of imperialism.

20.3 LU DINGYI: THE HUNDRED FLOWERS CAMPAIGN, MAY 1956

During the first seven years of the People's Republic, widespread enthusiasm for the new era of peace brought about by the Communist unification of China insulated the new government from criticism. The party also used programs of "thought reform" and "reeducation" to win over potential opponents. In the first, "honeymoon" phase of Communist rule, the power of the party was absolute; the leaders of the party and many common people believed in the scientific truth of Marxism–Leninism–Mao Zedong Thought and the party elite ruled with a self-assurance rarely challenged from below.

In 1953 and 1954, the first cracks began to appear in the edifice of Communist control. Power struggles and internal purges shook the party. A number of prominent Chinese Communist regional leaders were removed from power, and leading writers and intellectuals were persecuted. In addition, the death of Stalin in 1953 initiated in the Soviet Communist party a cautious reassessment of Soviet history from 1928 onward that lead ultimately to Khruschev's textured renunciation of the Stalinist system during the Soviet twentieth party congress in February 1956. In the fall of the same year, the Hungarian uprising provided further proof that all was not well in the socialist world. The tragedy in the streets of Budapest showed that a powerful *popular* sentiment for the reform of Stalinism now confronted Communist states throughout the world.

In China, the early years of Communist rule, with the attendant application of "thought reform" and the party's self-proclaimed monopolization of political truth, created a hunger for greater democracy. Many Chinese, but particularly intellectuals, felt dissatisfied under the "people's democratic dictatorship." Recognizing that an outlet was necessary for these passions and feeling that it was better to confront criticism head on, a number of party leaders began to advocate a campaign to ease pressure by lifting the lid on dissent.

The result of this debate was the short-lived Hundred Flowers campaign. The opening of the campaign was heralded by a historic speech delivered in May 1956 by Lu Dingyi, the director of the powerful Propaganda Department of the Central Committee of the party, in which Lu argued the need for a careful opening to dissent and for more creative freedom for intellectuals working in all fields.

After almost a year of reticence, intellectuals, prodded by party workers to address problems that concerned them, began launching sharp attacks on the deficiencies they saw during the early years of Communist rule. The June 1957 denunciation of the party and party leadership by two Shenyang Normal University professors, reproduced below, was mild in comparison to some critiques. However, its challenge to fundamental aspects of Communist rule and critique of the party's transformation into an arrogant and privileged elite suggests why party leaders saw a throat in the literary "flowers" brought to bloom by the Hundred Flowers policy.

"LET FLOWERS OF MANY KINDS BLOSSOM, DIVERSE SCHOOLS OF THOUGHT CONTEND!"

MAY 26, 1956

Mr. Guo Morou, President of the Chinese Academy of Sciences and Chairman of the All-China Federation of Literary and Art Circles, has asked me to speak on the policy of the Chinese Communist Party on the work of artists, writers and scientists.

To artists and writers, we say, "Let flowers of many kinds blossom." To scientists we say, "Let diverse schools of thought contend." This is the policy of the Chinese Communist Party. It was announced by Chairman Mao Zedong at the Supreme State Conference.

In applying this policy we have gained some further experience, but it is still far too scanty. Furthermore, what I am saying today is merely my own personal understanding of this policy. You here are scientists specializing in the natural and social sciences, doctors, writers and artists; some of you are members of the Communist Party, some friends from democratic parties, and others non-Party friends. You will readily see how immensely important this policy is in the development of Chinese art, literature and scientific research—the work you yourselves are engaged in—so if you think I am mistaken on any point, please don't hesitate to correct me. Then we can all do our bit to promote the common cause.

I. WHY THIS POLICY, AND WHY THIS EMPHASIS ON IT NOW?

If we want our country to be prosperous and strong, we must, besides consolidating the people's state power, developing our economy and education and strengthening our national defense, have a flourishing art, literature and science. That is essential.

If we want art, literature and science to flourish, we must apply a policy of letting flowers of many kinds blossom, letting diverse schools of thought contend.

Literature and art can never really flourish if only one flower blooms alone, no matter how beautiful that flower may be. Take the theatre, an example which readily comes to mind these days. Some years back there were still people who set their face against Peking opera. Then the Party decided to apply the policy summed up in the words "let flowers of many kinds blossom side by side, weed through the old to let the new emerge" to the theatre. Everybody can see now how right it was to do so, and the notable results it led to. Thanks to free competition and the fact that the various kinds of drama now all learn from one another, our theatre has made rapid progress.

In the field of science, we have historical experience to draw on. During the period of the Spring and Autumn Annals (722–481 B.C.) and of the Warring States (403–221 B.C.) more than two thousand years ago, many schools of thought vied with each other for supremacy. That was a golden age in the intellectual development of China. History shows that unless independent thinking and free discussion are encouraged, academic life stagnates. And conversely, when they are encouraged, academic growth speeds up. But, of course, the state of affairs existing in those ancient times was very different from what it is in present-day China. At that time, society was in turmoil. The various schools of thought did vie with each other, spreading their ideas; but they did so spontaneously, with no sort of conscious, organized leadership. Now the people have won a world of freedom for themselves. The people's democratic dictatorship has been set up and consolidated. There is a popular demand that nothing should be allowed to impede the onward march of science. That is why we consciously map out an all-embracing plan for scientific development and adopt a policy of letting diverse schools of thought contend to give vigor to academic growth.

One cannot fail to see that in class societies art, literature and science are, in the last analysis, weapons in the class struggle.

This is quite clear in the case of art and literature. Here we can see things that are obviously pernicious. The stuff written by Hu Feng[1] is one such example. Pornographic and gutter literature that debauches people and turns them into gangsters is another. Still another example is the so-called literature summed up in phrases like "let's play mah-jong and to hell with state affairs," "the moon in America is rounder than the moon in China," etc. It is perfectly right and proper for us to look on literature of this pernicious kind as a par with flies, mosquitoes, rats and sparrows and rid ourselves of it all. This can only benefit, not harm our literature. Thus we say there is art and literature, for instance, that serves the workers, peasants and soldiers, and art and literature that serves the imperialists, landlords and bourgeoisie. What we need is art and literature that serves the workers, peasants and soldiers—art and literature that serves the people.

The existence of class struggle is also fairly clear in the philosophy and the social sciences. Hu Shi's views on philosophy, history, education and politics have been held up to public odium. The repudiation of his views is a reflection of class struggle in the field of the social sciences. We are perfectly justified in denouncing Mr. Liang Shuming's[2] ideas. We are also right in criticizing other philosophical schools of bourgeois idealism and bourgeois sociology.

Now let us see how things stand in the field of natural science. All scientists have their own political viewpoint, although natural science itself has no class character. Formerly some who specialized in the natural sciences blindly worshipped the United States, while others tended to be "non-political." It is right and proper to criticize all such things as undesirable—and such criticism is a reflection of class struggle.

We cannot fail to notice too that although art, literature and scientific research have a close bearing on the class struggle, they are not, after all, the same thing as politics. Political struggle is a direct form of class struggle. Art, literature and the social sciences give expression to the class struggle sometimes in a direct, and sometimes in a roundabout way. It is a one-sided, rightist way of looking at things to assume that art, literature and science have nothing to do with politics and that "art for art's sake," or "science for science's sake" is a justified standpoint. To look at things in that way is certainly wrong. On the other hand, it is one-sided and "leftist" to oversimplify things and equate art, literature and science with politics. This view is equally wrong.

"Letting flowers of many kinds blossom, diverse schools of thought contend" means that we stand for freedom of independent thinking, of debate, of creative work; freedom to criticize and freedom to express, maintain and reserve one's opinions on questions of art, literature or scientific research. . . .

1. Marxist literary critic (1903–1985). Hu was heavily criticized in the 1950s and later as a counterrevolutionary and imperialist.

2. Leading opponent of the New Culture movement and exponent of cultural preservation in the May Fourth period.

II. STRENGTHEN UNITY

Let flowers of many kinds blossom, diverse schools of thought contend: that is a policy to mobilize all the positive elements. It is also, therefore, a policy that will in the end strengthen unity.

On what basis are we to unite? On the basis of patriotism and socialism. What do we unite for? To build a new, socialist China and combat our enemies both at home and abroad.

There are two kinds of unity: one is built on mechanical obedience and the other on our own conscious, free will. What we want is the latter.

Are those engaged in art, literature and science united? Yes, they are. Compare the situation in the days when the Chinese People's Republic was just founded with what we have now and you find we now have a far closer unity among artists, writers and scientists. This has come about as a result of our work for social reforms and changes in our ways of thought. It would be wrong to deny or ignore this. But even so, we cannot say that our unity is all it should be: there is still room for improvement. . . .

We hope, too, that writers, artists and scientists who are not Party members will also pay attention to the question of securing closer unity. And here I would like to repeat part of what Comrade Zhou Enlai said in his "Report on the Question of Intellectuals."

"We have already pointed out that there is still a certain distance between some intellectuals and our Party. We must take the initiative to remove this. For this distance, both sides usually bear responsibility. On the one hand, our comrades do not approach to try to understand the intellectuals; on the other, certain intellectuals still have reservations regarding socialism or even oppose it. There are such intellectuals in our enterprises, schools, government offices and society as a whole. Failing to differentiate between friend and foe, between the Communist Party and the Guomindang, between the Chinese people and imperialism, they are dissatisfied with the policies and measures of the Party and the People's Government and hanker after capitalism or even feudalism. They are hostile to the Soviet Union and unwilling to learn from her. They refuse to study Marxism-Leninism, and sneer at it. Despising labour, the laboring people and government workers who come from families of working people, they refuse to mix with workers and peasants or government cadres of worker or peasant origin. Unwilling to see growth of new forces, they consider progressives as opportunists, and often stir up trouble and hostility between intellectuals and the Party as well as among intellectuals themselves. They have enormous conceit, thinking themselves Number One in the world, and refusing to accept anyone's leadership or criticism. Denying the interests of the people or of society as a whole, they view everything only from their personal interests. What is to their personal advantage they accept, what is not to their personal advantage they oppose. Of course, there are very few intellectuals today who have all these faults; but not a small number have one fault or another. Even some of the middle group often hold some of the wrong views mentioned above, let alone the backward intellectuals. And not a few progressives are still guilty of such faults as narrow-mindedness, arrogance, and the tendency to view everything from their personal interests. Unless such intellectuals change their stand, however hard we may try to approach them, there will still be a distance between us and them."

That is to say, we must call on Party members and, equally, on people outside the Party to make a great effort, to strengthen our unity....

III. CRITICISM AND STUDY

In regard to criticism, our policy of letting flowers of many kinds blossom, diverse schools of thought contend means freedom to criticize and freedom to counter-criticize.

Some of the criticism we have today is of the thunder-bolt variety; some of it is milk and water. How do we tackle this question?

There are two kinds of criticism. One is criticism directed against the enemy—what people call criticism that "kills at a blow," criticism with no holds barred. The other is criticism directed against the honestly mistaken—well-meant, comradely criticism, made in the cause of unity, intended to achieve unity through struggle. In making this kind of criticism, one must always bear the whole situation in mind. The critic should rely on reasoning, and his aim should be to help others.

We must have a broad range of general knowledge.

In medical science, agronomy, philosophy, history, literature, drama, painting and music, etc., China has a rich heritage. This heritage must be studied seriously and accepted critically. The point is not that we have done so much in these fields, but that we have done too little, and have not been serious enough in our approach. There is still this attitude of belittling our national heritage, and in some spheres it is still a really serious problem.

What kind of heritage are we to accept and how?

If we were to accept only what is perfect by present-day standards, there would be nothing left for us to take over. On the other hand, if we were to accept our cultural heritage uncritically, we should simply be taking the attitude summed up in the phrase "everything Chinese is best."

We suggest that in dealing with our cultural heritage the principle should be: Carefully select, cherish and foster all that is good in it while criticizing its faults and shortcomings in a serious way. At present our work suffers because we do neither well. There is a tendency to reject offhand even what is good in our cultural heritage. At present that is the main trend. The recent performance of the Kunshan opera *Fifteen Strings of Cash* shows how wrong it was to say there was nothing good in Kunshan opera. And if there is such a tendency in the theatre, what about other branches of art, literature and scientific research? We must admit that there are similar tendencies in them too, and we must do something about it. At the same time, we can also see a tendency not to criticize or even to gloss over shortcomings in and blots on our cultural heritage. This attitude is neither honest nor sincere, and that we must alter, too.

Workers in art, literature and science need to learn from the people. The wisdom of the people is inexhaustible. There are still many treasures among the people that have not yet been discovered or, though discovered, not made good use of. Take medical science for instance. In the past, needling and cautery and special curative breathing exercises were scorned; only now are they being taken notice of. Both other "popular" healing methods such as osteopathy, massage and herbal medicines have even now not received the attention due to them. . . .

As they come from the people things are often not systematically developed or are crude or lack theoretical explanation. Some of them have more than a bit of the "quack" about them, or a taint of the superstitious. There is nothing surprising about that. It is the duty of our scientists, artists and writers not to despise these things but to make them, to select, cherish and foster the good in them, and, where necessary, put them on a scientific basis.

We must have our national pride, but we must not become national nihilists. We oppose that misguided attitude known as "wholesale Westernization." But that does not mean that we can afford to be arrogant and refuse to learn good things from abroad. Our country is still a very backward one; we can make it prosperous and strong only by doing our best to learn all we can from foreign countries. Under no circumstances is national arrogance justified.

We must learn from the Soviet Union, from the People's Democracies, and from the peoples of all lands.

To learn from the Soviet Union—that is a correct watchword. We have already learnt a little, but much remains to be learnt. The Soviet Union is the world's first socialist state, the leader of the world camp of peace and democracy. It has the highest rate of industrial development. It has a rich experience in socialist construction. In not a few important branches of science it has caught up with and surpassed the most advanced capitalist countries. It stands to reason that it is worth our while to learn from such a country and such a people. It is utterly wrong not to learn from the Soviet Union.

Nevertheless, in learning from the Soviet Union we must not mechanically copy everything in the Soviet Union in a doctrinaire way. We must make what we have learnt fit our actual conditions. That is a point we must pay attention to. Otherwise, we shall run into trouble.

Besides learning from the Soviet Union, we must also learn from the People's Democracies. Every People's Democracy has its own special merits. Some of them have advanced further than China in industry and scientific technique, others are more advanced in other fields. To learn from them all is well worth while. Arrogance in this connection is entirely out of place.

People in countries other than the Soviet Union and the People's Democracies have different social institutions and political systems. Social institutions and political systems may come and go, but the people will live on and continue to progress. It is not without good reason that this is so. We must therefore critically study all their good points—in art and literature, in science, in their customs and habits, in every sphere. Here too a feeling of superiority is quite out of place.

Apart from learning from our friends, we must see what we can learn from our enemies—not to learn what is reactionary in their systems but to study what is good in their methods of management or in their scientific techniques. Our aim in this is to speed the progress of our socialist construction, so as to build up our strength to ward off aggression and safeguard peace in Asia and throughout the world. . . .

20.4 PROFESSORS SPEAK OUT, JUNE 10, 1957

Chang Po-sheng and Huang Chen-lu at a "contention" meeting of the faculty members of the Shenyang Normal College on June 10, jointly made a long speech lasting about three hours . . . Chang Po-sheng is head of the propaganda department of the Communist Youth League in the Normal College and Huang Chen-lu is editor of the school paper . . .

They said: "The suppression of counter-revolutionaries was necessary and timely but too many persons were put to death . . . Many among the executed were formerly military and political personnel of the so-called Manchukuo and the Guomindang and landlords, but they were not guilty of heinous crimes, still less were they flagrant counter-revolutionaries; they were the product of history . . It is inhumane to put all of them to death . ."

They said: "If the cause behind the mistakes of the campaign for rounding up counter-revolutionaries is traced, it will be traced to the Party centre. The 5 per cent—Party centre's estimate of the percentage of counter-revolutionaries in the population—is a gross manifestation of subjectivism and bureaucratism. The idea is influenced by Stalin's erroneous theory 'the more developed the socialist cause, the more the enemy.' . . ."

Huang Chen-lu went on: "Socialist transformation is over-hasty all round. It is not a question of whether co-operativisation is called for but a question of how to do it. To this question no answer was given by Chairman Mao in his report to the Supreme State Conference. . . . Outwardly the movement was launched with a fanfare; actually, it was too early. It is not true that all the peasants consciously want to join the co-operatives; as a matter of fact, the majority of them are forced to join. That is why Agricultural Producer Co-operative cadres are short, their quality is not high, work is chaotic, non-productive personnel are too large in number and production enthusiasm is low." Huang Chen-lu proposed that, where conditions were not appropriate, co-operatives should be allowed to disband themselves and the state should concentrate on the state farms and permit purchase and sale of small holdings. . . . With the private industrial and commercial establishments coming under state-private ownership, large numbers of directors, accountants and cashiers—"leading personnel"—had appeared, and money had flowed into their pockets. Moreover, there had been more trouble for consumers. "Can there be any disturbance if they are allowed to run their business independently under the leadership of a powerful state economy?"

The central problem brought up in the joint speech by these two men was "doing away with the absolute leadership of the Party."

"Doing away with the absolute leadership of the Party," said Huang Chen-lu, "is aimed at strengthening the Party leadership and making the Party a vanguard. . . ."

Huang Chen-lu said: "Before the liberation the Party enjoyed high prestige, maintaining intimate connections with the people and uniting with the people, and there were no such contradictions as exist today. Since the founding of the Republic, particularly in the last one or two years, the Party has become superior to the people and has assumed privileges, praising itself for its 'greatness, glory and correctness' and placing itself above the state, above the people. For this reason, Party prestige is falling day by day. More and more persons with impure motives join the Party. They join the Party because they can win glory and acquire power, influence and money. Imbued with despicable individualism, they insinuate themselves into the favour of the Party, flatter the Party, bow to the Party and obey the Party on everything. . . . The Communist Party has 12,000,000 members, less than 2 per cent of the total population. The 600 million people are to become the obedient subjects of these 2 per cent of people. What sort of principle is this! The absolute leadership of the Party must be done away with. The privilege of Party members must be done away with!"

Supplementing this point, Chang Po-sheng said in his speech: "Now that the Party is in a privileged position, Party members of mediocre talent are found everywhere occupying high positions. Old Party members, forgetting the tradition of working for the nation and the people, are fond of flattery and loath to accept criticism. The Party centre takes the lead, 'setting a bad example to those in low places.' The Press unanimously sings the praises to its meritorious service and virtue.

". . . We warn the Party; beware of organizational and ideological ossification!"

Huang Chen-lu said: "It was logical that the Party should exercise absolute rights of leadership and that Party members were put into important positions before and at the beginning of the founding of the Republic. Conditions have changed today and history demands the liquidation of the absolute right of leadership of the party and the privileges of the Party. Otherwise, the course of history will be obstructed." In their opinion, only when the privileges of Party members were done away with would genuine Communists join the Party and only such Party organizations could preserve their purity and lead the state with a correct policy; otherwise, the Party and socialism would be buried.

"There has been no socialist democracy in the years since the liberation, and what democracy there is is only in form and there is not even the pseudo-democracy of capitalist countries," Chang Po-sheng said. "The Constitution is a scrap of paper and the Party has no need to observe it. Outwardly we have democratic elections, a united front policy and non-Party people exercising leadership; actually, the Party exercises dictatorship and a few persons of the Political Bureau of the Party centre exercise absolute power. Since the election of people's deputies is not democratic, elections are actually a variety of appointment. Although some non-Party people occupy leading posts, they perform duties but have no power. . . . Nor is there democracy within the Party. The convening of the 8th National Congress, for instance, was a great event, but which Party member could put his views to the congress? . . . As to freedom of assembly, association and publication, that is just something written in the Constitution; actually, citizens can only become obedient subjects or, to use a harsh word, slaves. The Party is the emperor and an august and sacred body. Who dares to oppose it when it holds the bible of Marxism-Leninism in the one hand and the sword of state power in the other? You would either be labeled an anti Marxist-Leninist or handcuffed with 'unfounded charges.' "

"If this state of affairs is to be changed, a system of general election campaigns should be put into effect alongside the abolition of the absolute leadership of the Party. The people should be allowed freely to organize new political parties and social bodies, and to put out publications so as to open the channels of public opinion, supervise the government, combat cheap praises and encourage them to oppose an undesirable *status quo* even if it meant opposition to the Communist Party, provided they do not stand against the people and socialism. The Communist Party, if it really represents the people, will not be kicked out; if the Communist Party is kicked out, it means it no longer represents the people. Is it pitiable to have such a Party kicked out?"

Chang Po-sheng went on: "Whose words count in connection with state affairs? The Constitution lays down that the words of the National People's Congress and its Standing Committee count, but actually the National People's Congress is nothing but a mud idol while all power is in the hands of the Party centre. The National People's Congress merely carries out the formality of raising hands and passing resolutions. In all these years, one has seldom seen a Standing Committee member putting forward an important motion, though occasionally one has seen some of them publishing unimportant notes on inspection tours in the Press. Is this not laughable? Why did the National People's Congress deputies see no contradictions among the people during their inspection tours? They saw only what the Party said and saw nothing when the Party did not say anything. They did not see or they dared not say? Even more laughable is that the Chinese People's Political Consultative Conference, which is said to be representing the united front, spends most of its energy on work connected with organization of studies . . . Like two paper flowers the National People's Congress and the People's Political Consultative Conference decorate the facade of democracy . . . All kinds of important questions are decided upon by six persons—Chairman Mao, Liu Shao-ch'i, Premier Chou En-lai and those above the rank of the secretary general of the Party centre—at their table. The destiny of 600 million people is dictated by the pen of these six persons. And how can they know the actual situation? At best they can make an inspection tour of the Yellow River and swim in the Yangtze [in 1956]. Even if they talked with the peasants, the peasants would not tell the truth and could only say: 'Chairman Mao is great.' How can mistakes be avoided when such a small number of people take arbitrary action and recklessly issue orders? The Party centre has never criticized itself publicly since the founding of the Republic. If this dictatorial obstruction to national affairs is to be changed, the Party must be removed from its position of superiority to the National People's Congress and the government, the government must be placed below the National People's Congress and the National People's Congress must be made an organ exercising genuine power. . . ."

Chang Po-sheng said: "Personnel work is in a complete mess. Incompetent persons become leaders and competent ones become men without official standing . . . Full-time Party cadres should be drastically reduced. . . . One hears that the Young Communist League of Yugoslavia has only some 170 full-time cadres throughout the country, whereas our First Motor Car Plant alone has more than 100 full-time League cadres. This is indeed a laughing matter, a big laughing matter! . . . If a person is a Party member, he is made a leading cadre; if he is not a Party member, he is placed at a lower level. . . .

"Whether a post should be high or low should be determined by whether the person is equal to the post. How about the veteran revolutionary cadres who have worked for the revolution for several decades but whose cultural level is very low? They may be employed as grooms but, since they have rendered meritorious service to the revolution, we should respect them and grant them a service allowance . . ."

In conclusion, Chang Po-sheng explained that the views as expressed in their speeches were at the stage of fermentation in December 1956 and were only written down yesterday.

[*Shenyang Daily,* June 11, 1957]

20.5 DENG XIAOPING: THE ANTIRIGHTIST CAMPAIGN, SEPTEMBER 23, 1957

In late summer 1957, Mao Zedong, in a revised version of his speech "On the Correct Handling of Contradictions among the People," stated strict limits on dissent and took aim at critics who were too aggressive in their attacks on the Party and Communist state.

In the months that followed, a "rectification" campaign against "rightists," supervised by Deng Xiaoping, was launched in every city and every work unit in China. As a result of the campaign, many of the bold critics, within and outside of the party, who exposed their real feelings about politics and other issues between May 1956 and June 1957, were denounced and obliged to undergo either "thought reform" or "reform through labor." Others paid for their outspokenness with terms in prisons or labor camps. The lesson derived by party leaders from the Hundred Flowers campaign was that orthodoxy was preferable to freewheeling dissent and, in subsequent years, great efforts were expended to win unwavering support for the thought of Chairman Mao and the party's economic and social initiatives.

Deng Xiaoping, who was general secretary of the party during the antirightist campaign, was given responsibility for pursuing the lines set out by Mao Zedong in "The Correct Handling of Contradictions among the People." And it was Deng who oversaw the concrete implementation of antirightist activities. The excerpt that follows, from Deng's report in September 1957 to an enlarged Plenum of the Central Committee of the CCP, suggests the way in which the campaign against rightists was viewed in party circles and illustrates how Mao's rather abstract analysis of the problem of rightists emerged as policy.

ON THE COMMUNIST PARTY AND THE YOUNG COMMUNIST LEAGUE

At present our Party has 12,712,000 members (including 2,800,000 probationary members). Among them are more than 1,740,000 workers, more than 8,500,000 peasants, more than 1,880,000 intellectuals and more than 600,000 members with other backgrounds.

During the rectification campaign and the struggle against the rightists, the majority of the Party members behaved well. However, many problems have also been exposed.

Large volumes of matter relating to bureaucracy, sectarianism and subjectivism have been exposed during the campaign. One section of the Party members possess bourgeois individualism to a serious degree, zealously craving for personal enjoyment and keeping their minds on honor and position. There are also a very small number of Party members who have lost their revolutionary spirit or have even degenerated, become corrupt, and offended against the law and against discipline.

In the course of the campaign, the rightists within the Party have come into the open. The discovery of these spokesmen of the bourgeois class is of great significance for the consolidation and purification of our Party. In addition, there are still some Party members who have serious rightist ideology and are extremely discontented with the Party. Their views diverge from those of the Party over some important policy questions and they have shown political vacillation in the current struggle.

The rise of these serious problems within the Party has social and ideological origins. (1) The majority of the Party members are not from the working class; (2) The Party has grown rapidly without adequate attention having been paid to quality and the ideological and political work has lagged behind; and (3) What is more important is that the majority of Party members joined the Party in the days after victory. At the time when they joined, they lacked genuine socialist consciousness. After joining the Party, they have been in an environment of cooperation with the bourgeoisie for a long time without experiencing direct and acute class struggle against the bourgeoisie. The majority of the 1,880,000 intellectuals among the Party members have not experienced training in productive labor, nor have they gone through serious tests of the class struggle.

In the struggle against the rightists, the rightists within the Party must be treated equally and as seriously as the non-Party rightists. However, there are now some comrades who, in the struggle against inner-Party rightists, have exhibited to a more serious extent the trend of sentimentalism, and this is especially noticeable in the expressions of regret, the show of weakness, and the reluctance to take action in dealing with some veteran Party members who should be demarcated as rightists.

When the campaign proceeds into the third and fourth stages, it is more necessary to tackle carefully the task of rectification within the Party than outside. Apart from the errors of bureaucracy, subjectivism and sectarianism (including sectionalism and group exclusiveness) among leading functionaries which must be corrected in all seriousness, the rightist ideas among rank and file Party members must also be criticized. All kinds of bourgeois and petty-bourgeois ideology must be criticized.

The work of ideological and political education must be strengthened. During the current rectification campaign, a comprehensive ideological and political survey of every Party member must be made. The weaknesses of inadequate attention to ideological and political education, unhealthy organizational life and loose discipline must be seriously corrected.

During the rectification campaign, except for renegades and those who have gravely offended against the law and disciplinary rules, consideration should be shown to all Party members and Young Communist League members. Great efforts must be made to help them correct their errors and overcome their shortcomings, improve their working methods, and raise their working ability, their ideological and political level. The Party members and cadres must be educated to be vigorous, to have revolutionary will and to have the attitude of serving the people selflessly and whole-heartedly.

It is necessary to have a conscientious check-up of all the basic organizations of the Communist Party in conjunction with the rectification campaign. Through the rectification campaign, the purity of the ranks of the Communist Party and the consolidation of the Party organization must be achieved.

Rightists inside the Party should be dismissed from the Party. If their cases are less serious and they make a showing in changing for the better, and are not dismissed from the Party, their rightist "label" may be taken away.

All kinds of bad elements who have infiltrated into the ranks of the Party, elements who have seriously violated the law and Party discipline, those who have degenerated to the point beyond salvation, and those with serious bourgeois individualist thinking and acts who fail to repent after repeated education must be purged from the Party.

People who have lost their revolutionary will and cannot play the role of the Communist Party member and fail to reform after criticism and education, should be persuaded to resign from the Party or else be purged from the Party.

In deciding on the expulsion of a member of the Party, his mistakes must be verified, the prescribed procedure must be followed, and after his dismissal, concern should continue to be given to him politically and ideologically, special personnel assigned to maintain contact with him, to place him under observation and to educate him.

We must strengthen the education of probationary Party members, and carry out a rigid examination to prevent those who do not possess the full qualifications for Party membership from becoming into full members of the Party.

To ensure a constant readjustment of the composition of the Party membership and to infuse fresh blood into the Party, people who are really qualified for membership, particularly veteran workers and outstanding higher intellectuals, may be accepted into the Party in a selective manner on the basis of the rectification campaign and the anti-rightist struggle and on the condition that the quality of the membership is assured.

The rectification campaign and the anti-rightist struggle place each Party member, and particularly each functionary, to a test. It is necessary here to say something about the work of the Party relating to its functionaries.

Our Party has paid consistent attention to selecting outstanding workers, peasants and intellectuals closely linked with the masses of workers and peasants for various leading positions. This is the line of the Party's work regarding functionaries.

During a certain period in the past, we had assigned to leadership organs of various levels too large a number of young intellectuals who had not been steeled in production labor or tested in actual struggles. This was a defect.

Hereafter, we should continue to choose functionaries from among the excellent elements of the workers and peasants but these should be workers and peasants with a certain cultural level. We should likewise select functionaries from among the better elements of intellectuals, but they should be intellectuals who have been steeled in production work and struggle and maintain close connection with the workers and peasants. Those intellectual functionaries who have not been tempered in practical struggle and have no experience of working in an organization at the lowest level should be systematically sent to do production work in villages and factories for a few years, or to do practical work in an organization at the lowest level for a few years. All leading personnel in the Party, government and the mass organizations at various levels should be tempered in practical struggle and equipped with the experience of working at the lowest level. Those who are not should make up for it. This is also true of those working in the fields of literature, the arts, press, theoretical work and in other fields of propaganda.

An appropriate scheme should be worked out to enable graduates from universities and colleges and technical schools first to do manual work in organizations of production which are suited to their specialties. Only after one or more years of work, can they be assigned to jobs according to their specialties and their record in manual work.

Serious efforts should be made to create conditions to enable manual workers in production work to have opportunities to raise their cultural and technical knowledge and to enable part of them who can proceed to advanced education to enter universities and colleges.

Only by seriously carrying through this working line regarding functionaries can the Party and the state do the work of selecting functionaries on a reliable basis, and establish a force of functionaries dedicated to the cause of Communism and capable of weathering storms.

CHAPTER 21

Deepening the Revolution

21.1–21.3 THE GREAT LEAP FORWARD AND THE SINO-SOVIET SPLIT

The propaganda campaign in the spring of 1958 that prepared the way for the Great Leap Forward emphasized the originality and vast revolutionary contributions of Mao Zedong. The methods used to compel China forward in this massive ideological effort were deemed by supporters of Mao to be unique in the history of Marxism as a mode of "building socialism" and were seen as derived from the experience of the CCP in its years of revolutionary struggle under the Chairman's leadership. Chen Boda's[1] speech at Peking University in July 1958, with its emphasis on Mao's creativity and genius as a pilot of China's economic construction was a standard evocation of a set of themes that undergird the cult of Maoist leadership.

Two concrete goals of the Great Leap Forward, launched in the fall of 1958, were the increase of Chinese steel production and the widespread formation of "people's communes." Throughout China a campaign to construct "backyard blast furnaces" was actively pursued by local party authorities. Propagandists of the movement announced that in fifteen years China would be able overtake Great Britain's steel production and frenzied efforts went on to collect and smelt iron in the crude, earthen furnaces constructed by almost all work units.

Yin Zeming's account of accomplishments in central Hunan suggests how the steel production movement was promoted. A massive effort of

1. Secretary to Chairman Mao and party specialist in ideological matters (1905–1989). With the fall of the Gang of Four in 1976, Chen was toppled from his party positions and sentenced to sixteen years in prison. He was released in 1988 and died in October the following year.

will was to provide the impulse for the Great Leap in steel production and descriptions of the campaign and its attainments were suffused with a sense that anything was possible. In the end, much of the iron produced by melting pots and pans and other iron scrap collected to feed "backyard blast furnaces" was useless. In fact, the cost of building the furnaces and deploying massive numbers of workers to run them far exceeded any conceivable benefit to China's steel industry.

But during the Great Leap era, practicality was beside the point. The steel campaign provided a way of harnessing energies and directing them toward purposes construed as valuable by the state. It helped re-establish a chain of command between the party leadership and the people and it provided the illusion that the party was still the dynamic sponsor of programs of reform and construction it had always claimed to be.

Undoubtedly, the most sweeping program of the Great Leap was the party's plan to fully collectivize agriculture. The "people's commune" was designed to bring economic, political, cultural, and military affairs all under the umbrella of the commune. According to party theorists, private property would virtually cease to exist and the countryside would enter a new utopian age of socialist production. The September 3, 1958, *People's Daily* editorial reproduced below was a statement on collectivization derived directly from the writings of Mao Zedong. Its extreme optimism and the lack of any hint that the road before "people's communes" was fraught with difficulty were typical aspects of the rhetoric of the Great Leap era.

In the end, the Great Leap proved self-defeating. The mood of exhilaration whipped up by propagandists at the outset of the movement gave way to deep cynicism as it became apparent that the goals set for the Great Leap in all fields were unrealistic. In industry, some sectors of the economy ground virtually to a standstill and in the agricultural sector, drastic food shortages and widespread starvation put the lie to party promises that the accelerated collectivization of agriculture would result in huge increases in grain production. Within and outside of the party, the Great Leap Forward provided a lesson that "voluntarism" would not work and cast great doubt on Chairman Mao's abilities as the helmsman of China's economy.

21.1 Chen Boda: "Under the Banner of Comrade Mao Zedong," July 16, 1958

July 1 is the birthday of our party. It has been 37 years since the founding of our party. In these 37 years, the Chinese people and our party have traversed a tortuous path and won a series of great victories under the banner of Comrade Mao Zedong. Thirty-seven years is not a long time in the history of China but one can see that under the leadership of our party and the banner of Comrade Mao Zedong the Chinese people have realized an epoch-making revolution on their land and we are creating their own life by leaps and bounds at such a rate that "twenty years are concentrated in one day. . . ."

Comrade Mao Zedong is able to examine and explore the characteristics of China without being the least bound by formalism. Practice instead of formula is his point of departure. The most striking feature of Comrade Mao Zedong's thought is his ability to integrate the universal truth of Marxism-Leninism closely with the creativeness of the masses. He puts faith in the masses, relies on the masses, and respects the intelligence of the ordinary masses, thereby to increase the invincible power of Marxist-Leninist theory under new conditions and in new surroundings. . . .

The problems solved by Comrade Mao Zedong were many sided. Here I will take up several problems that were important to the cause of the Chinese people as a whole.

The primary and outstanding contribution Comrade Mao Zedong made to the Democratic Revolution was his theory of building and developing revolutionary bases in the countryside as the main form of alliance between the working class and the peasantry under the leadership of the Communist Party in the political, military, and economic fields, and of taking such bases as the starting points of revolution and nation-wide victory. In the past, many people, basing their view on the French bourgeois revolution of the eighteenth century and on the 1911 revolution and Northern Expedition in China, established the idea that revolution always began from big cities. And it was generally held that guerrilla warfare was merely a supplement of regular warfare. Comrade Mao Zedong rejected these old ideas that were not applicable to the conditions of the Chinese revolution. He set forth the new idea of placing guerrilla warfare in a strategic position in the Chinese revolution, and the new idea of arming all the people in revolution. These new ideas put forward by Comrade Mao Zedong gave the party leadership a new direction of struggle after the 1927 revolutionary failure. Later, during the period of anti-Japanese war Comrade Mao Zedong developed and enriched these ideas, and eventually the Chinese people and our party were enabled to win a nation-wide victory during 1949.

During the period of socialist revolution in our country, Comrade Mao Zedong creatively solved a series of fundamental problems of socialist transformation arising from transition from individual ownership to collective ownership, from capitalist ownership to popular ownership. During the time of establishing revolutionary bases, Comrade Mao Zedong had summed up the experiences of the mutual-aid organizations of the peasant masses. He saw germs of socialism in such mutual-aid organizations and popularized these mutual-aid organizations in his belief that such mutual-aid organizations could raise labor productivity to a considerable degree. After the nation-wide liberation, Comrade Mao Zedong continued to sum up new experiences of this and, shortly after conclusion of the agrarian reform, urged widespread establishment of temporary mutual-aid teams and year-round mutual-aid teams on a voluntary basis, and the gradual and massive development of agricultural producer cooperatives semi-socialist in character (land share, common labor, and unified administration) on the basis of mutual-aid teams. He took the view that such agricultural producer cooperatives semi-socialist in character were the main form of guiding the peasants voluntarily to full socialism, thereby breaking down the old view of some comrades that without agricultural machinery large-scale cooperativization of agriculture could hardly be realized.

On the question of capitalist ownership, Comrade Mao Zedong drew a distinction between ownership by bureaucratic capitalists and ownership by the national capitalists. Towards the former, a policy of expropriation was adopted at the time of liberation; towards the latter, methods of gradual transformation and various forms of state capitalism were adopted in order to transform capitalist enterprises steadily into socialist enterprises.

In short, whether in the case of agriculture and handicrafts or in the case of capitalist industry and commerce, coordination was achieved between revolution from the top and revolution from the bottom, and diversified forms of transition and different methods of transition were massively adopted. As a result, the socialist transformation of economy won an unexpected and rapid victory.

Comrade Mao Zedong broke down the old view that the solution to the problem of ownership would answer the question of outcome of struggle between socialism and capitalism. He held that, beside solving the question of outcome of struggle as regards ownership, we must go a step further and solve the question of the outcome of struggle on the political and ideological fronts—otherwise the results of socialist transformation as regards ownership could not be consolidated. The big debate held by the people over socialism and capitalism during 1957, when the bourgeois rightists launched a ferocious attack on the party, bore out Comrade Mao Zedong's viewpoint. When the masses have waged an all-out struggle against the rightists and the people have distinguished right and wrong through the rectification campaign, contention, and blossoming, a new situation has arisen in which the Communist ideology is set free.

As far back as the time when Jiangxi was used as a revolutionary base, Comrade Mao Zedong laid down a correct policy of combining revolution and construction. During the Anti-Japanese War, Comrade Mao Zedong continued to adhere to this policy. Following the rectification campaign which began in 1942, Comrade Mao Zedong promoted a large-scale production drive during 1943, which considerably increased the material strength of the people in liberated areas and provided a material basis for wiping out Chiang Kai-shek's counter-revolutionary army during the liberation war. Over the economic and financial problems Comrade Mao Zedong always placed the mass development of production in the leading position and criticized the error of one-sided financial and distribution viewpoints divorced from the development of production.

After the nation-wide liberation, socialist transformation and socialist construction are interlocked in their progress. In the course of socialist transformation, observing the signs that began in agricultural cooperation, Comrade Mao Zedong pointed to the inexhaustible and immense latent power of the Chinese working people to develop the productive force. Comrade Mao Zedong said in his comments in the *Upsurge of Socialism in China's Countryside*. "There will appear various things never conceived before and high yield of crops several, ten and scores of times greater than at present. The development of industry, communications, and exchange will be beyond the imagination of the predecessors. This will also be the case with science, culture, education, and public health." Therefore, he pointed out in the preface to the *Upsurge of Socialism in China's Countryside* that the questions confronting the party and the whole nation after solution of the problem of socialist transformation were the question of scale and rate of economic and cultural construction, the question of doing things regarded as impossible, and the question of criticizing the rightist conservative ideas. . . .

Mao Zedong's banner is a banner combining the Chinese Communists and the people, a banner integrating the universal truth of Marxism-Leninism with the concrete practice of the Chinese revolution, and a banner creatively developing Marxism-Leninism under the conditions of China. Therefore, Mao Zedong's banner is a banner of victory of the Chinese people's revolution and socialist construction.

Mao Zedong's banner is a red flag held aloft by the Chinese people. Guided by this great red flag the Chinese people will in the not distant future enter in the great Communist society.

21.2   Yin Zeming: "The Strength of the Masses Is Limitless," 1958

Iron smelting and steel making in the Shaoyang Special Administrative Region, Hunan Province, are rapidly developing on a mass scale. In a short period in the autumn of 1958, 12,378 local blast furnaces were built in this area. Of these, 4816 went into immediate operation, with a daily output of more than 2400 tons. The highest daily output has reached the 2438 ton mark, which is an average of half a ton a day for each local furnace in operation. In the first ten days of September, 1958, daily output of iron more than trebled (the daily output on September 1 was 595 tons). Now this region has already produced 50,000 tons of iron. Not only is there a "bumper harvest" in many places but the

Chinhua Iron Works in Shaotung County, "king" of local blast furnaces, has produced the remarkable record of almost three tons (5836 catties) a day.

At present, people in many districts are working with increasing enthusiasm to produce iron and steel, and as more and more effective measures are taken, it is anticipated that there will be even greater achievemen in steel and iron production in the near future.

The main reason for this remarkable progress in iron and steel production in such a short time in Shaoyang region is the fact that this region has fully carried out the Communist Party's directive to let the whole party and all the people work in iron and steel production, in keeping with the party's general line of socialist construction.

Iron and steel production is not simply a technical job; it is also a political task that has an important bearing on all other activities. Therefore, the first condition for the rapid development of production is for the party secretaries to take the lead and have the entire party membership mobilized. The party committees of Shaoyang region are all clearly convinced of the importance of the guiding principle of making steel production the first task, in order to hasten the progress of industry and agriculture and they gave iron and steel production priority. The first secretaries of different party committees all took personal charge, leading more than ten thousand government functionaries and nearly one million workers in this battle for iron and steel. Many government functionaries organized experimental units in the factories and workshops and they all took part in actual production. By joining the movement first the leaders not only set an example for the masses and hastened its progress, but they also learned much and became experienced workers. By the beginning of September, 1958, government functionaries in this region had set up a total of 2352 experimental blast furnaces and 500 experimental coal pits. In Lienyuan County 15 members of the county party committee and 29 township party secretaries have already mastered the technique of smelting iron.

In Lunghui County, deputy secretary of the county party committee, Hsieh Kuo, set up experimental furnaces at Shihmen, but failed to produce iron in 22 successive attempts. He persisted, studying and trying again and again and finally he produced iron in all five local furnaces. In Shaotung County, the head of Niumasze Township, Chao Lin-fu, stayed by the furnace, sleeping and eating on the spot. After 21 experiments he finally increased the daily output of each furnace from 300 to 2250 catties. Leaders of co-ops, peasants, men and women of all ages, workers, government officials, and soldiers are all trying their skill with experimental furnaces. Many peasants want to be capable of running agricultural co-ops and factories, capable of farming as well as smelting iron.

When they first began to work in iron and steel production, many people wanted to have big "foreign" blast furnaces. They were not interested in these small native furnaces. They thought it necessary to wait for elaborate equipment. Actually that line of thinking would result in producing less, slower, more expensively, and not so well and it would not lead to production on a mass basis. Under the timely guidance of the Central Committee and the provincial committee of the Communist Party, that policy was firmly rejected and the policy of putting iron and steel production on a mass basis, of mobilizing all the party members, and letting politics take the lead was carried out. From the beginning, Shaoyang region initiated a gigantic propaganda campaign. All the people were encouraged to voice their opinions in a general debate on such subjects as the following: Why must iron and steel production be developed? How can it be done? What is the relationship between the production of iron and steel and agriculture? Through voicing different opinions and public debates the masses achieved a clearer understanding and became convinced; thus their enthusiasm was aroused. Within a few days more than half a million written pledges were sent to the party in support of the campaign. The people felt elated and stimulated; millions of hearts had only one wish—to fight hard to achieve and surpass the goal of producing 300,000 tons of iron in 1958.

The strength of the masses is tremendous. All the problems of funds, raw materials, equipment, fuel, and geological survey of resources, which seemed hard to solve in the past, disappeared before the resourcefulness of the people. In honor of the anniversary of the Communist Party (July 1), 67,000 people in Hsinhua County worked for three days and nights on end and built 1025 blast furnaces. Many people hearing the news came from as far as 100 li away to join in the work, carrying timber and bamboo and their food and clothes. In Szetu Township, 53 couples came to put their names down offering to help in industrial production. Within a few days this county collected a fund of more than 1.6 million yuan. There was a 50-year-old woman who voluntarily contributed more than 200 yuan, her savings of many years, for the local industry. The people contributed 1280 pigs, more than 700,000 catties of vegetables, and 180,000 pairs of straw sandals for the people who were taking part in this industrial construction project. To solve the housing problem, the people of Tienping Township, in one morning, spontaneously vacated more than 500 rooms. The contributions from the masses became a mighty torrent, and the blast furnaces were set up very quickly. The people composed a song describing this event:

> The Communist Party is really wonderful.
> In three days more than a thousand furnaces were built.
> The masses' strength is really tremendous.
> The American imperialists will run off, tails between legs.
> The Chinese people will now surpass Britain.
> The East wind will always prevail over the West wind.

21.3 *"Hold High the Red Flag of People's Communes and March On," September 3, 1958*

People's communes, which mark a new stage in the socialist movement in China's rural areas, are now being set up and developed in many places at a rapid rate.

This movement has been spontaneously started by the mass of peasants on the basis of great socialist consciousness. When a small number of people's communes were first established, their success at once inspired many of the agricultural producers' co-operatives to follow suit. The movement gradually gained momentum. Now, with the encouragement and guidance given by the Central Committee of the Communist Party and Chairman Mao Zedong, it is making even greater strides forward. Dazibao [big-character posters][2] are appearing everywhere in the countryside, and a great number of applications have been made for the establishment of people's communities. Virtually all the peasants in Hunan and Liaoning provinces are now members of people's communes and the movement is in high tide in the provinces of Hebei, Heilongjiang, and Anhui. Meanwhile, preparations are being made in northwestern China, the Yangtse valley and provinces south of the Yangtse River to establish people's communes after the autumn harvest.

Where the people's communes have already come into existence, the peasants, beating drums and gongs, celebrated the occasion with great joy, and their enthusiasm for production has reached a new height. The poor and lower-middle peasants, in particular, rejoice in the formation of the commune and regard it as the "realization of a long-cherished dream."

The people's commune is characterized by its bigger size and more socialist nature. With big membership and huge expanse of land the communes can carry out production and construction of a comprehensive nature and on a large scale. They not only carry out an all-round management of agriculture, forestry, animal husbandry, side-occupations and fishery, but merge industry (the worker), agriculture (the peasant), exchange (the trader), culture and education (the student), and military affairs (the military man) into one.

People's communes so far established usually have a membership of 10,000 people each, in some cases 10,000 households. A commune generally corresponds to a township. If a township is too small, then several townships may be combined to form a commune.

Being big, they can do many things hitherto impossible to the agricultural

---

2. Long sheets of paper pinned to walls or bulletin boards during the Cultural Revolution that expressed political sentiments and sometimes became the vehicle for attacks on "revisionists" or others deemed guilty of political sins.

producers' co-operatives, such as building medium-sized water-conservancy works, setting up factories and mines requiring complicated technique, carrying out big projects of road and housing construction, establishing secondary schools and schools of higher learning, etc. As a matter of fact, many of these undertakings are being carried out by the large communes and the matter of manpower shortage also becomes easier to tackle.

The people's commune represents a much higher degree of socialist development and collectivization than the agricultural producers' co-operative. Its massive scale of production requires organization with a higher efficiency and great maneuverability of labour as well as the participation of all the women in production. Consequently more and more community canteens, nurseries, sewing groups and other kinds of establishments are being set up, and the last remnants of individual ownership of the means of production retained in the agricultural producers' co-operatives are being eliminated. In many places, for instance, the reserved plots, livestock, orchards, and major items of production tools owned by individual peasants have been transferred to the people's communes in the course of their organization.

Ownership of the means of production by the whole people has been instituted by a few people's communes on the basis of the full agreement of their members. In the method of payment they are making experiments on both the wage and supply systems. These experiments are necessary because they help to point out the road to the further development of the relations of production in the countryside.

As the people's commune has for its membership workers, peasants, traders, students and militiamen it is no longer a solely economic organization—it combines economic, cultural, political and military affairs into one entity. There is, therefore, no longer any need for the separate existence of township governments. The management committees of the people's communes are in fact the people's councils of the townships. There is also a tendency for the federation of people's communes in a county to become one with the people's council of that county. This facilitates unified leadership, closely combines the collective economy of the agricultural producers' co-operatives with the state economy of the townships and counties and helps the transition from the collective ownership to ownership by the whole people.

For this reason the people's commune is the most appropriate organizational form in China for accelerating socialist construction and the transition to communism. It will become the basic social unit in the future communist society as thinkers—from many outstanding utopian socialists to Marx, Engels, and Lenin—had predicted on many occasions.

China has now some 700,000 agricultural producers' co-operatives, mostly set up during the upsurge of socialism in 1955 and later gradually transformed into advanced co-operatives. They are undoubtedly far superior to individual farming, mutual-aid terms, and even the elementary agricultural producers' co-operatives, and have contributed enormously to the steady increase of China's farm out-put in the past few years. With the growth of agricultural production, especially the great leap forward in agriculture since last winter, these co-operatives have, however, gradually become inadequate to meet fully the needs of the day. The reason is as follows. These co-operatives are comparatively small in size. Averaging less than one hundred households in membership, they have but a small amount of manpower. The amount of their public reserve funds is small and the rate of accumulation slow. With these handicaps it is difficult for them to engage in many kinds of production.

To achieve a high-speed advance in agriculture, enable the countryside to assume a new aspect at an early date, and improve the peasants' living standards as quickly as possible, as facts show, it is necessary to carry out large-scale capital construction that will fundamentally change the natural conditions; to apply new farming techniques; to develop forestry, animal husbandry, side-occupations and fishery side by side with agriculture; to build industries that serve agriculture and the needs of the peasants as well as big industries; gradually to carry out mechanization and electrification; to improve transport, communications and housing conditions in rural areas; and set up educational, health and cultural establishments—to do all this is beyond the power of an agricultural producers' co-operative consisting of a few dozen or hundreds of households.

The agricultural producers' co-operatives which merged into the present Zhaoying People's Commune in Shangzheng, Henan Province, previously had little industry though they abound in natural resources. After the formation of the commune 2,500 cadres and 17,500 members were allocated to the work and in ten days steel and iron plants, and factories making machinery, chemical fertilizer, cement, etc.—4,530 all told—were built, of which 3,250 enterprises soon went into operation. Here, the superiority of people's communes is clearly visible.

In the work of building water-conservancy projects, afforestation, combating drought, and flood prevention since last winter, the agricultural producers' co-operatives in many places acutely felt the inferiority of small co-operatives and the incompetency of their original labour organization to develop potential power and raise labour efficiency. Hence many small co-operatives spontaneously joined hands, and socialist co-operation between co-operatives of different townships, different counties, and even different provinces was carried out. A series of measures have also been taken to "get organized along military lines, work with a fighting spirit, and live in a collective way." This shows that the agricultural co-operatives, which are small in size, meager in items of production and low in the degree of collectivization, are becoming handicaps to the further development of the productive forces.

It must be pointed out that the rapid growth of the people's communes definitely does not stem solely from economic causes. The keenness shown by the mass of peasants towards the people's communes speaks first of all of their greatly increased socialist and communist consciousness.

Through the 1957 debate among the rural population on the socialist and capitalist roads of development in the countryside, the Communist Party smashed the attack launched by the bourgeois rightists, landlords, rich peasants, and counter-revolutionaries, and overcame the capitalist trend among the well-to-do middle peasants. Later, through the rectification campaign, it fundamentally changed the relations between the cadres and the masses and eliminated the rightist conservative ideas in agricultural production. During the current leap forward in agricultural production and rural work the mass of peasants have witnessed not only a several-fold increase in agricultural production but also the happy future of industrialization and urbanization of rural areas. As a result, the prestige of the Party has become more consolidated than ever among the peasants. The peasants have shown an unprecedentedly firm determination to achieve socialism at an earlier date and to prepare conditions for the gradual transition to communism. While striving for the quickest advance in production and in culture and education, the peasants are trying to establish new relations of production and new organizational forms best suited to the development of the productive forces. Without political consciousness as a basis, development of the people's commune movement would be impossible and inconceivable.

The establishment of people's communes has provided good conditions for the further development of the relations of production in the countryside. The expansion of the people's communes and the merger of people's communes and townships into one entity, which facilitates the rapid advance of industry, mining, communications, culture and education in the rural areas, makes it possible gradually to eliminate the differences between rural and urban areas, between peasants and workers, between peasants and intellectuals, as well as between collective ownership and ownership by the whole people.

The present people's commune movement does not, however, require the immediate transformation, in all cases, of collective ownership into ownership by the whole people. Even less does it mean the transition from the lower stage of socialism which is based on the principle "from each according to his ability, to each according to his work," to its higher stage, i.e., communism, which is based on the principle "from each according to his ability, to each according to his needs."

Some people's communes may have gone farther than others, but generally speaking, the transformation of collective ownership into ownership by the whole people is a process that will take three or four years, even five or six years, to complete in the rural areas. Then, after a number of years, production will be greatly increased. The people's communist consciousness and morality will be highly improved. Education will be made universal and elevated among the people. Differences between workers and peasants, urban and rural areas, mental and manual labour—left over from the old society and inevitably existing in the socialist society—as well as the remnants of unequal bourgeois rights which are the reflection of these differences, will gradually vanish, the function of the state will be limited to protecting the country from external aggression; it will play no role in domestic affairs. By that time Chinese society will enter the era of communism, the era when the principle "from each according to his ability, to each according to his needs" will be realized.

Now the development of people's communes is growing into a mass movement more gigantic than the co-operative movement of 1955. The Party committees of various places must work out appropriate plans and give active guidance to the development according to local conditions. The development of people's communes will doubtlessly be different in time, scale, pace, and method in different places. Uniformity should not be imposed. People's communes must be set up on the basis of full discussion by the people concerned and it must be a matter of the people's own choice. No rash, impetuous, or domineering attitude should be taken, especially on the question concerning change in the ownership of the means of production.

At present, work in the autumn fields allows for no delay while preparations must be made for the farm work of the coming winter and next spring. We must give first priority to work related to production in all places, regardless of the condition whether people's communes have or have not been established.

21.4 "DECISION APPROVING COMRADE MAO ZEDONG'S PROPOSAL TO STEP DOWN," DECEMBER 10, 1958

The catastrophic failures of the Great Leap Forward sharpened the conflict between Mao Zedong and other leaders of the Communist party. Despite the mounting failures of collectivization and the ill-conceived steel production campaign, Chairman Mao was stalwart in his belief in the efficacy of mass movements and refused to retreat from the overambitious plans and catastrophic miscalculations of the Great Leap. Liu Shaoqi, the chairman of the National People's Congress, and Deng Xiaoping had made their careers in Party circles as loyal supporters of Chairman Mao; they had served in important capacities at the pinnacle of the Chinese state throughout the first decade of Communist rule and were enthusiastic and unqualified supporters of the Hundred Flowers campaign, the Anti-Rightist campaign, and, of course, the Great Leap Forward itself. Their power and influences were so well known that a common element of criticism of the party during the Hundred Flowers was that all power was held by a group of six senior leaders: Mao, Liu, Deng, Zhou Enlai, Zhu De, and Chen Yun.

Now, however, Mao was vulnerable due to the economic crisis brought about by misguided policies and Liu and Deng, in a political struggle still obscure in some of its dimensions, exercised their influence in the Central Committee to pressure Mao Zedong to step down from the chairmanship of the state. Mao Zedong remained the Party chairman but was deprived of actual participation in decision making. Liu Shaoqi replaced Mao as chairman of the state and the erstwhile chairman was encouraged, as the following document suggests, to concentrate on "Marxist-Leninist theoretical work."

Mao Zedong was unhappy with this forced departure from the frontline of political work and later complained that he was treated by Liu and Deng as a "dead man at his own funeral." Between 1958 and 1966, Mao restively inhabited the historical shrine constructed for him by his comrades-in-arms but the struggle for control of the state was still very much alive. During the Cultural Revolution, Mao Zedong would return to the stage with a vengeance and his opponents would learn the perils of confronting a living political legend.

In the past few years, Comrade Mao Zedong has more than once expressed to the Central Committee of the Party the wish that he should not continue to hold the post of Chairman of the People's Republic of China. Following full and all-round consideration, the Plenary Session of the Central Committee has decided to approve this proposal of Comrade Mao Zedong, and not to nominate him again as candidate for Chairman of the People's Republic of China at the First Session of the Second National People's Congress. The Plenary Session of the Central Committee deems this to be a completely positive proposal, because, relinquishing his duties as Chairman of the state and working solely as Chairman of the Central Committee of the Party, Comrade Mao Zedong will be enabled all the better to concentrate his energies on dealing with questions of the direction, policy and line of the Party and the state; he may also be enabled to set aside more time for Marxist-Leninist theoretical work, without affecting his continued leading role in the work of the state. This will be in the better interests of the whole Party and of all the people of the country. Comrade Mao Zedong is the sincerely beloved and long-tested leader of the people of various nationalities of the whole country. He will remain the leader of the entire people of various nationalities even when he no longer holds the post of Chairman of the state. If some special situation arises in the future which should require him to take up this work again, he can still be nominated again to assume the duties of the Chairman of the state in compliance with the opinion of the people and the decision of the Party. Party committees at all levels should, in accordance with these reasons, give full explanations to the cadres and masses both inside and outside the Party at appropriate meetings of the Party, sessions of the people's congresses of various levels, meetings of workers in industrial and mining enterprises, and meetings in people's communes, offices, schools and armed units, so that the reasons for this may be understood by all that there may be no misunderstanding.

21.5 "The Origin and Development of the Differences between the Leadership of the CPSU and Ourselves," September 6, 1963

The Chinese Communist party and the Communist party of the Soviet Union (CPSU) worked closely together after 1949 to rebuild China but by the closing years of the 1950s this collaboration was beginning to fray. The Chinese leadership resented the Soviets' provision of outdated or useless machines; rejected the Soviets' doctrine of "peaceful coexistence" with the United States, and were outraged by Khrushchev's secret speech at the twentieth congress of the CPSU and the subsequent process of de-Stalinization.

A major portion of the following 1963 *People's Daily* editorial focused on the issue of de-Stalinization and Chinese perceptions of Khrushchev's leadership. From the point of view of Mao and other Chinese leaders, "whipping the corpse" of Stalin served no purpose and invalidated the notion of a single center of authority in party work. The Chinese party, following the break with the Soviets, became increasingly dogmatic and sought, now independently of the Soviet Union, to play a leading role as a font of revolutionary theory.

It is more than a month since the Central Committee of the Communist Party of the Soviet Union published its open letter of July 14 to Party organizations and all Communists in the Soviet Union. This open letter, and the steps taken by the leadership of the CPSU since its publication, have pushed Sino-Soviet relations to the brink of a split and have carried the differences in the international communist movement to a new stage of unprecedented gravity.

Now Moscow, Washington, New Delhi, and Belgrade are joined in a love feast and the Soviet press is running an endless assortment of fantastic stories and theories attacking China. The leadership of the CPSU has allied itself with U.S. imperialism, the Indian reactionaries and the renegade Tito clique against socialist China and against all Marxist-Leninist parties, in open betrayal of Marxism-Leninism and proletarian internationalism, in brazen repudiation of the 1957 Declaration and the 1960 Statement and in flagrant violation of the Sino-Soviet Treaty of Friendship, Alliance and Mutual Assistance.

The present differences within the international communist movement and between the Chinese and Soviet Parties involve a whole series of important questions of principle. In its letter of June 14 to the Central Committee of the CPSU, the Central Committee of the CPC systematically and comprehensively discussed the essence of these differences. It pointed out that, in the last analysis, the present differences within the international communist movement and between the Chinese and Soviet Parties involve the questions of whether or not to accept the revolutionary principles of the 1957 Declaration and the 1960 Statement, whether or not to accept Marxism-Leninism and proletarian internationalism, whether or not there is no need for revolution, whether or not imperialism is to be opposed, and whether or not the unity of the socialist camp and the international communist movement is desired.

How have the differences in the international communist movement and between the leadership of the CPSU and ourselves arisen? And how have they grown to their present serious dimensions? Everybody is concerned about these questions. . . .

THE DIFFERENCES BEGAN WITH THE 20TH CONGRESS OF THE CPSU

There is a saying, "It takes more than one cold day for the river to freeze three feet deep." The present differences in the international communist movement did not, of course, begin just today.

The open letter of the Central Committee of the CPSU spreads the notion that the differences in the international communist movement were started by the three articles which we published in April 1960 under the title of *Long Live Leninism!* This is a big lie.

What is the truth?

The truth is that the whole series of differences of principle in the international communist movement began more than seven years ago.

To be specific, it began with the 20th Congress of the CPSU in 1956. . . .

The criticism of Stalin at the 20th Congress of the CPSU was wrong both in principle and in method. Stalin's life was that of a great Marxist-Leninist, a great proletarian revolutionary. For thirty years after Lenin's death, Stalin was the foremost leader of the CPSU and the Soviet Government, as well as the recognized leader of the international communist movement and the standard-bearer of the world revolution. During his lifetime, Stalin made some serious mistakes, but compared to his great and meritorious deeds his mistakes are only secondary. . . .

It was necessary to criticize Stalin's mistakes. But in his secret report to the 20th Congress, Comrade Khrushchev completely negated Stalin, and in doing so defamed the dictatorship of the proletariat, defamed the Socialist system, the great CPSU, the great Soviet Union and the international communist movement. Far from using a revolutionary proletarian party's method of criticism and self-criticism for the purpose of making an earnest and serious analysis and summation of the historical experience of the dictatorship of the proletariat, he treated Stalin as an enemy and shifted the blame for all mistakes on to Stalin alone.

Khrushchev viciously and demagogically told a host of lies in his secret report, and threw around charges that Stalin had a "persecution mania," indulged in "brutal arbitrariness," took the path of "mass repressions and terror," "knew the country and agriculture only from films" and "planned operations on a globe," that Stalin's leadership "became a serious obstacle in the path of Soviet social development," and so on and so forth. He completely obliterated the meritorious deeds of the Stalin who led the Soviet people in waging resolute struggle against all internal and external foes and achieving great results in Socialist transformation and Socialist construction, who led the Soviet people in defending and consolidating the first Socialist country in the world and winning the glorious victory in the anti-fascist war, and who defended and developed Marxism-Leninism.

In completely negating Stalin at the 20th Congress of the CPSU, Khrushchev in effect negated the dictatorship of the proletariat and the fundamental theories of Marxism-Leninism which Stalin defended and developed. It was at that congress that Khrushchev, in his summary report, began the repudiation of Marxism-Leninism on a number of questions of principle.

In his report to the 20th Congress, under the pretext that "radical changes" had taken place in the world situation, Khrushchev put forward the thesis of "peaceful transition." He said that the road of the October Revolution was "the only correct road in those historical conditions," but that as the situation had changed it had become possible to effect the transition from capitalism to Social- ism "through the parliamentary road." In essence, this erroneous thesis is a clear revision of the Marxist-Leninist teachings on the state and revolution and a clear denial of the universal significance of the road of the October Revolution.

In his report, under the same pretext that "radical changes" had taken place in the world situation, Khrushchev also questioned the continued validity of Lenin's teachings on imperialism and on war and peace, and in fact tampered with Lenin's teachings.

Khrushchev pictured the U.S. Government and its head as people resisting the forces of war, and not as representatives of the imperialist forces of war. He said, "... the advocates of settling outstanding issues by means of war still hold strong positions there [in the United States]," and "... they continue to exert big pressure on the President and the Administration." He went on to say that the imperialists were beginning to admit that the positions-of-strength policy had failed and that "symptoms of a certain sobering up are appearing" among them. It was as much as saying that it was possible for the U.S. Gov- ernment and its head not to represent the interests of U.S. monopoly capital and for them to abandon their policies of war and aggression and that they had become forces defending peace.

Khrushchev declared: "We want to be friends with the United States and to co-operate with it for peace and international security and also in the economic and cultural spheres." This wrong view later developed into the line of "Soviet U.S. co-operation for the settlement of world problems."

Distorting Lenin's correct principle of peaceful co-existence between countries with different social systems, Khrushchev declared that peaceful co-existence was the "general line of the foreign policy" of the U.S.S.R. This amounted to excluding from the general line of foreign policy of the Socialist countries their mutual assistance and co-operation as well as assistance by them to the revolutionary struggles of the oppressed peoples and nations, or to subordinating all this to the policy of so-called "peaceful co-existence."

The questions raised by the leadership of the CPSU at the 20th Congress, and especially the questions of Stalin and of "peaceful transition," are by no means simply internal affairs of the CPSU; they are vital issues of common interest for all fraternal Parties. Without any prior consultation with the fraternal Parties, the leadership of the CPSU drew arbitrary conclusions; it forced the fraternal Parties to accept a fait accompli and on the pretext of "combating the personality cult," crudely interfered in the internal affairs of fraternal Parties and countries and subverted their leaderships, thus pushing its policy of sectarianism and splittism in the international Communist movement. . . .

CHAPTER 22

The Cultural Revolution

22.1 LIFE AND DEATH OF LEI FENG, AN ADMIRABLE "FOOL"

In September 1959, Lin Biao, a veteran general and one of the ten great "field marshals" of the People's Liberation Army (PLA), succeeded Peng Dehuai as minister of defense. During the years prior to the opening of the Cultural Revolution, the army remained a powerful bastion of support for Mao Zedong and the Maoist line. As minister of defense, Lin Biao played a central role in organizing PLA support for the ex-chairman of the Chinese state and later, when Mao returned to power, was rewarded for his loyalty by being designated as Mao's successor.

One aspect of Lin Biao's political work was the creation of a cult around the figure of a PLA soldier named Lei Feng. For the Maoists of the army, Lei Feng epitomized the highest qualities of socialist man. He was devoted to Chairman Mao, he loved the people, he was frugal, he did good deeds, and was, in general, great because of his sheer ordinariness. Everyone could imitate Lei Feng; he was praised as a "rust-proof screw" in the machinery of revolution. In fact, even Lei's death, his species of revolutionary martyrdom, was humdrum: he died when a heavy pole, propelled by a skidding truck, crashed down on his head. The model of Lei Feng was designed to promote personal submission to the Party's leadership and incorporation of Mao Zedong thought into everyday life. After 1963, a "Learn from Lei Feng" campaign became a central element of army political training. The following excerpts, purportedly from Lei Feug's diary, create a vivid sense of the values Lin Biao and the PLA would promote with great energy before and during the Cultural Revolution.

I want to be of use to our people and our country. If that means being a "fool," I am glad to be a "fool" of this sort. (From Lei Feng's Diary)

Lei Feng made a box in which to keep the screws, bits of wire, toothpaste tubes, rags, worn-out gloves, and other scraps that he collected. He called this his "treasure chest."

And that treasure chest was extremely useful.

If a screw was missing from the truck or a part broke down, Lei Feng searched through his treasure chest and made do if possible with something there. Only in case of extreme necessity did he ask the leadership for a replacement. He washed the rags and old gloves and used them as dusters, returning the new dusters that were issued to him. As for the toothpaste tubes and wire, when he had collected a sufficient amount he sold it as scrap and handed in the proceeds to his unit.

When summer uniforms were issued, each man received two uniforms, two shirts, and two pairs of shoes. From 1961 on, however, Lei Feng drew only one uniform, one shirt, and one pair or shoes.

"Why not take two?" asked the officer-in-charge.

"There's still plenty of wear in this uniform I have on, if it's patched and mended. The patched clothes I'm wearing now are a thousand times better than the rags I wore as a child. I'd rather hand back the other clothes to the state."

It hurt him to see the least waste of state property. There was a time when their job was loading cement. During the loading and unloading, some of the paper sacks invariably burst, so that at the end of each trip the bottom of the trucks would be covered by a layer of cement. Lei Feng always fetched a brush to sweep this up. The others followed suit, with the result that by the time this particular job was finished, they had salvaged nearly 1,800 kilos of cement.

Lei Feng lived extremely simply, never spending a cent more than necessary. Every month, after paying his Party dues and keeping a small sum to buy more of Chairman Mao's writings or some daily necessities, he banked all the rest of his pay. His socks were darned and re-darned until little of the original material was left, yet still he did not like to throw them away. His basin and mug have lost nearly all their enamel, exposing large patches of the iron beneath, yet he refused to buy new ones.

One of the men asked. "Why skimp yourself, Lei Feng? You've no family to support."

"Who says I have no family?" Lei Feng retorted. "There are hundreds of millions of people in my family—the big family of the motherland. Chairman Mao has called on every one of us to go all out and struggle hard to change our country's poverty and backwardness. Am I wrong to economize?"

"What difference will those few yuan of yours make to a big country like ours?"

"Every little bit counts. If everyone saved ten cents a day, just figure out for yourself how much the whole country would save. Now that we're masters of the state, we ought to be good managers."

Another man said, "Lei Feng is a fool—and so stingy!"

He did not let himself be influenced by these taunts. In the past, he had wanted to dress smartly and live well. But his standards had changed. He had realized that labor and creation were true beauty, that lofty moral qualities were beautiful. To spur himself on, he made the following entry in his diary:

True beauty can be found in a soldier's faded, patched yellow uniform, a worker's grease-stained blue overalls, a peasant's rough, calloused hands, and the laboring people's swarthy, sun-burned faces, clamorous work chants, and tireless work for the building of socialism. All these things make up the beauty of our age. And anyone who sees no beauty in them does not understand our age.

After being called a "fool" he told himself, "If that's being a 'fool,' I'm glad to be a fool. The revolution needs 'fools' of this sort."

In reality, Lei Feng's actions were the best reply to those who called him "stingy" or a "fool."

Summer was just coming in all its loveliness when the people near the base held a rally, beating gongs and drums to celebrate the establishment of urban People's Communes. To support the communes, Lei Feng drew out of the bank the whole 200 yuan he had saved in the past few years in the factory and the army, and took it to the Party committee office of the Hoping People's Commune in Wanghua.

"I've been looking forward to this day," he cried, putting a pile of bank notes on the table. "Please take this small contribution as a token of my warm support for the people of Wanghua."

"We'll accept your good wishes, comrade," said the people in the office, deeply stirred. "But we can't take this money. Keep it to use yourself, or send it home."

The word "home" touched Lei Feng to the quick.

"The People's Communes are my home!" he exclaimed. "I'm bringing my money home. I was an orphan in the old days, but I've grown up in good times. Everything I have I owe to the Party and the people. Because this money comes from the Party, let it play a small part now for the cause of the people."

When they still would not take the money, Lei Feng went on pleading until he burst into tears. Then the comrades there, moved to tears themselves, agreed to take half. The commune Party committee, in a later report, wrote, "Comrade Lei Feng's love for the commune is an immense inspiration to all our cadres and commune members. It has made some of our members pledge to run the commune well to show our appreciation to the PLA. . . ."

The 100 yuan that the commune would not accept was the sum Lei Feng sent for flood relief to the Liaoyang Municipal Party Committee. . . .

AN IMMORTAL FIGHTER

I must always remember these words:
Treat comrades with the warmth of spring,
Treat work with the ardor of summer,
Treat individualism like the autumn wind blowing down dead leaves,
Treat the enemy with the ruthlessness of winter.
(From Lei Feng's Diary)

At 8:00 A.M. on August 15, 1962, a fine rain was falling when Lei Feng and his assistant brought their truck back from a mission. Lei Feng jumped out and asked the assistant to park the truck where he could overhaul it and wash the mud off.

The assistant slid across to the driver's seat and started up. The truck vibrated as the engine roared and churned up mud as it began backing. Lei Feng stood behind, signaling directions: "Left, left! Back, back . . ."

The puddles of rain on the ground were very slippery. As the truck turned, it skidded into a post in a barbed-wire fence. Lei Feng was absorbed in giving directions and did not see the post, which crashed down on his head. He fell unconscious . . .

The assistant company commander himself drove at top speed from Fushun to Shenyang, aware that there was not a moment to lose. A first-rate driver, he covered the distance in record time, bringing back the best doctors in Shenyang.

But it was too late to save Lei Feng. The local doctors had done all they could, but he had lost so much blood from his head injuries that he could not hear the assistant company commander calling his name, could not hear the anguished sobs of his assistant, could not hear the weeping of his comrades-in-arms.

Lei Feng gave his life in the execution of his duty.

He lived only twenty-two short years, but his life was a glorious one.

He was born in bitterness, but he grew up in sweetness, and his every action shed radiance in this age of Mao Zedong!

His whole life was militant. He was the living embodiment of the Communist spirit of loyalty to the motherland, to the people, and to the Party, of utter devotion to others without thought of self. He expressed his philosophy in these words: "I believe we should live so that others may have a better life . . . I will gladly put up with a few hardships myself if I can thereby help others and do some good deeds." This was his world outlook, his rule of life, his lofty revolutionary ideal.

The people honored him, but he never let it go to his head. He wrote in his diary:

Lei Feng, Lei Feng! Remember this warning: On no account be complacent. Don't ever forget that it was the Party that rescued you from the tiger's mouth, it was the Party that gave you everything...Any little job you can do is no more than your duty. Each trifling achievement or any slight progress you may make should be attributed to the party. The credit must go to the Party. Water has its sources, a tree its roots.

The source and roots of Lei Feng's spirit were Mao Zedong's thought and the teaching of the Party. He was keenly aware that "The more we study and the more deeply we delve into Chairman Mao's writings, the clearer our ideas will be, the broader our vision, the firmer our stand, and the more farsighted our views." He compared Mao Zedong's thought to food, to a soldier's weapon, to the steering wheel of a truck. He studied avidly and put all he learned into practice, making a creative study and application of Chairman Mao's works. This was the basis reason why Lei Feng—an orphan in the old society—developed into a hero and a Communist fighter in the new society.

Lei Feng was immortal. In the words of a poet:

> Death, do you boast that you have killed Lei Feng?
> In a hundred million hearts he still lives on.

To commemorate Lei Feng, our beloved and honored leader Chairman Mao wrote an inscription, calling on us to "Learn from Comrade Lei Feng!"

22.2 LIN BIAO: "LONG LIVE THE VICTORY OF PEOPLE'S WAR!" SEPTEMBER 1965

Lin Biao also pledged his devotion to the Maoist vision of "people's war." Like Mao, Lin believed that human beings, rather than complicated weapons systems or atomic bombs, were the essential element in warfare. Written in 1965, just as the United States was expanding its role in Vietnam, "Long Live the Victory of People's War!" was Lin Biao's attempt to crystallize his notions of revolutionary warfare and the contradictions existing between advanced industrial and rural countries. Extending Chairman Mao's military and political ideas to the international arena, Lin Biao argued that revolutionary forces in Asian, African, and Latin American countries would soon isolate, surround, and defeat U.S imperialism.

Overall, Lin Biao's political work helped provide a sense of devotion to Mao and the idea of a world revolution sponsored by China that would be of great value as the Maoist group opposed "revisionists" in the party. As the Maoists triumphed over rivals in the party in 1966 and 1967, the style of PLA political work, as laid in place by Lin Biao, was utilized throughout civil society.

IN COMMEMORATION OF THE TWENTIETH ANNIVERSARY OF VICTORY IN THE CHINESE PEOPLE'S WAR OF RESISTANCE AGAINST JAPAN. . . .

The International Significance of Comrade Mao Zedong's Theory of People's War

The Chinese revolution is a continuation of the Great October Revolution. The road of the October Revolution is the common road for all people's revolutions. The Chinese revolution and the October Revolution have in common the following basic characteristics: (1) Both were led by the working class with a Marxist-Leninist party as its nucleus. (2) Both were based on the worker-peasant alliance. (3) In both cases state power was seized through violent revolution and the dictatorship of the proletariat was established. (4) In both cases the socialist system was built after victory in the revolution. (5) Both were component parts of the proletarian world revolution.

Naturally, the Chinese revolution had its own peculiar characteristics. The October Revolution took place in imperialist Russia, but the Chinese revolution broke out in a semicolonial and semifeudal country. The former was a proletarian socialist revolution, while the latter developed into a socialist revolution after the complete victory of the new-democratic revolution. The October Revolution began with armed uprisings in the cities and then spread to the countryside, while the Chinese revolution won nationwide victory through the encirclement of the cities from the rural areas and the final capture of the cities.

Comrade Mao Zedong's great merit lies in the fact that he has succeeded in integrating the universal truth of Marxism-Leninism with the concrete practice of the Chinese revolution and has enriched and developed Marxism-Leninism by his masterly generalization and summary of the experience gained during the Chinese people's protracted revolutionary struggle.

Comrade Mao Zedong's theory of people's war has been proved by the long practice of the Chinese revolution to be in accord with the objective laws of such wars and to be invincible. It has not only been valid for China, it is a great contribution to the revolutionary struggles of the oppressed nations and peoples throughout the world.

The people's war led by the Chinese Communist Party, comprising the War of Resistance and the Revolutionary Civil Wars, lasted for twenty-two years. It constitutes the most drawn-out and most complex people's war led by the proletariat in modern history, and it has been the richest in experience.

In the last analysis, the Marxist-Leninist theory of proletarian revolution is the theory of the seizure of state power by revolutionary violence, the theory of countering war against the people by people's war. As Marx so aptly put it, "Force is the midwife of every old society pregnant with a new one."

It was on the basis of the lessons derived from the people's wars in China that Comrade Mao Zedong, using the simplest and the most vivid language, advanced the famous thesis that "political power grows out of the barrel of a gun...."

Comrade Mao Zedong's theory of people's war solves not only the problem of daring to fight a people's war, but also that of how to wage it.

Comrade Mao Zedong is a great statesman and military scientist, proficient at directing war in accordance with its laws. By the line and policies, the strategy and tactics he formulated for the people's war, he led the Chinese people in steering the ship of the people's war past all hidden reefs to the shores of victory in most complicated and difficult conditions.

It must be emphasized that Comrade Mao Zedong's theory of the establishment of rural revolutionary base areas and the encirclement of the cities from the countryside is of outstanding and universal practical importance for the present revolutionary struggles of all the oppressed nations and peoples, and particularly for the revolutionary struggles of the oppressed nations and peoples in Asia, Africa, and Latin America against imperialism and its lackeys.

Many countries and peoples of Asia, Africa, and Latin America are now being subjected to aggression and enslavement on a serious scale by the imperialists headed by the United States and their lackeys. The basic political and economic conditions in many of these countries have many similarities to those that prevailed in old China. As in China, the peasant question is extremely important in these regions. The peasants constitute the main force of the national-democratic revolution against the imperialists and their lackeys. In committing aggression against these countries, the imperialists usually begin the seizing the big cities and the main lines of communication, but they are unable to bring the vast countryside completely under their control. The countryside, and the countryside alone, can provide the broad areas in which the revolutionaries can maneuver freely. The countryside, and the countryside alone, can provide the revolutionary bases from which the revolutionaries can go forward to final victory. Precisely for this reason, Comrade Mao Zedong's theory of establishing revolutionary base areas in the rural districts and encircling the cities from the countryside is attracting more and more attention among the peoples in these regions.

Taking the entire globe, if North America and Western Europe can be called "the cities of the world," then Asia, Africa, and Latin America constitute "the rural areas of the world." Since World War II, the proletarian revolutionary movement has for various reasons been temporarily held back in the North American and West European capitalist countries, while the people's revolutionary movement in Asia, Africa, and Latin America has been growing vigorously. In a sense, the contemporary world revolution also presents a picture of the encirclement of cities by the rural areas. In the final analysis, the whole cause of world revolution hinges on the revolutionary struggles of the Asian, African, and Latin American peoples who make up the overwhelming majority of the world's population. The socialist countries should regard it as their internationalist duty to support the people's revolutionary struggles in Asia, Africa, and Latin America. . . .

Vietnam is the most convincing current example of a victim of aggression defeating U.S. Imperialism by a people's war. The United States has made south Vietnam a testing ground for the suppression of people's war. It has carried on this experiment for many years, and everybody can now see that the U.S. Aggressors are unable to find a way of coping with people's war. On the other hand, the Vietnamese people have brought the power of people's war into full play in their struggle against the U.S. Aggressors. The U.S. Aggressors are in danger of being swamped in the people's war in Vietnam. They are deeply worried that their defeat in Vietnam will lead to a chain reaction. They are expanding the war in an attempt to save themselves from defeat. But the more they expand the war, the greater will be the chain reaction. The more they escalate the war, the heavier will be their fall and the more disastrous their defeat. The people in other parts of the world will see still more clearly that U.S. Imperialism can be defeated, and that what the Vietnamese people can do, they can do too.

History has proved and will go on proving that people's war is the most effective weapon against U.S. Imperialism and its lackeys. All revolutionary people will learn to wage people's war against U.S. Imperialism and its lackeys. They will take up arms, learn to fight battles and become skilled in waging people's war, though they have not done so before. U.S. Imperialism, like a mad bull dashing from place to place, will finally be burned to ashes in the blazing fires of the people's wars it has provoked by its own actions.

22.3–22.5 THE FUTURE DIRECTION OF THE CULTURAL REVOLUTION

On August 5, 1966, while the Eleventh Plenum of the Central Committee of the CCP was debating the future direction of the Cultural Revolution, Mao Zedong launched his attack on Liu Shaoqi and Deng Xiaoping. His famous big-character poster, put up at the site of the plenum meeting within the Zhongnanhai official compound in Peking, indirectly, but with clear intent, denounced his rivals and set the tone for the subsequent decisions taken by party leaders attending the plenum meeting.

In the days that followed, the plenum issued a sixteen-point decision that would serve virtually as the charter for the Cultural Revolution and became a constant point of reference for Red Guards and other radicals. The plenum meeting was a crushing defeat for Liu Shaoqi and Deng Xiaoping. The policies they represented were repudiated; Lin Biao took second place in the party hierarchy; Liu Shaoqi fell to eighth place; and, having been identified by Mao Zedong as an appropriate object for "bombardment," the entire group of officials who had given Liu and Deng the political wherewithal they needed to push Mao to the sidelines were thrown into disrepute. The radical line was now clearly ascendant and the official communiqué of the plenum meeting left no doubt about how Mao Zedong and his contribution to Marxism should, henceforth, be viewed:

> Comrade Mao Zedong is the greatest Marxist-Leninist in the contemporary world. He has ingeniously, creatively, and totally inherited, defended, and developed Marxism-Leninism and elevated it to a brand-new stage. Mao Zedong Thought is the Marxism-Leninism of an age in which imperialism is approaching complete collapse and socialism is approaching total global victory. Mao Zedong Thought is the guiding principle for all the work of the entire party and nation.[1]

In the aftermath of the plenum meeting, Liu, Deng, and their allies came under attack from all sides. As the cult of Mao Zedong grew, Lin Biao consolidated his power within the regime, and Red Guard organizations became active throughout China, and the erstwhile pragmatists found themselves powerless to stem the tide of events set in motion at the Eleventh Plenum meeting. In October, 1966, Mao gathered national and provincial party leaders in Peking to instruct them about the future direction of the Cultural Revolution. The meeting lasted far longer than was originally anticipated and in its concluding days, Liu and Deng issued abject self-criticisms that were, in fact, symbolic declarations of political defeat.

The three documents that follow, Mao's big-character poster, selections from the "Sixteen-Point Decision," and Deng Xiaoping's self-criticism, trace this sequence of events. Cumulatively, they provide a sense of the process of policy reversal and purge that brought radicals to the forefront of party work and overthrew key "revisionist" leaders like Liu and Deng. For the Cultural Revolution to go on at the grassroots level, these changes were first necessary within the highest tier of the party.

1. Yan Jiaqi, *Zhongguo Wenge Shinianshi* vol. 1, (Hong Kong, 1986), p. 42.

22.3   Mao Zedong's Big-character Poster: "Bombard the Headquarters"

China's first Marxist-Leninist big-character poster and Commentator's article on it in *Renmin Ribao* (People's Daily) are indeed superbly written! Comrades, please read them again. But in the last fifty days or so some leading comrades from the central down to the local levels have acted in a diametrically opposite way. Adopting the reactionary stand of the bourgeoisie, they have enforced a bourgeois dictatorship and struck down the surging movement of the great cultural revolution of the proletariat. They have stood facts on their head and juggled black and white, encircled and suppressed revolutionaries, stifled opinions differing from their own, imposed a white terror, and felt very pleased with themselves. They have puffed up the arrogance of the bourgeoisie and deflated the morale of the proletariat. How poisonous! Viewed in connection with the Right deviation in 1962 and the wrong tendency of 1964 which was 'Left' in form but 'Right' in essence, shouldn't this make one wide awake?

22.4   The Sixteen-Point Decision

1. A NEW STAGE IN THE SOCIALIST REVOLUTION

The great Proletarian Cultural Revolution now unfolding is a great revolution which touches the very soul of the people; it is a new and deeper phase of the socialist revolution in China.

At the Tenth Plenary Session of the Eighth Central Committee of the CCP Comrade Mao Zedong said: "To overthrow a political power, it is always necessary to first of all, create public opinion, to do ideological work. This is true both for the revolutionary classes as well as for the counterrevolutionary classes." Practice has proven Comrade Mao Zedong's thesis to be entirely correct.

Although the bourgeoisie has been overthrown, it is still trying to use the old ideas, culture, customs and habits of the exploiting classes to corrupt the masses, capture their minds and endeavour to stage a comeback. The proletariat must do the exact opposite: it must meet every ideological challenge posed by the bourgeoisie head-on. Our present aim is to topple those in power who are taking the capitalist road, to criticize reactionary scholarly 'authorities,' criticize the ideology of the bourgeoisie and all exploiting classes. We must reform art and literature, reform all parts of the superstructure that do not accord with the socialist base of our country. Our purpose in doing this is to stabilize and develop our socialist system.

2. THE MAIN CURRENT AND THE TWISTS AND TURNS

The broad sectors of workers, peasants, soldiers, revolutionary intellectuals and revolutionary cadres make up the principal forces in this Great Cultural Revolution. Large numbers of revolutionary young people, previously unknown, have become courageous and daring pathbreakers. They are vigorous and intelligent. Through the media of big-character posters and through great debates, they argue things out, expose and criticize thoroughly, and launch resolute attacks on the open and hidden representatives of the bourgeoisie. In such a great revolutionary movement, it is unavoidable that they should show shortcomings of one kind or another; however, their general revolutionary orientation has been correct from the beginning. This is the main current in the Great Proletarian Cultural Revolution. It is the general direction along which this revolution continues to advance.

Since the Cultural Revolution is a revolution, it inevitably meets with resistance. This resistance comes chiefly from those in authority who have found their way into the Party and are taking the capitalist road. It also comes from the force of habits from old society. At present, this resistance is still fairly strong and stubborn. However, the Great Proletarian Cultural Revolution is, after all, an irresistible trend and there is abundant evidence that such resistance will be quickly broken down once the masses are fully aroused.

Because the resistance is fairly strong, there will be reversals and even repeated reversals in this struggle. There is no harm in this. It tempers the proletariat and other working people, especially the younger generation, teaches and gives them experience, and makes them see that the revolutionary road zigzags and does not run smoothly. . . .

4. LET THE MASSES EDUCATE THEMSELVES IN THE MOVEMENT

In the great Proletarian Cultural Revolution, the masses must liberate themselves, this is the only way and any other method must not be used.

Trust the masses, rely on them and respect their initiative. Cast out fear. Don't be afraid of disturbances. Chairman Mao has often told us that revolution cannot be so very refined, so gentle, so temperate, kind, courteous, restrained and magnanimous. Let the masses educate themselves in this great revolutionary movement and learn to distinguish between right and wrong and between the correct and incorrect way of doing things.

Make full use of big-character posters and mass debates to argue matters out, so that the masses can clarify the correct views, criticize the wrong views and expose all the witches and goblins. Thus, the masses will be able to raise their political consciousness in the course of the struggle, enhance their abilities and talents, distinguish right from wrong and draw a clear line between ourselves and the enemy.

5. FIRMLY APPLY THE CLASS LINE OF THE PARTY

The primary question of any revolutionary movement, including the Cultural Revolution is, who are our friends and who are our enemies.

Party leadership should be good at discovering the Left and developing and strengthening the ranks of the Left; it should firmly rely on the revolutionary Left. This is the only way to isolate the most reactionary Rightists thoroughly, win over the middle forces and unite with the great majority in the course of the movement so that in the end we shall achieve the unity of more than 95 percent of the cadres and more than 95 percent of the masses.

Concentrate all forces to strike at the handful of ultrareactionary bourgeois rightists and counter-revolutionary revisionists, and expose and criticize to the full their crimes against the Party, against socialism and against Mao Zedong Thought so as to isolate them as much as possible.

The main target of the present movement is those within the Party who are in power and are taking the capitalist road.

Greatest care should be taken to distinguish between the anti-Party, antisocialist rightists and those who support the Party and socialism but have said or done something wrong or have written bad articles or other works.

Greatest care should be taken to distinguish between the reactionary bourgeois scholar-despots and 'authorities' on the one hand and those who have the ordinary bourgeois academic ideas on the other....

8. THE QUESTION OF CADRES

Cadres fall roughly into four categories:

1) good;
2) comparatively good;
3) those who have made serious mistakes but have not become anti-Party, anti-socialist rightists;
4) the small number of anti-Party, antisocialist rightists.

In general, the first two categories (good and comparatively good) are the great majority.

The anti-Party, antisocialist rightists must be fully exposed, refuted, overthrown and completely discredited and their influence irradicated. At the same time, they should be given a chance to turn over a new leaf. . . .

10. EDUCATIONAL REFORM

One of the most important tasks of the Great Proletarian Cultural Revolution is to transform the old educational system and the old principles and methods of teaching.

In this great Cultural Revolution, the phenomenon of our schools being dominated by bourgeois intellectuals must be completely changed.

In every kind of school we must apply thoroughly the policy advanced by Comrade Mao Zedong of education serving proletarian politics and education being combined with productive labour, so as to enable those receiving an education to develop morally, intellectually and physically and to become labourers with social consciousness and culture.

The period of schooling should be shortened. Courses should be fewer and better. The teaching material should be thoroughly transformed, in some cases beginning with simplifying complicated material. While their main task is to study, students should also learn other things. That is to say, in addition to their studies they should also learn industrial work, farming and military affairs, and take part in the struggles of the Cultural Revolution to criticize the bourgeoisie as these struggle occur. . . .

14. GRASP REVOLUTION AND PROMOTE PRODUCTION

The aim of the Great Proletarian Cultural Revolution is to revolutionize people's ideology and as a result achieve greater, faster, better and more economical results in all fields of work. If the masses are fully aroused and proper arrangements are made, it is possible to carry on both the Cultural Revolution and production without one hampering the other, while guaranteeing high quality in all our work.

The Great Proletarian Cultural Revolution is a powerful driving force for the development of the productive forces in our country. Any idea of counterposing the great Cultural Revolution to the development of production is incorrect.

15. THE ARMED FORCES

In the armed forces, the Cultural Revolution and the Socialist Education Movement should be carried out in accordance with the instructions of the Military Commission of the Central Committee of the Party and the General Political Department of the People's Liberation Army.

16. MAO ZEDONG THOUGHT IS THE GUIDE TO ACTION IN THE GREAT PROLETARIAN CULTURAL REVOLUTION

In the Great Proletarian Cultural Revolution, it is imperative to hold aloft the great red banner of Mao Zedong Thought and put proletarian politics in command. The movement for the creative study and application of Chairman Mao Zedong's works should be carried forward among the masses of the workers, peasants and soldiers, the cadres and the intellectuals, and Mao Zedong Thought should be taken as the guide to action in the Cultural Revolution.

In the complexities of the current Cultural Revolution, Party committees at all levels must study and apply Chairman Mao's works all the more conscientiously and in a creative way. In particular, they must study over and over again Chairman Mao's writings on the Cultural Revolution and on the Party's methods of leadership, such as *On New Democracy, Talks at the Yenan Forum on Literature and Art, On the Correct Handling of Contradictions Among the People, Speech at the Chinese Communist Party's National Conference on Propaganda Work, Some Questions Concerning Methods of Leaderships, and Methods of Work of Party Committees.*

Party committees on all levels must abide by the directions given by Chairman Mao over the years, that is, that they should thoroughly apply the mass line of "from the masses, to the masses" and that they should be pupils before they become teachers. They should try to avoid being one-sided or narrow. They should foster materialist dialectics and oppose metaphysics and scholasticism.

The Great Proletarian Cultural Revolution is sure to achieve brilliant victory under the leadership of the Central Committee of the Party headed by Comrade Mao Zedong.

22.5   Deng Xiaoping: Self-Criticism

... My recent errors are by no means accidental or disconnected; they have their origins in a certain way of thinking and a certain style of work which has developed over a considerable period of time. Ideologically, I must confess that not only have I not raised high the banner of Mao Zedong Thought, but that I have not even lifted this banner up. As my office is very close to the Chairman, theoretically I should have ample opportunity to receive personal direction and help from him. However, I have a very inadequate grasp of Mao Zedong Thought, do little to propagate it and am not practiced at applying it in my work. Mao Zedong Thought is the soul of all of our work, and an aptitude in it or otherwise is the standard by which to judge the depth of a person's knowledge of Marxism-Leninism and the amount of a person's proletarian thinking.

If one does not make progress, then one will retrogress. If one does not study Mao Zedong Thought, then it is inevitable that the non-proletarian things in one's thinking will increase. The results of this is that one will make mistakes, and if unchecked, one will commit errors of a right opportunist tendency. In retrospect, my last few years have been marked by a steady regression and due to my laxity in the study and use of Mao Zedong Thought, I have made a number of mistakes. As the person in charge of the Secretariat of the Central Committee I must admit that the work of this department has been very badly done and that the areas of greatest error and fault are those departments under the direct leadership of the Secretariat. In matters concerning class struggle and struggle within the Party, I have consistently shown rightist tendencies. I am partly responsible for the rightist tendencies commited in 1962 which Chairman Mao mentioned in his big-character poster. Similarly, I must take some responsibility for the seemingly leftist but in essence rightist excesses of 1964, for though I was not in full agreement at the time, my objections were still not in compliance with Mao Zedong Thought. I also want to take this opportunity to make a thorough criticism of the numerous errors I made prior to 1962. My distancing myself from the masses and lack of contact with reality is directly connected with my failure to follow Chairman Mao and my lack of proper study. As a result, I have become accustomed to lording it over others and acting like someone special, rarely going down among the people or even to make the effort to contact cadres and other leaders so as to understand their working situation and problems. I have not been exacting in the execution of my office, continually failing to mix with the people and carry out investigatory work. The manner in which I deal with everyday problems has been too simplistic and sometimes quite inflexible. It is due to the above attitude that I have imprisoned myself in a mesh of subjectivism and bureaucracy over the past years. As a corollary to this 'imprisonment' I have made ideological and administrative errors with greater frequency and of increased gravity. A prolonged neglect of Mao Zedong Thought in the past has now developed into a salient opposition to it. Till recently I have not been aware of my attitude and still felt myself superior and infallible. Affected by such a viewpoint, I naturally have not taken great care in doing my work. Rarely did I ask for help or advice from other comrades or the people. Worse yet still is that I have rarely reported to and asked advice from the Chairman. Not only is this one of the main reasons for my errors, but is also a serious breach of Party discipline. In late 1964, Chairman Mao criticized me for being a kingdom unto myself. At first, somewhat shaken by this, I, however, consoled myself with the thought that I was neither a greedy person nore a power seeker, therefore delved no further into the origins of my faults. Thus unchecked, it was inevitable that I would commit an error involving political line, now or in the future. In the final analysis, my way of thinking and style of work is completely incompatible with Mao Zedong Thought. I have not raised high the great banner of Mao Zedong Thought, nor have I followed Chairman Mao closely, therefore I cut myself off from the leadership; in addition, my contact with the masses is infrequent and I am isolated from reality. I have shown myself not to be a good student of Chairman Mao and am absolutely unsuited to my present position of responsibility. Recent events have revealed me as an unreformed petit-bourgeois intellectual who has failed to pass the tests posed by socialism. Seeing myself thus reflected in my actions I am overwhelmed. I feel it would be damaging to the Party and the people for a person with my ideological level and political understanding to continue in my present position. What I need to do is reflect on my past actions, I need to earnestly study Chairman Mao's works, reform myself and correct my mistakes. By so doing, I hope to be of some use to the Party and the people in the latter years of my life and make up, in some way, for my past misdeeds. I firmly believe that with the help of my comrades and with my own determination, I will be able to correct my mistakes. Though I have gone astray on the road of politics, with the radiance of Mao Zedong Thought lighting my forward path, I should have the fortitude to pick myself up and go on. . . .

The above is a preliminary self-criticism. I hope all comrades present will give their criticisms and suggestions.

Long live the Great Proletarian Cultural Revolution!

Long live invincible Mao Zedong Thought!

Long live the great teacher, the great helmsman and the great leader Chairman Mao!

22.6 AND 22.7 LIN BIAO'S FALL

The fall of Lin Biao was the result of a power struggle that pitted Mao Zedong's anointed successor against the chairman. Although important aspects of this bitter conflict remain murky, evidence indicates that there was tension between Mao and Lin almost from the beginning of the Cultural Revolution. In part, these ill feelings were the product of their separate visions of the Great Proletarian Cultural Revolution, but a more practical source of tension was the political ambition of Lin Biao.

The largely invisible battle of political moves and countermoves by Mao and his "close comrade-in-arms" arrived at its sanguinary denouement in September 1971 with the death of Lin Biao, his wife Ye Qun, and their son Lin Liguo. The circumstances of their deaths are still far from certain, but their departure from life and politics marked the definitive victory of the Maoist forces.

The two documents that follow highlight the transformation of Lin Biao's reputation from honored political and military hero to the vilest specimen of traitor and hypocrite. The party spread elaborate explanations of Lin Biao's sins, as can be found in the communiqué of the Central

Committee concerning the September 12, 1971, "anti-party" incident, with its charges of skullduggery and complicated betrayals. The terse order from the Central Committee concerns the disposal of Lin Biao's literary legacy. It shows how the party leadership strove to abolish all memory of Lin and his crucial role in facilitating Mao Zedong's triumphs in the early stages of the Cultural Revolution. In countless artifacts of the Cultural Revolution, the ex-"close comrade-in-arms" Lin Biao was immortalized as a defender of Mao and the revolution. As this document suggests, the process of de-immortalization was, likewise, directed energetically and with scrupulous attention to detail.

22.6 *Official Explanation of Lin's Death*

COMMUNIQUÉ OF THE CENTRAL COMMITTEE OF THE CHINESE COMMUNIST PARTY CONCERNING LIN BIAO'S "SEPTEMBER 12" ANTI-PARTY INCIDENT (1971) TOP-SECRET DOCUMENT

On September 12, when Chairman Mao was making an inspection tour in the South, Lin Biao took advantage of the opportunity and attempted to blow up the train in which Chairman Mao was riding near Shanghai in order to accomplish his objective of assassinating Chairman Mao. When the plot failed and was exposed, Lin Biao hurriedly left Peking on the afternoon of September 12 and boarded a British-made Trident jet military transport, with the intention of surrendering to the enemy and betraying his own country. After crossing the national border, his plane crashed near Undur Khan in Mongolia. Lin Biao, Ye Qun, Lin Liguo, and the pilot were all burned to death.

Lin Biao, by his act of surrendering to the enemy and betraying his own country, invited his own destruction. Yet his death could not redeem his crime, and his notoriety will last for ten thousand years to come. What has been most intolerable is that Lin Biao stole a huge quantity of secret documents and foreign currencies and shot and wounded one of his long-time bodyguards. Lin Biao's sworn followers, Yu Xinye, Zhou Yuzhi and Chen Liyun took off separately in two military helicopters in an attempt to escape from the country. They were intercepted by the Air Force units of the Peking Region. Yu Xinye and Zhou Yuzhi shot the pilots to death and then committed suicide. Chen Liyun put up a fight and was seriously wounded. All the documents they had attempted to take with them aboard the two aircraft were recovered.

Lin (Toutou), daughter of Lin Biao, placed national interest above filial piety by refusing to escape with Lin Biao, and she reported the situation to the premier in time, which led to the foiling of her father's monstrous conspiracy. Lin (Toutou) has thus performed a great service to the Party and the state and helped the Party Central Committee smash a serious counterrevolutionary coup d'etat.

Central Committee of the Chinese
Communist Party
September 18, 1971

22.7   *Discarding Lin's Works*

NOTICE OF THE CENTRAL COMMITTEE OF THE CHINESE
COMMUNIST PARTY CONCERNING THE DISCARDING OF
THE "FOUR-GOOD" AND "FIVE-GOOD" MOVEMENTS AND
THE TURNING IN TO HIGHER AUTHORITIES OF THE
EPITAPHS AND PORTRAITS OF LIN BIAO (1971)
TOP-SECRET DOCUMENT

1. Resolved by the Central Committee of the Chinese Communist Party: Comparisons and competitions of the "four-good" and "five-good" movements be discarded from 1972 on, and the "Congress of Activitists for Living Study and Application of Chairman Mao's Works" as well as the "Meeting for Exchange of Experience on Studying Mao Zedong Thought" at various levels be disbanded.
2. Resolved by the Central Committee of the Chinese Communist Party: Copies of the "Constitution of the Chinese Communist Party," "Documents of the Ninth Party Congress," and "Long Live the Victory of the People's War" be turned in to the central authorities for disposal. Other works about Lin Biao, as well as Lin Biao's epitaphs and portraits, be collected by the basic levels and submitted to the *hsien* (county) authorities for disposal.

Central Committee of the
Chinese Communist Party
November 1971

CHAPTER 23

Reopening the Doors

23.1 AND 23.2 RAPPROCHEMENT WITH THE UNITED STATES AND THE INTERNATIONAL COMMUNITY

While the Cultural Revolution resulted in domestic chaos and constant purges within the party hierarchy, Premier Zhou Enlai struggled, at first with mixed results, to take charge of state affairs. China's foreign relations were greatly disrupted from 1967 to 1969. Many of China's ambassadors were called back to China and embassies were left with skeleton staffs; relations with the United States, escalating the war in Vietnam, were extremely hostile; and in 1969, border conflicts with the Soviet Union seemed about to erupt into a full-scale war. China grew increasingly isolated in global affairs, with only tiny, Stalinist Albania remaining a consistent friend.

In 1969 and 1970, this situation began to change. Mao Zedong, alarmed by the collapse of China's global position, was prepared to permit Zhou to play a more active role as the primary architect of China's foreign policy. At the same time, the new Nixon administration sought to consolidate a relationship with China and find a multilateral solution to the Vietnam conflict. The net result of ping-pong diplomacy, Kissinger's secret visit to China, and other initiatives was Richard Nixon's historic visit to China in February 1972. The Shanghai communiqué of February 28, 1972, the largely noncommittal document produced by the Nixon visit, led to momentous changes: within months Japan normalized relations with

China; the way was paved for China's acceptance into the United Nations; Taiwan was discredited as the government of all of China; and the People's Republic was drawn into the complex negotiations designed to produce an American withdrawal from Indochina.

The documents presented here, the Shanghai communiqué and Deng Xiaoping's speech at the United Nations, illuminate the shape of China's foreign policy as it emerged in the early 1970s. In the Shanghai communiqué the two sides agreed to disagree while pursuing mutually beneficial endeavors. This agreement established a basis for the normalization of relations with China during the Carter administration and a nonconfrontational American approach to the question of Taiwan's future. Deng's enunciation of Mao's theory of three worlds suggested the role China would seek to play among the nonaligned states of the world and in its competition with the two "superpowers," the United States and the Soviet Union.

23.1   The Shanghai Communiqué

JOINT COMMUNIQUÉ

The Chinese and U.S. Sides reached agreement on a joint communique on February 27 in Shanghai. Full text of the communique is as follows:

President Richard Nixon of the United States of America visited the People's Republic of China at the invitation of Premier Zhou Enlai of the People's Republic of China from February 21 to February 28, 1972. Accompanying the President were Mrs. Nixon, U.S. Secretary of State William Rogers, Assistant to the President Dr. Henry Kissinger, and other American officials.

President Nixon met with Chairman Mao Zedong of the Communist Party of China on February 21. The two leaders had a serious and frank exchange of views on Sino-U.S. Relations and world affairs.

During the visit, extensive, earnest, and frank discussions were held between President Nixon and Premier Zhou Enlai on the normalization of relations between the United States of America and the People's Republic of China, as well as on other matters of interest to both sides. In addition, Secretary of State William Rogers and Foreign Minister Qi Pengfei held talks in the same spirit.

President Nixon and his party visited Peking and viewed cultural, industrial, and agricultural sites, and they also toured Hangchow and Shanghai where, continuing discussions with Chinese leaders, they viewed similar places of interest.

The leaders of the People's Republic of China and the United States of America found it beneficial to have this opportunity, after so many years without contact, to present candidly to one another their views on a variety of issues.

They reviewed the international situation in which important changes and great upheavals are taking place and expounded their respective positions and attitudes.

The Chinese side stated: Wherever there is oppression there is resistance. Countries want independence, nations want liberation, and the people want revolution—this has become the irresistible trend of history. All nations, big or small, should be equal; big nations should not bully the small and strong nations should not bully the weak. China will never be a superpower and it opposes hegemony and power politics of any kind. The Chinese side stated that it firmly supports the struggles of all the oppressed people and nations for freedom and liberation and that the people of all countries have the right to choose their social systems according to their own wishes and the right to safeguard the independence, sovereignty, and territorial integrity of their own countries and oppose foreign aggression, interference, control, and subversion. All foreign troops should be withdrawn to their own countries. The Chinese side expressed its firm support to the peoples of Viet Nam, Laos, and Cambodia in their efforts for the attainment of their goal and its firm support to the seven-point proposal of the Provisional Revolutionary Government of the Republic of South Viet Nam and the elaboration of February this year on the two key problems in the proposal, and to the Joint Declaration of the Summit conference of the Indochinese Peoples. It firmly supports the eight-point program for the peaceful unification of Korea put forward by the Government of the Democratic People's Republic of Korea on April 12, 1971, and the stand for the abolition of the "U.N. Commission for the Unification and Rehabilitation of Korea." It firmly opposes the revival and outward expansion of Japanese militarism and firmly supports the Japanese people's desire to build an independent, democratic, peaceful, and neutral Japan. It firmly maintains that India and Pakistan should, in accordance with the United Nations resolutions on the India-Pakistan question, immediately withdraw all their forces to their respective territories and to their own sides of the ceasefire line in Jammu and Kashmir and firmly supports the Pakistan government and people in their struggle to preserve their independence and sovereignty and the people of Jammu and Kashmir in their struggle for the right of self-determination.

The U.S. Side stated: Peace in Asia and peace in the world requires efforts both to reduce immediate tensions and to eliminate the basic causes of conflict. The United States will work for a just and secure peace: just, because it fulfills the aspirations of peoples and nations for freedom and progress; secure, because it removes the danger of foreign aggression. The United States supports individual freedom and social progress for all peoples of the world, free of outside pressure or intervention. The United States believes that the effort to reduce tensions is served by improving communication between countries that have different ideologies so as to lessen the risks of confrontation through accident, miscalculation or misunderstanding. Countries should treat each other with mutual respect and be willing to compete peacefully, letting performance be the ultimate judge. No country should claim infallibility and each country should be prepared to re-examine its own attitudes for the common good. The United States stressed that the peoples of Indochina should be allowed to determine their destiny without outside intervention; its constant primary objective has been a negotiated solution; the eight-point proposal put forward by the Republic of Viet Nam and the United States on January 27, 1972, represents a basis for the attainment of that objective; in the absence of a negotiated settlement the United States envisages the ultimate withdrawal of all U.S. Forces from the region consistent with the aim of self-determination for each country of Indochina. The United States will maintain its close ties with and support for the Republic of Korea; the United States will support efforts of the Republic of Korea to seek a relaxation of tension and increased communication on the Korean peninsula. The United States places the highest value on its friendly relations with Japan; it will continue to develop the existing close bonds. Consistent with the United Nations Security Council Resolution of December 21, 1971, the United States favors the continuation of the ceasefire between India and Pakistan and the withdrawal of all military forces to within their own territories and to their own sides of the ceasefire line in Jammu and Kashmir; the United States supports the right of the peoples of South Asia to shape their own future in peace, free of military threat, and without having the area become the subject of great power rivalry.

There are essential differences between China and the United States in their social systems and foreign policies. However, the two sides agreed that countries regardless of their social systems should conduct their relations on the principles of respect for the sovereignty and territorial integrity of all states, non-aggression against other states, equality and mutual benefit, and peaceful coexistence. International disputes should be settled on this basis, without resorting to the use or threat of force. The United States and the People's Republic of China are prepared to apply these principles to their mutual relations.

With these principles of international relations in mind the two sides state that:

—progress toward the normalization of relations between China and the United States is in the interests of all countries.

—Both wish to reduce the danger of international military conflict;

—neither should seek hegemony in the Asia-Pacific region and each is opposed to efforts by any other country or group of countries to establish such hegemony; and

—neither is prepared to negotiate on behalf of any third party or to enter into agreements or understandings with the other directed at other states.

Both sides are of the view that it would be against the interests of the peoples of the world for any major country to collude with another against other countries, or for major countries to divide up the world into spheres of interest.

The two sides reviewed the long-standing serious disputes between China and the United States. The Chinese side reaffirmed its position: The Taiwan question is the crucial question obstructing the normalization of relations between China and the United States; the Government of the People's Republic of China is the sole legal government of China; Taiwan is a province of China which has long been returned to the motherland; the liberation of Taiwan is China's internal affair in which no other country has the right to interfere; and all U.S. Forces and military installations must be withdrawn from Taiwan. The Chinese Government firmly opposes any activities which aim at the creation of "one China, one Taiwan," "one China, two governments," "two Chinas," an "independent Taiwan" or advocate that the "status of Taiwan remains to be determined."

The U.S. side declared: The United States acknowledges that all Chinese on either side of the Taiwan Strait maintain there is but one China and that Taiwan is a part of China. The United States Government does not challenge that position. It reaffirms its interest in a peaceful settlement of the Taiwan question by the Chinese themselves. With this prospect in mind, it affirms the ultimate objective of the withdrawal of all U.S. Forces and military installations from Taiwan. In the meantime, it will progressively reduce its forces and military installations on Taiwan as the tension in the area diminishes.

The two sides agreed that it is desirable to broaden the understanding between the two peoples. To this end, they discussed specific areas in such fields as science, technology, culture, sports, and journalism, in which people-to-people contacts and exchanges would be mutually beneficial. Each side undertakes to facilitate the further development of such contacts and exchanges.

Both sides view bilateral trade as another area from which mutual benefit can be derived, and agreed that economic relations based on equality and mutual benefit are in the interest of the peoples of the two countries. They agree to facilitate the progressive development of trade between their two countries.

The two sides agreed that they will stay in contact through various channels, including the sending of a senior U.S. Representative to Peking from time to time for concrete consultations to further the normalization of relations between the two countries and continue to exchange views on issues of common interest.

The two sides expressed the hope that the gains achieved during this visit would open up new prospects for the relations between the two countries. They believe that the normalization of relations between the two countries is not only in the interest of the Chinese and American peoples but also contributes to the relaxation of tension in Asia and the world.

President Nixon, Mrs. Nixon, and the American party expressed their appreciation for the gracious hospitality shown them by the Government and the people of the People's Republic of China.

February 28, 1972

23.2 Deng Xiaoping: Speech at the United Nations, April 10, 1974

Mr. President,

. . . . This is the first time in the 29 years since the founding of the United Nations that a session is held specially to discuss the important question of opposing imperialist exploitation and plunder and effecting a change in international economic relations. This reflects that profound changes have taken place in the international situation. The Chinese Government extends its warm congratulations on the convocation of this session and hopes that it will make a positive contribution to strengthening the unity of the developing countries, safeguarding their national economic rights and interest and promoting the struggle of all peoples against imperialism, and particularly against hegemonism.

At present, the international situation is most favourable to the developing countries and the peoples of the world. More and more, the old order based on colonialism, imperialism and hegemonism is being undermined and shaken to its foundations. International relations are changing drastically. The whole world is in turbulence and unrest. The situation is one of "great disorder under heaven," as we Chinese put it. This "disorder" is a manifestation of the sharpening of all the basic contradictions in the contemporary worlds. It is accelerating the disintegration and decline of the decadent reactionary forces and stimulating the awakening and growth of the new emerging forces of the people.

In this situation of "great disorder under heaven," all the political forces in the world have undergone drastic division and realignment through prolonged trials of strength and struggle. A large number of Asian, African and Latin American countries have achieved independence one after another and they are playing an ever greater role in international affairs. As a result of the emergence of social-imperialism, the socialist camp which existed for a time after World War II is no longer in existence. Owing to the law of the uneven development of capitalism, the Western imperialist bloc, too, is disintegrating. Judging from the changes in international relations, the world today actually consists of three parts, or three worlds, that are both inter-connected and in contradiction to one another. The United States and the Soviet Union make up the First World. The developing countries in Asia, Africa, Latin America and other regions make up the Third World. The developed countries between the two make up the Second World.

The two superpowers, the United States and the Soviet Union, are vainly seeking world hegemony. Each in its own way attempts to bring the developing countries of Asia, Africa and Latin America under its control and, at the same time, to bully the developed countries that are not their match in strength.

The two superpowers are the biggest international exploiters and oppressors of today. They are the source of a new world war. They both possess large numbers of nuclear weapons. They carry on a keenly contested arms race, station massive forces abroad and set up military bases everywhere, threatening the independence and security of all nations. They both keep subjecting other countries to their control, subversion, interference or aggression. They both exploit other countries economically, plundering their wealth and grabbing their resources. In bullying others, the superpower which flaunts the label of socialism is especially vicious. It has dispatched its armed forces to occupy its "ally" Czechoslovakia and instigated the war to dismember Pakistan. It does not honour its words and is perfidious; it is self-seeking and unscrupulous.

The case of the developed countries in between the superpowers and the developing countries is a complicated one. Some of them still retain colonialist relations of one form or another with Third World countries, and a country like Portugal even continues with its barbarous colonial rules. An end must be put to this state of affairs. At the same time, all these developed countries are in varying degrees controlled, threatened or bullied by one superpower or the other. Some of them have in fact been reduced by a superpower to the position of dependencies under the signboard of its so-called "family." In varying degrees, all these countries have the desire of shaking off superpower enslavement or control and safeguarding their national independence and the integrity of their sovereignty.

The numerous developing countries have long suffered from colonialist and imperialist oppression and exploitation. They have won political independence, yet all of them still face the historic task of clearing out the remnant forces of colonialism, developing the national economy and consolidating national independence. These countries cover vast territories, encompass a large population and abound in natural resources. Having suffered the heaviest oppression, they have the strongest desire to oppose oppression and seek liberation and development. In the struggle for national liberation and independence, they have demonstrated immense power and continually won splendid victories. They constitute a revolutionary motive force propelling the wheel of world history and are the main force combating colonialism, imperialism, and particularly the superpowers.

Since the two superpowers are contending for world hegemony, the contradiction between them is irreconcilable; one either overpowers the other, or is overpowered. Their compromise and collusion can only be partial, temporary and relative, while their contention is all-embracing, permanent and absolute. In the final analysis, the so-called "balanced reduction of forces" and "strategic arms limitation" are nothing but empty talk, for in fact there is no "balance," nor can there possibly be "limitation." They may reach certain agreements, but their agreements are only a facade and a deception. At bottom, they are aiming at greater and fiercer contention. The contention between the superpowers extends over the entire globe. Strategically, Europe is the focus of their contention, where they are in constant tense confrontation. They are intensifying their rivalry in the Middle East, the Mediterranean, the Persian Gulf, the Indian Ocean and the Pacific. Every day, they talk about disarmament but are actually engaged in arms expansion. Every day, they talk about "détente" but are actually creating tension. Wherever they contend, turbulence occurs. So long as imperialism and social-imperialism exist, there definitely will be no tranquillity in the world, nor will there be "lasting peace." Either they will fight each other, or the people will rise in revolution. It is as Chairman Mao Zedong has said: The danger of a new world war still exists, and the people of all countries must get prepared. But revolution is the main trend in the world today. . . .

The hegemonism and power politics of the two superpowers have also aroused strong dissatisfaction among the developed countries of the Second World. The struggles of these countries against superpower control, interference, intimidation, exploitation and shifting of economic crises are growing day by day. Their struggles also have a significant impact on the development of the international situation.

Innumerable facts show that all views that overestimate the strength of the two hegemonic powers and underestimate the strength of the people are groundless. It is not the one or two superpowers that are really powerful; the really powerful are the Third World and the people of all countries uniting together and daring to fight and daring to win. Since numerous Third World countries and people were able to achieve political independence through protracted struggle, certainly they will also be able, on this basis, to bring about through sustained struggle a thorough change in the international economic relations which are based on inequality, control and exploitation and thus create essential conditions for the independent development of their national economy by strengthening their unity and allying themselves with other countries subjected to superpower bullying as well as with the people of the whole world, including the people of the United States and the Soviet Union. . . . .

Mr. President,

History develops in struggle, and the world advances amidst turbulence. The imperialists, and the superpowers in particular, are beset with troubles and are on the decline. Countries want independence, nations want liberation and the people want revolution—this is the irresistible trend of history. We are convinced that, so long as the Third World countries and people strengthen their unity, ally themselves with all forces that can be allied with and persist in a protracted struggle, they are sure to win continuous new victories.

23.3 CENTRAL COMMITTEE "OBITUARY" ON THE DEATH OF MAO ZEDONG, OCTOBER 1976

This New China News Agency obituary of Mao Zedong emphasizes his importance as a leader of the Chinese Communist party, his primacy as a figure in the history of Marxism-Leninism, and the "greatest Marxist of the contemporary era." Written shortly after his death in September 1976 and circulated throughout China, this memorial to Mao stresses his successful struggles against party opponents from the 1920s (Chen Duxiu and Qu Qiubai) to the 1960s and 1970s (Liu Shaoqi, Lin Biao, and Deng Xiaoping). The authors of this tribute, writing in the same elegiac terms as tributes to Mao penned during the Cultural Revolution, clearly did not foresee that Deng Xiaoping and other "revisionists" banished from public life would soon lead the party and country.

Mourning with Deepest Grief the Passing Away of the Great Leader and Great Teacher Chairman Mao Zedong

MESSAGE TO THE WHOLE PARTY, THE WHOLE ARMY AND THE PEOPLE OF ALL NATIONALITIES THROUGHOUT THE COUNTRY

The Central Committee of the Communist Party of China, the Standing Committee of the National People's Congress of the People's Republic of China, the State Council of the People's Republic of China and the Military Commission of the Central Committee of the Communist Party of China announce with deepest grief to the whole Party, the whole army and the people of all nationalities throughout the country: Comrade Mao Zedong, the esteemed and beloved great leader of our Party, our army and the people of all nationalities in our country, the great teacher of the international proletariat and the oppressed nations and oppressed people, Chairman of the Central Committee of the Communist Party of China, Chairman of the Military Commission of the Central Committee of the Communist Party of China, and Honorary Chairman of the National Committee of the Chinese People's Political Consultative Conference, passed away at 00:10 hours on September 9, 1976 in Beijing as a result of the worsening of his illness and despite all treatment, although meticulous medical care was given him in every way after he fell ill.

Chairman Mao Zedong was the founder and wise leader of the Communist Party of China, the Chinese People's Liberation Army and the People's Republic of China. Chairman Mao led our Party in waging a protracted, acute and complex struggle against the Right and "Left" opportunist lines in the Party, defeating the opportunist lines pursued by Chen Duxiu, Qu Qiubai, Li Lisan, Luo Zhanglong, Wang Ming, Zhang Guotao, Gao Gang-Rao Shih, and Peng Dehuai and again, during the Great Proletarian Cultural Revolution, triumphing over the counter-revolutionary revisionist line of Liu Shaoqi, Lin Biao and Deng Xiaoping, thus enabling our Party to develop and grow in strength steadily in class struggle and the struggle between the two lines. Led by Chairman Mao, the Communist Party of China has developed through a tortuous path into a great, glorious and correct Marxist-Leninist Party which is today exercising leadership over the People's Republic of China.

During the period of the new-democratic revolution, Chairman Mao, in accordance with the universal truth of Marxism-Leninism and by combining it with the concrete practice of the Chinese revolution, creatively laid down the general line and general policy of the new-democratic revolution, founded the Chinese People's Liberation Army and pointed out that the seizure of political power by armed force in China could be achieved only by following the road of building rural base areas, using the countryside to encircle the cities and finally seizing the cities, and not by any other road. He led our Party, our army and the people of our country in using people's war to overthrow the reactionary rule of imperialism, feudalism and bureaucrat-capitalism, winning the great victory of the new-democratic revolution and founding the People's Republic of China. The victory of the Chinese people's revolution led by Chairman Mao changed the situation in the East and the world and blazed a new trail for the cause of liberation of the oppressed nations and oppressed people.

In the period of the socialist revolution, Chairman Mao comprehensively summed up the positive as well as the negative experience of the international communist movement, penetratingly analysed the class relations in socialist society and, for the first time in the history of the development of Marxism, unequivocally pointed out that there are still classes and class struggle after the socialist transformation of the ownership of the means of production has in the main been completed, drew the scientific conclusion that the bourgeoisie is right in the Communist Party, put forth the great theory of continuing the revolution under the dictatorship of the proletariat, and laid down the Party's basic line for the entire historical period of socialism. Guided by Chairman Mao's proletarian revolutionary line, our Party, our army and the people of our country have continued their triumphant advance and seized great victories in the socialist revolution and socialist construction, particularly in the Great Proletarian Cultural Revolution, in criticizing Lin Biao and Confucius and in criticizing Deng Xiaoping and repulsing the Right deviationist attempt at reversing correct verdicts. Upholding socialism and consolidating the dictatorship of the proletariat in the People's Republic of China, a country with a vast territory and a large population, is a great contribution of world historic significance which Chairman Mao Zedong made to the present era; at the same time; it has provided fresh experience for the international communist movement in combating and preventing revisionism, consolidating the dictatorship of the proletariat, preventing capitalist restoration and building socialism.

All the victories of the Chinese people have been achieved under the leadership of Chairman Mao; they are all great victories for Mao Zedong Thought. The radiance of Mao Zedong Thought will for ever illuminate the road of advance of the Chinese people.

Chairman Mao Zedong summed up the revolutionary practice in the international communist movement, put forward a series of scientific theses, enriched the theoretical treasury of Marxism and pointed out the orientation of struggle for the Chinese people and the revolutionary people throughout the world. With the great boldness and vision of a proletarian revolutionary, he initiated in the international communist movement the great struggle to criticize modern revisionism with the Soviet revisionist renegade clique at the core, promoted the vigorous development of the cause of the world proletarian revolution and the cause of the people of all countries against imperialism and hegemonism, and pushed the history of mankind forward. . . .

Chairman Mao Zedong was the greatest Marxist of the contemporary era. For more than half a century, basing himself on the principle of integrating the universal truth of Marxism-Leninism with the concrete practice of the revolution, he inherited, defended and developed Marxism-Leninism in the protracted struggle against the class enemies at home and abroad, both inside and outside the Party, and wrote a most brilliant chapter in the 0history of the movement of proletarian revolution. . . .

The passing away of Chairman Mao Zedong is an inestimable loss to our Party, our army and the people of all nationalities in our country, to the international proletariat and the revolutionary people of all countries and to the international communist movement. His passing away is bound to evoke immense grief in the hearts of the people of our country and the revolutionary people of all countries. The Central Committee of the Communist Party of China calls on the whole Party, the whole army and the people of all nationalities in the country to resolutely turn their grief into strength:

We must carry on the cause left behind by Chairman Mao and persist in taking class struggle as the key link, keep to the Party's basic line and persevere in continuing the revolution under the dictatorship of the proletariat.

We must carry on the cause left behind by Chairman Mao and strengthen the centralized leadership of the Party, resolutely uphold the unity and unification of the Party and closely rally round the Party Central Committee. We must strengthen the building of the Party ideologically and organizationally in the course of the struggle between the two lines and resolutely implement the principle of the three-in-one combination of the old, middle-aged and young in accordance with the five requirements for bringing up successors to the cause of the proletarian revolution.

We must carry on the cause left behind by Chairman Mao and consolidate the great unity of the people of all nationalities under the leadership of the working class and based on the worker-peasant alliance, deepen the criticism of Deng Xiaoping, continue the struggle to repulse the Right deviationist attempt at reversing correct verdicts, consolidate and develop the victories of the Great Proletarian Cultural Revolution, enthusiastically support the socialist new things, restrict bourgeois right and further consolidate the dictatorship of the proletariat in our country. We should continue to unfold the three great revolutionary movements of class struggle, the struggle for production and scientific experiment, build our country independently and with the initiative in our own hands, through self-reliance, hard struggle, diligence and thrift, and go all out, aim high and achieve greater, faster, better and more economical results in building socialism.

We must carry on the cause left behind by Chairman Mao and resolutely implement his line in army building, strengthen the building of the army, strengthen the building of the militia, strengthen preparedness against war, heighten our vigilance, and be ready at all times to wipe out any enemy that dares to intrude. We are determined to liberate Taiwan.

We must carry on the cause left behind by Chairman Mao and continue to resolutely carry out Chairman Mao's revolutionary line and policies in foreign affairs. We must adhere to proletarian internationalism, strengthen the unity between our Party and the genuine Marxist-Leninist Parties and organizations all over the world, strengthen the unity between the people of our country and the people of all other countries, especially those of the third world countries, unite with all the forces in the world that can be united, and carry the struggle against imperialism, social-imperialism and modern revisionism through to the end. We will never seek hegemony and will never be a superpower.

We must carry on the cause left behind by Chairman Mao and assiduously study Marxism–Leninism–Mao Zedong Thought, apply ourselves to the study of works by Marx, Engels, Lenin and Stalin and works by Chairman Mao, fight for the complete overthrow of the bourgeoisie and all other exploiting classes, for the establishment of the dictatorship of the proletariat in place of the dictatorship of the bourgeoisie and for the triumph of socialism over capitalism, and strive to build our country into a powerful socialist state, make still greater contributions to humanity and realize the ultimate goal of communism.

Long live invincible Marxism–Leninism–Mao Zedong Thought!

Long live the great, glorious and correct Communist Party of China!

Eternal glory to the great leader and teacher Chairman Mao Zedong!

CHAPTER 24

Redefining Revolution

24.1 DENG XIAOPING: "EMANCIPATE THE MIND, SEEK TRUTH FROM FACTS AND UNITE AS ONE IN LOOKING TO THE FUTURE," DECEMBER 13, 1978

In the two years following the fall of the Gang of Four, Deng Xiaoping emerged as the most important leader within the hierarchy of the regime. China's nominal leader, Chairman Hua Guofeng, was marginalized in the reshuffling that occurred in party circles in 1978. When a dramatic program of national reform was launched at the end of 1978, it was clear that Deng and not Hua was its major proponent.

The speech that follows was made by Deng Xiaoping in the closing session of the Central Working conference of the Central Committee which was then preparing for the Third Plenum of the Eleventh Central Committee of the CCP. This latter meeting worked out the details of the program for the Four Modernizations, the modernizations of agriculture, science and technology, national defense, and industry, which subsequently, became the guiding blueprint for party work. Deng's speech, made just prior to this famous meeting, laid the groundwork for the discussions that followed. With its emphasis on freedom of thought, democracy, and pragmatism and its reversal of the verdict on the Tiananmen Incident (1976), the speech seemed a dramatic and hopeful departure from the previous style of party work. However, the speech's firm insistence on the importance of Mao Zedong Thought and Marxism-Leninism as the source of the party's "unity" as well as its stress on adherence to party line, centralized leadership, and democratic centralism were obvious signals that Deng's group still subscribed adhered to the authoritarian formulas of rule that had emerged early in the party's history.

Comrades,

This conference has lasted over a month and will soon end. The Central Committee has put forward the fundamental guiding principle of shifting the focus of all Party work to the four modernizations and has solved a host of important problems inherited from the past. This will surely strengthen the determination, confidence and unity of the Party, the army and the people of all of China's nationalities. Now we can be certain that under the correct leadership of the Central Committee, the Party, army and people will achieve victory after victory in our new Long March....

Today, I mainly want to discuss one question, namely, how to emancipate our minds, use our heads, seek truth from facts and unite as one in looking to the future.

I. EMANCIPATING THE MIND IS A VITAL POLITICAL TASK

When it comes to emancipating our minds, using our heads, seeking truth from facts and uniting as one in looking to the future, the primary task is to emancipate our minds. Only then can we, guided as we should be by Marxism-Leninism and Mao Zedong Thought, find correct solutions to the emerging as well as inherited problems, fruitfully reform those aspects of the relations of production and of the superstructure that do not correspond with the rapid development of our productive forces, and chart the specific course and formulate the specific policies, methods and measures needed to achieve the four modernizations under our actual conditions.

The emancipation of minds has not been completely achieved among our cadres, particularly our leading cadres. Indeed, many comrades have not yet set their brains going; in other words, their ideas remain rigid or partly so. That isn't because they are not good comrades. It is a result of specific historical conditions.

First, it is because during the past dozen years Lin Biao and the Gang of Four set up ideological taboos or "forbidden zones" and preached blind faith to confine people's minds within the framework of their phoney Marxism. No one was allowed to go beyond the limits they prescribed. Anyone who did was tracked down, stigmatized and attacked politically. In this situation, some people found it safer to stop using their heads and thinking questions over.

Second, it is because democratic centralism was undermined and the Party was afflicted with bureaucratism resulting from, among other things, over-concentration of power. This kind of bureaucratism often masquerades as "Party leadership," "Party directives," "Party interests" and "Party discipline," but actually it is designed to control people, hold them in check and oppress them. At that time many important issues were often decided by one or two persons. The others could only do what those few ordered. That being so, there wasn't much point in thinking things out for yourself.

Third, it is because no clear distinction was made between right and wrong or between merit and demerit, and because rewards and penalties were not meted out as deserved. No distinction was made between those who worked well and those who didn't. In some cases, even people who worked well were attacked while those who did nothing or just played it safe weathered every storm. Under those unwritten laws, people were naturally reluctant to use their brains.

Fourth, it is because people are still subject to the force of habit, the small producer, who sticks to old conventions, is content with the status quo and is unwilling to seek progress or accept anything new.

When people's minds aren't yet emancipated and their thinking remains rigid, curious phenomena emerge.

Once people's thinking becomes rigid, they will increasingly act according to fixed notions. To cite some examples, strengthening Party leadership is interpreted as the Party monopolizes and interferes in everything. Exercising centralized leadership is interpreted as erasing distinctions between the Party and the government, so that the former replaces the latter. And maintaining unified leadership by the Central Committee is interpreted as "doing everything according to unified standards." We are opposed to "home-grown policies" that violate the fundamental principles of those laid down by the Central Committee, but there are also "home-grown policies" that are truly grounded in reality and supported by the masses. Yet such correct policies are still often denounced for their "not conforming to the unified standards."

People whose thinking has become rigid tend to veer with the wind. They are not guided by Party spirit and Party principles, but go along with whatever has the backing of the authorities and adjust their words and actions according to whichever way the wind is blowing. They think that they will thus avoid mistakes. In fact, however, veering with the wind is in itself a grave mistake, a contravention of the Party spirit which all Communists should cherish. It is true that people who think independently and dare to speak out and act can't avoid making mistakes, but their mistakes are out in the open and are therefore more easily rectified.

Once people's thinking becomes rigid, book worship, divorced from reality, becomes a grave malady. Those who suffer from it dare not say a word or take a step that isn't mentioned in books, documents or the speeches of leaders: everything has to be copied. Thus responsibility to the higher authorities is set in opposition to responsibility to the people.

Our drive for the four modernizations will get nowhere unless rigid thinking is broken down and the minds of cadres and of the masses are completely emancipated.

In fact, the current debate about whether practice is the sole criterion for testing truth is also a debate about whether people's minds need to be emancipated. Everybody has recognized that this debate is highly important and necessary. Its importance is becoming clearer all the time. When everything has to be done by the book, when thinking turns rigid and blind faith is the fashion, it is impossible for a party or a nation to make progress. Its life will cease and that party or nation will perish. Comrade Mao Zedong said this time and again during the rectification movements. Only if we emancipate our minds, seek truth from facts, proceed from reality in everything and integrate theory with practice, can we carry out our socialist modernization programme smoothly, and only then can our Party further develop Marxism-Leninism and Mao Zedong Thought. In this sense, the debate about the criterion for testing truth is really a debate about ideological line, about politics, about the future and the destiny of our Party and nation. . . .

People both at home and abroad have been greatly concerned recently about how we would evaluate Comrade Mao Zedong and the Cultural Revolution. The great contributions of Comrade Mao in the course of long revolutionary struggles will never fade. If we look back at the years following the failure of the revolution in 1927, it appears very likely that without his outstanding leadership the Chinese revolution would still not have triumphed even today. In that case, the people of all our nationalities would still be suffering under the reactionary rule of imperialism, feudalism and bureaucrat-capitalism, and our Party would still be engaged in bitter struggle in the dark. Therefore, it is no exaggeration to say that were it not for Chairman Mao there would be no New China. Mao Zedong Thought has nurtured our whole generation. All comrades present here may be said to have been nourished by Mao Zedong Thought. Without Mao Zedong Thought, the Communist Party of China would not exist today, and that is no exaggeration either. Mao Zedong Thought will forever remain the greatest intellectual treasure of our Party, our army and our people. We must understand the scientific tenets of Mao Zedong Thought correctly and as an integral whole and develop them under the new historical conditions. Of course Comrade Mao was not infallible or free from shortcomings. To demand that of any revolutionary leader would be inconsistent with Marxism. We must guide and educate the Party members, the army officers and men and the people of all of China's nationalities and help them to see the great service of Comrade Mao Zedong scientifically and in historical perspective.

The Cultural Revolution should also be viewed scientifically and in historical perspective. In initiating it Comrade Mao Zedong was actuated mainly by the desire to oppose and prevent revisionism. As for the shortcomings that appeared during the course of the Cultural Revolution and the mistakes that were made then, at an appropriate time they should be summed up and lesson should be drawn from them—that is essential for achieving unity of understanding throughout the Party. The Cultural Revolution has become a stage in the course of China's socialist development, hence we must evaluate it. However, there is not need to do so hastily. Serious research must be done before we can make a scientific appraisal of this historical stage. It may take a rather long time to fully understand and assess some of the particular issues involved. We will probably be able to make a more correct analysis of this period in history after some time has passed than we can right now. . . .

The four modernizations represent a great and profound revolution in which we are moving forward by resolving one new contradiction after another. Therefore, all Party comrades must learn well and always keep on learning.

On the eve of nationwide victory in the Chinese revolution, Comrade Mao Zedong called on the whole Party to start learning afresh. We did that pretty well and consequently, after entering the cities, we were able to rehabilitate the economy very quickly and then to accomplish the socialist transformation. But we must admit that we have not learned well enough in the subsequent years. Expending our main efforts on political campaigns, we did not master the skills needed to build our country. Our socialist construction failed to progress satisfactorily and we experienced grave setbacks politically. Now that our task is to achieve modernization, our lack of the necessary knowledge is even more obvious. So the whole Party must start learning again.

What shall we learn? Basically, we should study Marxism-Leninism and Mao Zedong Thought and try to integrate the universal principles of Marxism with the concrete practice of our modernization drive. At present most of our cadres need also to apply themselves to three subjects: economics, science and technology, and management. Only if we study these well will we be able to carry out socialist modernization rapidly and efficiently. We should learn in different ways—through practice, from books and from the experience, both positive and negative, of others as well as our own. Conservatism and book worship should be overcome. The several hundred members and alternate members of the Central Committee and the thousands of senior cadres at the central and local levels should take the lead in making an in-depth study of modern economic development.

So long as we unite as one, work in concert, emancipate our minds, use our heads and try to learn what we did not know before, there is no doubt that we will be able to quicken the pace of our new Long March. Under the leadership of the Central Committee and the State Council, let us advance courageously to change the backward condition of our country and turn it into a modern and powerful socialist state.

24.2   HE SHIGUANG: "ON A VILLAGE MARKET STREET," AUGUST 1980

The Four Modernizations had an immediate impact on the rural economy and the life of the peasantry. The party's new emphasis on the formation of managerial personnel and the development of a wide array of profit-making enterprises was a sharp departure from past policies. During the Cultural Revolution, such endeavors were condemned as "following the capitalist road." Many peasants who successfully created thriving side enterprises were victimized by local party bosses and self-proclaimed "radicals." In essence, the decisions of the Third Plenum marked a return to schemes of partial privatization that had already been experimented with in the 1950s and early 1960s and were greeted with authentic enthusiasm throughout China's countryside.

In both rural and urban areas, however, the corruption and nepotism of the party elite, although diminished, remained a central feature of everyday life. In many places, local party notables who supported Mao Zedong and the Gang of Four, and used the Cultural Revolution to enhance their own powers, remained in place. Uncomfortable tensions persisted between individuals whose relations had been were poisoned by their roles in the tumultuous movements of the 1950s, 1960s, and early 1970s, and who still lived in the same villages and work units.

He Shiguang's short story, "On a Village Market Street," published in *People's Literature* in the summer of 1980, captures this facet of the process of modernization. Its hero, Uncle Feng, feels so emboldened by the government's new economic policies that he is willing to take the previously unthinkable risk of "speaking bitterness" against the well-connected local termagant Mrs. Luo and other abusers of power. Urged to "seek truth from facts," one of the clichés of the modernization program, Feng tells the truth and launches into a rambling but highly impassioned attack on those who have tormented him and others in the village. The other villagers, who listen on the sidelines, agree with him and roles are reversed as the once invincible Mrs. Luo becomes the laughingstock of the entire village. While this story ends with a rather syrupy note of optimism, it reflects accurately the hopeful mood of the early modernization period and the political skepticism that was now part of both of literature and everyday life.

On our market street in Pear Blossom Village, this small street in the Wumeng mountains, Uncle Feng, tall and fortyish, is a well-known drunkard, a penniless good-for-nothing farm hand. The devil only knows how he manages to survive the three hundred and sixty five days of the year but, in fact, this is a subject not worth much discussion on the market street. Just now, who knows why, he has been brought here. Grinning and laughing embarrassedly, he stands between two women as he waits for questions from the brigade party secretary. He is to testify as witness of a quarrel between the women and suddenly is transformed into a valued treasure. It seems so funny!

"Uncle Feng, just a little while ago, at breakfast time—that's to say, at Primary School morning break time—were you passing the market street with your ox?" Secretary Cao Fugui asks him.

The incident took place on the market street and so, of course, either Secretary Cao or Secretary Song of the market street should act as an arbitrator. But everyone here knows that Secretary Cao is on Mrs. Luo's side. In appearance this Secretary looks not much older or different from Uncle Feng. Cao, too, seems like just another farm hand wearing loose shirt and a bandanna wrapped around his head. But don't be fooled by appearances; he's a very wily character! Pear Blossom Village has only this one street, so short you can see it all in a glance, and living here is like being part of a big clan household. Everyone knows all there is to know about others.

Uncle Feng narrows his eyes and scratches his loose, wild hair. He giggles in an ingratiating way and replies:

"We all live on this street, why fuss?"

The bystanders burst into laughter. It's the leisurely time just after breakfast and nearly half the people living on the street have gathered here. Just as a little stone can disturb quiet reflections on the surface of a pond, so any small matter on this market street arouses the concern of everyone. Partly that's because the street is so small that anything happening here will probably pull you in and partly it's just because there's too little to see on the street. Uncle Feng's just playing tricks, right? He can't be a good witness!

"Well, did you go by or not? Speak up."

"You mean. . . . breakfast?"

"At the time of the morning break for breakfast!"

"Pulling my ox?"

"Yes, right!"

Uncle Feng scratches his head again and can't help but to start laughing. He opens his wide mouth and seems to be shy and this evokes another guffaw from the crowd.

Mrs. Luo, the short, stout woman standing by his side, laughs coldly toward the thin woman standing opposite her and says:

"Uncle Feng, everyone insists that you were there. You saw everything. Could you have seen a kid belonging to the Luo family acting so low class he wanted something not worth two cents? Did he really need to be beaten. . . ."

When this woman opens her mouth, the lively, happy atmosphere associated with Uncle Feng is dampened. People remembers things and feel stifled. In recent years, when people hear her voice, they feel as depressed and desolate as a harvested cornfield with broken stalks left soaked by the rain. To look at this woman you would think she was grimy and ridiculous, right? About thirty, it looks like she never washes her hair or face and her two wadded flannel shirts are spotted with grease. Elsewhere she would be laughable but here on the market street of Pear Blossom Village, she appears to be a noble woman because her husband is the accountant of the food station on the street and also the butcher. No one believes that the thin woman or her child could dare to provoke the Luo family. Her man is Big Ren, the honest but drab schoolteacher who has been teaching at the village primary school for many years. How can they measure up to the Luo family? Everyone has just lived through some bleak years and knows how differently honor and humiliation have been doled out to these two women on this little street. Although the past now seems as bizarre as a nightmare, the reality of it is like a stone. Everyone knows that Mrs. Luo is tormenting Big Ren's woman and they feel unsettled and concerned.

"Please say something fair Uncle Feng! My kid really didn't. . . ."

Big Ren's woman watches Uncle Feng in a timid, imploring way. This ill-fated woman is married to a teacher and will never be someone important on this street. Her clothing, like her house standing forlornly along the street, always needs mending. Her face is so shriveled that people only see her pointed chin and a pair of large, lusterless eyes. She has always been weak and submissive and, if it was not necessary, she would have never involved Uncle Feng. . . .

As for Uncle Feng, he pulls his head lower and lower and still stays silent. Oh, Uncle Feng is really being crushed and everyone feels sorry for him.

Mrs. Luo keeps swearing. This evil hen demon puts her hands on her hips, stamps the ground, and then slaps her thighs. She purses her lips and spits repeatedly at the ground in front of Uncle Feng.

"If I were you Uncle Feng," Secretary Cao speaks again, "I would 'seek the truth from facts' [*shishi qiushi*] and speak out! It has been four years since we smashed the Gang of Four. Everyone should 'seek truth from facts'!"

Goaded by this continuous persuasion, Uncle Feng finally makes a move and stands up.

"That's right," the Secretary says, "it's not your own business anyway."

Uncle Feng suddenly nods his head. Dragging his feet, he walks back and seems to be almost crying. He looks very strange. The saying goes that "you go against your conscience when you cannot do otherwise"; will he harm the family of the poor and timid teacher?

"Secretary Cao," his voice is quavering in a strange way, "you . . . want me to speak out?"

"Yes, we have been waiting for you for a long time."

Uncle Feng nods his head again and stands still.

Feeling quite uncomfortable and facing the crowd, he speaks slowly: "I, Uncle Feng, as everyone knows, do not even count as a man on this street. . . .

No one needs to make it clear that I'm like a dog here. . . . I am so poor I can't help it! . . . Everyone has seen it, I have lost all face. . . ."

What's happening to him? The people feel strange, they're silent and watch him.

"Last year," he continues, "if you add up the millet and corn combined, I got several hundred catties more than before. I figure that my family will have food until the Dragon Boat festival. I also have several dozen catties of glutinous millet and my woman has said that this year we could wrap a few millet patties with bamboo leaves for the kids. By that time the potatoes will be ready . . . for our vegetable seed garden, the country promises to sell some rice as a reward. In our private plots there is some wheat to harvest. . . . Last year we insisted that we should pull water into the wet fields to plant fast growing crops. The fields are full of water and so the responsibility falls on individuals and it is easy to make up the fields and transplant rise seedlings . . . As long as the seedlings can be planted, there will be millet and corn to pick in the future. . . ."

Mrs. Luo interrupts him: "You're going from the southern mountains to the northern sea; how far are you going to go?"

No one expects it but Uncle Feng suddenly turns around. He stamps his feet, and, with both eyes turning red, roars with all his might: "Secretary Cao, it's up to you whether I get my grain ration. But I don't care! This year, even without it, I, Uncle Feng, can still survive."

The people have never seen Uncle Feng so ferocious. Everyone is dumbfounded. His broad face is suddenly sunken and steely gray and he grinds his teeth. He is truly terrifying. "Do I, Uncle Feng, want to have a few ounces of meat?" He pounds his breast and replies: "I do! What about it? Buy it. After I sell my vegetable seed, I'll buy a few catties to feed my kids but I promise not to buy it from you Luo. Anyway, country people can now slaughter their own pigs and sell them. It's no longer a monopoly for your food station. It's open. It's only a few dimes more and you can even choose between the lean and fatty meat as you like. . . . Let me tell you, now it's different than it was before. Whoever refuses to sell this or that or whoever hides this under the counter or that behind the door can't even fulfill his sales quota. This year, your old dad . . ."

"Uncle Feng! You better have a cleaner mouth. Whose old dad are you?"

"What can you do? Do you dare to touch me? If you want to have a fight, try it today! For the past few years, your old dad has been neither a man nor a ghost! But I've had enough! It's fortunate that in these two years the country has untied us farmer's hands and feet. Who dares curse me? I won't be polite today!"

Secretary Cao now intervenes: "Now then, Uncle Feng—"

Uncle Feng immediately interrupts him. "Don't give me this! Pack up your nasty tricks and beat it! Send me to the correction camp? Send me to do irrigation work on New Year's eve? Forget it! You can't do it anymore. . . . Be a little official; if you're an official for ten years then I, Uncle Feng, won't steal a cow for ten years. I can make a living; the government allows it this time. Let's see what you can do to me."

"You, you . . ."

"You what? Didn't you ask me to come to be a witness? I was there all the time. You can't say only the Luo kid was raised by human beings. He took something from Big Ren's kid. When people asked him to give it back he said no and got nasty and cursed everybody out. *Who* beat him? The Ren kid didn't fight back or curse. Now am I speaking clearly?"

All of this comes so suddenly that everyone is stunned. Then laughter bursts from the crowd like thunder on a dry day and shakes the whole street. The thunder changes into the sound of noisy discussions which follow like the patter of rain on the market street. To use another figure of speech, it's like the dragon dance on the Lantern Festival that brings the happy sound of firecrackers to the little market street. All the time this fellow Uncle Feng was squatting there he was figuring this out! We always misunderstood him in the past. Things happen this way. Things should happen this way. It's as happy and comfortable a feeling as planting the whole basin with seedlings. . . .

Now he turns around and speaks solemnly to Big Ren's woman: "Tell Teacher Ren, the kid didn't hit Luo. I, Uncle Feng, saw it with my own eyes. We farm hands are not like those sons of turtles . . ."

Mrs. Luo screams out hoarsely: "Good, Uncle Feng, just you remember . . ."

But the grating sound of her voice is lost in the raucous laughter of the crowd. Only Uncle Feng's voice is clear and loud:

"As long as the government's policy does not go back to what it was in the past few years and so long as it doesn't change back and forth against us farm hands, I, Uncle Feng, with my strength and energy, what do I have to fear?"

And so, tramping off with his big feet, saying he is busy, Uncle Feng walks away. Watching his broad shouldered back, the people begin to remember that since last year Uncle Feng has changed. He doesn't drink so often and he has become more diligent. Didn't he buy that big pair of Liberation sneakers last winter? It's said that "When food is at hand, the heart is not anxious; with two feet on solid ground, one is truly happy." When he put on those Liberation sneakers, he liberated himself. The unfair days of the past were like a mist that was now scattering day by day. On this market street, sunshine is piercing through the gray fog. The situation is changing hour by hour and the backbones of the farm hands are straightening. This most ordinary quarrel makes the people of Pear Blossom Village very happy. No matter how Mrs. Luo fusses, the people laugh and, feeling contented, disperse. The spring is certainly a busy season; there is lots to be done and the whole group, men and women, all walk rapidly away.

24.3 Ye Wenfu: "General, You Must Not Do This!" 1979

Ye Wenfu's poem "General, You Must Not Do This!" criticized new abuses of power that surfaced following the Cultural Revolution. It was based on the apparently true story of a self-indulgent general who tore down a kindergarten to make room for his own home. The poem, is notable for its powerful condemnation of corruption, and its use of the Communist party's own vaunted moral standards to attack a party personality. Two generations of Chinese who had grown up after 1949 "under the red flag" had been trained in the party's schools. Through the party's propaganda they learned to to measure themselves and their world by a rigorously self-sacrificing code of socialist morality. After the massive suffering of the Cultural Revolution, acts of corruption undercut this standard and made the behavior of corrupt leaders seem a form of hypocrisy of the highest and most objectionable order.

Reportedly, a top-ranking general, who came into power again after being cruelly persecuted by the Gang of Four, recently ordered a kindergarten to be demolished to make way for his new mansion, which he lavishly furnished with modern facilities, costing the country a total of several hundred thousand RMB [renminbi, the currency of China]. And I . . .

> What can I say?
> And how shall I say it?
> You, my honorable elder
> And I, years your junior
> Between you and me
> Lie the gunsmoke years—
> The nineteen-thirties
> And forties.
>
> To criticize you
> Is something
> I never imagined,
> Because perhaps
> It may have been your hand
> That held the machine gun
> Which aimed deadly shots
> At the Old World
>
> It might have been your hand
> That snatched away
> The whip from my back—

You held me
In your blood-stained bosom,
As your teardrops fell
You touched the scars
Over my body,
Your thick lips trembling.

You said: "My child,
We are not liberated—"
And so I, bare footed,
Small-footed, treading
In your giant footprints
Walk into a New China. . . .

How sad, my battle-tired General
That forty or more years later
Your heroic stature should turn
To a limping gait,
Your achievements
And thunderous voice
Washed and shrunken
By the tide of time
To a weak note:
"To me. . . . To me. . . ."

Give you the Moon
But you say it's too cold,
Give you the Sun
But you say it's too hot!
You want the whole World
In one embrace, everything
To pick and choose . . .
For your amusement
Everything, you want all.
But why did you deny the oath
You swore to the party?

And why have you discarded
The mark of the true proletarian?
Must the flames of Jinggang Mountain,
Which even the Dadu River could not tame,
Be smothered by the cups of maotai
That adorn your banquet table?
And must the Red Boat,
That came through the storm
On the South Lake, be anchored in
Your comfortable armchair?
Must a member of the CCP
Create history as tragic as Niu Jinxing?

Must generation after generation
Start revolutions and pledge their lives
Only so you and your family
Can live in paradise?....

Can it be that Premier Zhou Enlai's
Good teachings no longer penetrate
The pores of your skin?
For your own "modernization"
You tear down the kindergarten
And send the children away!
Do you know, hoary-headed one,
Your happy years are few.
The children hold the future,
Yes, it is the children
Who hold the future!
Disown them, and who will be left
To carry your ashes?

Perhaps you proudly say:
"I have my son . . ."
Yes, you have your son—
If your son is a revolutionary
He will angrily stay away
From your mansion; If your son
Is a good-for-nothing parasite
The accusations that you reap
From the people will forever
Weigh upon his delicate hands!....

On the first Long March
You conquered the Dadu River
But as the new Long March
Begins, what are you contemplating today—
Fall back one step
And your end will be: the Dadu River!

No! Niu Jinxing's tragedy
Certainly will not happen again
Because the people
Will not remain silent!
And so may my lines
Become like thunder and with heroic force
Pound into your ears and heart,
while on our new Long March
Those who march after you,
And the Law, which also marches along,
Loudly join in unison: "General,
You must not do this!"

CHAPTER 25

Levels of Power

25.1 SPEECH BY HAN NIANLONG, APRIL 26, 1979

Long before the collapse of South Vietnamese resistance to Hanoi, China's relationship with Vietnam was fraught with difficulty. Centuries of rivalry between Vietnam and her powerful northern neighbor were put aside after 1949 as China emerged as the chief backer of the Vietminh struggle to defeat French colonialism and promote Communist unification of the country. Tensions between the two states remained, however, after the Geneva Accords of 1954 enabled a communist-dominated Vietnamese state to be founded north of the 17th parallel and were accentuated by the Sino-Soviet split in 1960. During the Cultural Revolution the Soviet Union took over as the prime backer of North Vietnamese efforts against the South and, at least for a time, China even carried its rivalry with the USSR so far as to forbid the passage of Russian arms and materials bound for the Vietnam front from passing through its territory.

After the fall of Saigon in 1975, the relationship between China and Vietnam continued to deteriorate. Vietnam's expulsion of thousands of overseas Chinese angered Peking as did acts which China saw as provocations on its border with Vietnam. When the Vietnamese entered Cambodia in 1978 to overthrow the Khmer Rouge regime of Pol Pot, a new nadir was reached and Chinese troops began to be transported south so that the Vietnamese could be, as Deng Xiaoping told American reporters in February 1979, "taught a lesson" for their disregard of China's interests.

China's military intervention occurred in March 1979 when thousands of Chinese troops crossed over into the northernmost provinces of Vietnam and were engaged in a short but bitter war with the Vietnamese army.

The armed conflict ground to a halt shortly but any illusions about a Communist solidarity in Asia were dispelled by the war. Vice Foreign Minister Han Nianlong's speech in Hanoi summarizes China's grievances and underlines the minimum conditions for a restoration of harmonious relations.

Your excellency Phan Hien, head of the government delegation of the Socialist Republic of Vietnam and colleagues of the Vietnamese government delegation:

... Early in 1977 when the Vietnamese authorities started a military buildup along the Sino-Vietnamese border in preparation for a war against China, they instituted measures to set up a cordon sanitaire, driving into Chinese territory large numbers of Chinese nationals and Vietnamese citizens who had lived in the border areas for generations. They later intensified their anti-Chinese activities throughout Vietnam, regarded Chinese nationals as enemies even when the latter had over the years contributed positively to the revolutionary cause in Vietnam, and cruelly persecuted and expelled them en masse. . . . Subsequently, instead of showing restraint in its persecution and expulsion of Chinese nationals, the Vietnamese side resorted to even more sinister means. Around the time of our delegation's arrival in Hanoi for the negotiations, the Vietnamese authorities expelled more than ten thousand Chinese nationals and Vietnamese citizens across the border into China's Guangxi and Yunnan provinces. Incomplete statistics show that the number of Chinese nationals and Vietnamese citizens driven by you into China has exceeded 200,000. The Vietnamese authorities must immediately stop their continued expulsion of Chinese nationals and Vietnamese citizens to Chinese territory.

Moreover, it was reported that in south Vietnam you have driven hundreds of thousands of Vietnamese of Chinese descent and Vietnamese citizens across the open sea to Southeast Asian countries and quite a number of other countries and regions in the world, causing great difficulties to those countries. The Vietnamese authorities have been for some time strongly condemned by world opinion and by the countries concerned for their "exporting" refugees. Yet in its speech, the Vietnamese government delegation has absurdly alleged that the massive expulsion of Chinese nationals and Vietnamese citizens to China was the result of Chinese incitement. This attempt to evade its culpability is entirely futile. People are bound to ask whether the expulsion of hundreds of thousands of Vietnamese refugees to Southeast Asia and other countries was also the result of incitement by those countries? That the Vietnamese authorities should resort to such gross misrepresentation of facts is indeed shocking!

Concurrently with their large-scale anti-Chinese activities, the Vietnamese authorities started to mobilize the party, government, and army for war and stepped up their military buildup along the Sino-Vietnamese border. In their directives to all lower-level organs, they openly referred to China as "the most immediate and dangerous enemy" and "their opponent in the next war," and issued the slogan: "Do everything for the sake of defeating China." They massed more than 200,000 troops in northern Vietnam and stationed many regular troops along the Sino-Vietnamese border. In its "Outline For Education On The New Situation And Tasks" issued on July 8, 1978, the general political department of the Vietnamese People's Army explicitly stipulated that "an offensive strategy" would be adopted against China, and that "a counter-attack and resolute offensive be carried out both within and beyond the frontier." The Vietnamese authorities built a great many fortifications and other military facilities in the border areas and stored large quantities of war material while clamouring for turning the border areas into "positions" and "fortresses" of war against China. The erstwhile peaceful and friendly Sino-Vietnamese border was turned by the Vietnamese authorities into a springbord for invading China. The erstwhile staging posts for receiving Chinese aid supplies were turned into strongholds for aggression against China. The rice which the Chinese people saved up through frugality, and sent as aid to the Vietnamese people became provisions for the Vietnamese armed forces in anti-China operations. The arms and ammunition China had given Vietnam for fighting its anti-imperialist wars were laid up for massacring Chinese armymen and civilians. It was from these posts that the Vietnamese armed forces constantly intruded into Chinese territory, bombarded and harassed China's border areas and created more and more armed provocations and bloodshed incidents. In 1978 the number of border incidents provoked by Vietnam rose sharply to more than 1,100. In the period from January 1 to February 16, 1979 alone the number reached 129. From the 1974 to the above-mentioned date, the Vietnamese authorities created a total of 3,535 border incidents. Vietnamese armed personnel frequently invaded and harassed our border villages, strafed and bombarded Chinese towns, schools, hospitals, dwellings, railway stations and trains, and killed Chinese border inhabitants and frontier personnel who had helped Vietnam with blood and sweat in its anti-imperialist struggle. In the short space of six months prior to February 16 this year, they invaded the Chinese border at 162 places and killed and wounded over 300 Chinese personnel. . . .

The Vietnamese authorities pride themselves on the large quantities of captured U.S. arms and ammunition and on Soviet-supplied planes, tanks and artillery and claim to be the "third strongest military power in the world" and "the strongest military power in Southeast Asia." Brandishing its might, Vietnam has carried out aggression and expansion and done harm to its neighboring countries. The Vietnamese authorities not only harbour the ambition to annex Chinese territory, but cannot wait to set up their long-dreamed of "Indochinese federation" as soon as the war ends and then proceed to dominate the whole of Southeast Asia. Toward this aim, they first brought Laos under their complete control, and then at the end of 1978 they brazenly launched the massive armed aggression against democratic Kampuchea and put it under their military occupation. . . .

To sum up, the Chinese government delegation has factually reviewed the problems existing in our relations in recent years, and particularly that of the armed border conflict, giving the true story and expounding its views. Facts show conclusively that the grave deterioration of Sino-Vietnamese relations is wholly the making of the Vietnamese authorities; it is the result of their pursuance of expansionist nationalism and a hostile anti-China policy with Soviet instigation and support. It has caused the Chinese government and people great pain and sorrow.

With a view to upholding the traditional friendship between the Chinese and Vietnamese peoples, and acting in the common interest of China and Vietnam and of the two peoples, as well as for the furtherance of peace and stability in Indochina, Southeast Asia and the Asia-Pacific region, the Chinese government delegation, animated by the sincere desire to settle questions, puts forward the following proposal of principles for handling the relations between China and Vietnam.

1. The two sides shall restore friendly and good-neighbourly relations between China and Vietnam on the basis of the five principles of mutual respect for sovereignty and territorial integrity, mutual non-aggression, non-interference in each other's internal affairs, equality and mutual benefit and peaceful coexistence. [These "Five Principles of Peaceful Coexistence" were enunciated by China at the Bandung Conference in 1955.] They shall seek a reasonable solution of the disputes and issues in the relations between the two countries through peaceful negotiations.

2. Neither side should seek hegemony in Indochina, Southeast Asia or any other part of the world, and each is opposed to efforts by any other country or group of countries to establish such hegemony.

   Neither side shall station troops in other countries, and those already stationed abroad must be withdrawn to their own country. Neither side shall join any military blocs directed against the other, provide military bases to other countries, or use the territory and bases of other countries to threaten, subvert or commit armed aggression against the other side or against any other countries.

3. The two sides respect the Sino-Vietnamese boundary line as delimited in the Sino-French boundary accords which shall serve as the basis for a negotiated settlement of their boundary and territorial disputes. Pending a settlement of the boundary question, each side shall strictly maintain the status quo of the boundary at the time when the central committees of the Chinese and Vietnamese parties exchanged letters in 1957–1958, and will not attempt to alter unilaterally and forcibly the actual extent to its jurisdiction along the border in any form or on any pretext.

4. Each side shall respect the other side's sovereignty over its twelve-nautical-mile territorial sea, and the two sides shall demarcate their respective economic zones and continental shelves in the Beibu Gulf and other sea areas

in a fair and reasonable way in accordance with the relevant principles of present-day international law of the sea.

5. The Xisha and Nansha islands have always been an inalienable part of China's territory. The Vietnamese side shall revert to its previous position of recognizing this fact and respect China's sovereignty over these two island groups and withdraw all its personnel from those islands in the Nansha group which it has occupied.

6. Nationals of one country residing in the other country shall respect the laws of that country and the ways and customs of the local people and shall endeavour to do their part for the economic and cultural development of that country. The government of the country of residence shall guarantee their proper rights and interests in regard to residence, travel, making a living and employment and safeguard their personal safety and lawfully acquired properties in that country.

   Each side shall treat all the nationals of the other side residing in its country in a friendly manner and must not persecute or illegally expel them.

7. The response to the legitimate wish for repatriation on the part of the Vietnamese citizens forcibly driven by the Vietnamese authorities into Chinese territory—the Vietnamese government should receive them back into the country and re-settle them in a proper manner as soon as possible. The Chinese government is ready to facilitate their early return in every way.

8. The restoration of railway traffic, trade, civil aviation, postal and telecommunication services and other bilateral ties shall be dealt with by the departments concerned of the two countries through consultations.

The above eight-point proposal put forward by us consists of fundamental principles for improving relations between China and Vietnam and for dealing with the relevant disputes. It is reasonable and practical, and it accords with the fundamental interests of the two people and meets with the wishes of the people of Southeast Asia and the world. If this proposal can be put into effect, it will remove the tension on the Sino-Vietnamese border, restore normal relations between the two countries, consolidate the traditional friendship between the two peoples and make a contribution to the maintenance of peace, security and stability in Indochina, Southeast Asia and the world. . . .

25.2 THE BACKGROUND TO *BITTER LOVE*, APRIL 1981

Bai Hua (b. 1930) was a PLA writer who joined the Communist party in 1949. He was criticized as a rightist in 1957 but after years of proscription as a writer was rehabilitated and returned to creative work in the late seventies. His screenplay for *Bitter Love* (Kulian) was one of the first works of art to explore the plight of intellectuals during the Cultural Revolution. Its stark portrayal of the fate of Chinese who returned from abroad to serve the Revolution caused it to be supressed and it was widely criticized and supressed in 1980.

In the article below, published by the *Liberation Army Daily* (Jiefangjun bao) in April 1981, Bai Hua was attacked for suggesting that the suffering of intellectuals in the Maoist era, attributed to the machinations of Lin Biao and the Gang of Four, was due, instead, to the socialist system and perhaps the Communist party itself. Bai, *Liberation Daily*'s critic suggested, was guilty of attacking the "motherland" by hinting that the love of intellectuals for China after 1949 was one-sided: "The more deeply you love the motherland, the more bitter your end will be."

The controversy over *Bitter Love* showed that the party was willing to examine the past on only its own terms. Party leaders were hostile to portraits of historical excesses that overstepped the definitions it provided; they were especially intolerant of works that dared to suggest, however indirectly, that Lin Biao, Jiang Qing, and other party renegades were not the only culprits when it came to the degradation of China's intellectuals.

As everyone knows, since the founding of New China, the Party has made tremendous achievements in its work concerning intellectuals. The Party Central Committee and Mao Zedong, Zhou Enlai and other leading comrades devoted a great deal of their energies and efforts to uniting with, winning over, transforming and training the intellectuals.

Of course, the Party has also made mistakes in policies towards the intellectuals since the founding of New China and should seriously sum up experience and draw lessons from them. Particularly during the "Great Cultural Revolution," vast numbers of intellectuals, as well as the Party's leading cadres at all levels and the masses of the people, suffered ruthless persecution by Lin Biao and the Gang of Four. This is a fact that remains fresh in people's memories.

. . . . Since the downfall of the Gang of Four, the Party and State have redressed many cases in which people were framed, falsely charged and wrongly sentenced and then had their names cleared. Facts have proved that the motherland [literally *zuguo*, the "ancestral land"] and the Party are concerned about and take good care of intellectuals and that the hearts of the masses of intellectuals have always turned to the motherland, the Party and socialism.

However, this is not the way "Bitter Love" describes them. One of the themes of the story is the relationship between intellectuals and the motherland. On the surface, the story does seem to describe the intellectuals' patriotism with bold strokes and striking colours. It describes how several intellectuals, filled with patriotic passion, returned to the motherland and how deeply each one of them was attached to the motherland. The author indeed has imparted to these characters quite a few patriotic words and deeds, even to the point of sometimes being touching.

However, this is not the point. The point is that by taking great pains to describe the love of a few intellectuals for the motherland, the author intends to contrast it with the motherland's lack of love for the intellectuals. Under the author's pen, not one of the returned intellectuals has had a happy experience and come to a good end. In short, the intellectuals' love for the motherland is merely one-sided, unrequited love. You love the motherland, but the motherland does not love you. The more deeply you love the motherland, the more bitter your end will be. Thus, the more vividly the story plays up the intellectuals' patriotic words and deeds, the sharper its condemnation of the motherland. This is the so-called "bitter love."

The depiction of this part of history is not intended to denounce and castigate Lin Biao and the Gang of Four but to accuse the ancestral land which suffered together with its 1,000 million sons and daughters. It is intended to equate Lin Biao and the Gang of Four, the handful of traitors, with the motherland and to sum up the crimes of Lin Biao and the Gang of Four in trampling on the patriotic intellectuals in the conclusion that the motherland does not love intellectuals. Thus, the intention is to reach the objective conclusion that the motherland is not worthy of love. How can this be called a hymn of patriotism? . . . .

First, "Bitter Love" confuses the essential distinction between the counter-revolutionary crimes of Lin Biao and the Gang of Four and the mistakes made by the great Marxist, Comrade Mao Zedong, in his later years. It points the spearhead of criticism not at Lin Biao and the Gang of Four but at Comrade Mao Zedong, the Party and the socialist system as a whole.

The story not only arranges for Xingxing, the painter's daughter, to flee the country in order to criticize the motherland's failure to love her sons and daughters but takes great pains to describe the tragic experience of the painter Ling Chenguang in the motherland in order to place the blame for the tragedy on the Party, the leader and the socialist system.

The finale as depicted in the script is a scene that develops like this: The time seems to be some time after the downfall of the Gang of Four. People are running in search of the missing painter. However the painter has already died a tragic death on the snow-covered ground. In the last moment of his life, he is seen carving with all his remaining strength a big question mark in the snowy ground, his cold body substituting for the dot of the question mark.

Thus, with its enormous question mark as the end, the script raises a question of major political importance before the audience. That is, who is to be blamed for the tragic life of Ling Chenguang? Although the author has not answered this question in so many words, he has offered a clear explanation through his overall portrayal. The work depicts Chinese society during the decade of the cultural revolution as a dark kingdom with no ray of light. What perplexes people even more, despite their repeated pondering over the matter, is that while the author has maintained that his work is about the 10 chaotic years, there is no scene in the entire script that can arouse hatred among the people for Lin Biao and the Gang of Four. Why is this? Instead, many devices like metaphors and insinuations are employed in the script to direct its spearhead squarely at the Party, Party leaders and at the socialist system.

Third, "Bitter Love" not only draws no distinction between socialist New China and semi-feudal and semi-colonial Old China, but it does not distinguish either between the different intrinsic characteristics of the socialist system and the capitalist system. As a result, while debasing the socialist motherland, it also enhances capitalist society and advertises the bourgeois idea of humanism. By employing methods peculiar to film-making, the work alternately describes Ling Chenguang's escape both in the period of the old society and in the period of the new society to liken New China to Old China and show that the new society is just as dark as the old society. . . .

To portray the great and tortuous course we have traversed in the 31 years since the founding of our country is undoubtedly an important task for the writers and artists of China. Yet it is also a very complex and arduous task. The Party Central Committee has earnestly given us this admonition: With regard to the appraisal of the Party's work since the founding of our country, we must fully affirm the tremendous achievements made over the past 31 years. Shortcomings and mistakes should be criticized seriously, but they must not be described as utterly hopeless. . . .

25.3 AND 25.4 DENG LIQUN ON PROPAGANDA

The era of the Four Modernizations brought China into increased contact with "greater China" and the rest of the world. Videotapes, records, pirated books and magazines, and works of literature from Hong Kong and Taiwan poured into China in a manner unprecedented since 1949. Within the Chinese Communist party, this was a confusing time. Many powerful figures in the senior tier of the party leadership remained wedded to ideological formulations of earlier eras and, although they were willing to tolerate a measure of dissent and criticism, they felt deep skepticism toward a variety of cultural forms produced in the capitalist world.

Deng Liqun, director of the Propaganda Department of the CCP, represented the view of the party old guard. When Deng Xiaoping, in a closed meeting with party leaders in the winter of 1983, denounced "spiritual pollution" (*jingshen wuran*), his propaganda minister was quick to provide an explanation of this term and how it might be employed.

The campaign against "spiritual pollution" was short-lived but it indicated the ambivalence felt by party leaders as they contemplated the vast cultural changes that started to transform China in the reform era. In the two documents that follow, Deng Liqun defines spirtual pollution and suggests how it must be accommodated to "Marxism–Leninism–Mao Zedong Thought."

25.3 Deng Liqun on Clearing Cultural Contamination, October 28, 1983

.... He [Deng Liqun in a meeting with reporters] cited four main categories of cultural contamination:

—Spreading things which are obscene or reactionary;
—Vulgar taste in artistic performances which do not give aesthetic enjoyment but rather make people feel disgusted;
—Efforts to seek personal gain, indulgence in individualism, anarchism, liberalism, etc. The Constitution expressly provides for the rights and obligations of the citizen and it follows that no individual is permitted to harm the interests of the collective, the society and the state. There are indeed some people inside the Communist Party who took advantage of their power and positions to further their personal interests to the detriment of others in the state and the society;
—Writing articles or delivering speeches that run counter to the country's social system which is explicitly laid out in the Constitution.

Activities under the first category involve criminal offences and must be banned in accordance with law.... The three other categories are all ideological problems and should be dealt with through education, criticism, and self criticism....

It is necessary to do a good job both in rectifying the Party and clearing away cultural contamination, he [Deng] said. The Central Committee has pointed out the need to overcome weak and slack leadership; such leaders underestimate the harm these elements have done to the Party and are not fully aware of the importance of clearing away cultural contamination, and have failed to take resolute measures. In this sense, [a] Rightist tendency is to be opposed....

There are worries among friends abroad that the Party consolidation might go perfunctorily or that it might take up the form of the "cultural revolution," he [Deng Liqun] said. But most of those leading the Party consolidation at all levels were themselves subjected to such methods during the "cultural revolution" and had suffered enough. "We will not do unto others what they did unto us," he said.

Deng Liqun traced the cultural contamination to domestic and foreign causes. On the domestic side, he said, the socialist system has been established in China and the exploiting class no longer exists as a class, but the influence of the old society still exists everywhere and has grown in the recent period.

China has followed a policy of opening to the outside world in the past few years. This policy has achieved remarkable successes but has also created new problems. Those Communist Party members and cadres who have been affected by outside influences should be educated, but eliminating cultural contamination will neither shake nor stop the open policy. Getting rid of decadence will only benefit the further development of China's economic and cultural changes with the outside world.

China has always insisted on an analytical approach towards things from the West, and will continue to accept the good while rejecting the bad, Deng Liqun said. Even advanced things should be adapted to China's national conditions rather than mechanically copied, he added. The open policy, he said, will be carried on and developed along an ever-broader path.

25.4 *Deng Liqun on the Scope of Spiritual Pollution, December 7, 1983*

.... Our ideological and political work has made some progress in the past few years, but it still has not become an important item on the agenda. We should firmly focus our work on economic construction and must not waver on this question. However, we must not think that as the economy is pushed forward, people will naturally increase their consciousness; and that even if we give up or neglect ideological and political work, we still can push economic construction forward. Ideological and political work is the lifeblood of economic and all other work. The correctness of this conclusion of Comrade Mao Zedong has been further proved by current practice. Ideological and political work must be strengthened, not slackened. If there is the slightest negligence in this respect, problems of one kind or another are hard to avoid in our economic, technical, and other fields of work. Neglecting ideological and political work is not in keeping with the character of our Party, our socialist state system and the basic theories of Marxism–Leninism–Mao Zedong Thought. We must never forget that while transforming the objective world, people must also transform their subjective world.

Prior to the victory of the revolution, we need to imbue the workers and people with ideas of scientific socialism and integrate scientific socialism with the workers' movement and the people's revolutionary struggle. After the victory of the revolution, we still need to imbue the people and workers and staff members with ideas of scientific socialism, Marxism–Leninism–Mao Zedong Thought and the Party Central Committee's line, principles, and policies. To do this, it is necessary to strengthen and improve ideological and political work. . . .

Spiritual pollution is, in essence, the spreading of decadent ideas of every description of the bourgeois and other exploiting classes and feelings of distrust of the socialist and communist cause and Communist Party leadership. Whatever spreads these ideas and feelings is spiritual pollution and must be eliminated. Other kinds of problems are not spiritual pollution and should not be arbitrarily regarded as spiritual pollution. A clear line of demarcation must be drawn and the target should not be enlarged. . . .

25.5 LIU BINYAN: A CASE OF PERSECUTION IN XI'AN IN DISREGARD OF CENTRAL INSTRUCTIONS, AUGUST 25, 1984

After 1979, a number of prominent "rightist" intellectuals who had disappeared from public life in 1957 were rehabilitated and again permitted to work in cultural fields within which they had earned their fame some twenty years before. One such intellectual was Liu Binyan (b. 1925), a famous investigative journalist and ace practitioner of the genre known as "reportorial literature" (*baogao wenxue*). Liu was a major target in the antirightist campaign and the reappearance of his byline on the pages of *People's Daily* was an indication that the party was willing to forgive those it castigated in the past for political errors and welcome their contributions in the new era of reform and modernization.

Liu Binyan emerged form obscurity with a critical spirit in no way diminished by years of persecution and hardship. His reports once again established him as a powerful and controversial figure in Chinese journalism and provided some of the most searching and acid portraits of everyday life that had ever appeared during China's years "under the red flag."

The following article, written between March and June 1984, indicates the problems faced by China—in this case in the setting of the Xi'an local government—as the legal system addressed grievances inherited from previous eras. As Liu's report indicates, former victims of Maoist-era politics, like Guo Jianxing and his family, were often at a disadvantage in court as networks of *guanxi* (relationships) came into play to prevent the reversal of confiscations of property and other illegal acts that occurred in the context of political movements of earlier decades. The article illustrates the imperfect separation of the party and judiciary that continued to frustrate legal reformers in the eighties. This article provoked an enormous controversy when it appeared and helped lead to Liu's expulsion from the CCP in 1987.[1]

"THE RIGHTS AND WRONGS OVER THE PAST 38 YEARS"

A reversal:

Because of China's enormous size many stories go unheard. Lately a seventy-two year old man named Guo Jianying became a defendant and the No. 2 branch of the Xian housing and land management bureau, which 12 years ago occupied the backyard of Guo Jiangying's house and robbed him of his property, took on the role of plaintiff. On 7th December 1983, the branch bureau gathered people together and sent dozens of armed men and a prison van to pull down a shed in the backyard of Guo's house (142, Qingnian Street, Xian city). By order of Liang Ping, Vice President of the Lianhu district court, they also brutally raided Guo's family.

There was a bigger reversal: Another reason why old Guo became the defendant was that in 1946, he lent a large sum of money to the New Fourth Army, which was in a difficult position in southern Shaanxi at that time, to help it solve a pressing need.

In 1958 [at the time of the antirightist campaign], the following logic was employed: If Guo Jianying could find so much money to support the revolution, was it possible that he was not a capitalist? The answer was no: He had to have been a capitalist.

This was the original theoretical basis for "transforming" his private house. In 1966, yet a new logic was applied: Why would a capitalist be willing to take out so much money to support the revolution? His support must have been insincere. And so Guo was thrown into a "cowshed" on the charge of "perpetrating a political fraud by misrepresenting himself." He and his family were in dire straits.

In 1972, a looter named Gu Laigen of the No. 2 branch of the Xian housing and land management bureau took over the backyard of the Guo house and built a posh five-room house with an exclusive courtyard for Zhang Jintang, a section-chief who controlled the city materials bureau. During the construction, the seepage pit in the backyard was filled in, two brick toilets were destroyed, eight trees were felled and Guo Jianping's property was stripped from him.

After ten years China entered a new historical period. But Gu Laigen was still able to ride roughshod over the Guos. Supported by a friend named Shi Zhaoyi, who was chief of the financial section of the city housing and land

---

1. Liu Binyan's investigation of Guo Jianying and its results are described in Liu Binyan, *A Higher Kind of Loyalty* (New York: Random House, 1990), pp. 179–190.

management bureau, Gu Laigen had the house with its exclusive courtyard pulled down. He wanted to construct a building for the provincial timber company by expanding the area of construction to the north. This meant occupying nearly the whole courtyard. Guo Jianying was driven beyond forebearance and, encouraged by the line of the third plenary session of the 11th CCP Central Committee, he rose in resistance against these people. He claimed an "unfulfilled correction."

Knowing that Leftist errors were often at the root of private legal interests and that in many cases houses and property were at stake, Vice Mayor Li Tingbi, who has been in charge of Xian urban construction for many years, decided to investigate six families. An investigation group led by Wang Jianpeng conducted a careful and practical investigation for four months and a conclusion was made that the socialist transformation of four of the houses in 1958, including that of the Guos, was wrong. At a routine affairs meeting of mayors on 16th June 1983, mayors and vice mayors maintained that mistakes should be corrected and property rights should be restored to the owners. But Zhang Huaide, chief of the city housing and land management bureau, who attended the meeting, raised an objection and proposed that the returning of two private houses should be postponed. Guo Jianying's house was one of the two.

In the twenty-six years since 1958, the members of the Guo family grew more numerous and Guo Jianying's children were now adults. Since 1980, the Guos applied twice to build a house in the courtyard. But the housing and land management bureau did not approve their application. The family had no choice but to build a twelve square meter shed in the backyard for the youngest son to dwell in.

Although this wretched little shed was far from the construction site [of the building for the provincial timber company], Gu Laigen insisted that the shed was hampering the progress of construction. Guo's family maintained that the construction was in itself illegal and that the property ruined and taken away in 1972 should be returned. Vice Mayor Li Tingbi supported Guo's family's reasonable and legal request. He instructed both sides to talk the matter over and suggested that construction projects should be suspended until the dispute was solved. Having strong backing, Shi Zhaoyi and Gu Laigen turned a deaf ear to the vice mayor's instruction. They lodged a suit with the Lianhu district court against Guo Jianying. Thus, a tug-of-war with great disparity in strength began.

"EVEN IF THE DECISION IS WRONG, IT MUST BE CARRIED OUT."

The plaintiff's superiority was clear: "It" was a "unit" and "organisation" safeguarding "state interests"; whereas the defendant was a family pursuing its private affairs.

Guo Jianying, however, had a rare, favourable condition: President Li Xiannian issued two instructions with regard to his appeal.[2] On many occasions, Comrade Ma Wenrui, First Secretary of the Shaanxi Provincial CCP Committee, instructed the Xian city CCP Committee seriously to implement President Li Xiannian's instructions. Comrade Wang Feng, a member of the Central Advisory Commission . . . was the most authoritative person who could stand witness to the problem concerning Guo Jianying's lending money. He instructed a responsible comrade to advise Comrade He Chenghua, Secretary of the Xian city CCP Committee, not to violate Comrade Li Xiannian's instructions so as to avoid committing mistakes.

On the night of 5th December 1983, Comrade Wang Feng, who was then at Xian, learned that the Xian city court had made a decision to pull down the shed in Guo's backyard the following day. He called Secretary He Chenghua, telling him to put off the decision. However, Secretary He Chenghua resolutely took the opposite step. He told Li Tianshun, his personal secretary, to inform Guo Jianying: "Even if the decision is wrong, it must be implemented. In the future, if the verdict passed on you is reversed, I will have the building which has been constructed pulled down. But for now the decision must be implemented." The reason was that "the Party must not interfere in judicial affairs."

What Secretary He Chenghua said was contrary to the fact. Without the interference by some Xian leaders, the case would not have been placed on file for prosecution. From the beginning, some comrades of the Lianhu district court maintained that the case was a dispute over property rights, involved the problem of implementing policies and should be handled by the Party and government departments concerned. They placed the case on file for investigation only after they had received instructions from some "city leaders." Also, only after the district court submitted the files to Secretary He Chenghu for approval was the judgment made.

With a high sense of organisation and discipline, the district court and the intermediate court fulfilled their tasks exceptionally fast. Not only did they turn a blind eye to the plaintiff's violation of civil lawsuit procedures, but they themselves also violated the procedures. They shortened the process of examination and approval so as to enable Gu Laigen and his followers to continue the projects as soon as possible, as Gu Laigen and his followers had been waiting impatiently. . . .

In late December, Secretary He Chenghua wanted to implement President Li Xiannian's instructions. He formed an investigation group for Guo Jianying's case. To investigate what? First, to investigate the problem of Guo Jianying lending the money in 1948. The three investigations made over the past twenty years and more, Comrade Li Xiannian's instructions and Comrade Wang

---

2. Here we see that intervention from the highest level of the central government failed to deter local authorities.

Feng's testimony did not count. Second, to investigate the problem of trans-forming Guo Jianying's private house. The former investigation was to be car-ried out by an investigation group of the city government and the conclusion made by the vice mayors of the city did not count.

By selecting testimony which had been negated by a witness who possessed first-hand materials and by relying on other testimony inappropriately obtained by a lawyer engaged by the housing and land management bureau, the city CCP Committee investigation group tried to prove that Guo Jianying was forced to "deliver" the money to the New Fourth Army instead of willingly lending the money to the army. To arrive at this conclusion, the investigation group distorted history and brought shame on the New Fourth Army. It asserted that the southern Shaanxi Party and army adopted the policy of "beat-ing rich people" and the method of "canvassing votes," which in fact they never did. It even went so far as to say that because Guo Jiangying informed against a guerrilla leader, the guerrilla leader was killed by the enemy. It did so in disregard of the fact that since 1958, this allegation was negated twice by a more reliable witness and that recently Comrade Wang Feng testified that the killing of the guerrilla leader had nothing to do with Guo Jianying.

In its scrutiny of the matter of private houses, the city CCP Committee's investigation group did no more than to negate the investigation carried out by the city government and to affirm the mistake in 1958, that is, houses in a compound with an entrance or entrances commonly used by the dwellers were regarded as houses being rented. The purpose of this regulation was to make up the figure of 150 sq.m., which was the minimum area fixed for "transfor-mation." [This technicality made it possible to take over the Guo property.] So the site in Guo's backyard was "transformed." Otherwise, the occupation of Guo's backyard would have been unreasonable.

To be perfectly safe, it was necessary to make an alteration on the class status of Guo Jianying. In 1980, in line with the Central (1979) Document No 84, the Lanzhou motor transport company of Gansu Province, where Guo Jianying worked, determined Guo's class status as "petty proprietor," which belongs to the category of the working people. But the city CCP Committee investigation group maintained that the classification was a little biased toward the "Right." So it started collecting materials concerning Guo Jianying in an attempt to prove that the classification had been carried out in a "minor key." It would be a good idea to determine Guo's class status as capitalist, as this would legalise the transformation of his private house in 1958 and would make unassailable every-thing done by the housing and land management bureau, by Gu Laigen, by the court and by the city CCP Committee.

This was how the principal leaders of the Xian city CCP Committee imple-mented the "practical" spirit of the third plenary session of the 11th CCP Central Committee and President Li Xiannian's instructions with regard to Guo Jianying's problem. A person is invincible if he has the power to distribute houses.

In this drama, which was focused on Guo Jianying, Gu Laigen played a very important part. Gu was a low-level cadre of the housing and land management bureau. Everybody knew that during the "cultural revolution," he commanded an attack on the city CCP Committee and that he was a "two-gun" tyrant. But in his files, there is not even a single line carrying records of his activities during the "Cultural Revolution," nor can a trace of his several years' imprisonment be found, (it was also struck off the table of contents). He often used the "house distribution tickets" he possessed to threaten or bribe people. He was good at using hard and soft tactics to force families out of the sites to be used for capital construction. Because of all this, many people dared not offend him, as he was quite useful to them.

In this affair, Gu Laigen just demonstrated his power. He could instruct the public security bureau to threaten Guo's family. He could hire some twenty gangsters to beat the Guo family and to carry out kidnappings. He could also control judicial departments. Why did Xu Pei, judge of the Lianhu district court, side with Gu Laigen, ignore the most rudimentary legal proceedings and shorten the process of examination? His purpose was to get a house, and indeed, he got one with two large rooms. Why did Yang Qingxiu of the city intermediate court overstep his authority to remove obstacles for Gu Laigen and to engage Liu so and so, lawyer of the Legal Advisory Department? And why did Liu so and so, a part-time lawyer, illegally open an introduction letter and take risks (because it was illegal) in investigating Guo Jianying's history and class status, which had nothing to do with the case? . . . Obviously, each had his own purpose.

What did Gu Laigen and his behind-the-scenes backer—Shi Zhaoyi, chief of the financial section of the housing and land management bureau—intend to have? The provincial timber company had long agreed to provide them with 15 houses and a fund of 300,000 yuan. In addition, Gu Laigen got another thing: He and his wife were transferred back to Shanghai to work in a Shanghai-based Shaanxi office. Dark forces and dirty tricks

Now we can faintly see a "united front" encircling Guo's family. . . .

Of course, Guo Jianying is not a hero. But, after all, he made some contributions to the victory of the liberation war. Also, he was a victim of "Leftist" mistakes. The CCP Central Committee has issued explicit policies and instructions with regard to his rewards and the way to treat him. But why does the Xian city CCP Committee still adhere to their "Leftist" principles in handling his case? Why does the Xian city CCP Committee persist in their Rightist principles in dealing with Gu Laigen and his followers, who have serious problems both in politics and morality and who rode roughshod in the 10 years of internal disorder? Can creators and supporters of this affair be regarded as persons keeping abreast with the CCP Central Committee politically?

25.6 THE JOINT AGREEMENT BY BRITAIN AND CHINA DEFINING THE FUTURE OF HONG KONG, SEPTEMBER 26, 1984

After 1949, Hong Kong and its tiny neighbor Macao remained the final colonial possessions on Chinese soil controlled by foreign powers. For decades they were permitted by the PRC to continue to exist because they played a useful role in the trade and commerce of China. Hong Kong, in particular, served as a door to the external world that could be opened and closed at will.

The some 400 square miles that constitute Hong Kong and the New Territories were defined by a set of treaties signed in 1842, 1860, and 1898. The last of these gave Great Britain a ninety-eight year lease on the New Territories that was due to expire in 1997. The imminent expiration of this lease triggered the negotiations between Peking and London that culminated in the Joint Declaration of 1984, which defined how Hong Kong would be reincorporated into Chinese society after July 1, 1997.

In these negotiations the Chinese stressed that Hong Kong would be treated, per the Chinese constitution, as a Special Administrative Region (SAR); it would maintain its own laws and economic Peking's system without interference from China. Two ruling slogans that summarized Peking's approach to reversion were: "No changes for fifty years" and "One country, two systems." As Hong Kong was restored to China the world watched expectantly to see whether the city's anomalous path to a postcolonial future would follow the guidelines laid out in the joint agreement.

The Government of the United Kingdom of Great Britain and Northern Ireland and the Government of the People's Republic of China have reviewed with satisfaction the friendly relations existing between the two Governments and peoples in recent years and agreed that a proper negotiated settlement of the question of Hong Kong, which is left over from the past, is conducive to the maintenance of the prosperity and stability of Hong Kong and to the further strengthening and development of the relations between the two countries on a new basis. To this end, they have, after talks between the delegations of the two Governments, agreed to declare as follows:

(1)

The Government of the People's Republic of China declares that to recover the Hong Kong area (including Hong Kong Island, Kowloon and the New Territories, herein after referred to as Hong Kong) is the common aspiration of the entire Chinese people and that it has decided to resume the exercise of sovereignty over Hong Kong with effect from 1 July 1997.

(2)

The Government of the United Kingdom declares that it will restore Hong Kong to the People's Republic of China with effect from 1 July 1997.

(3)

The Government of the People's Republic of China declares that the basic policies of the People's Republic of China regarding Hong Kong are as follows:

(1) Upholding national unity and territorial integrity and taking account of the history of Hong Kong and its realities, the People's Republic of China has decided to establish, in accordance with the provisions of Article 31 of the Constitution of the People's Republic of China, a Hong Kong Special Administrative Region upon resuming the exercise of sovereignty over Hong Kong.

(2) The Hong Kong Special Administrative Region will be directly under the authority of the Central People's Government of the People's Republic of China. The Hong Kong Special Administrative Region will enjoy a high degree of autonomy except in foreign and defense affairs, which are the responsibilities of the Central People's Government.

(3) The Hong Kong Special Administrative Region will be vested with executive, legislative and independent judicial power, including that of final adjudication. The laws currently in force in Hong Kong will remain basically unchanged.

(4) The Government of the Hong Kong Special Administrative Region will be composed of local inhabitants. The chief executive will be appointed by the Central People's Government on the basis of the results of elections or consultations to be held locally.

Principal officials will be nominated by the chief executive of the Hong Kong Special Administrative Region for appointment by the Central People's Government. Chinese and foreign nationals previously working in the public and police services in the government departments of Hong Kong may remain in employment. British and other foreign nationals may also be employed to serve as advisers or hold certain public posts in government departments of the Hong Kong Special Administrative Region.

(5) The current social and economic systems in Hong Kong will remain unchanged, and so will the life style. Rights and freedoms, including those of the person, of speech, of the press, of assembly, of association, of travel, of movement, of correspondence, of strike, of choice of occupation, of academic research and of religious belief will be insured by

law in the Hong Kong Special Administrative Region. Private property, ownership of enterprises, legitimate right of inheritance and foreign investment will be protected by law.

(6) The Hong Kong Special Administrative Region will retain the status of a free port and a separate customs territory.

(7) The Hong Kong Special Administrative Region will retain the status of an international financial center, and its markets for foreign exchange, gold, securities and futures will continue. There will be free flow of capital. The Hong Kong dollar will continue to circulate and remain freely convertible.

(8) The Hong Kong Special Administrative Region will have independent finances. The Central People's Government will not levy taxes on the Hong Kong Special Administrative Region.

(9) The Hong Kong Special Administrative Region may establish mutually beneficial economic relations with the United Kingdom and other countries, whose economic interests in Hong Kong will be given due regard.

(10) Using the name of "Hong Kong, China," the Hong Kong Special Administrative Region may on its own maintain and develop economic and cultural relations and conclude relevant agreements with states, regions and relevant international organizations.

The government of the Hong Kong Special Administrative Region may on its own issue travel documents for entry into and exit from Hong Kong.

(11) The maintenance of public order in the Hong Kong Special Administrative Region will be the responsibility of the government of the Hong Kong Special Administrative Region.

(12) The above-stated basic policies of the People's Republic of China regarding Hong Kong and the elaboration of them in Annex I to this joint declaration will be stipulated, in a Basic Law of the Hong Kong Special Administrative Region of the People's Republic of China, by the National People's Congress of the People's Republic of China, and they will remain unchanged for 50 years.

ANNEX I

Elaboration by the People's Republic of China of Its Basic Policies. The Constitution of the People's Republic of China stipulates in Article 31 that "the state may establish special administrative regions when necessary. The systems to be instituted in special administrative regions shall be prescribed by laws enacted by the National People's Congress in the light of the specific conditions." In accordance with this article, upon the resumption of the exercise of sovereignty over Hong Kong on 1 July 1997, the National People's Congress shall enact and promulgate a basic law of the Hong Kong Special Administrative Region stipulating that after the establishment of the Hong Kong Special Administrative Region, the socialist system and socialist policies shall not be practiced in the Hong Kong Special Administrative Region and that Hong Kong's previous capitalist system and life style shall remain unchanged for 50 years.

The government and legislature of the Hong Kong Special Administrative Region shall be composed of local inhabitants. The chief executive shall be selected by election or through consultations held locally and be appointed by the Central People's Government. Principal officials (equivalent to secretaries) shall be nominated by the chief executive of the Hong Kong Special Administrative Region and appointed by the Central People's Government. The legislature of the Hong Kong Special Administrative Region shall be constituted by elections. The executive authorities shall abide by the law and be accountable to the legislature.

LANGUAGE AND FLAG

In addition to Chinese, English may also be used in organs of government and in the courts in the Hong Kong Special Administrative Region.

Apart from displaying the national flag and national emblem of the People's Republic of China, the Hong Kong Special Administrative Region may use a regional flag and emblem of its own.

The Hong Kong Special Administrative Region shall maintain the capitalist economic and trade systems previously practiced in Hong Kong. The Hong Kong Special Administrative Region government shall decide its economic and trade policies on its own. Rights concerning the ownership of property, including those relating to acquisition, use, disposal, inheritance and compensation for lawful deprivation (corresponding to the real value of the property concerned, freely convertible and paid without undue delay) shall continue to be protected by law.

The Hong Kong Special Administrative Region shall retain the status of a free port and continue a free trade policy, including the free movement of goods and capital. The Hong Kong Special Administrative Region may on its own maintain and develop economic and trade relations with all states and regions.

The Hong Kong Special Administrative Region shall be a separate customs territory. It may participate in relevant international organizations and international trade agreements (including preferential trade agreements) such as the General Agreement on Tariffs and Trade and arrangements regarding international trade in textiles. Export quotas, tariff preferences and other similar arrangements obtained by the Hong Kong Special Administrative Region shall be enjoyed exclusively by the Hong Kong Special Administrative Region. The Hong Kong Special Administrative Region shall have authority to issue its own certificates of origin for products manufactured locally, in accordance with prevailing rules of origin.

The Hong Kong Special Administrative Region may, as necessary, establish official and semiofficial economic and trade missions in foreign countries, reporting the establishment of such missions to the Central People's Government for the record.

FINANCIAL CENTER

The Hong Kong Special Administrative Region shall retain the status of an international financial center. The monetary and financial systems previously practiced in Hong Kong, including the systems of regulation and supervision of deposit-taking institutions and financial markets, shall be maintained.

The Hong Kong Special Administrative Region government may decide its monetary and financial policies on its own. It shall safeguard the free operation of financial business and the free flow of capital within, into and out of the Hong Kong Special Administrative Region. No exchange control policy shall be applied in the Hong Kong Special Administrative Region. Markets for foreign exchange, gold, securities and futures shall continue.

The Hong Kong dollar, as the local legal tender, shall continue to circulate and remain freely convertible. The authority to issue Hong Kong currency shall be vested in the Hong Kong Special Administrative Region government. Hong Kong currency bearing references inappropriate to the status of Hong Kong as a Special Administrative Region of the People's Republic of China shall be progressively replaced and withdrawn from circulation.

The Exchange Fund shall be managed and controlled by the Hong Kong Special Administrative Region government, primarily for regulating the exchange value of the Hong Kong dollar.

The Hong Kong Special Administrative region shall maintain Hong Kong's previous systems of shipping management and shipping regulation, including the system for regulating conditions of seamen. . . .

DIPLOMATIC RELATIONS

Subject to the principle that foreign affairs are the responsibility of the Central People's Government, representatives of the Hong Kong Special Administrative Region government may participate, as members of delegations of the Government of the People's Republic of China, in negotiations at the diplomatic level directly affecting the Hong Kong Special Administrative Region conducted by the Central People's Government. The Hong Kong Special Administrative Region may on its own, using the name "Hong Kong, China," maintain and develop relations and conclude and implement agreements with states, regions and relevant international organizations in the appropriate fields, including the economic, trade, financial and monetary, shipping, communications, touristic, cultural and sporting fields.

The application to the Hong Kong Special Administrative Region of international agreements to which the People's Republic of China is or becomes a party shall be decided by the Central People's Government, in accordance with the circumstances and needs of the Hong Kong Special Administrative Region, and after seeking the views of the Hong Kong Special Administrative Region government....

POLICE POWER

The maintenance of public order in the Hong Kong Special Administrative Region shall be the responsibility of the Hong Kong Special Administrative Region government. Military forces sent by the Central People's Government to be stationed in the Hong Kong Special Administrative Region for the purpose of defense shall not interfere in the internal affairs of the Hong Kong Special Administrative Region. Expenditure for these military forces shall be borne by the Central People's Government.

Religious organizations and believers may maintain their relations with religious organizations and believers everywhere, and schools, hospitals and welfare institutions run by religious organizations in the Hong Kong Special Administrative Region and those in other parts of the People's Republic of China shall be based on the principles of non-subordination, noninterference and mutual respect....

25.7–25.9 FANG LIZHI AND THE PARTY

To achieve the Four Modernizations, the party had to win back the sympathy of China's intellectuals. Their expertise was a precondition for the success of the regime's ambitious reform scheme. But after the oppressions of the Cultural Revolution, intellectuals were wary of the party's overtures. Moreover, China's intellectuals considered the Four Modernizations a limited reform program. In 1978 and 1979, they began calling for a "fifth" modernization—a modernization of the entire legal, intellectual, and political framework of Chinese life. Reform, they argued, could not work without democracy. And democracy came to be synonymous with a withering away of the whole repressive apparatus of thought control produced by Maoism. In advocating a fifth modernization, intellectuals placed themselves on a collision course with the conservative Party elite who wanted change to occur only on their terms.

Fang Lizhi, an astrophysicist and, for a time, vice-chancellor of the prestigious University of Science and Technology in Hefei, Anhui, emerged in the mid-1980s as one of the most outspoken exponents of radical change. As his 1987 interview with Italian journalist Tiziano Terzani, given shortly after Fang's expulsion from the Communist party, shows, Fang's criticisms were clearly calculated to jangle the nerves of China's party elders. His views directly inspired prodemocracy demonstrations on the campus of the University of Science and Technology and other schools in 1986 and caused the party's leaders to see Fang as a dangerous trouble-maker. After being driven from the party, he was also stripped of his position in Anhui. Fang became a research fellow within the Academy of Sciences in Peking, where he continued to advocate reform and rallied support in the capital for a sweeping democratization of Chinese life.

Fang Lizhi argued that Marxism-Leninism was an outdated pseudoscience and that democracy was the only hope for a thorough reform. He vigorously criticized corruption in high places and called for laws to guarantee fundamental human rights. His articulate platform for change became an inspiration for the Tiananmen prodemocracy demonstrations in the spring of 1989. After the suppression of this popular movement, Fang Lizhi was obliged to seek refuge in the American Embassy in Peking.

In addition to Fang Lizhi's interview with Terzani, we have included two harsh criticisms of Fang printed in *People's Daily* in January 1987. They suggest the extreme irritation that his efforts to promote democracy and human rights provoked within officialdom. For the party leaders, Fang Lizhi's thinking was an intolerable type of heterodoxy; it struck at the very foundation of their power and subverted their worldview.

25.7   Fang Lizhi's Interview with Tiziano Terzani, 1987

Professor Fang, among Chinese students you are a hero. The international press has hailed you as China's Sakharov. Deng Xiaoping, on the other hand, calls you a "bad element." China's Communist Party maintains you are a victim of the disease called "bourgeois liberalization." What are you really?

A little bit of all of these. But in the first place I am an astrophysicist. The natural sciences are my religion. Einstein once said something of the sort. Previously I did not understand him. Now I know: we scientists have a belief and an aim, we have an obligation towards society. If we discover a truth and society does not accept it, this weighs on us. This is what happened to Galileo. That is when, as scientists, we have to intervene. With this mission I step into society.

What kind of mission do you have in China?

Democratization. Without democracy there can be no development. Unless individual human rights are recognized there can be no true democracy. In China the very ABC of democracy is unknown. We have to educate ourselves for democracy. We have to understand that democracy isn't something that our leaders can hand down to us. A democracy that comes from above is no democracy, it is nothing but a relaxation of control. The fight will be intense. But it cannot be avoided.

First you have attacked local Party cadres, then the Municipal Party Committee of Peking. Recently you attacked the Politburo. What is your next target?

Next I will criticize Marxism itself.

You go very far.

It is an undeniable truth that Marxism is no longer of much use. As a scientist I can prove it. Most answers given by Marxism with regard to the natural sciences are obsolete, some are even downright wrong. That is a fact. What Marxism has to say about the natural sciences stems from Engels' book *Natural Dialectics*. On nearly every page of this book one can find something that is either outdated or completely incorrect.

For example?

In the 1960s, with the aid of Marxism, the USSR and China repeatedly criticized the results of modern natural sciences. In biology they criticized genetics, in physics they criticized the theory of relativity and extended their criticism from cosmology to the development of the computer. Not even once has their criticism been proved correct. Therefore, how can one say today that Marxism should lead the natural sciences? It's a fallacy.

Have you ever believed in Marxism?

I certainly have! Immediately after Liberation [1949] and in the 1950s I firmly believed in Marxism. In 1955, when I joined the Party, I was convinced that Marxism would lead the way in every field and that the Communist Party was thoroughly good.

When, in 1958, during the Anti-Rightist Campaign, I was expelled from the Party, I made a very sincere self-criticism. I was convinced that I had wronged the Party. Now the Party has expelled me a second time, but this time I know that I was not in the wrong. Therefore I have refused to make a self-criticism.

Deng stated in 1979 that, in conformity with the Chinese Constitution, every citizen should be guided by the Four Basic Principles: the socialist road, the people's democratic dictatorship, leadership of the Party, and Marxism-Leninism and Mao Zedong Thought.

Marxism is a thing of the past. It helps us to understand the problems of the last century, not those of today. The same is true in the case of physics. Newton developed his theory 300 years ago. It is still valuable, but it does not help to solve today's problems, such as those related to computer technology. Marxism belongs to a precise epoch of civilization and that era is over. It is like old clothing that must be put aside. . . .

In 1978 something similar was said when the worker Wei Jingsheng wrote on a wall in Peking, which later became known as Democracy Wall: "Without democracy, there will be no modernization!" He got 15 years in prison for it. You, Professor Fang, are still free. Is it because you are a well-known scientist, whereas Wei Jingsheng was nothing but an electrician?

Of course. That's how things are in China. A worker who says something objectionable can easily be removed. Workers' unrest does not worry the government; workers are easily dealt with. Right now there are quite a few [workers'] disturbances, but the public is not aware of them. One knows nothing of them overseas, for these people have no international contacts.

Are things different in the case of the intellectuals?

Whenever it is students who demonstrate, the government is more concerned. It does not dare to take action as easily against students. That is why I maintain that the power of the intellectuals is relatively great. That is why I keep telling my students: he who has knowledge also has influence, and cannot be disregarded by the government. I advise my students not to say too much at first, but to study diligently. Those, however, who have successfully completed their studies must speak out. Wei Jingsheng spoke out ten years ago. Today I speak like he did. In another ten years perhaps other scholars may also speak up. People should be allowed to criticize their leaders without fear. This is a sign of democracy. . . .

What about human rights in China?

It is a dangerous topic. The question of human rights is taboo in China. Things are far worse than in the Soviet Union. Wei Jingsheng is a famous case, but there are thousands of others whose names are not even known. At least in the Soviet Union there are name lists. Not so in China. . . .

What is going to happen after Deng Xiaoping dies?

In the short run we might be worse off; in the long run, better. It's possible that after Deng's death Mao Zedong Thought will no longer be considered valid and then we will finally be able to make a radical reassessment of the past thirty years. That is probably just what General Secretary Hu Yaobang, who was demoted in January, planned to do. He once said that not one portrait of Mao should be left hanging in China. The last one hangs on the Tiananmen Gate, but Mao's Thought continues to dominate us.

Could the army play an important role in the future?

In our society, the army does plan an important role. But it is no monolith. People at different levels hold different views. I, for one, have received numerous letters of support from members of the army.

How many have you received in all?

Thousands. Often simply open postcards with the name and address of the sender—a brave deed in China. On one it even said: "If this postcard does not reach its destination, then there is no democracy in China." When, on the day of my departure, I passed through customs, the policemen on duty in the booths stopped working and came over to talk to me. "Are you Fang Lizhi? Are you all right now? Are you allowed to travel overseas? That's good!"

Are you sure that after you return to China you will not be arrested or exiled to some far away place?

I'm prepared for that possibility.

You could emigrate. . . .

I have seriously considered it in the past. Now it is impossible. Should I leave now, I would be abandoning my students and friends in China. I have been denounced by high-level cadres, yet I haven't emigrated, whereas the children of high-level cadres go abroad to study although they've never been criticized. . . .

What's happened to the students who took part in the demonstrations?

As far as I know, no students from the well-known universities have been arrested. However, we do known that all of them have been photographed and had their names registered [by the police]. Later, they will make them "wear small shoes,"[3] as we say in China.

The campaign against "bourgeois liberalization" continues. . . .

That campaign has shown us just how strong the resistance to the reforms is. It has shown us that we badly underestimated the strength of our opponents. We have been too optimistic. On the other hand, the campaign has convinced more and more people of the necessity of reform. We do not want a revolution, which would in the first place be very difficult to achieve, and secondly would not necessarily be a good thing. Therefore, the only option that left for China is reform. Democracy, education and intellectual freedom are the absolute and indispensable prerequisites of this reform. Without these last—be it with or without democracy—China has no future.

Professor Fang, we thank you for this interview.

25.8   On Fang Lizhi's Expulsion, January 20, 1987

On January 17 [1987], the Disciplinary Inspection Committee of the Anhui Branch of the Communist Party of China came to the decision that Fang Lizhi should be stripped of his Party membership.

Fang Lizhi was formerly the Vice-President of the Chinese University of Science and Technology. On January 12 he was dismissed from his post. In their report, "Regarding the Decision to Expel Fang Lizhi from the Party," the Disciplinary Inspection Committee pointed out that in recent years Fang Lizhi has on various occasions publicly encouraged Bourgeois liberalization, opposed the Four Basic Principles, defied the leadership of the Party, denied the socialist system, caused dissension between intellectuals and the Party, and incited student demonstrations, resulting in serious disturbances.

25.9   Explanation of Fang Lizhi's Errors, January 21, 1987

With regard to Fang Lizhi's errors of word and deed, the relevant Party organizations have subjected him to severe criticism many times, but he has always merely feigned compliance, admitting to some mistakes on one hand and on

---

3. To persecute them by making life as uncomfortable as possible.

the other continuing in his bad old ways, becoming in fact even more unbridled in his attacks on the Four Basic Principles and in his advocacy of Bourgelib (bourgeois liberalism). He has thrown Party discipline to the winds. Not to eliminate from the Party someone who has been so outspoken in his opposition is something that neither the Party nor the people can tolerate. Fang Lizhi is a middle-aged intellectual who has been nurtured by the Party. The Party had high expectations of him and had, moreover, entrusted him with an important post. He has disappointed the Party and disappointed his people, however, by falling into the muddy ditch of error, from which he is incapable of extricating himself. Now, although he has been dismissed from his post and expelled from the Party, the Party and government have arranged a position in scientific research for him, thus allowing him to bring his specialized vocational skills into play. If his actions indicate he has made a genuine change for the better, he will be welcomed back by the Party and the people.

Even though people like Fang are only a tiny minority within the Party, their negative example reminds us of the importance and urgent necessity of educating Party members at large to abide by the Party Regulations, and to implement Party discipline, particularly within the new historical conditions created by the policies of Reform and the Open Door to the outside world.

CHAPTER 26 | # Testing the Limits

26.1 AND 26.2 DEMONSTRATIONS FOLLOWING THE DEATH OF HU YAOBANG

The death of Hu Yaobang on April 15, 1989, initiated a cycle of massive demonstrations in Peking. This new popular movement took as its model the bloody April Fifth incident of 1976; an incident in which thousands of Peking residents and students assembled on Tiananmen Square to mourn the death of Zhou Enlai were dispersed by troops and security forces loyal to the "Gang of Four." After the fact, Deng Xiaoping himself had deplored this use of force and used it to discredit Hua Guofeng in his own ascent to power in 1978.

Tens of thousands of students from Peking's universities and training institutes launched demonstrations that used Tiananmen Square, in the political heart of the city, as their hub. Almost from the outset, the strongest theme of the demonstrators was their demand for freedom of speech and greater participation in China's political life. They implored the country's leaders to reverse the verdicts on Hu Yaobang's dismissal in 1987. In their eyes, Hu's fall symbolized the party's rejection of popular participation in government.

Sharpening the division between government and demonstrators was the publication of a harsh and perhaps intentionally provocative editorial in *People's Daily* on April 26 that reflected the Party hard-liners' view of the recent events in the capital. In the editorial, the demonstrators were attacked as "conspirators" and their political activities were declared to be a destructive and illegal form of "turmoil." In the political parlance of the party, these were fighting words that escalated the tension already prevailing in Peking.

A popular reaction to the party's view of the democracy movement came swiftly. On April 27, a huge new wave of student demonstrations brought over one million Peking residents, including factory workers, to the streets in sympathy with the students. As demonstrations continued, new issues that further jangled the nerves of the party elite were joined to those that inspired the early demonstrations. By the end of April, the placards and speeches of demonstrators decried the failures of some ten years of reformist economic policy, bemoaned China's rampant inflation, called for rule by law and human rights, and condemned corruption in the Communist party and on the part of family members of party leaders.

Reproduced below are the *People's Daily* editorial of April 26, 1989, and an official China News Agency account of the demonstrations that occurred on the following day. Visible in the latter document is an obvious sympathy for the demonstrators and, implicitly, a rejection of the construction placed on their activities by the party.

26.1 People's Daily: *"We Must Unequivocally Oppose Unrest,"* *April 26, 1989*

In the mourning activities commemorating the death of Hu Yaobang, vast numbers of Communist Party members, workers, peasants, intellectuals, cadres, People's Liberation Army soldiers, and young students expressed their grief in many forms and indicated that sorrow should be transformed to into strength, a strength that could contribute to the realization of the Four Modernizations and the revival of China.

During the mourning period, abnormal situations emerged. A tiny handful of people took this opportunity to fabricate rumors and openly attack Party and government leaders; they poisoned and bewitched the masses to attack the New China Gate of Zhongnanhai, the location of the Central Committee of the Party and National Council; there were even some people who shouted counterrevolutionary slogans such as "Down with the Communist Party!"; in the provincial capital cities of Xi'an and Changsha, rioters used the occasion to engage in serious instances of assault, vandalism, looting, and arson.

In its consideration for the deep grief of the vast masses, the Party and the government adopted a tolerant and restrained attitude toward some of the inappropriate words and deeds of those young students who acted in moments of emotional distress. Before the mourning service commemorating Comrade Hu Yaobang on April 22nd, the police did not, in conformance with past practice, clear Tiananmen square where some students had already gathered. The police simply asked them to behave in a disciplined manner so that all could mourn Comrade Hu Yaobang. Owing to the mutual efforts of all involved, the mourning service could smoothly take place in a solemn and dignified manner.

But after the mourning service, a tiny handful of people with ulterior motives continued to take advantage of the grief of the students to fabricate all sorts of rumors, poison people's mind, and used posters and handbills to slander, deprecate, and attack the Party and government leaders. They openly violated the constitution and encouraged opposition to the leadership of the Communist Party and the socialist system. In some institutions of higher education they formed illegal organizations to "wrest power" from student government associations and some of them even forcibly occupied school loudspeaker control rooms; in other schools, they encouraged students to boycott classes and teachers to strike and even used force to prevent students from attending class. Fraudulently using the name of workers' organizations, they circulated reactionary flyers and, moreover, began establishing contacts in all quarters in order to manufacture an even more serious incident.

All these facts indicate that this tiny handful of people are not really engaged in mourning Comrade Hu Yaobang. Their goal is not to promote the process of socialist democracy in China nor are they simply complaining because they are dissatisfied. They are waving the flag of democracy to destroy democracy and law and order. Their goal is to sow dissension in people's minds, to disrupt the entire nation, and to ruin an orderly and united political situation. This is a planned conspiracy; it is turmoil which, in essence, aims at negating the leadership of the Communist people and the socialist system. This is a serious political struggle confronting the entire people and all the peoples of the entire nation.

If this turmoil is appeased or tolerated, if it is allowed to simply develop, a serious and chaotic situation will emerge in the future. The reform, opening, good management, construction, development, control of inflation, betterment of living standards, anti-corruption, and construction of democracy and law and order that are hoped for by the people of the entire nation, including the vast majority of the students, will vanish like a popped soap bubble. Even the enormous accomplishments of ten years of reform could be entirely lost; the glorious hope of the entire people for the revival of China could become impossible to realize. A China with enormous hopes and a great future would be changed into a China in turmoil, a land without peace or future.

Therefore, the entire Party and the people of the entire nation should sufficiently understand the severity of this struggle. They should unite and unequivocally oppose this turmoil in order to defend our hard-earned political harmony and unity, to protect the constitution, and to defend socialist democracy and law and order. We absolutely will not permit the establishment of any illegal organization; we will resolutely halt all actions based on any pretext designed to encroach upon the rights of legally constituted student organizations. Those who intentionally fabricate rumors in order to slander others will be legally prosecuted to the extent of their criminal responsibility. Illegal demonstrations or parades are prohibited; forming contacts in factories, farming villages, and schools is prohibited. Those who engage in acts of assault, vandalism, looting, and arson will be punished according to the law. The legitimate right of students to attend class and study will be protected. The broad masses of the students sincerely hope to eliminate corruption and to advance democracy and these are also the demands of the Party and the government. These demands can only be realized under the leadership of the Party and through the strengthening of administrative structure, the active promotion of reform, and the amplification of socialist democracy and law and order.

All Party comrades and all the people of the nation must awaken and recognize that if we do not firmly halt this turmoil, our nation will never have a day of peace. This struggle is connected to the success or failure of reform, opening, and the achievement of the Four Modernizations. It is connected to the future of our nation and our people. Organizations at all levels of the Chinese Communist Party, the vast masses of Communist Party members, the members of the Communist Youth League, all democratic party members, patriotic democratic people, and all of the people of the nation should distinguish right from wrong and actively take action to firmly and expeditiously stop this turmoil.

26.2   *China News Agency: Report on the Peking Student Demonstration*

A huge number of student demonstrators from the colleges and universities in Peking, carrying thousands of red flags and horizontal banners, marched through Tiananmen Square on April 27. The total number of the demonstrators, including those city residents who jointed the students along the way, is estimated at several hundred thousand.

The students left their schools at about 8:00 a.m., to gather their forces at the Peking Institute of Nationalities. At 10:30 a.m., they reached their first blockade set up by police in front of the Friendship Hotel, and broke through it after being halted for a few minutes. These students from the northern part of Peking and those from the eastern part of Peking converged again on the No. 2 Ring Road near Chegongzhuang and then broke through another blockade line formed by hundreds of policemen, continuing their march along the same road. Throughout their journey, the students were warmly applauded by the local people gathered on skyways, saluted by the construction workers standing on scaffolds, and greeted by the hand-waving residents in the high-rise apartment buildings along the road. Some people sent food and drinks to the students; and several Buddhist monks dressed in kasaya, each holding a wooden box with both hands, volunteering to raise money for the students. Once, when some students saw a person put more than two hundred yuan into a box, they shouted to him, "Thank you for understanding and supporting us"; this man and others then shouted back, "We support the students."

At about 2:00 p.m., the procession of students turned onto the Avenue of Eternal Peace, the main road that runs from the east to the west of the city, and the traffic in the city was forced to a halt for a long time. To prevent the students from marching onwards, thousands of policemen formed a human barrier at Liubukou, a place near Zhongnanhai, the headquarters of the Chinese Communist Party. But even such a barrier was not strong enough to hold back waves after waves of students. Finally, the police gave up, and let the crowds of demonstrators stream in to Tiananmen Square.

At 4:15 p.m., thousands of soldiers formed one more barrier in front of the north gate of the Great Hall of the People, but again, it failed to stop the crowds. At 4:40 p.m., fifteen military trucks packed with soldiers appeared on the east side of the Square, and began to move towards the Great Hall of People. The convoy was stopped by local residents. Some of them shouted to the soldiers, "A people's army should love people," and then reached out to shake hands with the soldiers, and explained to them what the student movement is all about.

The Tiananmen Square had been sealed off from visitors since early morning, and large troops of police and soldiers were sent in by the authorities to prevent the students from storming the entrances of the Great Hall of People and Zhongnanhai, but the students were very well-organized, they did not even walk into the Square, but passed by the Tiananmen Gate tower and continued to move towards the east. Their procession then turned north at the Jianguomen Skyway, and moved onto the No. 2 Ring Road again to go back to their schools. It is said that it only took the whole procession one hour and forty-five minutes to pass by the Tiananmen Gate Tower.

According to a circular distributed by the organizers of the student demonstration, the purpose of this massive demonstration was not to overthrow the present Government, but to push the Government in a non-violent way to eradicate corruption. It also denies that the students have been manipulated by any conspirators. It points out that from a long-term point of view this student movement will accelerate the process of democracy in Chinese society.

This unprecedented student demonstration has found a strong echo in the hearts of the people of Peking. The slogans they shouted most frequently are "Long live the Communist Party" and "We support Socialism." These slogans are not only an expression of their political inclination, but also a repudiation of an inaccurate report which said the purpose of the students is to "overthrow the Communist Party." Some people said, "News coverage should be faithful to the facts. We don't believe that the students' intention is to overthrow the Party, because we have heard their slogans." A man dressed like a cadre said, "There was another massive rally in Tiananmen Square on April 5, 1976. During that rally someone shouted 'Down with Zhou Enlai' and was caught by the crowd. He later on confessed that he was sent by the 'Gang of Four' to create disturbances so that the authorities could find some excuses to crack down the massive protest movement. We must now also watch out for such troublemakers." An office worker standing in the Tiananmen Square said, "Before this student movement, I kind of felt that our country is hopeless. But now, when I see the patriotic enthusiasm of the students, I begin to realize that China's hope lies with these young students."

Many of the slogans created by the students are criticisms of the problems prevalent nowadays in the society, and proved to be very effective in gaining popular support for the demonstration. Some of the slogans written on the banners are "Our country should be ruled by law, not by privilege," "People cannot be fooled," "If Government officials do not work for the public, they should go home to cultivate their private plot," "People won't tolerate official speculators," "Prices must be stabilized," "Get rid of nepotism" and "Corruption must be uprooted."

Some Peking residents said, "We don't quite understand the students' talk about democracy, but if they demand to get rid of those officials who are corrupted or engaged in illegal speculation, we will support them."

The students also created some slogans to attack specific problems that have so far been neglected. For instance, "Official speculators get richer, peasants get poorer," "Peasants' interests must be protected," etc . . . There are also many slogans expressing the students' hope that the Government will understand them. One of the slogans regarded by the spectators as the most touching is written on a banner, "Mother, what we are doing is not wrong." Similar slogans included "We demonstrators would rather take a beating than let our country take it," "Dialogue with youth is dialogue with the future," "We are patriotic students," "The lowly are the most patriotic," "We are reluctant to quit studying, we want equal dialogue," "To express people's wishes is not to create disorder" and "We want China to be strong and prosperous, we want nothing for ourselves."

Some of the banners carried by the students displayed several statements quoted from the *Selected Works* by Deng Xiaoping, such as "The April 5 Movement is understandable," "The Chinese Communist Party is a party that values truth" and "If the old do not get out, the young cannot get in."

The students are also deeply concerned about the educational problem in China. Some of the slogans written on the small paper flags in their hands are "The strength of a country depends on education," "Teachers have a conscience," "Education is in crisis, the teachers' conscience is uneasy" and "Poverty threatens our teachers, educational crisis endangers our next generation."

Analysts here have said the Communist authorities in China must carefully deal with such massive demonstration staged by students and ordinary people. They believe that the best way to calm the situation is to begin a frank dialogue with the students as soon as possible.

26.3 "OPEN DECLARATION OF A HUNGER STRIKE," MAY 1989

Determined to carry their democracy movement forward at any cost, a core group of student activists that included Chai Ling and others, launched a hunger strike on May 13, 1989. In the first days of the strike, the participants refused all food and drink and soon press reports of weak and dehydrated demonstrators, willing to sacrifice their own lives for freedom and democracy, dramatized as no other symbol could the desperation and sincerity of the students' cause.

The manifesto that follows was typical of the many melodramatic last wills and testaments produced by the hunger strikers. Circulated prior to the hunger strike, it was apparently a committee document prepared by the "Hunger Strike Volunteers of Peking's Institutions of Higher Education." The hunger strike upped the political ante in the prodemocracy movement for now the students were also demanding, in addition to democracy and freedom of speech, concrete changes including the resignations of Li Peng and Deng Xiaoping. Both leaders were seen by the demonstrators as the spiritual (if not actual) authors of the *People's Daily* editorial of April 26 and the most important opponents of democratic change.

The hunger strike and the arrival of Mikhail Gorbachev in Peking that followed on May 15, complicated the political situation in China's capital. By declaring their willingness to become martyrs for democracy, the students were embarking on a collision course with a group of powerful government leaders who were increasingly threatened and discomfited by the students' activities.

In this May of glowing sunshine, we are starting our hunger strike. In this moment of beautiful youth, we must resolutely put behind us the beauty of life. But how unwilling we are, how unreconciled!

But out nation has come to a critical juncture: inflation is sky-rocketing, government corruption is rampant, power is in the hands of few high-ranking officials, bureaucrats are corrupt, a large number of patriots have fled into exile, and social order grows daily more chaotic. Fellow-countrymen, all fellow-countrymen of conscience, at this crucial moment for the survival of the nation, please hear our voice:

The country is our country!

The people are our people!

The government is our government!

If we do not dare to cry out, who will?

If we do not dare to act, who will?

Even though our shoulders are soft and tender, even though death is too heavy a burden, we are going, we must go, history demands this of us.

Our purest patriotic feelings, our most excellent innocent spirits, are said to be linked to "turmoil" and "ulterior motives" and it is said we are "used by a tiny handful of people."[1]

We ask all upright citizens of China, every worker, peasant, soldier, average person, intellectual, famous social dignitary, government official, policeman, and all of those who concocted the charges against us: Put your hands over your own hearts and ask your own consciences, what crime have we committed? Are we creating "turmoil"? We are boycotting classes, we are demonstrating, we are engaging in a hunger strike, we are in hiding but why, in the final analysis, are we doing all of this? Our feelings are repeatedly toyed with, we are enduring hunger in our search for truth, and yet we are viciously beaten by soldiers and police. . . . Student representatives knelt down to beg for democracy but were ignored; their demands for conversations on equal footing were repeatedly postponed. Student leaders are in danger. . . .

What must we do?

Democracy is the most noble feeling of human existence and liberty is a natural human right bestowed at birth. Can the Chinese people feel proud that here we must exchange our young lives for such things?

A hunger strike is a last resort but at last it must be done.

We use the willingness to die to fight for life.

But we are still children! We are still children! Mother China, please cast a serious eye on your children. Hunger is ruthlessly destroying our youth. Can you fail to be moved as death approaches us?

We do not want to die, we would like to live good lives, because we are at the most beautiful moment of our lives. We do not want to die, we want to go on studying, because our Motherland is still so impoverished. It seems that we are leaving our Motherland behind as we die and yet we do not want to die. But if the death of one person or a group of people can permit more people to live happily and allow our nation to prosper and flourish, then we do not have the right to go on living an ignoble existence.

Fathers, mothers, as we endure hunger, do not be sad for us! Uncles, aunts, as we bid good-bye to our lives, please do not grieve for us! We have only one wish and that is that our people can live more happily; we have only one request and that is that you will please not forget that our search was certainly not for death. Democracy is not a matter for a few people. The enterprise of democracy can definitely not be accomplished by a single generation.

Death comes in expectation of a vast and infinite echo.

1. All of these quotations are taken from a threatening April 26, 1989 *People's Daily* editorial that condemned the demonstrations as a form of "counter-revolutionary turmoil."

The words of someone about to die are spoken with good intentions. The cries of a horse about to die are filled with grief.

Farewell fellow students, please take care of yourselves! The dead and the living share the same faith.

Farewell lovers, please take care of yourselves! We cannot bear to leave you but it must end this way.

Farewell parents, please forgive us! Your child cannot reconcile loyalty to the nation and filial piety.

Farewell to the people of China! Please permit us to use this necessary means to show our loyalty to the country.

The pledge we write with our lives will surely illuminate the sky of the Republic.

The reasons for the hunger strike: 1. To protest against the cold and numb attitude taken by the government toward the Peking student's boycott of classes; 2. To protest the government's postponement of dialogues with the delegation of Peking's institutions of higher education; 3. To protest both the government's labeling of this democratic, patriotic student movement as "turmoil" and its entire series of distorted reports on the movement.

The demands of the hunger strike: 1. We demand that the government rapidly undertake substantial and concrete dialogues on equal footing with the student delegation; 2. We demand that the government must rectify the name of the student movement and give a fair evaluation that will confirm that it is a patriotic and democratic student movement.

Time of the hunger strike: Starting May 13th at 2:00 P.M.

Place of the hunger strike: Tiananmen Square.

This is not "turmoil"; immediately reverse this verdict! Start dialogue now! No postponement will be permitted! We are starting the hunger strike for the people! We have no alternative! Public opinion of the world, please support us! All democratic forces in society, please support us!

26.4 LI PENG'S ANNOUNCEMENT OF MARTIAL LAW, MAY 20, 1989

The student hunger strike and Gorbachev's visit sparked a spirited political debate in Peking and elsewhere in China. The inability of the security forces to regain control over Tiananmen Square was viewed by most as manifestation of "people's power" that would lead to "people's victory" over the party hard-liners. Moreover, the visit of the Soviet leader, whose program of "glastnost" contained elements missing in China's reform package, added fuel to the fire as Zhao Ziyang expressed dissatisfaction with the vertical style of Deng Xiaoping's rule. The demonstrations and parades of millions of democracy movement supporters that became a daily occurrence after May 17 touched off a feverish debate within the Party's top leadership about how to halt this increasingly uncontrollable mass "turmoil." Although the details of this debate are unknown, it is clear that Zhao Ziyang was an isolated voice calling for moderation, with Deng Xiaoping and Prime Minister Li Peng arguing that only military force could end this cycle of demonstrations and halt the spread of unrest to other parts of China. On May 20, 1989, martial law was declared, setting the stage for a violent collision between the students and the People's Liberation Army. The following document shows how the demonstration was viewed by the Party hard-liners and the strategy they would later use in justifying their actions against the student demonstrators.

The briefing by the Peking Municipal Party Committee Secretary Li Ximing shows that the capital is in a critical situation. The anarchic state is going from bad to worse, and law and discipline are being violated. Before the beginning of May the situation was beginning to cool down as a result of great efforts. But after that the turmoil revived again.

More and more students and other people were involved in demonstrations and many colleges and universities had come to a standstill. Traffic jams happened everywhere, the party and Government offices were affected and public security was deteriorating. All this has seriously disturbed the normal order of production, work, study and everyday life of the local people. Some activities on the agenda of the Sino-Soviet summit that attracted worldwide attention had to be canceled, greatly damaging China's international image and prestige.

Some of the students on hunger strike on Tiananmen Square are continuing their fast. Their health is seriously deteriorating, and the life of a few is in imminent danger. Actually a handful of persons are using the hunger strikers as "hostages" to coerce and force the party and the Government to yield to their political demands. In this regard, they have not one iota of humanism.

AN END TO THE CHAOS

The party and the government have on one hand taken every possible measure to treat and rescue the fasting students. On the other hand, they have held several dialogues with representatives of the fasting students and have earnestly promised to continue to listen to their opinions in the future, in the hope that the students would end their hunger strike immediately. But the dialogues did not yield results as expected. Representatives of the hunger-striking students said that they could no longer control the situation on Tiananmen Square, packed with extremely excited crowds who kept shouting demagogic slogans.

If we fail to put an end to such chaos immediately and let it go unchecked, it will very likely lead to a situation which none of us want to see.

The situation in Peking is still worsening, and has already affected many other cities in the country. In many places, the number of demonstrators and protesters is increasing. In some places, there have been many incidents in which people broke into local party and government organs, along with beating, smashing, looting, burnings and other undermining activities that seriously violated the law. Recently, even some trains running on major railway lines such as the Peking-Guangzhou line, a north-south trunk line, were intercepted, causing communications to stop.

This will lead to a nationwide turmoil if no quick action is taken to turn and stabilize the situation. The nation's reform and opening to the outside world, and the fate and future of the People's Republic, are facing serious threat.

STUDENTS' INFLUENCE

The party and Government have pointed out time and again that the students are kind hearted and they do not want to create turmoil. Instead, these patriotic students hope to promote democracy and overcome corruption, and this is in line with the goals the party and Government have strived to achieve.

Questions and suggestions raised by the students have exerted positive influence on improving the work of the party and Government. But demonstrations, protests, boycott of classes, hunger strikes and other forms of petition have upset social stability, and will not be beneficial to solving the problems. Moreover, the situation now is not developing in line with the subjective wishes of the students and is going in a direction that runs counter to their intentions.

It has become more and more clear that the very few people who attempt to create turmoil want to reach their political goals—negating the leadership of the Communist Party of China and the socialist system and violating the Constitution—goals that they could not reach through democratic and legal channels. They spread rumors and smear party and Government leaders. They concentrate their attack on Comrade Deng Xiaoping, who has made great contributions to China's opening to the outside world and adhering to the four cardinal principles.

Their purpose is to overthrow the people's government elected by the National People's Congress and to totally negate the people's democratic dictatorship. They stir up trouble everywhere, establish secret ties, set up illegal organizations and force the party and Government to recognize them.

In doing so they attempted to lay a foundation to set up opposition factions and opposition parties in China. If they should succeed, the reform and opening to the outside worlds, democracy and legality and socialist modernization would all come to nothing, and China would suffer a historical retrogression. A promising China would lose its hope and future.

POLITICAL CONSPIRACY

One important purpose, for us to take a clear-cut stand in opposing the turmoil and exposing the political conspiracy of a handful of people, is to distinguish the masses of young students with the handful of people who incited the turmoil. This is out of our loving care for the young students. Our extremely tolerant and restrained attitude in handling the student unrest earlier was out of the same wishes and purpose, that is: not to hurt good people, particularly not the young students.

However, the handful of behind-the-scene people, who were plotting and inciting the turmoil, took the tolerance as weakness on the part of the party and Government. They continued to cook up stories to confuse and poison the masses, in an attempt to worsen the situation. This has caused the situation in Peking and many localities across the country to become increasingly acute. Under such circumstances we are forced to take resolute and decisive measures to put an end to the turmoil.

CLEAR-CUT ANSWERS

It must be stressed that even under such circumstances, we should still persist in protecting the patriotism of the students, make a clear distinction between them and the very few people who created the turmoil, and we will not penalize students for their radical words and actions in the student movement.

Moreover, dialogue will continue in an active way through various channels and at different levels between the party and the Government on one hand and the students and people from other walks of life on the other, including dialogue with those students who have taken part in demonstrations, class boycott and hunger strike, so as to take full heed of opinions from all fields.

We will give clear-cut answers to the reasonable demands raised by the students, we will pay close attention to and accept their reasonable criticism and suggestions, such as punishing profiteering officials, getting rid of corruption and overcoming bureaucratization, so as to improve the work of the party and the Government.

Under extremely complicated conditions in this period, leaders, teachers and students of many colleges and universities have taken pains to try to prevent demonstrations and keep order for teaching and studying.

Public security personnel and armed policemen have made great contributions in maintaining traffic, social order and security under extremely difficult conditions, Government offices, factories, shops, enterprises and institutions have persisted in production and work, taking pains to keep social life in order. For all this, the party and the Government are grateful and the people will never forget.

Now, to check the turmoil with a firm hand and quickly restore order, I urgently appeal on behalf of the party Central Committee and the state council:

To those students now on hunger strike on Tiananmen Square to end the fasting immediately, leave the square, receive medical treatment and recover their health as soon as possible.

ORDERS TO END STRIKE

To students and people in all walks of life to immediately stop all demonstrations, and give no more so-called support to the fasting students in the interest of humanitarianism. Whatever the intent, further "support" will push the fasting students to desperation.

On behalf of the party Central Committee and the state council, I now call on the whole party, the whole army and the whole nation to make concerted efforts and act immediately at all posts so as to stop the turmoil and stabilize the situation.

Party organizations at all levels must unite the broad masses, carry out painstaking ideological work and play a role of the core leadership and fighting fortress.

All the Communist Party members must strictly abide by the party's discipline. They should not only stay away from any activities harmful to stability and unity but also play a vanguard role in curbing the turmoil.

THE PARTY'S DISCIPLINE

Governments at various levels must enforce administrative discipline and law, strengthen leadership and administration over their regions and departments and earnestly carry out the work of stabilizing the situation, reform and economic construction.

All Government functionaries must stick to their own positions and maintain normal work order.

All the public security personnel and armed policemen should make greater efforts to maintain traffic and social order, intensify social security, and resolutely crack down on criminal activities.

All the industrial and commercial enterprises and Government institutions should abide by work discipline and be engaged in normal production.

And schools of various kinds and at various levels should maintain normal teaching order. Those on strike should resume classes unconditionally.

MAINTAINING LEADERSHIP

Comrades, our party is a party in power and our Government, a people's government. To be responsible to our sacred motherland and to the entire Chinese people, we must adopt firm and resolute measures to end the turmoil swiftly, maintain the leadership of the party as well as the socialist system.

We believe that our actions will surely have the support of all members of the Communist Party and the Communist Youth League, workers, peasants, intellectuals, democratic parties, people in various circles and the broad masses, and have the backing of the People's Liberation Army which is entrusted by the Constitution with the glorious task of safeguarding the country and the peaceful work of the people.

At the same time, we also hope the people in the capital will fully support the People's Liberation Army, police and armed police in their efforts to maintain order in the capital.

Comrades, we must, under the conditions of resolutely safeguarding stability and unity, continue to adhere to the four cardinal principles, persist in the reform and opening up to the outside world, strengthen democracy and the legal system, eliminate all kinds of corruption and strive to advance the cause of socialist modernization.

26.5 DENG XIAOPING'S EXPLANATION OF THE CRACKDOWN, JUNE 9, 1989

Following the imposition of martial law, student hunger strikers and their supporters ignored the government's order to clear Tiananmen Square and impeded the movement of troops into the heart of Peking. Tense confrontations took place almost every day and rumors abounded as to the "real" attitude of China's army commanders and their troops. The protesters and the PLA circled each other warily; yet, despite the fact that millions of people were involved in overt defiance of government orders and the active obstruction of PLA deployments, no fatal accidents or serious injuries occurred prior to June 3.

At the same time, massive demonstrations of support took place throughout China, in Hong Kong, and among Chinese living abroad. To many analysts of Chinese affairs, it seemed that the government would be forced to seek a compromise solution or run the risk of civil war.

But in the end, the cruelly prophetic words of the *People's Daily* editorial of April 26 became a reality as the party decided to halt "turmoil" with the full weight of its armed forces. Under orders from Li Peng and

President Yang Shangkun, troops, tanks, and armored personnel carriers forced their way into the heart of Peking. The first clashes occurred on June 3 and after midnight, on June 4, tanks and soldiers armed with AK-47 assault rifles fired indiscriminately on demonstrating crowds. The demonstrators were methodically herded out of Tiananmen Square and in a day, the pro-democracy movement was over. The human cost, however, was high. Peking's hospitals were swamped with civilian casualties and makeshift morgues were set up at Peking University and elsewhere. The protest ended, and a period of active repression and arrests began.

For several days after June 4, it was unclear whether Deng Xiaoping was behind the massacre. Any doubt about Deng's role was dispelled, however, by his speech on June 9 to the commanders of the martial law forces. In this speech, Deng, in his capacity as chairman of the Central Military Commission, applauded the "martyrs" of the army who were killed in the fighting. The speech provided a sense of the apocalyptic fears of Deng and other aging veterans of the Party and suggested the sources of their willingness to use violence to crush dissent.

You comrades have been working hard.

First of all, I'd like to express my heartfelt condolences to the comrades in the People's Liberation Army, the armed police and police who died in the struggle—and my sincere sympathy and solicitude to the comrades in the army, the armed police and police who were wounded in the struggle, and I want to extend my sincere regards to all the army, armed police and police personnel who participated in the struggle.

I suggest that all of us stand and pay a silent tribute to the martyrs.

I'd like to take this opportunity to say a few words. This storm was bound to happen sooner or later. As determined by the international and domestic climate, it was bound to happen and was independent of man's will. It was just a matter of time and scale. It has turned out in our favor, for we still have a large group of veterans who have experienced many storms and have a thorough understanding of things. They were on the side of taking resolute action to counter the turmoil. Although some comrades may not understand this now, they will understand eventually and will support the decision of the Central Committee.

The April 26 editorial of the *People's Daily* classified the problem as turmoil. The word was appropriate, but some people objected to the word and tried to amend it. But what has happened shows that this verdict was right. It was also inevitable that the turmoil would develop into a counterrevolutionary rebellion.

We still have a group of senior comrades who are alive, we still have the army, and we also have a group of core cadres who took part in the revolution at various times. That is why it was relatively easy for us to handle the present matter. The main difficulty in handling this matter lay in that we had never experienced such a situation before, in which a small minority of bad people mixed with so many young students and onlookers. We did not have a clear picture of the situation, and this prevented us from taking some actions that we should have taken earlier.

It would have been difficult for us to understand the nature of the matter had we not had the support of so many senior comrades. Some comrades didn't understand this point. They thought it was simply a matter of how to treat the masses. Actually, what we faced was not just some ordinary people who were misguided, but also a rebellious clique and a large quantity of the dregs of society. The key point is that they wanted to overthrow our stand and the party. Failing to understand this means failing to understand the nature of the matter. I believe that after serious work we can win the support of the great majority of comrades within the party.

OVERTHROW OF THE PARTY

The nature of the matter became clear soon after it erupted. They had two main slogans: to overthrow the Communist Party and topple the socialist system. Their goal was to establish a bourgeois republic entirely dependent on the West. Of course we accept people's demands for combating corruption. We are even ready to listen to some persons with ulterior motives when they raise the slogan about fighting corruption. However, such slogans were just a front. Their real aim was to overthrow the Communist Party and topple the socialist system.

During the course of quelling the rebellion, many comrades of ours were wounded or even sacrificed their lives. Some of their weapons were also taken from them by the rioters. Why? Because bad people mingled with the good, which made it difficult for us to take the firm measures that were necessary.

Handling this matter amounted to a severe political test for our army, and what happened shows that our People's Liberation Army passed muster. If tanks were used to roll over people, this would have created a confusion between right and wrong among the people nationwide. That is why I have to thank the P.L.A. officers and men for using this approach to handle the rebellion.

The P.L.A. losses were great, but this enabled us to win the support of the people and made those who can't tell right from wrong change their viewpoint. They can see what kind of people the P.L.A. are, whether there was bloodshed at Tiananmen, and who were those that shed blood.

Once this question is made clear, we can take the initiative. Although it is very saddening that so many comrades were sacrificed, if the event is analyzed objectively, people cannot but recognize that the P.L.A. are the sons and brothers of the people. This will also help people to understand the measures we used in the course of the struggle. In the future, whenever the P.L.A. faces problems and takes measures, it will gain the support of the people. By the way,

I would say that in the future, we must make sure that our weapons are not taken away from us.

PASSING THE TEST

In a word, this was a test, and we passed. Even though there are not so many veteran comrades in the army and the soldiers are mostly little more than 18, 19 or 20 years of age, they are still true soldiers of the people. Facing danger, they did not forget the people, the teachings of the party and the interests of the county. They kept a resolute stand in the face of death. They fully deserve the saying that they met death and sacrificed themselves with generosity and without fear.

When I talked about passing muster, I was referring to the fact that the army is still the People's Army. This army retains the traditions of the old Red Army. What they crossed this time was genuinely a political barrier, a threshold of life and death. This is by no means easy. This shows that the People's Army is truly a great wall of iron and steel of the party and country. This shows that no matter how heavy the losses we suffer and no matter how generations change, this army of ours is forever an army under the leadership of the party, forever the defender of the country, forever the defender of socialism, forever the defender of the public interest, and they are the most beloved of the people.

At the same time, we should never forget how cruel our enemies are. For them we should not have an iota of forgiveness.

The outbreak of the rebellion is worth thinking about. It prompts us to calmly think about the past and consider the future. Perhaps this bad thing will enable us to go ahead with reform and the open-door policy at a more steady, better, even a faster pace. Also it will enable us to more speedily correct our mistakes and better develop our strong points. I cannot elaborate on this today. I just want to raise the subject here.

CLEAR ANSWERS SOUGHT

The first question is: Are the line, goals and policies laid down by the Third Plenum of the 11th Central Committee, including our "three-step" development strategy, correct? Is it the case that because this riot took place there is some question about the correctness of the line, goals and policies we laid down? Are our goals "leftist"? Should we continue to use them for our struggle in the future? These significant questions should be given clear and definite answers.

We have already accomplished our first goal of doubling the gross national product. We plan to use 12 years to attain our second goal of doubling the G.N.P. In the 50 years after that, we hope to reach the level of a moderately developed country. A two-percent annual growth rate is sufficient. This is our strategic goal.

I don't believe that what we have arrived at is a "left" judgment. Nor have we set up an overly ambitious goal. So, in answering the first question, I should say that our strategic goal cannot be regarded as a failure. It will be an unbeatable achievement for a country with 1.5 billion people like ours to reach the level of a moderately developed nation after 61 years.

China is capable of realizing this goal. It cannot be said that our strategic goal is wrong because of the occurrence of this event.

APPLYING THE PRINCIPLES

The second question is this: Is the general conclusion of the 13th Party Congress of "One Center, two basic points" correct? Are the two basic points—upholding the four cardinal principles and persisting in policy of opening and reforms— wrong?

In recent days I have pondered these two points. No, we haven't been wrong. There's nothing wrong with the four cardinal principles. If there is anything amiss, it's that these principles haven't been thoroughly implemented—they haven't been used as the basic concept to educate the people, educate the students and educate all the cadres and party members.

The crux of the current incident was basically the confrontation between the four cardinal principles and bourgeois liberalization. It isn't that we have not talked about such things as the four cardinal principles, worked on political concepts, and opposed bourgeois liberalization and spiritual pollution. What we haven't done is maintain continuity in these talks—there has been no action and sometimes even hardly any talk.

The fault does not lie in the four cardinal principles themselves, but in wavering in upholding these principles, and in the very poor work done to persist in political work and education.

In my Chinese people's political consultative conference talk on New Year's Day 1980, I talked about four guarantees, one of which was the enterprising spirit in hard struggle and plain living. Promoting plain living must be a major objective of education and this should be the keynote for the next 60 to 70 years. The more prosperous our country becomes, the more important it is to keep hold of the enterprising spirit. The promotion of this spirit and plain living will also be helpful for overcoming decay.

ON POLITICAL EDUCATION

After the people's republic was founded we promoted plain living; later on, when life became a little better, we promoted spending more, leading to wastage everywhere. This, in addition to lapses in theoretical work and an incomplete legal system, resulted in backsliding.

I once told foreigners that our worst omission of the past 10 years was in education. What I meant was political education, and this doesn't apply to schools and students alone, but to the masses as a whole. And we have not said much about plain living and the enterprising spirit, about what kind of a country China is and how it is going to turn out. This is our biggest omission.

Is there anything wrong with the basic concept of reforms and openness? No. Without reforms and openness how could we have what we have today? There has been a fairly satisfactory rise in the standard of living, and it may be said that we have moved one stage further. The positive results of 10 years of reforms must be properly assessed even though there have emerged such problems as inflation. Naturally, in reform and adopting the open policy, we run the risk of importing evil influences from the West, and we have never underestimated such influences.

In the early 1980's, when we established special economic zones, I told our Guangdong comrades that on the one hand they should persevere with reforms and openness, and on the other hand they should deal severely with economic crimes.

SOME INADEQUACIES

Looking back, it appears that there were obvious inadequacies—there hasn't been proper coordination. Being reminded of these inadequacies will help us formulate future policies. Further, we must persist in the coordination between a planned economy and a market economy. There cannot be any change.

In the course of implementing this policy we can place more emphasis on planning in the adjustment period. At other times there can be a little more market adjustment so as to allow more flexibility. The future policy should still be a marriage between the planned and market economies.

What is important is that we should never change China back into a closed country. Such a policy would be most detrimental. We don't even have a good flow of information. Nowadays, are we not talking about the importance of information? Certainly, it is important. If one who is involved in management doesn't possess information, he is no better than a man whose nose is blocked and whose ears and eyes are shut. Again, we should never go back to the old days of trampling the economy to death. I put forward this proposal for the consideration of the Standing Committee. This is also an urgent problem we'll have to deal with sooner or later.

In brief, this is what we have achieved in the past decade: Generally, our basic proposals, ranging from developing a strategy to policies, including reforms and openness, are correct. If there is any inadequacy, then I should say our reforms and openness have not proceeded adequately enough. The problems we face in implementing reforms are far greater than those we encounter in opening our country. In political reforms we can affirm one point: We have to insist on implementing the system of the National People's Congress and not the American system of the separation of three powers. The U.S. berates us for suppressing students. But when they handled domestic student unrest and turmoil, didn't they send out police and troops, arrest people and shed blood? They were suppressing students and the people, but we are putting down counter-revolutionary rebellion. What qualifications do they have to criticize us? From now on, however, we should pay attention to such problems. We should never allow them to spread.

ELEMENT OF PERSISTENCE

What do we do from now on? I would say that we should continue, persist in implementing our planned basic line, direction and policy. Except where there is a need to alter a word or phrase here and there, there should be no change in the basic line or basic policy. Now that I have raised this question, I would like you all to consider it thoroughly. As to how to implement these policies, such as in the areas of investment, the manipulation of capital, etc., I am in favor of putting the emphasis on capital industry and agriculture. In capital industry, this call for attention to the supply of raw materials, transportation and energy—there should be more investment in these areas for the next 10 to 20 years, even if it involves heavy debts. In a way, this is also openness. Here, we need to be bold and have made hardly any serious errors. We should work for more electricity, work for more railway lines, public road, shipping. There's a lot we can do. As for steel, foreigners judge we'll need some 120 million tons a year in future. We are now using some 60 million tons, half of what we need. If we were to improve our existing facilities and increase production by 20 million tons we could reduce the amount of steel we need to import. Obtaining foreign loans to improve this area is also an aspect of reform and openness. This question now confronting us is not whether the policies of opening and reforming are correct or not or whether we should continue with these policies. The question is how to carry out these policies, where do we go and which area should we concentrate on?

We have to firmly implement the series of policies formulated since the Third Plenary Session of the 11th Central Committee. We must conscientiously sum up our experiences, persevere in what is right, correct what is wrong, and do a bit more where we lag behind. In short, we should sum up the experiences of the present and look forward to the future.

That's all I have to say on this occasion.

CHAPTER 27

Century's End

27.1 DALAI LAMA AND "AHIMSA" FOR TIBET: THE NOBEL PEACE PRIZE LECTURE, DECEMBER 10, 1989

The awarding of the Nobel Peace Prize to the Dalai Lama (Tenzin Gyatso) in 1989 reflected global sympathy for Tibetan rights and, coming as it did in the wake of the suppression of the prodemocracy movement in Peking focused attention on the issue of human rights in China. The forcible reincorporation of Tibet into China in 1950 and its treatment as an "autonomous region" of the People's Republic of China came at the expense of the Tibetan people, their folkways, and their unique religion. In 1959 the Dalai Lama, Tibet's most important religious leader, fled Lhasa and entered a new phase of his life as a highly visible and respected advocate for the rights of his fellow countrymen.

In his Nobel address in Helsinki, the Dalai Lama discussed the plight of his people and established a program for the transformation of Tibet into "the Zone of Ahimsa" or a kind of "peace sanctuary" within which the human rights of Tibetans would be actively promoted and protected.

Brothers and Sisters:

It is an honor and pleasure to be among you today. I am really happy to see so many old friends who have come from different corners of the world, and to make new friends, whom I hope to meet again in the future. When I meet people in different parts of the world, I am always reminded that we are all basically alike: we are all human beings. Maybe we have different clothes, our skin is of a different color, or we speak different languages. This is on the surface. But basically, we are the same human beings. That is what binds us to each other. That is what makes it possible for us to understand each other and to develop friendship and closeness.

Thinking over what I might say today, I decided to share with you some of my thoughts concerning the common problems all of us face as members of the human family. Because we all share this small planet earth, we have to learn to live in harmony and peace with each other and with nature. That is not just a dream, but a necessity. We are dependent on each other in so many ways that we can no longer live in isolated communities and ignore what is happening outside those communities. We need to help each other when we have difficulties, and we must share the good fortune that we enjoy. I speak to you as just another human being, as a simple monk. If you find what I say useful, then I hope you will try to practice it.

I also wish to share with you today my feelings concerning the plight and aspirations of the people of Tibet. The Nobel Prize is a prize they well deserve for their courage and unfailing determination during the past forty years of foreign occupation. As a free spokesman for my captive countrymen and -women, I feel it is my duty to speak out on their behalf. I speak not with a feeling of anger or hatred towards those who are responsible for the immense suffering of our people and the destruction of our land, homes and culture. They too are human beings who struggle to find happiness and deserve our compassion. I speak to inform you of the sad situation in my country today and of the aspirations of my people, because in our struggle for freedom, truth is the only weapon we possess. . . .

The awarding of the Nobel Prize to me, a simple monk from far-away Tibet, here in Norway, also fills us Tibetans with hope. It means that, despite the fact that we have not drawn attention to our plight by means of violence, we have not been forgotten. It also means that the values we cherish, in particular our respect for all forms of life and the belief in the power of truth, are today recognized and encouraged. It is also a tribute to my mentor, Mahatma Gandhi, whose example is an inspiration to so many of us. This year's award is an indication that this sense of universal responsibility is developing. I am deeply touched by the sincere concern shown by so many people in this part of the world for the suffering of the people of Tibet. That is a source of hope not only for us Tibetans, but for all oppressed peoples.

As you know, Tibet has, for forty years, been under foreign occupation. Today, more than a quarter of a million Chinese troops are stationed in Tibet. Some sources estimate the occupation army to be twice this strength. During this time, Tibetans have been deprived of their most basic human rights, including the right to life, movement, speech, worship, only to mention a few. More than one sixth of Tibet's population of six million died as a direct result of the Chinese invasion and occupation. Even before the Cultural Revolution started, many of Tibet's monasteries, temples and historic buildings were destroyed. Almost everything that remained was destroyed during the Cultural Revolution. I do not wish to dwell on this point, which is well documented. What is important to realize, however, is that despite the limited freedom granted after 1979 to rebuild parts of some monasteries and other such tokens of liberalization, the fundamental human rights of the Tibetan people are still today being systematically violated. In recent months this bad situation has become even worse.

If it were not for our community in exile, so generously sheltered and supported by the government and people of India and helped by organizations and individuals from many parts of the world, our nation would today be little more than a shattered remnant of a people. Our culture, religion and national identity would have been effectively eliminated. As it is, we have built schools and monasteries in exile and have created democratic institutions to serve our people and preserve the seeds of our civilization. With this experience, we intend to implement full democracy in a future free Tibet. Thus, as we develop our community in exile on modern lines, we also cherish and preserve our own identity and culture and bring hope to millions of our countrymen and -women in Tibet.

The issue of most urgent concern at this time is the massive influx of Chinese settlers into Tibet. Although in the first decades of occupation a considerable number of Chinese were transferred into the eastern parts of Tibet—in the Tibetan provinces of Amdo (Chinghai) and Kham (most of which has been annexed by the neighboring Chinese province)—since 1983 an unprecedented number of Chinese have been encouraged by their government to migrate to all parts of Tibet, including central and western Tibet (which the PRC refers to as the so-called Tibet Autonomous Region). Tibetans are rapidly being reduced to an insignificant minority in their own country. This development, which threatens the very survival of the Tibetan nation, its culture and spiritual heritage, can still be stopped and reversed. But this must be done now, before it is too late.

The new cycle of protest and violent repression, which started in Tibet in September of 1987 and culminated in the imposition of martial law in the capital, Lhasa, in March of this year, was in large part a reaction to this tremendous Chinese influx. Information reaching us in exile indicates that the protest marches and other peaceful forms of protest are continuing in Lhasa and a number of other places in Tibet despite the severe punishment and inhumane treatment given to Tibetans detained for expressing their grievances. The number of Tibetans killed by security forces during the protest in March and of those who died in detention afterwards is not known but is believed to be more than two hundred. Thousands have been detained or arrested and imprisoned, and torture is commonplace.

It was against the background of this worsening situation and in order to prevent further bloodshed, that I proposed what is generally referred to as the Five Point Peace Plan for the restoration of peace and human rights in Tibet. I elaborated on the plan in a speech in Strasbourg last year. I believe the plan provides a reasonable and realistic framework for negotiations with the People's Republic of China. So far, however, China's leaders have been unwilling to respond constructively. The brutal supression of the Chinese democracy movement in June of this year, however, reinforced my view that any settlement of the Tibetan question will only be meaningful if it is supported by adequate international guarantees.

The Five Point Peace Plan addresses the principal and interrelated issues, which I referred to in the first part of this lecture. It calls for (1) Transformation of the whole of Tibet, including the eastern provinces of Kham and Amdo, into a Zone of *Ahimsa* (non-violence); (2) Abandonment of China's population transfer policy; (3) Respect for the Tibetan people's fundamental human rights and democratic freedoms; (4) Restoration and protection of Tibet's natural environment; and (5) Commencement of earnest negotiations on the future status of Tibet and of relations between the Tibetan and Chinese peoples. In the Strasbourg address I proposed that Tibet become a fully self-governing democratic political entity.

I would like to take this opportunity to explain the Zone of Ahimsa or peace sanctuary concept, which is the central element of the Five Point Peace Plan. I am convinced that it is of great importance not only for Tibet, but for peace and stability in Asia.

It is my dream that the entire Tibetan plateau should become a free refuge where humanity and nature can live in peace and in harmonious balance. It would be a place where people from all over the world could come to seek the true meaning of peace within themselves, away from the tensions and pressures of much of the rest of the world. Tibet could indeed become a creative center for the promotion and development of peace.

The following are key elements of the proposed Zone of Ahimsa:

—the entire Tibetan plateau would be demilitarized;
—the manufacture, testing, and stockpiling of nuclear weapons and other armaments on the Tibetan plateau would be prohibited;
—the Tibetan plateau would be transformed into the world's largest natural park or biosphere. Strict laws would be enforced to protect wildlife and plant life; the exploitation of natural resources would be carefully regulated so as not to damage relevant ecosystems; and a policy of sustainable development would be adopted in populated areas;
—the manufacture and use of nuclear power and other technologies which produce hazardous waste would be prohibited;
—national resources and policy would be directed towards the active pro-

motion of peace and environmental protection. Organizations dedicated to the furtherance of peace and to the protection of all forms of life would find a hospitable home in Tibet;
—the establishment of international and regional organizations for the promotion and protection of human rights would be encouraged in Tibet.

Tibet's height and size (the size of the European Community), as well as its unique history and profound spiritual heritage make it ideally suited to fulfill the role of a sanctuary of peace in the strategic heart of Asia. It would also be in keeping with Tibet's historical role as a peaceful Buddhist nation and buffer region separating the Asian continent's great and often rival powers.

In order to reduce existing tensions in Asia, the President of the Soviet Union, Mr. Gorbachev, proposed the demilitarization of Soviet-Chinese borders and their transformation into a "frontier of peace and good-neighborliness." The Nepal government had earlier proposed that the Himalayan country of Nepal, bordering on Tibet, should become a zone of peace, although that proposal did not include demilitarization of the country.

For the stability and peace of Asia, it is essential to create peace zones to separate the continent's biggest powers and potential adversaries. President Gorbachev's proposal, which also included a complete Soviet troop withdrawal from Mongolia, would help to reduce tension and the potential for confrontation between the Soviet Union and China. A true peace zone must, clearly, also be created to separate the world's two most populous states, China and India.

The establishment of the Zone of Ahimsa would require the withdrawal of troops and military installations from Tibet, which would enable India and Nepal also to withdraw troops and military installations from the Himalayan regions bordering Tibet. This would have to be achieved by international agreements. It would be in the best interest of all states in Asia, particularly China and India, as it would enhance their security, while reducing the economic burden of maintaining high troop concentrations in remote areas. . . .

Let me end with a personal note of thanks to all of you and our friends who are not here today. The concern and support which you have expressed for the plight of the Tibetans has touched us all greatly, and continues to give us courage to struggle for freedom and justice; not through the use of arms, but with the powerful weapons of truth and determination. I know that I speak on behalf of all the people of Tibet when I thank you and ask you not to forget Tibet at this critical time in our country's history. We too hope to contribute to the development of a more peaceful, more humane and more beautiful world. A future free Tibet will seek to help those in need throughout the world, to protect nature, and to promote peace. I believe that our Tibetan ability to combine spiritual qualities with a realistic and practical attitude enables us to make a special contribution in however modest a way. This is my hope and prayer.

In conclusion, let me share with you a short prayer which gives me great inspiration and determination:

> For as long as space endures,
> And for as long as living beings remain,
> Until then may I, too, abide
> To dispel the misery of the world.

Thank you.

27.2 WEI JINGSHENG: "THE WOLF AND THE LAMB," NOVEMBER 18, 1993

Wei Jingsheng became one of China's most well-known dissidents as his Democracy Wall "big-character posters" attacked the absence of a party program to expand the realm of popular participation in China's political life in 1978 and 1979. In the spring of 1979 he was sentenced to fifteen years in prison on trumped-up charges. When he emerged from prison in September 1993, after serving fourteen years of his term, he was no less acerbic in his criticism than before his imprisonment.

The following editorial was published in the *New York Times* on November 18, 1993. It was the first essay written by Wei after his release and reflects his view that the climate for human rights in China was in no way improved. Wei also sensed that the Clinton administration was about to retreat from an emphasis on human rights in its relations with China and speculated that the United States government might place economic interest ahead of defending the rights of a people whose needs and aspirations were unknown to many Americans. Shortly after this essay appeared, Wei was arrested once again.

Most Americans don't really understand China, just as most Chinese don't understand America. This leads the two Governments to make numerous miscalculations in their relations and leads the two peoples toward numerous misunderstandings of the opposing regime's conduct.

For example, the Chinese Government holds that America cares nothing for the fate or future of the Chinese people; this means that raising human rights issues becomes nothing but a political tactic used in laying siege to the Communist Party or merely an economic bargaining tool.

So China treats human rights as a problem of foreign relations. And the primary pretext for refusing to bend under international pressure on human rights is that China "will not allow interference in its internal affairs."

Furthermore, there is a tendency on the part of China to view the detention and release of dissidents as a hostage transaction, in which freedom for the prisoner is just a bargaining chip in an economic poker game.

The reason the Chinese Government is willing to make such unclean transactions is that it does not understand why the U.S. might be unwilling to continue lucrative trade relations if China's human rights environment does not improve. China doesn't understand, because it thinks this way: Is it really likely that Americans would befriend a people they are not at all familiar with?

Is it really likely that Americans would abandon an opportunity to make money just to protect the human rights of those they have befriended?

Is it really likely that the American people's determinations of right and wrong could ever influence the judgment of the U.S. Government?

It looks as if the Communist Party has answered these questions in the negative. So even though it may have realized that its own conduct might have been in error, it still firmly pursues a strategy of brinksmanship, giving ground only when absolutely necessary and always in the last five minutes of negotiations. For example, Chinese officials last week agreed to give "positive consideration" to allowing the International Committee of the Red Cross to inspect prisons.

The party holds that in such ways it will save face, and in the end will debunk Yankee protestations of seriousness over human rights, which the party believes are just an affectation. Pursuing this strategy, Peking believes, will free it to deprive the people of their freedom. It also seems that the U.S. Government has misunderstood the true mind-set of the Chinese Government. Washington evidently believes that the Communist Party resembles a bunch of slow-witted rulers of a backward culture and that China doesn't comprehend that violations of human rights are evil.

Therefore, the Clinton Administration now plans to abandon policies of pressure in favor of a policy of persuasion and "enhanced engagement"—a misguided shift to be symbolized in Seattle today by the handshake between Presidents Clinton and Jiang Zemin. Unfortunately, the reality is more like the Aesop's fable in which a lamb tries to reason with a wolf. After the wolf accuses the lamb of fouling his drinking water, the lamb protests: "I could not have fouled your water because I live downstream from you." The wolf eats the lamb anyway.

I fear that no matter how much the two countries debate, the old wolf in China will still complain about its drinking water. China not only doesn't understand reason but also does not intend to reason.

I'm unclear about the American people's understanding of changes in China-U.S. relations, but the Chinese people's understanding of their own Government is very precise. The present leaders were the most outspoken group of men, shouting their support of human rights and democracy before they ascended to power. But their subsequent dictatorship made clear that they have no intention of making good on the promises they once made to the masses.

The Chinese people's understanding of the new direction of U.S. policy toward China leads them to believe that the party was right all these years in saying that the American Government is controlled by rich capitalists. All you have to do is offer them a chance to make money and anything goes.

27.3 PRESIDENT CLINTON REEVALUATES HUMAN RIGHTS AS ELEMENT OF CHINA POLICY, MAY 27, 1994

In his first years in the White House President Clinton stressed human rights as an element of American foreign policy. However, when it came to pursuing this policy in the framework of the debate about the renewal of China's Most Favored Nation (MFN) status in the spring of 1994, the Clinton administration changed its tack: It decided to "delink" human rights and, instead, pursue a policy of "engagement" that was designed to perpetuate the expansion of economic ties with China while promising that moral suasion would continue to be employed to address rights violations.

Our relationship with China is important to all Americans. We have significant interests in what happens there and what happens between us.

China has an atomic arsenal and a vote and a veto in the U.N. Security Council. It is a major factor in Asian and global security. We share important interests, such as in a nuclear-free Korean peninsula and in sustaining the global environment.

China is also the world's fastest-growing economy. Over $8 billion of United States exports to China last year supported over 150,000 American jobs.

I have received Secretary Christopher's letter recommending, as required by last year's executive order—reporting to me on the conditions in that executive order. He has reached a conclusion with which I agree, that the Chinese did not achieve overall significant progress in all the areas outlined in the executive order relating to human rights, even though clearly there was progress made in important areas, including the resolution of all emigration cases, the estab-lishment of a memorandum of understanding with regard to how prison labor issues would be resolved, the adherence to the Universal Declaration of Human Rights, and other issues.

Nevertheless, serious human rights abuses continue in China, including the arrest and detention of those who peacefully voice their opinions and the repres-sion of Tibet's religious and cultural traditions.

The question for us now is, given the fact that there has been some progress but that not all the requirements of the executive order were met, how can we best advance the cause of human rights and the other profound interests the United States has in our relationship with China?

I have decided that the United States should renew Most Favored Nation trading status toward China. This decision, I believe, offers us the best opportunity to lay the basis for long-term sustainable progress in human rights, and for the advancement of our other interests with China.

Extending M.F.N. will avoid isolating China and instead will permit us to engage the Chinese with not only economic contacts but with cultural, educational and other contacts, and with a continuing aggressive effort in human rights—an approach that I believe will make it more likely that China will play a responsible role, both at home and abroad.

I am moving, therefore, to delink human rights from the annual extension of Most Favored Nation trading status for China. That linkage has been constructive during the past year, but I believe, based on our aggressive contacts with the Chinese in the past several months, that we have reached the end of the usefulness of that policy, and it is time to take a new path toward the achievement of our constant objectives. We need to place our relationship into a larger and more productive framework.

In view of the continuing human rights abuses, I am extending the sanctions imposed by the United States as a result of the events in Tiananmen Square. And I am also banning the import of munitions, principally guns and ammunition, from China.

I am also pursuing a new and vigorous American program to support those in China working to advance the cause of human rights and democracy. This program will include increased broadcasts for Radio-Free Asia and the Voice of America, increased support for nongovernmental organizations working on human rights in China, and the development, with American business leaders, of a voluntary set of principles for business activity in China.

I don't want to be misunderstood about this. China continues to commit very serious human rights abuses. Even as we engage the Chinese on military, political and economic issues, we intend to stay engaged with those in China who suffer from human rights abuses.

The United States must remain a champion of their liberties.

I believe the question, therefore, is not whether we continue to support human rights in China but how we can best support human rights in China and advance our other very significant issues and interests. I believe we can do it by engaging the Chinese....

The actions I have taken today to advance our security, to advance our prosperity, to advance our ideals, I believe are the important and appropriate ones. I believe, in other words, this is in the strategic economic and political interests of both the United States and China, and I am confident that over the long run this decision will prove to be the correct one.

27.4 JIANG ZEMIN'S NEW YEAR'S GREETING TO TAIWAN COMPATRIOTS, JANUARY 31, 1995

As the reversion of Hong Kong to China approached, Peking was eager to establish guidelines for the reincorporation of Taiwan, Republic of China (ROC) into the "ancestral land" of China. After the death of Jiang Jingguo in 1988, the relationship between the PRC and Taiwan changed in remarkable ways. China welcomed ROC businessmen and the flow of Taiwanese investment in joint enterprises on the mainland continued apace under a permissive policy adopted by both governments. In addition, cultural, educational, and touristic activities greatly expanded as many Taiwanese visited the PRC and were welcomed by their mainland compatriots. However, leaders of the CCP were unwaveringly committed to unification and insisted that the "one country, two systems" formula worked out for Hong Kong and incorporated into the language of China's constitution under the formulation for Special Administrative Regions could be successfully applied to Taiwan.

Jiang Zemin's New Year's greeting of 1995 lays out the key themes of Peking's position. The PRC was especially intolerant of the idea of Taiwanese independence and refused to renounce force as an instrument of policy if ROC leaders tried to follow this course.

Comrades and friends,

Following the celebration of the 1995 New Year's Day, the people of all ethnic groups in China are now seeing in the Spring Festival. On the occasion of this traditional festival of the Chinese nation, it is of great significance for the Taiwan compatriots in Peking and other personages concerned to be gathered here to discuss the future of the relations between the two sides of the Taiwan Straits and the great cause of the peaceful reunification of the motherland. On behalf of the Central Committee of the Communist Party of China and the State Council, I should like to take this opportunity to wish our 21 million compatriots in Taiwan a happy New Year and the best of luck.

Taiwan is an integral part of China. A hundred years ago on 17th April 1895, the Japanese imperialists, by waging a war against the corrupt government of the Qing dynasty, forced the latter to sign the Shimonoseki Treaty of national betrayal and humiliation. Under the treaty, Japan seized Taiwan and the Penghu islands, subjecting the people of Taiwan to its colonial rule for half a century. The Chinese people will never forget this humiliating chapter of their history. Fifty years ago, together with the people of other countries, the Chinese people defeated the Japanese imperialists. October 25th 1945 saw the return of Taiwan and the Penghu islands to China and marked the end of Japan's colonial rule over our compatriots in Taiwan. However, for reasons everybody knows, Taiwan has been severed from the Chinese mainland since 1949. It remains the sacred mission and lofty goal of the entire Chinese people to achieve the reunification of the motherland and promote the all-round revitalization of the Chinese nation.

Since the Standing Committee of the National People's Congress issued its "Message To the Taiwan Compatriots" in January 1979, we have formulated the basic principles of peaceful reunification and "one country, two systems" and a series of policies towards Taiwan. Comrade Deng Xiaoping, the chief architect of China's reform and opening to the outside world, is also the inventor of the great concept of "one country, two systems." With foresight and seeking truth from facts, he put forward a series of important theories and ideas concerning the settlement of the Taiwan question which reflect the distinct features of the times, and defined the guiding principles for the peaceful reunification of the motherland.

Comrade Deng Xiaoping has pointed out that the most important issue is the reunification of the motherland. All descendants of the Chinese nation wish to see China reunified. It is against the will of the Chinese nation to see it divided. There is only one China, and Taiwan is a part of China. We will never allow there to be "two Chinas" or "one China, one Taiwan." We firmly oppose the "independence of Taiwan." There are only two ways to settle the Taiwan question: One is by peaceful means and the other is by non-peaceful means. The way the Taiwan question is to be settled is China's internal affairs, and brooks no foreign interference. We consistently stand for achieving reunification by peaceful means and through negotiations. But we shall not undertake not to use force. Such commitment would only make it impossible to achieve peaceful reunification and could not but lead to the eventual settlement of the question by the use of force. After Taiwan is reunified with the mainland, China will pursue the policy of "one country, two systems." The main part of the country will stick to the socialist system, while Taiwan will retain its current system. "Reunification does not mean that the mainland will swallow up Taiwan, nor does it mean that Taiwan will swallow up the mainland." After Taiwan's reunification with the mainland, its social and economic systems will not change, nor will its way of life and its non-governmental relations with foreign countries, which means that foreign investments in Taiwan and the non-governmental exchanges between Taiwan and other countries will not be affected. As a special administrative region, Taiwan will exercise a high degree of autonomy and enjoy legislative and independent judicial power, including that of final adjudication. It may also retain its armed forces and administer its party, governmental and military systems by itself. The central government will not station troops or send administrative personnel there. What is more, a number of posts in the central government will be made available to Taiwan.

Over the past decade and more, under the guidance of the basic principles of peaceful reunification and "one country, two systems" and through the concerted efforts of the compatriots on both sides of the Taiwan Straits and in Hong Kong and Macao and Chinese residing abroad, visits back and forth by individuals and exchanges in science, technology, culture, academic affairs, sports and other fields have expanded vigorously. A situation in which the economies of the two sides promote, complement and benefit each other is taking shape. The establishment of direct links between the two sides for postal, air and shipping services at an early date not only represents the strong desire of vast numbers of compatriots in Taiwan, particularly industrialists and businessmen, but has also become the actual requirement for future economic development in Taiwan. Progress has been registered in the negotiations on specific issues, and the "Wang Daohan-Koo Chenfu talks" represent an important, historic step forward in the relations between the two sides.

However, what the entire Chinese people should watch out for is the growing separatist tendency and the increasingly rampant activities of the forces working for the "independence of Taiwan" on the island in recent years. Certain foreign forces have further meddled in the issue of Taiwan, interfering in China's internal affairs. All this not only impedes the process of China's peaceful reunification but also threatens peace, stability and development in the Asia-Pacific region.

The current international situation is still complex and volatile, but in general, it is moving towards relaxation. All countries in the world are working out their economic strategies which face the future and taking it as a task of primary importance to increase their overall national strength so as to take up their proper places in the world in the next century. We are pleased to see that the economies of both sides are growing. In 1997 and 1999 China will resume its exercise of sovereignty over Hong Kong and Macao respectively, which will be happy events for the Chinese people of all ethnic groups, including our compatriots in Taiwan. The Chinese nation has experienced many vicissitudes and hardships, and now it is high time to accomplish the reunification of the motherland and bring about its all-round rejuvenation. This means an opportunity for both Taiwan and the entire Chinese nation. Here, I should like to state the following views and propositions on a number of important questions that have a bearing on the development of relations between the two sides and the promotion of the peaceful reunification of the motherland:

1. Adherence to the principle of one China is the basis and premise for peaceful reunification. China's sovereignty and territory must never be allowed to suffer split. We must firmly oppose any words or actions aimed at creating an "independent Taiwan" and the propositions "split the country and rule under separate regimes," "two Chinas over a certain period of time," etc., which are in contravention of the principle of one China.

2. We do not challenge the development of non-governmental economic and cultural ties by Taiwan with other countries. Under the principle of one China and in accordance with the charters of the relevant international organizations, Taiwan has become a member of the Asian Development Bank, the Asia-Pacific Economic Cooperation forum and other international economic organizations in the name of "Chinese Taipei." However, we oppose Taiwan's activities in "expanding its living space internationally" which are aimed at creating "two Chinas" or "one China, one Taiwan." All patriotic compatriots in Taiwan and other people of insight understand that instead of solving the problems, such activities can only help the forces working for the "independence of Taiwan" undermine the process of peaceful reunification more unscrupulously. Only after the peaceful reunification is accomplished can the Taiwan compatriots and other Chinese people of all ethnic groups truly and fully share the dignity and honour attained by our great motherland internationally.

3. It has been our consistent stand to hold negotiations with the Taiwan authorities on the peaceful reunification of the motherland. Representatives from the various political parties and mass organizations on both sides of the Taiwan Straits can be invited to participate in such talks. I said in my report at the Fourteenth National Congress of the Communist Party of China held in October 1992, "On the premise that there is only one China, we are prepared to talk with the Taiwan authorities about any matter, including the form that official negotiations should take, a form that would be acceptable to both sides." By "on the premise that there is only one China, we are prepared to talk with the Taiwan authorities about any matter," we mean naturally that all matters of concern to the Taiwan authorities are included. We have proposed time and again that negotiations should be held on officially ending the state of hostility between the two sides and accomplishing peaceful reunification step by step. Here again I solemnly propose that such negotiations be held. I suggest that, as the first step, negotiations should be held and an agreement reached on officially ending the state of hostility between the two sides in accordance with the principle that there is only one China. On this basis, the two sides should undertake jointly to safeguard China's sovereignty and territorial integrity and map out plans for the future development of their relations. As regards the name, place and form of these political talks, a solution acceptable to both sides can certainly be found so long as consultations on an equal footing can be held at an early date.

4. We should strive for the peaceful reunification of the motherland since Chinese should not fight fellow Chinese. Our undertaking to give up the use of force is not directed against our compatriots in Taiwan but against the schemes of foreign forces to interfere with China's reunification and

to bring about the "independence of Taiwan." We are fully confident that our compatriots in Taiwan, Hong Kong and Macao and those residing overseas would understand our principled position.

5. In face of the development of the world economy in the twenty-first century, great efforts should be made to expand the economic exchanges and cooperation between the two sides of the Taiwan Straits so as to achieve prosperity on both sides to the benefit of the entire Chinese nation. We hold that political differences should not affect or interfere with the economic cooperation between the two sides. We shall continue to implement over a long period of time the policy of encouraging industrialists and businessmen from Taiwan to invest in the mainland and enforce the Law of the People's Republic of China for Protecting the Investment of the Compatriots of Taiwan. Whatever the circumstances may be, we shall safeguard the legitimate rights and interests of industrialists and businessmen from Taiwan. We should continue to expand contacts and exchanges between our compatriots on both sides so as to increase mutual understanding and trust. Since the direct links for postal, air and shipping services and trade between the two sides are the objective requirements for their economic development and contacts in various fields, and since they are in the interests of the people on both sides, it is absolutely necessary to adopt practical measures to speed up the establishment of such direct links. Efforts should be made to promote negotiations on certain specific issues between the two sides. We are in favour of conducting these kinds of negotiations on the basis of reciprocity and mutual benefit and signing non-governmental agreements on the protection of the rights and interests of industrialists and businessmen from Taiwan.

6. The splendid culture of five thousand years created by the sons and daughters of all ethnic groups of China has become ties keeping the entire Chinese people close at heart and constitutes an important basis for the peaceful reunification of the motherland. People on both sides of the Taiwan Straits should inherit and carry forward the fine traditions of the Chinese culture.

7. The 21 million compatriots in Taiwan, whether born there or in other provinces, are all Chinese and our own flesh and blood. We should fully respect their life style and their wish to be the masters of our country and protect all their legitimate rights and interests. The relevant departments of our party and the government including the agencies stationed abroad should strengthen close ties with compatriots from Taiwan, listen to their views and demands, be concerned with and take into account their interests and make every effort to help them solve their problems. We hope that Taiwan Island enjoys social stability, economic growth and affluence. We also hope that all political parties in Taiwan will adopt a sensible, forward-looking and constructive attitude and promote the expansion of

relations between the two sides. All parties and personages of all circles in Taiwan are welcome to exchange views with us on relations between the two sides and on peaceful reunification and are also welcome to pay a visit and tour places. All personages from various circles who have contributed to the reunification of China will go down in history for their deeds.

8. Leaders of the Taiwan authorities are welcome to pay visits in appropriate capacities. We are also ready to accept invitations from the Taiwan side to visit Taiwan. We can discuss state affairs, or exchange ideas on certain questions first. Even a simple visit to the other side will be useful. The affairs of Chinese people should be handled by ourselves, something that does not take an international occasion to accomplish. Separated across the Straits, our people eagerly look forward to meeting each other. They should be able to exchange visits, instead of being kept from seeing each other all their lives.

Our compatriots in Hong Kong and Macao and those residing overseas have made dedicated efforts to promote the relations between the two sides, the reunification of the country and the revitalization of the Chinese nation. Their contribution commands recognition. We hope that they will make new contributions in this regard.

The reunification of the motherland is the common aspiration of the Chinese people. The patriotic compatriots do not wish to see reunification delayed indefinitely. The great revolutionary forerunner of the Chinese nation Dr Sun Yatsen once said: "Reunification is the hope of all nationals in China. If reunification can be achieved, the people of the whole country will enjoy a happy life; if it cannot be achieved, the people will suffer." We appeal to all Chinese to unite and hold high the great banner of patriotism, uphold reunification, oppose secession, spare no effort to promote the expansion of relations between the two sides and facilitate the accomplishment of the reunification of the motherland. In the course of the development of the Chinese nation in the modern world, such a glorious day will surely come.

Sources

CHAPTER 1

1.1 Wen Bing, *Dingling zhulue* [A brief account of the Chongzhen reign], vol. 5, in Xie Guozhen, *Mingdai nongmin qiyi shiliao* [Historical materials related to peasant uprisings of the Ming era] (Fuzhou: Fujian renmin chubanshe, 1981), pp. 202–03.

1.2 Shen Zan, *Jinshi congcan* [Fragmented pieces on recent events], in Xie (1981), p. 204.

1.3 and 1.4 Song Yingxing, *Yeyi* [Unbridled comments] (Shanghai renmin chubanshe, 1976), pp. 5, 35–39.

1.5 Xie (1981), pp. 173–74.

1.6 Ji Liuqi, *Mingji beilue* [A brief account of events before 1644] (Beijing: Zhonghua shuju, 1984), vol. 19, pp. 339–413.

1.7 Baoyang sheng [a penname], *Jiashen chaoshi xiaoji* [An account of events in 1644], vol. 7, in Xie (1981), pp. 181–83.

1.8 Gu Gongxie, *Xiaoxia xianji zhaichao* [Selections from leisurely accounts to pass the summer], vol. 2, in Xie (1981), pp. 184–85.

1.9 Yang Shangsong, *Guer xutianlu* [An orphan's outcry], in Deng Zhicheng, *Gudong suoji* [Fragmentary records on relics] (Beijing: Zhongguo shudian, 1991), vol. 3, pp. 494–95.

1.10 Song Maocheng, *Jiuyue ji* [Nine flute collection] (Beijing: Zhonguo shehui kexue chubanshe, 1984), pp. 112–18.

CHAPTER 2

2.1 Jiang Liangqi, *Donghua lu* [Records of the Forbidden City] (Beijing: Zhongua shuju, 1980), p. 7.

2.2 Zheng Tianting, comp., *Ming-Qing shih ziliao* [Materials related to the history of the Ming and Qing dynasties] (Tianjin renmin chubanshe, 1980), vol. 2, pp. 2–3.

2.3 Zheng (1980), pp. 3–4.

2.4 Zheng (1980), pp. 6–7.

2.5 *Jiangnan wenjianlu* [Eyewitness accounts of the Jiangnan area], in Mingji baishi chubian [First compilation of an official history of the Ming era] (Changsha, Shangwu yinshuguan, 1938), vol. 19, p. 355.

2.6 *Jiangnan wenjianlu* (1938), vol. 19, pp. 355–56.

2.7 *Qing Veritable Records* [Qing shilu], Shizu, vol. V. Fifth Moon, Renyin Day, 1644. (This document and the second *bianzi* decree were provided by Professor Andrew Hsieh.)

2.8 *Qing Veritable Records* [Qing shilu], Shizu, Volume XIV, Sixth Moon, Bingyin Day, 1645.

2.9 Xu Chongxi, *Jiangyin chengshou houji* [A supplementary account of the defense of Jiangyin city], in *Zhongguo lishi yanjiushe*[Academy of Chinese history] comp., *Dongnanjishi* [Recorded events of southeastern China] (Shanghai: Shenzhou guoguangshe, 1951), pp. 81–85.

2.10 Yu Zizhan, *Jinsha xito,* in Xie Guozhen (1981), pp. 229–34.

CHAPTER 3

3.1 Jiang Lianqi, *Donghua lu* (1980), pp. 137–38.

3.2 Shi Lang, ed., and annotated by Wang Duoquan, *Jinghai jishi* [Records of pacification of the seas] (Fujian renmin chubanshe, 1983), pp. 80–91.

3.3 Reprinted by permission of the publisher from *Russia and China: Their Diplomatic Relations to 1728* by Mark Mancall, Cambridge, Mass.: Harvard University Press, Copyright © 1971 by the President and Fellows of Harvard College.

3.4 Fang Bao, *Fang Bao Ji* [Complete works of Fang Bao] (Shanghai: Shanghai guji chubanshe, 1983), vol. 2, pp. 709–12.

3.5 From *Emperor of China* by Jonathan D. Spence. Copyright © 1971 by Jonathan D. Spence. Reprinted by permission of Alfred A. Knopf.

CHAPTER 4

4.1 Wang Yupu, *Shengyu guangxun zhijie* [An extensive exposition of the Sacred Edict], new translation from Chinese text in F. W. Baller, *The Sacred Edict* (Shanghai: Shanghai Inland Mission, 1924), pp. 20–21, 74–87, 88–93.

4.2 Baller (1924), pp. 184–211.

4.3 *Shangyu niege* (Yongzheng Imperial Edicts to the Grand Secretariat), 27th day of 4th month, the 5th year of Yongzheng.

CHAPTER 5

5.1 Wu Jingzi, *The Scholars,* trans. Yang Hsien-yi and Gladys Yang (Peking: Foreign Languages Press, 1964), pp. 65–77.

5.2 Zhongguo diyi lishi danganguan [China number one history archive], Zhongguo shehui kexueyuan lishi yanjiuso [Chinese academy of social sciences history research center], *Qingdai dizu boxue xingtai* [Landlord exploitation during the Qing era] (Beijing: Renmin chubanshe, 1982), pp. 53–55.

5.3 Jiang Liangqi, *Donghualu,* vol. 1., p. 1.

5.4 *Ji Shen Zhilue* [A brief account of the execution of Heshen], in *Ming Wuzong waiji* [An unofficial account of Ming Wuzong] (Shanghai: Shenzshou gouguangshe, 1951), pp. 265–74.

CHAPTER 6

6.1 *Lord Macartney's Commission from Henry Dundas, 1792,* Watkinson Library, Trinity College, typescript of manuscript copy, pp. 1–14.

6.2 and 6.3 From Lord George Macartney, *An Embassy to China; Being The Journal Kept By Lord Macartney During His Embassy To The Emperor Ch'ien-Lung, 1793–1794,* edited by J. L. Cramner-Byng. Copyright © 1962 Addison Wesley Longman. Reprinted by permission.

6.4 and 6.5 *Changing China: Readings in the History of China from the Opium War to the Present*, edited by J. Mason Gentzler. Copyright © 1977 by Praeger Publishers. Reproduced with permission of Greenwood Publishing Group, Inc., Westport, CT.

CHAPTER 7

7.1 John Slade, *A Narrative of the Late Proceedings and Events in China* (Canton: Canton Register, 1839), pp. 1–5.
7.2 Slade (1836), pp. 18–26.
7.3 Slade (1836), pp. 34–35.
7.4 Slade (1836), pp. 135–39.
7.5 Sir Frederick Whyte, *China and Foreign Powers: An Historical Review of their Relations* (London: Oxford University Press, 1928), pp. 42–48.

CHAPTER 8

8.1 Qian Yong, *Luyuan conghua* [Discursive talks from Lu garden] (Beijing, Zhonghua shuju, 1979), Appendix, vol. 21, pp. 575–78.
8.2 Liang Fa, *Quanshi liangyan* [Good words to exhort the age] (reprint edition), in *Jindai shih ziliao* [Modern history materials] (Beijing: Zhonghua shuju, 1979), vol. 39, pp. 25–32.
8.3 Callery and Yvan, *History of the Insurrection in China,* trans. John Oxenford (New York: Harper and Brothers, 1853), pp. 100–06.
8.4 Lindesay Brine, *The Taeping Rebellion in China* (London: J. Murray, 1862), pp. 371–75.
8.5 Brine (1862), pp. 386–91.
8.6 Gentzler (1977), pp. 65–67.

CHAPTER 9

9.1 Yung Wing, *My Life in China and America* (New York: Henry Holt and Company, 1909), p. 109.
9.2 Yung Wing (1909), pp. 142–53.
9.3 W. A. P. Martin, *A Cycle of Cathay* (New York: Fleming H. Revell Co., 1897), pp. 301–03.
9.4 Sir Robert Hart, *These From the Land of Sinim* (London: Chapman and Hall, 1901), Appendix I, pp. 171–81.
9.5 Mrs. Archibald Little, *Li Hung Chang, His Life and Times* (London: Cassell and Company Ltd., 1903), Appendix A, pp. 333–39.
9.6 Kiyo Sue Inui, *The Unsolved Problem of the Pacific* (Tokyo: Japan Times, 1926), p. 286.
9.7 Inui (1926), pp. 333–41.
9.8 North China Herald eds., *The Anti-Foreign Riots in China 1891* (Shanghai: North China Herald Press, 1892), pp. 182–83.

CHAPTER 10

10.1 Reprinted with the permission of Scribner, a Division of Simon & Schuster, from *Modern China: From Mandarin to Commissar,* translated by Dun J. Li. Copyright © 1978 by Dun J. Li.
10.2 Tientsin Press, eds., *Verbal Discussions During Peace Negotiations Between the Chinese Plenipotentiary Viceroy Li Hung-Chang and the Japanese Plenipotentiaries Count Ito and Viscount*

Mutsu at Shimonoseki, Japan. March—April, 1895 (Tientsin: Tientsin Press, 1895), pp. 1–16.

10.3 John V. A. MacMurray, *Treaties and Agreements With and Concerning China, 1894–1919* (New York: Oxford Press, 1921), pp. 74–77.

10.4 Zhang Zhidong, *China's Only Hope, An Appeal By Her Greatest Viceroy, Change Chih-Tung,* trans. Samuel I. Woodbridge (Edinburgh and London: Oliphant, Anderson and Ferrier, 1901), pp. 55–62.

10.5 and 10.6 Shandong daxue lixhixi zhongguo jindaishi jiaoyanshi [Modern Chinese history section, History Department, Shandong University], *Shandong yihetuan diaocha ziliao xuanbian* [Selected collection of materials from an investigation of the Boxer rebellion in Shandong province] (Jinan: Jilu shushe, 1980), pp. 131–34, 66–70.

CHAPTER 11

11.1 Wu Ting Fang, *The Awakening of China: An Address Delivered before The Civic Forum in Carnegie Hall, New York City, May 5, 1908,* New York: The Civic Forum, 1908, pp. 3–13.

11.2 Feng Yuxiang, *Wode shenghua* [My life] (Zhongqing: Sanhu tushushe, 1944), pp. 88–92, 120–22.

11.3 Zou Rong, *Gemingjun* [The Revolutionary Army] new translation from Chinese text as reprinted in John Lust, *The Revolutionary Army, A Chinese Nationalist Tract of 1903* (The Hague: Mouton and Company, 1968), pp. 18–23.

11.4 Dun Li (1978), pp. 137–41.

11.5 Anon., *Diary of the Revolution* (Hankow: The Daily News, 1911), np.

11.6 B. L. Putnam Weale, *The Fight for the Republic in China* (New York: Dodd, Mead, and Company, 1917), pp. 393–97.

CHAPTER 12

12.1 Yuan Shikai, "Poem to the Soldiers," *New York Times,* November 18, 1912, p. 4.

12.2 Anon., ed., (pamphlet issued "By Authority of Republican Goverment of China"), *The "Peoples Will", An Exposure of the Political Intrigues at Peking against the Republic of China,* np., 1912, p. 20.

12.3 Wunsz King, *V. K. Wellington Koo's Foreign Policy, Some Selected Documents* (Shanghai: Kelly and Walsh, 1931), pp. 87–90.

12.4 Aisin-Gioro Puyi, *From Emperor to Citizen* (Beijing: Foreign Languages Press, 1964), pp. 85–95.

12.5 Cai Tingkai, *Cai Tingkai zizhuan* [The autobiography of Cai Tingkai] (Harbin: Heilonjiang renmin chubanshe, 1946), pp. 91–95.

12.6 George T. B. Davis, *China's Christian Army, A Story of Marshal Feng and His Soldiers* (New York: The Christian Alliance Publishing Company, 1925), pp. 9–21.

12.7 Edgar Snow ed., *Living China* (London: G. G. Harrap, 1937), pp. 222–25.

CHAPTER 13

13.1 Lu Yitian, *Lenglu zashi* [Random comments from a cool residence] (Beijing, Zhonghua shuju, 1984), p. 175.

13.2 Lu Xun, "My View of Chastity," *Selected works of Lu Hsun,* trans. Yang Hsien-yi and Gladys Yang (Peking: Foreign Languages Press, 1980), vol. 2, pp. 11–24.

13.3 Li Dazhao, "Bolshevism de shengli" [The victory of bolshevism], *Xin qingnian* [New

Youth], vol. 5, no. 5, November 15, 1918, in *Zhongguo xiandaishi ziliao huibian* [Materials on the contempory history of China] (Hong Kong, Wenhua ziliao gonxingshe, 1976), pp. 14–19.

13.4 Zhang Yunhou, Yin Xuyi, and Li Junchen, eds., *Liufa qinggong jianxue yundong* [The work-study movement in France] (Shanghai: Renmin chubanshe, 1980), pp. 157–58.

13.5 Qinghua University Chinese Communist Party Teaching and Research Group, *Liufa qinggong jianxue yundong shiliao* [Historical materials on the work-study movement in France] (Beijing: Beijing chubanshe, 1980), pp. 209–11.

13.6 The Peking United International Relief Committee, *The North China Famine of 1920–1922 with Special Reference to the West Chihli Area* (Peking, 1922), pp. 11–15.

CHAPTER 14

14.1 Guangdong geming lishi buowuguan [Guangdong revolutionary history museum], *Huangpu junxiao shiliao* [Historical materials of the Whampoa Military Academy] (Guangzhou: Guangdong remin chubanshe, 1982), pp. 44–56.

14.2 A. I. Cherepanov, *As Military Adviser in China* (Moscow: Progress Publishers, Moscow, 1982), pp. 82–83, 84.

14.3 Lo Wen Kan, V. K. Ting, Hu Shih, and K. L. Yen, *China's Case*, published by The Union of Chinese Associations (London: Caledonian Press, 1927), np.

15.4 Report Presented by Secretary of Foreign Affairs to Parliament, *Papers Respecting The First Firing in the Shameen Affair of June 23, 1925, China* 1 (1926): pp. 8–10.

14.5 National Kwangtung University, *Manifesto to The Peoples of the World Re The Deplorable Events which Took Place in Shanghai, Hankow, And Canton* (Canton: Waihing Printing Co., 1925), pp. 1–10.

14.6 Secretariat, the Kuomintang of China, *Nationalist China* (Canton: Central Political Council of Kuomintang, Canton Branch, April 1927), pp. 14–15.

14.7 and 14.8 Secretariat, the Kuomintang of China (1927), pp. 15–17, 25–26.

14.9 Soong Ching-ling, *The Struggle for New China* (Peking: Foreign Languages Press, 1952), pp. 7–11.

CHAPTER 15

15.1 Hu Shih, "Failure of Law in Nationalist China," Shanghai: *North China Herald,* June 22, 1929, np.

15.2 Tang Liang-li, *Suppressing Communist Banditry in China* (Shanghai: China United Press, 1932), pp. 97–98.

15.3 Japan Ministry of Foreign Affairs, *Relations of Japan with Manchuria and Mongolia,* Document B (Tokyo, 1932), pp. 126–29.

15.4 P. Ohara, Manchuokuo, *The World's Newest Nation: Facing Facts In Manchuria,* Mukden: *Manchuria Daily News,* 1932, pp. 97–98.

15.5 Department of Foreign Affairs, Manchuokuo Government, Series #2, *The Chief Executives' Proclamation, Organic Law of Manchuokuo, and Other Laws Governing Various Government Offices* (Hsinking, Manchuria, November, 1932), np.

15.6 Yosuke Matsuoka, *Japan's Interests Rights and Responsibilities in the Far East* (New York: Japanese Chamber of Commerce, 1934), pp. 4–10.

15.7 Hsi-Huey Liang, *The Sino-German Connection, Alexander von Falkenhausen between China and Germany 1900–1941* (Amsterdam: Van Gorcum, Assen, 1978), pp. 199–204.

CHAPTER 16

16.1 Yang Chengwu, "Lightning Attack on the Luding Bridge," in Lui Bocheng et al., *Recalling the Long March* (Beijing: Foreign Languages Press, 1976), pp. 88–110.

16.2 Madame Chiang Kai-shek, *General Chiang Kai-shek and The Communist Crisis* (Shanghai: China Weekly Review Press, 1935), pp. 55–73.

16.3 New Life Promotion Society of Nanchang, *What Must Be Known About New Life* (Nanjing, 1935), pp. 216–20.

16.4 C. W. H. Young, *New Life For Kiangsi* (Shanghai: China Publishing Company, 1935), pp. 104–08.

16.5 Zhongguo xiandaishi ziliao congkan [China contemporary history materials series], *Yierhjiu yundong* [The December 9 movement] (Beijing, Renmin chubanshe, 1954), pp. 44–50.

16.6 Mi Zanchen, *The Life of Yang Hucheng* (Hong Kong, Joint Publishing Co., 1981), pp. 118–20.

16.7 General and Madame Chiang Kai-shek, *General Chiang Kai-shek: The Account of the Fortnight in Siam when th Fate of China Hung in the Balance* (New York, Garden City, 1937), pp. 177–84.

CHAPTER 17

17.1 Japan Foreign Federation, *Official View of The Sino-Japanese Conflict* (Tokyo: Maruzen Company, Ltd., 1937), pp. 8–12.

17.2 Hirosi Saito, *The Conflict in the Far East,* reprinted from *World Affairs* (December 1937): pp. 3–7.

17.3 Chiang Kai-shek, *Generalissimo Chiang Speaks* (Hong Kong: The Pacific Publishing Company, June 1939), pp. 73–123.

17.4 and 17.5 H. J. Timperley, *Japanese Terror in China* (New York: Modern Age Books, 1938), pp. 33–35, 216–17.

17.6 Wang Jingwei, "Radio Address by Mr. Wang Ching-wei, President of the Chinese Executive Yuan," June 24, 1941, *Tokyo Gazette,* Vol. V, No. 2, (Tokyo, August, 1941), pp. 82–88.

17.7 Lui Shaoqi, *How to Be a Good Communist* (Peking: Foreign Languages Press, 1964), pp. 1–9, 45–47.

CHAPTER 18

18.1 Wang Kang, *Wenyiduozhuan* [Biography of Wen Yiduo] (Hong Kong, Joint Publishing Company, 1979), pp. 434–37.

18.2 Department of State Bulletin, Washington, D.C. (Jan. 19, 1947), pp. 83–85.

18.3 Chiang Kai-shek, "President Chiang's Statement on Retirement," *China Magazine,* vol. XIX, no. 2 (February 1949), pp. 7–8, 8–9.

18.4 Mao Tse-Tung, *Selected Works of Mao Tse-Tung* (Peking: Foreign Langauges Press, 1975), vol. IV, pp. 387–89.

18.5 and 18.6 Mao (1975), vol. IV, pp. 397–400, 411–32.

CHAPTER 19

19.1 "Treaty of Friendship, Alliance, and Mutual Assistance between the Union of Soviet Socialist Republics and the People's Republic of China, February 14, 1950," reprinted in

Hungdah Chiu, *The People's Republic of China and the Law of Treaties* (Cambridge: Harvard University Press, 1972), Appendix B, pp. 125–26.

19.2 The Marriage Law of the People's Republic of China as Promulgated by the Central People's Government, May 1, 1950, reprinted in C. K. Yang, *Chinese Communist Society: The Family and the Village* (Cambridge: MIT Press, 1972), Appendix, pp. 221–26; see also Albert P. Blaustein, *Fundamental Legal Documents of Communist China* (South Hackensack, NJ: Fred B. Rothman and Co., 1962), pp. 206–75.

19.3 Ding Ling, *The Sun Shines over the Sanggan River* (Beijing: Foreign Languages Press, 1964), pp. 308–18.

19.4 Hu Shih-tu, "My Father Is An Enemy of the People," *Hong Kong Standard,* September 24, 1950, p. 5. The Chinese text appears Ta Kung Pao, Hong Kong, September 22, 1950, pp. 1,3.

19.5 Chiang Kai-shek, *President Chiang Kai-shek's Messages,* October 10, 1954–February 14, 1955 (Taipei: The Fourth Department, Central Committee of the Kuomintang, 1955), pp.1–9.

CHAPTER 20

20.1 Mao Tse-tung, *Selected Works of Mao Tse-Tung* (Peking, Foreign Langauges Press, 1975), vol. V, pp. 152–53.

20.2 Mao (1975), vol. V, pp. 308–11.

20.3 Lu Dingyi, "Let Flowers of Many Kinds Blossom, Diverse Schools of Thought Contend," Beijing, *People's China,* 1956, pp. 3–14.

20.4 *The Hundred Flowers Campaign and the Chinese Intellectuals,* edited by Roderick MacFarquhar. Copyright © 1960 by Stevens & Sons Limited, London. Reproduced with permission of Greenwood Publishing Group, Inc., Westport, CT.

20.5 Teng Hsiao-p'ing, "Report on the Rectification Campaign to the Third Plenum of the Central Committee," September 23, 1957, trans. NCNA, October 19, 1957, in *Communist China 1955–1959; policy documents with analysis* prepared by Harvard University under the joint auspices of the Center for International Affairs and the East Asian Research Center (Cambridge: Harvard University Press, 1962), pp. 358–59.

CHAPTER 21

21.1 Chen Boda, "Under the Banner of Comrade Mao Tse-Tung," *Red Flag,* July 7, 1958, in Dan Jacobs and Hans H. Baerwald, *Chinese Communism, Selected Documents* (New York: Harper and Row, 1963), pp. 135–44.

21.2 Yin Tse-ming, "The Strength of the Masses Is Limitless," in pamphlet *Six Hundred Million Build Industry* (Beijing: Foreign Langauges Press, 1958), in Jacobs and Baerwald (1963), pp. 106–08.

21.3 *Renmin Ribao* editorial, September 3, 1958, "Hold High The Red Flag of People's Communes and March On," in *Communist China* (Beijing: Foreign Languages Press, 1958), in *Communist China 1955–1959; policy documents with analysis* (1962), pp. 460–62.

21.4 Sixth Plenary Session of the Eighth Central Committee of the Communist Party of China, "Decision Approving Comrade Mao Zedong's Proposal That He Will Not Stand as Candidate of Chairman of the People's Republic of China for the next Term of Office" (Beijing: Foreign Langauges Press, 1958), pp. 50–51.

21.5 "The Origin and Development of the Differences Between the Leadership of the CPSU and Ourselves—Comment on the Open Letter of the Central Committee of the CPSU, by the editorial departments of People's Daily and Red Flag, September 6, 1963" as reprinted in *Peking Review,* VI:37, September 13, 1963, pp. 6–23, in William E. Griffith, *The Sino-Soviet Rift* (Boston: MIT Press, 1964), pp. 388–420.

CHAPTER 22

22.1 *We the Chinese: Voices from China*, edited by Deirdre and Neale Hunter. Copyright © 1971 by Praeger Publishers. Reproduced with permission of Greenwood Publishing Group, Inc., Westport, CT.

22.2 Lin Biao, "On People's War," *Peking Review* 36, (September 3, 1965): 9–30.

22.3 and 22.4 *Peking Review,* August 11, 1967, reprinted in Jaap Van Ginneken, *The Rise and Fall of Lin Biao* (New York: Avon Books, 1977), p. 80.

22.5 Reprinted in Chi Hsin, *Teng Hsiao-ping, A Political Biography* (Hong Kong: Cosmos Books, 1978), pp. 54–64.

22.6 and 22.7 Michael Y. M. Kau, *The Lin Piao Affair: Power Politics and Military Coup* (White Plains, N.Y.: International Arts and Sciences Press, 1975), pp. 69–70, 76–77.

CHAPTER 23

23.1 "Joint Communique," *Peking Review* 9, (March 3, 1972): 4–5.

23.2 Foreign Langauges Press, translation of Deng's address at the United Nations in Chi Hsin (1978), pp. 163–75.

23.3 "Mourning With Deepest Grief the Passing Away of the Great Leader and Great Teacher Chairman MaoTsetung," *Peking Review* 3, (September 13, 1978), pp. 6–11.

CHAPTER 24

24.1 Reprinted in Teng Hsiao-p'ing, *Speeches and writings of Deng Xiaoping* (New York: Pergamon, 1984), pp. 62–74.

24.2 He Shiguang, "Xiangchang shang" [On a village market street], *Renmin wenxue* 8, (August 1980), pp. 18–23.

24.3 Lee Yee, ed., *The New Realism, Writings from China after the Cultural Revolution* (New York: Hippocrene Books, 1983), pp. 86–91.

CHAPTER 25

25.1 Han Nianlong, Text Of Speech By Chinese Government Delegation Head at Sino-Vietnamese Negotiations in Hanoi, Xinhua General News Service, April 26, 1979, Item No: 042620. LEXIS-NEXIS.

25.2 Anon. " 'Liberation Army Daily' Examines Background to *Bitter Love,*" The British Broadcasting Corporation, BBC Summary of World Broadcasts, May 21, 1981. LEXIS-NEXIS.

25.3 and 25.4 Deng Liqun, "Clearing Cultural Contamination," November 1983 and "Scope of Spiritual Pollution," The British Broadcasting Corporation, BBC Summary of World Broadcasts, December 17, 1983, China II; FE77519/BII/1, LEXIS-NEXIS.

25.5 Liu Binyan, "A Case of Persecution in Xian in Disregard of Central Instructions," *People's Daily,* August 25, 1984, The British Broadcasting Corporation, BBC Summary of World Broadcasts, September 8, 1984, China II; FE7743/BII/1, LEXIS-NEXIS.

25.6 The Joint Declaration by Britain and China Defining the Future of Hong Kong, September 26, 1984.

25.7 Geremie Barmé and John Minford, eds., *Seeds of Fire: Chinese Voices of Conscience* (New York: Hill and Wang, 1988), pp. 329–37.

25.8 and 25.9 Barmé and Minford (1988), p. 336.

CHAPTER 26

26.1 Anon., "Bixu qizhi xianmingde fandui dongluang," [We must unequivocally oppose turmoil], *Renmin ribao* [People's daily], overseas edition, (April 26, 1989): 1.

26.2 China News Agency, "Demonstration on April 27," np.

26.3 "Open Declaration of A Hunger Strike, May 1989," *Jiushiniandai,* June 16, 1989.

26.4 Li Peng "Transcript of Remarks by Chinese Prime Minister Announcing Crackdown," *New York Times,* May 20, 1989, Section 1, p. 6.

26.5 Deng Xiaoping, "Deng's June 9 Speech: 'We Faced a Rebellious Clique' and 'Dreg's of Society,' " *New York Times* (June 30, 1989): A6.

CHAPTER 27

27.1 Dalai Lama, "The Nobel Peace Prize Lecture, Oslo, Norway, December 10, 1989," in Sidney Piburn, *The Dalai Lama, A Policy of Kindness* (Ithaca, NY: Snow Lion Publications, 1993), pp. 15–25.

27.2 Wei Jingshing, "The Wolf and the Lamb," *New York Times,* November 18, 1993, Section A, p. 27. Copyright © 1993 by The New York Times. Reprinted by permission.

27.3 William Clinton, "Remarks by President Clinton during the Announcement of the Renewal of MFN Trade Status for China," May 26, 1994, CNN transcript #406-2, LEXIS-NEXUS.

27.4 Jiang Zemin, "Continue to Promote the Reunification of the Motherland," January 31, 1995, NCNA English trans., The British Broadcasting Corporation, BBC Summary of World Broadcasts, China II/FE/2215/G, LEXIS-NEXIS.